Polar Exploration

This series includes accounts, by eye-witnesses and contemporaries, of early expeditions to the Arctic and the Antarctic. Huge resources were invested in such endeavours, particularly the search for the North-West Passage, which, if successful, promised enormous strategic and commercial rewards. Cartographers and scientists travelled with many of the expeditions, and their work made important contributions to earth sciences, climatology, botany and zoology. They also brought back anthropological information about the indigenous peoples of the Arctic region and the southern fringes of the American continent. The series further includes dramatic and poignant accounts of the harsh realities of working in extreme conditions and utter isolation in bygone centuries.

Journal of a Voyage in Baffin's Bay and Barrow Straits in the Years 1850–1851

In the mid-nineteenth century, British Arctic exploration was focused on the search for the missing expedition of Sir John Franklin. Physician and geologist Peter Cormack Sutherland (1822–1900) served as surgeon on William Penny's 1850–1 search expedition, which was instructed to concentrate on Jones Sound, Wellington Channel and Barrow Strait in the Canadian Arctic. Sutherland's illustrated eyewitness account, first published in two volumes in 1852, tells of appalling weather conditions, notes the hazards of navigating icy seas, describes the wildlife and geology of the region, and offers observations on the Inuit. Sutherland also recounts the poignant discovery of Franklin's winter quarters at Beechey Island and the graves of several of his crew. Franklin's fate, however, was yet to be discovered. Volume 2 contains insightful details relating to sledging journeys and crew diet. The volume concludes with the return voyage to Britain.

Journal of a Voyage in Baffin's Bay and Barrow Straits in the Years 1850–1851

Performed by H.M. Ships Lady Franklin and Sophia Under the Command of Mr. William Penny in Search of the Missing Crews of H.M. Ships Erebus and Terror

VOLUME 2

PETER CORMACK SUTHERLAND

CAMBRIDGE
UNIVERSITY PRESS

University Printing House, Cambridge, CB2 8BS, United Kingdom

Published in the United States of America by Cambridge University Press, New York

Cambridge University Press is part of the University of Cambridge.
It furthers the University's mission by disseminating knowledge in the pursuit of education, learning and research at the highest international levels of excellence.

www.cambridge.org
Information on this title: www.cambridge.org/9781108072083

This edition first published 1852
This digitally printed version 2014

ISBN 978-1-108-07208-3 Paperback

The original edition of this book contains a number of colour plates, which have been reproduced in black and white. Colour versions of these images can be found online at www.cambridge.org/9781108072083

J COVENTRY, LITH. M & N HANHART, IMPS

REST. ENCAMPING DRAGGING.

ARCTIC TRAVELLING.

JOURNAL OF A VOYAGE

IN

BAFFIN'S BAY AND BARROW STRAITS,

IN THE YEARS 1850—1851,

PERFORMED BY

H. M. SHIPS "LADY FRANKLIN" AND "SOPHIA,"

UNDER THE COMMAND OF MR. WILLIAM PENNY,

IN SEARCH OF THE

MISSING CREWS OF H.M. SHIPS EREBUS AND TERROR:

WITH A NARRATIVE OF SLEDGE EXCURSIONS ON THE ICE OF WELLINGTON CHANNEL;

AND OBSERVATIONS ON THE NATURAL HISTORY AND PHYSICAL FEATURES OF THE COUNTRIES AND FROZEN SEAS VISITED.

BY PETER C. SUTHERLAND, M.D. M.R.C.S.E.

SURGEON TO THE EXPEDITION.

IN TWO VOLUMES.—VOL. II.

WITH MAPS, PLATES, AND WOOD-ENGRAVINGS.

LONDON:

LONGMAN, BROWN, GREEN, AND LONGMANS.

1852.

London:
Spottiswoodes and Shaw,
New-street-Square.

CONTENTS

OF

THE SECOND VOLUME.

CHAPTER XVI.

PREPARATIONS FOR TRAVELLING.

CHAP. XVII.

TRAVELLING PARTIES.

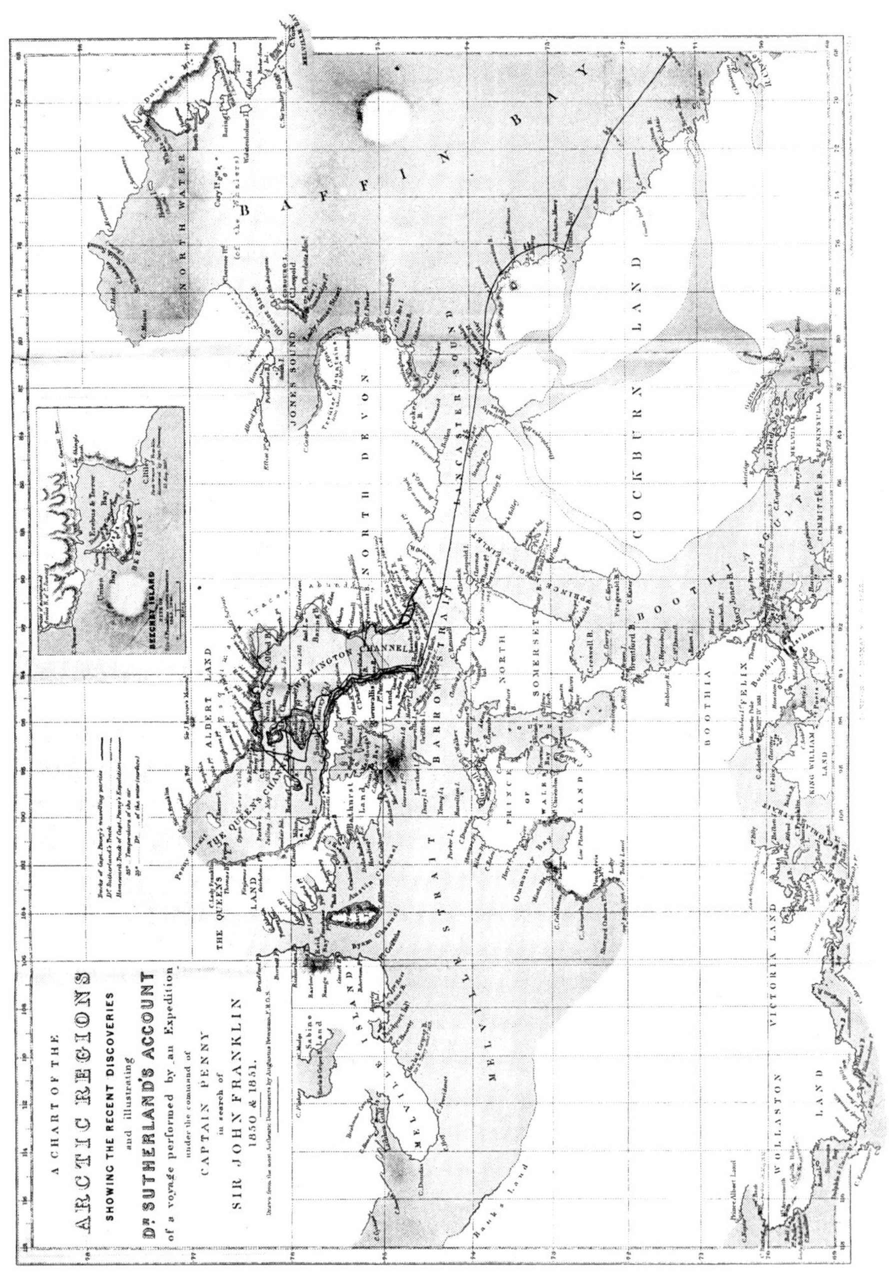

The material originally positioned here is too large for reproduction in this reissue. A PDF can be downloaded from the web address given on page iv of this book, by clicking on 'Resources Available'.

VOYAGE IN SEARCH

OF

SIR JOHN FRANKLIN.

CHAPTER XVI.

PREPARATIONS FOR TRAVELLING.

Provisions. — The last of our fresh Potatoes. — Preparations for Travelling. — Snow removed from the Deck. — Bear Hunt. — A Man falls into the Water. — The Weather. — A most violent Storm. — Form of Government among the Esquimaux Dogs.— The late Storm. — Light admitted into the Cabins. — Barrow Straits frozen over. — Snow melting on a black Surface. — View of Barrow Straits. — Party from Griffith's Island. — Outline of Plan of Search. — Proving the Sledges. — Bear Hunt. — Disturbed Depôts. — Tide Gauge discontinued. — Resolve to travel during the Day. — High Responsibility of the Commanders of Travelling Parties. — Travelling commences. — Leaving the Ships. — Parting Cheers. — Temperature above Zero.

March 12*th.* — The Expedition was most munificently supplied with preserved vegetables, which still remained as fresh as when they were put into the tins. The allowance of them that was served out proved most ample at all times, and no one seemed to have any "longing" for succulent vegetable food. The time, however, for this "longing" was only approaching; for, up to this time, we had the use of fresh potatoes, which, be it observed, grew in 1849, passed through a summer and a winter in the Arctic Regions, in addition to one winter in the climate that produced them, and still retained their nutritious properties unchanged. They always deserved and got the preference, and now, that we had just used the last of them at dinner, we should have felt glad to have transferred the high esteem that had attached to them in the fresh state, to the patent preserved potato of Edwards; this, however, we could not do, in the presence of succulent carrots and turnips. The fresh potatoes sometimes became frozen, and, if they were permitted to thaw without being used immediately, fermentation commenced and in a very short time they became quite sweet: if, however, they were put into the vessel to be boiled, without first being thawed in cold water, they invariably became quite tough, so that they might be boiled into shreds, without removing the fibrous structure which they seemed to have assumed. A remark was made to the cabin steward, on one occasion, that the potatoes were not sufficiently boiled; his reply was, that they had been kept in boiling water for three hours. This reminded us of what

Mr. Darwin observed in the lofty Andes, when his guides were blaming the new pot for not boiling the potatoes; the true cause being the lowering of the boiling point of water, from the immense height which they had attained, but of this they had no conception. Now that our fresh potatoes were at an end, too much could not be said of the quality of all our preserved and salted provisions. The name of Hogarth was often mentioned, and not without reason; for the firm of Hogarth & Co., Aberdeen, had carried the art of preserving meat to such an extent and degree of perfection, that even herrings were supplied to our Expedition, at a very low price, and scarcely deficient of their original freshness and flavour. The health of the crews of both ships was particularly good. The diseased finger which has been alluded to already, as affording a sort of key to the health of the Expedition, began to assume an active state, and it did not forbid the idea that another month or two might heal it up altogether. The crew of the "Felix," generally, were also in tolerable health, although still there were symptoms of the old disease.

Our preparations for travelling were advancing with great glee. Canvas boots, with leather soles, were made by those of the seamen who had a little knowledge of shoemaking; and where their knowledge happened to be at fault, close application and willing minds afforded a ready compensation. Moccassins, large enough to receive the feet with three or four pairs of stockings, were made of strong canvas; and some of the men put gutta percha soles to them to prevent wearing out so speedily in the event of walking over rough shingle. The sailmakers had to make the tents, of which we required seven; sledge-covers eight, of which two were for dog-sledges; forty-four haversacks; seven luncheon haversacks; eight ammunition bags; and forty sets of dog harness, including two pairs of canvas "boots" for each dog, to protect their feet from the rough ice, after being several days out. The blacksmith and carpenters had to prepare the sledges, and shod them with iron: tent-poles, each of which would be made to answer some other purpose besides being a tent-pole; each tent required five; two of these were to have ice-chisels, one would be fitted with a boat-hook, and one with a lance: eight conjurors or cooking utensils, the chief parts of which were made of sheet iron, while the part corresponding with the pot or kettle was nothing else than one of the six pound meat tins: eight pick-axes, one for each sledge: and thirty tins, each of which would require to hold a gallon; and, being intended for the spirits, it will be obvious that, however difficult it might be to solder up old tin vessels and make them air-tight, there could not be the slightest deviation from this property, otherwise we should necessarily lose our favourite beverage, — a glass of rum on a cold morning.

The persons who had charge of the stores had to draw up scales of victualling, and prepare the meat for use. The pork required to be soaked to remove the salt, boiled, bones removed, and then it had to be packed carefully in canvas bags made for the purpose; the pemmican required but to be allotted; bread, tea, sugar, tobacco, had to be weighed out carefully and put up neatly in canvas bags; fat for fuel, the refuse of the cooks, which they had been carefully preserving as a perquisite, and very inferior stuff for most part, had to be melted down and poured into canvas bags, each of seven to contain forty pounds; and, what would be necessary and was still more difficult, arrangements had to be made on board ship for leaving depôts or cachés of provisions for the return of the advancing parties.

Powder, shot, ball, guns, and percussion caps, as well as nipples and key, included in the stores, came also under the supervision of the store keepers. The surgeons had to make provision as they thought proper for diseases and casualties. Each man, and every person in our Expedition except two was included in the number, had to prepare his own blankets or sleeping bag, fill up his haversack, prepare all his clothing, and contribute a few needles, thread, buttons, and pieces of cloth, for mending his clothes, to the tent "ditto" bag. The captain of each sledge had to furnish a hammer, nails, pricker, gimblet, two files or rasps, sail needles, twine, and some cord, to the sledge "ditto" bag; and he also had to attend to the wolfskin or felt blankets, as well as to the wicks for the conjurors, which last required a cooking "ditto" bag.

The sledges were each about twelve feet long, and the runners an inch and a half to two inches in thickness, varied in height from eight to eleven inches, but I do not think any of them were so much as a foot. The under surface of the runners had a tapering rise at both ends, which occupied nearly a foot, and presented a decided convexity, which resembled a portion of a cycloidal curve. From the points at which each of these curves terminated, where the floor of the runner commenced, to the middle, there was a rise of one-eighth of an inch to the foot. If the rise was more than this, the resistance was increased about the centre of the runner; and if the rise was less than this, the resistance was increased at the extremities, especially the fore extremity. This was very clearly proved by the different forms that had been used. The shoeing of the runners was either of malleable iron or iron hoop; the latter promised to answer well from its smoothness, but there would be difficulty in fixing it on, owing to its thinness not affording sufficient metal to countersink the nails, which, of course, ought to be screw-nails; the former could not be made smooth enough, the batons of the hatches affording the only material out of which this kind could be made. The malleable iron shoeing was superior to the rolled iron in being thicker, and consequently conveying greater firmness to the runner on which it might be placed. The upper edge of each runner was perforated by a number of holes, through which the seizings of the cross-bars or "stretchers" were fastened; and, lest the runner should be weakened by these openings or perforations, a slip of fir-wood, the same as the runner itself, was nailed firmly along the upper edge of its inner side. The stretchers, two feet and a half in length, were generally hard wood, or this alternating with others made of fir. The sledge cover consisted of two parts, sewed closely together, the bottom or floor lying over the stretchers and the sides, the latter had eyelets in the upper edge for lacing, after the contents of the sledge were all in their places. In the fore part of the runners there were two small openings, through which the ends of the span were passed, and a knot applied. To the span the track-ropes, generally seven in number, were spliced in with an eye, which permitted of slipping a little either way, as might be necessary, if the sledge should require to be dragged a little to either side.

The tents, like the sledges, were fitted each for seven men. Their length was ten feet, and breadth a little more than six feet. The two ends were triangular, and the height was barely seven feet. One of the ends was close, and the other was open from the base upwards, about three and a half or four feet. Both sides of this doorway had a number of eyelets for a lacing, and one of them had a lapel or flap, which prevented the admission of snow. All the seams of the tent were single, except where the canvas was double, which generally happened around the foot, where there was a part which overlapped the snow, and was intended to receive snow upon it, to keep the whole tent down and secure it against the wind. At the two extremities of the ridge, there were two oblong pocket-looking appendages resembling asses' ears, for the reception of the upper extremities of the tent-poles. There was a square of canvas, ten feet by six, called a floor-cloth, intended for a covering over the snow, upon which our wolf-skin or felt blankets were to be placed. With the exception of the rope to steady the tent, and the two pegs to drive into the snow or shingle, when stones or blocks of ice might not be at hand, nothing has been omitted belonging to the tents. Each tent was to be supplied with two wolf-skin or felt blankets, which I may remark, in passing, were the only provision that had been made in the way of travelling equipment for our Expedition, before leaving home.

The blanket bags were made of a single blanket, covered with black or any kind of calico, to prevent the admission of snow into the long and woolly nap of English blankets. They very much resembled a corn sack, with the exception that some of them had hoods, while others had one-half the mouth sewed across the top, at the same time opening out the side seam sufficiently for the convenient admission of the individual intended to occupy it. There was an order that the weight of each should not exceed seven pounds.

There were seven haversacks for each sledge, one of which was a knapsack. Each man had to provide boot-hose, stockings, socks, flannel or other woollen drawers, mittens or mitts, of each, one pair, one flannel shirt, comb, towel, and soap, which, with two pairs of canvas moccassins, two pairs of blanket squares for wrappings to the feet, and the haversack supplied by the ship, was ordered not to exceed seven pounds weight. Some of them, however, weighed eight or nine pounds. The standing clothes of each man included one pair of socks, stockings, boot-hose, double drawers, trousers, and canvas boots, one flannel shirt, and one guernsey frock, or two of the latter, one vest with sleeves, one comforter, sealskin cap, welsh wig, two pairs of mitts, one of which was generally sealskin in the form of gauntlets, or only extending to the wrist, and a canvas overall called a "jumper," which resembled a shirt, except that it was not quite so long. In addition to this suit, each had a great-coat, south-wester, one pair of sea-boots, and one pair of cloth boots in the sledge. For occasional use, each person would require to have a veil, and gutta percha or wooden goggles.

The luncheon haversack contained seven pannikins and spoons, a half and a quarter gill measure for serving out the spirits, a small tin can or bottle to receive the daily allowance of spirits, and two small canvas bags containing pepper and salt.

The ammunition bag contained powder and balls of each two pounds, shot No. 1. five, and No. 4. four pounds, caps, wads, nipples and screws, two pounds. Each sledge was to have three single-barrelled or one double and one single-barrelled gun.

The fuel store or "ditto" bag contained a quantity of slow match, wicks, consisting chiefly of dry rope cut up into pieces one to two inches in length, a tin box containing half a dozen boxes of lucifer matches, with a candlestick adapted to the upper end or lid, and a larger tin box containing two pounds of candles.

Each of six sledges was to be provisioned for forty days, with slight modifications for the convenience of making depôts, and the daily allowances per man were, pork $\frac{3}{4}$ lb., pemmican $\frac{3}{4}$ lb., bread 1 lb., tea $\frac{3}{4}$ oz., sugar 1 oz., rum $\frac{1}{2}$ gill, and tobacco $\frac{1}{2}$ oz.

The amount of weight upon one sledge equipped for forty days and drawn by seven men, was as follows: —

	lbs.
Sledge and cover - - - - - -	130
Tent, with rope for steadying it - - -	50
Five tent-poles - - - - - -	30
Two wolf-skin blankets - - - -	32
Three guns and ammunition bag - - -	40
Pickaxe and shovel - - - - -	8
Cooking apparatus - - - - -	14
Fuel store bag - - - - -	8
Sledge store bag, spare cordage - - -	7
Quadrant or sextant - - - -	6
Luncheon haversack - - - -	12
Seven blanket bags - - - - -	45
Seven haversacks - - - - -	56
Seven pairs of sea-boots - - - -	35
Seven pairs of cloth boots, with cork soles - -	21
Seven great coats and south-westers - -	50
Tent store bag - - - - -	4
Medicine store bag - - - - -	4
Packages - - - - - -	40
Amount of constant weights	592

PROVISIONS.

	lbs.
Pork - - - - - -	210
Pemmican - - - - - -	210
Bread - - - - - -	280
Rum 4½ gallons, in tin cases - - -	48
Sugar - - - - - -	17½
Tea - - - - - -	13½
Tobacco - - - - - -	9
Fuel - - - - - -	42
Amount of weight of provisions	830
Amount of constant weights	592
Total weight of one sledge	1422

In estimating the weights of all the above articles, the lowest was taken as the standard; for example, owing to a little difference in the covers of the blanket bags, some of them weighed eight and some only six pounds; and, owing to a similar cause, the haversacks varied from seven and one-half up to nine pounds. The weight which each person had to drag was two hundred and three pounds; but, it will be observed, that this was just as the sledge was packed on board ship, when everything was dry and free from drifting snow, which we had no doubt might probably increase the weight per man to two hundred and twenty pounds. Little as the space occupied by the whole might be when packed carefully upon the sledge, which was only ten or twelve feet long by two and one-half feet broad, we began to learn that it was equally difficult to fit out for travelling this season, as it was last season to fit out the entire Expedition. The preparation of the fat for fuel would cost three or four persons at least a week's work, after it had been settled that, with the utmost care in the use of it, twenty ounces would be necessary for each sledge per day. We found that with our "conjurors" twice the weight of spirits of wine as of even our inferior and much adulterated fat would be necessary. This, coupled with the danger of its being lost by leakage, and the small quantity we had on board, was a sufficient inducement to give up all ideas of taking anything except fat for fuel in our travelling parties.

Each of the two ships had three sledges to fit out according to the foregoing plan, under the directions of the commanders; but, besides these, there was also a dog-sledge to be fitted out from each ship under the superintendence of Mr. Petersen, to whom we were deeply indebted on many occasions for his valuable experience in the Arctic Regions.

In the end of February the snow had been removed from the deck of the "Sophia," which reduced her to the condition in which the "Lady Franklin" had been all the winter. Since then the weather became much colder than it had been previously; notwithstanding, the temperature on board became very little reduced, and we had the comfort of a walk on the bare planks of the deck instead of on the snow, which often became very slippery, or hollowed out into depressions, which endangered the safety of our ankles.

March 17*th.*—We had violent gales, accompanied by closely drifting snow from S. E., for two or three days between the 12th and 15th. This was followed by a smart gale from N. on the 15th, and yesterday the weather was particularly pleasant, although the temperature varied from $-33°$ to $-22°$. The sky was very clear and cloudless, and at noon the temperature increased to $-22°$. There is no doubt the increase was owing to the influence of the sun's rays on the stratum of air close along the horizon.

A bear paid us a visit in the evening, and was announced by a party of strollers, who had been taking their Sunday walk along the beach. Our guns being at hand, and having collected a few of the dogs with Sultan * at their head, the chase was commenced, and carried on with vigour until the bear increased

* A cross between the Danish and Esquimaux breeds, which was a great favourite among the crews of the three ships, and was instrumental in saving the life of one of the seamen, I think, belonging to the "Felix;" who lay down upon the floe in a state of stupor during night, with the temperature about $-30°$.

the distance ahead of us so much, that to get up within musket shot was impossible, and he made his escape from the dogs by getting into the open water in the offing, which he swam across, and took to his heels over the ice on the other side of the water. He did not get out of the water for some time, because the dogs crossed to the loose ice on one or two pieces which linked the one ice to the other; however, as soon as their patience began to give way, he came out of the water, shook himself dry, and made his escape as some of the men were just coming to the water's edge. It was a novel scene when the bear was bounding across the icy plain, making the snow, firm as it really was at the time, fly like smoke from his heels, now springing to the top of some of the highest hummocks, and looking with fearful grins and horrid fierceness at the dogs which menaced him on every side, now taking a sally after some mettlesome cur, while Sultan, famous for his noble prowess, and his gallant followers rushed up to his heels, which were not cold, although the thermometer was $-30°$. There must have been a great exhibition of ivory on both sides, and this royal plantigrade had reason to feel proud of the display he had made of the insignia of his family. Some of the men followed up in the chase with so much eagerness that most oppressive anhelations came on, which forced them to walk very slowly to the ships. I felt as if in every inspiration the acrid fumes of cayenne pepper or sulphur entered my lungs. A feeling of constriction of the most painful nature across the chest, aggravated most intensely by every inspiratory effort, reduced the quantity of respired air to less than one-third its ordinary amount.

March 18th.—The thermometer exposed to the sun's rays rose to + 22° from — 26° in the shade, being the highest that had hitherto been observed this season. Soon after sunrise, two prismatic parhelia appeared on either side of the sun, at a distance of 22°, and continued till noon, when the sky became overcast, and the fine cirrus clouds gave way before threatening cumuli, mist, and a gloomy appearance of the atmosphere. Towards evening the wind was from S.E., and there was a little snow.

March 20th.—As one of our men was attempting to get hold of a seal he supposed he had shot dead in the water, he fell in and narrowly escaped being drowned, without capturing the prize he so eagerly grasped at. On his return in this wet state to the ships, several of his companions went out to the water, to make an attempt at getting the seal, but, like his, their endeavours also proved fruitless.

During the early part of the day cirrus clouds were spread over the sky towards the zenith, but along the horizon there was a misty haze which was partly caused by snow-drift. In the evening there was a prismatic halo around the sun, in which there was a deficiency on the western side. Towards night the wind increased, and blew keenly from northwest; the sky was clear and starry, and the thermometer fell to $-26°$ at 9 P.M. from $-10°$, which it was at at noon; the barometer had been rising gradually from 29·96 at noon, with the north wind. Our preparations for travelling were progressing fast towards completion, the boots and moccassins were all finished, and many other articles were brought in and approved of by the commanders.

March 23rd.—On the 21st and 22nd we experienced one of the most violent storms of the season. At 3 A.M., and since midnight of the 21st, there was a remarkably white appearance on the northern and north-eastern horizon over the land. Before 6 A.M. of the same day the gale commenced, the sky was overcast, and the snow fell fast, and, drifting in dense volumes which obscured objects even close at hand, it accumulated into dense wreaths which threatened to overwhelm our ships. The awning had to be cleared of that which collected on the lee side, for fear of accident from the increased weight: the deck, too, was very much encumbered by the snow that sought its way through even imperceptible chinks and fissures; but we were able to keep them clear by collecting it into heaps. The door or gangway was completely snowed up; and when we went into the open air, or returned from it, we had to pass through a large window in the awning on the quarter, which had a hinge door in it. At 2 P.M. the gale was at its acme, and then the thermometer was down to −41·75° or −42°, and the barometer was at 30·17. The wind veered at that time from northwest to north 22° west, and the barometer continued to rise steadily. There was a temporary lull at 7 P.M., when the wind veered again to northwest. On the following day, the 22nd, the gale moderated a little, and the temperature was up to −19°, having increased steadily since 2 P.M. yesterday, with the exception of a single deflection at 7 P.M., when there was a partial lull, followed by wind as strong as before. The wind came now in squalls, with intervals in which there was only a gentle breeze; the sky was still overcast and gloomy, and there were few or no signs of a return to decidedly better weather. To-day, however, there were signs of better weather, for we could discern distinct clouds on the sky, the wind had fallen to a force represented by 3, and the temperature was up to −13°, the barometer having descended considerably after rising to 30·335 during the gale.

The dogs had to be taken on board through fear

their kennel should become snowed up. One of the young ones had a deep cut several inches in length in its neck, which must have been inflicted by some of its own kind, in one of their constant struggles which should be master. The Esquimaux dogs must have a king among them; and when two separate packs, such as the two ships possessed, come together, they fight fiercely for which of the two sovereigns shall be in the ascendency; and if they are not interfered with, the dispute is settled, but this is only for a short time, if the two packs do not merge into one, in which case there will be but one king. If we rushed in to put down the riot, we were invariably successful, without any danger of being bitten; but ten to one if they did not resume it the moment we turned our backs upon them. In each pack the young dogs had a distinct understanding among themselves as to rank and prowess; and if the true and understood position of an individual became disputable in the least degree, it behoved to be settled by a keen engagement, which frequently resulted in the infliction of serious wounds. Their teeth are so sharp that the wounds they leave are scarcely discernible from wounds inflicted by sharp-pointed iron weapons.

During the violence of the gale, when the temperature was so remarkably low as 74° below the freezing point of water, frost-bite happened almost the instant any part of the bare skin was exposed to its influence. Owing to this, great caution was necessarily taken against undue exposure. Without incurring considerable risk in this way, it was found impossible to keep the tide line clear, every clearing requiring about five minutes, in which the individual thus engaged would be exposed to the concentrated violence of the blast as it swept around the ship's stern.

The equinox has been remarkable for violence of storms in point of severity and duration. The amount of snow which accumulated in the form of wreaths in sheltered parts was very great. Our ships bore testimony to this fact, for they were almost buried out of sight. About midships, the "Sophia" was so buried, that the dogs following the snow could run right over the ridge of the awning from side to side. This was cleared away as soon as the weather permitted. To account for the low temperature during the first and most severe half of the gale, and its gradual rise until it reached $-13°$ towards the termination of the gale, would prove exceedingly interesting if one could only be certain of being correct. The idea of far distant polynia, as the source of heat even in the depth of Arctic winter, was fully comprehended; but the low temperature at first, and gradually increasing subsequently, was an objection to the idea of open water to the northward being the cause, unless upon the supposition that the water, at the commencement of the gale, had on its surface a film of young ice, which, during easy weather, might retard evaporation and the escape of heat, but which during a violent storm would be broken up and drifted to the lee side of the water, leaving its surface exposed to the air, to which a great amount of heat would be imparted even by the congelation of a very small portion of the water. There are but two sources whence the increase of temperature could have come,—polynia more or less encumbered with drifting ice to the northward, and a more southern latitude. In the event of it being the latter, the northerly-going current of comparatively warm air, must have advanced northward at a considerable height above the earth's surface, to a much greater distance at the commencement than at the end of the gale. The air having passed over a greater extent of land or ice, which had been cooled down previously, would necessarily be colder than air passing over a less extensive refrigerating surface.

March 25th. For the first time this season, the sun's healthy rays were admitted into our dark, although candle-lit, cabins. The awning was traced up on the south side of the ship, and certainly the effect with which it was accompanied inspired every mind with feelings of gratitude for having been preserved from every harm, during days of violent storms, weeks of intense frost, and months of comparative darkness. The men were busily employed for a few days after the recent storm, clearing away the immense accumulations of snow which had threatened the safety of our awning for a longer time than could have been wished. In the evening, some of them went out to the water to shoot seals, after their usual custom in fine weather; but, to their dismay, not a drop of open water could be seen. Where they expected the recent gale should have made open water, by drifting the loose ice in a body to the opposite shore, there was an unbroken hummockless floe, varying in breadth from two to four miles, and extending westward in the direction of the south point of Griffith's Island, and eastward in the direction of Cape Hotham. During easy weather on the 18th, young ice formed on the water; but the loose pack moving about in Barrow Straits, and often coming in contact with the ice which lined the coast, squeezed up the young ice, and, shifting off, left open water. This happened throughout the whole winter as well as on the 18th. The wind prevailed for two days, chiefly from the eastward, and with the exception of moving to and fro a few hundred yards, the loose ice remained stationary; but when the violent gale of the 21st and the two subsequent days came on, the entire pack moved under its powerful influence to the southward, and pressed with equal violence on the south shore, as it would have done on the north shore had the wind been from the opposite quarter. The effect of such a decided shift of position, was a space of open water along the north shore of Barrow Straits, which, with the extremely low temperature during the gale, and the easy weather, and stillness of the pack subsequently, became covered over with a sheet of ice increasing rapidly in thickness, and acquiring sufficient strength in a few days to resist effectually the tendency to move, which the pack had enjoyed throughout the winter, and up to this time. If such a space of water as Barrow Straits, being only thirty-five miles, if so much, in breadth, can possess its polynia during winter, and a part of spring, by allowing the ice in it to drift about, there seems to be no reason why a less proportion of a space of water in a higher latitude, but of much greater extent, should not also remain open,—not throughout the winter months and up to the vernal equinox, but throughout the whole year, which includes the Arctic winter of perhaps ten months duration.

The ice formed on the 23rd was very rough on its upper surface, and a white efflorescence, abounding in saline matter, rendered walking over it rather heavy, especially if there was a thin coating of snow, which generally became very soft, and maintained this state independent of almost the lowest temperatures. There were brilliant parhelia and parhelic circles almost every day; and now the sun's rays had acquired sufficient power to melt snow on stones on the land, and on the black-painted bulwarks of the ships, although, in the shade, the thermometer was $-23°$ to $-28°$. The dogs could be seen basking in the hot sun on the south side of the ships, or licking the melting snow as the icicles formed, and drops of water called into existence but for a moment, trickled down the black-painted planking.

The only means the dogs possessed during winter of allaying their thirst, was by eating snow. They were frequently observed, during the early part of winter, burrowing to various depths, and lapping up the snow which had been taken from a depth of eight or ten inches beneath the surface. Now, with fine sunny weather, they licked it from the surface. The reason in both cases will be very obvious; and one cannot help admiring the instinct they displayed in thus choosing the material to allay their thirst which was sure to contain the least amount of cold. In cold weather the Esquimaux dog lies rolled up into a ball, with his muzzle deeply buried in the long and shaggy fur of his tail, which really imparts all the advantages of a respirator; and if there is snow, he never rises to shake the accumulating wreath from his side, or to clear the drifting snow which mats his hair. If he is accosted by his master, he deigns to open his eyes, but not to raise his head, or move a limb, unless the former persists in ordering his immediate attendance, or deals a kick, which is not unusual among the natives. In warm weather he lies stretched out at full length, and is up on his legs in a moment after he is called.

March 31*st.*—By this time our preparations for travelling had made great progress. Three sledges were ready to be packed. Some of the provisions were put up into packages suitable for *cachès;* and to preserve the bread from water, which might be expected to percolate through the soil before all the *cachès* would be taken up, we found gutta percha likely to suit very well. About twelve hundred and sixty pounds of boiled and "boned" pork would be required from our Expedition; and, to produce this quantity, at least sixteen hundred and fifty pounds of the raw meat would be necessary. It was not without great regret that we saw so much of our ship's stores using up; but this regret gave way before the fact, that, while using those now removed from the stores in the travelling parties, our stores on board ship would be spared. With the utmost care we could not expect but that our entire stock of provisions should be shortened from two to three months by the increased consumption dependent upon the travelling. We had remarkably fine weather for a few days. On the 28th, especially, the sky was remarkably clear; consequently, there was a correct view of the most distant objects. From the S.E. point of the harbour one could see the whole of the southern shore of Barrow Straits, from Cape Walker eastward to Leopold Island, and across to Cape Riley. From our feet stretching E. and W., and from shore to shore, nothing but one continuous sheet of ice lay before us without a single interruption. In vain did we look with our telescopes for seals upon it, or anything to break the spell of universal whiteness which pervaded it throughout its whole extent. There was no refraction, for the reason, that the air was not unequally heated. The snow which had fallen during the recent storm was of sufficient density to resist the sinking tendency of sledges; and, as a matter of course, this was very satisfactory to us, who expected to be very soon marching over it with ours laden heavily enough.

The maximum and minimum temperatures for the month were —4° and —41·75° on the 30th and 21st; and on the 28th the sun's rays received on Pastorelli's spirit of wine thermometer, raised it to +40°, while the air in the shade was −16°. We had numerous proofs that snow and shingle, with a southern slope, became heated considerably above the temperature of the ambient atmosphere in clear sunshine and calm weather. Plants, whose habitats are in such exposures in high latitudes, must possess immense advantages that would be denied to them in level plains.

April 3rd.—A party of two officers arrived from Griffith's Island, and reported favourably of the health of the squadron under the command of Captain Austin.

Great preparations were making for the intended routes which the parties proceeding from that squadron were to take. If there can be an excuse for repetition, I may state in detail, that Cape Walker, Bank's Land, Melville Island, and all the indentations eastward of the latter, in the North Georgian Islands, were to be examined, and no fewer than one hundred and twelve persons, and fourteen or sixteen sledges, were to be actively employed for two months at least in carrying out the great work of humanity. The time for starting had not been fixed when the officers left, but it was fully understood it would be early. The experience of Dr. Rae in travelling during cold weather (temperature −10°) was considered of great importance, and it seemed to merit being followed. There were few or none in our Expeditions in Assistance Bay, except one or two persons in the "Felix," who deviated from the general opinion, that there was nothing objectionable in leaving the ships early in April, for reasons that it was both safe and necessary if we desired to accomplish the object we had in view. The Wellington Channel was looked forward to by our crews with longing eyes, and great hopes were entertained our efforts should be carried out and sustained with spirit; and although it was a privilege we dared not expect nor demand, yet there were many secret, and perhaps some expressed, desires, that we should be the means, through Providence, of rescuing our long lost friends, or solving their fate. That we possessed those secret feelings, and expressed those desires, was not altogether incompatible with a faithful discharge of duty: indeed, in the eyes of not a few, it appeared essential; and, to be candid, I must acknowledge it was difficult, almost impossible, to be neutral, although it was very clear that the possession of those feelings led to a questioning of probabilities, which, in its turn, made the individual the unhappy slave of circumstances, destroyed his resignation, and ultimately assailed the strongholds of Hope.

April 5th.—Our three sledges were fully equipped

and ready to start, the crews of each were appointed long since, and each person had made his haversack preparations in his leisure hours. In supplying the sledges with all our requirements, the weight was never lost sight of; and even the tent poles and sledge runners, the most important parts of our outfits, were reduced to the least possible weight that could be considered compatible with strength and security.

The weather was always very favourable, although at times the sky was overcast, and there was a little snowdrift. Yesterday the thermometer in the shade rose to +2°, and on the preceding day it was +34° in the sun's rays. The temperature of the water had not varied for four months, except perhaps half a degree: and now it was 29·25°. In the glooming twilight, about ten o'clock, a bear was announced close to the ship's quarter: and certainly there he was, standing in the immediate vicinity of some casks which afforded shelter to the sleeping dogs. The old dogs fled to the top of the awning as the bear approached; but the young ones, I suppose not knowing any danger, stood eyeing him narrowly, while he as narrowly eyed them. In the short space of time in which we were certain he would take to his heels on seeing so many formidable enemies, only one gun could be got ready, and that was fired, but without effect, as the distance was too great. He set off at great speed; and as the dogs saw us sallying after him, they took courage, and were soon at his heels. They frequently brought him to bay, but he invariably got off before we could get up within rifle shot. The chase was kept up for two hours, but without success, owing to the faintness of the light and to the rapidity with which he distanced his eager pursuers, to whom his carcass would have been a prize worthy of a desperate struggle.

April 7th.—Captain Penny gave orders to prepare several bags of 120 to 180 lbs. each of dogs' food, to be taken out on the travelling parties. It was made of a large proportion of oatmeal mixed with melted fat, and a very small proportion, perhaps one-sixth or one-eighth, of "soup and boulli." The bags were made of canvas, adapted so as to lie quite flat, in which shape their contents were permitted to harden with the cold. There was no danger of fermentation taking place, so long as it remained in this frozen state; and before the temperature should rise so high as to thaw it, the greatest part of it would be used: the fat also would tend to retard fermentation among the meal. The use of much vegetable matter was very frequently hurtful to the poor brutes, but we had little else to give them. The young dogs, reared on board, suffered much less from it than the old ones which had been accustomed to different fare among the Danes and the Esquimaux of West Greenland.

April 8th. — The six fully equipped sledges were taken to the floe, and the crews of each were in readiness to try them. Each sledge had its name and number, the latter from one up to six. The names included such as these, with their mottoes: — "Union," *Dum spiro spero;* "Sylph," *Palmam qui meruit ferat;* "Perseverance," *Pas à pas on va bien loin;* and others which I forget. The flag of each sledge was hanging loosely to the pole, as there was no wind to blow it out. We all started at the same time; and, as may be supposed, no person lacked dragging, that he might, if possible, keep up with his neighbours: this, however, was found impossible, although the weights in each were nearly equal. No. 4. required eleven men to move on with the same ease, as seven men with No. 2.; No. 6. required eight men; and some of the others required less than their complement. After proceeding about half a mile from the ships, we made a large curve with the sledges, and commenced to return. Those which dragged heavily were allowed to come up, an exchange of crews took place, and then there was another fair start: the result was the same as before; for the same sledges again fell behind, although their crews had been changed. It was clearly proved that it was not a difference of strength between the crews that had been the cause of falling behind; all that the crew of No. 2. could do at No. 4. failed to keep it up with No. 2., which was dragged along very easily by the crew of No. 4. The eye could not detect any difference in the form of the runners of Nos. 2. and 4., but there was a difference; in the one the rise of the curve of the floor was not quite one-eighth of an inch to the foot; in the other, it was fully a quarter of an inch. In a sledge twelve feet long, the curves at each end occupying one foot, and for five feet on each side of the centre, the rise being one-sixteenth of an inch to the foot, seemed to be the model that suited best. Doubtless there is an exact proportion of length, to curve which, a sledge ought to have to carry a constant weight, with the least possible amount of friction, over snow of uniform resistance; in the same manner as there is a proper model for a ship, by which the resistance of the medium in which she moves is reduced to the lowest possible degree. The surface over which our sledges should have to move, varies in density; therefore, that model would suit best that could accommodate itself most easily to soft snow, hard snow, and ice. The carpenters received orders to alter the form of the runners of No. 4., making it, if possible, an exact resemblance of No. 2., which seemed to be the most perfect model among the six. It is a mistake to have the iron on the runners convex on the surface next the ice, for in this form it acts exactly like a wedge, and increases the friction very much; whereas, square or flat, the form used by the Danes, it rests upon, not in, the snow, and moves easily over it. The Danes and Esquimaux protect the runners of their sledges with bone, which is put on very neatly. Bone being highly porous becomes filled with ice, which gives it the character of nearly an icy surface.

The two officers belonging to the other squadron resolved to return to Griffith's Island, and Mr. Petersen accompanied them with the dog-sledge. The evening became a little misty; but there was not the slightest fear of them losing their way, for the dogs, having gone over the ground so often, knew it so well that they hardly required a touch of the whip during the whole journey. Mr. Petersen was the only person in our Expedition who could use the whip to the dogs. We often made attempts to learn the use of it, but they never were persisted in sufficiently to enable any of us sitting on the sledge to drive the dogs over a new and trackless journey.

April 9th. — Every day was most favourable for our preparations. The weather was generally fine; and when it happened to be stormy, our work on board went on very rapidly. At midnight there was now a long twilight, in which the thermometer in the open air could be read off with great correctness in clear weather. Last night the temperature fell to —21°, and laid a veto upon our intentions to start early. Sledge No. 4. was altered in the form of the runners, and also of the iron which protected them; the rise from the centre to the ends was reduced, and hoop was substituted for the iron of the hatch-batons, which the blacksmith had wrought up for that purpose. When it was reloaded and taken to the floe, we found that a great improvement had been made. After starting it, one person could continue moving it for a short distance, three persons could walk away with it at the greatest ease, and six stepped out with it with the utmost cheerfulness.

Mr. Petersen returned from Griffith's Island accompanied by Lieutenant Sherard Osborne, who reported favourably of all in that quarter. He said that they had been all ready to commence their journeys a few days previously, and that favourable weather would be the signal for starting within a very short notice.

A bear was seen in the entrance of the bay in the evening, and, as there was no necessity for haste, the greatest caution was used until guns and lances were in readiness. Men and dogs commenced the chase, and kept it up with great spirit for two hours. Poor bruin was brought to bay by the dogs, and wounded by the unerring aim of Mr. Petersen and Captain Stewart, and, escaping into a hollow on the top of a high citadel-like hummock, he stoutly defended his position, until, weakened by loss of blood, he yielded up his life to his more powerful pursuers, to whom his carcase, weighing six or seven hundredweight, proved an invaluable prize. A few days' good feeding upon bear's flesh would put the dogs into high spirits at the commencement of their journey; and, besides this, there would be at least two hundredweight of flesh without bones on each of their two sledges at the time of starting. I examined the stomach of the bear, and found nothing in it: the intestines also were quite empty, but the gall-bladder was tense with bile. The men who removed the skin from the carcase said that if the whole animal had been boiled down, six pounds of oil would not have been obtained. This is at variance with what is generally believed of polar bears, when they are supposed to be, as it were, buried in fat. If this one had been sucking his paw throughout the winter, it is not improbable that all the fat in his huge bulk had been sucked through it!

April 10th.—Mr. Petersen, who had accompanied Lieutenant Osborne to Griffith's Island, returned on the same day, having gone over at least forty-five to fifty miles. He brought from the "Resolute" a spirit of wine thermometer which Captain Austin was so kind as to let us have; and he reported that Mr. M'Dougall and his party, who had been sent out to examine the indentation between Bathurst and Cornwallis Islands, had returned, he believed, without completing the exploration upon which he had been sent, in consequence of finding that a depôt laid out in autumn had been disturbed and almost entirely destroyed by bears and foxes.

April 12th. — The anniversary of our day of sailing from Aberdeen would have been well commemorated by the commencement of our travelling; but, as it had been always observed that the weather became turbulent at the critical periods of full and change, it was resolved, that we should remain till Tuesday, the 15th. Mr. Petersen, whose opinion with respect to the weather always merited confidence, approved of this proposal, for his keen eye was beginning to perceive something portentous in the appearance of the sky. The temperature varied from $-7°$ to $-27°$, and the sky was cloudy: there was very little wind, and it was northerly. The barometer was very high and disposed to rise, having risen from 30·00 yesterday morning to 30·375.

The tide-line was discontinued by Captain Penny's orders, because there would be no persons on board to attend to it after forty-four had left upon travelling parties. It had been kept going since the 1st of October, with only one or two interruptions owing to bad weather. The merit of thus keeping it going is in great measure due to Mr. Mason, mate of the "Sophia," under whose superintendence it was begun and conducted. Although it was interrupted at present, we expected that on the return of some of the travelling parties it should again be set agoing, and kept in that state in the month of July, to ascertain the relative differences of rise and fall when the sea is covered with ice fixed from shore to shore, and when it is only partially covered with drifting ice.

It was resolved to commence our travelling in the daytime, contrary to the practice to be adopted in Captain Austin's parties. After being out a few days the change from day to night-travelling would be introduced by little and little as the men became inured to the change. Travelling by day would expose us to the risk of snow-blindness, and travelling by night would expose us to still greater risks of a greater evil—frost-bite,—which might happen during the dull hours of night, and not be discovered till next morning, when, in all probability, it should be too late. In speaking of conducting travelling parties, Captain Penny stated that he held those who had the charge of parties not only responsible for the duties of the parties, but also for their safety, for their health, and, above all, for their fingers and feet with respect to frost-bite. Our experience during winter proved very clearly that nothing but carelessness could be brought in as an excuse for frost-bite. He said he should charge not the suffering seaman, but the officer, with the carelessness of which any accidents of this description might be the result.

April 17th. — For a few days we had rather stormy weather, the wind, accompanied by snow, was from south-east, the sky was very much overcast, and the temperature having risen above zero was up at $+29°$, a degree of heat which we hardly expected so early, being $23°$ above what had been observed up to the same date in Sir Edward Parry's voyage to Melville Island. The snow which fell was soft and unresisting, both to men's feet and to the sledges. Although the temperature was high, the weather was very unfavourable for travelling, and we had reason for congratulating ourselves upon not having started on Tuesday. The crew of the "Felix," or a part of her crew, went with a sledge to Cape Hotham for some provisions and spirits from the depôt that had been left there by H. M. S. "Assistance" in Autumn, and, both going out and coming home, they experienced great difficulty from the disagreeably thick weather, and the softness of the snow. They returned early this morning, just as the weather began to improve, and we had come to the resolution of commencing our journey.

The whole of our crews—men and officers—assembled on board the "Lady Franklin" by Captain Penny's orders; and after prayers were read by him, and a few words were addressed to us with respect to our duties, we were ready to set out. There was not a drooping spirit among us, for every face beamed with delight, and each seemed to feel proud of the laborious duty upon which he was entering. The sledges were upon the floe with their flags flying, or rather drooping I should state, for there was very little wind to blow them out. The order of marching was according to the numbers of the sledges: No. 1. advancing, of which Captain Stewart had special charge; and No. 6., of which Mr. Reid had the charge, bringing up the rear; the other four being in the same line under the charge of the other officers of the Expedition. There was no distinction between the officers and the men in point of dragging, for the former were expected to pick out the best road, and drag at the same time. There was an exception to this, however, in the foremost sledge, for the person in charge of it had often to leave his track rope as the pioneer of the whole party.

The whole crew of the "Felix" accompanied us, and certainly the good feeling of the seamen of that ship towards their comrades in our expedition, and of Sir John Ross, Commander Phillips, Dr. Porteus, and Mr. Abernethy were fully displayed in the assistance they lent us crossing the rugged hummocks in the entrance of the bay, and in the three hearty cheers, and one more for good luck, with which they parted from us to return to their ship: Sir John Ross did not accompany us out of the bay: there is, however, an excuse for him at the advanced age of seventy-four. I shall never forget the venerable appearance of his grey locks, as he waved his hat, or fur cap, with its light blue veil, and joined heartily in the cheers of those we left on board.

The snow was very soft, for the temperature was up to +34° at noon, and +37° at 4 P.M., the first time this season it had risen above the freezing point of water. The smooth floe outside the hummocks was reached, and found to be very soft on its upper surface, and the snow on it, unless carefully collected from the very surface, when melted in our cooking apparatus, produced water which was sensibly salt, and could not be used with safety. The cause of this has been already observed.

Our first encampment was on the same floe, within

two miles of the land, eastward of Assistance Bay, at a distance of about seven miles, having travelled at least nine miles in seven hours and a half. Captain Penny and Mr. Petersen were to leave the ships in a day or two, and Mr. Manson, mate of the "Sophia," was to be left in charge of the ships, with only two persons, who were to attend to duties specified by Captain Penny.

CHAP. XVII.

TRAVELLING PARTIES.

First Encampment. — Difficulties. — Cape Hotham. — Deep Snow. — Eating Snow. — Barlow Inlet. — The Channel. — Prayers in the Open Air. — Hummocky Ice. — Violent Weather. — Snow-Blindness. — Darkened Tents. — Water freezing in Tents. — Depôt. — Fatigue Party sent back. — Frost-Bites avoided. — Precautions. — Point Delay. — Return of the entire Party. — Keen Appetites. — Weather in April. — Preparations. — Reports. — Travelling on the second Journey. — Upper Depôt. — Division of the Party. — Crossing the Channel. — President Bay. — Division of the Party. — Cape Grinnel. — Cape Osborne. — False Cairns. — Point Eden. — Baring Bay. — Hares burrowing. — Esquimaux Ruins. — Latitude and Bearings. — Character of the Seamen. — Point Davidson. — Point Hogarth. — Prince Alfred Bay. — Prince Albert Land. — Cape Simpkinson. — Return of the fatigue Party. — Seal Island. — Fissures in the Ice. — Birds. — Running Water. — Boots. — Stewart's Prospects. — Meet Captain Penny. — Open Water. — Parting. — Wading. — Stores exhausted. — Wet Ice. — Arrival. — Gloomy Aspect. — Indisposition. — Bill of Fare. — Captain Austin. — Death of Malcolm. — Report. — Return of Commander Phillips. — Set out again. — Meet Goodsir. — Difficulties. — Storm. — Advancing. — Forced to return. — Seals. — Arrived at Ships. — Stewart's Arrival. — Sir R. H. Inglis Bay. — Report to Captain Austin. — Health. — Party sets out. — Return. — Open Water at Cape Hotham.

April 18*th.* — Our encampment on the ice was exceedingly damp, and some of the blanket bags were a little wet after the moisture soaked through the canvas floor cloth and wolf-skin. This was a serious inconvenience, both with respect to comfortable blankets and the weight of our loads. The weight of each sledge was little below 1500 lbs., for a bag of dog's meat was placed upon each subsequent to their being loaded with the weights which have been enumerated in another place. The additional weight by accumulations of snow among our clothing, especially our great coats, and by the water soaking through the floor cloth from the wet floe, was felt on the sledges after one day's march. The sledge which I commanded had some of the nails in the iron on the runners started: by this our duties on the track-rope became all the more difficult, and we often fell astern of the other sledges in spite of our utmost efforts to keep up with them. The perspiration which flowed from us would really astonish a person already possessed of the idea that among ice, and exposed to low temperatures, we ought to feel cold. Thirst became unendurable, and the sledges had to be brought to a stand, to set the cooking vessels to work to prepare water. This was a feature in our travelling, for which no provision had been made in the way of fuel, and it was evident that what had been intended for only two meals a day could not prepare three. The tins which served as kettles required to be very carefully used; two were already thrown away as useless, from carelessness in putting in the snow when over the fire. Snow cannot be put in large quantities into a soldered vessel over the fire, at a temperature of something like $-20°$, for the water which the snow in contact with the bottom of the vessel produces becomes absorbed by the cold snow above it, and leaves the bottom of the vessel dry, in which state exposure to the heat of a flame, equal in size and heat to that of four or five candles, can hardly fail to melt the solder, and cause a leak.

In the course of the day we were overtaken by Captain Penny and Mr. Petersen with two dog sledges, and having followed up after them until we reached the farthest west of two table bluffs in the vicinity of Cape Hotham, we encamped on the smooth floe, close to the edge of the hummocks which lined the coast, and were two or three hundred yards in breadth at this point. The floe here was as soft as it was at our former encampment, and it evidently appeared to be ice of but one month's formation.

The men seemed to like this new life that they had begun to follow. Their jokes could be heard even when their thirst was excruciating, and when the sledges were sticking fast in the snow, or among the hummocks. The cooking was a duty which they took by routine, and the officer of each sledge was exempt from it. Each person had one day of cooking out of six. Sitting in the tent writing up my notes it was exceedingly amusing to hear the conversation in which the cooks engaged: it was a very common feature in their language to use irony, and always represent circumstances better than they were; for example, "Well, Lucas, how is your conjuror doing during this cold night among the drifting snow?" "Oh! it has just gone out three times, but I have managed to light it again; and now our fellows have had their second kettle; but how are you getting on yourself, Samuel, for you seem to have a comfortable shelter behind that bank of snow and hummocks?" "Yes, I have a comfortable place here; and I am just making off a little water, to be a drink in the tent, after we have had our smoke, for we have finished our hot pemmican and tea half an hour ago; but don't you hear them in that tent with the flute? Findlay tells me they have all turned in for the night." The truth was that not one of their conjurors had made the water lukewarm for the first kettle of tea, and there seemed to be no chance of having supper for probably two hours.

After the sledges halted and the tents were pitched, the officers went to reconnoitre the way round Cape Hotham. Some went in to the beach, and others went to the offing. Captain Stewart and I took the former route; and, after ascending to a height a little above the position of a flag-pole erected by H. M. S. "Assistance" in autumn, as a mark for the depôt, whence we commanded a view of several miles to the offing, we went to the eastward along the beach; thence, after striking through the hummocks, we went to the ice in the offing, where there appeared to be some floes of considerable extent among the much broken up ice. In vain did we endeavour to discover a connection between those floes, by which, threading our way, we might round the cape outside the heavy ice upon the beach. Mr. Petersen went still further eastward along the beach than any other person, except Captain Penny, and, from what he thought we had reason to expect, our route lay in that way, although he said the snow was rather deep in some places. When we returned to the tents, the supper was ready to be taken; and after a little conversation with the men about their feet and other parts exposed to the cold, we went to sleep. I am almost certain we forgot it was Good Friday, for I heard no person make mention of it. Perhaps it was not forgotten, although no person intruded his recollections of it, and the ideas he associated with respect to it, upon his neighbours on the track-ropes.

April 19th.—The morning was very gloomy, but not cold; the lowest temperature through the night was but +20°; the sky was overcast, and there was a slight fall of snow, but there was very little wind, so that we could get under way with our sledges, and be moving along. The dogs, during the night, broke into the sledge of which Mr. J. Stuart had the command, and scarcely left a trace of seventy pounds of bears' flesh. This, however, did them no harm, for it amounted to little more than four pounds to each. We had to regret the extravagant use of so much valuable meat, for the poor brutes had to feed for several days afterwards on the oatmeal and fat exclusively. After getting up and breakfasting the sledges were packed up, and our hard labour was commenced. Our course through the hummocks until we reached the beach was really difficult; twenty men to each sledge will give an idea of the relative roughness of the road; but the sailors always said that they would require "to put a stout heart to a stiff brae," and I have no doubt this helped us through many a deep wreath along the beach. Sledging is rendered much easier in bad roads by having an extra pull ready before the sledge comes to the sticking point. This can be easily explained by the inertia of the moving body being increased in proportion to the resistance.

To-day thirst was more intolerable than on either of the two previous days, but there was none of the men who attempted to allay it by eating snow, except one person, who soon got sick, and had to lag on behind the sledge to which he belonged. Of this, although I had abundance of sympathy for the poor man, I was very glad; for it was but the just reward of his rashness, and it proved a most wholesome warning to all whose weak control over themselves was liable to fail in resisting the temptation to act in disobedience to orders when they knew that no one could discover their fault.

After rounding Cape Hotham, and advancing within two miles of Barlow Inlet, we encamped for the day where Captain Penny and Mr. Petersen, having advanced with the dogs, had appointed. We had to regret the extreme thickness of the weather, for a view of the Wellington Channel, which we had just entered, was denied us: however, we expected the weather would soon clear up. The temperature was very high during the day, and snow falling upon our clothes and upon the sledges melted, but soon became frozen again. The temperature on board the ships in Assistance Bay at this time was so high, that water appeared in the beds and cabins to a great extent, and any snow that lay on the decks became quite soft. We hardly knew what to think of such a decided rise of temperature so early in the season: surely it could not continue to increase, until summer should establish it, at the rate which it had shown for nearly a week. If it should, we certainly would discover that we had not started early enough by one month. Towards night the snow thinned away a little, and the temperature fell with a gentle wind that came down the channel; the sky appeared as if disposed to clear up, and fond hopes were cherished that we should get a full view of the channel, from shore to shore, on the following morning.

April 20th. Easter Sunday. — Our expectations of seeing the land on the opposite side of the channel were fully realised, for it was plainly discernible from Cape Spencer several miles northward. A seal was seen upon the ice in the channel; it appeared to be exceedingly large, owing to a peculiar state of the atmosphere, in which distant objects appear very large, and as if they were at a great distance. This is the condition which proves most injurious to the eyes, and it seems to defy all sorts of preservative means, for neither neutral tint, nor black or green veils, afford even a slight compensation for undue exposure. With the exception of two ravens which we saw at Cape Hotham, perching upon the rugged precipices, and croaking portentously over us, dogs and all, as we passed underneath them, the seal was the only living creature we saw since leaving the ships. As we had no spare hands nor time, he was permitted to take his wind upon the ice, and to retire in peace into the water, which he had inhabited comfortably through the winter.

According to our intentions before commencing travelling, we started at a very early hour, for the purpose of bringing round night travelling, to prevent snow-blindness as much as possible. After getting breakfast, and packing up the sledges, just as we were about to put our belts over our shoulders, we were summoned together, by the orders of Captain Penny, to hear prayers read. The sailors all uncovered their heads, and appeared to be deeply attentive. No sight could be more appropriate; one and all invoking the Divine protection under the blue canopy of heaven, while, the vaulted arches of lofty and magnificent cathedrals, and the unceiled roofs and unsculptured walls of humble country churches, yielded their echoes to the words, "That it may please Thee to preserve all that travel by land or by water," as they issued from the hearts as well as from the lips of millions of devoted worshippers of Him the winds and the seas obey. What consolation ought we not to have received from the knowledge of this alone, that we were the objects of His care, to Whom ascended, specially in our behalf, the united prayers of Christendom. Although we had to drag heavily at the sledges, and had often to wipe the large drops of sweat from our faces as they trickled down our cheeks, while our friends and relations at home were meeting quietly, and greeting each other upon the joyful events of the day, we hoped humanity, whose glorious banners we had unfurled, would stand between us and every inculpation that might arise from our travelling on Sunday.

After getting to the northward of Barlow Inlet, at a short distance from the land, we came to a range of very rugged ice, which stretched to the opposite side of the channel, and appeared to present no means whatever of enabling us to advance northward, except by proceeding through them right in for the land. The ice to the southward of this range of hummocks was almost without a single hummock, and it evidently was of recent formation from the softness of its upper surface. In going through the fearfully rough ice between us and the land, we required twenty men to each sledge. One can easily conceive the danger the sledges were in while coming through such a "sea-way" of ice, now rising, as it were, on the crests of the waves, the runners resting on a mere point, and next moment sinking half out of sight in the wreaths, as if it were in the trough of the sea. The men had to make frequent journeys over the white snow; and, owing to this, some of them complained a good deal of not seeing very well. Indeed, this was very obvious from the tumbles they got among the snow. They had little or no pain, however, and I ardently hoped that a few hours of darkness would go far to relieve the congestion which, as yet, only applied to the nervous part of the eye. Our encampment was not on the land, although certainly we could have wished it very much, owing to the constant damp that was oozing through the canvas floor-cloth from the snow beneath, which evidently contained a large impregnation of saline matter. When I say large, I do not mean more than a mere trace compared with sea-water. A watch of one man was set to prevent the dogs doing any harm to the sledges. He had to remain out but half an hour, when he called some other person, and in this way the watching went on with the utmost harmony.

April 21*st.* — Last night the wind appeared disposed to come down the channel, and to increase in force; the temperature was falling, although not very rapidly, and the sky was very much overcast with blue and portentous clouds. Early this morning, however, it was beyond doubt impossible to face the strong north wind, and the penetrating drift. The tents were all formally called, and breakfast was prepared and taken, but the increasing violence of the weather forbade to start. Had the wind been behind us, we could have gone on well, or had it been in our sides, we might also have been moving; but directly a-head, we dared not attempt it with impunity. From bad it went on to worse; for at midnight the wind howled fiercely, and the drifting snow thickened the air, and sought into our tents, which were flapping about our ears, and shaking an impalpable snowy powder over our heads. The temperature of the tents was about $-16°$, while outside it was $-25°$. The poor men who complained merely of not seeing yesterday, had superadded to this to-day, violent pain and swelling in the eyes. The conjunctiva was deeply congested, and the eyelids were in a highly tumefied state. The most partial admission of light into the eye by separation of the eyelids, was accompanied by excruciating pain, as streams of water gushed from them, and became frozen upon the faces of the poor sufferers. Captain Stewart, who had to leave the sledges to pick out the best road, when we were under way yesterday and the previous day, suffered, I believe, more than any other person. He wore neutral tint glasses set in horn, very pretty things indeed, but quite unfit for what they were intended. The escape of vapour from the eyes caused an accumulation of hoar-frost around and on the glass and horn; but it extended to the skin around the eye, and often implicated the eyelashes, causing very great irritation. Besides the irritation which arose from particles of frost, there was also a heated state of the eye, owing to want of freedom in the circulation of the air. I believe both these difficulties may be diminished by the use of wire gauze instead of glass. Mr. Goodsir attended to as many of the men as belonged to the "Lady Franklin," and the remainder were under my charge. It was very clear that keeping them in the dark was a matter of the first importance. It could only be accomplished by each drawing himself into his blanket bag, or tying up his eyes with a napkin. Either mode was objectionable, because the eyes became over-heated; and the suggestion at once arose, that the cloth of the tents might have been tanned brown, like the sails of French fishing-vessels, or of some of the herring fishing-boats on the north coast of Scotland. This would not only be a relief to those whose eyes were already affected, but it would also prove an additional security to those that would be exposed to the same exciting cause during the hours of travelling. Wine of opium and water, made a collyrium which became very reputable; more, I dare say, from the fact that persons suffering, and very anxious to recover, must have recourse to means, than that it proves really useful. It was always made very weak, lest the assiduous application of a strong "wash," should prove hurtful instead of beneficial.

April 22nd. — The temperature was down to – 30° in the air, and – 25° in the tent. How water could be kept from freezing in the tents, when the temperature was 57° below the freezing point, is best known to those who made the attempt. A tin flask half full, which the person who had the cooking for the day took into his blanket bag, and a gutta percha flask holding two pints, which I took into my own blanket bag, and kept on the outside of my vest, within two folds of woollen cloth and my skin, became frozen quite hard, and it was not without considerable difficulty that we got the ice thawed out afterwards. The tin was put over the flame of the cooking apparatus, which soon dissolved the ice in it, but the gutta percha could not be so dealt with. One of the men tried one of the flasks in this way, and, as might be expected, the side of it opened out, so that it became useless. I took the one that belonged to my tent into my arm-pit for two or three successive nights, before the ice became all dissolved, the water being always removed as it was produced. As a detail of our proceedings will be found in the Appendix, I shall pass over it here, and merely touch upon the most important points in connection with it.

Captain Penny resolved that two of the sledges should be returned, for the provisions were disappearing in due proportion to the number of men, without any advance being made to the northward. As there were appearances of better weather, we turned out, and felt very much relieved by getting to our legs again. The snow still drifted about, but the blue sky could be seen, and that was a great relief to our eyes. After advancing a few miles northward, a depôt was made of the provisions in two sledges; one of them was exchanged for No. 4., which had received some damage, and after three hearty cheers, a section of the party was on its return, under the command of Mr. J. Stuart. Those who composed it were such persons as would be most useful on board the ships, and others who were affected with snow-blindness; but not all who were suffering from that severe complaint, for the confinement during the storm, and the disappearance of the misty snowy haze, followed by the reappearance of the vivifying azure tint, encouraged hopes that snow-blindness, bad as it might be for the time, was speedily recovered from, in healthy constitutions free from every scorbutic taint. After encamping a few hours at Cape Hotham, the returning party reached the ships in safety, with the exception of frost-bites, which only implicated the skin, and healed up in two or three days. They left the sledges, however, within three miles of the ships, and this looked a little as if they had been done up, which one might hardly wonder at after such fatiguing work.

On the 23rd, the weather proved still more favourable, both for travelling and for the eyes, than it had been on the previous day. Snow-blindness had entirely disappeared, but frost-bites of the cheeks and nose became very common, and it was not unfrequent in the feet, especially where leather boots had been used. One or two poor fellows had to cut off their boots piecemeal, but fortunately timely friction restored the circulation. Their feet were never exposed, so that the friction had to be applied by means of the hands over the stockings, which were generally pretty thick. We had proved very clearly, by what came under our observations at this time, the truth of Captain Penny's words, that it belonged to the officer of every party to watch over his men; and I am happy to observe they were watched over so carefully, that not so much as a finger nail was lost by one of them, although the temperature for three successive days was generally 60° below the freezing point of water. This care can be exercised without any hindrance to the party, nothing being easier than to ask the men who are moving within a few feet of their officer, also on the track-rope, if they feel their toes and fingers, and if they do not, then it will be proper to request them to count them by sensation. If this want of sensation does not disappear by increasing the motion of the feet and toes in the boots, which to be safe must be "roomy," it may be necessary to stop the sledge. This, however, with large canvas boots, such as we had, or carpet boots, or moccassins, in which the feet were at freedom, with three pairs of stockings, ought never to be necessary, and it happened in our party only where leather boots had been used as a trial. The strictest examination ought to be made after the tent is pitched, and every man ought to be inquired after individually, not omitting to be particular about the feet, for the hands and face speak for themselves. We had often heard glycerine vaunted as a specific in frost-bite, and we had seen it applied, even before the circulation had been restored, by placing the affected part in water, or by friction; such a course of treatment was worse than childish, for glycerine can only act beneficially on the same principle as hog's lard, by protecting parts where there may be abrasion of the cuticle, from the irritation arising from free exposure to the air. It was necessary to be very careful also with our drinking cups. Tin never suited, for it always adhered to the lips, and took a portion of the skin along with it. A dog attempting to lick a little fat from an iron shovel, stuck fast to it, and dragged it by means of his tongue, until, by a sudden effort, he got clear, leaving several inches of the skin and subjacent tissue on the cold metal. One of the seamen endeavouring to change the size of the eye of the splice in his track-rope, put the marling-spike, after the true sailor fashion, into his mouth; the result was, that he lost a great portion of the skin of his lips and tongue. Gutta percha suited remarkably well for drinking cups, for being a bad conductor of heat, it could be applied to the lips at almost any temperature, even when ice taken into the mouth adhered to the moist surface for a short time. The result of the constant application of the cold air, and the occasional application of cooled bodies to the lips, was excoriation to a very great extent, which entirely prevented laughing, and required the protection of a thick coating of hog's lard, in a good supply of which the stores of the medical officers were not deficient. I had a small tin box, which I carried in my pocket, and often sent round from one to another of my sledge crew while dragging, that they might renew the coating they had applied before starting. This practice often caused a laugh, from its resemblance to snuff-taking under more favourable circumstances. When we encamped, we found that the dog-sledges were about two and a half miles ahead of us, at a point which Captain Penny called Point Delay, from the circumstance that we had to come to a stand before coming up to where he then was. On the following day, after travelling north along the beach, inside the hummocks, a distance of probably seven miles, we encamped at the commencement of a fall of snow. After a consultation, it was decided we should return, for the reasons that our preparations were not so efficient as would make Arctic travelling safe. It was not easy for me to reconcile the necessity of returning with the extensive preparations we had made. There was, however, in the fuel, a decided deficiency which could hardly be overcome. The allowance of sugar and spirits, also, was too little; but we could get on with it. The cooking apparatus was very defective, and it was feared we should not be able to supply ourselves with better, even after returning. It was very clear that the short allowance of fuel was the chief cause of this unexpected event; and this brought the experiments I had conducted, to ascertain the amount of fuel that would be necessary, into disrepute. In making these experiments, we never had the slightest idea that thirst would have been so loud in its demands, without there being any chance that ever we should become inured to it. For two meals a-day there was a sufficiency of fuel; but the additional amount of water that was necessary, required at least as much fuel as the cooking. We might expect that the season, as it advanced, would have a warming effect upon the snow, so that less fuel would be necessary; but, even with this in view, we had too little by twenty pounds for each sledge.

Captain Penny and Mr. Petersen made a depôt of the provisions they had on the dog-sledges, and commenced their return the same evening, at 5 P.M., and arrived at the ships early on the following morning. Although the distance, as the sledges had to come, was not far below fifty miles, measuring it by latitude and longitude it would not exceed forty or forty-five miles.

Early next morning we made a depôt, and proceeded down the channel with two sledges, thirteen men to each. The walking was very cheerful, with the wind behind us, and the sledge light. In four hours we reached the depôt left by the two sledges that first returned, and at noon we took luncheon in Barlow Inlet, after we had passed beyond the high land on its north side. The sky at the time was divided into sections, which a number of parhelic circles cut out with the utmost beauty and regularity.

It was owing to the same cause as parhelia of the ordinary description, particles of frozen vapour floating thinly in the atmosphere, which polarize the light. After rounding Cape Hotham, and proceeding about five miles westward of it, we encamped for the night; and on the following day, the 26th, we arrived at the ships, where we were received with three hearty cheers from those who had come home before us. About an hour before coming into the harbour, when we were taking a refreshment, some of the men used soap and snow, for the purpose of removing a part of the thick coating of sooty matter from their hands and faces. The temperature at the time was $-8°$ or $-10°$, the result of which was, that patches of skin came off before this uncomfortable wash was over. It is generally believed that a frost-bite will be removed by being rubbed with snow: and so it will, if the snow be melting at the time; but if it be 40° below the freezing point, as was the case at this time, instead of "taking out the frost," to use a popular expression, it will send it farther in, and implicate parts which before were in a sound state. In applying snow to frostbitten parts, the temperature must be considered, otherwise the circulation may be retarded instead of being restored.

After coming on board the ships, we got refreshments in ample supplies, until our appetites, both with respect to "eatables" and "drinkables," were satisfied. It was astonishing how much each person could eat. I do not think it would be any exaggeration to say a pound and a quarter of preserved meat for the first meal; but probably some may have eaten three quarters of a pound more. There could not have been a better sign of the extreme fatigue and exhaustion which are inseparable from long-continued exercise at low temperatures. The day of our arrival being Saturday, no work was demanded of us; but plans were laid for the duties of the ensuing week, and expectations were entertained we should be able to start afresh, fully equipped, at the commencement of the following week. During the gale we experienced down channel on the 21st, 22nd, and 23rd, the temperatures, which were registered by Mr. Manson in Assistance Harbour, were a few degrees higher than those we had in the channel. They were nearly the same at the commencement and termination of the gale; but, during the violence of it, there was a considerable difference.

April 30th.—The winds during this month prevailed chiefly from the northward; but there were frequently smart gales from S.E. and S. The weather was generally clear with the former, and the temperature was low; but, with the latter, the weather was almost invariably dull and gloomy, and the temperature was comparatively high. The minimum was $-31°$, and the maximum $+37°$. On the 21st, the change was rather sudden; for, in less than twelve hours, the thermometer came down from $+5°$ to $-25°$ The results of this sudden change might have been disastrous to us at the time, for we were encamping on the open floe. On the day after we arrived at the ships, the weather was very violent, and we had reason to be thankful that we had returned. The temperature, however, was not so low by 9° as we had it on some of the days we were absent.

May 6th. — The sledges were refitted. Those that had been returned as unfit to be taken farther were repaired, and there appeared to be a great improvement in the model of No. 4. The runners were made a little higher by the addition of a strip of hard wood on the lower surface, which obviated any tendency the fir wood had to be "pitted" when crossing over rugged hummocks. This pitting of the under surface of the runners, would result in a slackening of the iron, and probably, also, the nails might draw. Iron bolts, passing through the whole depth of the runners, assisted to fasten on the iron, in addition to screw nails two inches in length. We regretted very much that we had not wood to make new sledges, for those we had were evidently too short by four feet, although they were all not less than twelve feet, with the exception of one, which was only eight. The refitting went on rapidly; and, after the first few days in May, we were ready to start with double allowance of fuel and spirits, and an additional half allowance of sugar. Our cooking apparatus was vastly improved by appropriating, for the benefit of the Expedition, two square tins, each holding a gallon and a half, which belonged to the cook of the "Sophia," and to which a casing was made of galvanised sheet iron, for which we were indebted to the kindness of Sir J. Ross. Every suggestion that could be made by way of improvement was carried out; even the wicks of the conjurors were not omitted. On the morning of this day a party returned which had gone from the "Felix" to Griffith's Island for supplies of provisions, and, if I mistake not, with a man who had relapsed into scurvy since the commencement of spring, after giving signs of recovery during winter. They brought reports of the return of some, if not most of the fatigue parties from the direction of Cape Walker and the S. shore of Bathurst Island; but no news of the missing ships. As every avenue to the discovery of Sir J. Franklin was closing up elsewhere, it was opening out in the Wellington Channel; and each in our Expedition looked forward to a rich harvest of discovery. We heard with exceeding regret of the numerous disasters by frost-bite which had occurred in the travelling parties from Captain Austin's expedition on the memorable days of April 21st, 22nd, and 23rd, when we were in the Wellington Channel. Although some of the sufferers had to be brought in on the sledges, and appeared to be alarmingly affected, mortification of some parts having already taken place, in the absence of a proper medical report we did not lay great stress upon the verbal statements which reached us, but rather looked upon them as exaggerations arising from the ugly appearance which frost-bitten parts assume after sloughing commences, even in slight cases, where only toes may be implicated. Like ourselves, they suffered from snow-blindness; and if the reports could be credited, much more than we did; for some individuals required to be led along for three or four successive days.

In the evening, as the weather proved favourable, and everything connected with our travelling was ready, we started, having first assembled on board the "Lady Franklin" for purposes mentioned elsewhere. When it was settled in the forenoon we should commence our journey in the evening, all hands were ordered to bed to refresh them for their nightly duty. The crew of the "Felix," as before, accompanied us to the outside of the south-east point, and after three hearty cheers we parted from them. Up to this time from leaving the ships, the drum was beating a-head of the foremost of the sledges, and the effect which accompanied the cheering sounds of even this rough species of music was very pleasant; however, sailors are not fastidious with respect to music and its refinements. The crews of five sledges were dragging three, making a complement of twelve to two, and eleven men to the third. This made walking very easy and not at all uncomfortable, at the rate of two and a half or three miles an hour. Our first encampment was at Cape Hotham, whence we were forced to send a man back to the ships for a floor-cloth, which No. 1. had forgotten to pack up before starting.

Captain Penny and Mr. Petersen were to follow us in a day or two, with the dogs and sledges as before. Before leaving Assistance Bay, we learned that the crew of the "Felix" were to make an overland journey to the north side of Cornwallis Island, if they should find it practicable. The party was to be under the command of Commander Phillips, and it was to set out on the 15th of May. They were to take advantage of frozen lakes or snow on the land, without which they would find it impossible to advance with sledges. To us it really appeared a hopeless task, depending so much upon chance, that little encouragement or inducement could be held out in entering upon it. If, however, the island should happen to be less than sixty miles in breadth, they might succeed in gaining its opposite shore, whence a view could be obtained of ice or land beyond it, as the case might be; but no hopes could be entertained of their being able to search the coast east or west, for their provisions would be all expended, except such as should be necessary for their return. Considering all the circumstances connected with it, I believe the party which was about to undertake it, deserved more credit than any other that set out upon the search. If the route was not encouraging, it was not their fault, and should it turn out satisfactory even to a limited extent, the more praise would be merited.

May 7th. — After a most comfortable sleep, preceded and followed by meals, which were both abundant and palatable from our new cooking apparatus, although at the expense of two and a half pounds of fat per day, we proceeded round Cape Hotham, and after manœuvring a bear without success, we proceeded to Barlow Inlet, where we took luncheon on the morning of the 8th; thence our course lay close along the beach, until we reached the lower depôt, where we encamped. The depôt had been disturbed by bears or foxes, or very probably by both, for they seem to be often in each other's company, if one can judge from the recent foot-prints. It snowed hard, but the tents were very warm, and there was not one among us whose face did not glow with satisfaction as the reeking pemmican was handed round, followed by a glass of rum, which invigorated us for the weary march. The depôt was repaired, and no waft was left upon it. When we started in the evening, the sails were got up, and some of the men sat upon their sledges occasionally, when the ice between the hummocks and the beach was smooth. On the following morning the other depôt was reached, and found to be quite safe.

May 9th.—After encamping, we had a comfortable sleep in our tents. Captain Penny and Mr. Petersen were heard shouting to their dogs, as they were flying over the ice and snow towards us. The dogs appeared to be glad to overtake us, for they generally met with a great deal of caressing and attention among the seamen.

The depôt was opened out, and every sledge selected its own materials. I had the "Perseverance" as before, and her weight, when fully packed, was fifteen hundred pounds, which included the forty pounds of fuel, in addition to the former allowance. After making some observations, and receiving a summary of our instructions from Captain Penny, we commenced our journey across the channel, having first gone up along the land for nearly two miles, until we came to a place favourable for embarking. This was opposite a deep cut in the land, where a large quantity of water must escape every season into the channel. On the south side of this broad ravine there is a low point, which Captain Penny called Point Separation, from the circumstance that the party here made its first division, according to previously arranged plans. Captain Stewart's division consisted of three sledges, one of which, under the command of Mr. J. Stuart, was to proceed to Beechey Island and Cape Hurd, from a point northward of Cape Bowden; the other two were to advance to the northward, following the line of coast E. or W., as it might be found trending. In all our operations a latitude was afforded, with which we might use freedom when the safety of the men was likely to suffer.

Mr. Goodsir's party was to keep along the west coast, and Captain Penny, accompanied by Mr. Petersen and one man, with the two dog-sledges, was to strike due north or keep to the westward, as circumstances might render it necessary. The divi-

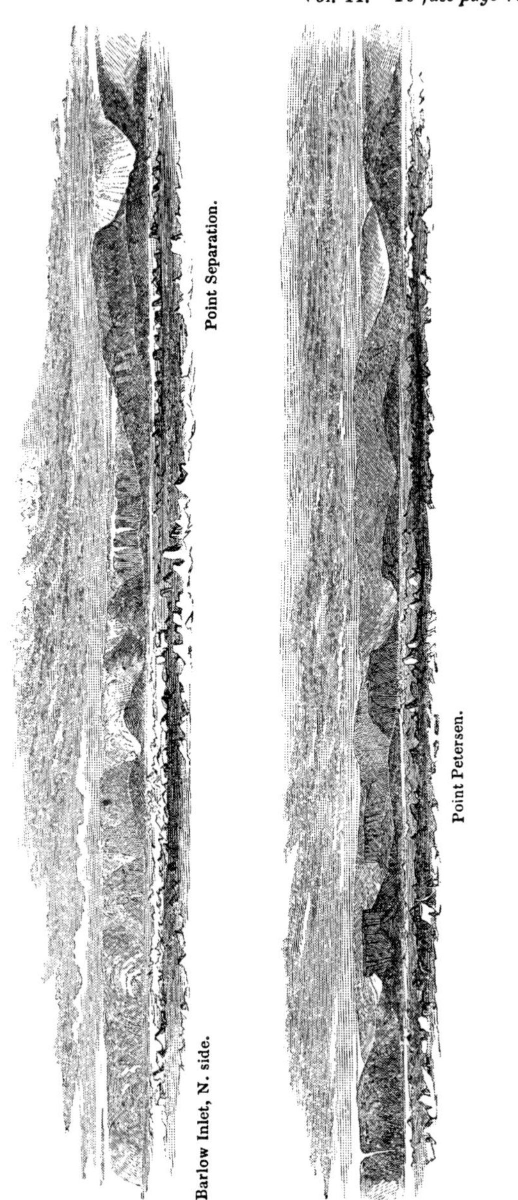

Barlow Inlet, N. side.

Point Separation.

Point Petersen.

sion under the command of Captain Stewart, to which I was attached, set the floor-cloths as sails, and were soon lost sight of by the other division, which kept close along the land.

May 13*th.*—In crossing the channel several floes of old ice had to be crossed. They were readily recognised by the appearance of the surface, and by the comparative freshness of the snow on it and of the ice itself, especially at the surface, upon which the sun must have been beating throughout the previous summer. When we arrived at the opposite side of the Wellington Channel, a bay was discovered on the north side of Cape Bowden, which was subsequently named President Bay by Captain Penny, after the president of the United States.* After making a small depôt for our return, Mr. J. Stuart, according to orders, parted company with us, and proceeded down the channel along the land, first exploring and surveying the bay. The depôt was made in a cairn of heavy stones, owing to that mode being more secure than the shingle; the latter, however, was frozen so hard together, by means of water percolating into it in the previous season, that one could hardly get a single

* I may state that the same thing obtained with respect to other newly discovered points and bays, &c., the names by which they are distinguished having been given by Captain Penny.

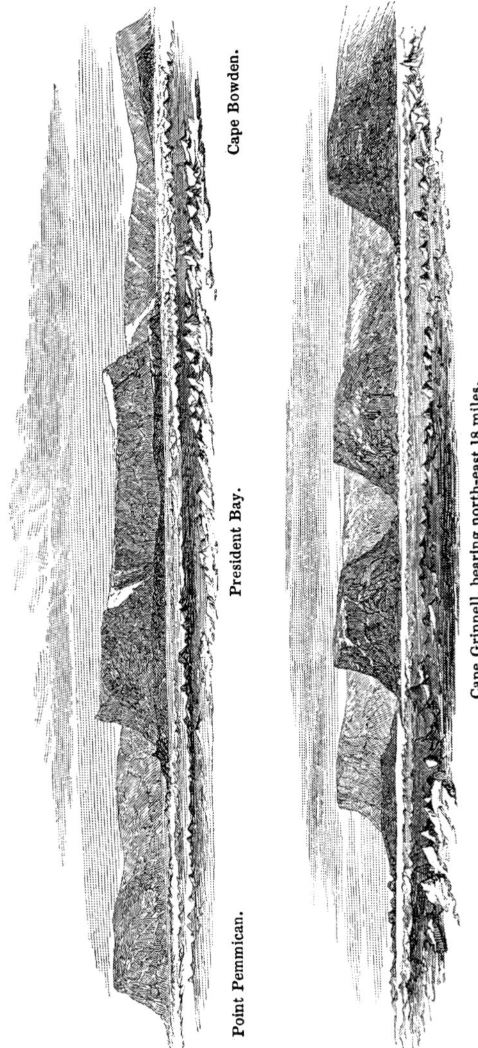

Cape Grinnell, bearing north-east 18 miles.

shovel full, even with the assiduous application of the pick-axe, which was in danger of being broken. Of Mr. J. Stuart's proceedings I shall take no farther notice, except that he arrived at Cape Hurd on the 22nd of May, and at the ships on the 6th of June, without finding any traces of the missing expedition. By the order in which he brought in the party under his command, and the manner in which the duty entrusted to his execution was discharged, the efficiency of the equipment of his party and their good behaviour, together with his own enthusiasm in the search, are fully displayed.

Our journey lay about due north, but trending a little westward, until, on the 14th, we were abreast of a point, which is the northernmost land that can be seen on the east side of the channel from Cape Bowden, or a continuation of the coast southward. From this point the land trends a little to the eastward of north, and on both sides of it, north and south, there are a great many bluffs or table hills, which have generally shallow bays between them; but sometimes they are so close together, that two appear to join; those we generally designated double bluffs. This point, which is a continuation of the talus of one of the bluffs, is in latitude 75° 17′, being about the narrowest part of the channel. It was named Cape Grinnell, after Henry Grinnell, Esq.,

New York, whose munificent liberality and earnestness in the search for Sir John Franklin, are well known. On the 15th, as we were about to start, a ptarmigan was seen flying in towards the land. This was the first bird we had seen this season, with the exception of the ravens at Cape Hotham. As we proceeded northward, Captain Stewart and I went in towards the land, and having travelled along it, a cairn was erected, and the usual note, of which a copy will be found in the reports in the Appendix, was left. The coast is in all respects the same as that extending eastward and northward of Beechey Island; bluffs and shingly beaches alternate with the utmost regularity. The ice leading along it was of one year's formation. Its surface was composed of a great number of angular fragments, which had been raised up by pressure, when there was but a thickness of two or three inches, or varying from that up to half a foot or foot. The ice, however, beneath this fragmentary surface, presented no such structure, but one continuous blue mass, which was generally about seven to eight feet thick.

In the evening we came to what appeared to be the northern extremity of the eastern boundary of Wellington Channel. This was called Cape Osborne after Lieutenant Sherard Osborne, an

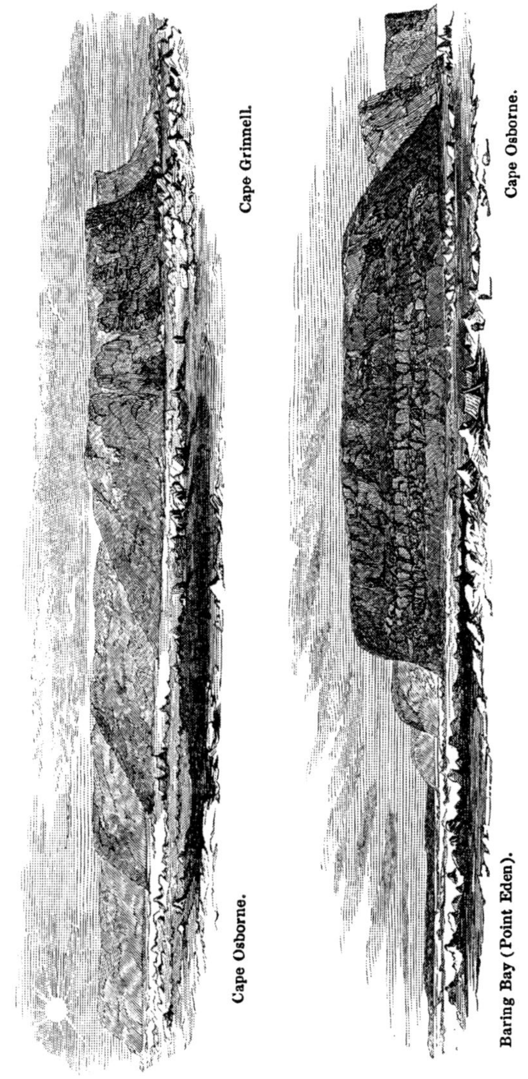
Cape Osborne.
Cape Grinnell.
Baring Bay (Point Eden).
Cape Osborne.

officer in H. M's. navy, and in command of one of the ships of Captain Austin's squadron. From this headland, which is in latitude 75° 27′ or 30′ (there being no observation at the time, owing to thick weather), we could see another point bearing about north-east, which was named after Captain Eden, private secretary of the First Lord of the Admiralty. The ice around Cape Osborne was exceedingly hummocky, some of them being at least thirty feet above the level of the water. They appeared to have been thus raised from their bed in autumn. A very good proof of this will be found in the fact that fresh-water ice was found among them, which was only three to four inches in thickness. The ice of last season did not all dissolve, nor did it drift out of those seas; and as the large floes with pools of fresh water upon them, part of which became frozen over, were carried by the drifting process against the land, the fresh-water ice could not escape being piled up along with the ice upon which it was borne along. After the severe frost of October had set in, it appears to me, from the smooth floe on the outside of the squeezed up hummocks on the beach, that the whole pack north-west of Cape Osborne shifted westward. This shift might have been much later, however, than the end of October, for the smooth ice referred to as the result of it might present similar features even if it had formed in November or December.

The land changed its aspect a little as we advanced eastward; the bold terraces were exchanged for sloping and undulating beaches rising gradually to a height inland equal to that of the table bluffs. It was not unfrequent to be deceived by cairn-like resemblances of hard limestone, which protruded above the surface. If one of those appearances continued to be conical all the time that it remained in sight, after its bearing had been considerably changed as we walked on, we could not rest satisfied without examining it. The seamen were afforded amusement by the wild goose chases their officers had after cairns. I had many times great difficulty in recognising, after reaching the land and the whereabouts, the objects that had attracted me away from the party. After passing some enormous blocks of ice, at least thirty feet above the surface of the water, our day's work being done, we encamped, and a party of two, of whom I happened to be one, went to the land to erect a cairn, by the orders of Captain Stewart, who had to remain at the encampment to take observations, for latitude, &c. &c., as the weather was very clear. After reaching Point Eden, I erected the cairn and left the note. To the eastward of this point there is a splendid bay, which was called after the Right Honourable Sir Francis T. Baring, the First Lord of the Admiralty. From an elevation of two hundred and fifty feet, in latitude 75° 32′, I could see no land extending across the top of Wellington Channel, a circumstance which we were led to think of by the report which we had from H. M. S. "Assistance," together with the report of Mr. Manson on the 26th August 1850. From the same point I could see the land on the west side of Wellington Channel trending to the westward until it dipped beneath the horizon. A ptarmigan and a hare were seen and fired at, but not shot. The hares burrow in the snow; one burrow which I saw measured eight feet in length in a southern exposure, but it never was more than five or six inches beneath the surface. From the appearance of the snow which must have been removed in the process of excavation, it was my impression that the burrow had been open during winter, and this will give rise to the idea that the creature which inhabited it remained in its neighbourhood throughout the winter. The bones of whales found imbedded in the frozen shingle or soil, at a height of two hundred and fifty feet above the sea level, and the cooking places of the Esquimaux long since deserted, can be associated, and the same date can be applied to both. It may appear strange that the Esquimaux should remove to so great a height the refuse of their labours. Such a procedure is quite at variance with what is known of this race at the present time. They might, however, have laid them out to that distance to be a sort of trap for foxes; or probably wolves might have dragged them to places where they could pick them clean, or gnaw them at their leisure, without molestation from persons at the encampments, which appeared to have been at the beach.

On the following day, the 17th, the latitude was 75° 41′; it was 75° 34′ on the previous day. By means of latitudes, which could be depended upon, as being correct within a mile or two, and by bearings from the sun, which guides without permitting any chance of error, there was no difficulty in ascertaining the distances travelled, and our watches, including a chronometer, for which we were indebted to the kindness of Sir John Ross, afforded the time, which enabled us to make out our rate of travelling per hour. Till now I never knew by experience what snow-blindness was. When one requires to haul at the sledge and be led at the same time, he must guard against sprains and fractures, as he plods over the rough hummocks, and goes to his knees among the snow in fissures in the level ice. On the 18th my sledge got out of order, and came to a dead stand. It was unpacked, and two of the stretchers or cross bars were found broken in the middle. They were soon repaired, however, and after resuming our march, in a few hours we landed on the north-east side of Baring Bay, at a distance of one hundred and fifty miles from the ships. Here we laid down a depôt of five days' provisions, and several other things which could be spared, such as sea boots and foul clothes. It was remarkable with what eagerness the seamen rid themselves of everything cumbersome for the purpose of lightening the sledges. To say the least of them, they behaved very well indeed on all occasions. One thing which we had doubts about before leaving the ships the first time was spirits; this, however, we found as safe in the keeping of the men as if it were under lock and key. They have a thorough understanding with respect to equal right, and to freedom from partial dealings. This is well exemplified in the system they often adopt of sharing out by lot their messes, or anything among them requiring impartial division.

May 19th.—This was a day in which our march had to be cut short owing to violence of weather, and the following day was, if possible, worse, about twelve miles being all that had been accomplished in two days. On the 21st we were able to move onwards, and in two hours' march we came to a point where there are a great number of Esquimaux ruins. It has a very rough appearance when viewed from the southward, and there is a ravine about three miles eastward of it: following it still further in the same direction, it merges gradually into the flat undulating land in the bottom of Baring Bay. It was named Point Davidson, after a gentleman well known in Aberdeen, who has been long connected with the Union Whale-fishing Company of that city. To the westward of Point Davidson we observed the resemblance of an island, but the weather again became quite thick in

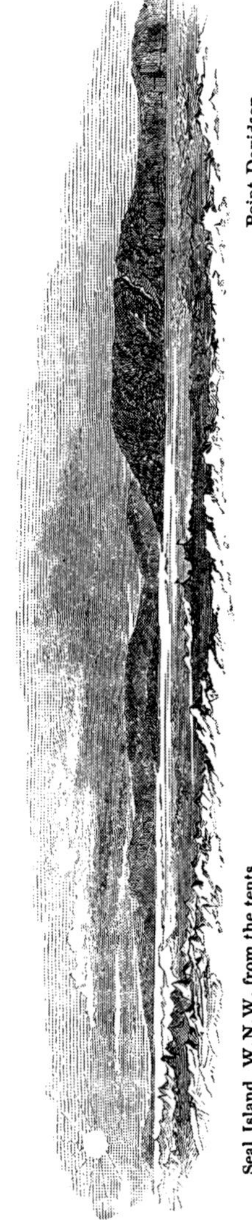

Seal Island, W.N.W. from the tents.

a few minutes, and caught it away from us before we had a glimpse of it. After making a circuit of a deflection of the coast beyond Point Davidson, and after arriving at a blunt point, where we encamped, we again saw it bearing south. The latitude of the encampment was 75° 55′. The observations were very good, for the sky cleared up, and the horizon became quite distinct before mid-day. The men were at this time remarkably cheerful; each washed his face and hands with soap and snow. The snow melted with the heat of the hands and face sufficiently to make a good lather; and although a little remained undissolved, its roughness and coldness increased the glowing heat and redness which followed. The temperature was up to +31°. On the 22nd we crossed a long flat beach, which extended several miles inland, but never lost sight of the hummocks at the outside of it. By their assistance in pointing out the coast line, there was no danger whatever of falling into a mistake with respect to which was beach and which was sea, as we afterwards learned had happened to some of the parties from Captain Austin's squadron. Some of the hummocks appeared to be raised to an elevation of forty feet; and, what is more important still, the pressure to have effected this must have come from about west, and at some period since the beginning of last autumn. On the 23rd we were again detained on the beach in latitude by observation 76° 3′. The weather was very bad indeed, and the snow drifted with great violence. We often thought the extra *spells* we had of the blanket bags did no good, but, on the contrary, great harm, for every person was as stiff as possible after twelve or twenty-four hours' detention.

May 24th. The weather cleared up, and being the Queen's birthday, we were not behind our neighbours in wishing our beloved sovereign a long and a happy reign. About two hours after starting, we came to a low point, where we built a cairn with stones from Esquimaux ruins, which were very numerous. The point was named after William Hogarth, Esq., Aberdeen, to whom our Expedition was deeply indebted, as has been already noticed. It is the southern boundary of a magnificent bay, twenty miles in breadth, and three fourths of that in depth, which was called Prince Alfred Bay, after the youthful scion of the Royal Family. The ice in this bay was very thick: in some parts along the eastern side it was not less than thirteen feet, and closer still to the land it was fourteen to fifteen feet. Such an enormous thickness does not indicate degrees of cold, so much as stillness of water. The latitude at noon where we encamped was 76° 9′, making Point Hogarth in 76° 5′, or thereabout. On the two following days we were crossing Prince Alfred Bay, and after a few hours' march on the 26th, we encamped within five miles of land, stretching to the westward in latitude 76° 25′. The coast does not present a straight line; the deflections occasionally vary in latitude from 5′ to 7′. The newly discovered land was visited and taken possession of; but it is doubtful to whom the honour of naming it belongs, if it be the same land seen by Captain Ommanney of H. M. S. Assistance and Mr. Manson, mate of the Sophia, on the 26th August 1850. This matters little, so long as it bears the illustrious name of His Royal Highness Prince Albert, with which Captain Ommanney honoured his discovery. If the expedition under the command of Mr. Penny cannot claim the privilege of naming it, it can that of exploring it, and, so far as we know, of first landing upon it. Several hares were seen the moment we landed, and two of them were obtained subsequently. Very extensive Esquimaux ruins were observed, and, among the stones, Arctic plants were beginning to put out their green leaves. During a very sunny day some of our men went to the land, and saw the

Land at the bottom of Prince Alfred Bay.

Distant view of Prince Albert Land. Taken from Point Hogarth.

larvæ of *Lepidoptera* creeping over the mosses and lichens. One of the lichens observed was of a beautiful orange colour (*Lecanora elegans*), and, being abundant, it variegated the rocks very much, and produced a highly picturesque appearance. The bottom of Prince Alfred Bay is surrounded by very rugged land, in which the salient and retiring angles are very distinct. In one part, the depression is so great, that rather a close view is necessary before the land is discovered, closing up the bay to the eastward. From the bottom of this bay, the land trends away about west, at first a little rugged, then presenting two large table bluffs, with intervening shallow bays, after which there is a gently sloping point, which has been called Cape Simpkinson, after the late Sir Francis Simpkinson, a near relation of Lady Franklin.

After considering matters fully, Mr. Stewart came to the resolution of filling up the "Perseverance," and sending me to the ships with the "Sylph," with orders to examine the bottom of Prince Alfred Bay and the island on the north side of Baring Bay. On the 28th, after completing the arrangements that were necessary, with parting cheers each took his route. In the bottom of Prince Alfred Bay, and at Point Hogarth, I met with limestone of a much more compact structure than any that had hitherto been seen in North Devon. Perhaps a formation slightly different commences at Point Hogarth, and runs north-eastward until it merges into the rugged hills at the bottom of Prince Alfred Bay, which not only bound and close in this bay to the westward, but may also close in Jones Sound to the eastward, or deflect it northward from its apparently western course. After examining the bay and crossing the point, we made the best of our way, in thick snowy weather, to the island, which we reached on the 31st of May, and where we were detained by a southerly storm for nearly two days. The island is in latitude 75° 49′, about three miles westward of Point Davidson. Its greatest length is from east to west, and, from the circumstance of seeing a seal upon the ice near its western extremity, the best name it can get is Seal Island. On the 2nd of June the depôt in Baring Bay was reached, and thence we proceeded towards Cape Osborne, which we rounded on the 5th, and proceeded down the Wellington Channel, where we encountered severe gales of southerly winds, accompanied by soft snow. On the 6th we came to several cracks in the ice about six miles south of Cape Osborne. Some of them were upwards of eighteen inches wide, and the ice was not less than nine feet in thickness. We observed at one of the cracks which led off from the land several sea-fowl, such as glaucous (two of which species were seen on the 28th of May in Prince Alfred Bay, flying eastward), Sabine and ivory gulls, and other birds, such as ducks, brent geese, &c., were on their flight up the Channel. Bears and foxes, too, were on their way up the Channel, several of both having been frequently seen; indeed, sometimes much oftener than the seamen had any desire. Our tent became a temporary shower-bath on one occasion, from the snow melting outside, and passing through it. This was the first time we had observed the mean temperature at +32°. Our second depôt, on the north side of President Bay, was found to be in safety; and, after being detained a single day through bad weather, we commenced our march across the channel, direct for Point Separation, where we arrived on the 11th. The ice in the Channel was beginning to assume a blue appearance, especially where it was of one year's growth; but the old ice did not so readily yield to the temperature, which was hardly sufficiently high to melt fresh snow or fresh water ice, which the old ice so much resembles in that particular. Our blanket bags were quite wet; and those of the party who could spare a few hours to dry them in the sun, were

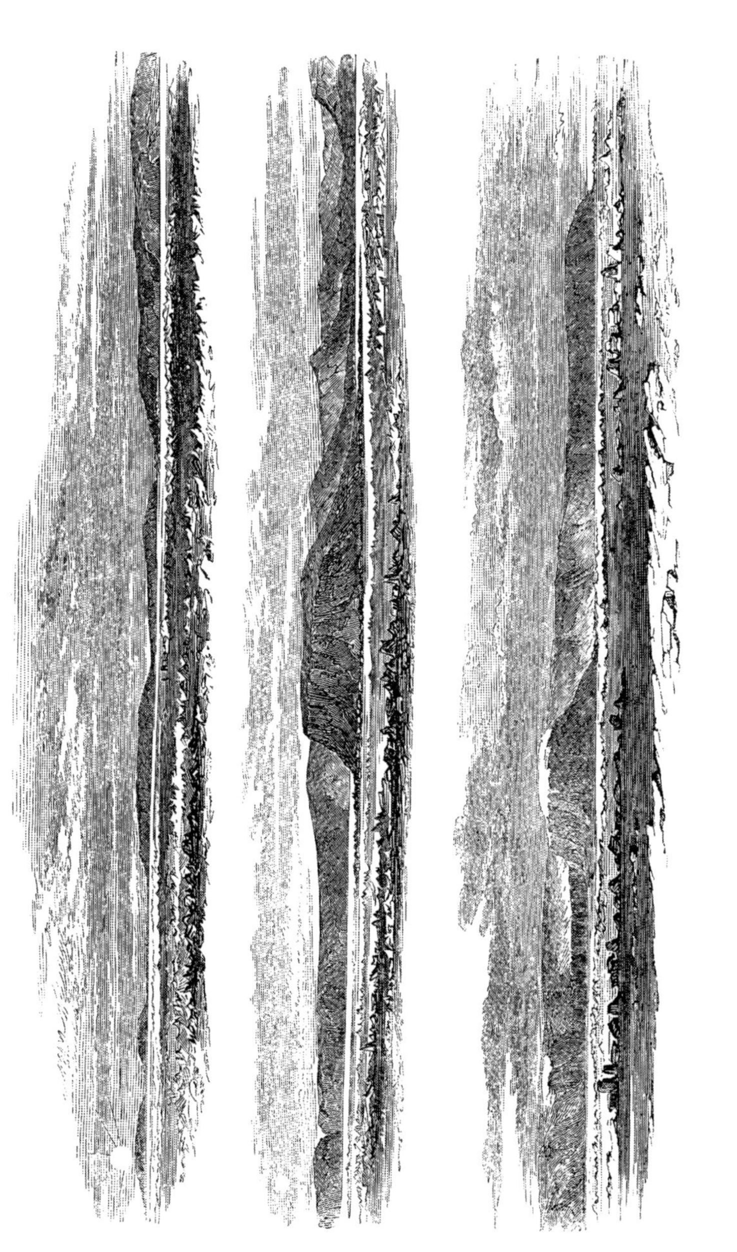

wisely enough employed. Our stockings were now beginning to be in great demand, for our feet generally became soaking wet in less than an hour after the commencement of every march, and they continued in that state until we encamped, when, of course, it would be highly desirable to put on something dry, suppose it were only a pair of blanket squares. It was not uncommon to keep the wet stockings for wet use, and the dry for the blanket bags. The sensation was rather a chilly one, when the wet, and, perhaps, frozen, stockings had to be put on in the morning. No boots of any description kept out the water. Leather, if possible, was worse than the canvas moccassin, for it retained the water which transuded through it; but the latter allowed it to pass through as it entered. India rubber boots, such as are prepared by Cording, I believe, may suit well; for that substance is not permeable by water so long as it continues without holes. Next to india-rubber, seal-skin moccassins or boots suit very well; but only so long as the oil remains in the substance of the skin, after which they become as porous as ordinary leather. I have seen the Esquimaux on the west coast of Davis Straits, after a journey over the wet ice, require to take off their boots, and wring the wet wrappings of their feet. These wrappings were generally birds' skins, which, I must acknowledge, were not improved in appearance by the process of wringing. I know nothing connected with Arctic travelling so insurmountable, and that has such a bad effect upon men, as having to walk with wet feet: they may, and doubtless must, keep them somewhat comfortable, by walking smartly, but they cannot keep them warm; and although it is a nice thing to wet one's feet at the commencement of a long day's journey over land, during which they will dry before night as perfectly as if they had never been wet, it is quite a different affair among snow and water; and, however little men may make of it at the time, it produces, if long continued, lasting impressions upon the strongest and most hardy constitutions. If travelling in those regions must be conducted on an extensive scale, such as from Lancaster Sound to Behring's Straits, it must be begun early, if boats are not to be used; and even with boats, it would be a good thing to be early out, on account of the clear and dry weather.

When we were collecting the scattered remains of a small depôt that had been left for our return, and raising up stones to erect a cairn, a great number of small insects were observed on the under surface of the stones, where their cocoons could be seen in abundance. There were, at least, three species; and some of them were so small that it was difficult to detect them with the naked eye. One of the species appeared to belong to the family *Thysanoura*, and to the genus *Podura;* a description of which, and other specimens of natural history, will appear in another place.* The temperature at noon in the shade was very high, probably owing to the high and almost overhanging cliffs in the immediate neighbourhood. The early and perfect development of the insects may be owing to a local high temperature. I left a note in the cairn intimating the route that had been pursued by Captain Stewart's party; but we had no idea where the parties might be who followed the western route until the morning of the 12th, when we met our commander on his way up the channel with a whale-boat mounted on a sledge, to examine several islands surrounded by water, which he discovered on the 16th of May. His party consisted of twenty men, who were divided between two ordinary sledges with provisions and the boat; two men, however, had to attend to the two dog sledges, which also carried provisions. It will be obvious, as only three or four persons were left on

* For the names of these insects I am indebted to the kindness of Adam White, Esq., of the British Museum.

board the ships when we commenced our travelling in May, that so large a party could be made up only by the return of part of the western party and the party that had gone to Cape Hurd. Mr. I. Leiper, second mate of the "Lady Franklin," who commanded Mr. Goodsir's fatigue party, was detached on the 22nd of May, and arrived on the 29th of the same month. The whole party appeared to be in high spirits; so high, indeed, that although the duty they had commenced looked formidable in the face of even twice their number, they seemed to think the boat would be launched into the water in a few days. In my party we thought we had been doing wonders, boasting of our miles and our encounters with bears; but all our doings sunk into insignificance before the gigantic task of taking a heavy whale-boat over upwards of one hundred miles of rough and hummocky ice before it could be launched into the water. Some of my party volunteered to join Captain Penny; but he could not receive them, owing to the difference even a few additional persons would make to the provisions of his party. He gave me orders, however, that we should follow up his party, with provisions to be left as depôts for his and Captain Stewart's return, along the coast from the lower depôt up to the N.E. point of Cornwallis Island. I furnished Captain Penny with a verbal abstract of the proceedings of the party from which I had been detached, and a rough tracing of the coast that had been discovered up to the time I had parted with Captain Stewart. I also gave what information I possessed with respect to Captain Stewart's intentions. When I stated that he intended to proceed westward or northward, as the land might lead, and the safety of his party permitted, with provisions of which he could avail himself for thirty-seven days' longer absence from the ships, Captain Penny at once said that a few days' march from Cape Simpkinson would bring him to the water, which would put an end to his journey, and force him to return. This was to be regretted very much; but we expected that the boat would reach the water in safety, and accomplish what we should have done with our sledges, to the extent of four hundred miles from our ships, had not the most unexpected presence of water without ice disconcerted all our plans. What did Wrangell say when he stood on the edge of the ice with the blue and open sea at his feet, the limits of which were beyond the powers of vision? The same hopeless prospect presented itself to all our advancing sledge parties; but here, mounted on a sledge, there were the means to overcome that hopelessness, so far as might be consistent with the advanced state of the season.*

At 8 P.M. both parties were under way, and, after three hearty cheers on both sides, and one more on mine for good luck to the hearty fellows who were yoking themselves to the boat, and whom we really envied, we parted, and, as evening advanced, my party crossed Barlow Inlet, and proceeded onwards to Cape Hotham. The weather was not unpleasant, for the sky was clear, and there was very little wind. In the shade of the high land on the north side of Barlow Inlet, and again at Cape Hotham, everything around us assumed a very gloomy appearance, and would have imparted the same to us, had it not been for the amusement which was afforded, when some of us, and not unfrequently all, had to wade through water, with ice in the bottom of it, which often came over the tops of our sea-boots, and required our great coats to be tucked up, to save them from the water. The constant renewal of the water to our feet precluded the possibility of their ever becoming warm; if, however, by walking fast over snow, which sometimes had to be crossed, they began to be com-

* For an account of Captain Penny's sledge and boat expeditions see the following chapter, which is almost a copy of the journal he kept.

fortably warm, it was only to be plunged into the water, probably deeper than before. It was most amusing to see how they fared who took to either of the sides where there was shallow water, when a sudden increase in depth had to be crossed; their track ropes were tight, the sledge was moving along, and there was no alternative but to dash onwards, through thick and thin, heedless of everything, except tumbles and coat-tails. The accumulation of water so close to the beach was owing to a ridge of heavy ice, which pressure had raised up on the beach, at the water-marks in autumn, and which caused a lodgment of the water set free in the almost perpendicular cliffs above. As the hummocks, however, disappeared with the advance of the thaw, the water established channels, by which it made its way through them into the sea. Our case, now contrasted with what it had been but six weeks previously, when intense thirst had to be endured, and not a drop of water could be obtained, except what we prepared by artificial means from snow or ice; not only had we as much as we could drink now, but also a sufficient depth and extent for a bathe, had we been inclined to luxuriate to so great an extent in the element, which for a time had been sealed from us.

On the 13th, at an early hour in the morning, we

encamped at Cape Hotham, and, after a most comfortable sleep and a meal, which exhausted the last of our stores, we started in the evening for the ships. The sky became overcast, and the two bluffs, westward of Cape Hotham, were enveloped in dense blue clouds, which I had never before seen on Cornwallis Island, and reminded me of another climate. Although they were surly enough looking, yet the resemblance they had to what our eyes had been accustomed to among the hills on the sea-coast of Great Britain had a genial effect upon our minds as light showers of rain fell around us. At the time of starting, we were overtaken by a dog-sledge, accompanied by Mr. Petersen, who was unwell, and Mr. J. Stuart, on their way to the ships, which they reached two hours before us. The ice seemed to have been covered with a little water a few days previously; but, being of recent formation, and having thawed early on the surface, on that account it became permeable, and readily transmitted the water through its substance. There were several small cracks W. of Cape Hotham, which we crossed very easily, for the ice was about four feet thick. These were the only cracks we had seen in the ice in the channel, or Barrow Straits, except those seen at or near Cape Osborne on the 5th and 6th of this month. On coming into Assistance Bay the ice there, which was seven feet nine inches thick, was covered with one continuous sheet of water, which varied in depth from one to six or eight inches. Where there were hummocks, they were surrounded on all sides with water, and the snow, which had accumulated in their shelter during winter, was so soft, that not unfrequently did we sink to the middle, when our way lay through them. Every thing in Assistance Bay had a dismal aspect; the land around it was of a black appearance, except where there were patches of snow in hollows; and it too had lost its whiteness, owing to the upper part having thawed, and left the dust, &c., exposed that had been blown into it during winter. The hills were enveloped in thick misty clouds, and there was a sort of vapour falling, which puzzled one to conclude whether it was snow or rain: the thermometer, however, being at + 39°, left no doubt that it was rain. The ships looked exceedingly black and out of sorts, and the snow and ice all round them, for twenty or thirty yards, was covered with filth of all description —straw, fragments of shingle, meat, tin, iron hoops, that became buried in the snow, or were thrown away as useless, several heaps of ashes, and the sites of the dog's kennels.

During winter and spring every thing around us was as neat as one could have wished, to make it pleasant to the eye. We had convenient closets upon the ice, and we thought that great attention had been paid to keeping the ships and the space around them free from accumulations of extraneous material. But the searching influence of summer brought to light so much that the white surface of the snow became almost entirely hid out of sight. Even in this state, and without any to hear our cheers or respond to them, when we arrived at the ships, and brought our sledge, that had been dragged for forty days over four hundred and fifty statute miles, to a stand, the ships and Assistance Bay had peculiar attractions. The former had been our home for a considerable time; and their awnings, although black with the soot of the funnels, had afforded us shelter during many a stormy night: the latter protected us from the pressure of the ice and the influence of currents, when, had we been exposed, we should have been carried out of Barrow Straits, and far from the place where anything could be done to throw light upon the route of the missing expedition; here was our home; and I hope we all felt grateful to Him by whose "Almighty and most Gracious Protection" we were brought back to it in safety. On our way from Cape Hotham one of the men complained a little; but there could not have been much, or at least anything alarming, the matter with him, otherwise he would not have been able to accomplish a distance of fifteen miles in six hours and a half. I expected that a few days' rest would restore him to his usual good health.

In conducting ice travelling, as well as in preparing for it, the most minute detail must be entered into in the choice of the men and their clothing; from their caps, down to their boots and stockings; in the choice of the provisions, and its careful use; in the form of the sledge, and the arrangement of the weights placed upon it, together with the careful choice of the road; and, above all, in the constant and watchful eye which the officer keeps over his men, guarding them, and caring for them, as if they were parts of himself, yet without being too familiar with them; these are points of the deepest importance, and upon these the success of a party will depend.

June 14th.—On our arrival on board the ships, Mr. Manson gave orders that the men should receive fresh meat for several successive days, to compensate as much as possible for the want that had been sustained in that respect. The pemmican was nothing but meat preserved without salt, which possessed all the properties of fresh meat, and always afforded wholesome meals to us when mixed with pounded bread and water, after it had been placed over the fire for a short time, until the whole became intimately mixed; but, even with the liberal allowance of three quarters of a pound of it, we felt a great craving for vegetable substances—such as carrots and Edward's preserved potatoes—and, above all, for Mr. Hogarth's "Hotch Potch," which was the best preserved soup we had in the expedition. It was also Captain Penny's orders that the allowances of the parties should be liberal on their return to the ships. To say the least of the travelling, there was not a person engaged in it who was not reduced in flesh, although all did not suffer alike in that respect. It occurred to us before starting, that it would prove interesting to ascertain the weight of every person, so that we might have in figures the exact loss each sustained by the travelling. This, however, was found impracticable, owing to want of proper weights and other convenInces.

At the usual breakfast hour, I had the pleasure of meeting Captain Austin, who paid a visit to our expedition, and took up his residence for a few days on board the Lady Franklin, in compliance with the request of Mr. Penny. It was not without extreme regret, that we learned from Captain Austin, that one of the severe frost-bites which happened on some of the memorable days of April, between the 21st and 23rd, proved fatal to George Malcolm, the captain of the hold of H. M. S. "Resolute," a person whose fate all lamented. His body is buried on the east side of Griffith's Island in the frozen shingle.

I furnished Captain Austin with a verbal account of the proceedings of Mr. Stewart's party up to the time I parted with him, and also stated the course Mr. Stewart intended to pursue, together with Captain Penny's fears he should not go far, owing to the water. There was, however, some doubt in my mind as to the direction of the coast-line west of Cape Simpkinson, because there appeared to be a northern trend in the land, when viewed from Prince Alfred Bay: this trend might lead to the northward, and out into Jones's Sound. Captain Austin said with respect to this, that he hoped Captain Stewart would be able to draw within narrow limits the search in that quarter; and, although we had found nothing relating to the missing ships, he expressed his satisfaction in the operations that were going on upon our side, and a feeling of confidence, that the search would come to a conclusion this season. Starting from the point of the first winter quarters of the missing expedition, there was hardly a direction in which they could have advanced but was undergoing examination by widely spread travelling parties; and it was lamentable to reflect upon the painful fact that one after another was beginning to return without the much-desired "news." Preparations were at once begun to carry out the orders of Captain Penny; but the weather was very unpromising: the clear and keen atmosphere of April and May, and the beautiful fleecy clouds and prismatic parhelia which adorned the clear blue sky, were exchanged for angry clouds, which constantly enveloped the hill tops, and for a densely loaded atmosphere over Barrow Straits. It does not require a second thought, that travelling could have been conducted with greater safety to health and more satisfactorily in the first week in April than at this time.

June 16*th*.—At an early hour in the morning Commander Phillips and his party arrived from their overland journey. They were exceedingly fatigued from the extreme difficulty there was in walking over the land, which by this time was very soft on the upper surface. In some parts one would sink half up to the knees in the muddy shingle which covered the surface of the frozen soil; and in other parts, he would sink to the waist in sludgy snow in the hollows. Such an interchange as soft snow and shingly mud could not fail to destroy the best means that could have been used to protect the feet. Although the party had not travelled above one hundred miles, which occupied them a month, they were almost barefoot on their return; and had the journey been protracted but a few days longer, it is very questionable whether they could have stood it out. The highest latitude attained by the party was 75° 29′, which must have been within a few miles, probably ten or fifteen, of the N. side of the island. They saw no signs of approaching its northern shore early, and their provisions intended for the outward journey being exhausted, no alternative remained but to return. The interior of the island is flat and generally covered with snow. Commander Phillips, being asked for a sketch of it, drew that of a tent and a sledge on a plain wilderness of snow. He completed the picture by placing a man in the tent-door, who is in the act of driving away from the provisions in the sledge the little dog, the only companion in their journey, which they had left outside to keep watch (from I know not what) during the time they should be asleep.

I intended to have set out with the provisions according to the orders of Captain Penny; but the backward state of the weather did not permit of that since the return of my party. I found, too, that two of the men were unable to accompany me immediately; they would require at least a whole week to recover from the fatigue of the journey they had just completed before they could be taken out again to endure the hardships of the wet ice over which the present journey had to be made. This forced me to modify my original plan of taking out the same party again; and after consulting Mr. Manson, who virtually was in command of the Expedition at the time, it was resolved to take out the dog-sledge that had returned on the same day as ourselves. Mr. Petersen thought well of this arrangement, but could not accompany us, although he soon began to recover after his return to the ships. When Captain Austin observed that our first plan had been departed from, he remarked, that if we should require assistance, he would certainly lend any in his power, after the return of his parties should enable him to do so. The provisions were divided between the dog-sledge and a long sledge drawn by six persons, of whom Mr. J. Stuart was one, and one of the seamen drove the dog-sledge. On the 17th we started in the evening, and Captain Austin and his party left Assistance Bay about the same time.

We had not proceeded far until we were met by Mr. Goodsir and his party on their return. They had met Captain Penny's party with the boat a few days ago, and their opinion was, that by this time they should be at the water, which was considerably nearer now than when Captain Penny first saw it, owing to the ice breaking up at the edge and drifting away to the N.W.

Mr. Goodsir was absent forty-three days from the ships, in which time he accomplished a journey along the N. shore of Cornwallis Island as far W. as the 99th degree of longitude, where he found it impossible to advance any further, owing to open water. The water was first seen by him about the 20th of May from the vicinity of Disappointment Bay; and from that time to the 1st of June he continued to advance, keeping close along the land for fear of getting adrift among the loose ice, or of falling through where it was very much decayed. Seals and walruses were seen by him and his party both in the water and on the ice; and they also saw a great many bears, hares, and deer, of all of which they succeeded in shooting some. After the beginning of June they saw sea-fowl in abundance; but, previous to that time, chiefly ptarmigan, although occasionally glaucous gulls were also seen at the water. They found drift-wood in a bay on the N. side of a narrow isthmus, which connects Cornwallis and Bathurst Islands. It was very much bleached by the action of the weather, and appeared to be very old; but it formed no part of Esquimaux implements, like most of the driftwood that has been picked up along the S. shore of the same island. Mr. Goodsir gave us very little encouragement with respect to the state of the ice in the Wellington

Channel, which he said was covered with water from N. to S. and from shore to shore. We had abundance of wading in prospective.

June 18*th*.—After crossing the small cracks, eastward of Dungeness Point, we arrived at the largest of the two bluffs, where we found the dog-sledge had been drawn up by the man who attended to it, having arrived there at least two hours before us. Part of the provisions were taken from the large to the dog-sledge, and the driver and I started with it, expecting that the dogs could reach the lower depôt with safety in one start. The large sledge, lightened a little, could be drawn along easily by five persons. We went outside the squeezed-up ice at Cape Hotham, because travelling along the beach was impracticable. There were several cracks in the floes, in which a few dovekies were swimming about. They were crossed very easily; but the dogs were very anxious to go after the birds, and were not restrained without great difficulty. We used a sort of drag made of rope, which we threw over one of the runners of the sledge at its forepart, where the friction on the snow could be increased so much, by one leaning with all his weight upon it, that the sledge could be brought to a stand in a short time, in spite of all the efforts of the dogs, going at a galloping pace. All control over

Esquimaux dogs is lost in a sledge the moment they see an object of pursuit. Mr. Petersen says he rarely succeeds in bringing them to a stand with the whip alone, if once they see a black object upon the ice, when they are in high spirits. The young dogs, which had been accustomed to see hardly anything extraneous upon the ice around the ships or elsewhere during the whole winter, became very much excited on seeing a few birds or a seal on the ice, and could hardly be kept back by the driver and myself leaning with all our weight upon the sledge; while the drag underneath the runner was leaving a broad and rough groove in the hard crust of snow which covered the surface of the floe. After proceeding to the northward of Barlow Inlet, we had to strike in through the heavy ice to the beach, where there was one continuous sheet of water, which the dogs were not, in many parts, able to cross, owing to the depth. Here our difficulties were very much increased, because our way lay through the water. On the one hand, the rugged hummocks, on the other, the shingly beach, and between them a sheet of water, in which a boat afforded the best means of advancing. I need not state that we had to shift our stockings when we encamped.

June 19*th.*—After a whole day and night of a violent storm, from which we sought shelter in the face of a cliff, under a few shreds of a black calico tent, we crawled out to the edge of the beach, to see if the large sledge, under the command of Mr. J. Stuart, had arrived from Cape Hotham, where we had left him and his party encamped; but there were no signs of their arrival. The dogs were let loose, that they might have a run about the beach to warm themselves, for the poor brutes had been shivering all night, although we and they lay huddled in a heap beneath our slender covering. They soon put the ravens to flight, which had been croaking over us; and after half an hour of chasing each other on the beach, they all disappeared. It was probable they might have set out for the ships, or the party at Cape Hotham: either supposition would prove awkward for the driver and myself, because we expected to carry out the provisions, solely by their assistance, from this place, to the north-east point of the island. In a short time one of them returned, and it was soon followed by the others; lest they should again decamp, they were put into their harness, and the driver was left in charge of them, while I went down the channel to meet the large sledge, which was expected to come in sight every minute. After proceeding about a mile, I came upon the party, whom I found sound asleep in their tent, having arrived four hours previously. The water which we had to make our way through with the dog-sledge presented an obstacle, which they did not think proper to attempt. I roused up two of the men, and, with their assistance, got the provisions conveyed to the dog-sledge, which was thus loaded to the amount of four hundred and twenty pounds, and included two blanket bags and a gun, with ammunition. The remainder was buried in the shingle for the use of Captain Penny and Captain Stewart's parties on their return.

As soon as we were ready, Lawson — for that was the driver's name — and I started with the heavily laden dog-sledge. Our way, at first, lay through very rough hummocks, which lined the beach, and presented deep chasms, communicating with the water underneath; but after passing through them, we came to a smooth floe, which, like the floe in the channel southward of this, and along the south shore of Cornwallis Island, had relieved itself from the water which had accumulated on its surface. The sledge moved on tolerably well for the first ten or twelve miles, where the floe was smooth and without much water; but after opening out Point Separation, it frequently stuck in the soft snow among the hummocks, and often came to a dead stand; while the dogs were sprawling helplessly in sludge and water. We persevered, however, until Point Petersen bore well to the westward, and we were within twenty-five miles of our destination. Here we found it impossible to advance any further, for the floe was covered with water to such a depth in some parts, that the sledge was more than half immersed. To persevere to the north-east point was not impossible, as far as our ability was concerned; but it would be of little value to arrive there with damaged provisions; therefore we resolved upon making a depôt of them at Point Separation, with the intention of coming out with a large sledge, and after the floe should have relieved itself from the surface water. I shall not describe the difficulties that were encountered before the hummocks were reached, or those of carrying all the provisions through a quarter of a mile of hummocks, which lined the coast, and appeared formidable, even without seventy pound bags of bread, and hosts of six pound tins of meat: suffice it to state, that the depôt was made in the centre of a cairn, which occupied as conspicuous a position as we could assign to it, and that we returned the same evening to the place we had left in the morning, where we found it absolutely necessary to remain for the night, owing to the extreme fatigue of the poor dogs and their bleeding feet. There were two cracks extending right across the channel, between the lower depôt and the one at Point Separation. The one was crossed at the part of it which was first reached, but the other required to be skirted for a quarter of a mile, before a part was found sufficiently narrow to enable us to cross safely. Several seals were seen on the ice in the channel; and in the two cracks a few dovekies, which often attracted the notice of our dogs.

June 20th.—At an early hour we resumed our journey down the channel, and arrived at Cape Hotham, where about a score of dovekies were shot to feed the dogs. There were in the cliffs at Cape Hotham a great number of glaucous, sabine and ivory gulls, and terns, and also not unfrequently flocks of brent geese, were seen flying up Barlow Inlet and along the coast westward of Cape Hotham. Undue exposure during the previous twenty-four hours brought on a severe attack of snow-blindness, so that poor Lawson and myself had to grope like blind men during the rest of the journey. On our way from our weary encampment at Cape Hotham, the dogs often went after seals, and the sledge was frequently in danger of being dashed to pieces against the hummocks. It was amusing (although we could hardly see) to observe them set out at full gallop, in the direction of a wary seal, lying asleep, but "wide-awake," on his icy bed. The sudden approach of so formidable a force produced as sudden an evolution on the part of the seal, as it went plump head-foremost into the water through its hole in the ice. After reaching the spot where it was seen, the dogs came to a dead stand, and were amazed at the disappearance of the object they had seen but a moment before. On the evening of the 21st we arrived at the ships, and found that Mr. Stuart's party had arrived nearly thirty-six hours previously, having come at one march from the lower depôt to the ships. I delivered to Mr. Manson a verbal report of our proceedings, and consulted him as to the measures to be taken to advance a part of the provisions the remaining twenty-five miles. From the report of Mr. Goodsir, who met Captain Penny, we had every reason to believe that fatigue parties, returning from the latter, would be on their homeward route, and probably already to the southward of the north-east point. Captain Stewart might be expected daily, and then we would command a large force, to carry out any measures that might be necessary, according to the instructions which Captain Penny had given before leaving on the boat expedition.

June 22nd.—A party of two persons arrived from Griffith's Island, bringing intelligence of the arrival of all the travelling parties, except those engaged in the search of Melville Island. No accidents had befallen any of them since the frost-bites were returned, but all were more or less reduced in flesh, and required a few days to recruit their strength, before they were called upon duty. Cape Walker and the adjoining land were examined by a division under the command of Captain Ommanney; and the southern shores of the Parry group, except Melville Island, were examined by the western division, including the fatigue parties, and one extended party under the command of Lieut. Aldrich. The same dark mystery hung over the fate of the missing ships, as there was before the travelling commenced. Party after party was coming in, but the same report was received from all, "they had seen nothing of the missing Expedition." Early on the following morning, Captain Stewart arrived, having been absent forty-eight days. Since he and I parted on the 28th of May, a few miles eastward of Cape Simpkinson, he proceeded to the westward along the coast, to a distance of about forty miles, where he met with open water, which forced him to retrace his steps with the same doleful intelligence as those who had arrived before him, "no traces of the missing ships." In the coast westward of Cape Simpkinson there is a bay, where there appeared from Point Hogarth to be an opening leading northward. It was named Sisters Bay; and to the westward of it there is a second bay, which was named after his Majesty Frederick VII., King of Denmark, to whose government and country the Esquimaux in West Greenland are very deeply indebted. To the westward of this bay there is a very prominent headland, which was named Cape Majendie, after a gentleman related to Sir John Franklin's family, who has done much in assisting and encouraging the search for the missing ships. On the east side of the same bay there is another point, but less prominent than Cape Majendie; it was called Point Alexander, after a son of Captain Hamilton, R. N., Secretary of the Admiralty. At Captain Stewart's extreme distance westward, there is a headland, from which the coast trends to the N. W., until it is lost sight of from a height of seven to eight hundred feet. This headland was named Cape Becher, out of compliment to Captain Becher, R. N., one of the gentlemen engaged in the hydrographic department of the Admiralty. A few miles N. W. of Cape Becher a bay was discovered, which, should it be required, might suit well as a place of shelter to ships from pressure among the ice. It was named after Sir R. H. Inglis, M. P., who has always been interested in the search for Sir J. Franklin, and has watched over its progress with the true spirit of philanthropy.

After remaining a few days at or near Cape

Becher, Mr. Stewart commenced his return to the ships, calling at the two depôts on the east side, and crossing the channel from the north side of President Bay to Point Petersen. He describes the ice in his journey from Cape Becher to the middle of Wellington Channel as being very wet; in many parts the depth of water was very great, and when much snow had to be crossed, it was so soft and "sludgy," that the men generally sank through it until their feet reached the hard ice underneath. As they came down the channel, however, there was considerably less water, and it was beginning to establish small hollows and channels in the ice for its own reception. For further remarks with respect to the observations of Captain Stewart at Cape Becher, reference must be made to his travelling report, which is inserted in the Appendix.

A party was just about to leave Assistance Bay for Griffith's Island. It was to proceed from the "Felix," under the command of Commander Phillips; and its object was to get supplies of provisions. As Mr Stewart was a good deal fatigued, with his permission I water a letter to Captain Austin, which contained an abstract of what had come under Mr. Stewart's observation to the westward of Cape Simpkinson. I endeavoured to make all the circumstances connected with the open water as clear as possible to Captain Austin, so that he might be able to judge of the efficiency of our operations in the search for Sir J. Franklin. Captain Stewart was put in possession of all the facts connected with the boat expedition; and the result was, that he resolved to start in a few days, as soon as his party had recruited a little, to advance the provisions to the north-east point, according to Captain Penny's instructions to me. Captain Stewart's entire party might have proceeded on a journey the very next day after their arrival, for they appeared to be in excellent spirits, and almost equal to any amount of fatigue; however, as there was no necessity for such extreme haste, a few days were to be allowed to pass for the purpose already stated.

June 25th. — In the afternoon two sledges drawn by dogs, and attended by two persons, were observed coming round the S.E. point of the bay; and over the lowland, to the northward of the point, a large party of men were observed coming towards the ships. We soon learned they were Captain Penny's fatigue sledges which he had sent back on the 17th, but eight days previously. On that day the boat was launched into the water and lost sight of by the returning party with its sail set standing to the westward, at a short distance from the free edge of the ice. At the water the fatigue parties shot as many birds (chiefly dovekies) as supplied themselves and the dogs until they arrived at the depôt I had laid out at Point Separation. They also shot a few at Cape Hotham, which they brought to the ships. Although the weather had been rather wet for two or three days, they seemed to have improved by their journey; and in that respect there was a contrast between them and all the other travelling parties that had started from our Expedition. They reported that the ice in the top of the channel had relieved itself from the water, and that travelling over it could now be accomplished with great ease as compared with the state in which I and Mr. Stewart found it on the 19th and 20th. We received a note from Captain Penny, requesting that the provisions should be advanced from the N.E. point to another point six or eight miles W.N.W. of it, which he called Point Decision. Captain Stewart, with Mr. Petersen's concurrence and assistance, resolved upon attempting to advance the provisions from Point Separation to Point Decision with the dogs, of which now there was a choice out of eighteen or twenty. In this respect there was a wide difference from the half dozen lame ones with which Lawson and I succeeded so far in the same journey on a former occasion.

June 27th.—Late in the evening Mr. Stewart

and Mr. Petersen left the ships with the fully-equipped dog-sledge, and were lost sight of in a very short time, proceeding to the eastward at a rapid pace. They would reach Cape Hotham in three hours; and before another six hours they would be encamping at Point Separation. After twelve hours' rest there, and taking the provisions upon the sledge, they would start for the N.E. point and Point Decision, which they would reach in probably six hours more, going at the rate of five miles an hour. Soon after Captain Stewart and Mr. Petersen started for Cape Hotham, two officers belonging to H.M.S. "Assistance" left the "Lady Franklin" to proceed to Griffith's Island. Although they were not furnished with official despatches to Captain Austin, which, in the absence of Mr. Penny, no person took the authority to draw up, inasmuch as there seemed to be no immediate necessity for such a procedure, they were in possession of a thorough knowledge of all the proceedings of our travelling parties that might have reached us since my letter to Captain Austin explained the circumstances connected with Mr. Stewart's return. After proceeding about a mile and a half from the ships, a disaster occurred which forced them to return. One of them fell into a deep hole in the ice along the beach, and narrowly escaped drowning. It must be confessed there was danger, in spite of all the laughing that ensued, when he sank to the ears in sludge and water where no bottom could be felt, without his companions possessing any ready means of assistance, except such as endangered their own safety.

June 28th. — At an early hour in the morning our watch was aroused by the unexpected return of Captain Stewart and Mr. Petersen. After reaching Cape Hotham they found that the ice in Barrow Straits, eastward of and around that headland, had begun to drift away. Several seals were seen in the water among the angular pieces of ice. One was shot, and picked up by means of Halkett's boat, which Captain Stewart had taken along with him for the purpose of using it in the water at Point Decision in picking up birds or seals he might shoot while there, for the use of the dogs, and perhaps, also, for the use of his party. He also shot eider ducks and dovekies. The stomach of the former contained abundance of chitons and other molluscs, while that of the latter only contained crustacea of the genus *Gammarus*, which are very abundant in Barrow Straits, as well as all other parts of the known polar sea.

The carpenters were set to work forthwith to prepare a boat to be mounted on a sledge, which also had to be got ready: our wood had become so scarce, that there was not so much on board as would make a sledge sixteen feet long to receive the boat. Two of the other sledges were made into one, by cutting off the obliquity at one end of the runners, and bolting them together as firmly as possible. It was at one time contemplated to send a boat from the "Lady Franklin" to Pond's Bay to communicate with the whalers; if this boat should not be necessary for going up the channel to assist the returning parties, it might suit very well to go to Pond's Bay.

CHAP. XVIII.

CAPTAIN PENNY'S TRAVELLING REPORT.

Leaving the Ships. — Overtake the Party. — Division of the Party. — Snow-blind Bay. — Point Decision. — Hamilton Island. — Cape Washington. — Cape Scoresby. — Haddo Bay. — Open Water. — Birds. — Cape Crozier. — Prince Albert Land. — Walruses. — Forced to return. — Course Homeward. — Arrival. — Fitting out a Boat. — Fatigue Party come in. — Bear shot. — Boat Expedition starts. — Second Part comes in. — Detention to the Party. — Commenced the Journey. — Sutherland's Return. — Parting Cheers. — Scudding with a strong Breeze. — Goodsir's Return. — Wet Blanket Beds. — Reindeer seen. — Reach the Water. — Fatigue Party sent to the Ships. — Violent Weather. — Victoria Channel. — Disappointment Bay. — Open Water. — Opinion upon the Currents. — Getting clear. — Irksome Navigation. — Unsuccessful Explorations. — Shooting. — High Spirits. — Dundas Island. — Cape Fitzjames. — Heavy Pressures. — Explorations. — Piece of English Elm. — State of the Ice. — Shot a Seal. — Contrary Winds. — Reach Margaret Island. — False Cairns. — Bearings laid down. — Mr. Stewart's Cairns. — Reach Baring Island. — Cape Becher. — Channel running N. W. — Return. — Landing upon Cornwallis Island. — Abandon the Boat. — Sleeping in the Open Air. — Fording Ice-cold Streams. — Down the Wellington Channel. — Arrival at the Ships.

May 9th. — This being the day on which I intended to leave the ships with the two dog sledges, according to my arrangement with Mr. Stewart, although there was a good deal of snowdrift and

C. COVENTRY. LITH M. & N. HANHART, IMP.

THE MEETING IN WELLINGTON CHANNEL JUNE 14TH 1851

a smart breeze, I determined to start, and push on after the men at all hazards. At four o'clock in the morning, all of the crew that were on board were called; and at six, Mr. Petersen and I started, accompanied by Thompson, one of the seamen whom I had appointed to attend to the dogs, and also by one of Mr. Goodsir's sledge crew, who had been sent back to the ships for a floor-cloth that had been forgotten. After eight hours of uninterrupted driving I arrived at the advanced depôt, which was at least forty-five miles from the ships, where I found encamped the entire party that went on before me, having left the ships on the evening of the 6th.

At a quarter-past 2 P.M., we encamped and had dinner. The five sledges, exclusive of the two dog sledges, were filled up out of the depôt, and were ready to start at 8 P.M. I accompanied them up along the land, and parted with the three that were to cross the Channel to the east side, having given them their instructions, with every caution to be careful of the peoples' feet from frost-bites and other accidents. At 11 P.M. started again, and advanced six miles further, where we encamped at a distance of fifty-one miles from the ships. The three sledges that started to cross the Channel had a fair wind, and were lost sight of with their sails set. Temperature -3° to -10°.

May 10*th.*—At $1\frac{3}{4}$ A.M., I passed Mr. Marshall, mate, and Mr. Goodsir, surgeon, in charge of a party of two sledges. They had most laborious work of it among deep snow, for the sledges were very heavily laden, and required double journeys to be made until they reached my encampment. They accomplished seven miles before they halted. At noon the sun was obscured; however, at half-past 3 P.M., we got sights for the time-piece. Our encampment was on a low flat point, in the vicinity of the entrance of a remarkable ravine. The point I called after Mr. Petersen, to whose services the expedition which I commanded is very much indebted. At half-past 6 P.M. we started from Point Petersen and had a splendid drive, passing a deep bay, which I named after Dr. Kaine, a highly intelligent medical officer in the American Expedition. On the north side of Kaine Bay we came to three table bluffs, which had between them two shallow bays. These also were passed, and then we opened out another bay, on the north side of which we encamped. Our eyes were very much affected, consequently the bay in which we were encamped was called Snow-blind Bay. The ice over which we had to make our last journey appeared to be at least three years old. The distance must have been about thirty miles, following the sledge track. Temperature +9° to

+11°. We had an unsuccessful hunt after a bear around the north-east point of Cornwallis Island. This point forms the northern boundary of Wellington Channel on this side.

May 11*th.* — Poor Petersen and I snow-blind; eyes very painful; dull heavy weather, winds westerly, from which causes we were prevented starting. The Wellington Channel extends due north, to latitude 75° 22′, to the above-mentioned headland, which was named Cape de Haven, out of compliment to the Commander of the American Expedition, who so nobly came out in search of our lost countrymen. From Cape de Haven, the land trends away to the westward and northward for about ten miles, where there is a second prominent point. Temperature +9° to +11°; weather still cloudy, and sky overcast at midnight.

Monday, May 12*th.*—There was a very bright sunshine and a powerful glare, which affected our eyes very much, so that we were obliged to put off starting till evening. At 7½ P.M. we started, and proceeded round Cape de Haven, and to the point beyond it, which we reached in two hours. At this point I ascended a hill about four hundred feet high, from which I could see land stretching from the opposite side of the Wellington Channel northward to a point bearing about N.E., and appearing to be continued north-westward, as if it should join the land on which I stood, which stretched away about N. W. There was, however, a space to the eastward in which the land was lost sight of. Here, as well as between the points N. E. and N. W., there might be openings out of this newly-discovered sea. I came to the resolution of proceeding northward, leaving instructions for Messrs. Marshall and Goodsir to continue along the line of coast leading to the north-westward. The point from which I had this view was called Point Decision. To the eastward of Point Decision, there is a deep bight running a considerable distance into the land, which appeared to terminate in a water-course, or a ravine. It was named Helen Haven. To the north-westward of this point, at a distance of about ten miles, a second prominent headland appeared: it was named Point Phillips, out of compliment to a valued friend and hearty companion in winter-quarters, Commander Phillips, R. N., who accompanied Sir John Ross in the "Felix," and whose zeal in search of the missing expedition was then about to be thrown away in a useless journey across the trackless and barren top of Cornwallis Island. Temperature in shade, during the last twenty-four hours, varied from +8° to +20°.

Tuesday, 13th.—Blowing from north-west, accompanied by snowdrift, which was so violent, that Petersen said the dogs could not face it; however, nothing could satisfy me but to start, and after proceeding about two miles we were obliged to return and encamp. This was about midnight.

Wednesday, May 14*th.*—At 4 A.M. the weather moderated a little, but just as we began to pack up, the dog Sultan was off after a bear; Petersen, Thompson, and I started after him, and after a chase of five miles, we were obliged to return unsuccessful; but it was long before the dogs returned, for all of them set out in the chase, and when they did return they were completely done up. At 5 P.M. the weather was still more moderate, and we started, and had to run after the sledges a great part of the way. Our course was N.W., and by N., and the distance twenty-five to thirty miles. At midnight we encamped, and served out two pounds of meat to each of the dogs. The temperature during twenty-four hours was +5° to +18°; winds north-westerly. From our encampment a large island was seen bearing about N.W., which was named after Captain W. A. B. Hamilton, R.N., Secretary of the Admiralty.

Thursday, May 15*th.*—Fine soft snow on the ice, on which we slept very comfortably; for six hours' incessant labour running after the sledge seemed to have taken great effect upon Mr. Petersen, who had been little accustomed to such fatiguing work for a long time. Our dog's-meat was within four days of being done. At half-past 1 P.M. we packed up and started over new ice. The rate we came at was very fast; and at half-past 7 P.M., when we reached Hamilton Island, the distance we had come from our last encampment was at least twenty miles as the sledges had come, which left a track as straight as Mr. Petersen could make it with his great experience in driving dogs over ice and snow. The moment we landed I set out to a bold headland, or I should say rather the south-east point of the island; but I found no traces of the missing ships; and from this my inference was, that Sir John Franklin had kept along the north land, which I saw from Point Decision. The south-east point of Hamilton Island I called Cape Washington, out of compliment to Captain Washington, R. N. The Channel leading westward, and a little northward between this island and the north shore of Cornwallis Island, is about fifteen miles wide, and for distinction from other channels I called it South Channel.

May 16th.—The ice in the South Channel seemed to be very much decayed, and there were several large lanes of water in it. Beyond it, at a distance of twenty miles bearing about W. and W.N.W., there were two islands, the nearest, which could be seen sufficiently distinct, was named after Admiral H. Stewart, one of the Lords Commissioners of the Admiralty. At Cape Washington I obtained a meridian altitude, which gave latitude 75° 44′; but as my eyes were at this time very much inflamed, I could not depend upon its correctness within a mile or two. The compass here was exceedingly sluggish, and indeed of no use; I placed my whole dependence upon the sun, and with ordinary foresight in laying down courses and bearings, by his assistance there was little fear of falling into egregious mistakes. At 6 P.M. we again started round the east side of the island, and after rounding Cape Washington, we found it turned away about N.N.E. At 10 P.M. we came to the termination of the N.N.E. trend, from which the side of the island leads away N.N.W. Here there is a very prominent point which I called Cape Scoresby, after the Reverend Dr. Scoresby, whose elaborate and graphic descriptions of the Arctic Regions will ever continue standard works. On the north side of Cape Scoresby there is a large deep bay, which was named Haddo Bay, out of compliment to Lord Haddo. Immediately to the northward of Haddo Bay, we found that water had also formed in this direction. Mr. Petersen called out "Birds," and sure enough there were a few burgomasters. At a quarter-past 11 P.M. we landed on the side of the island, and drove along upon the land terrace, for, at a short distance off, the ice was too decayed to support the dogs, and a little farther on there was open water at the very edge of the terrace. The snow became very deep, and we were obliged to stop. Petersen and I set off to a point several miles farther along, making sure that we should find traces of the missing ships in the shape of a cairn. The point is a very low one, and there was immensely pressed up ice upon it. But, lo and behold! to our surprise a strait, and nothing but clear water, opened out before us. The tide seemed to be going at a very rapid rate, I should say not less than four knots. This channel or strait is about eight miles in breadth, and ten miles in length from east to west. The point on which we then stood was called Point Surprise, from the sudden appearance to our view of so large an extent of water. Bearing north-west at a distance of eight miles, the breadth of the strait, there is a bold table headland, which I named after B. Smith, Esq., whose zeal in the search for Sir John Franklin has been most amply displayed in the abundant supplies of kites and their materials, which at great expense he afforded to our Expedition. Leading westward from

Cape Benjamin Smith, one comes to a second point which bears also from Point Surprise, W. ½ N. about twelve miles distance, where the land on the north side of the strait terminates, or turns to the north-west or north; but this I could not determine. This point was named Cape Crozier, after Captain Crozier, R. N., the second in command of the missing expedition. South-west from Point Surprise, on the south or same side of the strait, there is also a prominent headland, which was named after Captain Fitzjames, R. N., the third in command of the missing expedition. At a distance of about thirty miles bearing, the north end W. ½ S., and the south end S. W., there appeared to be an island, which I at once named after the Right Honourable Sir Francis T. Baring, the first Lord of the Admiralty. To the north and north-east, the land could be seen very bold at a distance of about twenty miles, and its deep bays could be distinguished very clearly. As the first idea of there being land in this direction occurred on the 26th August, 1850, on board H. M. S. "Assistance," and also on board the "Sophia," our discovery is doubly entitled to be named after H. R. H. Prince Albert. At a considerable distance from the coast-line in Prince Albert Land, there is a range of rugged hills, which in one part rises high above the ordinary level of the land, and appears to be the most northern point that could be discovered from the position which I occupied. This I named Sir John Barrow's Monument, out of compliment to the late Sir John Barrow, who for forty years filled the office of Secretary of the Admiralty, and during all that time devoted his utmost zeal and interest, as well as most distinguished talents, to the advancement of Arctic discovery. The moment I passed over Point Surprise, the expression that escaped me was, "No one will ever reach Sir J. Franklin; here we are, and no traces are to be found:" so we returned to the sledges very much disappointed.

May 17*th*. — At 2 A.M. we turned in into our sleeping bags, and had eight hours very comfortable sleep. After breakfast, which was prepared by Thompson, and a comfortable wash, which was equally necessary, I got a meridian altitude, which gave the latitude of Point Surprise four miles farther north, about 76°, that of our position being 75° 55′ 43″. Sir James C. Ross said he would give one thousand pounds for ten days' provisions; I certainly should have given five thousand pounds for a boat, to follow up the search for Sir J. Franklin. How pleasant to the eye it is to see the blue open water! Mr. Petersen and I set out again for Point Surprise, and while I was laying down the bearings of the points and islands by the compass card and the sun, I sent him back to let Thompson, our only attendant, see the expanse of water, from this point, whence only the strait could be opened out. As we were thus employed going back and fore, and making a tracing of the coasts, two walruses sailed past, upon a piece of ice, at the rate of at least three knots. Two eider ducks and some burgomasters flew past at the same time. Here we had creatures that we could only have expected ten degrees farther south, at such an early date. I shall never plume myself upon experience again. Light ice and twenty-five miles (all the way to Baring Island, and far beyond Cape Crozier) of open water; and from the appearance of the sky, at least twenty-five miles more beyond the north point of the strait. To have proceeded northward could only be accomplished by making a very large circuit; and for this we had but barely two days' provisions for the dogs. Our own provision might last for twelve days; but should we be under the necessity of serving it out to eighteen or twenty ravenous dogs, it would certainly not last three days. We might shoot seals or walruses, and birds in the water; but where was the boat to pick them up in such rapid tides. No alternative remained but to return to the ships, and see if, by any means, a boat could be got into the open water, which was so unexpectedly discovered. At 9½ P.M. we started for the ships. The sky was dark and lowering, and the wind was coming away from the westward.

Sunday, May 18*th*.—The wind blew smartly from N. W., and was attended by snowdrift; but as it was fair, we carried on. One of the dogs, an old female, gave in, and we were obliged to shoot her, both for food to the others, and for the reason that we could not think of leaving her upon the ice. At 4½ A.M. we encamped, and tried the dogs with the flesh of the one we had shot, but they would not deign to taste it.* Mr. Petersen was very much done up, driving the headmost sledge; I, also, felt very wearied; but had we been advancing instead of retreating, I do not believe we should have felt the

* I am informed by Mr. Petersen, that at one of their encampments at or near Hamilton Island, one of the dogs which had been let loose brought him the paw of a young bear, which appeared to have been dead but a few days. As there is no animal in the Arctic regions which can possibly attack and destroy the young Polar bear, defended stoutly and affectionately by its mother, he thinks it most probable that the old males, when hard pushed by hunger, as they must often be during winter and spring, attack and devour their young in the same manner as the old Esquimaux dogs destroy their young under similar circumstances. The violent chase which I observed between two full-grown bears and a cub in Prince Alfred Bay on the 29th May seems to bear out the same opinion. See Travelling Report in the Appendix E.

fatigue nearly to the same extent. At 8 A.M., after onr meal, we turned into our sleeping bags; and after eight hours most comfortable sleep, by which we were much refreshed, we turned out, and having dined, this being the Sabbath, we had worship; and on the solitary waste of snow, we returned our grateful thanks to our Maker for our preservation in health, and all His other mercies and blessings which we enjoyed. At 9 P.M. we started, and came over very good ice; but as Thompson was attached to my sledge, I was often under the necessity of running behind it for hours together, until with perspiration I had not a dry stitch upon me.

Monday 19*th.*—The gale and thick snow continued, but it was fair, being from N.W. The very dogs knew they were on their way home. Poor brutes! they had nothing to eat for the last twenty-four hours. Had any member of the Royal Humane Society seen us, I fear very much our conduct would not have met with his approbation, for it did not meet with our own; but necessity has no laws, and no human foresight could have thought we should not have got a bear, when so many were seen. In a hunt which I had, after one in which I was assisted by the dogs, I ran until sheer exhaustion brought me to the ground. I was never so disappointed with the loss of a whale worth a thousand pounds, as with the loss of that bear. Having encamped opposite Cape de Haven early in the forenoon, after we had a sleep, we turned out, and divided Mr. Petersen's sealskin dress (which was not so good as mine) among the dogs. At 9 P.M. we started, and it was blowing a gale in right good earnest. There was also violent snowdrift, accompanied by strong squalls; nevertheless, on we went, although the dogs had eaten nothing for two days, with the exception of Mr. Petersen's dress.

Tuesday, May 20th.—After we got fairly into Wellington Channel, the wind followed us down. At 2 A.M. we came to the depôt at Point Separation, where the dogs did get a feed of the small quantity of "dog pemmican" that had been left there for our return. This we knew to our experience, for after one hour's rest they would hardly move. It was very hard work for us to get them to advance even homewards. At 8 A.M. we came to a halt, two miles south of Barlow Inlet; and at 8 P.M. we started, and reached the ships at midnight, where we found no person moving about.

*Monday, May 26th.** — Strong north-west wind

* From the time of Mr. Penny's arrival on board the ships to the 23d, the weather was exceedingly stormy. On that day he and one of his men drove over to Griffith's Island, and acquainted Captain Austin with his proceedings up to that

with drifting snow, nevertheless the chief carpenter of the "Sophia," the only carpenter on board, was busily employed fitting up our only sledge to receive our largest six-oared whale boat.

Wednesday, May 28th.—Weather cloudy. The carpenter was very actively employed about the sledge and boat. The sailmaker, also of the "Sophia," was getting ready a housing cloth for the boat, as I was determined that her crew should have no other shelter in the shape of a tent. Thompson was preparing forty days' provisions for sixteen men, whom I daily expected in from the advancing travelling parties to which they had been auxiliaries.

Thursday, May 29th.—The wind still continued northerly, but it had become unsteady. At 5 A.M. Sir John Ross's Esquimaux returned from his auxiliary trip with Commander Phillips. He had left Sir John and his party encamping inland, some four miles from the harbour. At 7 P.M. I received the pleasant intelligence that Mr. Leiper, my second mate, was in sight with his party, having been detached from Messrs. Goodsir's and Marshall on the 20th, at a point bearing about due south of

time. On the 25th he returned to Assistance Harbour with the determination to get a boat ready to be taken to the water which he had discovered, as soon as the return of a sufficient number of his men should enable him to set out. See Appendix E.

Hamilton Island, whence they were to proceed westward. They had then thirty-five days' provisions, and had shot two bears, seen several more, and a great number of burgomasters. They also had seen the open water to the northward and westward before he commenced his return.

Tuesday, May 30th.—The carpenter was actively employed with the sledge, Mr. Manson was preparing provisions for the boat expedition. The wind was northerly and variable. At 4 A.M. Sir John Ross returned, and I had the pleasure of his company at dinner on board of the "Lady Franklin." He was in very high spirits, and appeared to be quite delighted with his journey of thirteen days, and indeed he looked well.

Saturday, May 31st.—Wind from the southward, with flying showers of snow. A bear was shot by Mr. Petersen and Thompson. It was very fortunate for us, and came just in time to put our dogs into good condition for the work that was before them.

June 1st.—Southerly wind, with soft thick weather. Had all the people that were at the ship assembled to public worship on board the "Lady Franklin."

Monday, June 2nd.—South-east wind and clear weather. The carpenter and sailmaker and every other person are all busily employed preparing for the boat expedition. Mr. Petersen is preparing the dog-sledges as auxiliaries.

June 3rd.—This was the first day on which the eider duck and brent goose made their appearance at Assistance Bay. The weather was very mild. Carpenter and blacksmith most actively employed. Mr. Manson preparing to start with the boat expedition.

June 4th.—The sledges and boat were now ready, and at 9 P.M. they started under the command of Mr. Manson, as I intended to follow them up in a few days. They got the assistance of those of the crew of the "Felix" that were on board to take the boat over the hummocks in the entrance of the harbour.

The party consisted of fifteen persons; indeed, all the people that were on board, except Mr. Petersen, the clerk in charge, and myself: and they were divided between the boat mounted on its sledge; another sledge, the one that had returned but a few days previously; and the dog sledge. The dogs were also to assist the men in dragging the boat and sledges along. The snow was very deep and soft, and on this account they made but little progress. I could see that it suited very ill to have dogs tackled to the same weight along with men. Their steps do not agree, and the dogs become useless.

June 5th.—Fine mild and warm weather. Sir John Ross went out to hunt to-day. In the afternoon the wind came away from the northward. Two officers from the squadron at Griffith's Island arrived at Assistance Harbour. They had a sledge and a party, and appeared to have been hunting.

June 6th.—South wind with snow. Mr. J. Stuart arrived with his party from Cape Hurd and Beechey Island. He parted with Captain Stewart on the 13th May to the northward of Cape Bowden, and proceeded down the channel to Beechey Island, and eastward to Cape Hurd, examining all the intermediate coast. His journey out and home included about two hundred and sixty miles, and was accomplished in thirty-one days, having occupied one day more than had been allotted to him. No further traces were found by him in his explorations, with the exception of a few at Caswall Tower similar to those already found north of Cape Spencer, and at Cape Riley. He and his party were ordered to get ready to start with their sledge as soon as possible, that they might accompany and augment the strength of the boat expedition.

June 7th.—The weather continued mild and warm. Mr. J. Stuart was actively employed preparing his sledge, and at 11 P.M. he started with twenty days' provisions, having been on board the ships only thirty-four hours. Mr. Petersen and I had a hunt after a bear. Mr. Petersen shot him. One of the officers of the other squadron wondered to whom it should belong, although my dogs had been in chase of it for six hours, and it had been shot by Mr. Petersen.

Sunday, June 8th.—The weather was very mild and warm. At 6 A.M. Thompson and the blacksmith returned from Cape Hotham, where the party was encamping, with a message from Mr. Manson, stating, that the sledge on which the boat was mounted did not answer the purpose for which it had been intended.

Monday, June 9th.—Fine mild weather. I wrote a note to Sir John Ross, requesting him to let me have his carpenter to make a sledge of the proper dimensions, as my own carpenter was at Cape Hotham with the party. He very kindly sent over both his carpenters, whom I at once set to work along with my own blacksmith to make the sledge.

June 10th.—The sledge was making great progress, and a splendid one it was. There seemed no fear but the boat should reach the water. At midnight it was ready, and we started for Cape Hotham.

June 11th.—At 3¾ A.M. we came up with the party. It was a very great disappointment to me to learn that three days and a half had been spent without advancing, actually lost; since an addition of six men had been made to the party. The travelling seemed to have tried Mr. Manson, who said that he hardly slept any since he had left the ships. The roads were very soft, and the first sledge on which the boat had been mounted was too short, so that it buried itself in the snow. There was no help for the detention. At 5 P.M. all the people were called, and at 7½ P.M. we started, and passed Cape Hotham at 9 P.M. The arrangement of the party was as follows: five men to each of two sledges, Mr. Petersen and Thompson (the latter a most active fellow) to the two dog sledges, and the remaining eight or nine to the boat. The weight which each in the entire party had to drag was not less than two hundred pounds, and this had to be performed over very soft snow. The ships were left with but one person on board; however, as Mr. Manson and the steward of the "Sophia" were to return this night, there was no danger; every duty in Assistance Bay would be attended to as satisfactorily as could be accomplished by so few hands. At midnight we passed Barlow Inlet, and the spirits of the people rose with the remarkable progress we had made.

Thursday, June 12th.—At 2 A.M. came to a halt

and encamped at the site of the lower depôt. At 4 A.M. we were most agreeably surprised by the return of Mr. Sutherland, surgeon of the "Sophia," and his party, who had been auxiliary to Captain Stewart. He reported that he had parted with Mr. Stewart on the 28th May, at a distance of two hundred and twenty statute miles from the ships, following the coast line that had been examined, with twenty-seven days' provisions on his sledge, besides ten days' more provisions in depôts. He carried a note from Captain Stewart, and furnished a rough outline of the newly explored coast. The highest latitude he had attained was 76° 25′, that in which he parted with his commander being 76° 20′. Mr. Stewart intimated by his note that he was to follow the coast to the westward or northward, as the case might be, until want of provisions should force him to think of returning. The same was reiterated by Mr. Sutherland. I ordered the returning party to proceed to the ships, rest over Sabbath, and start again with a supply of provisions to be laid down for the use of my party on its return at Cape de Haren, and at one or two places between it and Cape Hotham. He reported his party to be in good health and high spirits. Some of them, however, appeared to have lost flesh, but that was no hindrance to them in the discharge of their duty, and most of them volunteered to join my party immediately; indeed, I believe all of them would have done so, although they had been thirty-eight consecutive days in the track-belt. At 5 P.M. all hands were called, and at 7½ P.M. we started, parting with Sutherland and his fine fellows with three British cheers. How pleasant it is to see with what enthusiasm they perform their duty! The water upon the floe and the land terrace was now about knee-deep; however, we went on at a good rate.

Friday, June 13*th.*—At 2 A.M. we were obliged to come to a stop, having made only ten miles. Although the channel runs due north and south, in travelling over the ice we made the distance gone over at least one fourth more, choosing the best road and going round the rugged hummocks. At 2 P.M. the people were again called. The provisions of one of the dog sledges were transferred to the boat and the other sledges, as Mr. Petersen's health had given way under the heavy work of running after the sledge in water up to the knees. Mr. Stuart also was ordered to accompany him upon the sledge to the ships. As soon as everything was clear, and Mr. Petersen and his companion had started for the ships, we got under way, and made a first-rate journey of it; I should say not less than sixteen miles. We had a fair wind up the channel, accompanied by small rain.

Saturday, June 14th.—It blew a gale from about south right up the channel, and there was rain. We were very anxious to take advantage of the fair wind; but it came to rain heavily, so that we were necessarily delayed until 10 h. 45 m. A.M., when we set out under sail. Sometimes all or most of the men sat upon the sledges, as they scudded before the wind at the rate of five knots. Since the return of Mr. J. Stuart and Mr. Petersen, there had been but eight persons, including myself, dragging the boat; however, we got on very well, for the men were enthusiastic; and when the wind lulled, those who were on the sledges jumped off and ran alongside. There was none but had his share of the dragging.

At 2 P.M. voices were heard in shore of us; and who could the party be that was thus hailing us? The sledges and the boat were stopped. I went in shore directly, and found the party to consist of Messrs. Marshall and Goodsir, with six men, on their return. Mr. Goodsir stated that they had proceeded westward until the island, which I had seen on my former journey, and called Houston Stewart Island, bore about N. E. He also stated that they could have advanced much farther west, had it not been for the open water, which obliged them to return. The wisdom of this step will be very clear, I have no doubt. They found no traces of the missing ships.

They got each a glass of spirits out of our stores, for their own had been exhausted; and after ten minutes' detention, we again parted with three hearty cheers. How pleasant it was to see such a lot of fine fellows, and to know that each had performed his duty! But still it was a great disappointment that no traces had been found of Sir John Franklin and his brave companions. The wind continued to blow violently. We took it by turns to sit upon the sledges, and to run alongside. The water was in many places more than knee-deep. At 10 h. 30 m. P.M., Point Decision was reached. Since starting, we had come at least thirty-five miles. The work was very laborious, especially when continued for twelve hours; the wind was fair, and not one of the poor fellows ever complained.

Sunday, June 15th.—The people being very much fatigued, we continued in our sleeping bags for twelve hours. At 5 h. 45 m. P.M., we started, and had to pass over six miles of old ice. It was most laborious; and after 9½ hours of hard toil, we managed to make but fifteen miles. Our course was N. W. and N. N. W.

Monday, 16th.—At 3½ A.M. we encamped upon the floe under a ridge of hummocks, where we got some dry snow, or at least which appeared to be dry, from its great depth. Our floor-cloths, which were but porous canvas, were quite wet, and so, likewise, were the men's sleeping bags. There was no complaint, for every one seemed to think it rested with himself to solve the fate of our missing countrymen. The government of our country held forth a handsome reward; I did most sincerely hope that my deserving fellows might reap that reward; but I must say, that I never once heard them utter such a thought, and they seemed to be actuated by far higher motives.

At 2 P.M. all hands were called, but many of the men, as well as myself, had slept or rested very little, owing to cramps. At 5 P.M. we started, and, after proceeding about twelve miles, having seen a large herd of deer on the land to the southward, we halted, and I left the party to encamp, while I went after the deer.

Tuesday, June 17th. — After three hours' travelling and running after the deer, I ascended a high headland, and, behold, the water was within twenty miles of the boat! clear open water! The wind having prevailed for the last twenty-four hours from N. N. W., the ice, of course, had been driven into the south channel. At 3½ A.M. I reached the encampment, got supper, and turned into my sleeping bag. Fine clear weather. At 11½ A.M. called all hands. The first person that turned out called out "The water! the water!" There was no waiting for dressing. The water was distant somewhat less than ten miles, bearing about W. N. W. at the nearest part. At 2 P.M. we were all packed up and starting. The wind was fair; being off the land, we set our sails, and got on rapidly. At 5 P.M. we reached the water, and launched our boat into it, and in an hour it was loaded with provisions for forty days; however, I said we should manage for fifty days. The fatigue party received orders to proceed to the ships without loss of time, taking with them all the dogs. The wind was blowing strong from W. S. W. We close-reefed our sail, and set off like a courser, but not with a very bold side. As the course was W. and by N., the wind was shy; we had to take down our sail and ply with our oars, first right ahead of the wind, and then along the land. The party consisted now of seven men besides myself, and their names were,—

John Leiper, second mate, "Lady Franklin."
Daniel Henry, carpenter, „
James Knox, cook, "Sophia."
James Davidson, A. B., "Lady Franklin."
William Bruce, A. B. „
Alexander Thompson, A. B. „
James Hodgston, A. B. „

We continued to tug at the oars until 11 P.M.,

when the wind came to blow strong from W. and by N., and we were obliged to bear up for a bay on the south shore of the South Channel. Here we landed, and determined to remain until it should moderate; indeed, it was so violent, that we could not help ourselves.

Wednesday, June 18th. — It blew a perfect gale all night, with thick snow. The ice poured into the South Channel, and what was open water yesterday, was now covered with ice to an extent of twenty miles. Beyond this the water could be seen in the direction of Baring and Hamilton Islands, and beyond them again there was a dark watery sky to the utmost limits of vision. As it continued to blow a gale, I kept the people under cover.

June 19th. — Thick snow, but more moderate. At 7 A.M. we were surprised by a motion in the ice. Every one jumped to secure the provisions; and it was well we did so, for in ten minutes it would have reached them, and exposed them to the risk of being lost. There was but a small hole of open water; but the strong wind set in a motion, among the ice from it. At noon an altitude was obtained by the artificial horizon, which gave the latitude 75° 36′ 13″. As there was no prospect of an early lead to the westward or northward, every one was sent out to hunt and to examine the coast. Several deer were seen; but we were all equally unsuccessful in the chase. At 9 P.M. the ice opened out a little along a bit of land ice. We started to W.N.W. for six miles, when we came to a large floe, which was pressing in against the land ice, and raising blocks not less than one hundred tons in weight. As this was not a secure place for a boat, and as there was no passage, for it was completely blocked up, we were obliged to set our sail, and run back to our old station. The wind increased towards midnight as we ran down and landed. Both on the 17th and yesterday, as well as to-day, seals, walruses, white whales, and narwhales were seen in the open water, and occasionally in the small openings among the pack which the wind brought down upon the coast. They were very numerous, and the latter appeared to be going to the southward; for they headed that way as they came to the surface of the water at the edge of the ice. I could have counted them in numbers of twenty and thirty at a time; and in all respects their movements and manner in the water resembled those of the same animals in Davis Straits or Baffin's Bay.

Friday, June 20th. — This left-handed sort of wind was a great disappointment; and now it was again blowing a gale, after I fully expected it would have moderated. It was N. W., accompanied by showers of snow. The ice was packing down upon the north shore of Cornwallis Island, and nothing but water could be seen to the northward of Houston Stewart Island. The newly-discovered channel leading to the N. W. from Hamilton Island was honoured with the name of our illustrious and much-beloved sovereign. Our four muskets were in requisition, as three deer were seen; but none of them was shot. We succeeded in killing one hare.

Saturday, June 21st. — It still blew strong from the N. W. After breakfast I ascended a hill to see what could be seen. One immense floe had toggled across the channel on Hamilton Island, and a little hole of water had made under lee of it to the W. N. W. The people took their guns, and went out a hunting. Nine deer were seen, but not one of them was shot.

Sunday, June 22nd. — The wind still continued from N. W. and N. N. W. The bay in which we lay was named Disappointment Bay, from the circumstance that we had to remain so long in it, while nothing but open water could be seen around Baring Island. After *morning service* the people went out with their guns, it being considered a work of necessity. However, they returned unsuccessful. A small still voice whispered to me. "Is it a work of necessity?" I feared it was not. The meridian altitude by artificial horizon was 75° 16′ 20″, which gave nearly the same latitude as that obtained in the same place three days previously, the altitude then being 75° 16′ 30″.

Monday, June 23rd.—There being still no prospects of getting away, as the ice was pressed closely in upon Cornwallis Island, I took my gun and ascended a hill, I should say at least one thousand feet high. The bold table land bearing about N.N.E. was seen; and from Baring Island to the northward nothing but open water was to be seen, not even a bit of ice. To the W. and W.S.W. the range of vision was not so extensive; I should say about ten miles.

Tuesday, June 24th.—Again there was a strong wind from N.N.W. right down Queen Victoria Channel. The tides flow regularly; but when the wind prevails from this quarter, they continue tide and half tide, the flood coming from the westward, and at a much greater rate. While upon this subject I may as well mention what fell under the observation of the officers of the American Expedition last autumn. We had little else but S.E. winds right up Barrow Straits from the 20th of August till the 6th of September, and especially on the 1st, 2nd, and 3rd of the latter we had strong gales from about south, and a little easterly. Their two ships were made fast to the lee side of a floe brought up on Cape Spencer. The rush of water up through the Wellington Channel continued during all those gales, and it was observed by them while lying in safety at the lee side of the floe. We were now placed under exactly the same circumstances; for had the tides ran regularly, we should have been able to coast along during the ebb. On the 5th of the same month, two or three days later, I ascended Cape Spencer, which is about seven hundred and fifty feet high. It was a fine clear day, and the refraction was highly favourable for beholding objects at a great distance. I had my best telescope with me; and on looking up the Wellington Channel I could see nothing but open water beyond the barrier of what we whalers call land ice. I hoisted a flag to direct the attention of Captain Austin to the water; for his ship and her tender were lying off Cape Spencer at the time. I put my glass into the hands of Mr. Stewart, commander of the "Sophia," and Mr. Goodsir, who also said they could discern it very plainly. I believe the winds which then prevailed from the eastward had blown all the ice through the channel which since then has been discovered, leaving open water beyond the barrier in the Wellington Channel.

After breakfast at 8 A.M. we set about lashing our small sledge, which we had taken along with us in the boat. It was but a dog sledge; however, we expected it would be useful in dragging our provisions over broad floes when the boat might require to be launched. There was a small lane of water under lee of the large floe that had become toggled across between Hamilton and Cornwallis Islands. We launched our boat into it, and with the sledge we took our provisions from the land across a mile and a half of ice, and having stowed the boat with them, we started against a strong "head" wind. It would have been very dangerous to be caught among the drifting ice with such rapid tides. At 1 P.M. we plied the boat to the lee side of the floe and there set our sail, and at 3 h. 45 m. P.M. we reached Hamilton Island. The log was hove during the passage. We came at the rate of 5½ knots, but the sail was not set more than three-quarters of an hour. The course we made from Disappointment Bay to Hamilton Island was about due north, and the distance twelve or thirteen miles. The south side of this island had a ridge of pressed-up hummocks along it leading to the eastward. We had some trouble in getting a place to haul the boat up, having taken an hour to cut a slip.

Wednesday, June 25th. — The wind still continued but as we had got upon new ground our hopes were raised that we should find traces, although the weather should prove unfavourable. At 6 A.M. we had breakfast, and every one started over the island eager in the search for relics of the missing. The points and headlands were carefully examined without finding anything, not even so much as a bit of wood. At 9 A.M. we made sail towards the east end of the island, with the view of rounding it to advance to the northward by that route, as the ice still kept close at its western extremity. It was blowing a gale with thick snow from the N.W., and there were very heavy squalls. The log was hove, and we found the boat was going at the rate of 8 knots. We ran an hour and a half due east until we were near Cape Washington, and could get no further from the close state of the ice. The boat was hauled up on the ice that was fixed to the land. At 6 P.M. the people turned into their sleeping bags, and at 9 P.M. I went out to have a look before I should turn in. It was well I did so, for the ice on which we had landed was adrift, having driven off 100 yards, owing to the high tides which were caused by the violent gales from the westward. Our great fear was for our provisions, for we were always obliged to discharge the boat before hauling her upon the ice. At midnight we got the boat upon a secure landing-place or terrace; it was, however, at the expense of a good wetting with sleet and snow. The land was completely covered with soft snow.

Thursday, June 26th.—It was still blowing a perfect gale, with heavy squalls, which shook and agitated the boat's housing-cloth so much that not one of us could sleep. At 5 P.M. it moderated, the cooks were called, and breakfast was prepared. A great many birds were seen, and every person set off to hunt and explore; but, as usual, we were very unsuccessful. Our guns were anything but good, and the wet weather, and sea spray in the boat, had not improved them. The only person that had any success at all was Mr. Leiper, second mate of the "Lady Franklin." The weather still continued stormy and showery, and there was a little frost towards night.

Friday, June 27th.—It was very hard indeed to be so much delayed by bad weather. We only took two meals a day on account of our fuel. The tide was higher this day than we had yet seen it. It blew a perfect gale from the north, but it occurred to me that a valley near us inclined it more to the northward.

Saturday, June 28th.—It blew a gale until 4 A.M., when it began to moderate. At 6 A.M. the cooks were called, and after breakfast several parties were sent out to hunt and explore. They were more successful than before, for they brought in twenty-nine kittiwakes. At 8 P.M. it was calm, and there were appearances as if we were to have an easterly wind; an easterly wind in Barrow Straits I had no doubt, from the heavy clouds that hung over Cornwallis Island. We could not get under way, for the ice was close whichever way we turned. At 10 P.M. the tide turned to the westward, and the ice slacked along with it.

Sunday, June 29th. — The long and tiresome walking we had over the land yesterday made us sleep very soundly. No watch was kept. A smart breeze was heard rustling past. I looked out at 5 P.M. to see from what direction it came; and sure enough it was from the N.E. A large space of water was observed opening out under the lee of the island. Every one was out, and, in a few minutes, actively employed carrying the provisions to the water's edge. What a cheerful effect this change had upon the seamen's spirits, and upon no one more than myself; for I expected that even yet we should be able to accomplish a long search. After worship, we started on our mission with a single-reefed sail. Our course for ten miles was due W.; and after passing a small bay W. N. W., we went at the rate of 7½ knots. The west point of Hamilton Island was passed, and named Cape Graham Gore, after the first lieutenant of the "Erebus," one of the ships of the missing expedition.

On the south side of the same island, there is a prominent point, which was seen very plainly from the west point: it was named after H. T. D. Le Visconte, second lieutenant of the "Erebus." From Cape Graham Gore to Cape Fitzjames, on the same island, the course and distance is about N. E. ten miles. The wind being about N., the loose ice was packed down upon Cape Fitzjames. This put a stop to our progress, and we had need, for we had pulled all the way from Cape Graham Gore nearly against the wind. The moment the boat landed, I ascended this cape. It is a bold, almost perpendicular, headland, and commands a splendid view. The north point of Baring Island, which I named Cape Reid, out of compliment to the ice-master of the "Erebus," could be seen very plainly, bearing W. ½ N. The south point of the same island could also be seen distinctly; it was named Cape Blanky, after Mr. T. Blanky, the ice-master of the "Terror." Mr. Blanky spent upwards of four years, along with Sir John Ross, in the Arctic regions; and during the greatest part of that time, he and his companions were given up for lost; let it be hoped that the circumstances peculiar to his case then, may again occur in the Expedition that is still missing. Cape Crozier forms the south-west point of an island, situated on the north side of the eastern extremity of Queen Victoria Channel. This island was named after Admiral Deans Dundas, one of the Lords Commissioners of the Admiralty. Cape Benjamin Smith, on the north side of the same channel, but farther to the eastward, is the south-eastern point of a small island, which rises to the southward in the form of a square block, and runs away to the N. W., where it terminates in a long flat point. This island was named Margaret Island, and it is separated from Dundas Island by a narrow strait, which opens out very distinctly, when viewed from Cape Fitzjames. Beyond Dundas and Margaret Islands, the coast runs to the westward, and presents deep bays and rugged indentations, which vary in height from seven hundred to eight hundred feet. From a point (Cape Becher), it flies away more northerly, as far as the eye can reach. Two cairns were observed to the northward. I erected a cairn, and left a document in it, and then returned to the boat. There was a fresh northerly breeze. We hauled the boat upon an immense block of ice, which pressure had forced into shallow water, got supper, and turned in at 8 P.M. Hitherto we had found no traces; but when I mentioned to my poor fellows that I had seen two cairns, they were quite beside themselves with ardent hopes that they should prove to have been built by those for whom we had hitherto sought in vain.

Monday, June 30th.—A partial opening took

place at 5 A.M. Called all the people, and put into readiness for starting; but we were detained by a point until 9 A.M., when we started. Our course was to the eastward, around and along Cape Fitzjames. This is a bold and perpendicular headland of a very remarkable appearance, from the blocks of rock, of a black colour, which jut out among the white snow or ice. Very little snow can lie in the face of the cliffs without being actually beaten into them, which gives them more the appearance of glaciers than projections of land. This must be owing to the strong N. N. W. storms, with drifting snow, which prevail to such an extent during winter. We reached about half across the channel, when we were obliged to return, and on reaching the north side of Hamilton Island, which we had left but a short time before, we had very great difficulties in finding a secure place for the boat. As we rounded the headland, the wind followed us, until it was back to its old quarter, W. by N. Our landing-place was about four miles east of the cape, and it was anything but a pleasant situation. But it was the best that we could get; indeed, I may say the only place where a boat could be hauled up from the mercy of the drifting ice. On the one hand we had a perpendicular snowy cliff, on the other the ice pressing up and squeezing in two fathoms water, with a loud grinding noise, and tumbling over in huge blocks upon the terrace, on which we had taken shelter. The tide was very rapid, and the ice always continued in motion; no one slept, owing to the terrifying and groaning noise which it kept up all night. At 8 P.M. we were all in our sleeping bags.

July 1st.—The wind was light and variable. The channel completely blocked up with ice. Our spy-glasses were frequently occupied examining the two cairns to the northward, and some said they saw "the poles" in the centre of them. Every person was out searching along the coast. The headlands and beaches were all well examined. The tides are very rapid in this channel. The grinding of the ice on the shoals along the beach, and the squeezing up which takes place, emit a sound which may well be compared to distant thunder. At 9 P.M. two hares were brought in by the hunting parties.

Wednesday, July 2nd.—The first few hours of morning we had a partial breeze from the eastward, which brought the ice out of the channel. It came tearing along the land at a fearful rate, turning up immense hummocks in its progress. I felt very restless and could not sleep. The boat began to move a little. I took it into my head that there was a bear outside. My hand was upon my pistol, and all ready for action: I put out my head beneath the lower edge of the covering of the boat, and it was well I did so at the time, for immense hummocks were tumbling over and over, with the pressure within a few yards of us. No one waited to put on his clothes, for each flew to the provisions, and conveyed them up to the face of the precipice, and then to the boat to attend to its safety. The ice on which it rested was broken into several pieces, and thrown very much from its level, by the pressure among the hummocks around it. In the middle of the channel it was truly fearful, and could be compared to nothing but an earthquake. Some pieces were rising to a height of twenty feet, and tumbling down with tremendous crashing and rending. We again turned in beneath our covering; but little sleep was obtained, for every one was peeping from beneath the housing-cloth. Our situation was rather awkward, I must confess. About a mile and a half eastward there is a fine bay, which I named Robert Bay, after a son of Captain Hamilton, Secretary of the Admiralty: towards it we commenced launching the boat. After proceeding about three hundred yards with her, we returned for our provisions: by a little trouble in this way we reached Robert Bay, where we reckoned ourselves in comparative safety. The wind was again from W. N. W., attended with thick fog. Three of us were suffering severely from inflammation of the eyes, I suppose owing to the constant use of the spy-glass. I issued strict orders it should not be used, except with my permission.

Thursday, July 3rd.—At 4 A.M. all hands were called, and several parties were formed to go in various directions, that the coast might be thoroughly explored. The weather was so backward that it threatened to baffle our utmost endeavours, but we were determined to persevere to the last, trusting to an overruling Providence for guidance and a safe return to our ships. Blowing a gale from W. N. W.

Friday, July 4th.—It continued to blow a gale with heavy squalls at times, which made the boat shake again and again. At 2 A.M. it began to moderate, and before 4 A.M. it was calm. We were up and had breakfast, and as there was no change in the ice, several parties went out again to explore. I do not think there is a spot of Hamilton Island but has been gone over. We had a partial breeze from the eastward. Oh! for a week of strong easterly winds. In this I was not gratified, for westerly winds seemed decreed to prevail. At 8 P.M. blowing from N. N. W.

Saturday, July 5th.—After breakfast, off we again started to hunt and search. William Bruce and I took the beach. A bit of English elm quite fresh was picked up, and also a piece of driftwood. The elm had not been long in the water, but it was much reduced in weight, and weatherworn by exposure to the atmosphere. It could never have come in contact with ice. On every headland we erected cairns.

Sunday, July 6th.—We still lay closely beset in Robert Bay. There was a strong breeze from W. by N., which continued until about 4 P.M., when it died away. A light breeze sprung up from north-east; and there was a strong tide running to the westward. We packed up, and were in readiness for an immediate start, but the ice continued to pour down along the land, and on to the westward. Towards midnight there was heavy rain.

Monday, July 7th.—There was a strong breeze from north-east, with a constant torrent of rain. I put on an oil-skin dress, and went to the hill-top to look for a lead among the ice. The water extended as far as Point Surprise, and half across to Margaret Island. I returned immediately, and got the boat into the water. The covering was kept up to protect us from the heavy rain. There was a strong flood tide running in our favour. At noon we got the boat hauled upon the ridge of pressed up ice on the pitch of Point Surprise. There appeared to be very little difference in the state of the land ice since Mr. Petersen and I had been on the same spot on the 17th of May. Its edge was about the same distance (fifteen miles) from the island to the eastward. Parties were sent in several directions to explore. At 5 P. M. we all returned, and each was soaking wet. The rain still continued, but our easterly wind had failed; for it chopped in to the N. W., and blew strong from W. N. W. at midnight.

Tuesday, July 8th.—Strong W. N. W. wind and squally, with passing showers. The westerly wind made about a mile of open water around the east side of the island. Our fuel, of which we had on leaving the ships but a scanty supply, and of a very inferior description, was done. We launched the boat into this small space of water. There were a great many ducks (both eider and king ducks) in the water. Two of them and a small seal were shot. These added much to our comfort; but we should have got a great many more had the water free from drifting ice been of sufficient extent to render the boat safe in such rapid tides. The only spot where we could venture with the boat was in the eddy under lee of Point Surprise.

Wednesday, July 9th.—Still squally, with heavy clouds rising from the westward. I ascended a hill about four hundred and fifty feet in height above the level of the sea. Nothing but a dark black sky could be seen over the pack ice to the westward as far as the eye could reach. We thought this pack extended only so far to the westward, and that beyond it, from the indications of the sky, there was open water. In our narrow escapes with the boat, I often thought of Mr. M'Cormack, and the wise decision of their Lordships in not approving of his plan, and sending him out in an open boat, for they might as well have signed his death-warrant and that of those under his command. At 6 P.M. we had soft snow and a smart gale from about west. Notwithstanding all the care that had been taken, and all the patching and mending that had been practised, our boots and shoes were about done; indeed, one need hardly wonder at this, for we walked over the rough shingle from morning till night along the unknown coast, seeking for traces.

Thursday, July 10th.—The wind still continued westerly, accompanied by sleet and snow. The channel was tightly blocked up with ice, and there was heavy pressure among it very often. This need not be wondered at when the tide goes at the rate of four miles an hour. The water was still to be seen very clearly under Baring Island.

Friday, July 11th.—The weather at last became clear and dry. We launched the boat into the water at the lee end of the island, and shot some birds.

Oh! for an easterly wind. At noon, got an altitude by the artificial horizon, which gave the latitude of Point Surprise about 76° 4′. There was, between this and a former observation on the 17th of May, not at the point itself, but a few miles north of it, a discrepancy of four miles. This is to be regretted; the mean, however, of the two observations will, to a certainty, be within a mile or two of being correct. Towards evening there was a light air from E. N. E.

Saturday, July 12*th.*—The easterly wind did not last long, for at 8 A.M. it shifted to W. and W.S.W., and came away a perfect gale. At noon, however, it fell calm again, and began to come from the eastward. A crack opened half across the channel. An attempt was made to get across, but it failed, and we were glad to get back again.

Sunday, July 13*th.*—Blew a gale from N.W. with thick snow. We had *worship*, and the seamen were very devout; as, indeed, we all ought to be for such merciful preservation. There was a strong flood-tide running, no doubt influenced very much by the wind, for, as I have already remarked, it appears to run tide and half tide to the east. The rise and fall is not more than five feet.

Monday, July 14*th.*—The gale had turned a large portion of the ice in the Strait to the northward of us round the west point of the island,

and had left small holes of water in it. A small cask was filled with bread, and our knapsacks were kept uppermost in the boat; each had his duty allotted to him in case the boat should be caught between two floes. The best lead that began to open out on this side of the channel by the tide was at Point Surprise. We started at half-past 7 A.M., and proceeded northward along a large floe piece. At half-past 9 A.M. we got beset and hauled the boat upon the ice, and attempted to launch her; but it would not do, the ice was too much decayed in some parts. The ice again took a favourable turn; we launched the boat: the poor fellows were very active, for they knew the danger, and at noon we reached Margaret Island. This island presents a bold table bluff to the southward which runs east and west. The water is shallow at the east end of it. While dinner was getting ready I ascended this table island. The long-seen cairn was now within four miles of me, on the east end of Dundas Island.

Tuesday, 15th July.—After two hours and a half searching without finding any traces, I returned to the party loaded with fossil remains, in which the island is very abundant. Its extent from north to south is about five miles, east to west three miles, and the height of the southern extremity westward from

Cape Benjamin Smith is about four hundred feet. From S. E. to N. W. its length is about seven miles, and it slopes away in the latter direction to a low spit. It is divided from Dundas Island by a strait six miles in length, and one and a half in breadth running N. and by W. I erected a cairn upon it, and left a document. We had some fresh soup for dinner, which was made of birds that had been shot at this bluff. At 3 P. M. we started with a favourable tide, and washed down along the edge of the pushed up hummocks, which were in parts at least twenty feet high. There was no place where we could have landed, until we reached Dundas Island at 4h. 30m. P. M., and then we had to cut a slip before the boat could be got upon the land terrace. Immediately upon landing I set off, accompanied by one of the men, to examine the cairn-like objects, which had for such a long time danced before our eyes and tantalized us. When I was within one hundred yards of it, I felt so engrossed with what I was to discover, that even then the deception was not detected. It was a disappointment in real earnest, but it was much less felt, owing to the fact that we had been inured to such, ever since I came to Point Surprise, on the 17th of May. From this object we struck across the land, and after three hours' travelling a channel was discovered leading W. and by N., and from ten to twelve miles in breadth. This proved the correctness of the ideas I had when this island was named. The channel was named North Channel, to distinguish it from the South Channel, which had been discovered in my first journey. After crossing the island we coasted along two beautiful bays: one of them was about a mile deep from north to south, and it had no pressed up ice in it along the beach. It would suit well for a winter harbour. The N.W. extremity of this island is seven to eight hundred feet high; it was named Cape Liddell, after the first lieutenant of the "Terror." The opposite or north-eastern point of the same island was named Cape Collins, after the second master of the "Erebus." Although it rained hard, it was clear along the horizon, and this made me all the more anxious to push on to have a good look to the westward from the north-west bluff. Just as I was within one hundred yards of the top, the curtain dropped and everything was obscured. I ascended, thinking it might clear again; but it did not, and rain poured down in torrents. A cairn was erected, and as I and my companion descended, we came out of the fog or mist which rested on the hill-top. We had no difficulty from thick weather in finding our way back to the boat; but, as usual, we were without traces.

July 16th.—We reached the boat at 1½ A.M., after eight hours and a half hard walking, quite wet. In our journey we were joined by other two, who had left the boat to look for us, thinking that we must have found something. We were all wet and fatigued alike; but none of the fine hearty fellows ever complained after eighteen hours' hard labour, and not a dry stitch upon them. At 4 A.M., after a short rest, called the people out again, as we had still the west side of the island to examine. At 8 A.M. we started; and as the weather was perfectly clear, the chart was taken to the highest hill-top and spread out. The compass being next thing to useless, the card of it was taken, and, by its assistance, bearings were taken and positions assigned to every point of land and island, with, I believe, considerable accuracy, from the sun. They might be a little out; but as every precaution was observed to secure accuracy, it must have been little. From Cape Becher on the north shore, the land could be seen trending away to the N.W. to a distance of sixty or seventy miles. It is very bold land. The land on the west side of Queen Victoria Channel appeared to extend due north from the north side of Bathurst Island, which by this time had been proved to be continuous with Cornwallis Island to the eastward. At the remotest distance that could be seen in Prince Albert Land, we again observed the snow-clad mountains often enveloped in clouds which had been named Sir John Barrow's Monument. It was seen several times since Hamilton Island had been reached with the boat; but at no time had we so clear a view of it as on this day. Nothing but water was seen to the N.W. in Queen Victoria Channel as far as the eye could reach. The South and North Channels, and the eastern extremity of Victoria Channel, were fairly blocked up with ice, which extended about eight or ten miles to the westward of Hamilton Island, where the boundless water stretching to the N.W. appeared to commence. At 2 P.M. we returned to the boat, taking the western beach, along where there was very hard work, climbing over the pressed-up hummocks in the face of the perpendicular headlands. Two pieces of driftwood were picked up on the S.W. end of the island. Had dinner. At $2\frac{3}{4}$ P.M. we started, and plied up between Margaret and Dundas Islands with a favourable tide. However, our sail was set only for a short time. After getting about half up this strait or channel, two cairns were observed on the south shore of Prince Albert Land. We thought surely there could be no mistake this time; but could it be possible that Captain Stewart could have reached such a distance westward? Our disappointment was very great when we found it absolutely necessary to bear up and return to Margaret Island. It was fearfully grand to see the floes carried along, huge blocks turning over and over, and disappearing with crashing which was really tremendous. We had several narrow escapes before we reached Cape B. Smith, which was the only place where we could haul the boat up. Several birds were shot. The wind was W. N. W.

Thursday, July 17th.—Strong W. N. W. wind. What an extensive search we should have made had we been but favoured with easterly winds! My hopes of accomplishing one thousand miles with the boat, where were they? I had to submit to this as to a dispensation of Providence. At 10 A.M. we had the slack of the tide; and as there was a partial opening in the ice, an attempt was made to cross the channel obliquely to the west end of Hamilton Island, where water was seen from the top of Margaret Island. Robert Bay was reached, and a landing effected, just as the weather was becoming quite thick. During the passage we had to launch over several floes. Thick weather, strong W. N. W. wind.

Friday, July 18th.—Strong W. N. W. wind, with very thick fog. At 4 A.M. got breakfast, and were ready for a start, watching the state of the ice in the channel. At 8 A.M. a lead was observed in the sailing ice through a partial clear in the fog. Off we started for Baring Island, as the opening in the ice led in that direction. The sail was set most of the time, the wind being from N.W. The course steered was W. and by S. At $5\frac{1}{4}$ P.M. we landed on Baring Island. The passage to it occupied nine hours, the distance being about thirty miles. We sailed and pulled occasionally, and also made traverse courses. The above distance is estimated; but it is most probably under the real distance than above it. The moment we landed, every one set out to search for traces as well as for ducks' eggs. I calculated that I should have got as many eggs on this island as would last fourteen days; and I believe so we should, had not the continued rains kept the ground so wet and cold, that the ducks could not lay upon it. Their nests were to be seen in hundreds, and they appeared to be in an advanced state of preparation to receive the eggs. Only a dozen were found. These were a little help when our provisions were getting so nearly exhausted. After the half of the island had been explored without finding any traces, and being wearied, at 8 P.M. we turned into our sleeping bags.

July 19th.—At 2 A.M. got breakfast. There was a strong breeze from the northward, right in our faces, as we had to proceed in that direction. After breakfast I went to explore the north end of the island, while the party was preparing the boat. On its northern extremity I erected a cairn, and laid down the position of several points and islands, as usual, with the compass card and the chart, taking the bearings from the sun, whose bearing I always knew from having the time, which was generally within one or two minutes of being correct. Baring Island is about ten miles long and five broad. Its height is about two hundred feet, and the top is flat, with several lakes upon it, one of which I named Leiper Lake, after the second mate of the "Lady Franklin." James Knox picked up several pieces of driftwood, which appeared to be very fresh, on the east side of the island in a small bay which I named Driftwood Bay. Towards the south end of the island there is a deep indentation, which would suit for a harbour; it was named Fairholme Harbour, after one of the lieutenants of the "Erebus."

At 7 A.M. we started for the north side of Queen Victoria Channel, as our search here, as well as elsewhere, had proved fruitless. Our course was N. E., and the distance not less than thirty miles. We had not proceeded far on our passage across, until two seahorses were observed close to the boat; and thinking there was a chance we should be able to kill one of them, for the sake of fuel, we bore down upon them, and, after putting a ball into the mouth of one, we got fast to him with the harpoon and line. A good deal of firing ensued; but we were forced to draw close up and run a lance through him, for the balls took no effect whatever, except to increase his fierceness, and our danger in approaching him. We required to be very cautious in this respect, for his large tusks might easily have torn a plank out of our boat. The blubber proved of great value as fuel, and some of the seamen thought the thick hide would have suited for moccassins, as their shoes were very near done. I used part of the flesh, and relished it very much, but only so long as it was fresh and sweet; the least taint in it, I could not taste it. After twelve hours plying with our oars, for it fell calm, we reached Cape Becher. The moment we landed, I ascended to the top of the hill to examine the cairn, which proved to be Captain Stewart's farthest, and a good journey he must have made. While I was examining this cairn, Thompson, who had accompanied me so far, hailed the rest of the party not to go to examine the other cairn, that had been seen on a distant point. They mistook his meaning, and thinking that traces had been found of Sir John Franklin, they all ran to the top of the hill, where I was engaged laying down the coast. To have seen their faces when I told them it was Captain Stewart's, would have made any one sorry, they looked so disappointed. After travelling about five miles farther north, I opened out a splendid bay (Sir Robert H. Inglis Bay), which would suit well for a winter harbour. From the point where I stood, at an elevation of six to eight hundred feet, nothing could be seen to the N. W. but open water and a watery sky. The coast was bold, and led away N. W. The most distant part of it that I could discern was named Cape Sir J. Franklin, and it appeared to be a few miles beyond latitude 77° and longitude 100°. To the south-eastward of this cape the coast disappears for upwards of twenty-five miles, until it reaches a second bold point, which I named Cape Sophia, after the niece of Sir John Franklin. From Cape Sophia it could be traced to Cape Becher, in the vicinity of which I stood. In Victoria Channel, about longitude 100°, off Cape Sophia, I observed the southern shore of a small island, which was named after John Barrow, Esq., son of the late Sir John Barrow, to whom Arctic discovery is so deeply indebted. Immediately to the southward of John Barrow Island there is a second island, not quite so large as the former; it was named Parker Island out of compliment to J. Parker Esq., M. P., the Secretary of the Admiralty.

The northernmost point of the western shore of Queen Victoria Island I named Cape Lady Franklin. It does not appear to extend so far north as 77°, and its longitude is about 102°. From Cape Lady Franklin, the land stretches southward in one continuous coast. In this coast line there is a small inlet or indentation, which was named after Henry Goodsir, Esq., assistant-surgeon and naturalist in the missing expedition. I erected a cairn, and took another view of the expanse of water that was before my eyes — oh, to have been here only with my two little vessels, what could we not have done in the way of search? but I greatly fear, if we had, the missing ships are beyond our reach. That there is a large Arctic Sea beyond this channel, in which the ice is constantly in motion, there can be no doubt: for where could all the ice have gone to? where does the comparatively fresh driftwood come from? It must be from America or Siberia, and that through a body of drifting ice. Had Sir John Franklin left documents, surely he would have done so upon this headland or Dundas Island. We found none; Mr. Stewart was in the same state; we were all in the same predicament as when winter-quarters were discovered by us in August 1850. At midnight we turned into our sleeping bags.

Sunday, July 20th.—Little sleep was obtained,

owing to the heavy squalls, and the noise of the grinding and crashing of the ice, as it poured out of the channel past Cape Becher, the wind being very strong from E. N. E. At 5 A. M. all hands were called. I ascended the hill while they were preparing breakfast. Where there had been so much clear water yesterday, had now a stream, thirty miles of drifting ice, in it, which had come from the eastward. Would it be prudent to continue to proceed farther, with only one week's provisions? It was a severe struggle to leave the search, but there was no other course left. That the missing ships had gone beyond our reach, I had no doubt; for if they had not, then we should have found traces of them about some of the Bird Heads or Duck Islands, which had been surrounded with water ever since the 17th of May, in fact during the whole winter; for it is my opinion that the ice in Queen Victoria Channel kept in motion all that time. After worship, we started on our return to the ships, with a fresh breeze from the N. N. W. We often hove the log, and found that we came with sails and oars at the rate of 5½ knots. We were two hours and twenty minutes in crossing the north channel to Dundas Island. From Cape Liddell, its north-western promontory, we ran to Cape Crozier in one hour, and thence to Hamilton Island in two hours. We were six hours in getting round the west end of Hamilton Island; and after reaching its south shore, four hours more were spent in reaching the north shore of Cornwallis Island. We were fifteen hours and a half in crossing from Cape Becher; our courses were a little traverse, owing to the cross state of the ice; and the distance we had come in that time, under our single reefed sail, was about eighty miles. I had often to land, for the purpose of choosing the best leads among the ice.

From Hamilton Island and from Disappointment Bay, an island was observed to the westward of Houston Stewart and Baring Islands. It was named Milne Island, out of compliment to Captain Milne, R. N., one of the Lords of the Admiralty. Its northernmost point was named Cape M'Donald, after one of the medical officers in the missing expedition, who had accompanied me to Davis Straits during two or three voyages, previous to his entering Her Majesty's service. When I looked back upon the many escapes we have made, considering our experience with boats among ice, I again felt thankful that I did not take out Dr. M'Cormack and his boat's crew, when the expedition I commanded left home.

Monday, July 21st.—At 1 A.M. we turned into our sleeping bags, and, after six hours and a half, at

7½ A.M., we turned out and had breakfast. The boat-sledge left at Abandon Bay, the part of Cornwallis Island which we had just reached, was unlashed, and a runner was hauled up on each side of the boat's gunwale, and with this arrangement we got under way. Our course was along the land, over ice which was very much decayed. The boat broke through, and it began to press up around her, so that there was some difficulty in saving her. We hauled her to an old floe, lashed the sledge again, and got her upon it, and commenced dragging her along. The pools of water on the ice sometimes took us to the waist. Nevertheless, the poor fellows tugged away with their usual good will, and never once complained. After four hours' hard toil we gained about two miles. This showed the utter impossibility of taking the boat along with us. I at once decided that she should be left upon the land, and that we should travel to the ships by the coast, over a distance of upwards of one hundred miles. The wind was again from the westward. It was fortunate that we reached Cornwallis Island, for had it not been so at that time, a fatal termination might have been the consequence. Each was preparing for our return, mending shoes and patching knapsacks, &c. &c.

Tuesday, July 22nd.—Wind northerly, with fine

weather. The ice was all broken up along the north shore of the island, only waiting a strong south-east wind to clear it out. The long-continued westerly and northerly winds kept it stationary. At 6 A.M. I called the people out, and got breakfast; packed up six sleeping bags to be taken with us, stowed away all our spare clothing, felt blanket, tent, &c., in the boat; thirty pounds of bread and a broken case of pemmican were also placed in the boat, and the whole was covered over with the housing-cloth of the boat. A tent-pole was balanced, and the knapsacks were weighed, each being of the same weight. The bay where the boat was left is very properly called Abandon Bay. To the westward of it there is another bay, the one in which we were detained for such a length of time after getting the boat into the water; and still further to the westward there is a third bay, which was named after the Honourable Harriet Hamilton, the wife of Captain Hamilton, Secretary of the Admiralty. Lady Hamilton Bay is separated from the bay to the eastward of it by a prominent point, which was named Cape Austin, out of compliment to the commander of the Expedition with which we had to co-operate in the search for Sir John Franklin.

At noon we started each with his load, and at 3½ or 4 P.M. we came to a rapid and deep stream. We had to strip and ford it. Overheated by travelling, we felt the cold of the ice-cold water most intensely painful. There is an inlet here which I named Stuart Bay, after the assistant-surgeon of the "Lady Franklin." The watercourse at the top of it comes from a large lake a short distance from the coast. It was named Eleanor Lake, after a daughter of my much esteemed friend Captain Hamilton. We continued to push on at a rapid rate. Four miles to the eastward of the stream we had a fine view from a hill-top. The chart was again taken out, and the coast-lines, lakes, and bays were laid down as accurately as possible. We continued our journey for nine hours and a half, when we were obliged to come to a stand from fatigue. The night was cold, and the hoar frost could be seen on the wet sleeping bags and knapsacks. Two kept watch, as we had only six sleeping bags.

Wednesday, July 23rd.—Cold as the night was, the poor fellows slept soundly and were refreshed. At 7 A.M. they were called to begin their hard toil. We expected this would be our last day's journey to the depôt at Cape de Haven. The distance travelled yesterday was about thirty miles. We crossed Helen Haven, a securely sheltered bay, which would suit well for a winter harbour, and arrived at the depôt at 11 A.M. We found that it had been laid out for our use by Captain Stewart. At noon I had an altitude by the artificial horizon, which gave latitude 75° 22′. We had a most comfortable meal of warm coffee, which was followed by a glass of spirits, the first we had had for nearly three weeks. There was drizzling rain with close weather, but it was not cold. I allowed the people to rest until 5 P.M., when we repacked our knapsacks and started. We preferred travelling during the night, on account of the greater safety from cold during the day, when we should halt for rest. There was a cold S. S.W. wind, with passing showers. At midnight we had to strip for a broad and rapid stream. Its violence must have been very great when it first broke out this season, for stones, weighing upwards of a hundred weight, had been carried by it to a distance of two miles out upon the ice in Wellington Channel. Had a sledge party passed at the time, the results would have been fatal. At a short distance inland several lakes occur which appear to be the source of the stream; at all events its waters pass through them. They were named Laura Lakes, after a daughter of Captain Hamilton.

Thursday, July 24th.—It continued to rain, and we continued to push on drenching wet. At 2 A.M. we halted, but no sleep was obtained. At 11 A.M. we started again, and crossed another stream, but had not to strip. We then crossed a deep bay upon the ice, which was very much decayed, owing, probably, to the fresh water from the land. There were pools of water on it in some parts. At 8 P.M. we were again obliged to come to a halt, having travelled about twenty-five miles. As usual, we lay down upon the beach, but slept none. This was the worst halt we had felt since the commencement of our journey.

Friday, July 25th.—The rain continued to pour down with a strong S. S. W. gale, and we were still fifty miles from the ships. Some of the people would be laid up by such another night; and all of them were very much fatigued. There was nothing for us but push on at our best. At 4 A.M. came to a stream at Point Separation, which was too deep and too broad to be crossed. We had to cross upon the decayed ice in the Wellington Channel; while doing this two of us got a dip, but we got all safe to the land again. At 9 A.M. we found a boat hauled up at the mouth of a large run of water. Here again Captain Stewart's foresight had agreeably surprised us. As soon as the men had all come up, we launched the boat into the water, and plied southward for seven miles against a "head" wind. On the north side of Barlow Inlet we struck in with the boat, where we came to the conclusion we should leave her, and proceed to the ships on foot. This was owing to the strong wind that was blowing right in our teeth. We had a hearty luncheon of warm coffee, and at 3 P.M. we set out for the ships. It rained all the way, and every body was wet to the skin. After six or seven hours, having travelled twenty-five miles, we reached the ships at 10 P.M., and felt thankful to our Maker, by whom we had been enabled to surmount all the difficulties and perils of our journey, without immediate injury to our health. We were almost barefoot. John Leiper*, poor fellow! second mate of the "Lady Franklin," had actually been walking upon his bare soles for some time, although his feet appeared to be protected.

* He died in March, six months after the return of the Expedition to this country. His disease was an affection of the lungs, of which the first symptoms appeared or were detected early after the Expedition was paid off.

CHAP. XIX.

RETURN OF ALL THE TRAVELLING PARTIES EXCEPT MR. PENNY'S.

Open Water in Barrow Straits. — Boat Party setting out. — Proper Runner for a Boat Sledge.— Shooting Seals and Birds.—Diseases. —Commander Phillips from Cape Hotham.—Party from Griffith's Island. — Return of all the Travelling Parties except Mr. Penny's. — Abundance of Animals. — Melville Island. — Vegetation. — The Musk Ox. — Opinions respecting the Missing Expedition. — Appearance of the Ice.—Debacles.—Vegetation.—A Chain of Lakes. — Peculiar Mode of Thaw. — Brent Geese. —Recreation.—Jelly-like Plant. — Insects. — Experiments. — Sea-fowl. —Dredging. — Open Water.—Ballasting the Ships.—Journey to Griffith's Island. — The half-way House. — Water upon the Ice. — Red Snow. — Arrival. —Anxiety for Captain Penny.—Health of the Expedition. — Chart-making. — An Inspection. — Intelligence from Assistance Bay. — Return to Assistance Bay. — Small Fishes in the Ice. — Drifting Ice.—Relics of the Esquimaux.—Esquimaux Nomadic.— Softness of the Soil. — Stores of the Boat Expedition. — State of Barrow Straits. — Vegetation fading. — Insects. — A Party from Griffith's Island.—A Party adrift upon the Ice.—Looking anxiously for Captain Penny's Return.

July 1*st.*—The report brought from Cape Hotham by Captain Stewart was hailed with glee by all in our expedition, and frequent visits were made to a hill on the east side of the harbour, from which an extensive view of Barrow Straits could be obtained. There appeared to be very broad lanes of open water extending across the whole breadth of the strait. The ice was in very extensive sheets, and had our ships been a little nearer the edge of the water, which was only a mile and a half from the bottom of Assistance Bay, we might get clear in a few days, and proceed down the sound or across to the opposite shore. We saw that we had taken up a position for winter-quarters, which would prove *extra* safe by preventing us getting clear sufficiently early to take advantage of the first chances of navigating Barrow Straits. There was a fringe of ice along the south shore of Cornwallis Island, about a quarter of a mile in breadth; and at the edge of this fringe the water, varying in breadth from a few yards up to two miles, could be seen extending eastward to Cape Hotham, and westward to the south point of Griffith's Island. After such a length of time as we had been without an extensive sheet of blue water, to gaze upon the sight before us was exceedingly agreeable, and none less so on account of the fears which Sir John Ross was continually expressing, that we should not get clear of the ice till late in the season, if indeed we should get clear this season.

Captain Stewart and his party were ready to start with the boat, and as Commander Phillips was to proceed to Cape Hotham with a party for provisions from the depôt, laid down by the "Assistance" in autumn, both parties set out together.

Mr. Stewart had seven or eight men in his party; it was feared, however, that he would find them incapable of dragging the heavy boat over the barrier of ice in the Wellington Channel, which, from the water at Cape Hotham to the water which Captain Penny was then navigating, was not less than seventy miles, by the crookedness of the road, owing to the hummocks. On its passage to the edge of the water over the ice in Assistance Bay, the boat dragged very heavily, and the runners of the sledge which supported it appeared to yield and bend when an elevation had to be crossed. This was owing to the runners being made of two pieces joined in the middle, instead of one solid and unyielding plank. The more unyielding the runners of a sledge are, the less the friction will be, among rough ice as well as on the smooth ice. Suppose that a boat mounted on two sledges, the one before the other, and joined by a hinge, came among rough ice; it could not fail to happen often that one of the sledges would be on the one side of the hummock, while the other would be on the opposite; that is to say, the foremost would be burying itself in the snow in its descent, while the other would still be ascending. The chief features in making a sledge are, rigidity of the runners, very smooth and flat iron for shoeing, rolled being much better than hammered: the rise of the floor ought to be in proportion to the length and the weight; in a sledge sixteen feet long, a gradual rise of half an inch on seven or eight feet will be about the proportion which will suit best. After the experience we had in sledging, we occupied a position which enabled us to see at a glance what form of sledge and arrangement of weights would suit best.

The party from the "Felix" also had a boat, but it was very small, and capable of carrying only a few persons. When both boats were launched into the water, it was a delightful sight to behold them pulling away to the eastward, frightening seals and walruses, king, eider, and long-tailed ducks, loons, dovekies, gulls of two or three species, and terns, all of which were in abundance in the water. The surface of the sea was as smooth as oil, for there was no wind, and everything around us breathed an air of tranquillity and happiness inexpressible. Some of the men who accompanied the boat to the edge of the water, but did not belong to her crew, amused themselves at the water shooting seals and birds in it; but the want of a boat was very much missed to pick them up. The Esquimaux had his kyack, and often endeavoured to pick up something for himself in the way of food; but he appeared to be very cautious in going far from the edge of the ice, for fear he should be attacked by walruses. He said that on one occasion, having embarked to pick up a seal, he had to make his escape as fast as possible out of the water from one of those formidable looking animals, which appeared disposed to take a little pastime with his frail canoe.

During the absence of Dr. Porteus, the surgeon of the "Felix," one of the crew of that ship consulted me about a disease of which he complained. His legs were swollen and livid, and his thighs appeared as if diffused inflammation had supervened upon very extensive contusion of all the tissues, both deep-seated and superficial. His gums were spongy, but there was not present that languor and lassitude which is present in scurvy. He was one of the party who had accompanied Commander Phillips in his fatiguing overland journey, and there is no doubt the symptoms he had were the result of the excessive fatigue he had to undergo, as well as the privations that had to be endured. The treatment that was adopted was of a decidedly tonic character, and the good results of it were beginning to be apparent in eight or ten days. Those of our men who had been hard tried in the travelling, and were not able to accompany me in laying out the depôt for Captain Penny's return, were in all respects fit for duty in a week or ten days. They had all the symptoms of "purpura," which is a disease closely allied to scurvy in some respects, but is often brought on by excessive fatigue in travelling.* There were only two or three such cases, and there were never present such painful symptoms as prevented them going to the land in quest of game, where six or seven successive hours were frequently spent, in chase of hares and brent-geese, which were beginning to be hunted off the ground around our winter-quarters.

July 3rd.—At an early hour in the morning Captain Phillips and his party arrived from Cape Hotham. They were not able to bring a large supply with them from the depôt, owing to the small size of their boat; however it would serve until a larger should be obtained by means of a larger boat. They reported to us that they had parted company with Mr A. Stewart, rounding Cape Hotham, at 6 P.M. of the preceding day. They also said that there was abundance of open water to the eastward, but that the drifting ice in Barrow Strait often came in contact with the fringe along the south shore of Cornwallis Island. This was not a sign of great abundance of water; however, it was of sufficient extent to enable us to proceed east or west with the ships had they been ready for it, by being near the edge of it. The

* Statistical Nosology, 1845, p. 17.

weather was pretty clear for a few days, and the temperature ranged rather high. The ice in the bay was beginning to suffer considerable reduction from the upper surface, and the water as it was produced percolated through it. There were small pools in which it accumulated in the day time, but at night, when the temperature might be below the freezing point of water, they were generally dry, and a film of rough ice formed on the surface and at the sides as the water sunk gradually through the highly porous ice underneath.

July 5th.—A party was observed coming from the west point of the harbour, and in a short time we discovered it was made up of Dr. Porteus, who had been on a protracted visit to the Expedition at Griffith's Island, two officers from H. M. S. "Pioneer," and one of the officers of the "Sophia," who also had been on a visit to Captain Austin's squadron. The party brought reports that all the travelling parties had returned without having found anything that could bear upon the route pursued by the missing ships, except negatively. Melville Island, Cape Dundas, Bushnan Cove, Winter Harbour, and every other spot in the far west was examined by the indefatigable M'Clintock and Mr. Bradford, who had just returned after an absence of eighty days. The former picked up numerous relics of Captain Parry's expedition, and, among other things, a portion of the cart-wheels which had been used on the overland journey to Bushnan Cove from Winter Harbour in 1820. He saw abundance of game, and succeeded in shooting four musk oxen, the flesh of which proved of inestimable value to him in enabling him to carry out the search in that quarter with perfect safety to his party. The jaw-bone of a musk ox has been found on Cornwallis Island, but it appears to be very old. These animals, which inhabit the Parry Group, seem in great measure to be restricted to Melville Island, where vegetation is much more luxuriant than it is on Cornwallis Island. The plants of the former include upwards of one hundred and sixteen species, while those of the latter amount probably to little more than half that number. From the description given by Captain Parry, vegetation is much more luxuriant in the less calcareous soil of the western portion of the North Georgian Islands than in its eastern portion, which, so far as I know, does not present a single deviation *in situ* from one continuous and unbroken tract of secondary limestone. Such a difference in the number of species as well as in the development of the plants, is sufficient to account for the choice which the musk ox makes of the locality where its food is most abundant. It has been doubted whether this animal migrates. Its long hair and clumsy form seem to indicate how well adapted it is for passing the most inclement weather among the snow, and how ill adapted it is for journeys of probably one or two hundred miles over a frozen sea. The Esquimaux on board H.M.S. "Assistance," whom Captain Ommanney took on board at Cape York, says that he heard that the Esquimaux, who inhabit the coast in the vicinity of Whale Sound, in the top of Baffin's Bay, clothe themselves with the skin of the musk ox (Umingmak). This statement, if true, would lead one to the idea, that the musk ox inhabits still more northern regions than Melville Island — regions whence they cannot return into a more southern latitude with the close of the season, owing to the open water in the top of Baffin's Bay throughout the whole winter. And, moreover, it may lead to the inference that such regions as can maintain the musk ox throughout the year in so high a latitude as 77° and upwards, must present features with respect to temperature which are peculiar only to regions in the vicinity of an extensive sea. Those points are highly conjectural; and it is not improbable that the tradition with respect to the ancestors of Erasmus York having worn dresses made of the skin of the musk ox has been handed down through successive generations since the time that they inhabited the North Georgian Islands and the newly-discovered Prince Albert Land, places of which we have the most abundant proofs that they were inhabited by Esquimaux, but are now left alone to the bear, fox, wolverin, wolf, musk ox, deer, hare, and lemming, all of which roam at large without ever being in danger of being molested by man, except when, civilised, he dares to brave the dangers of so inclement a region.

The travelling party under the command of Captain Penny in the Wellington Channel and beyond it was now the only one out. As each of the others returned from time to time it was to receive and augment the universal and lamentable report. There were several opinions as to the course the missing ships might have pursued after leaving Beechey Island. Some out of so many could not fail to be right. There was none, however, more positive in his assertions than Adam Beck, who seemed to sneer at the disappointed travellers returning from distances out and home of upwards of seven hundred miles, and who often said that it was vain to look for Franklin here or elsewhere, except somewhere about or north of Wolstenholme Sound, where, he said, his ships' cables are still to be found. He had his abettors; but it was enough for the majority of those who could give reasons for their opinions that the "North Star" had seen nothing of the missing ships in that quarter, and that neither Mr. Petersen, who had examined the Esquimaux at Cape York, nor York Ommanney could be induced to favour what appeared fabulous and absurd. Every man in both expeditions was looking with wistful eyes and throbbing heart in the direction of the Wellington Channel, where both Mr. Penny and Mr. Stewart were engaged in the cause of humanity, and no one appeared to be more anxious about their safe return than Captain Austin, who expressed the strongest wishes that every avenue which might lead to the discovery of the missing ships should be examined this season.

The open water was very near the ships, being within a few hundred yards of the south-east point of the bay, which is about a mile from where the ships lay. The last floe that went off took a portion of the January hummocks with it. The floe in the harbour had by this time lost a foot and a half of its upper surface. It was remarkably dry, for the water was withdrawing itself into pools, the surface of which was generally on a level with the water-line of the ice. The colour of the ice was bluish, except when the temperature of the air was below +32°, and then it was whitish. Local fogs capping the hills were very common, the sky was frequently overcast with dense blue and angry looking clouds, and there was generally heavy rain with south-east winds.

July 6th.—The heavy rain of the preceding night caused an accumulation of water in some of the lakes around Assistance Bay, which the snow in the water-courses leading from them was unable to dam up any longer. There had been some water making its way to the sea from the lakes through the ravines which were full of snow, but it was not in great quantity, for the channel which it had established for itself was not sufficient to carry it off in due proportion to the accumulation in the reservoirs above. Probably there might have been a temporary blocking up of the channel by snow, which would certainly account for the accumulation. At an early hour in the morning we were roused by the sound of an advancing stream. A small lake on the east side of the harbour burst open the barrier of snow which opposed its exit from its tranquil bed, and its contents dashed with impetuous violence to the harbour, carrying masses of snow from the sides of the ravine through which it had to seek its way. A portion of the harbour was inundated, but a wide crack in the ice permitted the water to pass through without spreading over the whole harbour. At the part where the water issued from the beach the ice was covered with blocks of snow, five or six feet high. This ought to give an idea of the depth of water which would be necessary to float such huge masses. However, all these blocks did not float down, for their course was of a more destructive character, both to themselves and the bottom of the stream. Standing at the border of the roaring stream, which we knew would not continue above a few hours, we could watch the descent of the large cubes of snow as they were hurried along, now coming to a stand and damming up the water as it went foaming over them, now sliding along the bottom, as if they were reluctant to leave the place which had afforded them shelter for so long a time, and now rolling over and over, until they came to a dead stand by the water shallowing as its surface became more extensive. We visited the lake, and found that it was almost dry. Its situation was one favourable to a violent *débâcle,* such as we had just witnessed. In the evening a similar occurrence took place on the opposite side of the harbour, but of much greater extent. A chain of small lakes beyond Prospect Hill burst open, and rushing with great violence along the hitherto almost dry water-course, tearing up masses of rock, and bearing down a burden of white mud, set free among the rolling stones at the bottom, they spread their contents over the whole of the harbour, for there was no crack in the ice which could transmit such a large body of water into the sea. The sounds of running streams had become so familiar to our ears that no notice was taken of this sudden discharge, until a person went on deck, and exclaimed, that the ice in the harbour had all disappeared, except the hummocks, which were still to be seen above the surface of the water. "Surely," he continued "the ice must have sunk." A moment's reflection, however, convinced him that it was all a delusion. The white colour of the water thus spread over the ice in the harbour appeared in very striking contrast with the blue sea in the offing. On the following day it had all disappeared, and the ice through which it had percolated was covered with a coating of the mud which it had brought down. We could have wished this to have been at an earlier period, for it proved useful in setting the ships clear, by facilitating the thawing of the ice. Where there was an accumulation, however, to the extent of half an inch in depth, the ice was protected by it, and in a few days elevations began to appear where the ice had been disappearing uniformly up to this time. Nothing could be more pleasant than a walk on the land in the afternoons when the weather was fine, and distance permitted such wholesome recreation. Saxifrages, and one or two Cruciferæ were in full bloom, the catkins of one or two species of willow were beginning to show themselves, caterpillars were still crawling on their bellies and gnawing the leaves of the *Dryas integrifolia*, but many of the gnats and flies had gone through their metamorphic stages, and become denizens of the air.

July 7th. — The weather was generally pleasant, although it was often rainy and cloudy, when the wind prevailed from the eastward. Since the middle of June mists were very common, and we rarely had twenty-four hours of uninterrupted clear weather. The lakes in the neighbourhood of Assistance Bay had all, except Kate Austin Lake, been pretty well drained out. On visiting the chain of lakes from which such a rush of water came a few days ago as inundated the whole bay, we found that blocks of ice seven to eight feet thick (part of the ice which had formed during winter) had been floated by the stream that passed through the lakes, and were left dry on their banks considerably above the level which the water was at throughout the season. It was wonderful to see the deep impressions that had been made in the gravel composing the bottom and borders of the lakes by the force with which the ice had been driven against it, and no less wonderful was it to see two or three flolds of this heavy ice piled up piece above piece to a height of fifteen or twenty feet, when the greatest extent of water did not exceed the fourth part of a square mile. There are but three lakes in this chain, and the disturbed condition of the ice, which at one time covered them, was confined to the two lower. This at once points out that the commotion which the water of the upper lake caused when it burst into the middle and lower ones, was the cause of the changed position of the ice which we had witnessed. While standing at the side of some of these massses of, in every sense of the word, fresh water ice, and the result of the congelation of water itself, not a mixture of snow and water which became solid by subsequent congelation, after the manner of the icebergs, I was struck by the mode in which it appeared to be thawing; in a most peculiar manner it was divided, wherever there was an exposed part, into a number of small fragments, which varied in length from two or three inches up to a foot or more, and in thickness from a mere spiculum up to half an inch. This division into fragments was invariably at right angles with the line in which the ice had increased. At one time it occurred to me that it might be owing to the water, as it was set free on the surface by the action of the sun percolating into its substance. But this was completely disproved by the fact, that when the position in which it had formed was changed even to right angles, the fragments were then not vertical as before, but horizontal. A portion of ice placed flat on the surface of the snow often in a few hours resembled an immense number of rough needles, falling to their sides at the margin of the mass where they had no support, but standing over end in the centre; and if an individual were standing within a space sufficiently near, he would hear a noise as if a number of similarly shaped fragments, of some metallic substance, were falling to their sides with a peculiar tinkling sound. I can hardly arrive at conclusions as to the cause of this mode of dissolution. I believe it is owing to the presence of air in the ice, but air is present in berg ice as well as in every other ice, and it does not dissolve in the same manner. On looking at a piece of the same ice in autumn or during winter before thawing commenced, the air in it could be seen in the form of oblong vesicles, which in many cases were drawn out into perfect threads. Probably the different conducting properties of the air in those drawn out canals, and of the ice, may give rise to a corresponding difference in the process of thawing.

The lakes were inhabited by flocks of brent geese, which we had every reason to believe were breeding upon a small island in one of them. Their enjoyment while swimming gracefully up and down the water, and diving occasionally in quest of salmon, I suppose their favourite food, was really enviable; and so was his, who could sit at his ease on the brow of a neighbouring hill, eyeing them intently with the view of making a detour which would bring him unobserved within musket shot, or contemplating the natural and chaste beauty of every object around him. Here there was nothing to molest his thoughts; far from the habitations of civilized human beings, and the rolling din of crowded cities, he had nothing to fear, and he could tread the hitherto untrodden soil and pick up flowers, whose beauty increased with their minute size, and whose fragrance was reserved for those whose hearts responded to their hidden beauty, and who willingly stooped to admire the delicate tints with which Nature unobtrusively adorned the bleak world within fifteen degrees of the Pole.

A tremulous jelly-like plant was found in great abundance on the surface of the soil, when there was a good deal of moisture. The same substance was found in a much more entire state, in deposits of brown mould, the result of decaying vegetable substances, and also among mosses. It was seen in almost every stage of its growth, from the size of a minute pullet, perfectly spherical, and of an olive green colour, up to a large lobulated disc two inches in breadth. The plant of last season was very abundant, and resembled fragments of the leafy parts of seaweed (*laminaria* and *alaria*).

As there was nothing objectionable in its appearance after washing the mud from it I ate some of it, and if one can judge of the nutritious properties of any organic substance by its consistence and taste, certainly this appeared to possess far higher recommendations to the hungry palate than the dry "tripe de roche," which Sir John Franklin, Sir John Richardson, and their companions used as food for a considerable time. When this plant was examined with the microscope a beautiful structure was exhibited. It appeared to be composed of threads of perfectly spherical cells, of a less diameter than $_{\overline{1}}\,^{1}$ of an inch, and scattered loosely throughout the entire pond. The lenses I used did not magnify sufficiently to detect the structure of the tissue which intervened between the threads of cells; probably it is some sort of inspissated glutinous substance which is thrown out or secreted, by the parts of the plant, which, with the magnifying power I used, presented a distinct structure. There may have been more than one species, indeed this seems not improbable, for the circumstances under which it was found were very different; the spherical when young, but discoid, and lobulated at a more advanced stage of development, was generally found in peaty deposits or among mosses, which did not necessarily require to be saturated with moisture, and the other plicated form of the plant, which may be merely a state peculiar to undergoing decay, was confined to the muddy localities where there was a constant oozing of water.*

The bottom of every running stream and pool was covered over with a green slime made up of filamentous *Confervæ*, which, as well as the gelatinous plant already alluded to, abounded in the larvæ of insects, which crawled about in thousands. Of these, there appeared to be four species, or at least two species and two varieties of each. There was also infesting the gelatinous plant, especially that in the moisture localities, a species of insect of wonderful agility and exceedingly abundant. And it was so wary, that it was not without considerable difficulty that I succeeded in obtaining specimens. I generally used a thick solution of mucilage, which I took with me on my excursions, and which by entrapping them suddenly enabled me to get more than was necessary ; by this mode, there was no risk whatever of destroying their delicate structure, as they were consigned immediately to spirits of wine and water, in which they were to be brought home for examination.

In travelling over the ice in the lakes, both before and after the famous *débâcles*, our attention was

* Since returning to England, through the kindness of Sir William J. Hooker, I have learned that this plant belongs to the genus *Nostoc*, not uncommon in Britain.

frequently attracted by portions of the gelatinous plant, seen on the land. By the action of the sun it had sought its way to a depth of one or two inches in the ice; and what struck us as remarkable was, that it always abounded in those active and leaping insects. Portions of it were picked up on the surface of the ice in Barrow Strait at a distance of one or two miles from the land, whither it had been blown in a dry state by the winds during winter; and here, too, scores of these little creatures, which appeared to be inseparable from it, could be seen leaping with the utmost alacrity, and evidently unaware of the doom that was awaiting them. The plant becomes dry after the frost sets in, and any part of it that may have become detached from the mud or medium, on or in which it was growing, will be subject to be blown about by the winds, far from its habitats, to the middle of the lakes, or to any distance from the land. Before those insects could be present upon it, whether formed on the ice over the sea, on the ice over the fresh water of the lakes, or on the land, it is very evident that the ova which produced them must have been deposited the previous season. It was truly an agreeable duty to sit beside the purling rivulet and watch these creatures in their dance over the water. Truly wonderful is the power with which life endows matter before it can endure with impunity the intense cold of such high northern latitudes and be called into a short-lived existence to perform its functions in the economy of nature — to leave its germ — the future itself, and to die. But life is essential to this condition, and when there is a deviation from the laws by which nature controls matter there is invariably a failure. At the beginning of winter I took a portion of cheese which abounded in mites (*Acarus domesticus*) and divided it into three portions, one of which was exposed at once to the intense cold of winter, another was dried and then exposed along with the former until the return of summer, the third portion was preserved at a temperature which never was less than probably twelve or fifteen degrees below the freezing point of water. On the return of summer and warm weather the three portions were exposed to exactly the same circumstances, but they were not permitted to come in contact. The two portions which had been exposed to intense cold, after two months' exposure to a temperature ten to twenty degrees above the freezing point of water, did not exhibit the slightest signs of life, while the last and third portion was swarming with mites in the most active state. The cheese, which belonged to the ship's stores, was often during winter exposed to $-10°$ or $-20°$. Before winter it gave signs of possessing the germs of an abundant race of mites; but having passed through the winter, after two months and a half of a temperature above the freezing point of water, frequent and careful examinations with a microscope invariably failed to detect any signs of returning life. This may be deemed irrelevant, but it may perhaps assist those who have taken up their position in the defence of truth against the advocates of spontaneous generation.

A party went often out to the water, and not unfrequently we had a good deal of sport in it, shooting sea-fowl. A light clinker-built boat, belonging to Mr. Stuart, which had often sailed up the Aberdeen harbour, was very useful, and it was light for launching over the edge of the ice, as we had to haul it to a distance over the ice, in case it should go adrift with any portion of the latter that might become detached during our absence. Loons were the most abundant, and perhaps also the most useful birds that we succeeded in shooting. We frequently had soup made of them, and they proved exceedingly palatable in this way. While skinning a loon on one occasion my collection had one specimen of a parasitical insect added to it, which was found among the feathers of that bird. At the edge of the ice in the bay there was a sort of "bore," caused by the mixing of waters of different densities; that from the harbour being fresh, and that in the offing being comparatively warmer than the former; it was what one might naturally expect, although at first we certainly thought it was a strong tide setting out of the harbour. A large mass of ice, drawing eight or nine feet of water, which became detached from the ice in the bay, floated loosely from its edge, but was not carried away to any distance, when to appearance it ought to have been out of sight in less than two or three hours.

June 11th.—A crack appeared in the ice right across the harbour, about three quarters of a mile from the ship, and as it held out inducements to try the dredge, I got the assistance of the Esquimaux this evening, and went out to it. We were not very successful, owing to the rope being apt to get entangled at the edge of the ice, especially where the crack was narrow. Adam seemed quite delighted to work with me, without any inducement in the way of reward being held out to him. I often saw his ingenuity displayed in overcoming difficulties most skilfully. In this he exceeded anything that I expected from him, and gave unequivocal proofs that he exercised reasoning powers to a greater extent than even some of our seamen were capable of. He endeavoured to explain to me the "true" nature of the report he had set on foot at Cape York, and he had kept up since then by the assistance of others: as he could not stand an examination with respect to such gross fabrications, I evaded the subject as often as he introduced it.

The depth of the water was twelve to fifteen fathoms, the bottom shingly and abundant in animals, of which the most common were, sea-urchins, starfishes, and Crustacea. I observed one large shrimp, fully four inches and a half in length, and hundreds of smaller Crustacea of the genus *Scorpioides;* there were also great numbers of Ophiuridæ, and a great variety of Annelides. I had reason to regret the tender structure they possessed; for, with the utmost care I could use, some of them were destroyed. This was very common with the genera *Terebella, Amphitrite, Nereis,* and *Syllis,* of which I endeavoured in vain to get good and entire specimens. On going to the hill top, on the east of the harbour, and looking east and west in Barrow Strait, nothing could be seen but water. The opposite shore was as plainly discernible as I had ever seen it, and there was no refraction. As far west as the utmost limit of vision could extend, there was nothing but water. There seemed to be less ice now than there had been at a period two months later the previous season. Where the ice had gone to was very strange to not a few in our expedition. There was no way in which it could have gone, except to the eastward through Lancaster Sound, which way would convey it ultimately to Davis Strait. There was still a large quantity of ice holding on in the bays, and spaces between the islands along both shores. From Assistance Bay westward to the side of Griffith's Island, and still farther westward along the south shore of the Parry group of islands, the ice would not break off for some time, at least a week or ten days, unless a heavy swell should set up the strait, a very improbable occurrence at so great a distance from a sufficient extent of sea, to raise a swell such as we often experienced on the east coast of Davis Strait. From the state of Barrow Strait at this time, as far as one can judge from the highest land on the south side of Cornwallis Island, navigation could be accomplished with very little trouble, and there seemed to be no obstacle to making a passage to Melville Island in the ships or steamers, if they were but clear of winter quarters.

The storehouse and blacksmith's shop, which had been built of snow on the land, had fallen long since, and the provisions and other articles that had been stored up were removed from their ruins, which, by this time, had all disappeared. The crews of both ships were busily employed in taking off ballast from the land, for the ships would certainly be too light without at least thirty to forty tons. Water was also taken from the land; and, as there were abundance of casks for the purpose, the "Lady Franklin" was ballasted with it. Both ships were caulked and blackened, and the rigging, both running and standing, was carefully examined; the ships were looking as neat as fiddles, and every person in the harbour was longing for a cruise in the open blue sea. Our dogs became exceedingly useful in taking off shingle from the beach. Over the smooth ice, their load often weighed from six or seven hundred weight up to half a ton. They seemed to have improved by the travelling, during which they suffered much from hunger, and not a little from fatigue; however, they devoured the flesh of three bears in that time, which must have contributed greatly to their present good condition. Some of the young ones, which were not yet twelve months old, were producing their second breed.

July 19*th*.—At the request of the officers of H.M.S. "Pioneer," and with the concurrence of Mr. Manson, upon whom the command of the expedition devolved in the absence of Mr. Penny and Mr. A. Stewart, I paid a visit to the squadron at Griffith's Island. The first ten miles were over the land until we reached the east side of the bay eastward of Cape Martyr; this was crossed, after which we came to a half-way tent, where a hearty refreshment was obtained. The distance to the ships was about seven or eight miles over ice, which was still in many parts inundated with water, although now much less so than it had been even a few days previously. We had to wade through some pools which came up above the knees. It is difficult to account for so much water being on the surface of the ice between Griffith's Island and the adjacent coast of Cornwallis Island, at a period after the ice in the channel between the latter and North Devon, in a corresponding latitude, had relieved itself of all the water, and had established channels all over its surface, in which the water accumulated and lodged at the same level as that of the water on which it was floating. It was a common feature in the pools to have miniature whirlpools when the water was escaping from them through openings communicating with the sea beneath. This gives rise to the idea of there being a sort of rise and fall of the water upon the ice, but I do not know a single other fact which tends to corroborate it. The rise and fall of the tide averaged from three to five feet, although at times the range might be greater or less. Presuming the ice where Captain Austin's squadron wintered to have been fixed immovably, without the freedom of rising and falling with the tides, at one time it would have several feet of water on it, and in a few hours it would be left dry. I cannot conceive the possibility that a breadth of seven miles of ice could be fastened down so immovably as not to rise and fall with the tide; its buoyant property is so great, and its resistance so little, when even a breadth of half a mile is considered, that it appears absurd in the extreme to suppose it now to be suspended like a bridge over the water, and next tide to be overwhelmed. Were these conditions present, one might expect the tidal wave to advance over the free edge of the ice where it floats lightly upon the water, or, failing this, the openings in the ice would be alternately performing the functions of fountains and drains. I do not know that any person had observed the water boiling up through the openings, nor did I observe it myself during a stay of five days. Upon the supposition that the floe here was not free to rise and fall during winter, let the question be put, what thickness would it have acquired under the influence of such alternations? It seems most according to reason, that the amount of water on the ice in this locality was owing to the thawing process; and if the hourly or daily escape was not always uniform, neither was the process by which it was set free. The fact that no such thing was observed until thawing commenced, is in itself sufficient to give a correct idea of the real cause.

After crossing the bay east of Cape Martyr, and landing on the beach not far from a cairn which was built by some of the surveyors from Captain Austin's squadron, we observed a pool a few feet above the level of the sea, which reflected the light from the sky, and appeared to be of a blood red colour. On approaching it we found the water as pure and clear as possible, but the small stones which composed its bottom were grown over with a most perfect coating of the red snow plant (*Protococcus nivalis*). Some of the water appeared either to have drained away or evaporated, for the stones around its margin were left dry, but they had the same coating of "red snow" adhering to them as those that were still in the water. In the water the plant was of a beautiful crimson tinge, but that on the dry stones was slightly darker, resembling dried blood, except that it was a little more granular when closely examined. The bottom of this and other pools containing the "red snow," contained the larvæ of insects; they exactly resembled those found on *Confervæ* in the vicinity of Assistance Bay, and it was very likely they should soon be left dry by the water evaporating from them, and this would doubtless accelerate their transition through those stages of their short-lived existence, which still confined them to the slime in which their parents had most probably given them birth.

After arriving at the ships, the party to which I had attached myself was met by Captains Austin and Ommanney, whose first inquiries were—"What of Penny." We had to state that he had not come in, and that he might not be expected for some time, as he then (the 14th) had two weeks' provisions, if the calculations made in provisioning the boat should prove correct. Those two officers, and indeed all the officers under them, seemed to have as much anxiety about our commander's return, as we had ourselves. Their anxiety however was only of a certain kind—it related to themselves only, and not to its source. If Mr. Penny should not return soon, it was clear we should find it necessary to go to look for him. This might involve three-fourths of our whole force, and before they would find it possible to return, having accomplished the object for which they started, the anxiety of Captain Austin for their safety could not fail to move him to send assistance to Assistance Bay. Moreover, such protracted researches might be continued so long that his expedition could not get home this season. Every day increased his anxiety for Mr. Penny, because the delay breathed of a feeling of fear, that the work in which the latter was engaged was more than he should find means equal to; and as messenger after messenger left for Assistance Bay, and returned to his squadron, in which now one hundred and seventy-nine persons (for one man had died) were engaged, the unwelcome news that Mr. Penny had not yet returned, tended much to increase the pain of dwelling upon the fact. The fact, too, that not a single trace had been found of the missing ships to the westward of Cape Hotham, led our ideas up the channel where alone Mr. Penny and Mr. A. Stewart, the two commanders in our little expedition of forty-six men, with their two boats' crews, were at this time engaged in that most interesting part of the search. A party might hourly be arriving with intelligence, painful or joyful, of the fate or rescue of those we had come so far, and toiled so hard, hitherto in vain, to find.

There were several invalids in the squadron at this time, the chief cause being frost-bite and the ulcers which followed. The treatment which the medical officers adopted was not effectual, for the sores looked sluggish and indisposed to heal, in spite of the most powerful antiscorbutic and restorative treatment that could be adopted in the expedition.

There seemed to be a general depression of tone both in health and spirits, which no one sought to conceal. When the summer was approaching, and daylight was increasing, and the travellers were setting out full of hope, there was a glow in every person's face I met; but now, after the sun had commenced his southward career, and every day was sensibly shorter than the one which came before it, when the travellers had almost all returned and hardly any hope was left we should find the missing expedition, a powerful reaction took place that could be read in every face, from the highest to the lowest. Every one looked in the direction of home, if Mr. Penny did not on his return take upon him to keep them all out a second winter. Captain Austin looked upon those under his command, one hundred and seventy-nine men, like a fond parent, and with the opinions of his medical officers, written or expressed before him, he could not but shrug his shoulders at the chilling ideas of a second winter. He could not be blamed for saying that we might look forward to a large mortality among those who were invalids, and who had suffered much as the result of their exertions in travelling, if circumstances should require a protracted stay to carry on the search for another year. There was hardly a severe frost-bite which had healed quite up, and of those there was a considerable number. The presence of so many invalids, and the grave of a beloved comrade who had died from frost-bite, had not the best effect upon the healthy and hearty in Captain Austin's squadron; and that he knew well and duly appreciated in the event of being called upon for a decision on the return of Mr. Penny. I was the guest of Lieut. Osborne, of whose kindness, and, in truth, of all the squadron, it becomes me to be both ashamed and proud. I shall ever cherish the warmest feelings of gratitude for their courtesy. It was the first visit I had made to Captain Austin's squadron, and certainly I wished it should not be the last. The officers who had returned last from their journeys had not completed their travelling reports and their charts. The others, however, had almost all given in theirs.

It was amusing to trace how inadvertently mistakes in chart-making managed to creep in. This officer's compass has turned out ill; that officer's chronometer has altered its rate, and lost time egregiously; while a third cares neither for compass nor chronometer; valuing nothing but the meridian sun and his sextant, which, with an ordinary time-piece, are quite sufficient for all ordinary purposes in travelling in the Arctic regions during cold weather. At noon the latitude ought to be obtained, if possible, but if not then, by ex-meridian altitudes at other times; bearings ought to be taken, and the course for the first march ought to be shaped at the earliest opportunity after the party encamps. I have often, by doing this, been able to commence my journey when the weather at the time of starting was as thick as possible. There is little danger of making serious mistakes, when an officer trusts to courses and distances taken from the sun, and brought into nice check by his meridian altitude in a fine day. A discrepancy of one or two degrees between two charts, extending over a space of three hundred miles, may appear an egregious blunder, until it is stated that it only amounts to thirty miles of longitude; and taking the mean between the two, which is fifteen, one cannot be far out of the reckoning. No such blunders can occur, when a party has to make northing or southing; for then the latitudes will prove a valuable check upon the estimated distances. It is only when whole weeks are spent travelling on the same mile of latitude, E. or W., that mistakes occur most readily; for then one must place his sole dependence upon his chronometer, which he will often find a treacherous friend. With the utmost care that can be taken, it often happens that the low temperature of April deranges the best chronometer when taken out on a journey, although it may have proved a most correct instrument while kept in a comfortable place in the cabin of a ship, where the temperature, solely for the sake of the chronometers, is generally kept about +60°.

During my stay on board the "Pioneer" her crew was mustered for inspection by Captain Austin, and her steaming machinery was carefully examined by that experienced officer. The last part I did not witness; the former, however, was exceedingly gratifying, for all the crew, I believe, were up and fit for duty, with the exception of one man, whose toes had been frost-bitten; yet, although not upon duty, he generally walked about the decks. Each man, as his name was called, doffed his cap to his commander, and walked across the deck from port to starboard. Captain Austin complimented Lieutenant Osborne, the commander of the "Pioneer," for the order which his ship displayed was in every department. The health of the crew entitled the medical officer to due approbation; the steam-engines, and all that belonged to them, were praised very much, for the order in which they were kept, and the engineers were warmly eulogized for their extreme attention to them, while the rigging of the ship herself was all as neat and tidy as could be; and the master, who, perhaps, expected the first compliment, got the last, which, there is no doubt, pleased him as much as the whole pleased me, a disinterested onlooker, to whom the inspection of a man-of-war in the Arctic regions was as novel a scene as it was to the majority of those who were engaged in it.

The following day, after my arrival at Griffith's Island, Captain Ommanney set out for Assistance Bay, to wait the arrival of Mr. Penny from his explorations beyond the Wellington Channel; next day another party set out for the same place, and yesterday they returned bringing intelligence of the return of Captain Stewart from the point intended for the depôt, without having seen anything of Captain Penny. He did not succeed in getting the boat up to the point, for reasons which were anticipated before she was launched into the water on the 1st of this month. The provisions were placed where Captain Penny requested; and as Mr. Stewart could be of no benefit to Captain Penny, he returned to the ships. He stated that the ice in the Wellington Channel had relieved itself from the water that had been on its surface, and that a large portion of it had drifted away, the free edge being now a little to the southward of Point Delay. At the same time as the last large detachment of ice took place in the Wellington Channel, a similar took place between Griffith's and Cornwallis Islands. The breadth of ice between Captain Austin's squadron and the water was not above four miles, if quite so much. It was contemplated to commence sawing and blasting forthwith. I suspected they would find this stiff work, especially when they had to look forward to three or four miles of solid immovable ice.

On my return to Assistance Bay, I was accompanied by one of the officers of the "Pioneer," whom Captain Austin permitted to leave his expedition for a week. The floe was considerably drier than when I crossed it a few days before. On coming in towards the land, we made for Bruce Bay, — for that is the bay on the east side of Cape Martyr, — where we found the ice quite dry, but appearing to be very thick, and at least of a second year's growth. To the southward of Bruce Bay, about, I should say, two miles from its entrance, there was an extensive crack in the ice leading towards the land, from the free edge of the ice in which Captain Austin's squadron was still fixed. The one side of the crack was the margin of an extensive floe, part of the large sheet that went off a few days previously. The other side was the fixed ice, on which we walked across from the ships to Cornwallis Island. Looking into this crack, where it was three to four feet wide, the ice appeared to be at least six or eight feet thick; but the lower half was composed of a kind of soft spongy ice holding in its substance great numbers of frozen in, and also masses of a whitish substance, which evidently was of a vegetable nature, probably accumulations of Diatomaceæ, which in their white colour differed very much from any of that family of Algæ that I had seen before. How the fish were caught will appear very soon; only I may observe here that several of the same species were often seen coming to the surface of the water in pools on the floe, which had a communication with the sea beneath. They were so slow and unwary that a person could catch them with the hand as if they had been half dead; and so lean, with the head quite out of proportion to the body, that I question whether even the snow-bird would stoop to make them its prey.

After coming to the land we proceeded eastward along the coast, first taking a hearty luncheon and shifting our stockings, for we were wet to the knees after leaving the ice. The evening was very clear for an hour or two, and we had a good view of the ice in Barrow Strait. There was no longer present an extensive sheet of blue water without ice, as we often had it in the first ten or fourteen days of July. The S. E. wind invariably brought in from the eastward large patches of ice, which saved the fixed ice, both in Assistance Bay and between Cornwallis Island and Griffith's Island, from the swell which one might expect where there was so much open water as we knew to have been at that time in Barrow Straits.

The whole of the south shore of Cornwallis Island

is remarkable for the immense number of Esquimaux ruins which one meets. There is no doubt they are the relics of Esquimaux, for there is a very striking resemblance between the remains of some of the bone instruments found here and the instruments which I have seen the natives at Ponds' Bay and Hogarth Sound use in their daily avocations. At Cape Riley, I picked up a portion of a bone harpoon, which I found buried in a deposit of turfy soil. It resembled a portion of a similar instrument, which five years previously one of the officers of a whaling ship in which I served cut out of the back of a whale, where it might have lain for several years, having been driven into this monster of the deep by the daring Esquimaux in his kyak. There were portions of whales' ribs near the ruins, which had been used as a protection to the runners of sledges; each had holes neatly perforated in it, by means of which, with wooden pins, it was fastened to the runner which it was intended to protect. And small fragments of wood containing holes, which had been burned out for receiving fastenings, were very common. It undoubtedly was part of some coniferous tree, but it was more than could be solved here to what species or varieties of species it belonged: this had to be remanded, like many other things, until we should arrive in England. The remains of their houses or huts were merely circular arrangements of stones, which often varied in dimensions, from several up to fifteen or sixteen feet. Fox-traps which they had used were still standing, appearing as if hardly a single stone had fallen from them; they resemble those the Esquimaux build on the Island of Keimooksooke and the adjacent coast, on the west side of Hogarth Sound, from which I have seen the uncivilised Esquimaux remove the blue and the white fox. In these points the former inhabitants of the north Georgian Islands, as well as those of the North Devon, the coast of which from Cape Riley to Cape Becher we found in a manner strewed with ruins, resemble the present inhabitants of the west coast of Davis' Straits. There is, however, a point in which they differ widely, and it is not unimportant to notice it, because it may lead to the elucidation of facts hitherto unknown. On the coast of West Greenland, from Cape Farewell to Whale Sound, and from the Coast of Frobisher's Straits round into Davis' Strait and up to Possession Bay, where the Esquimaux are still in existence, one always finds their graves, substantial oblong arrangements of stones containing entire skeletons, unless by age some of the smallest bones have decayed into a brown mould. From Cape Martyr to Cape Hotham, and from Cape Riley to Cape Becher, where there is of coast abounding in other Esquimaux remains nearly two hundred and fifty geographical miles, there was not a single human bone seen. Mr. Stuart, who performed the journey by Cape Spencer, said that his men reported to him having examined what they took to be a grave; but as there was no substantial proof of it being a grave, for I do not believe they saw the bones, this is not an exception to what obtains on all other parts of the coast. To arrive at any conclusions with respect to the date of the ruins is impossible, as it may be two hundred or two thousand years ago. And it is equally impossible to conclude what they did with the bodies of the dead. Their mode of sepulture differed essentially from that of their descendants, and may not also their religious ideas have differed, although in other points they appear to be the same?

In those parts the bones of other animals were very abundant, from birds up to the common black whale. We often spoke of the Esquimaux remains; and there were persons who held the opinion that they were those of Nomadic races, which they said accounted for the absence of graves. But the Esquimaux, wherever they are in a state of uncivilisation, are Nomadic.

In the autumn of 1846 at Keimooksooke, the place of birth of Enoolooapike*, on board the St.

* Enoolooapike was a native brought to Aberdeen by Captain Penny in 1839, where he remained a whole winter,

Andrew of Aberdeen, under the command of Mr. Penny, I spoke to two Esquimaux, whose recollections of boyhood included some ideas of two ships that wintered at Igloolik, whence they had travelled to Hogarth Sound. On inquiring what time they had taken to accomplish the journey, I was told that they did not know, for they had been travelling all their lives. There was another person who had come all the way from Ponds' Bay in latitude 72° 40′ to Hogarth Sound, round by Saunderson's Tower, a bold headland on the north side of the entrance of that sound in or about latitude 64° 40′, and longitude 63° 30′. And many, indeed I may say all the Esquimaux, including not fewer than one hundred

and received a little education. He gave a map of a large inlet, which was put into the hands of Admiral Sir Francis Beaufort, the hydrographer of the Admiralty. In the following year Mr. Penny visited the inlet, and landed Enoolooapike on the Island of Keimooksooke, or some island in its immediate neighbourhood; and, on his return to Aberdeen, a more extensive and correct map, made by observations and bearings obtained on the spot, was transmitted to the hydrographer. The name Tenudiakweek, by which the natives distinguish the inlet, and which means "Whale and Rapid Tide Sound," was changed for Hogarth Sound by Mr. Penny, to whom the discovery, through the Esquimaux, belonged. In some of the charts Hogarth Sound is called Northumberland Inlet, by a Captain Wareham, in 1841. Dr. M'Donald, the surgeon of Mr. Penny's ship at the time, but now in one of the missing ships, published a small volume on that voyage.

and twenty, whom I saw that year at one time at Keimooksooke, had been at considerable distances from the places where they were born. From this there can be no doubt that the Esquimaux are all of a Nomadic character, so that this attribute is not a sufficient reason for the absence of graves and human remains on the now deserted tracts of North Devon, Albert Land, and the shores of the North Georgian Islands. They must have possessed some means of disposing of their dead which has fallen into disuse among their descendants.

The land along the coast was in some part very soft, and one often sunk into muddy deposits to a depth of several inches. These deposits are the result of water oozing down from melting snow over the surface of ice which is beneath the surface of the soil. Where there are large fragments of rock, of course the water as it is set free makes its escape very readily, but where there is finely divided material on a slope, or elsewhere where water remains fluid at the surface during a part of summer, it becomes very soft and acquires a gradual downward motion, which accounts for a very peculiar arrangement which fragments of shingle on the surface assume. When the descent is above 30° the fragments are set upon their edge in nearly straight lines running up the declivity, but when it is less than this, the same position is assigned to each fragment, while the arrangement is in the form of little pentagonal or hexagonal divisions, which are remarkably uniform, both with respect to size and appearance. At the foot of a talus, which is by no means uncommon where there are so many bluffs, large fragments are set upon edge by the same downward motion of the loose muddy soil or debris, and a very rough condition of the surface is the result, which often extends over spaces several hundred yards in length, and fifty or sixty in breadth. In making a journey along the coast when one has to walk over the land, such places rough, dangerous to the ankles, and extremely fatiguing, as they may be, are often preferred to smoother localities where one may be in danger of sinking half up to the knees. It was late in the evening before we arrived on board our little ships in Assistance Bay. They looked as neat and trim as if they had been newly launched. The "Sophia" had risen out of the ice, consequently she appeared to be much bolder in the hull than she was when we left the harbour a few days before. Her rudder had suffered slightly from a sudden spring which she took before it was entirely relieved; a few hours' work however of both carpenters would soon repair it. The anxiety about Captain Penny's return was daily increasing, and we examined the men which composed his fatigue party, as to the efficiency of the boat, its tightness and other capabilities, and more especially with respect to the provisions of which he could avail himself, in those unknown localities which he had to explore.

The following is an account of the stores he had on the 12th of June, with which Mr. J. Stuart furnished me when I reciprocated with him in his anxiety for the party that was still out. He was detached from that party on the 13th, and consequently he must have known, or have had the means of knowing, the exact quantities of each article which it had, more especially as he had been with the party for upwards of a week. I give the exact form in which the account reached me from Mr. Stuart.

Provisions contained in the whale-boat, and two long sledges: —

Bread - - - -	300 lbs.
Pork - - - - -	176 lbs.
Pemmican - - - -	180 lbs.
Preserved meat - - - -	107 lbs.
Sugar - - - - -	21 lbs.
Tea and coffee - - - -	17 lbs.
Tobacco - - - - -	6½ lbs.
Spirits (Rum) - - - -	8½ gals.
Fuel - - -	80 lbs. perhaps 100 lbs.

Additional on dog-sledge 340 lbs., of which 120 is bread.

Out of those provisions Mr. Penny's party of nineteen persons and ten dogs, had to be fed from the

12th to the 17th, the day on which the boat was launched into the water. And from that day up to the 22nd, the day on which the returning or fatigue party arrived at the depôt at Point Separation, the entire party had to receive supplies from the same stores. This reduced the stores of which Captain Penny and his party of seven men could avail themselves, to about thirty-five days' provisions from the 23rd of June. By Mr. Stuart's calculation, they would have no bread after the 27th of July, and in two or three days more, their preserved meat, pemmican, and pork would also be exhausted. In making these calculations, the feeding of ten dogs from the 13th to the 20th, is not included, and doubtless they required part of the provisions intended for the men, as those (half a dozen lame ones) did in the journey which I made to Point Separation. Considering this, the provisions could not last down to the 27th, at the farthest. We expected, however, that their resources in the water might prevent them starving, if circumstances should compel them to run the risk of being thrown upon the mercy of what they could obtain with their ammunition.

July 22nd.—The weather was generally rainy and disagreeable, and easterly winds, which were not uncommon, almost always produced an overcast sky. The ice in Barrow Strait drifted westward and appeared to render a passage in that direction or southward, much more difficult now than it would have been a fortnight earlier, had we been in readiness to attempt it. Captain Ommanney and his party, who had been about a week on board the "Lady Franklin," accompanied by Mr. A. Stewart, set out for Griffith's Island. A boat was taken part of the distance, it being expected that the remainder could be accomplished over the ice which lay between Captain Austin's squadron and the water. After the party disembarked upon the ice, the boat commenced its return to Assistance Bay, and arrived in a few hours. A boat was left at Depôt Point, Wellington Channel, for Captain Penny's use, whenever he should have advanced so far on his homeward journey. The south-east point of the bay was very rarely without some person taking a searching glance to the eastward, as far as Dungeness Point, and not unfrequently, parties of half a dozen men travelled as far as Cape Hotham, and had a look up the Wellington Channel, expecting they should meet their commander returning.

Excursions on the land became exceedingly interesting. Some of the flowers, especially those on the southern slopes, were beginning to fade, but the same species on the northern slopes and at elevations of four to five hundred feet, were only coming into flower. If one stooped and took a view close along the surface of one of the many almost level plains, which extended in patches, from the beach to the rising ground, of the bluffs, he would behold such an array of yellow poppies as could not fail to infuse a charm into everything around him. If again, he wished to amuse his palate, he might feed *ad libitum* upon the leaves of crucifers in full bloom, sorrel, and scurvy grass. Of these plants, especially the former, I believe persons labouring under scorbutus ought to obtain a sufficient quantity to effect a beneficial change in the disease. It often occurred to me, that the resources of the climate in the way of plants might be made available to prevent scurvy. Although a basket full could not be obtained in one or even two hours by one person, handfuls could, and this operation extended over several hours, by an increased number of men, would go far to appease the insatiable cravings of scurvy for vegetable food. There was no apparent craving in our expedition for the green leaves of Parrya Arctica; indeed, it was quite impossible any such want could be felt, with the liberal supply which our crews had of turnips and carrots, which had not lost a trace of their original taste, flavour, or nutritious elements in the process of preservation.*

* There was but one tin of damaged carrots, and one or two of damaged herrings, found among all the preserved meats that had been used on board the "Sophia."

The most beautiful plant that one could see in a whole day's walking around Assistance Bay, was the spider plant (*Saxifraga flagellaris,*) from its striking resemblance to a large spider when it first appears above the surface, before the stem begins to rise from the spherical arrangement of the leaves, or the flagellæ begin to creep to any distance from among them to the soil around. This plant was rather late of coming into flower, but the poppy was still later. The Ranunculus frigidus had a very beautiful little flower, but it did not admit of comparison with the other two that have been mentioned. The purple saxifrage (*Saxifraga oppositifolia*) vied with, and perhaps in the estimation of some exceeded, the spider plant in beauty; its chaste purple colour assisted this very much; but I do not think that this, which is mere colour, admits of comparison with the charm which is imparted to the other by its likeness to a creature so famous for its diligence. Lepidopterous, and three other species of winged insects, could be seen very frequently; probably they may be the same as those found by the Expedition under the command of Sir Edward Parry at Melville Island. The lepidoptera were generally seen flying, but the others were most frequently found in tufts of grasses and carices, where there were accumulations of the dung of hares, foxes, ptarmigan, and owls, the latter containing entire

C. S. SPOONER, FECIT. J. COVENTRY, LITH. M & N HANHART IMP.

PART OF THE VIEW REPRESENTS ASSISTANCE HARBOUR, WITH THE 3 CAIRNS,

1.1. Oxyria reniformis	4, Dryas integrifolia.	7 Saxifraga oppositifolia	10. Papaver nudicaule.
2.2. Saxifraga nivalis	5, Parrya arctica.	8 Polygonum viviparum	11. Cerastium alpinum.
3.3. Draba alpina	6 Saxifraga flagellaris.	9 Alopecurus Alpinus	12. Cochlearia fenestralis

13, Ranunculus frigidus

LONDON; LONGMAN, & Co 1852.

skulls and skeletons of the lemming in great abundance. In the same tufts could be found two species of spiders, very abundant. The connection between the spiders and the flies was not more remarkable than that between the creatures which visited those luxuriant patches of vegetation, to feed upon the grasses and their seeds, and to drop their dung to stimulate vegetation, and feed a colony of flies, which in their turn are attacked by spiders. The smallest of the flies and gnats, of which there were at least three species, resembles the common blood-sucking mosquito, and was found on the under surface of stones, whither it, I suppose, had retired for shelter. The other two species were invariably found in the tufts of grass, &c. already alluded to. I could not see a single larva crawling on the shingle, as they had been seen two or three weeks previously, and the pools along the beach were beginning to dry up, where the larvæ of flies were very abundant among immense accumulations of *Confervæ*.

July 23*rd*.—Late in the evening, two persons were observed coming towards the ships from the offing. At first we could not distinguish them, for there was a very thick mist; but as they approached the ships, we found they were Mr. Stewart and Lieutenant Aldrich, who had come from the squadron at Griffith's Island. Their journey was the same as that which I made a few days before, with the exception that they took the use of a small boat for the last six miles; and this accounted for their approach to the ships directly from the margin of the ice at the offing. Mr. Stewart, who accompanied Captain Ommanney and his party to Griffith's Island, said that they narrowly escaped being drifted down Barrow Straits, after the boat was sent back by them, having reached the floe, over which they intended to travel to the ships. The weather was very thick, and as they thought that a short cut could be made across the ice, which I told them was only four miles in breadth to the ships, they disembarked and commenced their march. After they had been travelling three hours, I believe, in what they thought was the direction of the ships, for they could not see above three hundred yards through the mist, they came to the north edge of the ice, and found a lane of water extending from E. to W., about three to five hundred yards in breadth; so broad, indeed, that they could only catch a faint glimpse of the ice on the opposite side. They must have looked into one another's faces, when they were thus arrested in a thick mist on a drifting floe. However, *nil est desperandum mortalibus:* they looked first at one another, and then up and down for a fragment of ice of sufficient dimensions to ferry them across to the opposite side.

In this, too, they were almost foiled, for the floe on which they stood, presented a straight edge, with hardly a single loose fragment. At length, by dint of perseverance, a detached piece was found, that appeared suitable, and on this the whole party, I think, of five persons embarked, first stripping to a single covering, that they might be in readiness to save themselves by swimming, if the frail boat, to which they entrusted their lives, should yield them up to the deep blue water by which it was borne. They used their guns as paddles, and the utmost caution was observed, lest a sudden motion should upset them; each took his place and dared not move from it, although his feet, protected only by stockings, were excruciatingly cold. It would be difficult to know whether they were shivering from cold or fear. Stewart told me that one of the party said, on reaching and landing on the opposite ice, "Thank God! that makes one think of his wife and weak family." They arrived at the squadron in a short time, and so terminated, safely, like all the others, one of the visits to Assistance Harbour.

Letters and reports reached us from Griffith's Island, which conveyed only a reiteration of what we all knew before, that every eye in that squadron was upon Assistance Bay. As day followed day in rapid succession, and the wheels of time were hurrying us on towards a second winter, the anxiety of almost all in that squadron for Mr. Penny's return was increasing in a geometrical ratio; while our side again was full of hope that he had good reasons for being so much longer out than he expected. I again read a note I had from him, dated June 17th, in which he said he should probably be back before the 12th July, when Captain Stewart would be ready, according to orders, to start for Ponds' Bay. There was everything unfavourable for him and his party in the weather, if it was the same with him in the newly discovered channels as it was with us on board the ships. Twenty-four hours' incessant rain was by no means uncommon; and it was very rare, indeed, to have the same length of time of clear weather.

July 24th. — In some of our excursions on the land collections of plants were made from time to time. The features which vegetation presented all round the harbour were highly favourable to the botanist. At the sea-level, or a little above this, and on the southern slopes, they appeared to flower simultaneously; but at greater elevations, and on the northern slopes, many plants were only beginning to bloom, while in the other and more highly favoured localities they were fading. The *Oxyiria reniformis* was exceedingly stunted, and it and a species of Polygonum were never found below an elevation of between three and four hundred feet, while the Ranunculus was confined to mossy and humid patches, at elevations not above one hundred feet, where it could send its long white roots into a thin layer of dark mould, the result of only partial decay of vegetable matter, and between the fragments of stones which were covered by the latter.

CHAP. XX.

RETURN OF MR. PENNY. — GETTING CLEAR OF WINTER QUARTERS.

Preparations for sawing out. — Views respecting Mr. Penny's Party. — Return. — No Traces. — Piece of English Elm. — Mr. Penny's Proceedings. — Route of the Missing Ships. — Cause of there being Open Water. — Idea of a Second Winter. — Drifting Ice. — Resources of our Expedition.—Probability of returning Home.—Party to Griffith's Island.—The Ice in Barrow Straits.—Sunday Service. —Heavy Rain.—Sawing out.—Snow upon the Land.—Remarks upon the Weather and the Climate. — Migration of Birds and Quadrupeds.—Increase and Decay of the Ice.—Table showing the Increase during Winter and Spring.—Heaps of Gravel upon the Ice.—Young Ice.—Clothing.—Boots.—Health of the Crew.—The South-west Bluff.—Captain Austin's Squadron. — Facilities for navigating Barrow Straits.—Rapid Motion of drifting Ice.—No Icebergs in Barrow Straits.—Fossils.—Water percolating through the Shingle. — Elevation of the Beaches. — Tertiary Deposits. — Early Navigation. — Sending off Pigeons. — Prospects of getting clear.—Dredging.—The Ice breaking loose in the Harbour.— Vegetation. — Distances travelled.—Barrow Straits encumbered with Ice. — Attempts to reach Griffith's Island. — Red Snow. — Captain Penny's Opinions. — Captain Austin's Squadron. — Consultation.

July 25th. — THE ships were fully prepared for sea, ballast and water had by this time been taken on board, and they were in readiness to be drawn out of the harbour the moment an opening in the ice should occur. There was a breadth of at least three-quarters of a mile of ice between us and the open water in the offing. As almost every other duty had been attended to and brought to a conclusion, we now began to think of sawing a canal to the outside, and with this in view the saws and triangles were got ready, and the seamen began to look out their long boots, for there were large pools on the ice, in which they would have to stand while engaged at the saws. Barrow Strait was often so free from ice that ships could navigate it in all directions with almost the same ease as if they were in the North Atlantic. The bays, however, were still unnavigable, owing to the ice in them not having left its fixed position to the land.

Mr. Stewart had returned from the north-east point of Cornwallis Island eight or nine days ago, without having seen any thing of Mr. Penny. Winds and violent storms, rainy, thick and gloomy weather prevailed to an alarming extent; hence it need not be wondered that our anxieties for the safe return of our commander, and his party of seven men, were daily increasing. From the calculations we had made of the provisions he had, even upon the supposition that no part of them should become damaged in a leaky boat, we found that in one or two days they would all be exhausted with the exception of a little salt pork, which we feared might become rancid during the hot weather of summer. We again had to fill up the dreadful hiatus of exhausted supplies by hoping that the resources of the localities through which he might have to pass would not fail him. This, however, depended upon his guns and ammunition, which might meet with accidents in the boat among the ice. The rivers, which two months previously were quite dry, were now discharging continuous streams into the sea, and often after heavy rains they were considerably swollen, so that there might be some difficulty in crossing them. There was, however, less danger in this respect now than when débâcles from lakes and pent up accumulations were taking place. In making a short journey along the coast, or even round Assistance Bay, where there are three rivers or streams I should say, one had often to strip off shoes or boots and stockings and to take the water bare-footed. The ice-cold water applied to the overheated feet and legs produced a most painful sensation, which was repeated at every step. The land was still so soft in many parts that walking over it for any length of time was exceedingly laborious, even when taken as a recreation. Such was the prospective view we had of Mr. Penny's party, and the circumstances under which they might be placed. I need not state that the south-east point of the bay was rarely without some person taking an anxious look towards Dungeness Point and Cape Hotham, the direction in which we fully expected the party would return.

About five o'clock in the afternoon Mr. Petersen and I took a stroll in the direction of the south-east point in spite of the constant and heavy rain. The sky was very gloomy and overcast, and there was a strong and constant breeze from south-east. The ice had come in from the eastward and blocked up the Straits, except a small space between Assistance Bay and the south point of Griffith's Island, and this space also was filling up very rapidly. We had a view of the coast as far as Dungeness Point, but owing to the overcast sky and murky atmosphere it was imperfect.

At 10 P.M., as good friends were parting with "good nights," a party was observed coming over the S.E. point, where it begins to join a rising hill to the N.E.; and for a few minutes we thought it was composed of some of the men who often, in spite of bad weather and fatigue from their day's work, took an evening excursion to the eastward; but as the party approached, and a telescope was levelled upon it, Captain Penny was recognised. Up went the St. George's or British ensign, and in a few minutes we were among the party. He at once told us that he had seen nothing of the missing ships except a bit of elm, which might have belonged to them, and that his opinion was they had gone away to the north-westward far beyond his reach. The men and their commander were drenched to the skin, and most of them had either their toes or heels exposed through their boots to the ice, or the rough and sharp-pointed fragments, of which the surface of the land is composed, over which they often had to perform their weary march for whole days. All of them had lost flesh considerably, but they were in the best of spirits, and seemed to be less disappointed by the want of success which attended their arduous and trying labours than those who had been comfortably housed on board the ships. It was exceedingly gratifying to see them all safe on board after so long an absence and during such unfavourable weather, although they had not earned the laurels for which they had endured such hard toil, and had been exposed to such imminent dangers. An account of their proceedings, taken from Captain Penny's Journal, has already appeared in Chapter XVIII. He had joined his track with Captain Stewart's at Cape Becher in latitude 76° 30′, or near that latitude, from which he proceeded to the westward and southward, examining several islands surrounded on all sides by open water, but subject to be beset with drifting ice. After carrying on the search as long as it was prudent, with due respect to the safety of his party, he landed on Cornwallis Island, and leaving the boat, he and his party travelled with knapsacks eastward until the depôt so recently laid out by Captain Stewart at Cape de Haven was reached; thence down the Wellington Channel, calling on the several depôts, until he arrived at Cape Hotham, whence he proceeded to the ships. With his arrival the last of the travelling parties in search of Sir John Franklin came in, and the same dismal shade which veiled the mysterious fate of our long-lost countrymen still remained as it had been when we commenced our travelling.

Examining what has been done this season in, I may say, every possible direction, a question arises, What can be done further in the same cause, and what probable route has the missing expedition taken from winter quarters? The Wellington Channel was before Franklin and his adventurous followers during the autumn, winter, spring, and part, if not the whole, of the summer; and in that time he would be afforded an opportunity of judging of its merits in holding out prospects of a north-west passage being made through it. The influence of tides and winds upon the ice in it, and the probable changes which they might bring about to facilitate the progress of ships desirous of passing through it, would doubtless be well considered and discussed. Let me take a short retrospect of what we have observed with respect to the Wellington Channel; for the missing expedition would, at the end of the summer following their first winter, have very probably arrived at similar conclusions, provided that their observations were equally extensive with our own.

When we crossed the Wellington Channel last season, in autumn, the ice was then only beginning to start in the narrowest part of it, which is to the northward of latitude 75°; and at that time it is very improbable we should have got through it with our sailing vessels, for in a single day of calm weather we might probably be so encumbered with young ice, that all our efforts to get clear would be in vain, and we should be exposed to the mercy of the winds and tides in a drifting pack. Until we recrossed it again in May and June, it was very doubtful whether all the old ice had cleared out. Then it was proved that all the old ice had not cleared out of it; but it was also proved, that the barrier which had opposed our progress to the northward in September, had opened out and shifted its original position in the form of large floes; to what extent this had taken place, and whether sailing vessels could have plied up among the detached floes, or steamers could have advanced ahead of wind, or in calm weather, among them, was still doubtful, although the latter was exceedingly probable, for steamers can move on among bay ice in calm weather, and in narrow leads ahead of wind, when sailing vessels are reduced to utter helplessness. Captain Penny, Messrs. Goodsir, Marshall, and Leiper, and also Captain Stewart, discovered open water on the 17th, 20th, and 31st days of May respectively, as they approached the newly discovered Queen Victoria Channel at the three different points, Hamilton Island, Disappointment Bay, and Cape Becher. The cause of there being open water so far to the northward at such an early period, and when Barrow Straits, and probably also a part of Lancaster Sound, were still full of fixed ice from shore to shore, at once appeared strange and problematical. About the same date as Captain Stewart had been arrested at Cape Becher by open water extending to the westward beyond the utmost limits of vision from a hill six to eight hundred feet in height, Mr. Stuart, standing also on an elevation of considerable height at Cape Hurd on the north shore of Barrow Straits, could see not a drop of water,—nothing but an unbroken icy plain, on which he could make sure journeys east, west, or south. Cape Hurd, in latitude 74½°, taking round numbers, within one hundred and fifty miles of a very extensive arm of the Atlantic, Baffin's Bay, is closely surrounded by ice, to which the eye can assign no bounds. Cape Becher, in latitude 76½°, nearly within three hundred and fifty, or probably four hundred miles of the same sea, is surrounded by open water, which washes and ripples upon the pebbles on the beach, and to which the eye also can assign no bounds to the north-westward. This is a feature in Arctic discovery which is truly anomalous, if we except the top of Baffin's Bay and the Greenland Seas, where even in the depth of the long Polar winter there is open water. Had the ice in the Wellington Channel been a loose pack, one could easily account for the open water at and beyond Cape Becher, and Queen Victoria Channel would then be reduced to the same condition as Baffin's Bay. But instead of being in this form, it is a fixed barrier for eleven months and I suppose three-quarters, every year. Were the ice in Davis' Straits fairly arrested in its progress to the southward, which I believe is more rapid during spring and the first six weeks of summer than at any other period of the year, we should never find such an extent of open water in the top of Baffin's Bay, unless an exit should also be found for the ice in some other direction. From our own observations upon the ice in Barrow Straits, it is very clear that an extensive drift being allowed to the ice during winter, it may not have closed up from shore to shore when the season has arrived for it to open out again. In this way Barrow Straits did not close up till the 20th of March. Had the winter, however, been a more severe one, it might have closed up at a much earlier period. The rapidity of the tide, too, has great influence upon the formation of ice. Particle after particle of water, which must be of a higher temperature than ice, unless its salinity be very much increased, coming in contact with the ice, which covers it in rapid succession, cannot fail to prevent rapid congelation. On the other hand, in still bays, where the same, or nearly the same water advances and recedes during the whole winter, the tidal wave being at right angles with the coast, not parallel with it, the thickness which the ice can attain may be very great. In some of the fiords of West Greenland there is open water throughout the whole winter, owing to the rapid tides. In the middle of Davis' Straits, and in Baffin's Bay, the ice moving along with the water attains a considerable thickness. In Prince Alfred Bay, and also in Baring Bay, I observed the ice eleven to thirteen feet thick, and I had no doubt it was one year's formation, from its peculiar and highly characteristic structure. Having premised so much, I may allude to the probability of there being an extensive sea beyond Victoria Channel. If the presence of open water there at so early a period, and probably also throughout the winter, be attributed to rapid tides, thus proving its analogy at once with the fiords of West Greenland, those tides must come from the westward, that is, there must be in that direction an extensive expanse of water, in the same manner as there is off the Greenland coast. Supposing no such sea to exist to the westward, the whole rush of the tide to fill Victoria Channel, and the extensive space beyond Cape Osborne on the east side, and Cape de Haven on the west side, would necessarily pass through the Wellington Channel; and the effect of this would be the disappearance of the ice in the latter at a much earlier period than at points much more remote, where the water might only have to rise and fall instead of having to rush along a coast-line. I need not state that exactly the opposite of this obtains, and that the Wellington Channel is the very last place in which the ice gives way. The open water so unexpectedly met with in Victoria Channel, may be owing to an extensive drift being allowed to the ice to the westward of it; and the facts already noticed, with respect to the channel to the southward of it, bear out the same conclusion. From the simple fact that walruses, white whales and narwhales were seen in this newly discovered channel when Barrow Straits and Wellington Channel were one continuous sheet of ice, there need hardly be any doubt that the ice did not close up in it during the whole winter.* What happens in one winter, when it relates to the instinctive habits of animals, must happen every winter, otherwise those animals whose existence depended so essentially upon circumstances of which the

* I am informed by Mr. Petersen, whose experience with respect to the habits of Arctic animals is most extensive, that white whales and narwhales, which generally go to the southward at the close of the season, sometimes appear at an opening in the land ice, which they prevent closing by coming to it in great numbers to breathe; in such numbers, indeed, that in a comparatively short time the fortunate settlements in the neighbourhood of so favoured a spot begin to be short of casks to receive the oil or blubber; and that the value of dogs to transport the blubber and skin over the ice to the settlements increases four or five hundred per cent. At one of these openings, which are called "souces" by the settlers, a very common thing it is to see two or three of these animals in their dying struggles, surrounded by perhaps three times their number of others pressing eagerly to the surface of the water for the purpose of breathing, little thinking that the cold iron of the Esquimaux is just about to pierce their smooth skins, and to open out the capacious reservoirs of blood which, from the length of time they may have been under water, are beginning to be gorged with the dark blood of the right side of the heart. Souces are not common; and when one does occur, the animals either leave it, or are all killed, and in a few weeks the spot which it occupied becomes frozen over, and can hardly be recognised in the floe, except by the oil and filth on the ice around it. These animals do not, like some of the seals, keep open holes for breathing; and when a souce occurs, it probably was begun when the ice was very young, and consequently weak.

inclemency of the season might deprive them would have been exterminated in the course of a single winter. The thickness of the ice in all parts of the Wellington Channel about the 1st of June, when it began to decay on its upper surface, was nearly the same as that in Assistance Bay, and upwards of three feet thicker than that which extended along the south shore of Cornwallis Island within half a mile to a mile of the land. This does anything but lead to the idea of there being rapid tides in the Channel; on the contrary, it tends to exactly an opposite idea, corroborating the observations of Captain Penny, with respect to the flood tide in Queen Victoria Channel, which he says comes from the westward. The flood tide in Barrow Straits coming from the eastward, and proceeding so far up the Wellington Channel, must meet the rising tide advancing from an opposite quarter. This, however, I fear is too hypothetical to be admitted into the category of anything like sound reasoning; I therefore leave to others to judge for themselves.

If the missing ships passed up through the Wellington Channel, it probably was late in the season, at a time when there might not be much ice to retard their progress to the westward, and with a favourable wind. The latter condition is one that they would have found most essential to safe navigation late in the season. A few hours of calm weather in the sea beyond Victoria Channel during the second week of September would reduce them to utter helplessness by surrounding them with bay ice, which the unwearying exertions of their hardy crews would fail to clear out of their way. To look for them in any other direction except through the Wellington Channel, after what had been done in every other direction they could possibly have taken, was out of the question (at least so Captain Austin said, for he considered that nothing remained to be done westward of Cape Hotham, along the line of Barrow Straits, and its numerous indentations and bays). After what Captain Stewart had done on the eastern shore, and round to Cape Becher, Mr. Goodsir on the west and south shore, and Captain Penny in the New Channels, and on a whole host of islands in them, without finding traces of an unequivocal description, it became very questionable indeed how far we should be justified in risking a second winter for the sake of following up the search. What were our inducements? The piece of elm picked up by Captain Penny on one of the islands might have been driven from a great distance among ice. He says, very distinctly, it could never have come in contact with ice, meaning, no doubt, that it had been dropped where it was picked up, or carried there and thrown up by a wave or left by a high tide. Being weather-worn and reduced in weight, implied long exposure to the atmosphere; and being found on the north side of Hamilton Island, might naturally give rise to the idea, that the missing ships had dropped it on their passage to the westward. As Captain Penny had the best opportunity of judging, with respect to the probable source of this piece of wood, from the fact that he had been so long in the neighbourhood of the spot where it had been found, his opinion was of greater importance than that of those who had been placed under less favourable circumstances. He had but one idea on the subject, and that was, that it had come from the missing ships, which he believed had gone to the westward in clear water, far beyond the most distant point that he had been able to reach with his boat. Without doubting for a moment his opinions with respect to the circumstances under which the piece of elm found its way to its resting place, it is not impossible it might have been carried there by drifting ice. Suppose that late in the season, when there is most probably in the Polar Seas the greatest extent of water free from ice, which consequently must then drift with the greatest rapidity, a piece of wood had been dropped by a ship in Lancaster Sound, at the commencement of an easterly gale, and that it had alighted on a bit of ice at the edge of a "stream," the gale would carry the ice westward into Barrow Straits, at the rate of three or four miles an hour, and before its termination the bit of wood might be at Cape Hotham or Cape Riley, still reposing upon the ice and waiting a fair wind to drift it up Wellington Channel. The ice bearing it along might even be detained at either of these two places or at any other place for a whole season, and it might take one of many directions the following year; westward to Melville Island with an easterly wind, eastward into Baffin's Bay with an opposite wind, southward into Prince Regent's Inlet, or northward and westward into Wellington and Victoria Channels, just as the wind might favour it. The oar picked up by Lieutenant Cator of H. M. S. "Intrepid" at Cape Hotham, bearing the whaling ship's name by which it had been lost many years previously, is a clear proof of those facts, but it does not in the slightest degree affect the observations of those who have shown that there is a constant set or current out of Lancaster Sound. The condition which is essential to this conveying process is open water, affording a free and extensive drift to the ice.

The almost constant barrier in the Wellington Channel is highly unfavourable to the idea that the piece of wood found by Captain Penny had drifted from the southward; it does not, however, render it impossible, for the barrier sometimes gives way. The most probable direction whence it could come (upon the supposition that it had drifted at all), is W. or N. W., where the missing ships may have dropped it, or where they may have been wrecked or destroyed among the ice, and where years may be spent in fruitless attempts to find them. There was one decided objection to the probability that the missing ships had gone through the Wellington Channel, and that was the entire absence of signs of any description (with the exception of the bit of elm wood), on both sides of the channel, and on the group of islands beyond it, of British seamen having ever visited those hitherto unknown regions. There was also another objection, of perhaps not less importance than the above, "the chances there are that the channel persists from year to year in presenting a barrier of impenetrable ice, until the season is too far advanced for navigating the, to a certain extent, unencumbered seas to the N. W." It was not for me to decide the question, shall we follow them? and shall we have a second winter? My answer was with the majority, Give us hope, and the chances of doing anything likely to throw the faintest ray of light upon Franklin's dark fate, and a second winter will be entered upon and spent with the utmost cheerfulness. The health of our crews was excellent, and the utmost hilarity prevailed throughout both ships; and from this my inference was, that we should get through a second winter with comparative safety. What could we accomplish with our sailing vessels? Upon the supposition that the missing ships had passed through the Wellington Channel, to follow them with similar means as they possessed, with the view of rescuing them, would only be throwing ourselves away and jeopardising the cause; and with travelling parties the following spring and summer, we should just be going over the same ground as we had now explored and discovered. Indeed, it is probable we might not be able to go over an equal extent of ground, for on board both ships there was not so much spare wood as would make a single sledge. It is true, we should not have to follow the same route in every particular. From Beechey Island we should have to proceed north-westward, by means of boat and sledge-parties through Queen Victoria Channel, to a distance of at least two hundred and fifty miles, before we might expect to accomplish any good at all, it being very probable that no traces of the missing ships would be found within that distance; and even if this distance were accomplished without finding traces, it would be but a sorry compensation for a second winter. We had not the means in our expedition even to go so far; and suppose we had, it was doubtful whether we should have advanced, without first consulting Captain Austin, whose expedition would necessarily become involved in our proceedings. In this respect Mr. Penny's position was rather irksome; for on the one hand, he would have to say that all farther search through the Wellington Channel was hopeless; or, on the other, to take upon him the responsibility of keeping the two expeditions engaged in the Arctic Seas another year, which might even lead to a third, and, perhaps, a fourth year. The search had assumed an entirely new feature. To be conducted safely and satisfactorily, steam-power would require to become an essential element; and this we did not possess, but Captain Austin did; and before it could be made available, that officer would require to enter deeply into consultation with Mr. Penny, upon the expediency of still prosecuting the search.

Previous to Mr. Penny's return, Captain Austin's frequently expressed opinion was, that nothing of which he then knew, his travelling parties having all returned unsuccessful, could induce us or any of us to remain out a second winter, or even risk circumstances that might tend to that as their result. He anticipated that a second winter would shake very materially the health of the crews of the vessels under his command, which had been affected very considerably since very soon after the commencement of the spring travelling. Mr. Penny, whose resources for carrying on the search were completely exhausted, and depended entirely upon Captain Austin and his steamers, as far as a continuation of the search was concerned, had to adapt and mould his opinions to those of that gallant officer already expressed; and although they had not yet met to deliberate over matters *in extenso*, it was beginning to ooze out, that all further search would be hopeless, and that, for us at least, little remained but to proceed home, making this, however, entirely dependent upon the condition in which we should find the Wellington Channel after getting out of winter quarters. Preparations for sawing a canal in the ice, which had been begun previous to Captain Penny's arrival, were to be completed: that most laborious work was to be commenced forthwith, and it was ardently hoped that ten or at most fourteen days would set us clear of the ice in the harbour, and find us once more sailing pleasantly upon the rippling blue water north-westward, in the further prosecution of the object of the Expedition, or homeward,—not to be crowned with the laurels for finding Sir John Franklin, but to receive, if possible, a still greater boon — the warm sympathy of our friends to soothe the smarting pain of disappointed hope.

July 26th. — The officer belonging to H. M. St. S. "Pioneer," and the seaman belonging to H. M. St. S. "Intrepid," who had been a week on board the "Sophia," took their leave for Griffith's Island, bringing only verbal reports of Captain Penny's proceedings, owing to his unfit state from fatigue to draw up official reports which require very deliberate consideration. I accompanied them to the western point of the bay. The distance from the ships to that point was not more than a mile and a half in a straight line, but owing to the deep pools on the ice and large broad holes in it, communicating with the sea beneath, we had to make it probably three times as great. We had to leap over some of the holes and cracks, wade through some of the pools, and make long detours for others, as we wended our way along. A pole assists one very much in crossing some of the pools; by placing the lower end in the bottom of the pool, and then springing over, a space of twelve to fourteen feet can be cleared at one bound without touching the water, but it requires agility. A person accompanied us from the "Lady Franklin," but in consequence of falling in and getting a sound drenching, he had to return to his ship before our two guests were seen safe on the land. This was not accomplished without great difficulty, owing to the irregularly wasted state of the ice close along the beach, and it could only be done at one or two places around the whole harbour. Although they used every precaution and took great pains in picking out the best and safest way, they were wet above the knees, and in this state they had to perform a journey of twenty miles.

Mr. J. Stuart was sent to Barlow Inlet in a boat, but with two boats' crews to bring the boat to the ships which Captain Penny had left on the previous day. The weather was very clear, the sky was almost without a cloud, and there was a smart breeze from W. S. W. The trip would be very pleasant to and from Barlow Inlet, and there was no doubt it would be enjoyed. From the hill top the water in Barrow Straits appeared to be of unlimited extent east and west, as well as to the south shore. In all those directions there seemed to be no obstacle to navigation, and in this respect there was a remarkable contrast with the preceding year, when even six weeks later we found it impossible to advance in almost any direction. It is very probable that the ice then had cleared out, and that it or some other ice had drifted back again with the easterly winds which prevailed. Unicorns, walruses, seals, and white whales could all be seen sporting about in the water at the edge of the ice in the harbour. Everything around us breathed of a happy and tranquil air, owing doubtless to the more pleasant weather and the safe return of our commander.

July 27th, Sunday. — The weather was again rainy and squally, the sky was overcast and gloomy, and the wind was about S. S. E. This favoured the return of the two boats from Barlow Inlet, whence they arrived at the ships at nine o'clock in the morning. Our "Morning Service" was attended as usual, but there was a slight difference made which seemed to attract the notice of the seamen very much. The 107th Psalm, found in the "Form of Prayers to be used at Sea," was superadded to those proper for that morning of the month; the beautiful coincidence of the former with the latter, and especially with *Nisi quia Dominus,* blended with hearty gratitude, rendered the Service for this day something not to be readily forgotten. The delight of having Morning Service (although only on Sundays) on board ship, tends very much to break down the huge barrier that lies between the condition of the rough and hardy sailor and that of the happy and regular church-going landsman.

In my visit to the squadron at Griffith's, I had the pleasure of being present at Evening Service on a week-day on board H. M. S. "Resolute." It was conducted by Captain Austin, and all the officers who were present joined heartily, and uttered the responses audibly. The effect of the whole was really beautiful, and the two services every week-day, and four every Sunday, would perhaps produce impressions which would never be effaced. But in spite of the devoutness and praiseworthy regularity with which those services were attended to by Captain Austin, and the officers and crews of the ships of his squadron, I was struck with the fact that it had not been deemed necessary to appoint a chaplain to an expedition in which one hundred and eighty men were serving; and it was all the more striking when it occurred to me that no fewer than six medical officers were serving in the same expedition. I do not for a moment doubt the expediency of the above number of medical officers, for the duties to which they might have to attend would very probably extend far beyond the precincts of medicine. They had to travel, and to conduct whole parties for months together. This, and other duties which the medical officers had to discharge in the Expedition, were quite beyond the pale of their honourable profession. The chaplain to such an expedition would not stand aloof from similar duties. He surely would not prove less able to encourage men in their difficulties, to conduct parties, to make himself useful, than medical officers. He ought to have got the trial, but above all he ought to have been there for the sake of his sacred office, and that the crews of the four ships might benefit by his administrations during the long and dreary polar winter.

July 28th.—The weather continued rainy all night, and early in the morning it still rained on. The eclipse was to have been watched, but all hopes of seeing it was given up, owing to the gloomy and violent weather. The floe in Assistance Bay was quite blue, and the pools on it were increased very much in extent and depth. This was owing to the water accumulating on its surface, from uninterrupted precipitation of rain, more rapidly than the porous ice could permit it to pass through. The rivers were pouring continuous streams of muddy water into the bay, which whitened the sea in it from side to side. They carry down great banks of stones, which attrition along their beds has deprived of their rough corners. In the evening the wind became squally, and distinct clouds began to appear. The "Sophia" leaned over before the gale. This was the first time for ten months and a half that she had yielded before the blast.

At the mouths of the three rivers which enter Assistance Bay, and a little beyond their places of exit into the sea, the ice was wasted away very much, and not unfrequently we saw seals, walruses, and white whales in the open spaces of water, which were the result of the decaying influence of water in rapid motion upon ice. It is most likely these animals frequented the open spaces at the mouths of the rivers for the sake of the salmon, which they might find escaping from the lakes into the sea with favourable overflowings of the streams.

July 29th.— Sawing was begun to day, and before six o'clock in the evening, Mr. Manson, with one well wrought saw, managed to cut a single draft three hundred and sixty yards in length, where the average thickness of the ice was four feet. In the same time Mr. Marshall also, with a well wrought saw, cut only two hundred yards, but the thickness of the ice with him was six feet; this was at the outer edge of the floe in the harbour, while Mr. Manson was at its inner edge in the fair way of the largest stream. Some of the men engaged at the saws fell into the water, and got good duckings: this, however, was less likely to happen at the saws than in going to them and in returning again; and it was also more frequent close in shore near the open water at the mouths of the rivers than farther out at the offing, where the ice was considerably stronger and thicker.

July 30th. — The weather was still squally, and

there was rain and also snow occasionally. The land was sometimes quite white with snow, already assuming a most wintry aspect, while a few days of the extremely short summer still remained. While walking over the land, along the long and undulating beaches around Assistance Bay, the snow lying on the ground after a heavy shower, I was often struck with the drooping appearance of the poppy, as it hung its large and hardly yet fully expanded flower, and seemed desirous of casting aside its large and pale yellow petals, and of hurrying on to maturity, in obedience to the beckonings of "all subduing frost," which already began to make nightly visits to the almost level or gradually southerly sloping plains, having hardly ever left the bleak and almost barren wastes a few hundred feet higher up which sloped in an opposite direction.

About the end of May and the first week of June, the weather changed in a remarkable manner. Instead of the keen bracing atmosphere, the clear blue sky, and the northerly winds generally accompanied by low temperatures, there was a densely overcast sky, the clouds were heavy, gloomy, and portentous, and the winds prevailed from the southward, accompanied by a constant falling of soft snow, and comparatively high temperatures. On the 6th of June, I was in latitude 75° 15′ in the Wellington Channel, the mean temperature for twenty-four hours was + 32·25°, being the first time that it had been about or above the freezing point of water this season. There was a strong south-easterly gale, accompanied by constant precipitation of soft thick and flaky snow. Snow began to melt, for the first time, on the canvas of our tent; and foreign substances, such as bits of rope, tins, &c., sunk into the snow on the floe during an overcast sky. At this time birds, brent-geese and a species of plover, were observed, for the first time, to have migrated so far north; but ptarmigan and sea-fowl were seen at a much earlier period on the same side of the channel. On the 7th, at President Bay, water was observed on the land for the first time during cloudy weather, but frequently before then the snow on the stones of the beaches and hill tops and sides which sloped southward could be seen melting in the bright sunshine, when there happened to be but a very thin coating of it; how ever, it always froze again, and could be found on the surface of the stones in fragments partly ice and partly snow. So early as the 14th of May, at a height of upwards of four hundred feet on a southern slope in the neighbourhood of Cape Grinnell, I observed the snow melting on the surface of a tuft of the purple saxifrage, which, fully exposed to the vivifying influence of the sun in such a highly favoured spot, seemed disposed to put forth its stunted green leaves in acceptance of such a warm invitation. On the 9th of June, the floe in the Wellington Channel, which had formed during the previous winter, presented blue spots, owing to the snow on its surface melting; but the snow on old floes still resisted the increase of temperature, and they retained their white appearance until a later period. At this time thousands of eider and king ducks were observed migrating up the Wellington Channel; but the tracks of neither deer, hares, nor musk oxen were seen on the floe, although those animals, except the latter, had been seen ever since the middle of May on the land to the northward of latitude 75°. On the 11th and 12th of June, on the west side of the same channel, the maximum temperature for the season, in the shade, was registered at noon in latitude 75° during calm and mild weather and a perfectly cloudless sky. I feared, however, that +55° in the shade was more than the latitude could produce; the instrument was secured from the influence of solar and local radiation as much as was possible under the circumstances; but to protect it from the latter was utterly impossible, for the small stones all along the beach were quite dry and actually warm to the touch; the almost perpendicular cliffs above were particularly favourable to irregular distribution of heat. On board the ships in Assistance Bay, at the same hours, the temperature was +40° and 49°. The air felt so warm at this time that the men took their blanket bags out of the tent, and slept basking in the sun, or in the shade of the tent, for some of them complained of the heat as being oppressive, which it really was. In the tent at the ridge rope the thermometer was +80° or above it. On the 4th of the same month the minimum +10° was registered during clear weather and a gentle breeze off the land, which was within two miles of our position in latitude 75° 35′. On board the ships at the same time it was +16° during south-east winds.

On the 14th the first rain for the season fell at the same time at Cape Hotham, Assistance Harbour, and Cape de Haven; and at Assistance Bay on the 22nd, small streams began to cut subterranean passages in the snow, and to escape into the sea. However, several days before this time, a large quantity of water had been set free along the west side of the Wellington Channel at the foot of the high land in that quarter, and had made its escape into the sea by cutting channels and passages through the high hummocks which lined the whole coast. So early as the 27th of May a caterpillar was found crawling over mosses and lichens on the south shore of Prince Albert Land, in lat. 76° 26′, and the same creatures were, up to the first week in July, to be seen gnawing the green leaves of the *Dryas* on the land around Assistance Bay, nearly two degrees further southward. These creatures seemed to have had a long summer of it. By the first week of July, flies and gnats were on the wing; but some of their larvæ could be seen among Confervæ in pools and streams on the land for two or three weeks longer. About the third week in July, birds' eggs were found on the land in the vicinity of Assistance Bay, and on Baring Island in Queen Victoria Channel. About the middle of June the ice in the Wellington Channel and in Baring and Prince Alfred Bays became covered with an extensive sheet of water. The same thing was observed in Barrow Straits, but a few days earlier. Towards the last week in June, the ice had released itself of the superincumbent water; this taking place earliest where the ice was of the most recent formation. Where there was old ice, the water continued a much longer time on its surface than on the new or that of one year's growth. As the season advanced, and July was pretty well through, large and deep pools appeared on the ice, and not unfrequently a film of young ice formed on their surface during night; and when this happened, there was generally in the smaller pools much less water present in the mornings than had been the previous evening. The floe was undergoing rapid decay on its upper surface during the high temperature and bright sunshine in the daytime, and the water, which was the result, did not pass through the ice with the same degree of rapidity as it was set free; consequently, the pools filled up during the day and drained away in the night, especially if it happened to be frosty. This was observed so frequently, that no one could be mistaken as to its real cause, and there could be no possibility for setting it down as a rise and fall of the tide upon the ice. I believe, however, that there were some in the searching expeditions who held the opinion that there was a rise and fall of tide on the ice in some parts in the vicinity of the winter quarters of the ships. Rains and easterly winds prevailed to a great extent in July. The maximum temperature was +50°, and the minimum +29°.

I had a most accurate proof of the modes in which ice forms and decays. During winter and spring I conducted a series of measurements of the ice as it went on increasing in thickness from day to day and week to week, until the return of summer heat put a stop to its growth. Through each hole that was made in the ice the thickness was taken, and a piece of spun yarn was passed to the under surface of it, having attached to it a bit of wood, which came across the hole the moment its motion in the water became free. To the upper end of the spun yarn another piece of wood was secured also across the hole, but at its upper surface, and the whole was left in this state throughout the autumn, winter, spring, and summer. Upwards of sixty different marks were laid down in this way in parts of the ice where there were no hummocks nor accumulations of snow. It will be seen from the following table at what rate the increase took place, and the meteorological abstracts in the Appendix will give the corresponding temperatures. All the surface markings from September to May could be seen at once, although the increase in that time was not less than seven feet. This proves beyond a doubt that salt water ice, as well as that of fresh water, however soft it may be on the surface, increases in thickness from below. One by one the lowermost bits of wood appeared as the floe decayed with the advance of the season; and at the end of this month, those that had been put down when the ice was between four and five feet thick were on the upper surface. There could not be any doubt here, again, with respect to the mode of decay. The greatest thickness it had attained was seven feet nine inches; and of this upwards of four feet had already disappeared from the upper surface. The question which was suggested by this result was, Where did the water go to that had been set free by the decay of so much ice? There is no way in which it could have escaped except by passing through the ice into the sea. The temperature of it was frequently ascertained, and always found to be +32°; while the temperature of the sea previous and subsequent to the ice closing together in Barrow Straits in March until, and, I suppose, after the thaw commenced in June on the surface, was not above +29·5°. In still bays, where there is not a rushing tide, the water of the sea doing little more than merely rising and falling, less than a due proportion of fresh, or, I should say, comparatively fresh water, such as melting floes afford, mixing at a temperature of +32° with sea water of the usual density, and at a temperature of +29.5°, will become congealed, owing to the degree of dilution not being in a proportion to maintain the whole in a fluid state, or at least a portion of it, the remaining fluid portion having its density increased. It may appear rather a strange process that the ice dissolving so rapidly on the upper surface should be increasing nerly as rapidly on the opposite by a sort of transfer of the same water; and it is so far hypothetical; but there is no other way of accounting for what I observed on the east side of Cape Martyr, on the 19th of July, in a deep and still bay, where the ice was then about eight feet thick, nearly the whole of the lower half being a loose spongy mass, in which scores of small fishes had been caught, cruelly detained, and "starved" to death, and myriads of infusoria and siliceous algæ luxuriated in the utmost profusion.

MEASUREMENTS in inches of the thickness of the floe in Assistance Bay, showing the rate at which it formed, its water-line, and the depth of snow upon it.

The distance from the beach was about two hundred yards and the depth of water seven fathoms.

a, entire thickness from lower to upper surface, including the coating of snow.

b, depth of ice beneath the water-line.

c, space above the water-line, including

d, the depth of snow on the ice where the hole was made.

1850.	*a.*	*b.*	*c.*	*d.*	1850.	*a.*	*b.*	*c.*	*d.*
Sept. 26	10½	-	-	1	Nov. 3	30	25	5	2½
28	11½	-	-	1	12	34	28	6	3
30	13¾	11¼	2½	1	13	34	29½	4½	2¾
Oct. 2	15¾	12½	3¼	2¼	15	34¾	29¾	5	3
4	15¾	12½	3¼	2¼	19	34½	30	4½	1¾
7	16½	12½	4	2¾	29	36½	31	5½	2½
9	16½	13	3½	1½	Dec. 3	40½	34½	6	2¼
11	17¼	13½	3¾	2	11	43	37	6	2¼
14	21	15	6	4	19	47	41	6	2¼
16	20¾	16	4¾	3½	1851.				
19	21½	17½	4	2¾	3	51	44	7	3
21	21¾	18¼	3½	2	24	58½	49½	9	4½
23	23½	18½	5	3½	Feb. 1	64	54	10	4
25	24	19½	4½	2½	13	68¼	60¼	8	2¾
28	25	21	4	2½	March 3	72¾	63	9¾	4
30	26	22	4	1¾	April 3	85	74½	10½	3
Nov. 1	28½	23½	5	2¾	May 10	91			

Very soon after thawing commenced in June, we observed large heaps of shingle on the surface of the rough ice which fringed the coast east and west of Assistance Bay, but it did not extend into the latter. Allusion has been already made to accumulations of shingle on and in the floe ice. In autumn we saw the ice in the very act of digging up the loose mud and gravel, which heavy grounding ice had raised into elevations varying from one to three feet in height. We now began to see a part of the gravel of those heaps exposed, and as they protected from the action of the sun the ice on which they rested and were borne upon the water, they gradually appeared to rise higher and higher by the disappearance of the ice around them, and before the end of that month the whole coast looked as if a great number of carts had been at work distributing heaps of shingles over the ice to a distance of probably thirty yards from the shore. It not unfrequently happened that a fissure ran right through some of them, exposing the edge of a solid floe probably six feet thick, and the surface of the water, where the depth would vary from one and a half to two fathoms. In that part of the floe which was immediately underneath a heap there appeared to be very little shingle in its substance, as one might have expected had the ice been raising it from the bottom during the whole period of its growth; and where there was no heaped up shingle, the edge of the ice, even in the same fissure, was as free from adventitious substances as if it had formed at a distance of ten miles from the land. There is no doubt but fragments of rock may be raised from the bottom by becoming frozen to the ice, when the tide is out, and that too on an extensive scale, but not nearly to the same extent as we observed in autumn from quite a different process. It very frequently happened that persons thought themselves close to the beach, when such an array of heaps of shingle sticking up on the ice was approached. But I have often been disappointed on walking ten yards farther on towards the land by coming to a broad chasm, which I could not leap, and in which the bottom could not be discerned, owing to the depth of the water. The mud and gravel, thus exposed to the sun, became quite dry, and the finest parts of it were subject to be carried away by the wind.

July 31*st.*—The weather still continued squally accompanied by showers of snow. A considerable formation of bay ice took-place on the surface of pools on the floe since last night, and the draft of the saw was found so stiff, that there were very great fears we should profit very little by sawing away at the ice when it became frozen before next morning. Mr. Manson was not certain whether pressure or a slight yielding among the ice might not have been the cause of the stiffness and the difficulty there was in introducing the saw into its place when he commenced the work in the morning. The tides appeared to be very high, and owing to this the ice all around the bay became detached from the land and considerably broken up, so that at high water there was great difficulty in effecting a landing.

The greatest part of a second suit of clothes, and a second pair of sea boots, were served out to every man in the Expedition. The provision that had been made for us with respect to clothing was more than enough, for each person had supplied himself almost sufficiently for three winters, independent of the Government Stores. The boots, however, were very much in demand, especially since the wet work of sawing had been begun. They did not keep the feet dry; and all the skill of the seamen was completely baffled by the want of something to rub over them "to close the pores of the leather," as they very properly remarked. Various substances and compound substances were used. Tar, oil, pitch, and fat, variously combined, were all used together, but the results were nearly the same in the use of all, for no one's feet were dry at night. As might be anticipated, a good deal of coughing in some cases, and cramps of the legs in others, became very common.

These, however, were merely the results of the sudden exposure to the depressing causes already noticed, which we would be away from before material harm could happen to any one. All in the Expedition except three or four "idlers," and they were the medical officers, were engaged in the sawing.

August 1st.—Three or four of us took a boat at high water to the beach, and launched her into the water, which I already remarked lay between it and the ice which still filled the whole harbour in one continuous sheet from side to side. She belonged to Sir John Ross, and drew very little water, a peculiarity which adapted her for the purpose we had in view. We had no difficulty in proceeding with her to the west side of the harbour, and could have gone much further had not the tide gone back and left us dry upon the beach. We ascended the south-west bluff by climbing on hands and knees among the rubbish of which the talus is composed. From the top of the hill which surmounts the bluff, we had a good view of the squadron at Griffith's Island. The ships seemed to have shifted their relative positions to one another or to Griffith's Island very little, and there was a bar of ice three miles and a half in breadth between them and the water to the southward, or south-eastward, and probably also the same distance to the north-westward. Its position appeared to be a few miles to the south-east of the north-western extremity of Griffith's Island, and it occurred to us it had been caused by the N.E. winds having sent out the ice which lay between Somerville and Griffith's Islands into Barrow Straits, which had been clear of fixed ice for nearly a whole month. If the winds should continue to prevail from the same quarter, it appeared more probable that the Expedition would get clear of the ice round the west end of the island than at its south-eastern end. The water was ruffled by the wind and had a very dark appearance, and the sky beyond it was of that peculiar tint which never fails to indicate the presence of open water. From our elevation about five hundred feet, we could see at least twenty-five miles, and the sky conveyed a decided idea that there was very little ice in Barrow Straits far beyond the limits of vision. The wind had been from the westward for a sufficient length of time to clear the ice away to the eastward, which had been floating loosely on the whole surface of the strait. The rapidity with which floes and loose pack ice move before a strong breeze, is remarkable. A floe has been observed at Cape Hotham coming to the westward before a strong east wind, at a distance of a few miles from the coast. In three or four hours it passes the harbour, and in the same number of hours it goes out of sight to the westward; probably a space of thirty miles in six or eight hours.

We did not venture to descend among the rugged turrets, for that would have been much more difficult and dangerous than the ascent was; and, moreover, we wished to examine and collect fossil remains in those ravines a short distance to the eastward, also on the west side of the harbour. We found the Cephalopods represented by very perfect specimens of the genus and family *Orthoceras* in which the siphuncle could be distinguished very clearly; the Brachiopods, which were very abundant, might be said to have at their head very perfect specimens of the genus *Pentamerus*, which exhibited sections showing the septum very distinctly; and the Crustaceans, as usual, had the *Trilobites*. There were corals also, and beautiful impressions of marine algæ. Altogether the excursion was one of great interest in a geological point of view. While coming down the ravines which had small streams in them, I observed that at the bottom of each the water of the streams which were almost dry owing to the advanced period of the season, made its escape by disappearing among large accumulations of fragments of the disintegrated strata above. After descending a considerable distance through a sort of subterranean passage formed partly by rocks, and partly by snow or ice, it sometimes re-appeared for a short space, and then again disappeared, by sinking among heaps of fragments much smaller than those seen further up, which probably great rushes of water had brought down. There appeared to be little reason to doubt but the water which thus sunk among the rubbish would find its way to the sea. Its course lay through fragments of rocks which were imbedded in ice impregnated with mud and debris, and if it did not reach the sea, that must have been owing to its being arrested by the cold, in which case it could not fail to add to the height of the land, especially if the same process of arrest were continued for an indefinite period.

That part of our excursion which included the banks of the two large streams was not less interesting than that which applied to the ravines and the west bluff with its turrets. On the west side of the stream which enters the bay from the eastern extremity of Kate Austin Lake, and from the land beyond it, there is a large bank of finely divided earthy material, which the water is removing gradually every season. It extends from the foot of Prospect Hill to within a few hundred yards of the beach, and its depth, from its upper surface to the bed of the river, varies from fifteen to twenty feet.

It contains rounded fragments of rocks and shells imbedded in the finer material, of which it chiefly consists. The shells are of various species, and some of them are very much worn. I could distinguish the same shells in this deposit as were found at considerable elevations, both on this island and on North Devon. The most common forms were *Mya truncata* and *Saxicava rugosa,* both of which, especially the former, were taken up from the bottom with the dredge.* This bank is evidently of a tertiary character, and although it is undergoing removal by the stream, a similar bank is being deposited from its remains in Assistance Bay, which will some day possibly be affording shells to the geologist of species which now exist, as well as of those which existed when the present bank was deposited; and those shells may be in the closest contact with each other. The other rivers, especially the one on the west side of the harbour, have their banks of tertiary deposit, also abounding in shells. The beach at this time was quite bare all along the coast, and that part of it which extended round Assistance Bay was strewed over with shells and marine plants in very great abundance, which, I suppose, the waves in the previous autumn had cast up.

* For the names of the above I am indebted to Professor Edward Forbes.

When we entered Barrow Straits last season there was not a yard of the coast without hummocks aground upon it, and frequently we observed them piled up to a height of twenty to thirty, and in some cases, even forty feet; and every particle of ice thus raised up and thrown upon the coast had evidently been all floating loosely in the strait that season. From this, I consider that the strait was open long before we entered it, and that the ice had decayed and drifted away from the coast, exactly as it had done under our own observation this year. Had it not been thus we should have found the whole coast lined with old ice, which could not be mistaken; and the hummocks on the beach, instead of appearing as fresh as if they had been turned up a few days before, when we travelled so often along the coast with our sledges, would have been rounded off, and reduced and altered by the action of the sun so much, that there could not be a doubt as to the age being more than one year. It matters not what sort of ice, whether of one or two years' formation, came against the open coast; so long as the pressure had taken place in the previous autumn it could be detected by the above characters in the ensuing spring. If, then, the analogy of the two seasons can be proved up to this time, it is very clear that we did not enter Barrow Straits for the purpose of early or easy navigation by six weeks at least. It is melancholy to think that this time had been spent closely beset in Melville Bay, when, probably, with our ships we should have been able to accomplish what has cost the other expedition a great amount of very severe toil. We could not, however, have done anything in the Wellington Channel; and up to this time, although Barrow Strait had been open a whole month, it was still a perfect barrier, and probably would continue so for some time.

When we arrived on board the ships we learned that the two remaining pigeons belonging to the "Felix" had been sent off, loaded with letters, in a basket, which was suspended to two balloons by means of slow match. The wind was fair for a passage into a more genial climate; and by the time that the rope had burned up to the basket they would be at least seven hundred miles to the south-east of the ships, where they would have to commence their homeward flight. It was to be regretted, however, that the amount of gas in the balloons was not quite sufficient to carry their neat little car, soaring in the air out of sight. After the fastenings were let loose they ascended to a short distance, and were carried directly before the wind; but this did not continue long, and they began to descend, until they touched the ice, which imparted a slight impetus upwards; they again and again descended, and I fear the basket met with rough usage among the hummocks.

The dogs, ever on the look-out for objects worthy of their attention, could not but observe what attracted universal attention; in a few minutes they were in chase, followed by the men, whose extreme anxiety to save the pigeons was a sufficient inducement to leave the saws. Pools on the ice hindered neither men nor dogs; the latter had the precedence, and were just up with their prize, when, fortunately, it cleared the edge of the ice in the mouth of the bay; but where it went to after this I do not know.

August 2nd. — The weather was mild but close, and there was a constant fall of soft snow. The land was completely white — quite its winter garb again, while the ice, too, had a coating of snow on it, which would considerably retard the process of thawing. Our saws met this morning, but it was only in one saw-draft. The ice was breaking up at its outer edge, and a large space of water had made at each of the mouths of the three streams. This was owing to the increased temperature of the water coming down from the land. Reasonable hopes were entertained we should get clear next week, and they were very cheering, for the nights were by this time beginning to look gloomy, and to assume their sombre hues.

August 7th.—The saws were making great progress, and the canal was fast approaching towards the ships. It was exceedingly laborious work, and was also much more protracted than we expected it would be. This was owing to some of the sawing requiring to be done over again, the first saw-draft having frozen. A lesson was taught by this occurrence, not to saw a yard more in one day than could be made available in floating out the ice. The ice between the ships and the land became broken into large fragments, so that it was by no means easy to get to the beach; but it was still entire between the ships and the open water in the offing.

Where the action of the running water from the streams had made openings in the ice in the harbour the dredge was plied until the bottom was fairly exhausted, that is, until new or different forms of animals ceased to be found. The bottom was muddy, and the depth varied from five to ten fathoms. In four fathoms, close to the mouths of the streams, the mud was displaced by shingle, which, as I have already remarked, they carry from the land over which they have to flow, hollowing out their passages, whether they are over the solid strata, or in a bank of once soft mud, shells, and rolled pebbles. The mud was exceedingly abundant in animal life. The same forms that had been brought up in the previous autumn were again brought up, and also many more. There were three genera of the sea slug (*Holothuria*) family, the smallest of which, with their young, were the most abundant of all the varieties of creatures that came into the dredge. The other two genera of the same family were very rare; the one was about four inches in length, of a dark inky colour, and possessing the same number of rows of cirri as the smaller and more abundant genus; and the remaining genus had a hard rough covering, which did not, however, prevent partial contraction and expansion of the whole animal; it was deficient in the regular rows of cirrhi, but they probably were confined to a portion of its side, which resembled a disc, and it differed in its bright orange colour from either of the other two, the former of which was nearly of the colour of the human skin. I regret that specimens of the two rare genera did not come into my possession. It was very common to see these creatures discharge their complex digestive and respiratory organs when cold sea-water was poured upon them to wash away the mud. Next to the sea-slugs, the brittle star-fishes were the most abundant, and then came a species of *Saduria*; but taking three of the great divisions of the animal kingdom, the

Mollusca were the most numerous, then the *Radiata*, and last the *Crustacea*, which represented the *Articulata.* By going out to the entrance of the bay, where the depth is twenty fathoms, the order was changed, the *Mollusca* took the place of the *Crustacea*, while the *Radiata*, from the immense numbers of sea urchins, took the first place. The beauty of the annelidans, or worm-like creatures, found at a depth of fifteen to twenty fathoms on the shingly bottom, was worthy of the utmost admiration. In this respect, it was almost impossible they could excel creatures of the same class which had to crawl in the mud and slime further in shore. The iridescent hues of the setæ, and of the under surface of the elytra, or scales, of the *Aphrodite*, could be placed in competition with the beautiful tints of the rainbow. In the deep water at the mouth of the bay, acorn-shells (*Balanus*), nearly an inch in breadth, were found adhering to the fragments of stone which came up in the dredge. The same stones were also encrusted with *Escharella*, and beautifully variegated with lime-secreting vegetable forms (*Nullipora*). Very perfect specimens of *Actinia** were also taken up from this depth, but some shreds of an *Ascidia*, adhering to fragments of stones, were hardly worth preserving. I regretted very much that

* For the name of this family of *Algæ* I am indebted to the kindness of Dr. Dickie, Queen's Coll. Belfast.

an *Aphrodite*, the scales of which came up in the dredge, and were of large size, was not obtained. Upon the whole, the dredging, although laborious, and by no means clean work, amply repaid us; and there is no doubt those who follow in the same field will find much that we missed to repay their toil.

I regretted very much that an attempt to dredge Kate Austin Lake proved ineffectual. We should certainly have found something very interesting, for the food of the salmon that inhabited it throughout the winter was still a great mystery to us, although we had often examined their stomachs; its water, or muddy bottom, would necessarily yield something to them in the shape of food. One or two were caught descending in the stream a few weeks ago. They were very lean, and so weak, that the person who caught them had no difficulty whatever in seizing them in the running water, and they appeared as if all their strength was necessary to keep them steady as the stream carried them towards the sea. The seine net, a dredge, and Halkett's boat, were brought to the lake, but as there was fully more than one-half the ice still remaining, our operations would necessarily be limited to the borders, where the water is shallow. The first person that went afloat in the boat tumbled out while attempting to land upon the ice, and narrowly escaped being drowned. The net was tried several times, but nothing was caught. If there were fish in the lake, they occupied deeper water than we could reach, owing to the ice. From the small size of the stream, I think it very likely they must have ascended it, and taken up their quarters for the winter, for every day now would be diminishing its size, until ultimately it would dry up altogether.

At this time I observed that the gnats had almost entirely disappeared, but on turning up fragments of stones they were found in great numbers, in a torpid state, adhering in pairs. They were in greatest abundance where the surface of the stones on which they reposed was tinged a little green with some microscopic vegetable form. Dryness of situation seemed also to attract them. Their long winter was setting in; they had performed their functions in the economy of nature, and their offspring, in an undeveloped state, having passed with impunity through the extreme cold of such a high northern latitude, would be called into active existence at the same time as plants, and by the same influence—the vital influence of the heat and light of the sun.

August 8th.—The ice in the bay broke loose at the east and west points, and moved off about two hundred yards. The sawing that had been carried on vigorously for nearly a fortnight proved altogether superfluous; but had not the ice all started and broken loose, we should have got clear by sawing about the 11th. The weather was sometimes rather stormy, and falls of snow were not unfrequent, whichever way the wind came; the land was very often white, but this rarely withstood bright sunshine for a single hour. If one happened to be on the land and among the hills on such an occasion, he could still see bunches of flowers, in the more elevated situations, peeping through the snow as it melted away, and appeared in large drops among the white petals of the widely diffused *Cerastium Alpinum*, and he would be reminded of other days in a more genial climate when the first snow-drops of the season hung their drooping heads over the white snow; as I have already remarked, this was peculiar to the poppy and a few other plants which are late in coming into flower. I had a flat box, about two feet by one and a half, carefully filled with living plants, which were taken up with their roots in the soil and packed side by side. One can form a good idea of the stunted development of the flowering plants of Cornwallis Island, when a complete collection of them, with sufficient room for each to grow, was comprehended within the above mentioned space. In a much higher latitude, on the eastern shore of Davis's Straits, plants attain to a much larger size, and are more numerous than they are here; and it is not improbable, that animals are also more numerous. It is difficult at present to decide whether this peculiar preponderance in favour of West Greenland is owing to the different character of the rocks, or to the immediate vicinity of the coast with water throughout the greatest part of the year. It has been already remarked, that Melville Island has a more abundant and highly developed Flora than this island. The difference of temperature between the two places must be little, if there be any; consequently one is forced to seek for the true cause and source of the difference in the rocks and the soil. Melville Island, containing sandstone in great abundance, is highly siliceous, and West Greenland partakes also of the same character, in perhaps a degree still higher; but Cornwallis Island is almost altogether deficient in this material. Here, then, probably is the real cause, and the next question is with respect to its *modus operandi.* Where the rocks are hard and flinty, water from rain or melting snow must either pass over them in a running stream, or remain on the surface and submit to be congealed, if the degree of cold be sufficiently low. And, again, when the soil is composed of fragments of a hard and gritty character, water falling upon it as before, from melting snow or rain, will pass through very readily, and by this means the surface will be left comparatively dry. But when the soil is argillaceous, or composed of a marly, pasty material, water may lie on its surface, or sink into it, and swell it up into a bog, over which one will not be safe to walk without sinking to the knees. It will be very clear that in the first two instances I have given, vegetation will be favoured by the condition of the soil in which it must take root, with the exception of this in the first, when snow and water may be detained to form glaciers. And it will be equally clear that in the last instance, while the soil is wet and boggy, the very opposite condition to warmth and comfort, vegetation cannot be favoured as in the other two, and a difference may obtain, both with respect to the number of species and the degree of development, which may be found analogous with that between the coast of West Greenland and Melville Island, and Cornwallis Island, the conditions and circumstances of which, favourable in the one case, and unfavourable in the other, I have endeavoured to lay down. There may, however, be plants suited for wet localities only, found on Cornwallis Island, which may be entirely wanting in the drier localities. This I consider well exemplified in the jelly-like plant (*Nostoc*), which is very abundant in this quarter, but has not been found, so far as I know, on Melville Island or Greenland.

August 9th.—A large cairn was erected on Prospect Hill, and two tin cylinders were left in the top of it, containing documents relative to our proceedings up to this time. One document, in particular, contained a detailed account of the miles travelled by each person in the Expedition. It will appear incredible when I state that the amount of all our separate parties was about 2000 miles. Seven hundred and ten miles of this were newly discovered, and had to be added to the charts of the Polar Seas. This distance may appear great; but when it is considered that the islands in and to the westward of the New Channel were all examined and circumnavigated, and that the coasts from Cape Bowden to Cape Becher, and from Point Delay to Lady Hamilton Bay or Goodsir's Farthest, were followed round every bay and indentation, it will not appear to be over-estimated. And when I state that there were double and triple journeys to Point Separation, Cape de Haven, and Point Surprise,—it will be also readily seen that two thousand miles, accomplished by distinctly separate parties, are not above the distances travelled over the ice with sledges, including the distance accomplished by the boat in the newly-discovered channel. The weakness of our force rendered double journeys absolutely necessary, before the provisions could be advanced sufficiently to enable the advancing parties to go on with safety.

All our communication with the shore had to be carried on by means of boats; and any spare articles that might have been left on the beach till now were taken off also by boats. From the top of Prospect Hill, Barrow Straits appeared to be a good deal encumbered with ice. The wind had been for some time from the eastward, and the loose ice in that direction came pouring to the westward along with it.

This was what we might, and did expect, for the large inlets on both sides of the strait would now be opening out, and spreading their ice over the adjoining seas; the ice from only a small portion of Prince Regent Inlet and of Wellington Channel would be quite sufficient to encumber that portion of Barrow Straits which is between Lowther Island and Cape Hotham, in such a manner as to render navigation impossible. The distance from Lowther Island to Cape Walker is not above twenty-four miles, and that from Griffith's Island to Cape Baring not above thirty; two or three not very large floes, and one or two smaller ones, such as might be set free in the two inlets to the eastward which have been just noticed, would easily form a barrier at either of the above places during an easterly or south-easterly wind, and the much broken-up ice following up after the larger fragments and floes, would render it altogether impenetrable. It is highly probable that in such a barrier, extending to the eastward twenty-five to forty miles along the south shore of Barrow Straits, the expedition under the command of Sir James Clark Ross got beset on or about the first days of September, 1849, during an easterly wind, and drove out of Lancaster Sound with opposite winds and the regular set of the currents, until it was set at liberty off Ponds Bay by a slight swell, which, even up there, was sufficient to reduce the close into a loose pack.

August 10th.—The heavy masses of clouds which loaded the atmosphere yesterday disappeared, and the south-east wind died away. Towards noon it was calm, and the ships lay motionless at anchor, except when the tide swung them round and round. The ice in the entrance of the bay was shifting about a good deal, but it had not yet completely disentangled itself from the land. It is probable we should have got out of the harbour had we made an attempt; but no good could come from this, as Barrow Strait was unnavigable, and our intentions, on getting clear, were to proceed to Griffith's Island to consult Captain Austin with respect to our future operations. An attempt had been made to visit his squadron by Captain Penny and one of the officers of H. M. S.

"Resolute" in a boat, but there was a large quantity of loose pack ice at the edge of the barrier in which the ships were still fixed, and it was impossible to walk over it, while the boat could not be bored through it. The Esquimaux on board the "Felix" left the harbour on the 11th in his kyak with the view of going to Griffith's Island. He intended to accomplish part of the journey on the water, and when that failed him, he was to carry his canoe on his shoulders, until, by alternate paddling and walking, frequently repeated, he should reach the ships. From the circumstance that he had not returned, it was presumed that he reached them safely. Mr. Penny was rather anxious, from not having sent Captain Austin anything more than a verbal report of his return from Victoria Channel; however, he felt easier from the fact that the means of communication had been cut off, and that no chance had been afforded for sending letters, except the one by Adam Beck, and that was of a very doubtful nature.

After dinner, as the weather was very pleasant, although quite thick and foggy, I accompanied Captains Penny and Stewart to the land, and had a most pleasant walk on the beach. We had not gone far when we came to a pool, eight or ten feet above the high water-mark, which had but an inch or two of water in its bottom. It appeared to have had much more water a short time before, but by escape through the shingle and finely divided earthy matter, or by evaporation, this had almost all disappeared, and it would be perfectly dry in a few days. The stones in the bottom and sides of it were encrusted or coated over with the red snow plant (*Protococcus Nivalis*). The incrustation on the dry fragments was of a dark red, but the coating of those that were still moist and under water was of a bright red colour, and the under surface of both had the plant of a decidedly green colour. The green may be quite a different plant from the red, but to me they appeared to differ only in the colour. From having found forms of animal and vegetable life (the minute leaping insects, the jelly-like plant, and the above) in considerable abundance on this part of Cornwallis Island, which are peculiar to the rugged slopes, precipitous cliffs, and extensive glacier ranges of the Alps, I went on during the rest of our walk musing upon the interesting analogies I should see drawn by some competent person, between objects from 74° 40′ N. latitude, and other objects, very probably the same, from an elevation 11,000 feet on Mont Blanc, in latitude 45° 49′ 58″*. My two commanders were holding a conversation about

* The latitude is taken from Professor Forbes's Travels through the Alps, p. 122.

remaining out a second winter. Captain Penny appeared to me to be in a sad dilemma. He had, on the one hand, to contend with the possibility, and even the probability, that much ought still to be done in search of the missing ships, and on the other hand, he saw coming upon his shoulders the responsibility for the lives of all engaged in both Expeditions. Again and again he said that he would neither be responsible for bringing the search to a close, nor for jeopardizing the lives of upwards of two hundred and twenty men, by leading them up the Wellington Channel in the very footsteps, as he believed, of the unfortunate Franklin and his adventurous companions. He could not convince others to the same extent as he believed it himself, that the missing ships had taken that route. But he looked forward to an early meeting with Captain Austin, and said that after he had given an outline of what had come under his observations in the Victoria Channel, he should at once propose a continuation of the search by means of one of the steamers and the "Sophia" through the Wellington Channel, so soon as the ice in that channel should open. Mr. Penny alone knew all the circumstances connected with the newly-discovered channel. Mr. Stewart, of the "Sophia," from being at Cape Becher, knew much however, and afforded materials, which assisted those obtained by Mr. Penny, in making out a map. I still felt much for Mr. Penny; and although his course was plain, at least to a certain extent, and although it was probable that Captain Austin would share the responsibility with him, still there was no proof of this; for Captain Austin had made up his mind, to my knowledge, long before now, with respect to the western routes which his parties had been exploring; and as he had with one bold stroke put an end to the search in that direction, although there was still unexplored a gap, two hundred miles in width, to the eastward of Bank's Land, it was equally probable he would not reciprocate with Mr. Penny, but leave him to act in the matter, between the two difficult and perplexing points with which we started, solely upon his own responsibility.

August 11*th.* — The morning was uncommonly pleasant, the sky was clear and almost cloudless, there was hardly a breath of wind, and distant objects along the horizon could be seen very distinctly. The temperature of the air in the shade varied from +34° to +43°, and the barometer at noon was up to 30·51. At noon there was really hot sunshine, and the pieces of ice which the tide had left dry upon the beach were melting away very rapidly. Mr. Goodsir and I, with one or two men and a boat, tried the river with a seine net in the entrance of the middle stream, but our success here was in all respects the same as in the lake, with the single exception of a *Merlangus*, which was so weak that it could hardly seek its way out of the meshes of the net, although they were sufficiently large to permit it to pass through.

The ice in the bay was quite open, and our ships could have been taken out very easily early in the morning, but there was little wind, and the pack in Barrow Straits was still near the land; consequently it was thought proper to remain where we were until circumstances should prove favourable for going outside.

In the afternoon Captain Austin's squadron came steaming into the harbour, and dropped anchor. The commander of the "Sophia" was immediately sent on board the "Resolute" to wait upon Captain Austin with letters from Mr. Penny; and in a short time the latter also went on board that ship to enter into a deliberate consultation with her commander, to go over what had been already done, and to shape the future operations of both Expeditions. It was a most important duty in which they at that moment were about to engage. Not only did the destinies of our fleet of six ships and their crews hang upon the decision to which they should come, but also the fate of those who might still be looking for help, whose eyes might be dim with daily scanning the far distant horizon, with watching the rise of every little cloud and the illusory appearance of anything that might encourage the hope that release from the icy wastes and chilly waters around them was at hand. The piece of elm was in requisition; and the carpenters of H. M.'s ships examined it with great care, and delivered their opinion upon it to Captain Austin. The latter, if conversation—if articulated expressions afford a key to the secret workings of the mind, appeared to share with Mr. Penny in a due consideration of the chances there might be of accomplishing anything to further the object of the Expeditions by following the so-far explored route through the Wellington Channel. The piece of elm failed; and from the absence of deposited records, all that Mr. Penny could or did say, failed to convince him of even the faintest probability that the missing ships had taken that route. He gave his opinion, that had he done exactly what Mr. Penny's Expedition had done, and were he placed in the position which Mr. Penny occupied, he should not hesitate to conclude at once that the search for the missing ships need not be prosecuted to the north-west of their winter quarters at Beechey Island,—a direction which he believed they had never taken. Mr. Penny had no means of satisfying Captain Austin with respect to the opinion he (who had been in and beyond the Wellington

Channel) entertained of the route they took from their winter quarters. This opinion he could not base upon anything more substantial than ideas suggested by the experience he and those engaged on the same route had acquired. To all appearance, it had no tangible relation whatever with the missing ships; and not a single unexceptionable fact could be brought in to substantiate it.* It has been remarked elsewhere, that without Captain Austin's co-operation our Expedition, dried up in its resources, could effect nothing by remaining out a second winter. This caused the absolute necessity of coming into the most intimate relation with that distinguished and highly-experienced officer, and deprived us of that freedom of action which would have enabled us to hold out strongly in defence of our opinions, however vague they might be in the estimation of equally, if not also more competent persons. The result of their deliberations enabled me to enter the following remark in my journal at the time: — "After the heads of the Expeditions had considered matters fully, we were given to understand that little remained to be done but proceed to England. Captain Austin was satisfied that the missing Expedition need not be searched for to the due west or north-west;

* See in the Appendix the report of Sir John Richardson on the piece of elm.

and Mr. Penny, uncertain whether they had proceeded up the channel, could hold out no hopes of our being able to accomplish anything deserving the almost inevitable risks of a second winter." I did not learn, however, till next morning, that Mr. Penny, in reply to frequent solicitations from Captain Austin with respect to the further prosecution of the search, had granted a note, stating that he had accomplished all that could be necessary within the bare limits of the Wellington Channel, and adding a question, "What more can be done?" This I heard from my commander, who had been present at the writing of the letter, and at almost all the recent deliberations of Captain Austin and Mr. Penny, the results of which he related to me with that gentlemanly frankness which always marked his manner towards his intimate acquaintances.

CHAP. XXI.

PASSAGE TO ENGLAND.

Leave Winter Quarters. — Pass Wellington Channel. — Old Ice. — Progress Eastward.—Refraction.—Loose Ice in Barrow Straits.— Favourable Wind. — Character of the Land. — Misty Weather. — First Icebergs seen. — Crepitation of Ice. —Absence of Glaciers on both sides of Barrow Straits. — Compasses slow of Action. — Thick Weather.— Cape Hay. — Glaciers. —Course down Lancaster Sound. — Icebergs numerous. — Changes which Icebergs undergo. — Button Point. — Luxuriant Vegetation. — Ponds Bay. — Whales. — The Esquimaux. — The Effects of Intercourse with Shipping. — The Effects of Civilisation in Greenland.— West Coast of Davis Straits inaccessible.—Outline of a Plan for Settlements. — Course Southward. — Icebergs of a dirty Colour. — Illusions. — Trim of the Ships. — Coming in among the Ice. — Thick Weather. — Crossing through the "Middle" Ice. — Little Auks. — The "East" Water. — Models of Sledges. — Mr. Petersen. — Lose Sight of "Lady Franklin." — Prospects of being sent out to make a North-west Passage.— Crossing the Arctic Circle.—Fishing.—Drift Wood.—Luminosity of the Sea. —Aurora Borealis. — Cape Farewell. —Final Departure. — Violent Gale. — One of the Crew in great Danger. — Favourable Weather. —Rainy Weather. — Currents. — Foul Wind. — Birds seen. —First Ships seen. —Make the Land.—Arrival of the "Lady Franklin."— American Expedition. — Baffling Calms. — Luminosity of the Sea off Whitby. — Serious Accident. — Conclusion of the Voyage.

August 12*th*.—It was rather a strange coincidence that we should be leaving Assistance Bay exactly eleven months after we had dropped anchor in it,

This was a long period to be confined to one place with our ships, without having in our power to hold any intercourse with the inhabited parts of our Planet, or to see a face, but the chosen few who were engaged as ourselves. Our associations, however, were extensive, and few or none suffered from *ennui*, monotony scarcely found a resting place among us, and each person seemed to be bent upon some favourite theme; even among the seamen there was a desire to make the voyage subservient to some general good, as far as could be accomplished with due respect to their discharge of the duties to be exacted daily by their commanders. The spare hours that many of them devoted to the wholesome recreation both of mind and body, in walking among the hills and along the sloping beaches in the vicinity of, and around Assistance Bay, left cheerful impressions upon their minds which would never be forgotten. The entrance into it being so wide and roomy, and the gradual and undulating slopes of the land, as seen from the ships, imparted by their openness an elasticity of spirit, and a buoyancy of disposition, to which we owed much of the good health and happiness we had enjoyed for so long a period. Doubtless there was not a person on board who did not feel most thankful for being again released from the ice; but equally, doubtless, there was not one who did not feel somewhat reluctant to leave a place so happy and so comfortable as Assistance Bay. The sky was cloudless, and there was no wind; there was a film of young ice on the whole surface of the harbour, and the large fragments of old ice that were drifting about with the tides were breaking it up with a well-known noise, which we had not heard for a long time. A little before midnight the sun went out of sight at the back of the west shoulder of Prospect Hill, and now he was beginning to deck with his golden rays the western flank of the hill to the north-east, and to burst forth, dispelling the shades which his bright presence beyond the hills had thrown around us. The snow (or rather ice) in the face of the south-west bluff, illuminated by the radiant stream which flowed

Prospect Hill.

to it, while the harbour was still in the shade, changed its pale white colour to a light dazzling yellow. The dogs, which were still upon the pieces of ice that floated loosely round the ships, seemed to have an instinctive idea that we were about to leave the harbour, and as some of them ran about from one piece of ice to another, uttering peculiar whines to get on board, others took the water and swam along side, where some of the seamen picked them up. This was the picture which Assistance Bay presented at two o'clock in the morning, when the sounds of the windlass pawls of the "Lady Franklin" and "Sophia" began to echo from the hills. The shrill sound of the boatswain's whistle issuing from each of H. M.'s four ships in succession, was superseded for a moment, and then followed such a clattering of pawls as our winter quarters had never heard before, nor, as we presumed, would ever hear again. Our two little crafts were soon under sail, standing out of the bay, and to the eastward. There was little or no wind, and as little chance of there being any till afternoon; however, we moved on by means of a boat ahead of each.

At 5 A. M. Captain Austin's squadron, with the "Felix" in tow, came up after us, and as cheers were exchanged on both sides ,they shot past, and were lost sight of for the last time, in the afternoon, to the westward of Beechey Island, standing on towards it. As the day advanced a slight wind sprang up, by which we crept to the eastward, and Cape Hotham was soon behind us, as the entrance of the

Wellington Channel was opening out. It was full of heavy ice, which pressed upon Cape Hotham, and appeared to extend up along the west side so far that, from its southern edge, we could not see water over it. Some of the floes were of very great extent, and they appeared to be in continuous sheets of ice, more than one year old. It was very doubtful whence they could have come, for they seemed to be larger than any of the same character that we had seen in the channel to the southward of Point Petersen and Cape Grinnell. As we approached the Beechey Island side the water seemed to be free from ice as far as one could distinguish from the crow's nest, but this did not extend beyond Cape Spencer, owing to the wide berth that we had to give Cape Hotham and the large floes which extended from it into Barrow Straits. In the evening the wind freshened up a little and filled our sails, and before midnight Beechey Island, Cape Riley, and Caswall's Tower were seen quite plainly on the north side, and on the opposite side, Whaler Point and Leopold Island could be seen at the same time. At 9 P.M. the moon rose over Leopold Island, and appeared to be very much distorted by refraction; the form was elliptical, following the direction of the horizon, and the colour was red, resembling that of the sun when viewed through very black glass. There was a patch of ice between us and the island, which probably may have assisted to increase the refraction in that direction, although it was exceedingly powerful in every other direction. The temperature of the air varied from $+31\frac{1}{2}°$ to $+34°$, and that of the water was the same. This was a mere coincidence, for there is not between the air and the water that specific relation which would make the temperature of both the same.

August 13*th.*—During the night there was a light northerly breeze, and the sky was very clear, but as morning approached it completely failed, and we lay motionless on the water, the ships bowing to the gentle swell, which even here could be observed very perceptibly. A patch of ice was seen, at a considerable distance from, and to the N. E. of, Leopold Island. It lay in the course we were making, and for a time we feared it would oppose our progress, but as we approached it we found that it was only loose streams. Some of the fragments were a little heavy, but they all repelled one another under the influence of the swell. With a light breeze we would have found no difficulty whatever in passing through them. The day was exceedingly pleasant, the weather very fine, the sky clear, and refraction most intense. The land on both sides of Barrow Straits was raised and rendered visible in a remarkable manner. Seals, white whales, walruses, and narwhals were often seen, but as we advanced to the eastward they became less frequent, until at length they were lost sight of altogether. The meridian altitude was 30° 9′, and in the evening observations were taken for longitude. At noon there was a light breeze from N. W., which helped us along; the east point of Prince Leopold Island bore S. 60° E., and at 3 P.M., three hours later, it bore S. 37° 22′ E., which marked very distinctly our eastward progress. The "Felix" was observed coming up astern at noon, but since we got the breeze she was dropping out of sight. In the evening the wind freshened up, and at ten o'clock our ships were leaning over before the strong gusts and squalls that came out of the large bays on the south shore of North Devon. The "Lady Franklin" had to take in her royals to wait for the "Sophia," which did not appear to have improved in her sailing capabilities during her fixed position in the ice. The latter, however, sailed remarkably well, although she was not a match for her consort.

At midnight we saw the land on the east side of Prince Regent's Inlet. The land on the opposite shore of Barrow Straits was also seen at the same time. Large blue clouds were beginning to rise over it to the eastward of Cape Fellfoot, and to drift rapidly before the wind. The land here changes its appearance very much; the regular rows of buttresses, the deep bays, with shallow water and long flat spites, and the level outline of the surface, at an elevation of six to eight hundred feet, with occasional undulations, so common eastward and northward of Beechey Island, are exchanged, before one reaches Croker Bay, or even Powell Inlet, for ascents without the slightest order in their arrangement, for long, rough, and iron-sided valleys, in which the glacier, by night and by day, shapes its resistless course, moulding and adapting its icy hardness to the still greater hardness which deflects its march, until it enters the deep waters, in which a progeny of icebergs can be seen floating in the face of the rocks, and for rugged ice-clad crags, rising irregularly fifteen hundred to two thousand feet, enduring and wild in the extreme; the soft and melting limestone, which alike shows that it had a beginning, and will also have an end, and thereby the true representative of Time, is exchanged for everlasting granite.

August 14th.—The wind kept up all night and morning; and at noon we began to discover that our position was not far to the west of Admiralty Inlet. At 6 P.M. we were to the east of its entrance; and the form of the land there, with which we had been made familiar on the 20th of the same month, the previous year, was at once recognised. The sky began to be murky and overcast, on the north side of the sound, at noon; but as evening came on, and the wind veered from W. to N., it also became hazy where we were; however, as there was a smart breeze, we glided along rapidly, the "Sophia," as usual, following in the eddying wake of the "Lady Franklin." The first icebergs, since we had left this spot the previous year, were seen; and portions of ice, which streamed away from one which we approached rather closely, could be heard crepitating in the water. This was a sound which had been quite familiar to us during winter, when a piece of ice, at a low temperature, was plunged into water, or when water was dashed upon the ice; but it never came under my notice, till now, at this season of the year; and, on inquiry, I found, that persons who had been visiting Davis Straits, during the summer and autumn, for nearly forty years, had never observed it; and it is remarkable, how the low temperature of the winter months should have remained, stored up in the ice, till now.

It is difficult to account for the entire absence of glaciers in the limestone district to the west of Lancaster Sound. The supposed cause of this has been already noticed, and I believe it must be sought in the peculiar character of the surface of the land.

Why the snow which falls on the extensive tracts of land on both sides of Barrow Straits, in latitude 72° to 77°, should escape into the sea whence it came, in running streams, while that which falls on the west coasts of Greenland, Davis Straits, and Baffin's Bay, including Lancaster Sound, should only reach the sea after a lapse of ages, not as streams of running water, carrying down mud and shingle into the immediately adjoining seas, but as streams of hard ice, slow in their motion but sure in their action, carrying, in addition to the mud and shingle of the other, immense boulders, which they do not drop in the adjoining sea, but distribute over an area of many thousand miles, is a problem difficult to solve. The difference between the two may rest in a few degrees of temperature, perhaps not more than the half of one degree, and the cause of this difference may rest in the character of the soil, the one being highly "animalised," and finely divided on the surface, the other presenting not so much as a trace of anything that had ever been endowed with life, and hard and crystalline on the surface. The disposition of things, however, is wisely arranged; for the shallow shores of Barrow Straits would so entangle icebergs, that, even in a few years, the passages which they might cut out for themselves would become blocked up, their exit would be impossible, and a frozen continent would be the result of a few small glaciers on the Parry group of islands. The various channels leading southward and northward of Barrow Straits would be blocked up. North Devon and Cornwallis Island would be joined by ice, extending to the bottom of the water in the Wellington Channel, and rising to the level of, perhaps, far higher than, Cape Spencer; the same ice, stretching across to Whaler Point, might probably extend a little to the east, in which case we should have a magnificent glacier entering Lancaster Sound, occupying the very sites of mountains the names of which I shall not mention, and sending out towering icebergs, which might accomplish distances half way to the equator, along with their neighbours from the opposite side of Baffin's Bay. Before bringing these speculations to a close, I must add, that one of the chief causes of the glacier accumulations is the more plentiful and more constant supply of material by evaporation, in the immediate vicinity of the localities where they occur, than there is where the distribution of land predominates over that of water. This, however, is not a sufficient cause for the entire absence of glaciers, for, according to it, we ought to have the accumulation in due proportion to the evaporation.

At 8 P M. we lost sight of the "Lady Franklin," owing to the dense fog that closed in around us. It was very difficult to steer, for our compasses were perfectly dead in their action, and they varied so much that we could not place the slightest confidence whatever in their separate or conjoint indications. The temperature of both the air and the water was about +35°.

August 15*th.*—The weather continued foggy all night and morning, and there was a gentle northwesterly breeze, by which we moved gradually to the east, as it were feeling our way, and groping in thick fog. It was not by any means uncommon to meet with icebergs, and to pass close by them. At 4 A. M. we caught a glimpse of the "Lady Franklin," but again lost her before we could rejoin her. She seemed to be much farther in shore than we were. At 9 A. M. she was again seen, and presently the signal 1479 was observed, which meant "come on board," and, as she was at a distance of two miles, coming up after us, it was very easy to obey the order. The weather was beginning to clear up, and the land on our right hand was seen very plainly. A boat was lowered, and, in a very short time, Mr. Stewart was seen safe on board the "Lady Franklin."

At noon Navy Board Inlet was passed, and, as the small island (Wollaston Island) was recognised, there were various conjectures whether we should land, with the expectation of finding orders from the

Admiralty, which some of the whalers might have taken from home and left there for us. There was an understanding, between Mr. Penny and the commanders of some of the whaling ships, that they should do their utmost endeavour to reach Cape Hay, where they would leave any Admiralty dispatches and letters that might be sent out for the Arctic Expeditions; but, failing to land them at this place, they were to land them at Button Point, Pond's Bay. We passed on towards Cape Hay, and at 7 P.M. we were abreast of it. Something like a cairn was observed, and a boat was at once dispatched to examine it. After landing and clambering up the rough rocks, the party found that the object of attraction was nothing but a mass of rock in a natural position. The boat soon returned to the "Lady Franklin."

At no great distance from Cape Hay, the coast in some parts rises almost perpendicularly out of the water, and, by this feature, the idea of very deep water close to the rocks is at once correctly suggested. In these precipitous cliffs, loons were exceedingly abundant, for it afforded to them a breeding resort of perfect safety. These birds are not less numerous in Davis Straits than the penguins are in the South Atlantic Ocean. We could see them, at this time, in hundreds of thousands, flying to and from the cliffs, by the constantly glistening appearance which was caused by the bright rays of the sun from the western horizon being reflected from the white plumage of their breasts and bellies, and, in this respect, they resembled crystals, which only become visible by light incident upon their planes.

To the eastward of Cape Hay, we observed a glacier, of not very large size, entering the sea from a valley, through which it could be traced until it was lost among the rugged, sharp-pointed, and bleak-looking almost inaccessible heights on both sides. The main valley appeared to be entered by smaller ones, which also contained ice; some of them entered at right angles, while others seemed to be a sort of division of the main one into smaller branches. The edge of the glacier protruded into the sea considerably beyond the coast-line, and it looked as if an iceberg was to be detached very soon. The water marked its side with lines corresponding with the high and low water-marks, and in this respect there was a striking resemblance with what we had often observed, on the sides of icebergs, on the eastern shore of Davis Straits, which had taken a firm lodgement on the bottom during very high tides. The protruding edge was quite perpendicular, just as it had been left by the last iceberg that had floated away from it, and it rose to a height of forty to fifty feet above the water; this would give the part under water about three hundred and fifty or four hundred feet. In many parts of its surface the glacier was very dirty, and masses of rock could be seen resting upon it, but there appeared to be very little order in their arrangement, except that, about the middle, the larger fragments followed the direction of the valley, and, at the west side, there seemed to be a collection of a dark colour and muddy consistence, which also followed the direction of the valley, but gradually thinned away as it ascended, while the east side was perfectly white, from the very edge, until it was lost sight of in the distance. From the appearance of the mud, I had no other idea than that it had been brought down by

Glaciers, near Cape Hay.

water in a running stream, which must have made its escape into the sea over the edge of the glacier. To the eastward of this glacier there is a second, which appeared to be a little higher, where it entered the water, than the former, and it was also of greater breadth. The surface was quite white, and did not appear to have a single fragment of rock upon it; the night, however, was coming on, and this precluded a sufficiently correct view to enable one to make out the presence or entire absence of foreign bodies. These two glaciers, although extending to the bottom at a depth of sixty to seventy fathoms, appear in very humble contrast beside the towering cubes which escape annually, through the deep valleys, from the immense glacier range of the Greenland continent into Davis Straits, and which in some cases (Claushaven, lat. 69°) rise to a height of nearly three hundred feet, and raise moraines, at the bottom, at a depth of the same number of fathoms.

As night approached, the blue sky began to appear, and clouds settled down upon the horizon, the wind increased hourly from W. and dispelled the remaining traces of the fog; and, as it had to come across a large body of water free from ice, its temperature was rather high, 37° being that of the water in the part of Lancaster Sound we now occupied.

August 16*th*.—Towards morning the wind increased and the sea began to be rough, for there was no ice on it to keep it down. Our course was eastward, close along the south shore of Lancaster Sound, which was narrowly watched, I suppose, with the expectation of seeing a cairn. A great many icebergs were passed, and all of them seemed to have turned over and over in the water since they came out from the glaciers. These revolutions happen to all icebergs in their passage down the straits, and each revolution is attended with great destruction, both to the icebergs themselves, and to the surface ice which may surround them. From this cause many icebergs never reach the entrance of Davis Straits.

After passing Possession Bay and Cape W. Bathurst, the wind followed us down along the bold and wild coast, which the floating icebergs appeared to approach so closely as almost to take masses of rock out of the face of the overhanging cliffs; and in the evening, about four or five o'clock, a boat went, from the "Lady Franklin," to Button Point, which is in the north side of Ponds Bay. Button Point looked as green as any English meadow, and the grass upon it was not one whit less luxuriant. The foxtail grass (*Alopecurus alpinus*) and the chickweed (*Cerastium alpinum*), and hosts of other grasses and herbaceous plants, grow among the bones of animals, and are stimulated, by the oil and animal matter which they contain, and by the filth which is inseparable from Esquimaux habitations, to a degree of luxuriance which no one would be willing to assign to the 73rd parallel of north latitude. The chubby Esquimaux boy, filthy and greasy as he is, takes his childish pastime, rolling on the downy plots which Nature provides for him, or watching, with his bow and arrows, and the cunning eye of a promising sportsman, the ill-fated mouse or lemming that may have lost its hole in the grassy banks which mark the sites of the huts that had been inhabited centuries ago.

Ponds Bay is one of the chief resorts (in Davis Straits) of the common black whale so far as is known at present. Here they are met with in thousands, in the months of June and July, lying quietly at the edge of the ice, which is then attached to the land, and is about fifteen miles in breadth. I have seen the horizon to seaward a perfect forest of jets of vapour (not water) which escaped from the capacious lungs of these huge creatures, and was rendered visible in a tenfold degree by the bright sun on the northern sky beyond. In less than half an hour the sea around us was literally swarming with them, and they could be seen in threes and fours at the edge of the ice, where they appeared to be in perfect safety. With enough men and material, fifty ships might be filled without appearing to thin them. This was in 1845, than which there has not been a better season for the whalers since Davis Straits became a whaling resort. In the following year every attempt to get into Ponds Bay was foiled, and the whale fishery, as far as Davis Straits was concerned, proved a great loss both to the adventurous seamen and to the owners of the ships. Some of the ships followed the usual routine of striking in for the west side of Davis Straits about Cape Searle, where they continued till the middle or end of October, picking up a whale now and again, as they pursued their usual course to the southward close along the land. Others of the ships proceeded still farther southward and entered Hogarth Sound, where whales are very numerous; and, at the same time, they are so wild, that it is almost impossible to approach them, even with the utmost caution. It is believed that this is owing to the want of ice; and there seems to be little room for any doubt on this head, for in the end of spring and in the first week or two of summer, when, according to the information given by the natives, there is land-ice stretching from shore to shore of the Sound, the whales, which are then very abundant, are as easily approached as they are at a later period in Ponds Bay.

It was proposed at one time to remain in Hogarth Sound with the ships during winter, that they might be ready to commence their deadly work among the whales early in the following season; and it was also proposed to establish a whale fishing colony or settlement: but an amount of caution, which does not always mark the career of British merchants, came into operation, and both the contemplated schemes were given up. I look forward to a flourishing settlement in that part; and it will not astonish me, at some future period, to learn that plumbago mines have been opened on the shores of Hogarth Sound, which bid fair to vie with those of Keswick, both with respect to the purity of the ore, and the returns which it brings in the market.

In less than an hour Captain Penny, who was one of the party, came off from Button Point; but they saw not a soul, for the natives had all gone away inland to the salmon fishing, I suppose. The splendid opening leading away to the westward from Ponds Bay through Cockburn Land, affords facilities to the Esquimaux for inland navigation in their frail kyaks and luggage boats, which are of infinite value to them. It is doubtful how far it goes to the westward; but as far as the whalers have gone, and that is at least fifty miles from its entrance, there appeared to be no signs of a termination: the idea obtains that it goes to join Navy Board Inlet, from the information conveyed to us by the Esquimaux, whose knowledge of the geography of their own native land entitles them to our confidence. There were no signs whatever that the whalers had been at Ponds Bay this season: had this been the case, it is very improbable that the Esquimaux should have left it so soon. When the whalers visit any of their resorts, they never think of any of their usual duties, such as fishing or sealing; nothing seems to go down with them then but excitement, and each endeavours to make the most of the intercourse that has been opened up with the white men. Enoolooapike, whom I have already mentioned, told me that a tribe of Esquimaux does not soon get over the visits of the whalers in the autumn. The excitement and the exposure to cold, the privations in the meantime, and those resulting from present neglect of duty, and in some cases the use of spirits, to which these poor creatures are rendered subject by their intercourse with us, are felt by them for a long time. If it were otherwise, it would be out of keeping with the state of the European colonies generally, where the poor savages are disinherited by their own choice, and where they to whom Nature has made her gifts as free as the air they breathe, wander about from place to place in the most destitute manner, the soil denying to them the subsistence which it had bountifully supplied to their progenitors. There is, however, to this tale of misery one bright exception; and it is in Greenland, among the Esquimaux. Here, the Established Church of Denmark has been planted by the Lutheran missionaries, who left the shores of their native land by the authority of the king, and with commissions bearing the seal of the Government. The native population is not decreasing, and they are almost all Christians; the prosperity of the settlements is steadily increasing, nor, so far as I know, have they ever been a burden to the mother-country. The rest of Europe may blush when Denmark, which may be considered but as a drop in a bucket, comes forward to show the true and proper channels through which the dawn and light of civilisation will be made to rise and burst forth upon the wretched and benighted heathen. Civilisation is a difficult task everywhere, and more especially so in some of the British colonies, where human existence is found assuming the most hideous and loathsome form; where man lives by plunder, rapine, and murder, following the beckonings of the foulest passions, and such as bid fair to exterminate his race. The Danes had but one object in settling in Greenland,—the benefit of the natives. This they have accomplished. Their resources are limited, but the laws which they impose upon others are stringent upon themselves; and the Esquimaux freely follow the example set before them by those who have settled among them. It is to be hoped that there is something good in store for the Esquimaux on the west side of Davis Straits, and that we will not lag behind the Danes in teaching these poor creatures the way of life, and the real blessings of a true system of civilisation.

This coast is less accessible than the coast of West Greenland, but still it is accessible, for the whalers reach it every season. From the circumstance that the ice in the Strait seeking southward presses against Cape Searle and the adjoining coast-line, it is generally about the middle of July or the first of August before the passage is clear in to the land, and even then it must be made through streams of ice. After the middle of August there is hardly any difficulty whatever in reaching it, for southerly winds have begun to prevail long before that time, which slacken the ice here, and render the coast nearly as navigable as opposite winds, together with the current, had done early in the season on the other side of the Strait. From the 63rd parallel of latitude up to the 73rd, extending over a space of six hundred miles, several settlements could be planted, which would not only be self-supporting, but would also return ample profits to the enterprising individuals who might establish them. The resources of these settlements would be much the same as that of the Danish settlements on the opposite side, adding, however, another most valuable commodity, which is almost unknown among the Danes, the produce of the black whale, which would include large quantities of valuable whalebone. The enterprising whalers who lose their ships in Melville Bay always make for the Danish settlements, where they are comfortably housed, clothed, and fed, and a passage is afforded for them to Denmark in the Danish ships. In this way not a few British seamen have been able to reach their native shores, who would to a certainty have perished among ice and snow, had it not been for the provision which was made for them at the settlements. And who knows what amount of good might not have accrued from similar settlements on the west side of Davis Straits, not only to the whalers, but also to those who have been so long absent in those cold regions from their mourning friends and relations? Who knows how many hundred thousand pounds, extravagantly wasted in search of a north-west passage, might not have been saved to the British Government? and who knows but the unsuccessful search for the "Erebus" and "Terror," conducted at such enormous expense, might not have been carried out more effectually, and at a fraction of the present expense, had there been but a few enterprising fellows in these settlements, planted on the coast south of Ponds Bay?

As soon as Captain Penny and his party came on board the sails were again filled, for the ships were lying with their yards aback, and our course was shaped for Cape Bowen on the south side of Ponds Bay. There was not a bit of ice attached to the land, and from the crow's-nests we could not discern the loose pack at the offing. There were, however, immense ranges of icebergs, which sometimes appeared to be so close that it was next to an impossibility to pass between them with the ships. There was a good deal of sea, and the waves were lashing against their sides; it was very common to see to leeward of each iceberg a whole string of fragments of ice floating away as they became detached by the action of the waves. Many of them were of a very dirty colour, from accumulations of mud, gravel, and larger fragments of rock which had taken place in them in the glaciers, and not unfrequently, very dark seams (the closed up crevasses) could be seen traversing them throughout their whole extent, causing the most illusory and fantastic appearances. These the whalers sometimes mistake for ships, and then they call them "country ships." Imbedded in the ice throughout the whole extent of huge icebergs, the rocks and mud of the valley traversed by the glacier, are often carried over a vast area; and sometimes they are dropped, probably in the middle of the Atlantic, upwards of two thousand miles from their source.

Although there was still a decided difference between the two ships with respect to rapid sailing, we found that both were in much better trim now, than at any time last season. It is very probable that the knowledge that had been gained of their respective peculiarities, and the draught of water with which they sailed best, had materially contributed to reach the proper mode of arranging and stowing the holds, so as to bring them to their exact water-lines. With a smart breeze in smooth water among sailing ice, I believe they would have done anything, and gone in any direction with unerring precision, so long as their length and breadth of water could be found among the floes.

At 9 P.M. we passed Coutts Inlet and Cape Bowen. There was a strong breeze, and the sea was running so high, that some of the spray was coming on board. The icebergs were still very numerous, but none of them were so large as some of those we had seen on the north side of Ponds Bay.

The weather was very cloudy, and the high land, as it led us down the Straits, was often enveloped in a white and passing haziness, which gave it a very gloomy and wintry appearance. The temperature of the air and of the water was about 36°.

August 17*th.*—Towards morning the wind fell considerably, but still there was enough to enable us to make about four miles an hour. In the forenoon we came in among loose sailing ice, which appeared to close in with the land. Here we expected to meet with some of the whalers looking out for whales; but the weather soon became quite thick, and it was not without a little difficulty that we wended our course among the floes. The temperature of the water fell 4° below what it was yesterday. Our close proximity with the ice was the cause of this change. Although icebergs were very numerous to the northward, the water was much warmer there than it was here, where there was surface ice, but fewer icebergs. There was rain at times, but it was not at all heavy, being of a drizzling character. The "Lady Franklin" was lost sight of for a short time, owing to the thick fog; but when it cleared away, and a sort of mist came in its stead, we again caught sight of her. In the evening we got out of the ice, and stood to the eastward. There was a slight swell discernible, and this we took for an indication that we were not far from the water on the east side of the middle ice. Here we again lost sight of the "Lady Franklin" in the thick fog that closed in around us.

August 18*th.*—At eight o'clock in the morning we again joined the "Lady Franklin" at the edge of a body of ice, which appeared to be rather close for navigation; and any obstacle to our progress which this offered was increased by the fog, which continued to be very close. Several long and flat icebergs were seen, and many of them appeared to be carrying very large masses of rock, which often resembled walruses and seals. Had their perpendicular sides, which generally rose sixty to eighty feet out of the water, not presented insurmountable obstacles to the ascent of these creatures, many of us would have often thought that masses of rock, weighing many tons, were seals of the smallest size.

After being among rather a close pack throughout the greatest part of the day, towards midnight it became so close that we had recourse to both windlass and capstan to assist us through it. The ice was heavy, some of it appearing to be eight to ten feet thick; and there were long tongues extending from the edge of some of the pieces to a distance of several feet under the water all round. Little auks were seen for the first time since we lost sight of them this day twelve months, while we were crossing the top of Baffin's Bay, going in an opposite direction. I shall not venture to give reasons for the entire absence of these birds in Lancaster Sound and Barrow Straits, and also on the west side of Davis Straits. They seem to be confined almost exclusively to the eastern shore of Davis Straits, and to the Greenland seas. It is not at all improbable that they follow the edge of the land-ice as far up as Sir Thomas Smith's Sound; and after they have visited their favourite resorts, they throw themselves into the edge of the southerly setting current, which assists very materially in hastening their progress down Davis Straits into a warmer latitude, where they pass the winter.

August 19th.— After passing the early part of the day among ice which sometimes brought us to a stand, at our breakfast hour a swell was perceived; and, although we could not see the edge of the pack, there was no room for any doubt that there was but a short distance between us and the "east water." The ice was in much smaller fragments, and it was scattered loosely over the whole surface of the sea; at times, however, there was a slight deviation from this, for it assumed the form of ill-defined streams. The temperature of the water was hourly increasing as we entered the open water, and at midnight it was 35°. The latitude had not been determined for several days by meridian altitudes, owing to the thick weather; by reckoning it was found to be about 70° at noon. It was exceedingly pleasant to feel the ships bowing and nodding gracefully to the swell, as the rotges could be heard chirping most cheerfully in the water and on the ice, which we were leaving fast behind. At midnight there was a slight fall of soft snow, which appeared to have a good effect in clearing the atmosphere.

August 20*th.*—In the morning expectations were entertained that we should have observations by which the latitude could be determined; and at noon they were not disappointed. The latitude was found to be 69° 56′. The wind was from S. W., and our course was S. E.; our progress up to this time was remarkably rapid, and in two or three days at the same rate we should cross the Arctic Circle if the course was not altered. It was at one time contemplated to go up with the "Sophia" as far as Uppernavik, for the purpose of landing Mr. Petersen, according to his agreement; but owing, I suppose, to the southing that we had made in crossing the middle ice, this appeared to be overruled; it still remained for him, if he chose, to be landed at any of the southern settlements, so soon as we should come in sight of West Greenland. I believe he had objections to this measure on account of the difficulties and impossibilities he should meet in attempting to join his family this season. Before losing sight of Mr. Petersen, it is due to him to state how extremely useful he had been in the Expedition, both with respect to travelling, and also to valuable suggestions which enabled us to adopt the best form of runner for our sledges. He made models of both kinds of sledges that we had used, and he introduced improvements which would certainly tend to facilitate the progress of Arctic travellers over ice, in the event of future expeditions being sent out to the Polar seas. But Mr. Petersen's usefulness does not stop here; for it must be remembered that at Cape York he brought out the truth in the fabulous reports of the Esquimaux Adam Beck, and clearly showed that the whole story was based upon the fact that H. M. S. "North Star" had wintered in that neighbourhood. This was a matter of the greatest importance at the time; for the report had taken such deep root in the minds of three-fourths of the officers in the searching squadron, that it was feared, by those who did not believe it, that the search would be brought to a close without advancing any further.

August 21*st.*—The weather was very foggy and

misty, and distant objects on the horizon could not be discerned. The "Lady Franklin" was lost sight of, bearing about S. S. E. Mr. Stewart had no written orders from Captain Penny, for it had not been anticipated that we should have parted company so soon. There was but one course left for the "Sophia," and that course was in the direction of home. The prospects of making a passage through the Wellington Channel into Behring's Straits by the aid of steam, afforded a constant theme of conversation; and there was not one person at the cabin dinner-table, nor I believe in the ship, but looked forward to be sent out with the view of following up the discoveries, of which those already made by our Expedition were merely the threshold. Of this our young commander felt too sanguine; and I am not certain that the oldest person in the ship, and indeed in the Expedition, did not allow his stray lucubrations to run in the same direction. These prospects, however, were kept in check by the caution which we knew Great Britain would observe for the future, in sending expeditions at enormous expense into the Polar seas. The winds were light in the early part of the day, and very little progress was made in consequence. The sea was quite free from ice, and there were very few icebergs. Sea-weed was very abundant, and some of the entire plants that were passed were upwards of twenty feet in length, while the thickness of their stems did not often exceed half an inch in diameter. The temperature of the water was about 39°, and that of the air varied from 44° to 35°.

The dogs were beginning to feel the effects of the rapidly increasing heat, and they often lay panting on the deck in the sunshine in a state of utter helplessness. In the evenings, after the sun went down, and they began to feel cool and comfortable, they generally commenced fighting, and nothing was more common than to see them rolling in heaps about the decks. The scene was anything but agreeable. We began to fear that disease might be the result of the sudden transition from cold to heat; therefore a resolution was come to by Captain Stewart, that a few of them should be destroyed. This was a great trial to the seamen, who were all exceedingly attached to them; and to the man who had charge of them, and who had watched over them during the long winter, it was a source of great grief and not a few tears. Although four were kept alive, and could still be heard running about the decks, and often seen fighting, there was not a person on board but felt ashamed of the deed of extermination that had just been perpetrated. I must confess that we might justly recoil at the idea that we had destroyed in a wholesale manner the poor brutes that had served us so faithfully, and had been our companions for such a length of time, the moment that they began to be troublesome, and their services were no longer required.

Towards evening a smart breeze came away from about W. N. W., which carried us southward at the rate of five or six knots. A few icebergs were passed, all much reduced in size, and appearing to be only the merest fragments of the huge masses that one can see in immense numbers farther up the country.

August 22nd.—To-day, as the ship was going at the rate of six or seven knots, she struck upon an immense rorqual whale, which happened to be crossing her bow. A tremulous motion was imparted to her by the shock, and although the cause of it was more yielding than an India rubber buffer, it was distinctly felt from stem to stern. Several of these animals were seen throughout the day. They did not appear to be on any particular route, although they were moving very rapidly. It is very probable that they were feeding, for the locality we were now entering upon is exceedingly fertile. The land was seen at noon, and then our course was shaped to the southward, it being a little easterly for the last two or three days.

August 23rd.—The wind always continued to favour us very much, and the weather was generally clear; at times, however, a sort of misty haze pervaded the atmosphere, but it never was so thick but distant objects on the horizon might be discerned. The sea was comparatively smooth, and if one can draw a safe inference from great numbers of sea-fowl, which doubtless were feeding, it must have been very abundant in minute animal forms. As we were crossing the Arctic Circle, the yards were backed, and one or two lines, baited with pork, were put down. A fine plump cod was hooked and hauled in. Its stomach contained shrimps in great abundance. A halibut was hooked and hauled to the surface, where a little scuffling ensued, the line gave way, and we lost our prize, with the hook in its mouth. It is hardly proper to say that we lost it, for Isaak Walton says "that we could not lose that which we never had." The depth was forty fathoms, and the longitude was 53°.

A piece of drift-wood was picked up. It was all grown over with a brown slime, and some parts of it were encrusted with barnacles. The slime presented an appearance which I had not observed in any part of Davis Straits to the north of the

Arctic Circle. It consisted of filamentous algæ, to the sides of which, at right angles, there were attached, by the finest and most delicate points, a whole array of minute forms of a siliceous character.* It contained the young of the barnacle, which might be seen by the assistance of a microscope, moving with the greatest freedom. It also contained great numbers of entomostracous Crustaceans, differing from any that had come under my observation since we had entered the Polar seas. These have the pouch of ova suspended by a very slender peduncle, from a point among the feet, about the middle of the body. Their antennæ are exceedingly short, and they move with equal freedom in the water itself, and among foreign substances in it. Their motions are regular and continuous, being caused by the action of several pairs of swimmerets. In this respect there is a striking contrast between them and the *Cetochilus*, for the latter moves chiefly by means of the long oar-like arms which work by successions of jerks. There is also a great difference between them from the fact, that the *Cetochilus* requires great freedom in the water, avoiding foreign substances with great care,

* By subsequent comparison, I found a slight resemblance between this Alga and Podosphenia Licomophora and Rhiphidophora, described and figured by Kutzing in his work on the Diatomaceæ.

while this creature is indifferent about all sorts of things that may be introduced into the vessel along with it. The wood itself was a piece of a very crooked birch tree. It is very doubtful whence it could have come. It came not from the Greenland coast to a certainty, because no wood grows there; and it came not from the American side, for in that case its course would have been against the current, that sets down along the American shores. I see no course so clear for it as the one from Spitzbergen, along the shores of the coast of East Greenland. The temperature of the water was 42°.

August 24th.—The wind continued fair, and the sea was very smooth. The rate at which we came down the straits was much more rapid than could have been at all expected. There were very few icebergs, and no surface ice, except "washen" pieces of icebergs, and they were dissolving very rapidly, from the combined effects of the direct rays of the sun and of the water. Sounding was tried, but no bottom was obtained at one hundred fathoms. At night, the sea was exceedingly luminous around the ship and in her wake. A little of the water taken up in a vessel and agitated, scintillated very much. Each successive shake produced, as it were, a shower of sparks followed by a state of repose. This was owing to the presence of Entomostraca of very small size. They could hardly be detected with the naked eye; but by the assistance of a lens their darting motions might be seen very distinctly. They resemble those found in Davis Straits, about lat. 70° to 75°, except that the latter are six or eight times larger. Fear may have some connection with the phosphorescence of these creatures, when the water is agitated. I always observed, that the moment the vessel with the water reached the deck, they all sunk to the bottom of it; and although the number often varied, it was common to find that twenty or thirty individuals had been drawn up in four pints of water. The water taken up during the day very rarely produced any. It is extremely difficult to account for this; and one is led by it to the idea, that these creatures retire from the surface during the day. The water, also, contained almost perfectly transparent Acalephs, of very small size. They might have been one of the causes of the luminosity around the ship; and it is highly probable, that from no other creatures could the phosphorescent balls have issued, which might be seen first in the agitated water at the ship's bow, and were lost sight of only in the eddying wake at her quarter and stern. To them, however, the scintillations in the vessel in the dark could not be owing, for they corresponded in a remarkable manner with the darting motions of the Entomostraca.

August 25th. — At noon the latitude was found to be 61° 58′. The wind, which had followed us so favourably down the strait, began to baffle us, and it ultimately blew freshly from S.W. We could afford this; for our distance from the Greenland coast was sufficiently great to enable us to stand to the eastward for a considerable time, before our approach to the land could force us to put upon the other tack. The temperature of the water was increasing almost hourly as we came down the strait, and now it was up so high as 47°, while that of the air was only 48°. In the evening there was much rain, and the sky was densely overcast. There were all the indications of a south-westerly storm; but towards midnight they all disappeared, the blue sky opened out, and a most brilliant Aurora Borealis danced from the horizon to the zenith. It was really pleasant to behold the broad gleaming bands folding like curtains of the richest and finest woven silken fabric. The colour varied every moment from red to white, and from yellow to a slight tinge of green, verging into purple, which became lost in the red. From the sudden appearance of this beautiful phenomenon, we hardly expected fine weather or a favourable wind, more especially as the barometer was too high for westerly winds.

August 26*th.* — If a calm day at sea can be pleasant, this one was extremely so; for there were few clouds, and the most remote objects on the horizon were plainly visible. A few fulmar petrels were attending closely upon us, and some of the seamen were making attempts to take them with baited hooks. One or two were caught in this way, and they were at once submitted to the hungry dogs, where such game always meets with a hearty response.

In the evening the wind veered round to N., and freshened up from almost a perfect calm to a smart breeze. The spars of the "Sophia" again began to feel it, as she scudded before it at the rate of five or six miles an hour. At midnight the whole sky was one living fire of Aurora Borealis. It far exceeded anything that we had seen in much higher latitudes during winter. The surface of the sea was sometimes illuminated so much, that had there been objects on the horizon at a distance of several miles, they would have been plainly visible.

August 27*th.*—The land, which we had not seen for a few days, came in sight this morning. It must have been the coast on both sides of Cape Desolation, extending as far southward probably as Cape Farewell.

There was a little refraction, and this tended to break it up, and to increase its already very wild and rugged appearance. We might now indeed feel that we were entering upon the Atlantic. Every preparation was made for the passage. The two boats were taken in on the deck, and firmly secured. The rigging was attended to, and made tighter as the hot weather slackened it. And no precautions were omitted by which the utmost safety to the ship and the crew might be promoted. The latitude at noon was 60° 48′. The temperature of the air was 45½°, and of the water 48°. The barometer was rising steadily during the north wind. The latter veered from north to south-east, and began to increase. The sky became overcast in the evening, and the clouds lowered portentously; the sea yielded a hearty response to the pressing invitation of the hourly increasing gale, and the fulmars were already upon the wing, as the disturbed water in the ship's wake attracted their attention.

At midnight there was a perfect gale from south-east. The ship had been snugged by little and little until at length she was "hove to," under the close reefed main-topsail. About eight o'clock, orders were given to stow the flying-jib, the foremast sail in the ship: two of the men went out to perform this duty. As one of them was feeling his way out, for it was as dark as pitch, he planted his feet on the lee foot-rope, and was almost precipitated into the yawning abyss. He caught hold of a rope in his fall, and struggled for a long time. It was very long indeed—not to him but to those who were watching his writhing form by the light of the boiling and phosphorescent waves beneath. I was on the weather bow at the time, and saw how his comrades behaved. No one spoke a word, for that might only diminish his chances of escape; there was no help for him if he failed to save himself. The man that was on the jib-boom with him, moved neither hand nor foot, and uttered not a word. At length he regained his footing, and proceeded to his duty. Had he been a minute longer swinging among the foot-ropes, he would have been swept off never to be seen, for the bowsprit was actually buried in the sea, while the two men were clinging with clasped arms to the yielding spar, on the strength of which their lives were hung. When they came in, having discharged the duty entrusted to them, I endeavoured to be near the one that had made such a narrow escape. As he stepped down upon the deck, he touched me by the merest accident. A trembling sensation passed through his whole frame, and a marked inspiratory effort carried gratitude to heaven from his breast. On the very threshold of home, we might have lost this poor fellow, after the Arctic winter and the intense frost, after the fatigue of travelling, and the excruciating thirst, had all failed to break our numbers.

August 28th. — The storm raged violently, and much of the spray came on board. Our little ship behaved remarkably well; but she sprung her jib-boom, and often threatened to carry away her main-top-gallant-mast. This was owing to the weight of the crow's-nest and the slackness of the rigging. The spars were really good, otherwise they would have given way long before now. Our leeway was about 2½ miles an hour. There was no ice in sight. The temperature of the air and of the water was about 47°. Well might we designate Cape Farewell the Cape of Storms. It is seldom passed, either in spring or autumn, without experiencing bad weather. Stormy petrels — very handsome, little, dark-brown birds — were very abundant. They were first seen in the morning, and then continued during the whole day. The sailors at once recognised them as "Mother Carey's chickens." They are fully as expert upon the wing as the fulmars, and can go in the face of the strongest wind without appearing to use their wings except in the most gentle manner.

August 29th. — At the commencement of this gale the barometer fell, in three hours, nearly half an inch. When it began to moderate, the barometer was disposed to rise, having fallen altogether about four-fifths of an inch. At six o'clock in the morning we made sail, and endeavoured to steer as carefully as possible over the high waves and the deep hollow troughs of the sea. The wind veered a few points to the westward. This favoured us very much, for we were able to keep away about north-east. It is not easy to estimate the exact course of a ship when there is much heaving motion.

August 30th. — Very little advance was made for the last two or three days. The wind was often foul and fair, and foul again. A foul wind is often better than the calm that succeeds a storm. This we experienced, for the ship was tossing about very much owing to the heavy swell. There was considerable difficulty in getting down the royal masts and the crow's nest. The jib-boom was found to be sprung; hence it had to be eased in, and the flying-jib was used instead of the jib. At noon the sun looked out, and a meridian altitude was obtained. The latitude was found to be 59° 17′. The weather began to look much better in the evening, and towards night the blue sky became visible, and some of the stars might be seen occasionally through the opening clouds. About midnight a light breeze sprung up from the north-west. This was a fair wind, and we were very glad of it, for it assisted to put down the easterly swell.

August 31*st.*—The winds were very light, but so long as they were fair we learned to be content with them, and endeavoured to make the best of them. Studding-sails were set on both sides, and the "Sophia" was again gliding homewards. The swell from the eastward was fairly subdued, and a slight rising motion from the opposite quarter was perceived coming up after us. In the evening the wind increased, and squalls became very frequent. There were also passing showers, which made those who sought recreation in the open air betake themselves to their berths. The dogs were often seen licking the water from the painted hatches and bulwarks. They often did this after refusing the water that had been supplied to them out of the water we used ourselves. It is very probable that the casks imparted a taste or smell to it, which did not suit the Esquimaux dog. The box of living plants that I had collected were watered twice every day, and some of them were looking very gay, as if they inclined to put forth their flowers a second time. The dogs seemed to smell that portion of their native soil that I had under my care, and they made frequent attempts to get at the box, but it was put beyond their reach.

September 1*st.*—We made great progress since

yesterday. Nearly five degrees of longitude had been run down, and also the greater part of a degree of latitude. The longitude was 43° 5′, and the latitude was 58° 11′. The weather was always squally and showery. The temperature of the air was 46°, and that of the water 48°. The sky was for the most part clear and starry, although occasionally the showers were spread over it to a great extent.

September 2nd.—At the beginning of the middle watch there was a squall which continued nearly three hours. Ten knots were entered on the log-slate. Our progress eastward was incredibly rapid. Upwards of two hundred miles of longitude in twenty-four hours make a good and quick run across the Atlantic. At noon, the latitude was 58° 11′, and the longitude was 36° 25′. In the evening, the temperature of the water was found to be 52°. Our rapid progress accounts for the suddenness of the change. Two species of Entomostraca were very abundant, and the water always sparkled when agitated in the dark. There were also Acalephæ, but they were not nearly so abundant as the others.

September 4th.—At noon, the longitude was 25°. From this it will be very plain, how exceedingly favourable the wind must have proved. Some of the squalls were so violent, that eleven knots were entered on the log-slate. We frequently had showers of drizzling rain, but they never continued longer than the squalls they accompanied. The temperature of the air and of the water was 55°. Such a difference of temperature in the water ought to afford an unequivocal proof of the existence of a current of heated water from the equator towards the pole. It is very singular how this current, in all cases, follows the same direction. We find it on the east side of the Atlantic, before it enters the Arctic Circle. We find it on the east side of Davis Straits, and it is very probable we shall find it on the north side of Lancaster Sound, and on the east side of Wellington Channel.

September 5th. — During the westerly winds and the showers we had, for a few days back, the barometer rose remarkably high. To-day we had it up to 30° 44′, and then the wind shifted from west to east. There was a steady breeze from this quarter. This is a feature peculiar to east winds, for we never find squalls and showers coming from that quarter. The sky is generally very clear or densely overcast, and if there is rain, it is in continuous showers, with hardly any intermissions. Our studding sails were all taken in, and the ship was hauled close to the wind. The sea was smooth, the weather was very clear, and although the wind was foul, everything else contributed to render our situation exceedingly pleasant.

The latitude at noon was 58° 3′, and the longitude was 22°. In the evening the sky became overcast for a short time, after which it cleared up, and beautiful feathery clouds were spread over it. They diverged in pencils from a point on the south-eastern horizon, and followed a direction parallel with that of the wind. They resembled Aurora Borealis, and one could almost fancy that they were in motion. This form of cloud melts away, and again appears of the same or of a different form, so rapidly, that a beholder is at once struck with the analogy there is between it and the Aurora Borealis.

September 6th. — The wind still continued in our teeth, and there was a smart breeze. It was fortunate we had made southing with the westerly winds, for had we not, we should not have been able to keep the ship "clean full" without being carried into a parallel of latitude too far to the northward for the south-westerly gales which prevail about the equinox in the autumn. Our latitude was 59° 4′, and our longitude was 16° 40′. Large flocks of birds were seen. They were the harbingers of our approach to our native shores, and as such, they were readily recognised by all on board. At night the Aurora Borealis was very vivid, and its rapid movements might be discerned very plainly through the opening clouds that were spread over all the sky. The barometer had fallen a little in the morning, but it was again rising, and before midnight it was up to 30·475. The temperature of the air and of the water varied exceedingly little, being generally about 54°.

September 7th.—At noon the latitude and longitude were found to be 60° 2′ and 13° 40′. The wind seemed to have taken a firm hold of the south-east, for it was still blowing keenly from that quarter. The weather was pleasant, although at times the sky was a little overcast, and the atmosphere was lurid. The sea was remarkably smooth; in this respect it resembled that part of the Atlantic which is embraced within the north-east trade winds, where I believe large waves rarely occur. The temperature of the water was 53°, and that of the air was from 53° to 57°. With the results of careful and extensive thermometrical surveys of the ocean, it is very probable that ships might make passages between very distant ports, with no other instruments than the thermometer and the compass. It is to be hoped that the day is not far distant when the mariner will have the valuable assistance of the temperature of the water on which he is borne, both to ascertain his position, and to discover danger.

In addition to the gannets and gulls, and other birds that were seen so plentifully yesterday, we saw to-day the little puffin (*Mormon Fratercula*), and it afforded another proof of our rapid progress homeward. The presence of all these creatures, which we could not help associating with the seas that wash the shores of the British Islands, made each of us feel as if he was already at home.

September 9th.—The wind veered to the southward a few points, and increased in violence. The sky looked more gloomy, and clouds began to rise upon it and to drift rapidly to the north-westward. The sea became "cross," and occasionally a little of the spray came on board. We gave up all ideas of going through the Pentland Firth, owing to the northing we had made with the easterly winds. The course that was left for us lay through the Roost—the channel which separates the Orkney from the Shetland Islands. About 10 A.M. we saw a ship standing to the eastward, but at the same time she made sufficient northing to go round the Shetland Islands. Since we parted with the whalers in Melville Bay this was the first ship we saw, except those engaged like ourselves in the search for Sir John Franklin. At noon another ship, a brig, was observed on the same tack with ourselves. She was close-hauled, and appeared to be making for the Roost. The latitude was 59° 35′. Our course was a little southerly, for fear we should meet the wind from the eastward as we approached the land. At midnight we found the latitude to be 59° 24′. There was faint moonlight, which enabled us to carry on, although our distance from the land could not be above a few miles. The water became much smoother than it was in the forenoon, and its temperature was 53°, that of the air being 54°.

September 10*th.*—At 2 A.M. we saw the land. It was Noup Head, which is in latitude 59° 20′, and longitude 3° 4′. Comparing its position with our estimated longitude at noon of the previous day, we found that an error of a few miles had crept into our calculations made in crossing the Atlantic. It was very trifling, however, not exceeding half-a-dozen miles; and it is likely that it was made since the commencement of the easterly wind. After passing through the Roost, we endeavoured to work up to the southward close along the land, taking the utmost advantage of the state of the tide. The wind failed us in the evening; consequently very little progress was made. Had we been in Davis Straits, we should have got the boats out to tow.

September 13*th.* — After two or three days of baffling calms we arrived off Peterhead, where a boat came alongside. Some of her crew were recognised by their townsmen in the "Sophia"; and, as one can readily conceive, there were happy greetings on both sides. We learned from them that the "Lady

Franklin" had arrived, and that Captain Penny was on his way to London. No intelligence, throwing light upon the route of the missing ships had reached home since we left Aberdeen eighteen months previously, except that the "Prince Albert" had brought reports from Cape Riley, to the effect that they had touched there. We had to add to this, the discovery of their first winter quarters, which was almost all that the Expedition had accomplished. The reports of the results of the travelling parties were of a purely negative character. We received newspapers, which certainly revealed coincidences to us that no person could have imagined; a short report from Captain Penny, of the proceedings of the Expedition under his command, and the very first intelligence of the American Expedition, appeared side by side in the columns of the same paper. It appeared that the American ships got beset in Barrow Straits on the very evening that they passed Assistance Bay, in which state they continued throughout the winter, drifting to the eastward and to the southward, until they were set at liberty by the swell of the Atlantic, in latitude 65° or 66°, in the beginning of June. In the drifting pack, exposed to imminent dangers, and continually aroused by the groaning sounds of the rending floes, for a period of nine months, they certainly occupied one of the most unenviable positions that ever falls to the lot of the Arctic navigator. They drifted clear of the land in Baffin's Bay off the south side of the entrance of Lancaster Sound, and did not see any part of the west coast of Davis Straits until they were off Cape Searle, on the 19th of May. Scurvy appeared among them early, and kept them in a weak state throughout the winter; fortunately, however, they all came through, and were recovering slowly when the report was closed. After getting clear they proceeded to the Greenland side of Davis Straits, where they fell in with the whalers, by whom they were supplied gratuitously with such fresh provisions as in their weak state they greatly required. The Danes also granted such supplies as the settlements afforded.

Owing to calm weather our intercourse with Peterhead was more protracted than could have been wished; however, towards evening, a breeze sprung up, by which we were able to resume our course southward. There was a thick fog at night, which rendered it necessary to keep a good look-out.

September 19th.—For five days we scarcely had any winds, and the weather was generally thick. An occasional glimpse was caught of the coast, and a church spire, always the first object that meets the eye in a Christian country, often came into view, when nothing else could be discerned in the murky haze that hung over the land. It was truly tantalising to see steamers passing and repassing while we stood still in the calm. This, however, had lost the poignancy of envy from the long experience we had of it during the voyage.

Since we entered the German Ocean or the North Sea on the 10th, the temperature of the water varied very little indeed. It was generally about 54°, but as we advanced southward it increased, and for the last two days, since we came upon the English coast, it rarely fell below 55°, and was often up at 56°. The water was often luminous in the dark. Frequent examination, both with the naked eye and with a magnifying power, revealed the true cause and source of this beautiful phenomenon. That most extensively distributed genus of entomostracous Crustaceans, the *Cetochilus,* was exceedingly abundant; and the active little creatures belonging to it gave out showers of scintillations by successive and oft-repeated agitation in a vessel. They were exceedingly small compared with creatures belonging to the same genus found in Davis Straits. It was observed one night, off Whitby, that frequent agitation failed in a most signal manner to produce a luminous appearance in a quantity of water in a vessel. This was at once at variance with what had been observed in Davis Straits, in the Atlantic, and, up to this time, in the North Sea; hence I thought it would prove not altogether devoid of interest to ascertain its cause. In the bottom of the vessel, after agitation of the water, followed by a short period of repose, I found a great number of minute Crustaceans rolled up like chitons or hedgehogs. The more I persisted in stretching them out for examination, the more persistently did they draw "head" and "tail" together. A few were placed in a little water upon a watch-glass, under a low magnifying power, in a position to be examined without being disturbed. After ten minutes' repose they began to open out and to move about. The number of legs, the antennæ, and the segments of the body, enabled me to refer the creature at once to the order *Isopoda;* and the peculiar feature of rolling itself into a ball may include it in the genus *Tylos* of Latreille. Its length varied from half a line to a line, and its breadth was a little more than half its length. It was amusing to see the creature draw itself up into a perfectly spherical ball the moment that the fluid was disturbed. In the same locality, during the day, the *Oniscus Oceanicus* was found on sea-weed that floated on the surface of the water. This creature is about an inch in length, and it has three greyish yellow stripes down its back,—one in the middle and one at each side at the extremities of the segments.

September 20*th.*—A light breeze sprang up from the northward, which carried us on very favourably. Studding-sails were set on both sides, and many an ugly "collier" did we meet and overhaul. About noon we were off Flamborough Head, and if the wind would continue to favour us, we fully expected to be in the Thames on the following day. The temperature of the water was 57°, and that of the air was 55°.

At 6 P.M. one of the seamen met with a serious accident, which demanded immediate surgical interference. A sharp-pointed pocket knife entered his leg, and divided the main artery. The bleeding was most profuse, and in a few minutes he was in a state of syncope. The bleeding stopped for a little, but commenced the moment he recovered from the faint. It was permanently arrested, after a little trouble to me and not a little suffering to my patient, by putting ligatures on the extremities of the bleeding vessels.

The common seamen are most attentive to each other in cases of sickness, and their willingness to be of service to an unfortunate sufferer is an ample compensation for any roughness of manners and awkwardness of manipulation where delicacy may be necessary.

September 21*st.* — After passing several lights on the English coast, we came along with a strong breeze at a rapid rate. The weather was thick, and the coast rarely to be seen. This would have increased our difficulties a little had it not been for the experience of most of the crew, and of the officers of the "Watches" on this part of the coast. The painted buoys, the beacons, the light-ships, and all the other leading marks, appeared to be as familiar to them as if they had been serving on the English coast since they first went to sea.

At 3 P.M. a pilot or waterman came alongside from one of the light-ships, the main yards were braced by, and in a few minutes he was on board. It was agreed that he should pilot us up to Woolwich. After passing through whole forests of ships riding at anchor owing to the foul wind, at nine o'clock in the evening we were off Gravesend, where the wind met us, and the tide failed. We knew that on the following day we should reach our destination, and be paid off then or as soon as possible thereafter; in the meantime, however, the rows of lamps, the rolling sounds of carriage wheels, and the well-known sound of the chain upon the windlass as the anchor went down, all spoke loudly in our ears that our voyage in search of the "Erebus" and "Terror," and their gallant crews, was at an end.

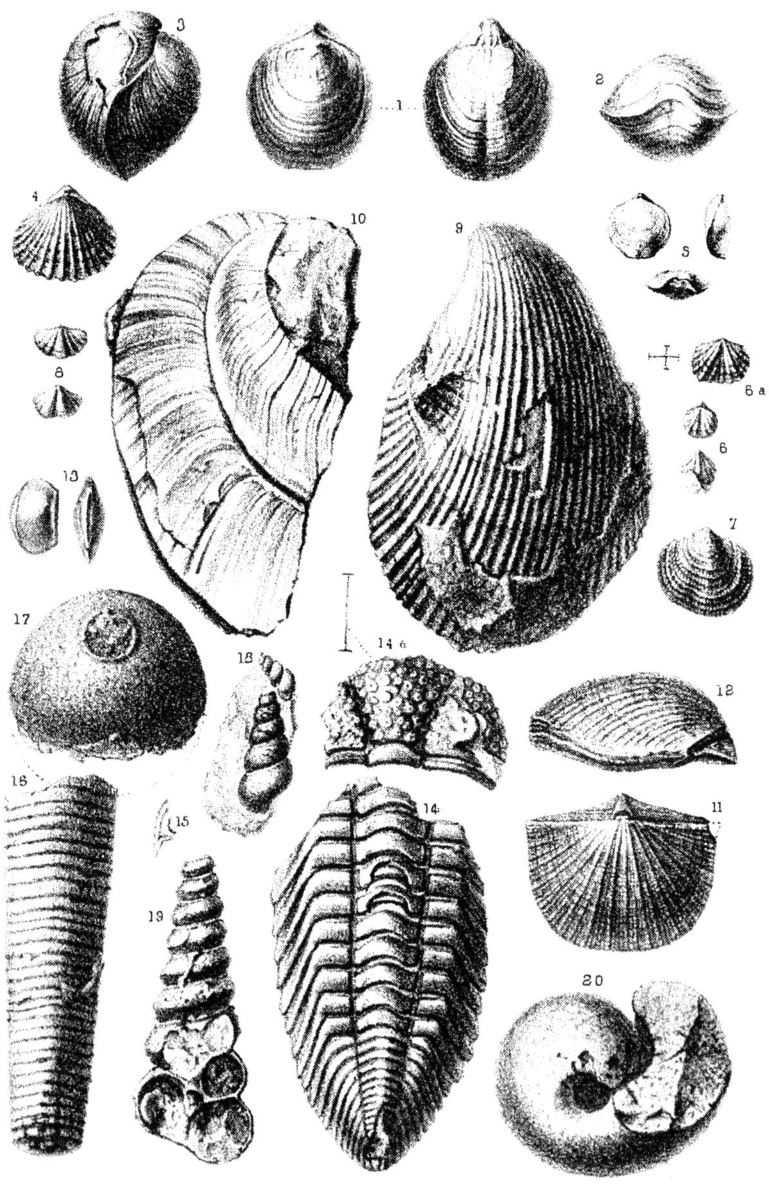

J. W. SALTER, FECIT.

M. & N. HANHART, IMP.

LONDON; LONGMAN & Co. 1852.

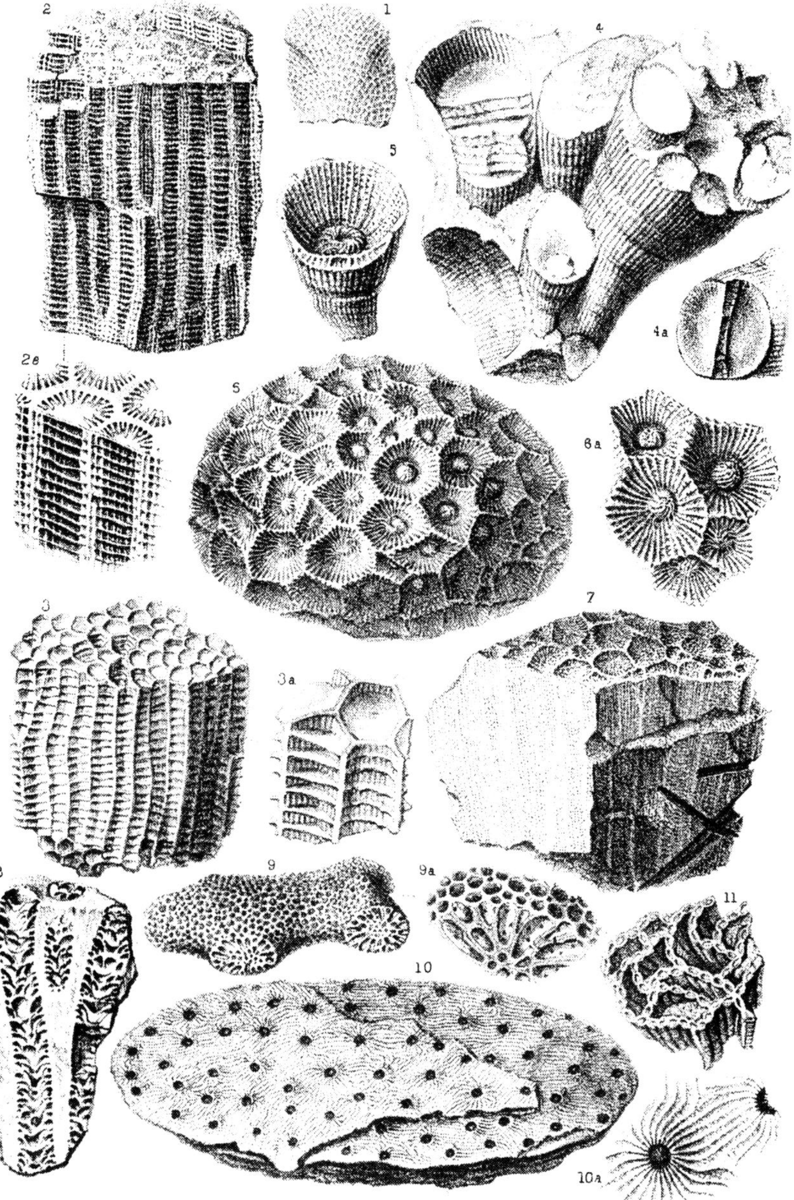

J. W. SALTER, FECIT.

M. & N. HANHART IMP.

LONDON; LONGMAN, & Co. 1852.

APPENDIX.

AN APPENDIX,

CONTAINING THE

DETAILED REPORTS OF THE TRAVELLING PARTIES,

SENT OUT

IN SEARCH OF HER MAJESTY'S MISSING SHIPS

"EREBUS" AND "TERROR,"

TO THE UNEXPLORED REGIONS IN AND BEYOND THE WELLINGTON CHANNEL,

FROM HER MAJESTY'S SHIPS "LADY FRANKLIN" AND "SOPHIA,"

IN THE SPRING AND SUMMER OF 1851;

ADMIRALTY PAPERS;

METEOROLOGICAL ABSTRACTS;

A REGISTER OF THE TIDES;

AND

ILLUSTRATED SKETCHES OF THE NATURAL HISTORY AND GEOLOGY OF SOME OF THE REGIONS VISITED DURING THE VOYAGE.

APPENDIX.

Report of the Proceedings of a Travelling Party from Her Majesty's Ship "Sophia," in search of Sir John Franklin, in the Spring and Summer of 1851.

April 17*th.*—Everything having been prepared for starting on our travels for a week back, we now took advantage of the first fine day, and at 8 A.M. both ships' crews were mustered on board the "Lady Franklin," when a prayer was read by the commander. Very soon thereafter we started out of the bay with three sledges, intended for the east side of Wellington Strait, and three for the west side of the same strait. The east side division, commanded by myself, was to strike off from the east side of Cornwallis Island, about the 75th degree of latitude, for the land on the opposite side of the channel, immediately to the northward of Cape Bowden, to which the Americans had travelled in the fall of 1850. The western parties, consisting of three hauling-sledges and two dog-sledges, under the superintendence of Captain Penny, were to examine the eastern and northern shores of Cornwallis Island, and any other land or islands that might be met with in that hitherto unexplored region.

On reaching the S.E. point of the bay, we had considerable trouble in getting the sledges over a tremendous ridge of hummocks. The snow, which had been falling heavily for three or four days before, was quite soft, and between the hummocks it was very deep, making the sledges heavy to be dragged along. After getting a quarter of a mile from the land we got to a floe as smooth as a bowling green, where we went along very well, although the snow was sometimes more than ankle deep, and still very soft. The temperature when we left the bay was +28°, and it was now about +32°. This was a decided change from what we had been accustomed to for a long time, and it felt uncomfortably hot. At half past 3 P.M. we encamped for the first time; and certainly the scene was a novel one to us,—six tents and six sledges, with the parties all striving who should have their tents first pitched, their stockings changed (for this was a stringent order), and who should be first into their sleeping bags, while the cooks for the day were busily engaged preparing the supper. I could not help admiring the spirit the men had, for they were deeply interested in the search they were about to make. 8 P.M. fine clear weather, with the wind from the S.W., and the temperature + 35°. People all in their bags asleep and comfortable.

Assistance Bay, W. ¾ N. 7 miles.

April 18*th.*—At 3 A.M. the cooks were called out to prepare our breakfast, and this occupied them not less than two hours. Our cooking apparatus, having been made on board ship, was found to be not so convenient or expeditious as was expected; but upon the whole the time they occupied was the greatest objection, although we also found that one pound of fat (our daily allowance) was not sufficient. After breakfasting, and getting the sledges packed up again, we proceeded along the land towards Cape Hotham, on a tolerably smooth floe. At noon we were overtaken by Captain Penny and Mr. Petersen, with the two dog-sledges; they left the ships in the bay at 8 o'clock in the morning, overtook us eleven miles out, and proceeded to the depôt of provisions left by Her Majesty's ship "Assistance" last autumn, where we reached them at 4 P.M. and encamped under some very heavy hummocks adjoining the land. The weather during the day had been very mild and close, with light winds from the southward, and at 8 P.M. we had it snowing very heavily. After the tents were pitched, and the people were comfortably in bed, I went on shore to look for a road for the next day, as the floe between us and Cape Hotham was very hummocky, and almost impassable for heavily laden sledges; for each, with forty days' provisions, including everything else, had weights amounting to 1500 pounds. The flag-post put up by the "Assistance" was still standing, and from it I saw the impossibility of getting along outside, the only way being to get the sledges over the heavy hummocks pressed home on the land, and proceed round the cape on the land ridge. At 8 P.M. I returned again to the tents. Thick snow, with a southerly wind, and a high temperature.

April 19*th.*—In the morning, after getting breakfast and packing up the sledges, we commenced taking them over the hummocks to the land one by one with all hands; and although with such a powerful force we got them over with very little trouble, we found that sledges, be they never so strong, will only endure for any length of time the fatigue that six men can give them. After we had got them all to the land, we proceeded along it round the cape, and got on very well, until we rounded the latter, and were fairly in the channel, where the snow became knee deep, and consequently the road was very heavy. After having had a good stiff pull we reached Captain Penny, who had gone on before us in the morning, and had pitched his tent immediately to the southward of Barlow Inlet, where we joined him, and encamped for the night. The weather was still snowy, with northerly winds, and a comparatively high temperature. The dogs were making a dreadful noise, and, from having committed depredation the previous night among the sledges, they were obliged to be watched.

Cape Hotham.

Barlow Inlet.

April 20th, Sunday.—2 A.M. we were up and at it again. Got our breakfast cooked with some trouble, but eaten without any. Packed up the sledges and commenced our march to the northward along the land towards Barlow Inlet, which we reached in an hour, and struck off from it, on to what appeared to be a good and smooth floe, and one on which we were likely to get along very well. After getting out through the hummocks lying at the mouth of the inlet, we got along very well for an hour or two, but then we were brought to a stand by very hummocky ice extending eastward from the land as far as we could see. The weather was very thick and disagreeable, and many of us were suffering from snow blindness. The sledges were stopped, while I went on shore with Captain Penny (who had gone on before us with the dogs) to see if we could get along on the land; and after getting up on the hills a little, we saw no other way of advancing except close along the land, and accordingly we at once commenced taking the sledges over the hummocks, two at a time, having to make the road with pickaxes in some places. After four hours' hard work we got the tents pitched on the inside of the ridge of hummocks, and encamped for the night close to the land. The weather, which had been thick and snowy all day, with variable winds, now began to clear up. The wind came from the northward, down channel, and the temperature from about $+20°$ began to fall rapidly. The pressure among the ice along the land must have been enormous; huge masses were turned altogether out of the water on to the beach, and our road lay between them and the steep land rising immediately from the beach, thus limiting our view from the sledges to a very narrow sphere.

On the 21st, at starting time, the weather was too severe to admit of advance; the wind was blowing a strong gale from the northward right ahead of us; we were glad enough to remain in our sleeping bags, and several of the people were suffering very severely from snow blindness. After having been confined to our tents for nearly thirty hours, the weather appearing disposed to moderate a little, we packed up and went on for five hours, but found that it was too severe for us to walk and pull in the face of a strong wind, with the thermometer from $-25°$ to $-30°$. It was very slow work, and after coming about four miles we encamped on a low point of the land, having got a gravel bed for the first time since leaving, although we came along the beach almost all the way. Here our arrangements were altered a little. Two of the sledges deposited their provisions and returned. One of them was commanded by Mr. John Stuart, from the "Lady Franklin," and the other by Mr. Reid, from the "Sophia." Mr. Stuart was to come out again in a fortnight, to cross over the channel to Cape Spencer, and to examine the coast as far as Cape Hurd. Mr. Reid was to join Dr. Sutherland's sledge, who was to accompany me to the eastern side of the channel, and assist in the search to the N.E. Dr. Goodsir and

Mr. Marshall were to proceed along Cornwallis Island, to the N.W.; and Captain Penny, with Mr. Petersen, was to go on before, and strike off to any land that might be discovered to the northward. These were the travelling arrangements that were made on the spot, in spite of the very slow pace at which we had been able to advance, and some little doubts were thrown upon them as to the results; for the northerly wind was still blowing strong, without any signs of abatement.

April 22nd.—In the morning one or two of the people were so ill with their eyes that they were obliged to be drafted into the return sledges, and, after having got everything put right, they started for the ships, while we packed up our baggage and went on to the northward, against a strong wind and a very low temperature. During the whole of the 22nd and 23rd the wind blew fresh from the northward; the weather was extremely cold, and consequently our progress was slow. On the night of the 23rd, we encamped at a deep and wide ravine, which had every appearance of sending out a torrent of water in the summer season. After the tents were pitched, it began to blow very hard, and about 8 P.M. it was blowing a strong gale, with thick snow-drift, and the squalls frequently threatened to bring the tents about our ears.

April 24th.—9 A.M. the weather had become more moderate; sufficiently so, at least, for travelling. We turned out, and had our pemmican, and then proceeded up along the land. Four hours after starting we came up to the flag-post put up by Captain Penny last autumn; and about five miles further on we encamped for the night. The northerly wind again freshened up, and the people required careful watching to prevent frost-bites.

Depôt Point. Here the officers of the expedition were called upon by the commander to give their opinions as to the prudence of continuing to advance, under the present adverse winds and circumstances. No one of the whole party, except Mr. Petersen, having ever travelled before, it need not be wondered that we found a few things deficient;—our cooking vessels were so small, and our allowance of fuel was so little, that many improvements, however small, had to be made; these, together with the inclemency of the weather, at once suggested the idea of returning to the ships for ten days to make these improvements, and then to start again stronger than ever, and more likely to perform the duties entrusted to us satisfactorily, than if we should advance at present. This was the opinion of Captain Penny; and it was such as no person, looking at things as they were, could say a word against. It was then settled that we should return to the ships for ten days; not that we were not both able and willing to go ahead now, but that we might make sure of doing our work well, and without a risk of failing. The provisions were to be left; and so, also, were two of the sledges; the other two were to be taken to the ships to get some alterations and repairs made upon them, and to bring out the fresh supplies to our present position, where each party would again have its sledge, to proceed on the different routes already noticed. After all the arrangements for returning were made, Captain Penny started with the dog-sledges, while we retired each to his tent to sleep, that we should be ready for the "track-belts" in the morning. Midnight, blowing a strong gale from the northward, with snow-drift.

April 25*th.*—In the morning we were busily engaged securing the provisions that were to be left against the attacks of bears (although they appear to be a scarce commodity in this quarter). We began by digging a hole in the gravel; but after getting down a foot and a half, we found it frozen so hard as to be proof against our shovels and pickaxes; so that we were obliged to gather everything together as closely as possible, place over them the two sledges, and then to cover them up with gravel, and over this we heaped up a depth of a foot of snow to prevent scent.

Expedition returned to the ships from Depôt Point.

After we had finished the depôt and had breakfast, we started with the other two sledges, containing three days' provisions and four tents. There were fourteen men to each sledge. This made the dragging so light and easy that it was scarcely felt, and certainly it did not delay us any. After five and a half hours hard walking, we halted at Barlow Inlet half an hour, and took some luncheon. Here we again started, and, ten hours from the time we commenced in the morning, we encamped about one mile S.W. of Cape Hotham, where we slept very soundly. We had fine weather under lee of the land; but it was still blowing, with apparently some snow-drift, in the channel.

April 26*th.*—Morning fine, clear and calm weather. Called the cooks out, had our breakfast *in bed*, and then packed up the sledges and started for the ships, which we reached after six hours' hard walking, and where we were received by those on board with three hearty cheers, which we as heartily returned, and then went on board all quite well, and with very keen appetites, after having been in the tents and on the floe, in almost as severe weather as we had hitherto experienced.

From April 27th to May 6th we were all busily engaged repairing damages, making improvements, and making everything ready for another start. The blacksmith made larger conjurers, the carpenters altered the two sledges, our allowance of fat for fuel and of spirits was doubled; there was also something additional to the allowance of sugar. On the night of the 4th of May everything was finished, and nothing was wanting to complete our travelling equipments, as far as we were able to judge by the ten days' experience we had gained; while the weather during that time was such as made us all fully alive to the prudence and almost absolute necessity for having returned. May 6th was the day appointed for our starting, and for it we were all waiting, and all prepared long before it came.

Expedition starts again.

May 6th.—8 P.M. As the season was now far enough advanced for night travelling, we commenced our journey at night, and soon after leaving the bay we had it blowing fresh from the northward, with snow-drift. We kept along the land ridges, and did not strike out to the floe until we were about six miles from the S.E. point of the bay, where we got out to the smooth floe with very little trouble, and proceeded along the land to the eastward (due E.) to the "Assistance" depôt, which we reached in eight hours, and where we encamped. Our distance was thirteen miles, and upon the whole the road was very good. Weather clear, with a fresh breeze from the northward, and the temperature about zero. On pitching the tents, it was found that one of the parties had come away without their *floor-cloth*, an article that could not well be dispensed with; and this obliged me to send a man back, to inform Captain Penny, who was to join us at the farthest depôt, that he might bring it out with him. In the meantime we contributed what spare canvass we had in the sledges, for a floor-cloth to the tent that was deficient.

May 7th, Wednesday.—7 P.M. we were again starting, and travelling round Cape Hotham. When about one and-a-half mile north of it, we saw a bear; I stopped the sledges, and made the people get behind them, while two or three of us creeped over the hummocks to get within shot of him; but he was rather knowing for us; for he soon set off to the eastward over the ice as fast as he could run. We followed him for a short time, but soon gave in and returned to the sledges. In the meantime the sledges started, and kept going along the land towards Barlow Inlet. Here we joined them, struck across the inlet, and again landed upon the beach, the floe on the outside being very heavy and hummocky.

Depôt Point.

2 A.M. on the 8th we reached the southernmost depôt, and found it torn open by a bear, probably the same one we had seen at Cape Hotham, for we had traced his footsteps nearly all the way up. However, no material injury was done, nothing having been touched but the gutta percha barrel in which the sugar, tea, and bread had been stowed, and only a pound or two of bread was destroyed. This circumstance made us pitch the tents and stop for the day, that we might get the provisions shifted and better secured. 4 A.M. strong gale from the southward, with thick snow-drift, and thermometer + 5.

May 8th.—4 P.M. more moderate. Commenced shifting the provisions to what I considered to be a better place; and after making them as secure as we could, we packed up the sledges and started to the northward along the land, to the upper depôt, which we reached in four hours and a half, and where we encamped to await the arrival of Captain Penny with the dog-sledges, who was to leave the ships on the 9th of May, and join us at the upper depôt. Fresh breeze from the southward, with snow-drift.

May 9th.—4 P.M. we were joined by Captain Penny and Mr. Petersen, with the dog-sledges; they started from the ships in the morning, and had come out without ever making a stop, further than to cook their own dinner, and probably, also, to give the dogs something to eat. They pitched their small tent along with us, and rested for a short time, while Drs. Goodsir and Sutherland and myself walked along the beach about five miles to the northward, to a remarkable looking headland, to make sure there were no traces of the missing expedition up to that point, before I should strike off for the east side of the channel. At 8 P.M. having opened the depôt and packed up the sledges, each with its own gear and fittings. Two were for the west and three for the east side of the channel; one of the latter, however, was to strike out to Beechey Island. We kept along the land for nearly two miles, before we could get out through a perfect wall of hummocks. Here we got a tolerably smooth place, and bidding the commander and western parties adieu, we struck off into the channel for a headland on the north side of a large bay on the east side, which we had seen from the top of the land over our last encampment. After getting out a few miles, we had to go southerly a good deal, to round some heavy hummocks that appeared to lie between the new and the old ice, and, after going in an E.S.E. direction for two hours, we were able to resume our course on tolerably smooth ice. After having travelled seven miles we encamped five miles from the land. At two o'clock in the morning, the wind was from the westward; there was a fresh breeze, and the sky was cloudy. I now found that my sledge, one of the two that were repaired, had been in a manner spoiled; from being the most easily hauled sledge of the whole six at one time, we now found her the worst; and with exactly the same weights as the others, she required almost double the former strength to drag her along, showing how very little in the shape of the runner, or in the polish of the iron, affects the sledge. Dr. Sutherland's sledge, which was in appearance exactly the same as mine, even when the runners were laid together and compared, was much lighter. However, having with us Mr. J. Stuart, who was going to Beechey Island and Cape Hurd, with only thirty days' provisions on his sledge, I transferred to his sledge a bag of pork weighing 77lbs. Besides this, he had 40lbs. of pemmican and 50lbs. of bread, which were to be laid down at our first landing-place on the east side of the Wellington Channel, to serve as a depôt for our return.

May 8th. Course from starting point to where we encamped, E.N.E., 5 miles.

May 10*th*.— Having arranged the sledges so that each might require nearly the same strength, at 9 A.M. we again started to the eastward, steering rather northerly. We came upon the old ice that remained in the channel since last year, and, finding it not such good road as the new ice, we again struck more southerly, and got over a ridge of hummocks to a tolerably smooth floe, upon which we went along until 7 A.M. of the 11th, when we encamped, having come ten miles E.N.E. The snow was very hard and dry under the tent cloth, even after we had slept upon it for twelve hours. Latitude observed, 75° 7′.

May 11*th*.—At midnight, having packed up the sledges and put everything again into marching order, we started for the headland on the east side of the channel, which we were now raising very fast, and we expected to reach before encamping. The road in some places was very hummocky, and we were often obliged to put both crews to one sledge and to get them along, one at a time. To-day we again passed over old ice, the surface of which was very uneven, but it was not from pressure; it appeared to be from the action of the sun last season having deepened the pools on its surface, and consequently raised the dry places, giving the whole surface of the floe an appearance of "round" and "hollow," resembling a *short sea*. There were only occasional detentions, and we got on very well until we were within three miles of the land, where we encamped for the night, having made a day's journey of twelve miles. The wind was from the northward, and there was a fresh breeze, with cloudy weather and a low thermometer.

May 12*th*.—Having had a most comfortable rest and a sound sleep, at midnight we were again ready for the road, and started, and after two hours' work we reached the land, and brought the sledges up outside a ridge of hummocks, while we went on shore to lay down our depôt of bread and pemmican for our return. We were now on new ground, a circumstance which, combined with the search for the missing ships, made our work doubly interesting, and made every stone look in our imagination like a cairn, so confident was every one that we should succeed in finding something of that kind as we went along. I felt sure of finding something from some travelling parties that might have been sent out from the winter quarters at Beechey Island. The land, as far as we could see to the northward, consisted of high and bluff headlands, with small bays between them, and some of the points were very rugged. Having selected a low but conspicuous point on which to leave the provisions, we set about securing them from the attacks of bears, which was no easy matter, when one might walk for a mile before he could get a stone much larger than his fist. It took us some time before we got them covered up safely, and a cairn built over them for a land mark. In this cairn I left one of the notices that were printed for the use of travelling parties. Here Mr. John Stuart left us to proceed to Caswell's Tower and Cape Hurd; and after we got to the sledges, we proceeded along the land to the northward for four miles, and then encamped under a high bluff, amongst some very heavy hummocks. There was a strong wind from the northward, with thick snow-drift; owing to this the tents were rather shakey. Some of us went on shore and took
Lat. 75° 10′. a long walk without finding anything worthy of note. Several
Cape Grinnel. traces both of deer and of ptarmigan were seen, but they were last year's traces, very likely, as it was too early in the season for either being so far north. A little after noon we got to the tent just as the supper was ready, and then we felt to the fullest

extent the value of our improved cooking apparatus, which answered admirably; certainly a "pannikin" of warm tea or coffee in such weather as we then experienced was no small matter, and our circumstances now with respect to meals afforded a striking contrast to the ten days we were out in April, when we scarcely had a warm diet the whole of that time. 8 P.M., blowing very strong, with heavy snow-drift. Wind from the northward.

May 14*th.*—9 P.M. on the 13th, at our time for starting, it was blowing so hard, and there was such thick snow-drift, that I was obliged to wait until the weather should moderate a little. At 6 o'clock in the morning, as the weather was more moderate, we packed up and proceeded along the land to the northward, keeping close along the shore, and examining closely, for traces of the missing ships, the several bays and headlands as we passed them; but all our examinations were without success. There are very old traces of Esquimaux along the coast. At noon we encamped close to the beach. The pressure along the land here must have been very heavy, in some places tremendous, for the blocks of ice that were turned up resemble portions of small icebergs. The floe outside was also very hummocky. Our track was on a strip of new ice running along the land, which was not more than 300 yards in breadth. The young ice formed during an off-shore wind, when the heavy and rough ice had been driven off to the above distance; in this way was afforded an easy road to the northward, which otherwise should have been difficult and tedious. The sledges had as yet been so loaded, that before halting time every one was too tired to dig a hole through the ice to ascertain its thickness; it being quite sufficient for our purpose to know that it was not less than four feet.

May 15*th.*—At 1 A.M. we were again on our march along the land, which here begins to trend more easterly. At 5 A.M. I went on shore and erected a cairn on a point, where I left the usual notice. We had fine clear weather with bright sunshine; several of the party were suffering from snow blindness, and all were suffering from thirst, which was almost the only thing we had to complain of. At noon we again pitched our tents, and were enjoying our rest after a hard day's work, our estimated distance being about 15 miles, and course N.N.E.

May 16*th.*—We travelled along the land to the north-eastward on a narrow strip of smooth floe, with very hummocky ice on both sides of it. We kept close along shore, but no traces were found. I sent Dr. Sutherland to the land to examine something looking very like a cairn, but he found it was a large stone standing out of the ground. These journeys after cairns were very numerous, but they always met with disappointment. If Sir John Franklin went this way, he left no traces, not even a chip or anything else equally minute. To-day a hare was fired at on the land; the fact that these animals were on the ground gave us hopes of being able to add a little to our provisions.

We soon found the land leading away much more to the eastward. At 10 A.M. we encamped. The weather was very fine, the sky was clear, and there was very strong refraction. A
Baring Bay. deep bay was discovered to the north-eastward. Our course was N.E. by N.½N., and the distance was about 16 miles. Sun's meridian altitude from the artificial horizon was 66° 40′. The wind was light and variable.

May 17*th.*—On the 17th, 10 P.M., we again started, and pursued our course to the N.E. The ice all around us was very hummocky, except the strip on which we were travelling, and it appeared to run well to the eastward into the bay already al-
Lat. 75° 42′. luded to. Some of the heaviest sea-water ice I have ever seen was passed during this day's march. At 5 A.M. we encamped close to some very heavy hummocks within four or five miles of the land. Our course made good was N.E., and our distance travelled was about 12 miles.

May 18*th*, *Sunday.*—At 8 P.M. we started, and got immediately to old ice, which proved a very indifferent road; however, we got on very well for five hours, until we were brought up by a ridge of hummocks, of which we could see neither the end nor the side. I saw that to travel over this would be very heavy work, therefore I immediately struck in for the land, over the narrowest place that could be chosen. Both crews were at one sledge, and even then we had a stiff job before we got them over the ridge and in to the land. The sky was quite overcast with a disagreeable white glare, which proved very injurious to the eyes, and some of the people were already suffering a good deal from it. Here the land was so low, that, everything being covered with snow, it was difficult to discern where the land ended or where the floe began; and had it not been for the long low ridges or spits of much broken-up limestone, we might have imagined ourselves upon the ice, when, perhaps, a mile and a half inland. At 3 A.M. on the 19th, we encamped on one of these low ridges. The weather was very thick and the wind was southerly. Altogether, it was a very bad morning. Here I determined upon leaving a depôt to take us on our return to the place where we had left the bread and pemmican in the Wellington Channel. I would rather have taken it out another day's journey, but the sledges were so heavy that, it was very plain, by leaving our ten-day depôt here, and also a deal of weight in extra clothing, we should be able to get on more easily and more rapidly. Each sledge had ten days' provisions for seven men in a gutta percha barrel; as we had come only five days' journey from the last depôt, it was agreed that I should leave a barrel to supply both parties for five days, while Dr. Sutherland was to carry the other one five days more. This, however, I determined upon only after getting his opinion.

May 19*th.*—Accordingly, on the morning of the 19th, we collected everything that was to be left besides the provisions, and put them on one of the sledges. They consisted of all our spare clothing, our sea-boots, one of our wolf-skins, together with some other little things which we found we could do without; and as we placed them all on one sledge, the remainder looked very small, and an idea obtained that we should find our burdens much lighter. We hauled the sledge thus laden about a quarter of a mile in shore, to the next ridge that was above the snow, where we buried both clothes and provisions, and built a large cairn to mark the place, so that we might not pass it in returning; this was rendered necessary by the land being so low and flat that there was nothing whatever to enable a person to know the place without some distinct mark. Our sledges were the highest objects in sight for miles and miles around, except the hummocks in the offing. Having finished making the depôt, we again started along the land. Our course was N.W. true. During the day we were sometimes a couple of miles inland, and sometimes on the ice, cutting over the low long points, and making the road as straight as possible. At mid-day we encamped on a low flat, eleven miles north of the depôt. It was blowing strong from the westward, and there was thick and hazy weather.

May 20th.—The weather was too severe to permit travelling, consequently we were confined to our tents for nearly forty-eight hours before we could possibly face it. The wind was from the N.W., and it was blowing strong, right along the land. The land was still very low and flat, and the ice in the offing was very hummocky.

May 21st.—3 A.M. weather more moderate. Packed up, and proceeded to the N.W. along the land, alternately on the land and cutting across the points. The only portion of distinguishable land in this neighbourhood, is a rough stony point, which is about four miles from our last encampment; and beyond this point to the N.W., there is the same low, flat, and shapeless land as we have been coming along from the last depôt. There are long, low spites of much broken-up limestone running out from the land, and, from the appearance of the ice along the land, there is shoal water for a considerable distance. A small island was discovered, which appears to be about five miles off the coast. At half-past 10, we encamped. No traces of the missing ships. Esquimaux traces were very numerous, and all along, the beach was strewed with whales' ribs and jaw-bones, but they all appeared to be very old, not less than 100 years. Tracks of hares and ptarmigan were occasionally seen, and also a few old traces of reindeer. The latitude, from observation, was 75° 55′.

May 22nd.—We were confined to our tents until midnight, by a strong gale, with thick snow-drift, from the N.W.; then (the weather being a little better) we packed up, and came along the land to the N.W. Having to make "detours" of the coast for good road, made the journey considerably longer. At 9 A.M. we encamped on a low ridge of much broken-up limestone, having made a N.W. course, and travelled about twelve miles (direct distance only nine miles). Still, there were no traces of the missing expedition. The wind was still from the northward, and the weather was very cold, the people, during this day's march, having required very careful watching to prevent accidents from frost-bite. The observed latitude was 76° 3′.

Near Point Hogarth.

May 23rd.—We were confined all day to the tents; it blowing hard from the eastward, with very stormy weather. I now began to think of sending Dr. Sutherland back to the ships, as these detentions by violent weather had not allowed us to get on so fast as I could have wished or expected. As far as I could judge at present, there was only one route which we could take, and, on that account, two sledges were less necessary; and it was very clear that the one, by loading up with the provisions of the other, might be able to make the eastern search, solely entrusted to me, much more extended. This intention I communicated to Dr. Sutherland, while we were lying storm-stayed, and he at once agreed to the necessity of the step; and although he would have willingly gone on to the last, he felt, at the same time, that it was necessary he should return early. We determined, therefore, that, so soon as we should have advanced fifty miles beyond the last depôt, he should transfer to me all the provisions he had, except as much as would be sufficient to take him to the depôt, and that I, with the extra supplies thus obtained, should prosecute the search to the N.E.

Point Hogarth. Prince Alfred Bay.

May 24th.—10 P.M. The weather having moderated, we turned out, packed up the sledges, and went on to the N.W. for four miles, when we came to a low rough point, where we stopped and built a cairn. Here there was a termination to the low land, for the coast turns away to the north-eastward, forming a deep and splendid bay; the land to the northward appeared to stretch far out to the westward. Two remarkable table bluffs were seen on the north side of the bay; we steered for the easternmost one, which bore N.N.W. true, and, at 6 A.M. of the 25th, we encamped in latitude 76° 8′.

May 25th.—We had fine clear weather, with a very hot sun, and intense refraction while crossing the bay proceeding to the N.N.W. There were appearances of land to the W.S.W. The ice was remarkably smooth, scarcely a hummock to be seen, and all of it being apparently new ice. Several of the party were suffering severely from snow-blindness, and the doctor's *Vinum Opii* was in great request. We found black net veils the best eye-preservers; they suited far better than green or blue, for both of these we also tried. Latitude observed, 76° 15′. Distance made good, nine miles (although the distance travelled was fourteen), and true course N.N.W.

May 26th.—At midnight we again got the sledges into pulling order, and commenced our journey to the N.N.W. against a strong wind and thick snow-drift. There were heavy squalls, and, being right ahead of us, the sledges came along very tardily. A little after starting we saw a bear, the first that had been seen since we left Cape Hotham, and we stopped the sledges to make an attempt to get within shot of it. On a nearer approach, it turned out that there were two, a mother and her cub. One of the men crawled out on the ice, imitating the motions of a seal, while the others were all concealed behind the sledges with muskets, ready to drop them when within shot; but after having come in a direct line for us for half a mile, the knowing dame stopped short, and set off again, urging the cub along with her, as fast as they could run; we followed them, but of course, in a very short time, we were left a long way astern. The wind freshened, and the snow-drift became so thick that we could not face it; consequently, we were obliged to encamp five miles from the bluffs for which we had been steering. The wind was blowing very hard from N.N.W., with heavy squalls and thick snow-drift.

May 27*th.* — At Midnight, the weather began to moderate, and before the end of four hours we had a fine clear and quiet morning, of which we were very glad, having been confined to the tents since the morning of the 26th. At 6 A.M. I divided the two sledge parties into parties of three each, and sent them on shore to examine the coast in the neighbourhood of the bluffs. I then went on shore myself to take some observations; and, having got to the top of the easternmost bluff, which is about a thousand feet high, I had a long look to the westward, for the land trended away nearly due west, where two islands were observed at a great distance. I saw three hares, and succeeded in shooting two of them, and, as a person may easily suppose, they were very acceptable, being a change from the pemmican.

Cape Simpkinson.

May 28*th.* — At 4 A.M., after the people had got a short rest from their land excursion, and after arranging everything according to the plan already proposed, both sledges were ready to start: we were to proceed westward with fully one month's provisions, while Dr. Sutherland's party, with whom I exchanged sledges, were to commence their return to the ships with only enough provisions to bring them to the nearest depôt. I gave Dr. Sutherland orders to examine all round the bay that we had crossed, and also, if he found it practicable, to view and examine the small island we had passed in about 75° 50′, and, after parting with cheers on both sides, I proceeded westward, making a little southerly at first, until I got round the point which forms the western limits of the north side of the bay; then I struck out over the land hummocks and kept my course close along the shore. The pressure along the land was very heavy, and the ice in the offing was also rough and hummocky; but close along shore we had very good road, and came along rapidly until noon, when we encamped. Calm clear weather, with a very bright sun. Latitude observed 76° 19′. Land trending W. ½ N., and the farthest headland about thirty miles distant. Two islands were also seen in the distance, the one lying south of the other, with apparently two channels between them and the coast.

Not marked in chart. Vide "June 12th examined by Dr. Sutherland."

Deans Dundas and Margaret Islands.

May 29*th*.—At midnight we were ready for starting; our course was along the land leading to the westward. During the day two bluff points were passed, the one steep and black, the other covered with snow. The floe was smooth where we were travelling, but outside of us it was exceedingly hummocky and uneven. At 10 A.M., on the 30th, we encamped upon the ice fifteen miles west of our last encampment. The sun was very bright, and refraction intense. There was a light breeze of southerly wind, with fine clear weather.

North Channel.

May 30*th*.—At 10 P.M. we started again, and, after travelling for ten hours over very good ice, we reached the headland already mentioned, and found, most unexpectedly, that we had come nearly to the end of our outward journey. The ice between the land and the island to the southward, having become broken up, appeared to have drifted to the westward, leaving no ice at all in the channel thus formed; on the side we occupied, close to the foot of the cliffs, the sea washed the base of the rocks. This was a most unexpected and astounding upbring; to have met with open water in this quarter at such an early period of the season I never once anticipated, and it was some time before I could bring myself to believe the fact. As we could not get the sledge over the water, it was certain that we were brought to a stand; and, before we encamped, we had to unload and carry all our things over some tremendous hummocks to the land. While the men were pitching the tent, I went to the hill head, about 700 feet high, to get a better look of the ice and the water to the westward, but the weather, that had been threatening all day, became thick just as I reached the top, and consequently at that time I was unable to see more than seven or eight miles, which along the land was all water, and in the offing very much broken-up pack sailing ice; between the island and the headland, a distance which I estimated at ten miles, no ice was to be seen, for open water washed the land all along in that direction. Here, then, there was an opportunity for going ahead, if we only had a boat; but wishing was useless, and at such a late period for ice travelling, at so great a distance from the ships, getting one was hopeless. All I could do, under those circumstances, was to remain for a day or two to examine the movements of the ice to seaward; in the meantime I sent Mr. Reid along the land a little, to see if there was any possibility of getting the sledge along, but on returning he reported that there was scarcely a footpath round the cape, far less enough room to get the sledge along. I then again determined on remaining for a few days where we then were, to observe what I could about this unlooked-for open water. To be stopped just as we were getting light and into good walking order, and having so much provisions on the sledge, without there being a chance of finding use for one-third of them on this trip, was very annoying indeed. A great many ducks were swimming in the water, and other sea fowl of various kinds were also nume-

Open water to the westward.

Limit of view 7′ or 8′.

rous; a number of seals were sporting in the water, while a bear, seen on the edge of the fast ice, ran away to the southward. On the east side of the island the weather was coming away thick with a southerly wind, and the temperature was something more than +32°. It was thawing, and, as we had no thermometer, I only knew the temperature when it was about the freezing point.

May 31*st.* — Morning thick, and blowing from the south-westward. Still lying at the cape waiting for clear weather. In the afternoon I went out over the hummocks to the edge of the ice, to shoot some birds, as they were very numerous, and succeeded in getting as many as made a fresh mess for all hands. I also shot a seal in the water, and got him; he turned out to be a very fat one, and this increased our fuel about 200 per cent., certainly a great boon, as we could then afford ourselves more water, the only thing of which we were in any want. In the evening a bear came up to the hummocks, and we sallied out to meet him, and to get some sport; tumbling about among the deep cracks, between the pieces of ice, we had some sport, and probably, also, a little fright, as the guns got full of water, and we had no other weapons of defence. However, we contrived to put two bullets into him, and this bruin did not like, upon which he took himself off faster than we were able to follow. Wind still from the southward, with thick snow.

Cape Beecher.

June 1*st.* — Thick snow continued the whole day, on account of which we were not able to look out of the tent, except when a bear came along; this, however, was not unfrequent, for we had no less than three visits from them to-day, but, as we never were able to kill them at first shot, they all escaped either into the water or to the ice, and we got none of them, although we had wounded three or four since our arrival here.

June 2*nd.* — Still lying at the cape. Weather very thick; and the wind from the S.W.

June 3*rd.* — The weather, which had been very bad for the last three or four days, now came to its height, and blew a strong gale from the S.W., with thick wet snow and sleet. The ice in the offing rushed into the channel, and pressed down all along upon the land; in some places the pressure was enormous. In the afternoon the loose ice left the fast edge of the ice to the eastward, and the land, and went away eight or nine miles to the S.W., against the wind, which, at the time, was blowing very fresh from the south-westward. Birds (loons, dovekies, and sea-gulls) were in great abundance. In the evening we had a bear hunt, but did not get within shot of him. At 8 P.M. still blowing hard with snow from the S.W.

June 4*th.* — At midnight the weather began to moderate, and before 8 A.M. we had a fine clear day. We then got out, had breakfast, laced up the tent door, and went out for a day's march over the land, to have a look as far as possible to the westward.

We started on our journey along the foot of the cliffs, but found it impossible there, owing to some heavy hummocks being pressed into the face of the precipice, where they still remained. We had then got to the top of the land, which was tolerably level; Sir R. Inglis' Bay. here we advanced very well, having had to cross two deep ravines before we got to a bluff, whence the land turned away and formed a bay, with an excellent harbour or inlet at the top. The land then stretched away to the N.W. as far as the eye could reach, and was entirely lost in the distance. Two islands J. Barrow and Parker Islands. were also seen; they lay about thirty-five or forty miles to the westward; everything else to be seen in that direction was water and ice. Apparently another island was seen to the S.W., but Baring Island. there was a white haze lying in that direction, and on that account I cannot speak with certainty. All along the main land, which we followed, there was so much water that a ship, or any number of ships, could have worked with safety. The ice outside was only loose sailing scattered ice; in fact, there was nothing to prevent a ship going in any direction from west to south. It was very much broken up, the edges were hollowed out, there were long jutting-out tongues underneath, and some of the pieces were a good deal washed, affording evident proofs that the water had been here for some considerable time, I should say a month at least. We built a large cairn here, and left a despatch in it, and, after getting some observations on the hill head, we started to return to the tent, which was about eight miles to the eastward of us. Two hares were seen on our return, but we got none of them. At 6 P.M. we arrived at the tent rather tired, the snow on the land being deep and soft.

Cape Beecher. *June 5th.*—At 4 P.M. we turned out and went to the top of the bluff headland, at the foot of which we had encamped so long a time; our object was to build a cairn, and, having accomplished it, I left a document relating the objects of there being so many expeditions in those seas, their positions, the names of their commanders, and also where depôts of provisions were to be found, together with the names of my sledge party.

North Channel. The ice again all cleared out between the land and the island.

At 9 P.M. we had our pemmican, and started on our homeward journey. The road during the first part of the day was rather heavy, owing to the immense quantities of snow that had fallen the week before; it was so deep and soft that we often sunk to the knees in it, and the sledge also sunk deeply in it. After travelling, at a rapid pace, for nine hours we encamped on the ice, about one mile from the land. This we had already searched so minutely, without having found any traces that might lead one to suppose that Sir John Franklin had been in that locality, that now, except that it was new ground, it presented nothing interesting to us. Very different were our feelings in coming out, for then each strained his eyes looking for cairns or anything else that might be seen in those hitherto unexplored regions. The temperature was high, the floe was wet, and so were our beds. South-west wind, and cloudy weather.

June 6th.—At 9 P.M. we were again under weigh, and went along the land to the eastward. Several cracks in the ice were crossed over, some of them not without a little trouble, but upon the whole the floe was very good and sound. After travelling fifteen miles we encamped on the ice about two miles off the land. Wind from the S.W., and cloudy weather.

June 7th.—At 8 P.M. we started and went along to the eastward; the floe was a good deal cracked, and through these cracks the thickness could be determined.

June 8th. — At 5 A.M. we encamped on the north side of the bay, where Dr. Sutherland and his party, under my orders, commenced his return to the ships. The sledge came along very lightly. The weather was so thick and disagreeable that we were not able to see above a hundred yards around us. Southerly wind blowing fresh.

After our usual rest we packed up again, and proceeded to the S. S. E. at a quick step. The floe was very good, and the wind helped us much, as we had our tent-cloth fitted and set for a sail. After travelling twelve and a half hours we reached the land on the opposite side of the bay, but owing to the thick weather we did not see it until we were within hail of it. The weather being so unfavourable we encamped, all a good deal fatigued, after having travelled upwards of twenty-two miles. At mid-day it began to blow keenly from the southward, and continued to do so, accompanied by thick snow, during the rest of the day.

June 9th.—At midnight there was a strong breeze, with thick wet snow. People all in the tent, as the weather was altogether unfit for travelling; this was the case more especially as we had no spare clothes to shift with in the event of getting wet. A few snipes were seen, but none procured. Morning, a little more moderate, but still snowing thick.

June 10th.—At 11 P.M., as the weather was better, we turned out, packed up our baggage, and came out toward the point of the bay, where we had built a cairn on the 24th of May on our outward journey. This we reached after walking four miles, and a note left by the doctor on the 30th of May was found, stating that he had examined the bay right round to the top, but with the usual success. His note, along with one of my return despatches, was placed in the cairn, after which we went on to the S.E. till 8 A.M., when we encamped on a low ridge of small limestone, having returned to the low land that proved so wearisome to us on our first coming out. The weather was very mild and warm, and the snow on the land was dissolving very fast. About an hour after starting in the evening we saw a deer, and put off some time trying to get within shot of him. He appeared to be a very large one, with a pair of splendid antlers, and possessed of more sense than to allow us to get within shot; we had to be content with a sight of this goodly animal, and returned from the chase unsuccessful. This was the only one we saw, although there were numerous traces of them on the land. Abundance of snipes were flying about the beach.

June 11*th.*—At 10 P.M. on the 10th we started with a fine night on an excellent road. The sledge came along at a quick pace for eight hours, until we came to the round hill and the rough point on the flat land, alluded to on our outward journey. As the weather, which had been thick ever since we commenced to return, cleared up, I encamped under the point to make a few observations. I went across the hill and shot a couple of hares, which to us were a great delicacy. There was abundance of fresh water to be got on the land; this proved of great relief to our fuel, which was getting very low. Snipes were numerous, but very shy.

June 12*th.*—At midnight we packed up and came along the land very fast, until we reached the depôt, where we stopped to remove our provisions, as there would have been little use in leaving them there, and as we were well able to take them to the ship. We had to encamp, owing to the tedious process of opening the depôt. The snow we had put over the small stones covering it had melted and ran down amongst them and the provisions, and had frozen the whole together, as hard almost as the solid rock. It was with a considerable amount of labour that we got them out; however, we found everything right, although wet when thawed. The doctor and his party had been there, and removed their share of the provisions. I also found a note from him, stating that he had visited the island, but found nothing. Blowing a fresh breeze from the southward, with showers of rain.

June 13*th.*—At 9 P.M. on the 12th we again started, and had a very bad day's work of it, striking out from the land through the hummocks, and wading almost up to the knees in water and sludge. Going a little southerly we came to some old ice, where we almost stuck, at one time going up to the middle in snow and water, and next time scrambling to a dry and rounded elevation. The sledge often sunk outright in it; consequently, it stuck every two or three minutes, and made very heavy work of it. Considering that we should be under the necessity of getting to the land before encamping, I struck right in for it; and after a deal of labour we reached it, and encamped on the side of a large ravine. The sites of several very old Esquimaux tents were found on the land; and there was abundance of bones, chiefly those of whales, strewed over the beach. We never once were on shore without seeing a great many very old bones of whales lying about, some of which were deeply imbedded in the ground, and a long way above the sea level.

June 14*th.*—Blowing strong from the southward, with heavy showers of rain and sleet. We were all inside the tent smoking our pipes or mending boots and stockings, &c. Thick wet snow all the latter part of the day; this was the worst possible weather for travelling.

June 15*th*, *Sunday.*—At noon it cleared a little, and, expecting that the weather was going to improve, we started. Our course was along the floe close inshore, and we were often up to and past the ankles in water. There was not a particle of snow on the ice; there were, however, large holes of fresh water in its surface, some of them almost of sufficient depth to float a boat. The sledge came along very easily, as the ice was perfectly smooth. We marched at a quick pace until 8 P.M.; the weather then coming away worse than ever, wet sleet and snow, with the wind from the southward, we hauled the sledge over the land hummocks, and pitched our tent under the farthest bluff seen when looking in this direction from the west side of the channel. This day ended with a fresh breeze and thick snow.

June 16*th.*—It blew a gale all day, with heavy showers of wet snow and sleet, and violent squalls came down along the hills, which often threatened to blow us away tent and all. The whole day was spent lying in the tent smoking, and mending boots and stockings.

June 17*th.*—Still disagreeable weather with snow and rain until 3 P.M. The weather then clearing a little, we packed up our baggage and came along the land on the east side of the Wellington Channel, towards the point on which we first landed on our outward journey. The ice was very smooth, for the snow had all melted from its surface, leaving it hard and smooth. We came along at a rapid rate for ten hours, until we arrived at the depôt left by Mr. John Stuart on his journey to Beechey Island, where we encamped. The weather had been fine, but threatening all the afternoon, and now it began to rain and to blow from the southward. The depôt was undisturbed, except by Dr. Sutherland, who had visited it, and had taken away some of the bread. I found a note from him dated 8th June, "All well."

June 18*th.*—Fresh breeze from the southward, with sleet and rain all day. All in tent patching up and mending boots, which suffered much from the soft state of the ice and walking on the land together. The land was very soft and boggy, and frequently we sank up to the ankle in mud at every step.

June 19*th.*—In the forenoon the weather cleared up, the wind came from the northward, and we had a fine day. Found the latitude by mer. alt. to be 75° 08′.

At 9 P.M. we packed up the sledge, took the bread and pemmican from the depôt, and struck off for the west side of the channel. It was a fine clear night, with a gentle breeze from the N.E. The ice was in first-rate order for travelling over it, and the sledge came along with three hands as fast as the others could walk. The ice to the northward appeared to be very hummocky. At 2 A.M. we came to an old floe, which had to be crossed over. In doing this we had three hours' hard work, although it was not more than two miles in breadth. Wading up to the middle in snow and water, and the sledge sticking every two or three yards, were common occurrences, and the source of not a little amusement. After crossing the old ice, we got to a smooth floe again, and went on at the same spanking pace as before. The ice was now in a state to prevent encamping on it, without sleeping in some three or four inches of water. I therefore only pitched the tent, and let the men have a cup of warm tea.

Crossed the ice in Wellington Strait.

June 20th.—We again started for the land on the Cornwallis side of the channel, and reached it, after a tight walk, at 1 P.M., having come right across the channel with a stoppage of only half an hour. Along the land the fresh water on the floe was in many places eighteen inches and two feet deep, occurring in large sheets, some of which extended two miles from the land. We encamped under the first headland to the northward of Point Separation, the point we had left on the 9th of May. The people were all a good deal fatigued, and our boots were much the worse from wearing. Fine clear weather and southerly wind.

June 21st.—After taking a good long sleep and having thoroughly refreshed ourselves, we started to the southward, keeping close outside the land hummocks. There was a great deal of water on the floe, and our road was very bad until we got round Point Separation, and then we reached the place where our sledges had been left in April. I was surprised to find a large depôt of provisions; and, looking at the notes that were left in a bottle, I learned that all the parties had returned, and that Captain Penny was again to the westward, with a boat and two sledges, altogether a party of twenty-one men; but a note written in pencil was so indistinct from having got damp, that I could barely make out its meaning. However, I saw enough to convince me that provisions were wanted, and, having twenty-six days' provisions on my sledge, I thought it as well to leave some of them; accordingly, the sledge was unpacked, and a fortnight's provisions for seven men were deposited along with what had been previously in the cairn. As soon as this was done, we started to the southward that we might arrive at the ships as soon as possible, for we had an idea that something was wanting. At 8 A.M. on the 22nd we encamped on the south side of Barlow Inlet, and, after resting for eight and a half hours, we again started for the ships. There was a strong breeze from the N.E., which we took advantage of by setting our sail. Four hands frequently sat on the sledge, while the others were steering her, as we were not able to keep up with her without three or four hands leaning on to increase the weight, thus taking a "sail" by turns. In seven hours we reached the ships in Assistance Bay, where we found all well, and learned that all the travelling parties had returned without finding the slightest traces of Sir

John Franklin. I also again learned that Captain Penny had returned on the 16th May, having discovered the water with the dog-sledges, that he was now out with a whale boat fitted up on a sledge, accompanied by only two other sledges and eighteen men to carry it and provisions to the water, and that all but a boat's crew were expected in daily. The provisions left at the upper depôt were to be taken to the N.E. point of Cornwallis Island; they were left there for a time only, owing to the quantity of water on the floe, which was likely to damage them on a low runner-sledge. I now waited anxiously for the return of the party from the boat (who were to leave her as soon as they reached the water), and refreshed my party, as I had determined on carrying out the provisions to the N.E. point of the island myself. Mr. Goodsir was also stopped by the water on the north shore of Cornwallis Island, and had returned to the ships only a few days before my arrival.

On the 25th the party returned from the water, having launched the boat into it, and, as they described, stood looking at her until she disappeared on the distant horizon under a double-reefed sail. They reached the water on the 17th, and had been walking along the beach from day to day since that time, on their return to the ships, the dogs taking the two sledges along on the ice. Captain Penny was now on the water, with thirty-four days' provisions and seven men. All that was to be done, being merely to take the provisions out to the N.E. point; and this I expected to do with the dogs after they had recruited a little, trusting to Mr. Petersen as the driver. I came to this determination from the circumstance that we required all our hands, to get the ships ready for sea. A note from Captain Penny stated that he would be on his return on the 12th July, so that there was plenty of time before then to carry out the depôt.

In the afternoon of the 27th I started, accompanied by Mr. Petersen, with one of the dog-sledges, containing as much provisions as should make up the quantity taken out of the depôt by the party returning from the boat. On getting a few miles to the eastward of the bay, we found the ice full of cracks, some of which were twenty feet broad, and, on proceeding as far as Parry's Bluffs, it was all so much broken up, that we found it utterly impossible to advance with the dogs. I went to the land and ascended the hill, and then saw that the ice in Barrow Straits was all adrift and broken up, to the utmost limits of vision assisted by a telescope. We turned round and drove home as fast as possible, and arrived at the ships at 6 A.M. on the 28th, and immediately set the carpenters to prepare a boat mounted upon a sledge, as travelling over ice so much broken up without a boat at such a late period of the season was impossible.

On the 1st July we had the boat ready, and in the evening we launched her down to the point of the bay. Since the 28th the ice had broken up still more, and had drifted from the land, leaving a lane of water from half a mile to a mile in breadth, extending to Cape Hotham; into this water we launched the boat, and made sail to the eastward. On reaching Cape Hotham I found the water leading right across the channel towards Cape Spencer, but the ice in the channel itself still remained fixed and apparently as strong as ever. Here we placed the boat on the sledge, and proceeded to the northward; but, finding that I should be unable to get the provisions to the appointed place at the time expected with the boat, I left her at Barlow Inlet, and proceeded with the sledge and party to the northward, calling at the depôts as I went along, and taking the provisions with me to the N.E. point, which we reached late on the evening of the 5th, and found that Captain Penny had not returned. Here we found the ice much decayed; along the land, large holes had wasted in it, although to seaward it still appeared to be strong and good. Having a few days' provisions to spare, we pitched our tent to remain for some time, to hunt deer, hares, or any other animals that might come within our reach, and to wait for the return of the boat party. With the assistance of a hare or two, and some birds, we remained a week at the point; but, not being able to wait any longer without encroaching on the provisions of the other party, we deposited them in a large cairn, and started for the ships. On coming to the southward we found the ice broken up and drifted away as far up the Wellington Channel as 75°, where the edge of the fast ice appeared to extend across from shore to shore. Here we left the sledge and everything on it, and, having travelled along the beach to Barlow Inlet, where we had left our boat, we returned with her for the sledge. On the 18th we reached the ships.

State of the ice.

State of the ice.

Barrow Straits now were all open water, and there was scarcely a piece of ice to be seen from the hill head. The ships were nearly all clear for sea. The carpenters and blacksmith were busily employed putting our ice-saws into cutting order, to saw a canal through about a mile and a half of ice that still remained between the ships and the entrance of the bay. On the 25th Captain Penny returned; his arrival brought the travelling to a conclusion, without any traces of Sir John Franklin or of his ships having been found.

Captain Stewart's opinion.

That Sir John Franklin may have gone up Wellington Strait is not at all impossible. I would (after having seen it), myself, if seeking a passage to the north-westward, seek for it in that channel. But the circumstance of the Wellington Channel and the shores and islands of the more intricate channels to the N.W. of it having been thoroughly searched, without finding any traces of the missing ships, goes a great way to refute the idea that they have gone in that direction. This circumstance, together with the late period at which the ice breaks up in the Wellington Strait, on one side, and the early period at which open water was found to the northward, coupled with the first winter quarters of the ships at the mouth of the Channel, on the other side, leaves the question in the same doubt and uncertainty as ever.

(Signed) ALEX. STEWART,

Commanding Her Majesty's Ship "Sophia," under the orders of Captain W. Penny, commanding the Expedition from Aberdeen in search of Sir John Franklin.

Names of the Men forming the party:

Alex. Stewart - - - -	Officer.
Alex. Samuel - - - -	Captain of tent.
Andrew Adams - - -	Seaman.
*John Eddie - - - -	Ditto.
John Dunbar - - - -	Ditto.
James M'Kenzie - - -	Ditto.
George Knowles - - -	Ditto.

---

* John Eddie returned with Dr. Sutherland, and Mr. J. Reid, second mate, was drafted in his room into the extended party.

A Detailed Report of the Proceedings of a Travelling Party from Her Majesty's Ship "Sophia," under the Command of Captain Stewart, in Search of Sir J. Franklin, by P. C. Sutherland, M.D., Surgeon. *April, May*, and *June*, 1851.

April 17th, Thursday. Leaving the ships. Accidents, &c.

Soon after 8 A.M. we assembled to prayers on board the "Lady Franklin," and, after that solemn service was over, Captain Penny addressed us with respect to the duty we were about to undertake. "He had no doubt we would overcome every difficulty, and brave every trial and privation attending it; and, whether or not we should be made, through Providence, the instruments for relieving our absent countrymen, or discovering their unhappy fate, he felt convinced, when our labours were over, we should possess the sweetest reward man can have, namely, 'minds conscious of having done our duty.'"

The men seemed to be in high spirits, and delighted with the idea of starting, for two days of bad weather had elapsed since we expected and intended to have commenced our journey.

The sledges had been drawn from the ships to the clear floe some time previously, and, as the cheering on both *sides* was over, we proceeded out of the bay at the rate of about two miles per hour, until we came to a ridge of hummocks which extended from the S.E. to the W.S.W. points of the bay, and required the sledges to be double and even triple manned before we got to the smooth floe outside.

We certainly had reason to feel grateful for the kindness of Commander Phillips, Dr. Porteous, and the greatest part of the crew of the "Felix," in accompanying and assisting us out of the bay, and after renewed cheers we again started, and proceeded to the eastward in the direction of Cape Hotham.

The floe was very soft from a great accumulation of snow and a high range of temperatures during the two previous days, but more especially from the circumstances of being of very recent *formation* during *low* temperatures, and consequently containing an unusually large proportion of the saline ingredients of sea water, which a *rapid* freezing process presses to the *upper surface.*

The sledges moved along very heavily, and profuse perspiration exempted no person; thirst too became so excessive that we were forced to make an early luncheon, and get the *conjurors* and kettles prepared and lighted to obtain water by melting snow. We soon observed how carefully the snow had to be taken from the surface of a layer not less than four to six inches deep, and when this was not observed the water was invariably brackish.

The iron on the *runners* of my sledge had been fastened on with a mixture of screw and plain nails. The latter started when we were crossing the ridge of hummocks, and increased the friction so much that it was impossible to keep pace with the other five sledges without assistance. I at once came to the conclusion of unpacking the sledge, and turning it upside down, to discover what was the matter, and have it repaired, if possible. Some of the nails were drawn a quarter of an inch, and bent over; those were dispensed with at once; but the others that had only been started were driven into their places, with the hope that they should maintain their hold of the wood, once it became thoroughly soaked with water. I ventured to prognosticate considerable annoyance, if not complete hindrance, from this simple cause alone.

Encamped at 4 P.M. Distance travelled, 9 miles. Hours, 7. Temps.: max. +37°, min. +23° mean of 5 readings, 31·2°.

We continued our march until we were at least nine miles from the ships. Our encampment was on the soft floe. The sky began to clear up beautifully, and the thermometer, which was up to +37° at 4 P.M., fell to +23° at 9 P.M.; but, in consequence of having to *haul* at the sledge with "belt over shoulder" all day, I did not turn out to read off the temperatures during the sleeping hours, perhaps more for the sake of the comforts of the blanket bag than for the fear of disturbing my tent companions and gruff messmates.

April 18th, Friday Packing up. Course to the eastward. Temps. +20° to +31°. Winds S.S.W.

We were aroused at an early hour to get breakfast, and resume our march. I could not help observing a remarkable change in the countenances of the "*cooks*." They left the ship as clean as could be, but now how black and sooty they had become! The sky was clear, and fleecy clouds could be seen in all directions. There was a gentle breeze from S.S.W., which raised a little snow-drift, but this was only for a few hours before 10 o'clock, when the temperature was low. After we had started we found the floe hummocky, and the sledges came along with great difficulty. No. 1. met with an accident, but it was very trifling. No. 2., the Sylph, went very easily; so much so, that one man could be spared to assist my sledge, which was generally falling behind, from causes already noticed. The conjurors and kettles were slung at the sterns of the sledges, and kept burning, "preparing water." Considering this, I thought we could congratulate ourselves on the twenty ounces of fat for fuel per day, which appeared to be a very liberal allowance when carefully used. The loss of one of the tins belonging to my sledge, from carelessness and inexperience in putting the snow into it while over the fire, was a source of regret to all of us, and at the same time a valuable lesson for the future.

Captain Penny and Mr. Petersen's

At noon, when we were taking luncheon, Captain Penny

arrival with two dog-sledges.

was observed, and heard hailing us from the hummocks inside. He and Mr. Petersen had come down along the land with two dog-sledges; but having found the way impassable in that direction, they came outside the hummocks, and went on as before until they arrived to the large bluff west of Cape Hotham, where we overtook them and encamped on the floe close by the hummocks that lay along the beach. This encampment, like the last, was very wet, for the snow on the floe melted by the heat of our bodies, and saturated the floor cloth and lower wolfskin, and even the under surface of our blanket bags. The sky began to be overcast with a gloomy haze, and before midnight we had a smart south-westerly breeze, accompanied by a considerable fall of soft snow.

Encampment about 4 P.M. Distance travelled, 7 miles. Temps.: max. +31°, min. +20°; mean, +24·2°. Winds S.S.W.

Mr. Stewart and I went to the land, and ascended as far as the flag pole left by H.M.S. "Assistance" in autumn, to the westward of a depôt of provisions. We could see the state of the ice to the offing, and certainly it seemed little likely to afford an easy road to the east and northward of Cape Hotham. Mr. Petersen gave his opinion that we should go along the land inside the hummocks. We kept no watch during the night. The dogs could be heard prowling about the tents and sledges; they were continually fighting, and next morning we discovered that they had broken into a sledge, and devoured not less than seventy pounds of bears' flesh, which had been carefully put up in a strong canvass bag before we left the ships.

April 19th, Saturday. Packed up, and started at 7 A.M. Course easterly, inclining to the northward and north, after rounding Cape Hotham. Temps.: midnight till noon, max. +31°, min. +20°; mean, +24°. Winds variable, generally southerly.

The sky was overcast during the whole day, and there was a heavy fall of soft snow; however, the gloomy appearances of last night disappeared, and we could discern the sun through the snow till late in the afternoon.

We crossed the hummocks with double or triple manned sledges, and proceeded with great difficulty through the deep snow that lay between the high hummocks and the shingly beach, both of which we had equal reasons for avoiding. The men were very thirsty, and perspired profusely, and from the time of our starting until we halted to encamp we drank *fourteen* pints of water, which had to be prepared during the travelling hours. Each man had an equal share, for every drop of it was carefully served out. I kept a watchful eye over my own party, for fear any one should attempt to allay his insatiable thirst by eating "snow;" but all were so imbued with the idea of the hurtfulness of that practice, that I never had occasion to check any of them.

Encamped at 8 P.M. Distance, 7 miles. Temps.: noon to midnight, max. +31°, min. +19°; mean, +37°. Winds variable, chiefly northerly.

From the large bluff to Cape Hotham the land trends away about E. 18° N., and after rounding the latter we found it inclining a few degrees to the westward of north as far as Barlow Inlet, which runs a little to the northward of due west. We rounded Cape Hotham at 11 A.M., and overtook Captain Penny and Mr. Petersen at their encampment about two miles to the southward of Barlow Inlet, where we also encamped at 3 P.M.

From the intense thirst we had to endure, and the profuse perspiration and other minor difficulties we had to encounter, I found I had much to learn with respect to Arctic travelling which I never imagined, nor could be got over but by patience and perseverance.

We found this encampment much better than the last, for it was on the dry snow on the land. The difference was so great that we determined for the future to avail ourselves of bivouacking on the land, if possible, even with a little trouble.

April 20th, Sunday. "EASTER DAY." Packed up, and started at 3½ A.M. Course up the channel. Temps.: midnight to noon, max. + 30°, min. + 19°; mean, + 25°. Winds light and variable, chiefly northerly. Overcast sky.

At 2 A.M. we were called, and had breakfast, but the allowance of tea was very scanty indeed. I increased mine considerably by putting in snow until the temperature of it was reduced from near the boiling point to 40° or 50°, and I continued to follow this practice until the insatiable craving for fluids was abated.

Before starting we assembled to prayers, and Captain Penny conducted that solemn and appropriate duty. The "sailors" uncovered their heads, and appeared to be deeply attentive. We kept close along the land, until we reached Barlow Inlet, and then crossed a hummocky floe in its entrance, after which we came to a smooth but *soft* floe, on which we were able to proceed to the northward at a slow and heavy pace. The sky was overcast all day, and at noon there was a white misty haze which proved very injurious to our eyes. We saw a seal *on the floe* to the eastward, and that condition of the atmosphere was present which made it appear as if at a great distance, and of very large size. This was the first time we observed the common seal (*Phoca vitulina*) on the floe this season. At 11 A.M. we came to a ridge of hummocks which seemed to extend to the eastward as far as the eye could reach, and *close* in with the land. This must have been from pressure between floes of unequal thickness, and at a season of the year when there was open water both in the channel and in Barrow Straits. Captain Penny and Mr. Stewart went in towards the land, and after ascending a short distance they discovered smooth ice to the northward of the hummocks, and they came to the conclusion, that the easiest way to reach it would be to strike in through the hummocks obliquely to the land. The sledges were triple manned; we had our *pioneers;* and after about two hours of violent labour we were half a mile farther along, at the edge of a smooth floe leading in the right direction along the land. Here we encamped at 2 P.M., having travelled at least seven miles by the circuitous route we had to follow. Our encampment was on the floe, for it seemed impossible to get to the land, in consequence of a wall of hummocks which was pressed up on the beach. Towards midnight the white

Encamped at 2 P.M. Distance travelled, 7 miles. Temps.: noon to midnight, max. + 30°, min. + 15°; mean of 4 readings, + 21·9°. Winds northerly. Snow. Overcast sky.

misty haze assumed a blue and angry appearance, the wind was increasing rapidly, and the thermometer fell to +15°. The air felt chilly, and, having perspired a good deal during the day, we did not feel as comfortable as could have been wished. Some of us were suffering from snow blindness, but as yet it had only commenced, and we expected a few hours of darkness in the blanket bags would go far to relieve the eyes from the congestion that had been brought on by too long exposure to a *perverse* state of the atmosphere, which could not fail to prove injurious to the most accommodating visual apparatus. A watch of one man had to be kept, to prevent the dogs breaking into the sledges.

April 21st, Monday. DETENTION. Temps.: midnight to noon, max. +15°, min. +5°; mean of ditto, +10°. Winds N.N.W. Violent storm.

Temps.: noon to midnight, max. +5°, min. −25°; Mean, −15°. Winds, N.N.W. Perfect gale. Violent storm.

We were aroused at the early hour of half-past 12, midnight, to resume our march. The weather was very gloomy and squally; there was a keen northerly breeze, and the snow drifted along, and annoyed us very much, seeking into the tents by the most minute openings about the door, and falling in an impalpable powder on the upper wolfskin and the blanket bags. The cooks had great difficulty in *lighting* their conjurors, and in keeping them in that state after they had succeeded. While these poor *unfortunates* were thus engaged in the open air, there were great risks of frost-bites, and more especially as the temperature was rapidly on the decrease. It was past 3 o'clock before we had breakfast, and then the weather was very stormy, and always becoming more so. Captain Penny considered it imprudent to start; consequently, we remained in our tents all day and the following night, during which time we came through a very violent storm. The temperature fell to −25°, and at 5 A.M. to −30°; but it might have been considerably lower than —30° between midnight of the 21st and 5 A.M. of the 22nd. At 7 A.M. some of us turned out, and had a ramble among the hummocks, and discovered very recent footmarks of a bear, that came down along the beach, and passed on unobserved even by the dogs. I suppose the poor brutes were so benumbed that they could not take sudden notice of such a valuable prize. Some of my party went to the land, and brought off a mass of fresh water ice, which was considered a great advantage in preparing water. One of them, the cook for the day, got his fingers slightly frost-bitten, but they soon recovered, and with no inconvenience to him in the discharge of his duty. Our boots were so hard that we could hardly get them on, and to thaw them in the tents, when the temperature was −25°, was a difficulty which we only overcame by taking them into our blanket bags, where we had to keep our tins and flasks full of water if we *would* have the comfort of a little to quench our thirst during the sleeping hours. I found it very effectual to place my boots, mittens, and boot-hose beneath my blanket bag; and I followed this practice until the increase of temperature as the

April 22d, Tuesday. Temps.: midnight to noon, max. −8°, —30°; mean of 3 readings, −21·3°. Winds north. Violent storm.

Temps.: noon to midnight, max. −8°, min. −30°; mean of 3 readings, −17·3°. Travelled 4 miles to the northward. Winds northerly. Moderate. Cloudy weather.

season advanced rendered such a precaution unnecessary. Towards noon the weather began to moderate, but still the snow drifted with great violence; the horizon was very obscure, and the temperature was too low to travel with safety AGAINST a strong wind.

Captain Penny resolved to make an attempt to get a few miles farther to the northward, that he might make a depôt of the provisions on Nos. 5. and 6., and send them back to the ships; and as the wind moderated towards evening, we packed up, proceeded along the land, and crossed the *grounded* hummocks, keeping between them and the beach, where there was a formation of almost perfectly fresh-water ice very smooth, and favourable for sledging. I discovered that my sledge had sustained some injury coming through the hummocks on the 20th; almost all the nails in the iron on the runners had drawn, the iron itself was bent to one side, and the bare wood was exposed to the floe. This increased our labours so much that we required the assistance of four additional men to enable us to reach the spot intended for the encampment. This sledge was exchanged for No. 6., and sent back to the ships.

Temps.: noon to midnight, max. −8°, min. −30°; mean of three readings, 17·3°.

John Gordon and Donald Sutherland were exchanged for Mr. Reid and John Lucas; and now I considered my party for the long journey made up. The sledge was also complete, and contained forty days' provisions, weighing about 1,500 lbs. The returning sledges made their depôt in the *shingle;* and as they gave us three cheers, which we responded to, we lost sight of them, proceeding down the channel at a rapid pace and with a fair wind. The sky was cloudy; but we could discern the beautiful azure tint, and this was a great relief to our eyes. There was a smart breeze, and occasionally volumes of snow were raised, and whirled about the rugged cliffs above us. We bivouacked on the shingle, and certainly our comforts far exceeded what we had experienced the two previous nights, although snow is much softer than stones. I took particular notice, that the depôt resembled one of the many heaps or mounds of shingle which have been raised along the beach by the action of *grounding* ice; but for distinction's sake a small waft was placed over it.

April 23d, Wednesday. Packed up, and started at 10 A.M. Travelled 3 hours up channel. Temps: midnight to noon, max. −13°, min. 30°; mean of 4 readings, −24·5°. Winds northerly. Sky cloudy.

We were roused out at 7¼ A.M., and at 10 we started. The sky was clear, and there was a smart breeze down the channel. The smooth ice along the beach inside the hummocks, which were very high, enabled us to go on easily some time at the rate of three miles per hour, but generally about two and a half. The temperature was low, ranging from −30° to −13°; and it was not uncommon to see noses and cheeks frozen to whiteness; then the rubbing that ensued was really amusing, if it could but be divested of the danger the bare hands were in while engaged in this affectionate duty. One man suspected his feet were suffering, and perhaps not without reason, for he had on leather boots, which had to be cut off, and before any mischief could have happened the circulation was restored by friction. The feet were carefully wrapped up in blanket squares, stockings, boot-hose, and moccassins; and the poor lad was as fit for his duty as if nothing had happened. On the 21st I strictly forbade the use of leather boots in my party; and those of us who were not supplied with canvas boots used moccassins or carpet boots, which answered even better than the canvas boots, for they were not so apt to slip.

I found it necessary to make frequent inquiries after feet, faces, and hands; and by thus directing the attention of the men to themselves it was not difficult to impress the idea how likely they were to be frostbitten, without the mere feeling of pain apprising them of it. The want of sensation altogether is the only criterion by which one can act safely.

Encamped at 1 P.M. Travelled 7 miles. Temps.: noon to midnight, max. −13°, min. −25°; mean of 3 readings, −20·3°.

The dog sledges started ahead of us, and when we were *forced* to encamp we saw nothing of them except the track on the snow.

Mr. Stewart and I went on, and after travelling about two miles and a half we overtook Captain Penny and Mr. Petersen, who had their tent pitched and their dinner cooked long before we came up to them, although they started nearly when we did, and we came along rapidly. This was a tolerable proof of what the dogs were able to accomplish when properly managed.

Mr. Stewart acquainted Captain Penny with his reasons for encamping so soon, and the latter acknowledged he had acted wisely under those circumstances.

The flag-pole Captain Penny had erected in autumn on a round hill was still standing, and could be seen plainly from his tent. We returned to the tents at 5 P.M., and soon took our places among the weary *sailors*. The sky continued cloudy, and there was a smart northerly breeze. The thermometer fell from −13° to −25°. The tents were very comfortable. In ours the thermometer at one time indicated +16°. Some of us were suffering *not a little* from severe excoriations of the lips, which were brought on by the application of vessels to the lips in the act of drinking water or spirits. It was always necessary to rub the edge of the vessel with the finger, lest one's lips should actually adhere to it; but even with this precaution the reaction that took place in the lips after exposure to intense cold invariably produced inflammation, which rarely failed to throw off the skin, and leave painful ulcers for some time. The accumulation of ice to our beards (although it had a manly appearance) was continually irritating the lips. I found nothing more effectual than the application of a little lard or cold

April 24th, Thursday. Packed up at 9 A.M. Course up the channel.

cream; but any applications will not make up for the careless and indiscriminate use of *tin* vessels.

Temps.: midnight to noon, max. −0°. min. −25°; mean of 4 readings, −15·2°. Winds north. Smart breeze. Clear sky.

We expected to have started at an early hour, but the extreme coldness of the weather rendered it dangerous, therefore we remained in our tents till 9 A.M. The sky was clear, and a keen piercing wind down the channel made us step out smartly to keep ourselves warm, and, although the sledges were heavy, when the road was at all good we went at the rate of two miles an hour. Soon after ten o'clock we came up to Captain Penny's tent, at a point which he called *Point Delay*, from the circumstances of our detention yesterday; and having received orders from him we carried on. One of the men belonging to sledge No. 2. had his toes frostbitten, but friction with the warm hand re-established the circulation, and no bad results accrued. We encamped at 1 P.M., just in time, for a heavy fall of snow was commencing, which continued till late in the afternoon. As we were pitching our tents, Captain Penny and Mr. Petersen came up with the dog sledges, and encamped. Mr. Stewart, Captain Penny, and Mr. Petersen walked a few miles to the northward, to examine the state of the (*roads*) ice. As the weather proved unfavourable for viewing distant objects, they returned in an hour or two, and reported favourably as far as they had gone.

Encamped at 1 P.M. Hours travelling, 4. Distance, 7 miles. Temps.: noon to midnight, max. −5°, min. −8°; mean of 3 readings, −6·6°.

Soon after Captain Penny's return we were called into his tent, and consulted as to the propriety of returning to the ships, leaving all our provisions, and coming out again in ten days or a fortnight, better provided, and with weather more suitable for travelling than we had since we left the ships on the 17th, only a week ago. He said, "I see your willingness and abilities to proceed *at present* in the journey we have undertaken, and I have no doubt we will be able to carry out to its full extent the object we have in view, even with the preparations we have at present, entirely to our own and the satisfaction of our country; but I think we will be able to do more, to go farther on, and with greater safety to ourselves, if we go back to the ships, remain a week or two, and resume our journey in all respects well provided and fitted by experience for every possible emergency in sledge travelling; our depôts are laid out before us, and we can come here in three days' march, fill up the sledges and start afresh, not from the ships, but nearly fifty miles on our journey." Each of us expressed his opinion, and all seemed to agree we should retreat, but only on the terms that by so doing we should be able to persist longer in the search for Sir J. Franklin, by making our preparations more complete than it was possible they could have been when we set out the first time. For my own part the reasons for retreating were very plausible indeed, although I had a strong inclination to the contrary, and a deeply rooted idea, that the present was the proper time for travelling; when the floe was unbroken, and the snow was crisp and hard, and resisting the sinking tendency of heavily laden sledges; and when the weather was generally clear, keen, and bracing; and, moreover, if we should find traces of the missing ships when we resumed our journey after a fortnight's delay, it might be at a time when the season would be found too far advanced to follow them out satisfactorily, — when the ice would be parting, and long narrow cracks might require to be skirted along for whole days before they could be crossed, — when the snow on the floe would be soft and unresisting, — when the land would be too soft to walk over it, in the event of being forced to that alternative, — when deep ravines and lakes would be sending sweeping and impetuous torrents into the sea, — and when soft, misty, and disagreeable weather might naturally be looked for for days without intermission. These ideas might appear extremely vague in the presence of the expectation that our travelling would be over, after starting a second time, long before such changes could take place.

Return of the party to the ships.

Captain Penny and Mr. Petersen made a depôt of the provisions that were on the dog sledges, and commenced their return to the ships at 5 P.M. Captain Penny left orders with Mr. Stewart to make a second depôt " of all our provisions, two of the four sledges, and all our spare clothing," and to commence our return to the ships, as the state of the weather would allow, early on the following day. The men were a little disconcerted at the idea of " turning back ;" but a few remarks soon put their minds quite at rest with respect to " bad luck " and future difficulties depending upon this unexpected change. There was a good deal of snow and a strong northerly breeze during the whole night. We entertained fears for Captain Penny; but as he had the dogs, and the wind was following him, we might rest satisfied he would arrive at the ships in safety. We began to unpack the sledges at 5 A.M., and having dug a trench as deep as the frozen state of the shingle would allow, our depôt was made according to the orders of Captain Penny. The spare tent poles were set up as marks, and lots of black *tin pots*, the relics of Arctic travelling, were distributed over every conspicuous point in the neighbourhood of the *depôt*. The sky began to clear up, the snow disappeared, the wind was from the S.E., and, from the general appearances of the sky, we had fair promises of tolerable weather for a few days.

April 25th, Friday. Made a depôt, packed up, and started at 7 A.M. Course down channel. Temps.: midnight to noon, max. +5°, min. −8°; mean of 3 readings, −2½°. Winds northerly. Clear sky. Snow.

At 7 A.M. we commenced our journey down the channel, close along the beach, at the rate of at least three and a half miles an hour. We had but two sledges, with about 500 lbs. on each; and thirteen men, with so little weight, could march on with an easy and quick pace, especially where the ice was hard and smooth. At 11 A.M. we passed the depôt made on the 22nd, and by keeping close along the land, we made a straight course to and across Barlow Inlet, where we had luncheon at 1 P.M. The atmosphere was very clear, and the most brilliant parhelia and beautiful arrangements of parhelic circles that I have ever seen were spread over the whole sky. A zone passing through the sun encircled the whole sky, and there were several smaller halos planted on and around it. The red, yellow, and white colours could be made out very distinctly; but there was a decided deficiency with respect to the violet, except in a small elliptical curve near the zenith, where all the colours could be seen very distinctly. There were eight or ten parhelia, and many of them, especially those at the greatest distance from the sun, were a pure white, increasing in brightness and prismatic tints the nearer they were to the sun. A bleak wind came across the floe from S.E., and there was a slight fall of fine snow. We apprehended an easterly storm; consequently we carried on our journey until we rounded Cape Hotham, and encamped to the eastward of the depôt at 4½ P.M. The parhelia at noon were still present on many parts of the sky. The evening was very pleasant, although cold, and there was a thin misty haze pervading the whole atmosphere. The temperature fell from + 5° at noon to − 22° at midnight, and there was a gentle southerly breeze.

Encamped at 4½ P.M. Distance 27 miles. Temps.: noon to midnight, max. +5°, min. −22°; mean of 4 readings, 11−°. Winds easterly. Clear sky.

During the night the blanket bags were very cold indeed. The temperature of the tent was −16°, owing to some carelessness in fastening the *door*, and the consequent admission of wind. An individual in one of the tents found his nose frostbitten in the morning, and had some difficulty in restoring the circulation. Desquamation of the skin (cuticle) was the only bad result. This ought to be a valuable lesson to those who "cannot bear" to sleep with their faces enveloped in the blanket bag. We started at 7 A.M., and proceeded along the beach until we came to the hummocks which we had crossed on our passage out; and having recrossed them without any difficulty, we directed our course (doubtless circuitous enough at times) for the ships. There was a smart breeze during the forenoon, and the snow drifted about a good deal. Before we came in sight of the ships, some, if not all of the men, attempted to wash their faces and hands with soap and snow. The attempt was so far successful; but if their hands and faces were cleaner, they were frostbitten to the bargain. However, we had a good proof of the desire they had to appear clean on their arrival on board the ships. As we came on towards the S.E. point of the harbour, we were met by one of the crew of the Felix, who reported all well in the harbour. After striking through the hummocks, we crossed the S.E. point, and stood on to the ships, which we reached at 1 P.M., and where we were received by Captain Penny, and those of the crew who were

April 26th, Saturday. Packed up, and started at 7 A.M. Course to the westward. Temps.: midnight to noon, max. −8°, min. −22°; mean of −16°. Winds S.E. Snow drift.

Hours travelling, 6. Distance, 18 miles. Arrival at the ships at 1 P.M.

on board, with three hearty cheers, and after a refreshment we began to consider what preparations would be necessary for starting a *second time.*

May 6th, Tuesday. Started from the ships at 7 P.M.

The preparations we engaged in during our stay on board the ships were of various kinds. The carpenters and blacksmith repaired the sledges Nos. 2 and 4, and made two large conjurors which would cook for all hands. They also repaired the small conjurors, which we also took along with us. Double our former allowances of spirits and fuel was provided, and also an additional half allowance of sugar; and as we found gutta percha flasks and drinking cups useful on our former journey, we availed ourselves of the opportunity we now had on board the ships to repair the old, and make *new*, if there was a deficiency.

Arrangements were made that four sledges should be able to remain out forty days from the "fifty mile depôt," and one sledge thirty days from the ships. The first separation was to take place at the depôt. Two sledges were to take the western route, while three were to cross the Wellington Channel, and having reached the opposite shore to the northward of latitude 75°, if possible, the thirty day sledge would proceed down the channel to Beechey Island and Cape Hurd, and examine all the intermediate coast. The other two sledges would carry on the *search* to the northward as circumstances would permit. Preparations were also made for travelling with the dogs by Mr. Petersen, whose extensive experience entitled him to a prominent position in all our arrangements.

Temps.: max. +11°, min. −4°; mean of 6 readings, +3°. Clear weather. Winds variable. Course easterly to Cape Hotham.

Our sledges were ready the day before; but as the weather happened to be unfavourable we were detained until it should suit our purpose. Early in the morning a party belonging to the Felix arrived from the squadron at Griffith's Island, bringing reports of the return of the fatigue parties from Cape Walker and other directions. The reports conveyed to us, that the parties had seen nothing of the missing ships, and that many of them were suffering severely from frostbites and snow blindness. The sky was remarkably clear during the day, and as there seemed to be indications of a continuation of good weather we started at 7 P.M., having first assembled to prayers on board the Lady Franklin. The greatest part of the crew of the Felix accompanied us out of the bay, and left us, with renewed cheering, at half-past eight, after we had fairly embarked on the smooth ice leading along the beach to Cape Hotham. Towards midnight the wind increased to a smart breeze, and snowdrift began to whirl about and to give us a little annoyance. After leaving Dungeness Point, we had to strike off to the smooth floe outside the hummocks. It was hard and crisp, and the sledges moved along very easily, for there were eleven or twelve

May 7th, Wednesday. Encamped at 4 A.M. Hours travelling, 9. Distance, 16 miles. Temps.: midnight to noon, max. +10°, min. −7°; mean of 5 read-

men to each, and the weights only amounted to about 140 lbs. per man.

ings, $+\frac{1}{2}^{\circ}$. Winds northerly. Snow drift.

At 4 A.M. we encamped at the base of the huge bluff west of Cape Hotham. The morning was squally, and there was a good deal of snow drifting. The temperature fell to -7°, but at noon it was up to $+10^{\circ}$. The sky was clear, and there were parhelia east and west of the sun. A man required to be sent back to the ships to bring out a canvas floor-cloth belonging to No. 1, when the dog sledges would start. Our new cooking vessels suited remarkably well, but the quantity of fuel which they required was enormous, being considerably above $2\frac{1}{2}$ lbs. per sledge per day. I found that my tent had undergone great improvement in Mr. Reid's hands, for the door, which would hardly meet before, now laced tightly up ; and when the pipes were lighted the temperature generally ranged from $+15^{\circ}$, $+25^{\circ}$, $+30^{\circ}$, and $+35^{\circ}$ to $+40^{\circ}$, and everything around us breathed an air of comfort which made one feel happy. We had abundance of water to drink, and during our resting and sleeping hours each could allay his thirst when he *chose*, although at times it was necessary to exercise a little patience, lest one should waken his sleeping companions in his attempt to search out the water flask, which was generally protected from the cold by being placed *between* the blanket bags

Packed up, and started at 7 P.M. Temps.: noon to midnight, max. $+10^{\circ}$, min. $+1^{\circ}$; mean of 9 readings, $+3\cdot6^{\circ}$. Winds westerly. Sky clear. Parhelia.

At 7 P.M. we started, and proceeded at a quick rate along the land. The snow was quite firm, and the sledges never required a *second pull*. The sky was very clear. The opposite shore of Barrow's Straits could be seen very distinctly. Two prismatic parhelia attended the sun, and were extended vertically so as to resemble portions of a halo. The temperature was about zero, and suited very well for travelling. Probably it would have been found too warm, but we were in the shade, for the sun had gone down behind the high land at Cape Hotham. Just as we were rounding that rugged headland, we observed a bear prowling among the hummocks, and as his curiosity seemed to encourage us to the chase, we stopped the sledges, and made attempts to get within musket-shot of him, but he soon took fright at so large a party, which could not have been hid from him, and bounded across the floe directly away from us. At 10 P.M. we saw the bold bluff on the north side of Barlow Inlet, and took luncheon at the foot of it at midnight. The land here begins to be very precipitous ; in some parts sloping at an angle of 50° to 56°, and frequently interrupted by perpendicular and even overhanging escarpments of the strata thirty to forty feet in height. By a rough guess I estimated the dip of the strata at 45°. As we were coming along from Cape Hotham to Barlow Inlet, the sun could be seen beaming from the northern horizon through that inlet, and his rays, striking the hummocks at right angles, produced a glazed ap-

May 8th, Thursday. Encamped at 2 A.M. Hours travelling 7. Distance, 17 miles. Temps.: midnight to noon, max. $+22^{\circ}$, min. $+1^{\circ}$; mean of 5 readings, $+7\cdot4^{\circ}$. Winds southerly. Strong breeze. Snow storm.

pearance which was well seen every moment as our eyes came within the sphere of the *reflected* rays.

Soon after midnight the wind came away with a constant fall of snow from S.W. Indeed we expected this, for the sky in that direction became overcast very suddenly an hour or two previously. We arrived at the first depôt at 2 P.M., and encamped on the shingle. The weather continued stormy, and the wind veered round a few degrees to the eastward of south. We found that the depôt had been disturbed by foxes, if not also by bears. Bread and pork bags were torn open, and their contents considerably destroyed. One of the latter, weighing 77 lbs., was dragged at least forty yards from the depôt, and pieces of the pork in it had numerous impressions of the teeth of the fox. The weather was very stormy all day. There was a smart gale from the southward, with a copious fall of soft snow. The tents were very warm, and some of the men turned into their blanket bags as they would have turned into their beds on board ship, yet they never felt the least cold.

Packed up at 9 P.M. Course up channel along the beach. Temps.: noon to midnight, max. +22°, min. +1°; mean of 5 readings, +10·2°. Winds southerly. Snow.

At 9 P.M. we packed up, and started. There was a strong breeze from the southward, accompanied by a constant fall of soft snow. We set sails on our sledges, and went on very fast. On the smooth ice, coming over wreaths of snow, one of the sledges was upset, but sustained no damage. It was righted without unpacking; and if the provisions, &c. had not shifted their position, it must have been owing to a well-adapted *cover*. Towards midnight the sky began to clear up, and the thermometer fell to −4°; the wind became more westerly, and violent gusts came down the deep ravines which we passed. In some parts of our track the recent snow-storms had raised up wreaths, which required a little unusual exertion before the sledges were got over them. About ten miles to the northward of Barlow Inlet the land begins to be less precipitous. Rounded hills, and a greater breadth of beach, begin to appear. The coast line runs about due north and south, with the exception of a few degrees east or west occasionally on either side of deep ravines. The strata have a dip of about 45 degrees.

At midnight we came up to and passed Point Delay, and at 2 A.M. we encamped at the depôt, which was exactly as we had left it on the 25th of April. After breakfast two or three persons went on, for a mile or two, in the direction we would require to follow, and on their return their report was not by any means encouraging with respect to the *road*. Deep snow among the hummocks and on the beach, we had no doubt would increase our labours very much, and more especially at that time when each sledge was to be completed for the forty days' journey out of the depôt. At 2 P.M. Mr. Petersen's well-known shouting to the dogs was heard, and in a few minutes Captain Penny's arrival, with two dog

May 9th, Friday. Encamped at the depôt at 2 A.M. Hours travelling,

sledges, was announced, and orders were received to open the depôt, and fill up the sledges, to be ready to start at 8 P.M. The evening was very clear, and beautiful fleecy clouds were dispersed over the whole sky. Prismatic parhelia could be seen on both sides of the sun till after midnight. There was a thin mist floating in the atmosphere; but withal distant objects were remarkably well seen.

5. Distance, 14 miles. Temps.: midnight to noon, max. −2°, min. −6°; mean of 4 readings, −3°. Winds westerly. Clear sky. Captain Penny's arrival.

A small party, of which I happened to be one, travelled about five miles to the northward, to explore the road, and discern the state of the ice across the channel. For the first two miles there was a great depth of snow; but after this, having crossed the termination of a deep ravine, where a large body of water must enter the sea on each return of the season, we came to a smooth sheet of ice running close along the beach inside the hummocks, and varying in breadth from fifteen to thirty or forty yards. We congratulated the western party on such good road, and hoped they would find it so to the end of their journey. At 3.45 P.M. we ascended an eminence, and commanded a splendid view of the Wellington Channel and the land on its opposite shore. We could see Cape Bowden quite distinctly, and the land to the northward of it. Close to the northward there appeared to be a deep bay, with a small island or table-like promontory in the south side of it. The sun shone in the face of the land, and from the numerous *black* spots we could see, our inference was, "that the season must have been further advanced there than on the *Cornwallis side*." The ice in the channel presented nothing to discourage us, although certainly it was hummocky enough in many parts. The sun bore per azimuth compass north 24° E. The north side of the bay distinguished by a small ravine, terminating in a heap beneath, in the face of a large bluff, bore south 16° W. On our return to the sledges we found them packed up, except the tents. The depôt had been dug up, and each sledge claimed its own provisions, &c. &c. Four sledges were fully equipped for forty days, each weighing at least 1500 lbs., and one sledge for thirty days, weighing about 1200 lbs. We ascended a hill with Captain Penny. It was about four miles south of the last position where a bearing had been taken. The north side of the bay bore per azimuth south 13° W.; south side, or Cape Bowden, south 20° W.; and Cape Spencer south 74° W. Captain Penny pointed out to Mr. Stewart the necessity there was he should keep a little southerly at first, and after proceeding eight or ten miles he would find the best ice leading him in the direction he wished to make good in crossing the channel.

Compass bearings, &c. Packed up, and started at 8 P.M. Course up and across the Wellington Channel. Temps.: noon to midnight, max. −2°, min. −9°; mean of 6 readings, −6°. Winds westerly. Moderate. Sky clear.

The tents were struck, and the sledges were fairly packed up. A depôt of one bag of dog pemmican, a small bag of bread, and one case, 90 lbs., of pemmican, was left, partly for our return, but principally because all the sledges had full allowance without them. At 8 P.M. we started, and by double manning the sledges for a mile and a half along the beach, we reached the ravine where the floe and hummocks offered the best chances of embarking with safety. Captain Penny bade all of us good-bye, by shaking hands with every individual; and after the usual cheering we parted, and stood across the channel, with the floor-cloths set as sails, to take advantage of a gentle breeze that sprung up from the westward. The floe proved very good, and certainly we required it, for the sledges felt remarkably heavy after the easy dragging we had been accustomed to for three days previously. I found the repairs No. 4., the "Perseverance," had received had improved it very much, but Mr. Stewart's sledge, No. 2., the "Sylph," which went very well on our former journey, was anything but improved by the repairs it required, and it proved a heavy drag until it was considerably lightened; indeed I may say to the end of the journey. Mr. J. Stuart's sledge, No. 5., being one of the two that had been left at the *depôt*, went very easily, and required little or no assistance to get through the worst hummocks we had to cross. There was a range of heavy ice leading to the eastward, which prevented us making a straight course for the north side of the *bay*. After making an offing of about ten miles, we encamped at half-past 3 A.M. The sky was overcast with a white misty haze, and there was a gentle south-westerly breeze. The floe we crossed was this year's formation, but early in the season it was covered with snow, in which the sledges did not sink above a quarter of an inch. Had it formed since the first of January, it would have been at a low temperature; and we should have found the snow on it soft and unresisting, for the reason, that salt in and on its upper surface would maintain that soft condition even at comparatively low temperatures.

May 10th, Saturday. Encamped at 3½ A.M. Hours travelling, 7½. Distance, 12 miles. Temps.: midnight to noon, max. +7°, min. −9°; mean of 4 readings, −1°. Winds westerly. Moderate. Overcast and misty sky.

9 P.M. started. Course N.E., but varying. Temps.: noon to midnight, max. +9°. min. −2°; mean of 6 readings, +4·73°. Winds south-westerly. Moderate. Misty overcast sky.

At 6 P.M. we were roused out, and after a hearty *meal* of tea and pemmican we started at 9 P.M., and proceeded to the north-eastward, as the state of the ice permitted. The accumulation of snow among the hummocks was a constant source of difficulty. The sledges frequently required double manning, and we were glad to encamp at 5 A.M., having travelled about twelve miles. The "Sylph," No. 2. required to have some weight transferred to the other two sledges. No. 5. took a bag of pork weighing 77 lbs., and No. 4. a bag of fat weighing 40 lbs. I could not help thinking she would have to yield up the palm, according to the motto in her flag, "*Palmam qui meruit ferat.*" One of the men picked up a small *amphipodous* crustacean, which puzzled me not a little to know how it found its way to the surface of the floe. Everything we saw at variance with the pure white colour of

May 11th, Sunday. Encamped at 5 A.M. Hours travelling, 8. Distance, 12 miles. Temps.: midnight to noon, max. +26°, min. −2°; mean of 5 readings, +10°. Winds south. Moderate. Weather misty. Temps.: noon to midnight, max. +26°, min. +4°; mean of 9 readings, +9·5.

the snow attracted attention. A flat cake of tarry looking substance in a frozen state was picked up from *among* the snow. It seemed to be the excrement of a bear, and was entirely made up of the *secretions* of the intestinal apparatus and biliary matters. We observed *old ice*, which could be distinguished by the rounded elevations and creamy or yellowish colour of its upper surface. It was so extensive that we could not see all around it, and the direction of the hummocks along its margin made our route very circuitous, trending, as it did, too little to the northward. After breakfast we went over the *Morning Service*, and having spent an hour or two in such conversation as might amuse and be useful, we went to sleep. The tents were very warm and comfortable. In one of them, the thermometer indicated +60°, and boots and stockings hung up on the ridge rope thawed and dried. The sky was overcast at noon, but towards evening it cleared up, and Mr. J. Stuart took bearings and angles by the azimuth compass. We supposed ourselves to be about mid-channel, but could not make up our minds as to the *exact* distance we were from either side. It was sufficient for our purpose at that time to lay down correct bearings, courses, and hours travelling, and ascertain the latitude when the weather might prove favourable.

Winds northerly. Moderate. Cloudy sky. Compass bearings: Cape Hotham, N. 23° W. 142° 10′. Bw. Inlet, N. 12° 40′ W. 150° 1′. Point Separation, N. 19° 20′ E. 181° 40′. Round Hill, N. 30° 26′ E. 192° 28′. North Point, N. 85° 20′ E. 259° 18′. North Bluff, S. 6° 10′ E. 336° 6′. Northernmost Land, S. 31° 30′ E. 310° 56′. North Cape, S. 2° 20′ E. 345° 10′. South Cape, S. 43° W. 29° 20′. Cape Bowden, S. 51° 30′ W. 39° 25′. Cape Spencer, N. 80° 50′ W. 77° 44′.

We were called out at 10 P.M., and at half-past 12, midnight, we commenced our march. The sky was overcast throughout its whole extent, except along the horizon, where the azure tint, always so charming, could be seen. The thermometer ranged about zero, and there was a gentle breeze. We passed along the edge of the *old ice* for a short time, and finding it leading to the northward we lost sight of it, and crossed a portion of new ice, which was a little hummocky, and required an extra pull at the sledges. We soon came to a second *old floe*, which we were forced to cross, because the north and south extremities of it could not be seen. The sledges came along it tolerably well; but the constant jerking, as the drag ropes tightened and slackened alternately, did not agree with us, after we had been accustomed to one steady and heavy pull on the level floe. We were about an hour in crossing the old floe, and from this its breadth was estimated at two miles. The next ice we came to was entirely the formation of last winter, for it did not present a hummock as far as the eye could reach. It was not unpleasant to move along at a steady and easy step. The step of the headmost party was always too slow for us by half a mile an hour, in consequence of the heavy dragging their sledge required. We had luncheon at the usual time, four hours after starting, and at 9 A.M. we encamped within six or eight miles of the land. At noon, and during this encampment, the temperature in the tents was about +50°, and our boots and moccassins that were hung up inside the tent were

May 12th, Monday. Started at ½ to 1 A.M. Hours travelling, 8½. Distance, 13 miles. Encamped at 9 A.M. Temps.: midnight to noon, max. +6°, min. −1°; mean of 9 readings, +39°. Wind moderate.

Temps.: noon to midnight, max. +6°, min. −1°; mean of 3 readings, +2½°. Winds northerly. Misty weather. Snow.

continually dropping water on our wolfskins and blanket bags. Towards afternoon, the sky became overcast with a misty haze, and there was a slight fall of snow; but as the evening advanced, the azure sky began to open out into view, and fantastic cobweb-cirro-cumuli beautified it to the north-eastward. The general appearances of the sky did not forbode favourable weather.

May 13th, Tuesday. Packed up, and started at 1 A.M. Landed at $3\frac{1}{2}$ A.M. Distance, 7 miles. Mr. J. Stuart made a small depôt, and parted company at $5\frac{1}{4}$ A.M. Course to the northward about 12° or 15° westerly. Encamped at $9\frac{1}{4}$ A.M. Distance from depôt, 6 miles. Hours travelling, $6\frac{1}{2}$. Temps.: midnight to noon, max. +11°, min. −5°; mean of 8 readings, $+2\frac{1}{2}$°. Winds northerly. Smart breeze. Weather gloomy. Snow drift.

At 1 A.M. we started, and found the snow on the floe quite firm as we proceeded in the direction of the bluff, on the northern side of the *bay*. The temperature at 3 A.M. fell to −5°, and there was a smart northerly breeze. The sky was generally overcast, but not unfrequently the clouds became detached and opening, and prismatic parhelia could be seen to advantage over the land we were approaching. At $3\frac{1}{2}$ A.M. we came to the edge of the hummocks extending along the land and halted. Mr. J. Stuart supplied about forty pounds of bread and thirty pounds of pemmican, which we left as a depôt to fall back upon, if *necessary*. A small cairn was erected on a conspicuous point on the top of the bluff, which is 650 to 700 feet high, and a second cairn was erected at the foot of the bluff, on a prominent point, thirty or forty feet above the level of the sea. The provisions were put into the lower cairn, and the following printed notice in a gutta percha envelope was left between two flat stones in the top of it:—

"13th day of May, 1851. Left by a searching party from H.M. brigs, Lady Franklin and Sophia, at present lying in north latitude 74° 40′, west longitude 94° 16′.

"AL. STEWART, Officer,
"Commanding party.

"Depôts of provisions, &c., at Whaler Point and Cape Hay on the south shore, and Cape Spencer, and five miles W. of Cape Hotham. Expedition under Captain Austin at Griffith's Island, one under Sir John Ross in harbour twelve miles west of Cape Hotham, along with the above brigs under Captain Penny. "SOPHIA."

There are two bluffs, with intervening bays, between this table bluff and a low point to the northward; the latter is shut in from this position by the northernmost of the other two bluffs; but it can be seen to the westward of and beyond them, from Cape Bowden, which in its turn bears to the westward of south from the cairn. On the low point where the depôt was left, we observed the footprints of a bear in the soil, which must have been left some time after the summer had been pretty well through, for from the middle of September to the middle of June, everything is possessed of icy hardness, and the frozen soil is able to support the weight of any creature without receiving impressions of its feet.

At half-past 5 A.M. we parted company with Mr. Stuart, who had instructions to examine and survey the *bay*, and proceed down the channel along the land, to Beechey Island, &c. We found the floe leading to the northward a little hummocky, but they were not of that huge size which would require great care to advance among them. This *superficial* roughness, and *brecciated* structure of the surface, must have been caused by pressure when the ice was only two to five or six inches thick, and maintained in this state by subsequent increase in thickness from below. The disturbed pieces assumed every shape, size, and position, and appeared to the *eye* as if the pressure had been but a few days previously. We had no doubt but the ice we were walking over was *new* ice, and our impressions were, that there had been open water in that part of the channel some time last season; but to what extent, and whether continuous with open water in Barrow Straits, were points full of interest, but involved in doubts which we hardly possessed the means of solving; with the exception, perhaps, of this single fact, that we had to cross *old ice* in our journey across the channel.

Temps.: noon to midnight, max. +11°, min. +2°; mean of 3 readings, +5½. Winds northerly. Smart breeze. Snow drift. Violent.

At half-past 9 A.M. we encamped at the second table bluff, in the *lee* of very high hummocks which prevented us getting to the beach. The wind had increased to a strong breeze, and the snow was drifting with considerable violence. Mr. Stuart and I went to the top of the bluff, which is about 700 feet high, and certainly the view we had of the ice in the channel repaid the hard toil we had in ascending. We observed the snow thawing on stones on the south side of the bluff, and the well-known purple saxifrage was beginning to show its stunted green leaves. We saw no game, but abundance of the dung of hares, deer, and ptarmigan; and one of the men picked up a deer's antlers, which he found partially imbedded in the shingle, thirty to forty feet above the beach. We expected to start at 10 P.M.; but the weather was so exceedingly violent, that it was considered prudent to remain in the tents until it should moderate.

May 14th, Wednesday. Packed up, and started at 6 A.M. Course along the land to the northward. Encamped at noon. Latitude, 75° 21′. Temps.: midnight to noon, max. +14°, min. +2°; mean of 5 readings, +7°. Hours travelling, 6. Distance, 11 miles. Winds northerly. Weather clear.

When we packed up, and resumed our journey, the temperature was +4°, and there was a keen breeze. The sky was clear, and the snow drift was beginning to cease. Some of the men suffered from slight frostbites of the face and nose; but as the day advanced, I ceased to detect anything of that kind. The snow on the floe was very firm, and when hummocks came in the way they were sure to demand an extra pull, if not double manning, before the sledges were got over. Our greatest distance from the land did not exceed one mile, but not unfrequently we were within a few hundred yards of it. Our eyes were continually examining the hitherto unknown coast; and they went over the ground oftener *than once*, as our weary feet trudged along the path-

Temps.: noon to midnight, max. +14°, min. +3°; mean of 6 readings, +10°. Winds northerly. Clear and pleasant weather.

less and snowy plain. As might be supposed, every object that appeared to possess the slightest deviation from the *natural* disposition of things attracted attention, with the fond hope that it might be some relic of our missing countrymen. We passed the low point alluded to on the 12th and 13th, and found the coast line trending to the eastward of north 12° or 13°; and there were several conspicuous table bluffs planted in it, until it seemed to turn suddenly to the eastward. After proceeding about four miles to the northward of the low point, eleven miles from our last encampment, we pitched the tents at noon, and found the latitude, by correct observations, 75° 21′. One of our conjurors was lost about an hour before we halted. We could have done without it; but the cook for that day was a determined person, and the idea of any bad results in consequence of his neglect were plausible enough reasons for permitting him to return to look for it. In less than an hour he arrived with the lost article, and there seemed to be a feeling that greater care would be observed for the future. As far as we could see from the sledges, the floe appeared to be very smooth in every direction, except along the land, where there were enormous hummocks. Some of the men were suffering from snow-blindness; but I expected a few hours' seclusion from light would restore them to their usual healthy state. The life we were leading with the track belt over our shoulders, and a heavy sledge to drag along, *seemed* to agree well with us, if sound sleep and a keen appetite be signs of good health.

May 15th, Thursday. Packed up, and started at 1½ A.M. Course north, a little easterly. Encamped at 9½ A.M. Hours travelling, 8. Distance, 12 miles. Temps.: midnight to noon, max. +22°, min. −2°; mean of 5 readings, +9½. Winds moderate. S.E. Weather clear.

We began to pack up at midnight, and at half-past 1 A.M. we were again moving along. The snow was very firm and resisting; the sledges came along very well, and we began to think them considerably lighter, although we had only used five days' provisions out of them. When the sledges were packing up, a bird flew past in the direction of the land; it was a ptarmigan. At 6 A.M., as we proceeded along the land. Mr. Stewart and I left the sledges to carry on, and went to the land, where we erected a small cairn, and left the usual *note.* The beach sloped gradually with wavy interruptions from the ordinary height of 600 feet at the bluffs and inland to the water's edge. The cairn is in one of the shallow bays which generally intervene between precipitous bluffs; and there are two such to be seen along the coast line to the northward before the northern extremity of the eastern boundary of the Wellington Channel is reached. This, for present distinction's sake, we called "The North Headland;" and as we came up to it, it was found possessed of a feature by which it cannot fail to be recognised afterwards (so long as that feature remains),—an isolated mass of rock rising in the face of the almost perpendicular bluff, and opening out when its bearing is north 15° to 40° E., and south 15° to 40° W. The bluff presents a bold and terraced appearance when viewed from the N.W.; and the rows of buttresses and lines of stratification are perfectly horizontal and conformable. It descends rapidly to the water's edge, and there is hardly any beach. (Perhaps the latter can be accounted for by the disintegrated rocks being conveyed away in great quantity by the drifting ice, which must attack so prominent a point with great force.)

The ice was raised into enormous hummocks close along the land; and at the N.W. point of the north headland the pressure to have raised such masses must have been very great. We encamped close to the hummocks, at the edge of a smooth floe which extended to the N.E. on the inside of a range of hummocky ice about a mile from the land. It is very probable that at an advanced period of last season the whole body of ice, both *old* and very recent, shifted to the westward and north-westward, during a violent storm, leaving a space of water open along the land, which became frozen over very suddenly in easy weather, and acquired sufficient thickness to resist the ordinary tidal pressure, until by further increase it might be capable of withstanding the pressure of the ice to the north-westward; which, in consequence of not having room to shift about, would be reduced to a state of perfect rest; but this is on the presumption that it meets with resistance to the north-west, which prevents it drifting away altogether when the shift takes place.

Temps.: noon to midnight, max. +22°, min. +5°; mean, +13½°. Winds south-easterly; moderate. Weather gloomy. Cloudy and overcast sky.

The sky became overcast at noon; there was no observation, and there seemed no chance of obtaining the latitude by ex-meridian altitudes. At 4 A.M. we packed up, and started. The sky began to clear up, and we could see very low land stretching to the northward at a great distance to the eastward. The smooth floe led us along the land at a distance of about a quarter of a mile, and we could see the raised beaches very distinctly, after proceeding about three miles to the north-eastward of the north headland. Mr. Stewart sent me to the land, to examine what appeared to resemble a cairn. It proved to be a conical mass of compact limestone, which by its greater hardness resisted the disintegrating action of alternations of heat and cold together with moisture better than the rock around it. I saw two ptarmigan, but my attempt to shoot them with ball was unsuccessful. I soon overtook the sledges, and fell into my place on the track rope. We passed some cubic blocks of salt-water ice which appeared to be at least thirty feet square above the ordinary level of the floe. The ice around them was a good deal broken up, and the pressure seemed to have been at some period since last summer.

May 16th, Friday. Packed up, and started at 4 A.M. Course N.E. and N. 55° E. Encamped at 10½ A.M. Hours travelling, 6½. Distance, 12 miles. Temps.: midnight to noon, max. +22°, min. +5°; mean of 6 readings, +10°. Winds south-westerly. Sky clear. Weather very fine.

After proceeding about twelve miles, we encamped at half-past 10 A.M. about a mile from the land; and as Mr. Stewart was under the necessity of remaining at the tents, to take observations at noon, I received orders to proceed to the land, and erect a cairn on a low round hill bearing about east of our encampment. Mr. Reid volunteered to accompany me. On landing we parted. I took to the eastward, and Mr. Reid went directly inland. In making the best of my way to the hill, I ascended to a height of about 250 feet; crossed extensive patches of vegetation; saw abundance of recent hares' dung; and, while crossing a patch of snow on a slope with a southern exposure, something attracted my attention. It proved to be a hare. I fired and wounded it, but it escaped, spinning away on its hind legs, and my time did not permit of continuing the chase. I examined where it had been lying, and found a burrow extending longitudinally about eight feet, but never exceeding five or six inches beneath the surface of the snow. After travelling about four miles, I reached the hill, and discovered a bay, but owing to the lurid state of the atmosphere in that direction on the horizon, it was impossible to make out its true extent. From the foot of the hill, which is about 200 feet high, the land inclined a few degrees to the southward of E., perhaps E. 11° S., then east, north-east, north, and north-west, until it seemed to sink out of view beneath the horizon, bearing about north of the encampments. I could see the raised beaches in succession extending to the opposite shore of the bight or bay; and there seemed to be very heavy ice in it from side to side. The atmosphere to the westward was very clear; I saw the land on the opposite side of the channel, leading away to the westward, with a slight trend to the northward; and from this point to about north, or north 20° W. there was a space in which nothing but a clear *ice-blink* could be seen. *So much for the continuity of land across the top of the Wellington Channel.*

Temps.: noon to midnight, max. +22°, min. +5°; mean of 3 readings, +10½°. Weather clear. Winds southerly. Latitude, 75° 34′.

On my return to the sledges along the gently undulating land, I found the bones of whales imbedded in the soil, and surrounded with vegetation, at a height of at least 250 feet above the level of the sea. How they came there, and were buried in the soil, or shingle, exceeds my comprehension, unless I begin to speculate, for which this is hardly the place. As I came down to the beach, and walked along at an elevation of twenty feet, circular arrangements of stone attracted my attention. They were two feet in diameter, and several of them that were examined, conveyed the idea that they were fire-places, for immediately beneath the moss, which always occupied the surface, there was a collection of ashes and burned bones, and beneath this, again, the stones which had not suffered from the fire were cemented together by a varnish-like substance, resembling the fluid parts of animal matter in a dry state. By whom they had been used, and when, were questions with which I scarcely ventured to tax myself, although it would have been highly interesting to follow out everything that might tend to throw light upon so dark a subject. At 3 P.M. I returned to the tents, and reported to Mr. Stewart what had come under my observations.

At midnight we packed up, and started. The floe proved very good, after a little trouble in getting through a ridge of sharp hummocks to the northward of our encampment. It was quite blue and glassy in many parts, although it seemed to have been much broken up when only eight to ten inches thick. The sharp angular fragments could be seen sticking up half a foot to a foot, and even two feet, above the surface. These small hummocks do not hinder a sledge, because it rests on three or four at a time. We encamped at a quarter past 9 A.M.; and certainly I was very glad, for yesterday's exposure for such a length of time to the intense rays reflected from the snow had reduced me to a state of almost utter helplessness by snow-blindness. Our latitude was 75° 41′, having advanced about fourteen miles.

May 17th, Saturday. Packed up, and started soon after midnight. Course about east, 30° to 35° north. Hours travelling, 9. Encamped at 9¼ A.M. Temps. max. +35°, min. +1°; mean of 6 readings, +9°. Winds northerly. Distance travelled, 14 miles. Latitude, 75° 41′. Packed up, and started at 10 P.M. Course to the eastward. Temps.: noon to midnight, max. +35°, min. +3°; mean of 4 readings, +12⅜°. Winds easterly. Lurid atmosphere.

At 10 P.M. we packed up, and started. The floe was anything but good. Our sledge felt unusually heavy, and we suspected some accident had happened to it. It was examined, and two of the stretchers were found broken. We patched them up with the stretcher of the tent; packed up afresh, and proceeded after the other sledge, which had got a good way a-head of us. We required double manning occasionally, until at 3 A.M. we landed on a low flat beach, and encamped, having travelled about six miles to the eastward. The sky was overcast, and there was a constant fall of soft snow. Some of us were suffering from snow-blindness. We estimated our distance from the ships at one hundred and fifty statute miles, following the winding course the sledges had made. After a hearty breakfast of coffee, bread, pork, and pemmican, and having gone over the *Morning Service*, we went to sleep. No watch was kept, and no danger was apprehended. Neither bears nor foxes excited the least alarm. Should they prowl about our tents and sledges during our sleep, perhaps they might get a warm reception from our muskets, which we took care to have close at hand. We intended to have started early in the afternoon, but the weather still continued thick; there was a constant fall of snow; and, above all, there was present in an intense degree that peculiar condition of the atmosphere which proves so injurious to the eyes; Mr. Stewart, therefore, thought proper not to start until the weather should prove more favourable.

May 18th, Sunday. Encamped at 3 A.M. Course about east. Hours travelled, 5. Distance, 6 miles. Temps: midnight to noon, max. +29°, min. +3°; mean of 7 readings, +12°. Winds south-westerly; moderate. Dense misty atmosphere. Snow.

At 10 P.M. we commenced to unpack the sledges, and to form a *depôt* of five days' provisions from Mr. Stewart's sledge. No. 4. supplied 22 lbs. of fat and two gallons of spirits, which went to form the depôt; we also left spare boots and clothing, a spare conjuror, and a wolf-skin blanket; altogether my sledge was lightened about 120 lbs., and Mr. Stewart's about 280 lbs. We had one great consolation, that

Made our first depôt, 150 miles from the ships. Temps.: noon to midnight, max. +25, min. +23°; mean of 4 readings, +20°. Winds south-westerly. Misty and snowy weather.

the weight of our sledges would be diminishing at the rate of eighteen to twenty pounds a day. We dug a trench as deep as the frozen shingle would allow, and having placed all the articles in it in the form of a heap, loose gravel was heaped up until everything was buried six or eight inches beneath the surface; and then snow was heaped over the shingle, pressing it together with the shovels. A conspicuous cairn was erected at the end of the mound, but not upon it, and for this reason: bears or foxes, or both together, might attack the provisions in the depôt, and in doing so the cairn would be in danger of being pulled down, and the consequences of our *mark* being destroyed might lead to difficulties in finding the *depôt*, if not to missing it altogether.

May 19th, Monday. Started at 3 A.M. Course about N. over the low land. Encamped at 9 A.M. Hours travelling, 6. Distance, 11 miles. Temps.: midnight to noon, max. +17°, min. +7°; mean of 8 readings +12°. Winds north-westerly; strong breeze. Stormy snowy weather.

Temps.: noon to midnight, max. +13°, min. +8°; mean of 5 readings +10°. Winds N.W.; strong breeze. Weather stormy. Snow-drift.

At 3 A.M. we started, and proceeded across the beach in the direction of a point which bears about north, or perhaps a few degrees to the eastward of north. It seemed to be near the edge of the hummocks, and the best thing we could do was to go straight for it, provided we should never lose sight of the beach while going over a point of flat land which could hardly be distinguished from the floe outside, except by the range of squeezed up ice that intervened between them. Very soon after we had started a violent snow storm came on. The snow drifted about, and annoyed us very much, and we had great difficulties in keeping our course. In this respect, occasional glimpses of *the point* proved very serviceable. We could see the ice along the beach at all times. The snow was deep on the land, and what had fallen *recently* allowed the sledges to sink the whole depth of the *runners*. We passed *Esquimaux ruins* which were recognised by their circular arrangement, and by accumulations of the vertebræ, jaw bones, and ribs of whales. At 9 A.M we were forced to encamp, after travelling only eleven miles. Some of the sailors thought the *old bones* should give out heat by burning, and could hardly be convinced to the contrary, until they tried them. We had clear sunshine at noon, but the horizon was obscured by the drifting snow, and consequently no meridian altitude could be obtained.

May 20th, Tuesday. 24 hours' DETENTION. Temps.: max. +13°, min. +9°; mean of 10 readings +11½°. Winds north-west. Strong breeze. Weather stormy. Snow-drift.

When we expected to have started the weather was very stormy; the wind blew keenly from the N.W., and the snow still drifted along with great violence. We could see the azure sky towards the zenith, but the horizon was always obscure. Our tents, blanket bags, amusing conversation, music, and sleep, were, each in their turn, taxed to pass the time, without allowing it to be tedious.

At 10 P.M. the blue sky began to open out *on the horizon* to the northward, and we could distinguish the land extending out so far as to bear about north 22° W. The point a-head, bearing to the eastward of due north, seemed to have a bay beyond it, and the land beyond it again could be traced out to the westward, but not so far as the N.N.W.

point, which gave the latter the appearance of an island. The sky cleared up soon after midnight, and cumulo strati and cirro strati appeared on the northern part of the sky; but the atmosphere still remained quite thick over the land to the south and south-west. The temperature fell to $+2\frac{1}{2}°$; the snow was quite crisp and resisting, and we expected the sledges would come along very easily. We packed up, and started at *four* A.M., and proceeded in the direction of the point which we *then* knew by the designation *Rough Point*. No sooner had we started than the snow came away again, and the wind veered round to S.W., and ultimately back again to N.W. We could hardly distinguish objects 200 yards before us. As the hummocks led along, we had to follow, however circuitous the route that might require to be made. We observed masses of half decayed grounded ice of last season standing as they had been raised by pressure from the westward and north-westward in *autumn*, *when* there must have been open water in this quarter. For four hours after starting the coast-line led away to the northward, and after this it flew away to W. 20° north, until we came to a point where we encamped at noon, and found the latitude 75° 55′.

May 21st, Wednesday.

Packed up, and started at 4 A.M. Course realised N.W. Distance travelled, 16 miles. Hours travelling, 8. Encamped at noon. Latitude 75° 55′. Temps.: midnight to noon, max. +31°, min. $+2\frac{1}{2}$; mean of 9 readings +12°. Winds N.W. Strong breeze. Snow.

As we crossed the *Rough Point*, a great many Esquimaux ruins were observed, and Mr. Stewart thought he saw some ptarmigan flying about them. Just as we were encamping, the weather began to improve; the thermometer rose to +31°, and the snow was melting on the side of the tent. The men had a very satisfactory *wash* with soap and snow; and after so much bad weather we felt so comfortable and so cheerful with prospects of better weather, that we began to think *nothing* of Arctic travelling. At midnight we began to pack up. A small cairn was erected on the point, and the usual note was left in it by Mr. Stewart. The weather still appeared unsettled. The sky was clear and open, except on the horizon to the southward. The sun was attended by two parhelia, but they were deficient in the prismatic colours, and we could see cirri and cirro-strati over all the sky, except to the southward. We could distinguish a small island bearing about south 6° or 10° east, and three to four miles to the westward of the rough point.

Temps.: noon to midnight, max. +31°, min. $+4\frac{1}{2}°$; mean of 3 readings +13°. Winds easterly, very light. Sky cloudy.

At 1 A.M. we commenced our journey. Our course was principally N.W., across a long flat beach, which seemed to extend at least ten miles inland, without an elevation of as many feet, and once or twice across what seemed to resemble lagunes, but it was very doubtful whether the sea flowed into them. The impression on my mind was, that it did not; for although there were *small* hummocks of ice and snow in them, it was not necessary that they should have been raised by pressure from the sea. There might have been a foot of water over the whole surface last season, in

May 22nd, Thursday. Started at 1 A.M. Course varying, chiefly N.W. Encamped at 8 A.M. Hours travelling, 7. Distance, 15 miles. Latitude 76° 3′. Temps.: midnight to noon, max. +21°, min. +6°; mean of 5 readings +12°.

Winds N.N.E.; smart breeze. Weather clear. Snow-drift.

which melting ice and snow would be at liberty to drift about; the heavier pieces would get aground, and portions of rock and mud would be turned up; as the season advanced the water would drain away, some portions of the ice and snow would still remain undissolved, and winter would close in the whole plain, which would become covered with snow, and these little eminences would be sticking up through it, affording proofs by their dirty colour that a *summer sun* had been beating upon them. We never lost sight of the coast line outside. It was quite impossible we could, for the ice along it was raised to very great heights. We observed some huge blocks, at least forty feet high, and thousands of tons in weight. The pressure to have raised them from their level bed must have been truly great, and there seemed no direction whence it could have come except west and north-west. At 4 A.M. we saw to north and north 20° west a range of land very different from what our patience had been tried with for a few days previously. The long and tedious flats were exchanged for rugged and precipitous hills, intersected by deep ravines, which, in many cases, could be called valleys, and the low points for towering table bluffs 700 or 800 feet high. We encamped at 8 A.M., having travelled at least fifteen miles. Our step was quicker and our luncheon halt shorter than usual, for the weather was very cold, and the snow drifted along with great violence.

Temps.: noon to midnight, max. +21°, min. +4°; mean of 4 readings +10°. Winds northerly. Weather clear.

At noon Mr. Stewart had observations. The latitude was 76° 3′. In the evening we found it impossible to pack up and proceed, owing to the extreme violence of the weather; and considering that this had been the third day we were to lose, we were impressed with the necessity there was for being careful in the use of our provisions. We discovered it was impossible the full allowance of provisions could be used, with the exception of fuel and spirits, which continued in great reputation till the end of the journey. At this encampment, which happened to be on the beach close to the hummocky floe, we picked up the feathers of glaucous gulls, and observed abundance of foxes' dung. The small eminences in the lagunes furnished our cooks with fresh-water ice, which suited much better than snow. The whole of the following day was spent in the tents, and really the blanket bags, however attracting after a hard day's work, were beginning to lose our favour. At noon the weather began to moderate, and the azure sky could be seen through the drifting clouds. During the clear intervals we saw the high and rugged land to the northward; and as the clouds drifted over it, and covered the hill tops, it had truly a wintry appearance.

May 23rd, Friday. DETENTION. Temps.: max. +16°, min. +4°; mean of 9 readings +11°. Winds northerly; strong breeze: squally. Weather stormy. Violent snow-drift.

At midnight the weather had improved considerably, and at four A.M. we packed up and started. Our course varied very much for two hours along the coast line, until we

May 24th, Saturday. Packed up, and started at 4 A.M. Course

arrived at a long low point where we discovered extensive Esquimaux ruins, which we dug up, and made a conspicuous cairn of the stones. From this point the land leads away about N.N.E., until it joins a chain of rugged hills which lead to the north-westward and westward, and form a sort of bay about twenty to twenty-five miles deep. The rock presented features which we had not observed previously in the limestone formation of North Devon; great hardness, with an even fracture, and a crystalline texture. After crossing the point, our course was north 11° west, in the direction of a table bluff on the opposite side of the bay. There was an extensive range of hummocky ice on and around the point, but we were able to take our sledges through it without double manning them. Beyond the hummocks the floe was very smooth, and the sledges came along admirably. We had no doubt the ice was the formation of last winter, for in some parts it had suffered from pressure when it was only six to eight inches thick. The surface of such parts presented the usual *brecciated* structure, and many of the pointed angular fragments were sticking up at least a foot above the snow, and of a light blue colour, which it was impossible they could have, had the sun been acting upon thom during a whole summer.

northerly. Hours travelling, 8. Distance, 12 miles. Temps.: midnight to noon, max. +18°, min. +6°. mean of 4 readings +12°. Winds variable. Weather clear. Encamped at noon. Latitude 76° 9′.

The day was very warm, and the men were very thirsty, but no attempts were made to allay their insatiable craving for *water* by eating snow. We could see land raised by refraction to the westward and north-westward. It presented numerous indentations where it was lost, and it disappeared altogether about north 35° or 40° W., until it opened out again two points farther to the eastward in the direction of the land we were approaching. The hills to the eastward and north-eastward were rendered obscure by a lurid atmosphere, but there was no distortion of the land by refraction in that direction. We encamped at noon, and found the latitude 76° 9′. After our breakfast of hot tea and pemmican, an extra half allowance of rum was served out, and this enabled us to show our attachment to our beloved Queen, by wishing her "a prosperous reign, and many happy returns of the 24th of May." During the evening the wind veered round to E.S.E., and blew keenly, but died away at midnight, when we were about to start.

Temps.: noon to midnight, max. +21°, min. +17°; mean of 3 readings +12°. Winds easterly; moderate. Weather clear.

Our course was considerably to the westward of north, at least 25° or 30°, towards a prominent bluff, where Mr. Stewart contemplated I should leave a five-day depôt, or proceed homeward after filling up his sledge. The sledges came along smoothly, for by this time they were considerably lighter. The sky was very clear, and almost perfectly cloudless, and the land to the westward could again be seen raised and distorted by refraction, even when the hills to the eastward were beginning to be enveloped in a dense mist.

May 25th, Sunday. Packed up, and started at midnight. Course N.N.W. or N. 30° W. Encamped at 9 A.M. Hours travelling, 8. Distance, 12 miles. Temps.: midnight to noon, max. +16°, min. +4°; mean of 7 readings $+9\frac{1}{2}°$. Winds variable. Weather clear. Latitude, 76° 15′.

After travelling eight hours, we encamped at 9 A.M. Our tent was very warm. A vessel hung up to the ridge rope full of snow prepared copious supplies of water; and although there was a constant dropping from the bottom of the vessel by condensation of vapour, we rarely allowed the ridge rope to be without a vessel, and by adopting this plan we were enabled to save fuel, and our supplies of water were more liberal. The latitude by meridian alt. was 76° 15′.

Temps.: noon to midnight, max. +21°, min. +16°; mean of 4 readings $+18\frac{1}{2}°$. Winds N.W.; fresh breeze. Weather gloomy. Snow.

At midnight we again started. The sky was overcast and gloomy, and the wind was freshening up in our faces; the snow was beginning to drift about, and we feared this would be a short day's march. A bear was observed and manœuvred, but without success; and as we were pitching our tents at 4 A.M., within five miles of the land, a fox passed close by the sledge, and was shot. The colour of its hair was beginning to change around the neck, and the general appearance of the creature was altogether wretched. Immediately after breakfast, one of the men and I went on towards the land. The floe was very hummocky, but upon the whole we went at least at the rate of three and a half miles in the hour. Soon after landing we observed two hares, which we endeavoured to approach within musket shot; but the creatures were so wary, standing on their hind legs, and spinning away in this upright posture, with watchful eyes on all our movements, that all our efforts were fruitless. The bluffs agreed in every respect with the table bluffs on the eastern shore of the channel and the bluffs west of Cape Hotham, with the single exception of being about one hundred feet higher. As the weather began to be very stormy, and no object could be accomplished by remaining on shore, we came off to the tents at eleven o'clock, suffering a good deal from snow-blindness, and very much fatigued. We observed the footprints of bears of various sizes, all going to the westward. Instead of packing up and starting in the afternoon, it and the following morning had to be passed in the tents, in consequence of the extreme violence of weather.

May 26th, Monday. Started at midnight. Course N N.W. Encamped at 4 A.M. Hours travelling, 4. Distance, 4 miles. Temps.: midnight to noon, max. +32°, min. +19°; mean of 5 readings, +23°. Winds N.W. Latitude 76° 20′. Distance from the ships, 220 miles. Temps.: noon to midnight, max. +32°, min. +17°; mean of 5 read- +25°. Winds northerly. Squally. Snow.

May 27, Tuesday. DETENTION. Temps.: max. +21°, min. +8°; mean of 9 readings, +15°. Winds northerly; moderate. Weather clear. Ashore examining the coast. Preparation made for the return of half the party.

About noon, Mr. Stewart and a large party of men went ashore to examine the coast, and to take bearings and angles. The latitude at the tents was 76° 20′; at the land, it would be 76° 25′. At 6 P.M. the party returned, bringing off two hares which Mr. Stewart had shot. They were male and female; the latter was in an advanced stage of gestation, and contained six well developed leverets. After Mr. Stewart's return to the tents, he examined the sledges, and found that all due preparations had been made for my *return*, according to the orders he had given in the forenoon. The sledges were exchanged. No. 4., the "*Perseverance*," very appropriately, became the advancing sledge, while No. 2., the "Sylph," was to return. The former had twenty-seven days' provisions, and the latter eight. Mr. James Reid was transferred from my party, and John Eddie, carpenter's mate, received in his place. I had orders from Mr Stewart to proceed to the south-eastward, and examine the bottom of the bay, about which there was a little doubt, whether there was not an opening leading to the eastward: after this, I was to make the best of my way to the ships, calling at the island, and taking supplies of provisions, &c., out of the depôts as I passed them.

May 28th, Wednesday.

PARTING.

Packed up, and started at 7 A.M. Course E. 33° S. Encamped at noon. Hours travelling, 5. Distance, 12 miles. Temps.: max. +16°, min. +5°; mean of 7 readings +7½°. Winds N.E., moderate. Weather clear.

At 7 A.M. we packed up, and took opposite directions. Our course for the first three hours was E. 22° south, and for the two remaining hours, until we encamped on the opposite shore, it was S.E. Our encampment was about seven miles from the bottom of the bay, which we could see very plainly. The latitude was 76° 13′; but I placed no confidence in the observation, for I believe it might be a few miles in error.

The floe we had come over was very smooth; and our sledge was *light*. Where the snow was *hard* I thought twelve miles a safe estimate in five hours. Some of the men endeavoured to raise a fire with tufts of dry saxifrage and masses of moss, but their attempts produced little else than smoke. The land sloped gradually from the elevated land behind to the edge of the ice, but there were occasional interruptions which caused a wavy appearance of its outline. The rocks were very hard, and presented an even fracture and crystalline texture, similar to what had been observed at the point a few days before. I erected a cairn on one of the ridges, about 250 feet above the level of the sea, and left the usual note. As we were packing up the sledge, a smart breeze came away from the N.E., and, as might be supposed, the *sailors* hoisted the floor cloth on the tent poles for a sail, and as we got clear of the hummocks which lined the beach a beautiful *blue* floe presented itself, leading exactly in the direction we had to proceed (a fortunate coincidence with a fair wind). For nearly three hours, we could hardly keep up with the sledge, although running nearly as fast as we could, and receiving great assistance from holding on by the *braces*. I am certain we travelled at least fourteen miles in three hours, being a little more than four miles an hour.

May 29th, Thursday. Started at 1½ A.M. Course S. 30° W. Sail set. Hours travelling, 8. Distance 20 miles. Temps.: max. +30°, min. +9°; mean of 7 readings +19¾°. Winds northerly: smart breeze.

At half past four A.M., as we passed along the land, I observed a mass of rock which resembled a large cairn, without examining which I could not rest satisfied, although the distance to it was not less than two miles and a half, or perhaps three miles. I started from the sledge, taking one of the men carrying the gun along with me. We soon reached the land, and were satisfied that the object of attraction was a deception. On our return to the sledge, we met the men in a state of alarm at three bears (two full grown ones and a cub), which swept furiously close by the

Encamped at 9½ A.M.

sledge, and showed off their ivory to advantage. I allayed their fears in the best way I could, by saying that bears were never known to attack even two or three men together, where attempts were made to keep them off by shouting, &c. &c. It was hardly proper, however, to have left the sledge without a gun that could have been depended upon; for the ship's gun that belonged to it was one that Mr. Stewart had rejected but a few days before. After putting everything to rights again, we started at 6 A.M., and travelled for three hours and a half, at the rate of about two miles an hour. The bears went to the west or north-westward at a very rapid rate, as if they had been chasing one another. A fox was seen at the same time. Can the fox be to the bear what the jackall is to the lion? From what we have already seen, the analogy wants little to complete it.

Ice 15 feet thick.

The floe had a good deal of snow on it as we came to the southward, and we observed numerous wide fissures, in which we could reach the water at a depth of two feet beneath the surface; these fissures were at right angles, or nearly right angles, with the land, and between two and three miles from it. Where we were, there were no hummocks nor raised up ice, and the thickness of snow on it was about six inches. Allowing the six inches of snow to be equal to two of ice, and applying the rule based upon the specific gravity of ice, then the thickness of the floe can be safely estimated. I made it 14 to 15 feet. We encamped at half past nine, not a little fatigued, having both by running and walking taken the sledge over a distance of twenty miles. In the evening the sky became overcast; there was a slight fall of snow. Some of the men were complaining of snow-blindness, and one of diarrhœa, which he had proved beyond doubt had been brought on by the use of pemmican, of which he was very fond. At midnight we began to pack up, and at half past one we started. The weather was very foggy, but we managed to keep our course by the sun, which could always be discerned through the fog. At 4 A.M. we arrived at the point, and left the usual note in the cairn; and at 8 A.M., having sighted our encampment on the 23rd, in latitude 76° 3′ we encamped on the beach, close by some mounds of ice thirty to forty feet high; how they attained this height must have been by some mysterious process of growth which I could not comprehend, for they did not seem to have been influenced by pressure for many years previously, but there was abundance of very high hummocks along the coast to their outside. The latitude was 76° 1′, two miles to the southward of our encampment on the 23rd. The sky became overcast in the evening, and a dense fall of snow commenced. Fortunately I laid down north and south marks at noon, otherwise it would have been puzzling to shape our course at 11 P.M. when we started, and could neither

May 30th, Friday. Packed up, and started at 1½ A.M. In 2½ hours travelled 4 miles. Reached the cairn, 194 miles from the ships. 26 from our farthest, by our circuitous route into the bay 36, making the home journey 10 miles more than the outward, which was 220. Encamped at 8 A.M. 6½ hours travelling. Latitude 76° 1′.

Temps.: max. +28°, min. +7°; mean of 10 read-

discern sun nor marks along the land, to enable us to shape a course.

After striking through the hummocks to the smooth floe outside, we kept going along them until the sun was seen, soon after midnight, and this enabled us to shape our course for the island, which we reached at 6 A.M., and after much labour taking the sledge through the hummocks, we landed and pitched the tent on a comfortable bed of dry moss, about 30 feet above the level of the ice, very near the top of the island. We observed a seal at a hole about a quarter of a mile from the S.W. end of the island, but all our schemes to get within shot of it were closely watched and completely foiled. Recent footprints of bears were observed around the hole. The floe at the end of the island was *brecciated*, and the angular fragments were sticking up through six inches of snow. The water line in the seal hole was nineteen inches below the upper surface of the snow, and from this the thickness of the ice was calculated at eleven feet; the depth of the water was twelve fathoms. The island is about forty feet high; its length from east to west 400 yards, and its breadth, north to south, 350 yards; the difference between length and breadth is owing to a long flat beach which is continued in an eastern direction, where there must be an eddy of the flowing tides. The opposite, or western extremity of the island is abrupt, and the water appears to deepen suddenly, from the enormous hummocks that are planted around it. The pressure to have raised and brought in such huge blocks could only come from between the points W.S.W. and W.N.W. The limestone, of which the island is composed, abounds in fossils peculiar to the silurian strata. Recent dung of hares and ptarmigan was very abundant, and I picked up the entire skull of a lemming in the castings of an *owl*. I observed depressions in patches of grass (*Junci*), which must have been hollowed out by ducks in the summer season, to answer the purpose of nests.

ings +15°. Winds variable. Weather thick and snowy.

Started at 11 P.M. May 31st, Saturday. Course S. 30° E., but often varying. Landed on an island, and encamped at 6 A.M. 7 hours travelling. Distance, 18 miles. Temps.: max. +31°, min. +15°; mean of 8 readings +20½°. Winds S.E.; smart breeze. Thick snow.

On Sunday morning the time for starting arrived, but the state of the weather was so violent that unless it had been absolutely necessary it would have been highly imprudent to have exposed ourselves to the inclement storm. At noon the sun appeared, and there were promises of better weather. I had a meridian altitude, which enabled me to lay down the exact latitude of the island, and a bearing of the *rough point*, which agreed pretty well with bearings taken on the evening of the 20th of May. Very soon after midnight we began to erect a cairn on the top of the island; the usual paper was deposited, and we started at 4 A.M. Our course for the first three hours was S.S.E., until we crossed the beach, and struck in upon the long *flat*, to the northward of the depôt, where we observed stuck up very conspicuously some of the relics of our encampment on the 20th May. From this we

June 1st, Sunday. DETENTION. Meridian altitude 36° 2′. Latitude 75° 49′, bearing of the rough point S. 50° E. Temps.: max. +32°, min. +16°; mean of 8 readings +23½°. Winds south-easterly. Violent snow storm.

June 2nd, Monday. Packed up, and started 4 A.M. Arrived at the depôt at noon. Encamped. Hours travelling, 8. Meridian altitude

36° 18′. Latitude 75° 41′. Temps.: max. +40°, min. +14°; mean of 9 readings +24°. Winds southerly. Weather thick and hazy.

made the best of our way to the depôt, which I feared we might have some difficulty in finding, from the circumstances that it had been laid down and left in foggy weather, without proper leading marks, except the hummocks along the beach. At noon we espied the cairn at it, and after coming to a convenient spot in its immediate neighbourhood we encamped. The sky cleared up, and enabled us to get a tolerable altitude. The depôt was found in a state of perfect safety, and the cairns that had been erected were still standing. Some of the men were suffering from snow-blindness.

June 3d, Tuesday. Began to pack up, and to open the depôt at 1 A.M. Started at 4 A.M. Hours travelling, 5. Course west, a little southerly. Encamped at 9 A.M. Temps.: max. +39°, min. +16°; mean of 8 readings +25½°. Winds southerly. Weather thick, and snowing. Started at 11 P.M.

At 4 A.M., after removing from the depôt our portion of the provisions, and our spare clothing, we proceeded to the westward at a rapid pace. The sledge felt heavy coming through the hummocks, but as soon as we got clear of them it came along very well. At 9 A.M., having travelled ten miles, we encamped. The weather was misty, and the wind veered to the westward. The temperature rose to + 39° from + 16° at 1 A.M.

At midnight the sky began to appear through the mist; distant objects became visible; cirro strati and cumuli were dispersed along and a little above the horizon; and as the temperature fell to + 16° the snow became hard and resisting. We could see the north headland very distinctly at a distance of at least twenty miles bearing S.W. We crossed several old floes, on which the rounded hummocks were very high, and we were much annoyed by the constant jerking of the sledge. We encamped at 5 A.M., about two miles N.W. of our encampment on the 16th of May. The day was very clear, but in consequence of not having an artificial horizon, I did not obtain a meridian alt., as the sun was over the land to the southward. At midnight we packed up, and shaped our course for the north headland. The floe was very rough in many parts, and those of the men whose eyes were a little affected were in danger of getting their legs broken or ankles dislocated in the deep cracks among the hummocks. We had luncheon at the north headland at the usual hour. Some of the men obtained some fresh-water ice, a little of which was brought along with us. After proceeding down the channel about five miles, the tent was pitched at 7 A.M., about a mile from the land. The ice at the north headland was cracked at right angles with the coast line, and the water-line in the fissures was eleven to thirteen inches beneath the surface, hence the floe was about nine feet.

June 4th, Wednesday. Course S.W. Encamped at 5 A.M. Hours travelling, 6. Temps.: max. +25°, min. +10°; mean of 9 readings +16°. Winds S.E.; light. Weather clear. Started at midnight.

June 5th, Thursday. Encamped at 7 A.M. Hours travelling, 7. Course S.W. and S. 11° W. Temps.: max. +36°, min. +15°; mean of 9 readings +27°. Winds S.E.; light. Weather clear. Cracks in the ice. Thickness about 9 feet, where no pressure had been.

At the spot of our encampment on the 15th of May, numerous footprints of foxes and bears were observed, and the dung also of these animals was in great abundance, many portions of the dung of the latter seemed to consist entirely of undigested grass, which maintained the shape of the intestine so well after it had been evacuated, that it resembled other than the evacuations of wild animals, and had not seals' claws been detected amongst it, I believe doubts would have remained with us respecting its true source. Towards midnight the sky was very clear, and bright parhelia attended the sun. There was a gentle breeze from S.E., but it quite baffled the skill of the sailors, who prepared their usual sail, to take advantage of it. The ravines between the bold bluffs we passed sent down violent gusts, which frequently put our tent poles into danger of being broken. At 3 A.M. the sky became overcast, the wind increased, and snow began to fall very thick; in short, there were all the appearances of an approaching storm. Several flocks of birds were observed flying to the north-eastward. They resembled red-throated divers in their flight, but I had reason to think afterwards that they must have been brent geese. A crack in the ice leading to the westward, two feet wide, was crossed, and the thickness was ascertained with tolerable accuracy. A number of sea fowl (gulls of several species) were sitting at it.

June 6th, Friday. Packed up, and started at 1 A.M. Course S. 11° W. down the Wellington Channel. Hours travelling, 7. Encamped at 8 A.M. Temps.: max. +41°, min. +20°; mean of 9 readings +32°. Winds south-easterly; strong gale. Weather very stormy. Brent geese seen. Thickness of the ice, 9½ feet.

At 8 A.M. we encamped close by a low point in the immediate vicinity of very high and precipitous bluffs, from which the wind swept down in violent gusts which threatened to carry away our tent. It blew very hard, and snowed all day. The snow was soft; and as the tent was sheltered by a range of high hummocks from the wind as it veered round to S.E., it accumulated on the canvas, and melted; and for a short time we had a shower bath, until the fibres had become swollen with the water, and ceased to transmit it in such great quantity. The snow on the floe became quite soft, and vessels placed on it sank into it. This was the first time we had observed any thing *seek its* way downwards by dissolving the snow *without clear sunshine*. In the evening the weather began to moderate; we could see Cape Bowden, and also a great part of the land on the opposite side of the channel; but the bluff at which our depôt had been laid down was shut in to the eastward. I went to a prominent part of the low point: erected a cairn, and left the usual note. It was nearly two hours before I overtook the sledge. The temperature having falling below the freezing point, the snow on the floe became resisting, and the sledge moved along very easily in consequence. We encamped at 6 A.M. at the edge, and in the shelter of a range of high hummocks close to the depôt we left on the 13th of May. There was a constant fall of soft snow, and a smart breeze from the S.W., which pelted in our faces on our march from the low point to the depôt.

June 6th, Friday. Snow dissolving on the tent, and dropping through.

June 7th, Saturday. Started at ½ to 1 A.M. Course S. 15° or 20° E. 5½ hours travelling. Encamped at 6 A.M. Temps.: max. +32°, min. +29°; mean of 9 readings + 30¼°. Winds S.W.; strong breeze. Soft snow. Arrived at the depôt.

During the whole of Saturday the weather was very severe, and on Sunday it was such that to have started across the channel would have been highly improper. We removed our portion of the bread from the depôt when we encamped, and secured the remainder in the cairn. Several brent geese

June 8th, Sunday. DETENTION. Temps.: max. +31°, min. +29°; mean of 8 readings +29¾°. Winds S.S.W.

Smart gale. Stormy and snowy weather. Started at 9 P.M. Thickness of ice, 7 to 8 feet.

were seen, and one was shot. While we were asleep three bears (a mother and two half-grown cubs) were heard prowling about the tent and the sledge, but as soon as we scrambled out they took fright, and ran away. We found that they had visited the conjurors, and everything which deviated from the pure white colour of the snow, with the exception of a crimson ensign that was waving in the breeze about ten yards from the tent door. I must acknowledge our *Whitsunday* was not so well spent as could have been wished; however, we went over the *Morning* and *Evening Services*, and engaged each other's attention in amusing if not also useful conversation. We began to pack up early, and started at 9 P.M. An occasional glimpse of the opposite shore enabled us to make a straight course for Point Separation, which bears about W. 30° S. Our pace was quick and light, for the snow was firm, and the sledge moved along it easily. After travelling about fourteen miles we encamped at 3 A.M. At noon the snow on the floe was very soft. Our tin vessels prepared *more* water than could be used; and it was not without very great reluctance, that a small remainder was thrown away. At 11 P.M. we started again; the floe was very soft, and blue spots were seen on it in every direction. The azure sky began to appear, but still there was a white misty haze, which affected our eyes a good deal. We saw Point Separation very distinctly, and our outward sledge marks were crossed several times.

June 9th, Monday. Course across the channel. Encamped at 3 A.M. Hours travelling, 6. Temps.: max. +40°, min. +29°; mean of 8 readings +38¼°. Winds, S.W.; moderate. Misty snowy weather. Packed up, and started at 11 P.M.

June 10th, Tuesday. Encamped at 5½ A.M. Hours travelling, 6½. Temps.: max. +34°, min. +31°; mean of 8 readings +32¼°. Winds S.S.E.; moderate breeze. Clear sky. Seals seen on the ice. Abundance of birds flying up the Wellington Channel.

Up to this time we were able to keep our feet warm, although not quite dry, without leather boots. Now we had recourse to them, but they were not proof against the water; for our feet were generally soaking wet in less than an hour after starting. We crossed an old floe, and found that the increase of temperature had, *as yet*, had no effect in changing its appearance. Several seals were seen on the floe, but no attempts were made to shoot any of them. Bears' footmarks were very abundant on the soft snow. We pitched our tent at half-past five A.M. about ten miles from Point Separation. Our blanket bags and wolf skins were very wet with floe or snow encampments since the weather became so soft. Large flocks of king and eider ducks were constantly flying northward. Brent geese, glaucous gulls, ivory gulls, ptarmigan, and snow buntings, had been seen since we commenced crossing the Wellington Channel. At noon I obtained a tolerable meridian altitude, and took the bearings of some of the headlands with a pocket compass and the quadrant. The floe was very soft, and although the sledge contained little more than our clothing, it sunk deep into the snow, and required good stiff pulling to bring it along. Our pace was quick, to keep our wet feet warm. I measured the thickness of the floe through several cracks, and found it was seven feet. As we approached the land something resembling a

Meridian alt. 37° 51′. Latitude, 74° 58′. Beechey Island, S.E. Cape Spencer, S. 55° E. Cape Bowden, E. 15° N. Point Pemmican, N.E. (North side of President Bay.) Low Point, N. 33° E. North Headland, N.N.E. North Point, W. side, N. 17° W. Point Separation, W. 38° S. Cape Hotham, S.S.W. Cape Hotham,

cairn was observed, but a still closer approach proved it was only one of the thousand deceptions we had already met with while looking for *cairns*.

After a comfortable luncheon on the beach at Point Separation we proceeded to the depôt, where we encamped, and expected to find reports of those of the western party who might have returned. The depôt was a perfect wreck; and as no reports were found, nor traces observed of any party having returned, our conclusions were, that *the entire* party was still out. The provisions, which bears and foxes had scattered about the beach, were collected and deposited in the centre of the cairn we built, along with a case of pemmican which fortunately happened to be proof against their teeth and claws. A paper containing a full report of the proceedings of Mr. Stewart's party was deposited in a bottle in the top of the cairn.

I observed several insects, chiefly *Poduræ*, running on the stones when they were turned up, specimens of them were obtained and brought on board the ship. After our usual rest, we packed up and proceeded down the channel along the land. The ice between the hummocks and the beach was a standing pool of water, which had to be waded; but there was ice in the bottom of it, and in many parts a thick formation of ice on the surface, which sustained the weight of the sledge, without breaking through altogether. The weather was very clear, and there was a gentle breeze from S.E.

At half-past four o'clock A.M. we arrived at the *first* depôt, where we met a party of twenty men under the command of Captain Penny, who had encamped but two hours before. The party had come from beyond Cape Hotham in the last day's march, and was proceeding to the northward with a whale boat mounted on a large sledge, to enable Captain Penny to carry out a proper examination of a number of islands surrounded by open water, which he had discovered about the middle of May, and which he had failed to examine satisfactorily, in consequence of the drifting state of the ice and open water. I received orders from Captain Penny to resupply my sledge with provisions as soon as I returned to the ships, and follow up after his party as the strength of my own party, the state of the ice and weather, might permit. I need not attempt to describe the expressions of feeling which the *sailors* exhibited on meeting with their old comrades, because they are such as can hardly be appreciated by any but those who have experienced them. After wading through pools of water along the beach, which reached to the knees, crossing Barlow Inlet and rounding Cape Hotham, we encamped at the beacon near the large bluff, at 2 A.M. The sky was beginning to be overcast, and there was a cold wind coming away from S.W. The ice

67° W. of Beechy Island,—by the quadrant. Bearings more or less doubtful; being, together with the latitude, only approximations. Packed up at 11 P.M.

June 11th, Wednesday. Encamped at 5 A.M. at the depôt on Cornwallis Island. Hours travelling, 6. Floe 7 feet thick. Temps.: max. +55°, min. +31°; mean of 8 readings +38°. Winds variable; light. Weather clear.

June 12th, Thursday. Started at midnight. Course down channel. Arrival at first depôt. Encamped at 5 A.M. Met Captain Penny: outward-bound boat party. Received orders. Packed up at 8 P.M. Hours travelling, 4½. Temps.: max. +55°, min. +29°; mean of 8 readings +43°. Winds variable; light. Weather clear.

June 13th, Friday. Course down the channel round Cape Hotham. Encamped at 2 A.M. Hours travelling, 6. Temps.: max. +40°, min. +29°; mean of 9 readings. +34°. Winds S.W.;

light breeze. Sky clear at first; gloomy towards night. Packed up at 10¼ P.M.

around Cape Hotham had changed remarkably; the hummocks had fallen down very much, and a dirty muddy colour had taken the place of what had been pure white snow a month before. Dovekies, terns, glaucous, sabine, and ivory gulls, and also brent geese and king ducks, were seen very frequently.

As we were packing up, and preparing to start, a sledge came in sight to the eastward. It was a dog sledge, and we could see two persons attending to it, coming through the soft and deep snow along the beach. When they came within a half a mile of our tent, they drew up to the shingly beach, and halted. Thinking a message might await me from Captain Penny, I proceeded immediately to the party, where I found Mr. J. Stuart and Mr. Petersen returning to the ships. The latter was unable to accompany the advancing party, in consequence of severe diarrhœa, and the former was ordered to accompany him to the ships, to make sure of his safe arrival, but no orders were conveyed to me by the party from Captain Penny. At half-past ten, we started, and got safely across some cracks in the ice to the westward of Cape Hotham. The floe was hard and smooth, and it had a blue appearance, for the soft snow had melted away from its surface. Our pace was quick and light; and at five o'clock we arrived at the ships, and welcomed ourselves with three hearty cheers, to which there were few or none on board to respond.

June 14th, Saturday. Course westerly. Hours travelling, 6½. Arrival at the ships: 40 days out. Distance, out and home, 450 statute miles. Temps.: max. +37°, min. +31°; mean of 3 readings +33°. Winds S.S.W.; smart breeze. Misty. Overcast sky. Rain.

On our march from Cape Hotham one of the men, Andrew Robertson, appeared to be suffering from severe pains in his legs, and great uneasiness and difficulty in making deep and protracted inspirations. He had suffered considerable reduction of muscle and energy, and he really appeared a little emaciated, but he was never behind his neighbours when his assistance was required; and the symptoms he complained of could well be attributed to wet and cold feet during the day, and damp clothes at night, in addition to long continued fatigue, which itself is an unexceptionable cause of similar symptoms under different and perhaps less depressing circumstances.

June 17th, Tuesday. Left the ships at 9 P.M.

Preparations were entered upon, immediately on my arrival at the ships, to carry out the orders of Captain Penny. But I found two of my former party unable to proceed along with me immediately, in consequence of fatigue, and a depressed state of health, brought on by long exposure to wet and cold. They might have been able to accomplish the journey, but as there would be risks in taking them out again when the encampments might probably be wetter than they were before, I thought it best to lean to the safe side. I had to request the assistance of Mr. Stuart for four days, and avail myself of the use of the dogs to take the provisions the last forty miles of the distance to the N.E. point.

The last step was one in which the opinion of Mr. Petersen coincided with an idea I had, that the dogs might be able to accomplish in two or three days what would occupy all our available force ten or twelve days, and expose them to the danger of encamping on the wet floe. Following this plan, the sledges were refitted; and we would have started on Monday the 16th, the day which Captain Penny had appointed, but the weather proved unfavourable, we had therefore to put off until the following day, when we left the ships at 9 P.M. with a fair wind. The dog sledge had 200 lbs. on it; there were seven dogs, two of which were lame; and John Lawson, from the experience he had had during winter and spring, took upon himself the responsibility of *driver*. The other sledge had weights to the amount of upwards of 750 lbs., and there were five of us to drag it along.

As we were proceeding to the eastward, we met Mr. Goodsir and his party, returning to the ships, from which he had been absent about forty-three days. They reported meeting and parting with Captain Penny a few days ago, within a short distance of the N.E. point. At 3 A.M. we arrived at the large bluff near Cape Hotham, where we overtook the dog sledge, and found Lawson lamenting the loss of one of his best dogs, which had been killed by the sledge running over it. The tent was pitched on the beach at the foot of the bluff, and after breakfast, having transferred upwards of 60 lbs. from the large to the dog sledge, Lawson and I started with the latter, rounded Cape Hotham on the smooth floe outside the squeezed-up ice (for travelling along the beach was quite impracticable), crossed Barlow Inlet, and reached the first depôt at half-past 7 A.M., where we remained under the shelter of a steep rock,—protected from the violence of the storm, snow, and rain, by a portion of a torn-up black calico tent that we had taken from the ships for that purpose. We kept the dogs close around us, and although they were often disturbed by two or three ravens that kept croaking over us from the cliffs, we were not altogether uncomfortable.

June 18th, Wednesday. Stormy weather. Arrival at the first depôt.

June 19th, Thursday.

About midnight Mr. Stewart arrived with the other sledge; and after leaving provisions to make a depôt, 350 lbs. were placed upon the dog sledge, in addition to other weights, which increased the weight of the whole to at least 420 lbs. Lawson and I commenced our part of the journey at 6 A.M., while Mr. Stewart, having accomplished his part, was to start for the ships in the afternoon. We struck through the grounded ice immediately to the northward of the depôt, and proceeded up the channel on the smooth but wet floe. The dogs did very well when one of us went on before them, but nothing without this way of leading them, for *we* had found it quite impossible to *drive them*. We opened out Point Separation with great difficulty, among deep snow and

Mr. Stewart's return to the ships.

Wet state of the floe damaging the provisions.

pools, in which the *cover* of the sledge was many times more than half immersed; and thinking the floe might be found more suitable at a greater distance from the land, we kept going off and north, until Point Petersen bore about W. 30° north, at a distance of not less than five miles, when the accumulation of soft snow among the hummocks, and the great depth of water on the floe, rendered farther progress in that direction impossible, without certain risk of seriously damaging the provisions. With painful reluctance I saw no alternative but to *return* to the ships, after making a depôt of the provisions, with the view of coming out with a more suitable sledge, and in sufficient time to reach the N.E. point before the 26th of June, which was the day appointed by Captain Penny I should be there.

Resolved to return to the ships.

We proceeded down the channel, and in towards the land; and in two hours and a half we reached the high hummocks about a quarter of a mile to the eastward of that well known spot, "Marshall's Depôt."* The sledge was unpacked immediately, and one of the bread bags was found quite wet on its lower surface. While we were engaged carrying the 320 lbs. of provisions to the land through the hummocks the dogs lay very quietly, and had a rest of five hours. We made a *secure* depôt at the cairn we had left but a week before, and proceeded down the channel to the first depôt, which we reached about midnight, and where we halted, because the dogs were hardly able to proceed any farther without resting. Next day we arrived at Cape Hotham, where we were detained twenty-four hours by snow-blindness; and, on the 21st, we arrived at the ships, quite disappointed that our attempts to carry out Captain Penny's orders had so far turned out a failure.

June 20th, Friday. At Cape Hotham.

June 21st, Saturday. Arrival at the ships.

P. C. SUTHERLAND.

---

* The place where the large depôt was made, about one and a half or two miles south of Point Separation.

"Pas à pas on va bien loin." Motto of Sledge.

"PERSEVERANCE." Name.

Sledge Crew.

John Gordon, A.B., exchanged for Mr. Reid, 22nd April.
George Thompson, A.B.
Andrew Robertson, A.B.
Alexander Smith, A.B.
John Lawson, A.B.

Donald Sutherland, sailmaker, exchanged for J. Lucas, 22nd April. May 6th.
M. James Reid, second mate, exchanged for Eddie, 28th May.
George Thompson.
Andrew Robertson.
Alexander Smith.
John Lawson.
John Lucas, A.B., "Lady Franklin."
John Eddie, carpenter's mate, in exchange for Mr. Reid, 28th May.

Mr. J. Stuart, "Lady Franklin." June 17th.
John Lucas, ditto.
John Eddie.
John Lawson.
Alexander Smith.

P. C. S.

Report of a Journey under the Orders of Mr. Goodsir, Surgeon.—Proceedings of a Travelling Party from Her Majesty's Brigs "Lady Franklin" and "Sophia" from 17th to 26th April, 1851.

First Journey.

17th April, 1851.

Our preparations have for some days back been all completed. One or two experimental exercising trips have been made round the bay, and the sledges, fully laden and packed, have been found to work very well. The men have been once or twice also exercised in striking and pitching the tents, and although we are all new to the work, yet every one is full of confidence as to what we will be able to do. Early this morning every one was astir, and immediately after breakfast the officers and crews of both ships were assembled on the quarter-deck of the "Lady Franklin," where prayers were read by Captain Penny, as well as a few words of advice and encouragement given to us all.

Wind, S.S.E., light and clear. Therm. +29°.

By 8 A.M. we were all ready, and after three hearty cheers the final start was made. The crew of the "Felix" were present, and lent us a hand out of the bay. Our six sledges made rather an imposing procession, each with their flag and little streamer flying, and one and all seemed to be in great spirits. Unluckily, for two days back, there have been repeated heavy falls of soft snow, which is now lying three or four inches deep on the ice: this makes our dragging very heavy; but we hope the first northerly wind and frost will improve the state of our roads. The six sledges are respectively commanded by Mr. Stewart, myself, Mr. Marshall, Dr. Sutherland, Mr. John Stuart, and James Reid, the second mate of the "Sophia," each having six men of a crew. In my own crew I think I am fortunate, as they are all fine young fellows, only two of them being above thirty: Richard Kitson, captain of the hold; Alexander Bain, sailmaker; Alexander Leiper, carpenter's mate; William Brandes, A.B.; George Findlay, A.B.; and Walter Craig, A.B. Officers and men alike drag at the sledges; and I hope that, by working well together, we may be able to search a considerable extent of coast. God grant that we may do so successfully, as far as regards our main object.

Captain Phillips, Dr. Porteus, and the crew of the "Felix," accompanied and assisted us over the hummocks at the mouth of the bay, and continued with us for a short distance along the smooth floe outside. They left us about ten o'clock, giving us three cheers, which were heartily returned. Pushing to the eastward, we found the dragging very heavy through the deep soft snow, although the floe we were on was perfectly smooth and level. This was the ice formed in the month of March, over the long lanes of water which were seen early in that month. Had it not been for these unfortunate falls of snow, for two or three days back, this would have been an excellent roadway for us. At half past 11, Sutherland's sledge got somewhat out of order, and a halt was called to put it to rights. Luncheon was taken at the same time; and we found the gutta percha water-bottles most acceptable companions, for we were all enabled to fully quench our thirst, which at this time was great, both from the comparative heat of the weather and the hard work. Starting again, after a halt of about thirty minutes, we carried on until about half past 3 P.M., when, the men beginning to show evident symptoms of fatigue, it was deemed advisable to halt for the day. This was not a very long "spell;" but the work was severe whilst it lasted, and it is scarcely prudent to push too hard at the first start, particularly taking into consideration the comparatively inactive life that all of us have been leading during this winter. It will be two or three days, I expect, before we get fairly into good working trim; we must consider ourselves, therefore, as in training at this, the commencement of our labours. The tents were soon pitched, and the conjurors under weigh to prepare our tea.

1st Encampment, 17th April, 1851. E.S.E. Clear. Therm. +27°.

The hard day's work gave the cold pork and biscuit a relish that had been almost unknown for months back, and every one was soon as much at home in the tent as if they had spent half a lifetime under canvas or duck. We certainly have had a favourable commencement to our travelling, for the evening was a beautiful one, and Cape Hotham, apparently about seven miles off, stands out in bold relief against the clear blue sky beyond, making a beautiful scene as viewed through our tent door. Tired as we were, it was difficult for some time to go to sleep, principally, I dare say, from the novelty to us all of our present position. More comfortable we could scarcely be, for the snow under our floorcloths and blanket bags formed a most inviting soft bed for us, and the thermometer over head hanging to the ridge rope was standing at +45°. A few airs on the flute from Richard, the captain of my sledge, and the sound of an accordion from a neighbouring tent, enlivened us before we finally ensconced ourselves in our blanket bags, in which novel bedding we spent our first night on the floe in the most sound and refreshing slumbers.

Therm. in tent +45°.

Two ravens have been the only animals seen during the day.

Found that the thermometer in tent had fallen to +25° at 1 A.M. Roused the cook at 4 A.M.; had breakfast comfortably, but our conjuror is rather small to supply seven. Huts struck, sledges repacked, and started at 8 A.M. Morning fine, though colder. Smart breezes occasionally from S.S.E. The snow is still soft, and dragging consequently heavy. We are all wishing for a northerly wind and hard frost to improve our roads. My sledge is rather low in the runners, and when we are crossing a snow wreath at all deep it drags very heavy. Better roads,

Friday, 18th April. In tent, +25°. Air, +15°.

however, I trust, in Wellington Channel. At 11 A.M., whilst crossing a ridge of hummocks, the after cross-bar of my sledge caught and was broken. This did not hinder us proceeding, however, at a good rate, as we had now got on a smooth bay floe, but on which the deep snow made dragging very heavy. Whilst halting for lunch at noon outside a range of very high and large hummocks off Dungeness, we heard the howling of the dogs inshore, and shortly afterwards perceived Captain Penny and Petersen on the top of the hummocks. We advanced to meet them, and they informed us that they had found the route we had pursued too heavy for them in consequence of the depth of the snow, and that they had struck inshore shortly after leaving the bay, where they had found a narrow ledge of ice comparatively free of snow. The dogs were behaving very well; they had some difficulty in getting over the ridge of hummocks to the floe on which we were, but they soon managed to join and get ahead of us. They halted, and waited for us a few miles further on, and at a quarter past three, we pitched tents for the night close under Parry's Bluffs, about five miles to the westward of Cape Hotham. It was now overcast and squally, and the thermometer was falling, so that we were all glad to get into our blanket bags for the night, after the hard day's work. We had to-night the first case of snow blindness in one of our crew, Bain, the sailmaker. He complained of his eyes being very hot and uncomfortable during the latter part of the day's march, but the immediate application of the proper remedies on halting gave him relief. We had a good many cases of this most painful affliction after this; but I shall in a separate sheet, to be appended to the end of this report, give an account of the very few ailings that we had during our travelling.

Wind, S.E., S.S.E., and light, Therm. at noon. +27°.

2nd Encampment, Parry's Bluff.

It continued gloomy weather and squally during the night, and the thermometer fell to 20°. In the tent, it ranged from 30° to 33°, and the snow being soft and wet underneath us, our floorcloth and bedding were rather damp in the morning.

Therm. 20° in air. 30° to 33° in tent.

Cooks called at 4 A.M., breakfast at 6, and were ready for a start by 7. Whilst breakfast was preparing, the most practicable route through the hummocks had been searched for, and it was determined to strike inshore at once. We accordingly started in this direction at 7, and, double manning each sledge, with considerable difficulty we reached the beach, where we found a road free of hummocks, but still covered with heavy wreaths of deep snow. It was ten minutes past 8 A.M. before we got all the sledges ashore, although the distance was not more than a hundred yards. During the early part of the day it was quite thick with heavy showers of soft snow, so that we were close under Cape Hotham before we saw it. We rounded it close under the rocky point formed by immense masses and blocks of stones, which have fallen from the cliff behind. It strikes me that this land slip must have taken place since Sir W. E. Parry's visit to it; for the cape seems to have a different appearance now when viewed from seaward,

Saturday, 19th April. Smart breeze, S.E. Therm. +24°. Soft snow showers.

Cape Hotham.

compared with his engraving of it. Many of the huge blocks, too, seem as if recently precipitated into their present position.

After passing the cape and opening out the channel, we continued our course close under the cliffs. For some miles we had somewhat of an ascent, and as the snow was excessively deep and blown into deep wreaths, the work was consequently very heavy. At 11 A.M. we halted for lunch for ten minutes. Started again, and carried on until 2 P.M., when we were all glad to see Captain Penny and Petersen about a mile ahead of us, where they had halted for us. By 3 we reached their position and camped for the night, all of us more fatigued than we had yet felt since leaving the ships. One of my crew was almost completely knocked up, our sledge being excessively heavy in dragging, in consequence of the lowness of the runners. Our camping place was about four miles north of Cape Hotham. For about a mile north of Cape Hotham, the limestone cliff descends sheer down to a narrow level beach, but little above the level of the sea; beyond this, and as far as Barlow Inlet, there is a steep bank of detritus, reaching fully two thirds up the face of the rocks. Along the whole distance between Cape Hotham and Barlow Inlet, the shore is covered with immense blocks of ice, upheaved in chaotic confusion. It was between these blocks and the steep bank that our tents were pitched this night. Whilst pitching, two ravens and a flock of snow buntings flew over us to the northward. We have come over about six miles this day; but, as the sledges had frequently to be double manned, the amount of labour was considerably increased.

Saturday, 19th April, noon. Temp. 24° to 27°

3 P.M. South. Gloomy. Therm. +31°.

Cooks called at 4 A.M. of the 20th. Breakfast, and ready to start by 5. Captain Penny read prayers to all hands, and we started at 5.30. The road continued much the same as on the previous day, and dragging the sledges was consequently very heavy. At 7.30 reached Barlow Inlet, on the smooth hard ice of which it was almost a relief to feel the sledges coming easily behind us, after the almost killing work of the last few days, at which, however, the men had scarcely ever grumbled. We now struck right out of the inlet, in order to reach the smooth floe outside. Captain Penny and Petersen with the dog-sledges kept inshore. We had some difficulty in getting across a ridge or bar of heavy hummocks stretching across the mouth of the inlet, but succeeded in reaching the smooth ice beyond, on which we pushed to the northward until 9 A.M., when we came to a stand, Petersen having here returned and reported to us that a very heavy barrier of hummocks was stretching in every direction ahead of us. This was for the time very annoying. Captain Penny and Mr. Stewart set off together to see if they could find a practicable route for us. In the meantime the men were ordered to put on their great coats, which I may here mention were always packed on the top of the sledge to be at hand for putting on the moment we halted at any time, and which we always found to be of the greatest comfort and ad-

Sunday, 20th April. N.N.E. Moderate and clear.

Barlow Inlet.

vantage to the men. For not only were they useful at these halts, but in the night-time in the tents they formed a most acceptable addition to the blanket bags and wolfskins. During this halt we took lunch. Every one suffered greatly from thirst, and water, being of course scarce, was equally valuable. At length Captain Penny and Mr. Stewart returned with the intelligence that they had found a practicable, though still very difficult road, through the hummocks.

N. by W. Gloomy weather. Therm. −15°.

By tackling three crews to each sledge we managed to get over about two thirds of a mile of hummocks; the sledges going through a very *heavy sea*, as the men said. Two or three hands going ahead with the light pickaxes improved the road somewhat for us. The weather was at this time very thick and murky, and as in going through the hummocks it was impossible for us to wear our veils, before all the sledges were over more than half a-dozen were complaining of their eyes. By 3 P.M. all the sledges had reached the little smooth patch of ice close into the land which had been fixed upon for our camping place. They were soon unpacked, and the tents were pitched for the night. A cup of tea made us ready for our blanket bags, with the exception of those whose bloodshot, hot, and stinging eyes made sleep unavailable. We were scarcely comfortable in the tents before it began to blow strong from the N.W., with heavy snow drift. The gale increased in violence during the night, and the thermometer hanging to the ridge rope in my tent fell to −30° at 11 P.M. Notwithstanding this, and the tent being of thin foreign duck, through which the wind blew sharply enough, all those who were not troubled with their eyes slept soundly enough. We were closely enough packed, and each helped to keep the other warm.

N.W. strong gale. Snow drift. Therm. −30° in tent.

21st April, Point Delay. Strong gale. Snow drift. Therm. −26°, −14°, −11°.

At 2 A.M. of Monday the 21st, when I awoke, I found the thermometer had risen to −26°, and it rose as high as −11° in the course of the morning. My left eye was slightly affected with snow blindness, which made me restless, but gave me a good idea of what pain those poor fellows must have been suffering who were in a much worse state. Every one was astir early and ready for a start, but not only did the state of the weather render it imprudent to stir, but the number afflicted with snow blindness, as well as others threatened with it, made a halt for the day almost imperative. Every one therefore set to make himself as comfortable for the day as possible, ensconcing himself in his blanket bag and lighting his pipe. Those who were inclined for a further indulgence in sleep did so, but the laugh and the joke resounded from tent to tent the greater part of the day. An attempt was even made to get up a little music, but the performers on both flute and accordion soon found it was too cold work for the fingers.

Tuesday, 22nd April. Smart breeze N.W. Clear.

It continued to blow hard throughout the night, but it lulled somewhat in the morning, and a start was determined on. We started at 10 A.M., leaving one tent standing with those afflicted with snow blindness in it, and the other hands who were unlikely to stand the long journey so well, intending to push on ahead a few miles, make a depôt, and send back two sledges. Poor Mr. Stewart of the "Sophia" had to be led to-day whilst dragging his sledge, as his eyes had been very much affected for some days back, and he has suffered accordingly. The smooth floe on which we had tented for two nights back continued favouring us, and the hard frost we have had for the same time having hardened the snow, the dragging was comparatively easy for us. At noon we were again obliged to strike inshore over the hummocks, which we managed with a little difficulty. On reaching the shore, a ledge of perfectly hard smooth ice, running inside the hummocks, and between fifty and one hundred feet broad, along which we pushed quite cheerily, after the almost killing roads we had experienced previously. About a mile further on we came to the first appearance of a beach that we had seen since rounding Cape Hotham, and we halted here in order to form a depôt of what remained of the lading of the three and six day sledges. Mr. John Stuart here left us, with orders to return to the ships without delay with the two sledges, and we camped for the night, as the weather was again threatening. We scarcely made out four miles this day, although we have come over upwards of six. It is exceedingly annoying the slow progress we are making; but it is impossible to control the weather. The men, poor fellows, all work with the greatest goodwill and cheerfulness, each exerting himself more than his neighbour. My own crew is an excellent one. The thermometer during the day has ranged from $-25°$ to $-30°$. In the tent at night it stood from $-11°$ to $-16°$.

Therm. $-17°$, $-20°$, $30°$.

1st Depôt. Therm. $-25°$, $-30°$. In tent $-11°$ to $-16°$.

It was 9 A.M. of the 23rd before we could start. The thermometer had stood as low as $-22°$ in the tent during the night. A very cold wind from N.N.W. was blowing in our faces during our march, if the slow progress we can make with our heavy sledges deserves the name. The road come over to-day was excessively slippery, and undulating in sharp ridges, so that it was almost impossible to keep one's footing. This difficulty was increased by most of us having put on, for the first time, our canvass boots, the smooth soles of which had no hold of the hard frozen snow. We were all, therefore, constantly experiencing awkward tumbles. The same reason made it exceedingly difficult to keep up a constant drag upon the sledge; in fact the whole day's work was a succession of "*standing pulls.*" The thermometer during the greater part of the day stood at $-30°$, which, with the smart breeze blowing, exposed our faces to constant frost-biting, whilst the rest of our bodies were bathed in perspiration. Whilst using my bare hands to thaw my own face and those of the men, it was all I could do to keep them from being *nipt.* Altogether the march was a very trying one for every one. At 3 P.M. we were crossing the outlet of a large ravine, out of which seemed to issue a large river, the course of

Wednesday, 23rd April. Therm. $-25°$ to $-30°$. In tent $-18°$, $-22°$. N.N.W.

Therm. $-30°$ Strong, N.N.W.

which could be tracked through the banks. It was 3h. 30m. before we reached the northern banks, when it was found absolutely necessary to encamp, as the men were all much fatigued and knocked up with the excessive cold. It had been arranged with Captain Penny in the morning, when he left us, that we should follow him up, and he was to halt at the first convenient camping place. This it was impossible to do. After the tents were pitched, Mr. Stewart walked on ahead, to see if he could overtake Captain Penny. On his return he informed me that he had found the captain's party about a couple of miles ahead of our camp, and that they were not astonished at our being unable to make out a greater distance. Also, that we were to start early in the morning; push on until we came to a favourable spot, when his party was to strike across channel to the eastward, leaving ours to follow up the west coast. It seems Captain Penny's tent is pitched exactly below our beacon and signal post of last year, which they have again examined, and found to have been untouched since we erected it. After this, therefore, it will be all new ground for us, and, of course, all the more interesting.

Strong, N.N.W. Therm. $-30°$, $-26°$. In tent $-19°$.

Thursday, 24th April. N.W., squally. Therm. $-26°$, $-28°$. In tent $-14°$, $-19°$.

The morning of the 24th was very squally, and we were late of rousing out in consequence. At 6 A.M., whilst they were preparing breakfast, Mr. Stewart and I walked a short way up the valley, which has a different appearance from any of the ravines we have hitherto seen in Cornwallis Island. Inside of the talus through which the stream makes its way in a deep winding narrow channel, the cliffs arise abruptly on either side, forming very bold features in the scene. Behind them the valley opens out into a pretty large area, the hills rising gently on each side. It was 9 A.M. before all was ready for a start. By a little past ten we came up to Captain Penny's tent, and, after halting a minute or two, pushed on. It came on to blow strong again as we proceeded, and every one suffered much from the cold.

2nd Depôt. Strong N. Therm. $-22°$.

At 3 P.M. we came to a point round which the snow-drift was driving with great violence, so that we were obliged reluctantly again to pitch our tents; but there was no help for it, seeing the state of the weather, and the thermometer standing at the time at minus 22°. Captain Penny and Petersen overtook us by the time we had pitched the tents, and he at once concurred in the necessity there was for halting at the time we did. He himself went on a little further with Petersen, taking advantage of a slight lull, to see the nature of the coast round the point. About 4 P.M., after he returned, he sent for us all to his tent, Mr. Stewart, Sutherland, Marshall, and myself, and informed us that he had come to the determination, from the unpromising state of the weather, and from Petersen's advice, to return in the meantime to the ships, after making a depôt of all the provisions we had here. Some of us did not like the idea of turning back at all at first; but a little consideration soon convinced every one that the measure was a wise one. We could look for nothing but unfavourable weather during the beginning of May, and getting on so slowly as we were doing was but consuming provisions. The risk of the men suffering from the exposure was besides great, and the season was yet early. There were also many little things that the few days experience we had gained had opened our eyes to, which might be remedied before we started again. There was, therefore, not a dissentient voice to the proposition; and after giving the necessary orders and resting for a short time, the captain and Petersen set off on their return to the ships; the poor dogs evidently knowing that their heads were turned homewards. The thermometer stood at minus 22° during the night, and in the tent about minus 9°.

Friday, 25th April. 2nd Depôt.

At 4 A.M. on Friday the 25th all hands were called, and whilst the cooks were preparing breakfast, we set to, to make a caché of all the provisions, &c. we had with us, with the exception of the tents and bedding, &c. After every thing had been securely buried in the gravel, and the two sledges turned over on the top, we had breakfast, and started with the remaining two sledges, laden with the four tents, bedding, clothes, &c. and four days provisions, with double crews of course. We set off at a good round pace, which we kept up steadily, with the exception of a few minutes halt at the first depôt, until we reached Barlow Inlet, which we did in six hours. We here halted for a few minutes for lunch; but only for a few minutes, as a bitter blast was blowing out of the inlet. Every one was thirsty, and water was scarce, although we had managed to keep a lamp going to melt snow, as we could spare a hand to look after it; and I noticed more than one poor fellow in anything but a good humour at himself for losing his allowance of water, by leaving it for a second or two in his pannikin whilst hastily eating his pork and biscuit. Started again, and pushed on round Cape Hotham until we were two miles to the westward of it. We had intended to reach the Assistance depôt this night; but by this time the people were so done up that a halt had to be called, and the tents were pitched for the night. This was a long and very rapid march, and must be very nearly thirty miles at least. I noticed last night that the dogs seemed to know that they were returning to more comfortable quarters. I think we ourselves to-day seem to have been equally well aware that we were homeward bound. The whole day's journey was on the ice inside the hummocks, between them and the beach. The day on the whole has been a pleasant one; a cold wind from N.N.W. in squalls, but enlivened by a strong sun, occasionally affording us heat sufficient to contrast strongly with the biting cold we have experienced for a week back. The thermometer during the day has ranged from minus 8 to 12. We had it in the tent during the night at *plus* 5.

Return.

Saturday, 26th April.

At 7 A.M. we started, and, after crossing the hummocks at

Return to Assistance Bay.

Parry's Bluffs, we gained the smooth floe on which we had travelled on the 17th and 18th. As it was now hard and clear of snow, we set off at the same pace as yesterday, and were not long of leaving Cape Hotham and Dungeness Point behind us. About 11 A.M. we were met by one of Sir John Ross's men, who informed us of the safe arrival of the fatigue party, and of Captain Penny. We entered Assistance Harbour about half-past 12, and by 1 P.M. we were again on board the "Lady Franklin," after a ten days absence without a single mishap, indeed I may say every one, thank God, improved in health. To conclude our first journey we had a kind and hearty welcome home.

Second Journey.

6th May, 1851. Departure.

Three sledges, with five crews, left the ships at 7h. 10m. P.M. We were escorted for a few miles by some of Sir John Ross's crew, who bade us farewell about 9 P.M. On this occasion we kept close inshore with the sledges instead of pushing out to the floe beyond the hummocks. This made little difference to us, as our sledges were double manned. The evening was clear and pleasant, though cold, the thermometer +4°. We made a quick march to the eastward, and halted at 4 A.M. of the 7th, under Parry's South Bluff, close to the flagstaff erected by the "Assistance" in the autumn of last year. The tents were pitched, and every one comfortable in their blanket bags by 5 A.M. We have come at a pace of fully two knots an hour, which will make the march eighteen miles.

Wednesday, 7th. Cape Hotham.

Cooks called at 4 P.M. All hands at 6. Breakfast, and started at 7. Rounded "Ragged Point*" at 8 or a little after it. Road rather heavy, but pushed on well until 11, when a short halt was made to lunch; and also to try if a shot could be obtained at a bear which was prowling amongst the hummocks, but it was soon found that it was losing time to follow him. About midnight we were crossing the mouth of Barlow Inlet. Halted a short way to the northward to dine, and then carried on until we reached our first depôt of the 22nd ultimo. The route pursued this day was immediately under the cliffs the whole day. The sledges were not so difficult to drag as on our first journey, and we only occasionally met with deep snow to impede our progress.

Thursday, 8th May. Barlow Inlet.

Besides the bear, a fox was seen to the south of Barlow Inlet, and two ravens at Cape Hotham. We reached the depôt at 2 A.M., which we found had been torn up by the bears and foxes. Luckily, however, not much damage had been done, although the bag of pork had been dragged on the ice and slightly torn. They had been gnawing at one corner of it, but

1st Depôt.

* Cape Hotham. Ragged Point by the seamen, from the heaps of rough and rugged rocks lying about.

fat pork did not seem to suit either bruin or reynard's taste. The latter part of this day's march was over a tolerably good road, but the weather was severe, and the blasts of snow frequent and heavy.

Breakfast was over, and all hands called at 7 P.M., when the depôt was re-arranged with more care as to its protection from plunderers. Taking on with us the "*dog* pemmican" which had been left here on the 22nd ultimo, we started at 10 P.M., and still keeping the hard snow of the beach we continued our course northward. We had a fair wind with us this day, and on Mr. J. Stuart's sledge they took advantage of this by hoisting their floorcloth as a sail, which proved of considerable use, until an unfortunate squall laid the sledge on her beam ends, much to the amusement of the crews of the others who had not been so adventurous in the use of their canvas. No damage, however, was done, and the rest of the march was performed without anything worthy of note happening, until our arrival at our second depôt made on our former journey, and our furthest point reached on that occasion. We found this caché quite undisturbed, and very soon all of us were snugly esconced in our tents, and busily engaged with our tea, pork, and pemmican. At 2 P.M. Petersen drove up with his dogs, and immediately afterwards Captain Penny also reached us. They had left the ships at 6 A.M. all well. They had been thus eight hours on the journey, and allowing that their rate of travelling will average five miles an hour, which is, I think, within the mark, this will make the distance of this point from our vessels in Assistance Harbour between forty-five and fifty miles. Captain Penny pitched his tent beside ours, and turned in whilst we took advantage of the fine clear afternoon to walk on ahead to examine the state of the roads and the coast to the northward. Mr. A. Stewart, John Stuart, and myself, pursued the coast along for about five miles. About a mile beyond our camp we crossed the outlet of a large watercourse, which I afterwards found issues from a small lake immediately behind the first or coast line of hills. The farthest point of land we reached at this time was one peculiarly marked and recognizable (since named by Captain Penny Point Petersen). Another watercourse had its outlet here, and from the extreme point we could see that a deep and extensive bay lay before us, in the bottom of which were seen three or four bold and precipitous outlying points. The coast here begins to take a slight westerly trend. As this was the point fixed upon by Captain Penny for the eastern parties striking across the channel, one of our principal objects in this walk was to remark the best spot at which it would be advisable to do so. It was pleasant then to us all to see that a very short distance north of our camping place there was a good outlet through the hummocks, and a smooth floe to the eastward, or at least comparatively smooth, as the hummocks were pretty widely scattered.

Friday, 9th. 2nd Depôt.

On our return to the camp the sledges were all packed, and we were ready for a start by 8 P.M. The sledges were now found to be very heavily laden, and it was necessary in consequence of the deep snow, to leave one behind, whilst with double crews we took the other on ahead. At half-past nine we reached the second ravine, where the eastern parties were to leave us. They struck out through the hummocks to the floe of the channel at 10 P.M. Mr. A Stewart, of the "Sophia," accompanied by Dr. Sutherland, and a fatigue sledge to examine the coast to the northward of Cape Grinell, and to follow it along in whatever direction it may trend. Mr. John Stuart with one sledge to go to the south-eastward in order to re-examine Beechey Island and its neighbourhood, as well as the coast as far as Cape Hurd in order to make sure that no trace of the missing expedition could have been passed over last year.

Saturday, 10th May. Port Separation.

We parted with mutual good wishes, and soon lost sight of them amongst the hummocks, where, however, they seemed to be making good way before a steady breeze, all three sledges with their sails set. We ourselves were not so fortunate, for during the rest of this march we had desperately heavy work, as the snow along the beach was soft and deep, and there was no practicable road outside the hummocks. We soon found it absolutely necessary to have again recourse to double manning the sledges, by leaving one behind and taking the other on ahead. This of course made it necessary to go over four-fifths of this day's distance three times, so that at the time for halting, although we had only made good some six or seven miles, we had yet actually gone over seventeen or eighteen miles of ground. About a mile to the southward of Point Petersen, to our great relief, we came to a piece of hard smooth ice, along which the sledges glided with great ease. When we reached Point Petersen we found that Captain Penny had encamped here, and the bag of dog pemmican was taken off Mr. Marshall's sledge and left here. We carried on for some hours longer, but the good road we had been so rejoiced to fall upon did not last us long, and we were soon again at "standing pulls." At 4 A.M. we picked out the best spot we could find at the inner edge of the hummocks for our tenting place, and pitched our tents on a soft bed of snow. Hitherto there having been five sledge crews, and on our former journey six, our encampments have had a very cheerful and lifelike appearance, but now our two little tents look solitary to our unaccustomed eyes. However, the hard day's work we had undergone made us all soon forgetful of such reflections, by the sound sleep enjoyed in our blanket bags.

Cloudy and variable. Therm. −7° to +8°.

The day has throughout been cloudy, with light variable winds. The thermometer ranging from minus 7° to plus 8°.

Point Petersen. Cloudy, variable. Therm. −7° to +8°.

I was up at 3 P.M. Called the cooks, and prepared to start at 6. Walked round the point with Marshall, and found that a deep bay lay before us, a smooth floe covering it outside, whilst the shores were covered with large and rough hummocks. We immediately saw that it would be advisable to strike off from the beach about three hundred yards north of our tents, and steer a course across to the bay. Captain Penny walked up to our tents before we were ready to start, and I again walked round the point with him, when he agreed as to the propriety of striking at once across the bay. We were under way by 6, and at 7 were overtaken by the two dog sledges. Captain Penny and Petersen are now accompanied by the man who has had charge of the dogs all winter, an active young fellow of the name of Thomson, who I hope will prove useful to them. They stopped for a minute or two and bade us farewell. We gave them three cheers, and wished them God speed on starting again. In less than an hour they were out of sight. They go at a great rate, but I am doubtful as to their supply of food. I trust, however, that they will get a sufficient quantity to enable them to do a good spell of work.

Sunday, 11th May. N.N.W., light. Therm. −4° to +6°. +15° in tent. 9 hours. 10 miles.

We had tolerably good ice during the whole march. Our sledges were heavy, but the work was not so trying as anything we have had for the few last days. Occasionally we had to cross low ridges of hummocks, but on the whole we got on well; there was but little wind, and the thermometer was only 4° below zero at midnight. At the foot of the bay there appeared two or three bold precipitous cliffs projecting a little. I had fixed upon the first of these as the probable extent of our day's journey, at least to get abreast of it; but at 4 A.M. we were still a little short of it. We halted here at 4 A.M. under the shelter of some large hummocks, having been ten hours under weigh; take from this an hour for stoppages, say ten miles of northing gained.

Called the cooks at 5 P.M. Struck tents and started at 8 P.M. Light breeze from N.N.W.; thermometer 6°. Crossed some heavier hummocks than any we had had yesterday, but the floe upon the whole good, although the sledges are too heavily laden to make satisfactory progress. At our first depôt I shall leave every article that can be possibly done without. At 11 one of the men pointed out something on the top of a large hummock, which, on examining, I found to be a cleft stick, in which was inserted a slip of paper from Captain Penny informing me that he had reached this spot in *two hours* after leaving us on Saturday night. We have thus been exactly *twelve hours* in doing what the dogs have gone over in *two*. But I think they had made a straighter course to this point than we have done. Petersen, I think, calculates his dogs' speed at eight miles an hour. Nothing worthy of note occurred during this journey.

Monday, 12th April. Squally. N.N.W. Therm. −1° to +4°. 9 hours' march, say 10 miles.

About midnight we passed the second headland; and about 2 A.M. of the 12th could see the northern termination of the Bay (since named Cape De Haven by Captain Penny) to be also bold and rocky, but with an apparently low point running out from it. It still appears a considerable distance off, and I

Cape De Haven.

expect will prove another day's march for us ere we reach it. The latter part of our road was rather heavy and hummocky, and progress slow. Halted under the lee of a large hummock at 6 A.M. when we tented. Ten hours under weigh,—say nine, after allowing for stoppages,—and about as many miles made good. We have had pretty sharp head winds during the journey; the thermometer $-1°$ to $+4°$.

Monday, 12th May. N.N.W., Squally. Therm. $-1°$ to $+6°$.

The day was throughout dull, cloudy, and overcast with occasional squalls from the N.N.W. The cooks were called at 6, and we started at 9 P.M. The floe continued hummocky, and our progress was rather slow. The horizon occasionally cleared to the northward, and we more than once thought we could see land stretching in every direction ahead of us, but very indistinctly. At 4 A.M. of the 13th we succeeded in getting within a mile of the point which had been in sight for two days back, upon which we found a broad range of high hummocks pressed up. At this time it blew very strong round the point with thick drift, so that I thought it prudent to call a halt and pitch tents, which was accordingly done in a snug corner under the lee of some of the largest hummocks. We have been seven hours under weigh, of which there has not been lost more than fifteen minutes from stoppages; say nine miles gained, as we are yet a mile from the point. After we had supper, and the men were comfortable in their bags, Marshall and I took advantage of a slight lull in the weather to walk to the point. Whilst crossing the hummocks to reach the shore, I perceived that the dogs had been in pursuit of a large bear. Before we halted we had also seen their footmarks, from which I take it for granted that Captain Penny and Petersen must have encamped somewhere near this. The tracks of bears were here very numerous, but we did not see any. However, we were happy to see these tracks, which makes it probable that Petersen may be able to procure a sufficient supply of food for his dogs, which will do away with the only difficulty in their way. When we reached the point, we could make out land to the N.W., apparently an island distinct from that we stand on, but our view was very indistinct. The continuation of this coast also seems now to take a more westerly trend. A low outlying point, apparently ten miles off, terminated our view in this direction. We had scarcely made out these particulars before it came on to blow with greater fury than ever from the N.W., so that we were fairly obliged to beat a retreat, and make the best of our way back to the tents, which we reached cold and tired enough. It continued blowing hard, with thick drift, during the whole day, and the thermometer did not rise above $+3°$.

Tuesday, 13th May. N.E. Point. Cape De Haven.

Therm. $-6°$ to $+3°$.

At the usual time for starting, found that the weather still continued too inclement to risk stirring in advance. The cooks prepared breakfast, after which every one composed themselves to sleep again as comfortably as possible. The early part of the 14th, therefore, was spent in forced inactivity. The people's appetites reminded them at 7 A.M. that it was their usual supper time, and the pemmican did not seem to have decreased the less on this occasion from the last twelve hours having been spent in the blanket bag instead of dragging the sledges. About midday it was a little quieter and calmer to walk out to see if I could discover Captain Penny's camping place in the neighbourhood. This I did not succeed in doing; but I had the satisfaction of finding that our next march would be on smooth ice, immediately outside the hummocks, and that these constant obstacles in our way were quite narrow at the most projecting part of the point, which would make it an easy matter to cross in to the gravel here in order to make our first depôt, which I intend to do before going further. The weather gradually improved after mid-day, and we prepared to make an early start. The sledges were packed, and we were in motion by 4 P.M. At half past five we reached the point, when we halted, unpacked both sledges, and deposited upon one everything we intended to leave here; this we, with some little difficulty, hauled over the hummocks, and about a hundred yards up the bank. It was a work of some labour excavating even a shallow hole in the gravel sufficiently large for our purpose. In this we deposited 70 lbs. of bread, 63 lbs. of pork, and two cases of pemmican. I besides left here every article that could possibly be done without, for too many things I now found were in both sledges. The whole was securely covered over with a mound of the limestone gravel, leaving of course a despatch paper as usual, enclosed in a gutta percha envelope. It was 8 P.M. before we had the sledges repacked and stowed, when we immediately set off to the low point seen to the westward. Shortly after we started the opening of a large wide valley or watercourse was seen in the bottom of the bight to the westward of N.E. point. I trusted to getting this examined on our return. The ice we passed over this journey was very fair; a few traverses had to be made for the hummocks, but our progress was rapid, and at midnight we were even half way between the points. At half past two A.M. of the 15th we fell upon the track of the dog sledges; following them up we arrived at the point at 4 A.M. where we found they had camped, as also a note from Captain Penny on the top of a high hummock, in which he informed me that in consequence of the appearance of land to the northward, he had determined to strike off in that direction. In this note he repeated his instructions that this party should follow up this coast, examine it thoroughly for traces of the missing expedition, and to push on as far as our means and the people's strength would with prudence allow. This last spell of work has extended over twelve hours, which, deducting four for stoppages and the time expended in making the depôt, leaves eight for the march, say ten miles gained. Ascending to the high ground behind the point, we could see that the coast now runs almost due west. It is changed in appearance also; there

Wednesday, 14th May. Storm stayed at N.E. point. N.W., thick drift. Therm. +5° to +8°.

N.E. point. N.W., squally. Therm. +5° to +8°.

Depôt at N E. point. N.N.W. light breeze.

Thursday, 15th May. Point Decision. Therm. +3° to +7°. N.N.W.

N.N.W., smart breeze, clear. Therm. +3° to +11°.

are now no bold rocky headlands in sight, such as we have been passing for some days back. Low outlying points have taken their place, and between them the coast rises in a gradual slope to a range of low round topped hills. Looking to the northward, the nearest land can now be made out to be, with little doubt, an island, but we cannot be certain as yet. There is, also, land to the northward of this, but apparently a great distance off. The east end of the nearest island is N.W. from this point of view. The northern horizon was at this time overclouded, so that our view in that direction was not the best to have been desired.

Light airs, N.W. Therm. +15° +23°.

At 5 P.M. called the cooks. Ready to start at half past eight; left a note for Captain Penny with the usual despatch paper in a cairn. Reached the outside of the shore ridge of hummocks at nine. The evening was cloudy and overcast, but the thermometer did not fall below plus 10°. We had very good smooth ice for some time, though the prospect ahead to the westward presented nothing but an uninterrupted wilderness of high hummocks. After passing over two or three ridges, however, we gained a narrow lane of very smooth ice, having on each side of it high ridges, along which we pushed rapidly for some hours. A ptarmigan, the first we have seen this season, flew close past us at this time, and alighted on the shore. A little before midnight the smooth ice which had been favouring us during the previous part of the journey was lost, the ridges here joining one another.

Friday, 16th May. Light airs, N.W.

We had here an hour's hard work, with the sledges double-banked, in getting clear of the hummocks, in doing which we had to strike more to the northward; after which we came upon some of last year's floe ice, easily recognizable, but apparently not of great extent, for during the next two hours we passed over various separate pieces. This is the first ice of last year's formation that we have yet seen, for since the 10th all the ice we have passed over has more the appearance of that which was formed outside Assistance Harbour in the middle of March than even ice formed in the autumn of 1850. At 3 A.M. we halted for ten minutes to lunch, when from the top of a high hummock I was glad to see a considerable extent of smooth ice stretching away to the westward, and from which we were only separated by a few ridges of comparatively low hummocks. Encouraged by this prospect, we were not long of reaching this smooth floe, and pushing on with increased speed. The nearest point of land had immensely high hummocks piled up upon it. It was apparently not more than four miles off, and I determined to push on and reach it before halting, but the longer we advanced the further off did it seem to be. At 6 A.M. we halted for a minute or two to breathe, but again started for another "spell," determined, if possible, to make out the wished-for point; but at half past seven it was still a considerable distance from us; and the sight of a pile of hummocks affording good shelter, with a soft

N.N.W., light airs. Therm. +10°.

bed of snow surrounding them, tempted us to halt and pitch our tents for the day, which was now clear with bright sunshine, wind from N.W., sharp, but thermometer + 10°. We have been thus ten hours and a half under way, say nine hours, allowing for stoppages; and as the greater part of the time we have been coming at a quick rate, I should say that ten miles is not above the mark.

We were all comfortable in our bags, and the cooks were just finishing their duties this morning, when one of them reported a bear close to the tent. We were not long of being ready for his reception; but too much noise being made, bruin took alarm, and made off before we could get a shot at him. N.W., light airs. Therm. +10° to +23°.

The cooks were called before 7 P.M., and we were ready to start at 9. The evening was pleasant, and the ice favourable. All the people in good health and spirits, so that we progressed to the westward rapidly for two hours. The shores still having the same appearance they have had since passing N.E. Cape on the 14th; viz., low round topped hills sloping gradually to the beach. At 11 P.M. an animal was seen moving slowly about on the sloping shore. This was at first taken for a bear; but on directing my glass towards it I found that it was a reindeer. As it was but a short distance off, I thought it worth while to endeavour to have a shot at it. Whilst the sledges proceeded, therefore, I went on shore, accompanied by Leiper, from Marshall's crew, and making a slight détour, gained the shelter of a watercourse, from which we expected to get within shot. Something alarmed him, however (probably the sledges on the ice), and he cantered off over the hills. Before he disappeared I saw that he was a fine large buck, with immense antlers. I advanced a short distance inshore, and found that in the hollows vegetation was somewhat plentiful, though scarcely yet showing any signs of spring. The tracks of reindeer in these hollows, where they had been scraping amongst the snow for the moss, were very numerous. The interior, as seen from the highest point I reached, seemed to be an undulating country of no great elevation, with here and there a round topped hill. The limestone gravel still prevails here, but the appearance of the country is not quite so desolate as we have hitherto had it, and the plentiful traces of game gave rise to more hopeful anticipations with regard to the fate of those we search for than we have had for some days back. I had scarcely rejoined the sledges, which I had some difficulty in overtaking, when a she bear, accompanied by two cubs, were seen making right towards us. Before they were within shot the watchful mother became suspicious, and made off. The cubs, excited by curiosity, stopped to look at us, rising on their hind legs, and gambolling about with great agility. Expecting in consequence to get within shot, we followed them a short distance, but the mother always took care, when they loitered too long behind, to give them most unmistakeable hints that they were in dangerous company, and that

Light airs, N.W.

Saturday, 17th May. A.M. W.

it was time to be off. We did not waste much time, therefore, in following them; as it was, we only did for the sake of the fuel which their carcasses might afford in the shape of fat. To make up for the time lost on these two occasions, we pushed on with greater speed for some time, which the state of the ice luckily allowed, although rough. There was scarcely a hummock high enough to stop us for a minute in our way during the rest of this day's journey. The early part of the 17th was bright sunshine and clear; the lowest reading of the thermometer was + 6, but it rose rapidly as the morning wore on. At 2 A.M. we passed a snow covered bluff, to the westward of which lay a small shallow bay. Another similar bluff was passed, and a second bay or small harbour opened out on the east side of which we pitched our tents at 7 A.M. We have thus been ten hours marching; deduct two for stoppages, will leave eight hours actually in motion. After the tents were pitched, I walked across the bay, accompanied by Mr. Marshall and Richard Kitson, and ascended the hill or high ground which forms its western side. This I calculated to be between four to five hundred feet high. The nearest land to the northward was now distinctly seen to be an island, apparently from fifteen to twenty miles off. Beyond this, but at a much greater distance to the northward, land could be seen, running as far to the eastward as we could see, but abruptly lost to sight almost abreast of us to the northward. There was, I think, a considerable amount of refraction at the time, which, perhaps, gave it the high and curiously peaked appearance, so different from that of the coast we then stood on. What astonished us most at this time, however, was the almost unmistakeable appearance of a water sky to the northward of the east end of the island. To Mr. Marshall's eye it had all the appearance of a water sky, and although it afterwards proved to have been actually so, yet at the time we were inclined to think that this peculiar appearance must have been caused in some other way.

The coast we are ourselves following along seems now to run almost due west; the furthest point we can see being a high bold headland apparently from thirty to forty miles off. On examining the ice for our future progress we were delighted to see that we would have a smooth floe, almost unbroken by a single hummock. It had a peculiar appearance altogether, the ice to the westward of this being more like a recently formed bay floe than anything else. All our previously formed ideas of the state of the ice to the northward of the Parry group have proved to be completely mistaken; for instead of the immensely heavy ice that we had anticipated it proves to be the very reverse. Indeed, except along the shores and across the mouths of the bays, we have as yet seen little or no heavy ice. In these places, to be sure, where there has been severe pressure, very heavy blocks are seen, but not heavier than those to be seen in Barrow's Straits. I was disappointed here in not being able to construct a cairn of any size, as I have more than once been before. The whole of the summit of the height on which we now stood was composed of limestone gravel, not a single piece of which exceeded the size of a shilling, and to even shovel up a pile of these was a matter of difficulty, from their being firmly compacted into a solid mass by the frost. In returning to the tent we struck at once outside the hummocks, and walked back on the smooth ice, which we were glad to find as level and free of hummocks as we had judged it to be from the top of the hill. During the afternoon it became cloudy and overcast, and at 8 P.M., by which time we had breakfasted, and were ready to start, it was blowing a sharp breeze from W.S.W., with occasionally a little drift. Thermometer + 5°. Until midnight we progressed rapidly along the level floe seen in the morning. This seemed to extend from the shore ridge of hummocks to about three miles off, between which and the island long ridges of hummocks running east and west were seen, but of small size. A good many seals were seen lying at their holes, but were too wary to be reached within shot. At one of these holes a large bear was on the watch; he allowed Leiper and I to come close to him before moving, but not within shot. The ice at this hole was not three feet thick. Shortly after this a ptarmigan alighted on the ice a short distance ahead of my sledge, which Leiper shot, being the first game of any kind we had as yet procured. The weather had now become quite thick and foggy, and every object loomed large, and seemed to be in motion in the misty atmosphere. Two large dark objects in particular, which were advancing rapidly towards us, we at first took to be the dog-sledges, which might have taken a circuit in this direction on their return. It was some time before we were undeceived, and every one was speculating on the chances of their having gained intelligence, when the closer approach of the objects made us aware that they were bears. Three others were seen at the same time, so that five were in sight at once. One of the nearest seemed to be rather suspicious of our intentions, and sheared off, but the other and largest kept steadily on, and passed within two hundred yards of us. Meanwhile Richard, the captain of my sledge, had walked quietly out towards him, and, when within forty yards, gave him a well-directed rifle bullet, which made him throw a very active somerset, and measure his length on the ice. Although severely wounded, and losing much blood, he was almost instantly up and moving off pretty smartly; so that I had to follow some distance before I could get a steady aim. He could not have gone much further, however, and the two additional balls, followed by one from Marshall, finished him. It was now past 3 A.M. of the 18th, blowing strong with thick drift, so that it was advisable, if not indeed quite necessary, to encamp at once. We had only been seven hours under way, one of which at least had been lost. The ice we had come over was favourable, and it is within the mark to say that six miles of

W.S.W. Therm. +5°.

Sunday, 18th May. W.S.W., strong squalls, drift. A.M. Therm. +6° to +8°.

W.S.W., squally, drift. A.M. Therm. +7° +8°.

westing was gained on this march. The sledges were, therefore, hauled at once under the lee of the nearest hummocks, and the tents pitched, not, however, before more than one had got wet feet by slipping into cracks through the soft snow. Taking the track belts from the sledges, we then hauled in the carcass of the bear to the neighbourhood of the tents, intending to bury the flesh for the dogs should they come this way. Whilst bringing it in we fell upon a small hole of water, about a couple of yards square, when the ice at the edges was extremely rotten, and scarcely eighteen inches thick. A strong current was here running to the eastward. The bear was skinned, and all his fat carefully preserved for fuel, which we were already beginning to get anxious about. We were fortunate enough besides to find in his maw the blubber of a seal, newly killed and devoured, so that he altogether yielded us between twenty and thirty pounds of fat. It continued to blow hard round the land ahead of us, with occasional thick clouds of drift during the day. The highest reading of the thermometer was +15°. We turned out between 3 and 4 P.M., quartered the carcass, and buried it in snow, as we thought securely, but as we afterwards found anything but so. Twice during the halt we had been aroused by the loud croaking of ravens, who had already been attracted by the carrion. Whilst the men were cutting up the carcass they found a large abscess in the groin, which I examined carefully, thinking that it might have been caused by an old gunshot wound, but there was no evidence to prove this.

Calm, overcast. P.M. +15° to +23°.

On the highest outside hummock I left a black bottle, in which was a note and paper for Captain Penny, should he come this way. From the number of bears we had now seen, however, I hoped that he and Petersen would be able to supply themselves amply with food for their dogs. At 7 P.M. we again started on our course to the westward. The evening was dull and overcast, but the thermometer had risen to +23°. As we advanced the ice evidently became weaker and weaker, and wherever a slight inequality or hummock on the ice had collected the snowdrift, it was soft, sludgy, and quite wet, with a strong saline taste. I have omitted to mention before, that for some days previous to this the cooks have had difficulty in procuring snow, which would yield water perfectly free of a brackish taste. It was only amongst the hummocks, where the snow was collected in deep wreaths, that it was quite fresh. In many places the ice was apparently so weak as even to give rise to an idea of insecurity. In many places there were short irregular rents or holes in the ice, where the sledges were raised, and sometimes slightly overlapped. Some caution was required in approaching these places, where a very strong current was seen running still to the eastward. The water seemed muddy and of a greyish colour, with all the appearance of a strong deep current which is running through a confined channel. This was not more than two hundred yards from the shore, the whole length of which we have come along

Monday, 19th May. A.M. N.W., squally. Therm. +8°.

during this march was steep slopes covered with deep snow banks. The tops of these, and similar snow banks whenever they occur, are formed by the drift into overhanging eves as it were, and, gracefully curling inwards, have the appearance in many cases of fine scroll work. Shortly after midnight, we were opening out a fine bay, the eastern headland of which presented a feature entirely new to us, — viz. a solid cliff of ice. Where the snow banks terminated this ice appeared stretching from eighty to one hundred yards to the westward. This ice had an almost perpendicular face to the northward, was distinctly stratified and of a dirty greenish colour. The strata running from east to west, and dipping towards the sea or to the northward, and having an inclination from west to east. Large blocks had fallen in different places, showing these features in this curious ice cliff, if one may use such an expression. Determined to examine this more minutely on my return, we kept on our course to the westward. Beyond this ice were bold and pinnacled limestone cliffs, the first we had seen since passing N.E. Cape on the 13th. A more remarkable pinnacle than usual on the summit of this cliff was so like a cairn that I was not astonished at the men taking it for one, and being doubtful of its not being one, even after examining it with my glass, for they had been more than once before taking these appearances for cairns.

Finding the bay, now that we had opened it up more fully, to be of some extent, I determined to walk round it, whilst the sledges proceeded on their course across it to the western point. I found some difficulty in crossing the hummocks to the shore, and sustained some awkward tumbles by plunging into the deep and soft snow drifts between these rugged masses. Bear tracks were to be seen in every direction, as well as numerous impressions of the footsteps of their usual companion the fox, the huge *sign manual* of the one contrasting strong with the tiny pad of the other. When I reached the beach I found it composed of the usual limestone shingle, with a considerable mixture of pieces of a cross grained dark red sandstone. There was some extent of low land in the bottom of this bay, ascending gradually to the southwards in terraces similar to those so well marked in Assistance Bay. These were cut through by the course of what must be a very large stream during summer, about midway between the eastern and western headlands.

The night had been all along gloomy and overcast, but the weather was now (2 A.M., 19th) assuming a more threatening appearance. Frequent snow showers, with heavy gusts from the N.W., obscured the prospect to the westward. I had lost sight of the sledges for some time; when last seen they were moving onwards almost abreast of me. When about three parts round the bay, I turned to see how they were getting on, and was not a little astonished to see that they had come to a halt. With the assistance of my glass I could see that three or four of the men were straggling about in different directions ahead of the sledges with tent poles and lances in their hands, and at the same time was not a little startled to see that this stoppage was caused by the ice being full of holes, water appearing in every direction in small pools, the floe, in fact, being completely "*honeycombed.*" From the way in which they were picking their steps too, I could easily see that they were anything but confident in the trustworthiness of the ice. I immediately turned and made the best way I could over the hummocks towards the sledges. Whilst doing so I passed two hummocks, which I had previously noticed from their immense size and peculiar form. They were fully thirty feet above the level of those surrounding them, and about fifteen feet square, standing close together, and forming a very marked feature in the view. The most brilliant blue colour of the more transparent parts of these huge ice blocks added to their picturesque appearance. These were near the outer edge of the ridge of hummocks running across the mouth of the bay, and I had not gone far from them when I narrowly missed a cold bath in a small hole which was merely covered with soft sludge. As it was I got wet feet. Rendered more cautious by this, I was as quickly as possible picking my steps towards the sledges, leaping from hummock to hummock amongst a number of small pools of water, when I was almost thrown off my balance by a loud noise and the sudden appearance, within a yard of my feet, of a hideous face with bright eyes and long protruding tusks. The poor walrus seemed nearly as startled as I was at our close proximity, for he at once made an unwieldy plunge out of sight. Within the next two or three minutes I noticed three large seals at these holes, and another walrus. I had not a little difficulty in reaching the sledges, and when I did so, found that Marshall, Leiper, and some of the others had been quite unsuccessful in finding any practicable route over this decayed ice, though they had examined it in different directions, and had found it weaker the further from the shore or further northward they went. There was now, therefore, no other course open for us but to retrace our steps for some distance, and take the best road we could over the hummocks to the shore, although the snow was deep, yet I knew we could advance to the westward without fear of any accident to our heavy sledges. Indeed it was only now, on turning the sledges, that we became thoroughly aware of the very frail state of the ice that we had latterly been coming over. Had either of the sledges broken through it might have been productive of very awkward consequences.

It was now blowing very hard from the N.W. with very thick snow, and before we had got more than a hundred yards over the hummocks we found it absolutely necessary to pitch the tents, two or three of the people complaining of their eyes, which had been much tried during the latter part of the march. The tents were pitched under the lee of a large hummock, on a soft bed of dry snow at half past 2 A.M., the thermometer + 9°. We have thus been seven hours and a half under way, of this, say six, actually advancing, and as the ice has been favourable and very level, it is not overstating to say that we have gained eight miles of westing. We were all glad to get under cover, for the drift and wind were now so violent that it was with difficulty the cooks could manage to prepare our suppers.

This unfavourable state of the weather continued throughout the day, and, if possible, become worse towards the evening. The thermometer rose to + 13° at midday. At 6 P.M. it was + 10°, the wind and drift still as violent as ever. The cooks were called, and breakfast prepared, but with little prospect of a speedy start. Those who could, composed themselves to sleep again, and the never-failing tobacco pipe lent its consolation to the restless.

Tuesday, 20th May. Strong gale, W.S.W. Therm. +10°+16°. Storm stayed.

The 20th commenced without the slightest amendment in the weather. The gale blows now from W.S.W., the drift so thick that no object was visible two yards from the tent-door. The land, though not one hundred yards off, was also, of course, quite invisible. The thermometer did not fall below + 10°, and in the forenoon was noted at + 16°. However carefully we closed and laced up the tent door, we found we could not altogether exclude the almost impalpable drift which was now coming down in showers upon us with every gust of wind from the roof of the tent, where it was hanging in thick festoons like the cobwebs in a flour mill. The usual time for starting again came round, but with little abatement in the gale and drifting snow. Every one was thoroughly tired of "*the bag*," which was now anything but comfortable, for from our long rest the heat of our bodies was beginning to have an effect upon the soft snow beneath us, and each was undergoing a very satisfactory course of hydropathy in his soaking blanket bag. This was only a source of amusement and joking to the men, however, for nothing seemed to come amiss to any one of them, and the only regret was that from their wet state the "*dunnage*" would be so increased in weight for the next march. At midnight it had, if anything, moderated somewhat, but the thermometer had fallen to + 1°, and the land was still invisible in consequence of the thick drift.

Wednesday, 21st May. Strong gale. W.S.W., drift.

The morning and forenoon, therefore, still found us close prisoners to the tent. At midday the thermometer had again risen to + 12°, the wind lulled at intervals, and occasionally the east head of the bay could be seen peeping out above the drift. Tired of the long inaction, and tempted by the more promising look of the weather at half past 12, I determined to walk to the land. Accompanied by Richard Kitson I did so; and although bitterly cold, yet we were fortunate enough to have two hours of tolerably clear weather. We made first for the eastern head of the bay, on reaching the summit of which I was startled, although I might have almost expected it, by the sight of long lanes and pools of open water stretching in every direction between us and the island to the northward. The whole ice in the straits before us apparently very weak and much broken up. I say I was startled, for the first consideration was the likelihood of Captain

Penny and Petersen with the dog sledges running the risk of being entangled or caught behind this now loose body of ice. However, I felt confident that Captain Penny was more likely to perceive the state of the ice before us, and take the necessary precautions accordingly.

I had thought it likely that I might here be able to make something out as to the nature of the curious ice cliff noticed two days before, and over which we were now standing. But I found it impossible to approach the edge in any direction, although I walked along a considerable distance, from the treacherous nature of the overhanging snow; which, as I have before noticed, projects like the eves of a house. I was satisfied, however, that the ice in no direction projected *above* the level of the land on which we stood, or *over* it.

Our view to the westward was entirely obscured as the drift snow was still blowing in thick clouds round the termination of the bay in that direction, and it was only at intervals that we could see far below us our little canvas home among the hummocks. To the northward, however, the air was so clear of drift, that we could make out the nearest shores of the island pretty distinctly, sufficiently to see that in some places the water, if not at them, was close to them.

We now turned inshore and walked for some distance in that direction. We crossed a hollow, in the bottom of which there was the appearance of a small lake, but so deeply covered with snow as to leave its shape, boundaries, and even the fact of its being a lake in doubt, had it not been for the outlet from it marking the course of a stream running towards the bay. This hollow or valley seemed to run to the eastward and northward, and very likely joins the coast in that direction. Beyond this, to the southward, we crossed a series of low undulations, on which in various places we saw the remains of last year's vegetation peeping through the snow,—grasses and moss. Here we fell upon numerous tracks of reindeer, their droppings appearing very recent. In different places, too, I noticed traces of ptarmigan. We separated as far as was prudent, considering the unsettled state of the weather, in order to have a better chance of falling in with game. As we advanced to the southward we found the ground gradually rising, intersected in every direction with deep watercourses, all tending towards the main one which issues from the bay we had left, and which must without doubt be a very large stream in the summer season. It was now getting very thick, and I was apprehensive that we had advanced as far as prudence would allow, when I saw Richard, who was somewhat in advance of me, making signs that he had seen something. In hastening to join him I narrowly missed being precipitated into a deep gully, from both banks being faced with steep walls of snow, the chasm between not being apparent to the eye until almost too late. On joining him I found that he had seen a herd of deer, and been almost within shot of them, but that they had

Storm stayed.

made off to the south-east at a great rate. We followed up quickly for some distance, the ground still continuing to rise, but our vision was very limited from the thick state of the atmosphere, when I noticed that the drift was rapidly filling up and obscuring our own footprints behind us, so that it was necessary at once to retreat. From this, our furthest, we could only make out that high land faced us in every direction to the southward. That we had not turned too soon we were convinced of before we regained the tents, for it was not only most bitterly cold, but the drift was almost blinding, and it was only by following the watercourses that we were enabled to grope our way back to the bay. We had some difficulty in making our way over the hummocks from the shore, but at last, at half-past 5 P.M., we found ourselves at the tent-door, nearly blind and very much fatigued. The weather was now nearly as bad as before, and the thermometer down to + 6°. I had been two or three times regretting that I had not taken the sledges on some distance instead of making this march inland, but I think, as it turned out, it was as well not. The men were saved the exposure, and the risk of incurring snow blindness with which I now found myself and companion threatened.

Thursday, 22nd May.

About midnight it moderated and cleared up. We immediately took advantage of this, and started, all of us very glad to leave our now wet-enough lairs. The tents were struck, and sledges packed, by a few minutes past twelve. It was absolutely necessary to take one sledge at a time over the hummocks with both crews. It was very difficult and tedious work, the cracks being so numerous and snow deep. In two hours we had the sledges on the beach, along which we struck to the westward, coasting round the bay. We had scarcely made out three miles, however, before it again began to blow violently from the westward, accompanied by a thick fall of hard sharp snow, which felt to our faces like so many needles, and which affected the eyes most acutely. Trusting that it would pass over, we persevered until it was impossible to keep our eyes longer open, when, much against our wills, it was found that we must again halt.

This was provoking enough, following close upon the loss of two days marching; for three miles is as much as we will have gained by this last move. We hauled up on a soft gravel beach, and the tents were not long of being pitched, for every one of the men, tired as they were of confinement to the "*bag*," were glad to escape from the sharp striking snow, or rather hail. By ten minutes to 4 A.M. we found ourselves again under the canvas; but this time with comfortable dry gravel under us, instead of wet, *slushy* snow; which, damp as our bedding was, was a change for the better. Thermometer at this time was noted at + 5°. Strong wind from the west and north-west, with very heavy showers of exceedingly hard particles of snow.

The time fixed for the fatigue sledge returning had now arrived; and, although I reflected that we had lost three days marches, and might take it further on on that account, yet the consideration that their turning now would save even a few days' provisions and fuel, induced me to come to the conclusion. Determining, therefore, to start the moment the weather permitted, I informed Leiper that he would now have to make the best of his way to the ships again, as Mr. Marshall would go on with me.

The weather continued most inclement all the fore part of the day: the thermometer did not rise above + 16°, and there was a continuous *fall* of snow until late in the evening. At 7 P.M., however, it had moderated so that all hands were roused out, both sledges unpacked completely, provisions for the return were put aside, and a depôt of pemmican, pork, and bread, made securely in the gravel. Mr. Marshall's haversack and blanket-bag were now transferred to my sledge, on which was packed the remainder of the provisions and other necessary articles.

When we were ready to start I was rather apprehensive, when I found the sledge to be exceedingly heavy laden. However, there was nothing for it but to push on as hard as we could. The men of the fatigue sledge, poor fellows, seemed very loath to turn back, and I rather suspect thought it was using them very ill, not taking them on as far as the rest. Indeed I more than once regretted the step myself, during the next two marches, when I found the sledge so very heavily laden; but it proved, in the long run, to have been as well as it was, for these very men constituted, with two exceptions, Captain Penny's crew in the boat expedition, arriving at the ship just in time to take their part in it, and having in consequence a still better opportunity of proving that they were as zealous as their comrades in the good cause.

They now proposed themselves, as they had a light sledge, and would be able to make rapid marches homewards, to assist and escort us for a few miles. One man was therefore left with the tent and sledge, the former being still standing, and we now commenced our onward journey with the one sledge. We kept along the beach for nearly a mile, the snow very deep, and dragging, consequently, very heavy. Here we found that we would be able to cross the remaining part of the bay, and get some distance round its western point on the ice, which was comparatively free of hummocks close to the shore. I sent Leiper to the top of the high land to the westward, in order that he might be able to report as to the appearances to the westward, on his return to the ships, and with instructions to come down and meet us, when he thought we had advanced as far as his men could accompany us. About 2 A.M. of the 23rd, he met us again, and his report of our road ahead was not very encouraging. We now parted with him and his men, and our regret at doing so was heightened by the idea that we had no intelligence to send by him of having found the slightest traces of those we were in search of. Our progress after they left us, was very slow and excessively fatiguing, from the soft state and depth of the snow. The shore here was a succession of high steep slopes faced with snow, the grounded hummocks coming close into them at the bottom. The only practicable road was between the hummocks and the bottom of these slopes, the sledge frequently having such a "*list*," that we were in momentary expectation of an upset; but such a casualty did not take place. Seeing two or three very large high hummocks about a mile ahead, I left the sledge and walked to them, thinking that I might be able to pick out a better road, but I could perceive no appearance of amendment. We managed to get the sledge as far as these hummocks, by which time it was close upon 5 A.M., and the men were very much fatigued, for the last two days spent in the tent were not at all calculated to increase their powers of endurance of fatigue. Although ten hours under weigh, I do not think we made more than five miles this day. Our now solitary tent was pitched for the first time by itself; and whilst the cook of the day was preparing our morning meal, I determined, although very much fatigued, to ascend to the high land above us, in order, if possible, to ascertain the nature of our marching ground in advance, for our slow progress to-day, as well as Leiper's report, had made me very anxious. Accompanied by Marshall, we climbed with some difficulty the high steep snow slope above the tent, and, gaining the level above, walked about two miles to the westward, when we found ourselves overlooking a very beautiful little bay of much smaller size than the one we had last left, but which had a very fine appearance as now seen beneath us. The sea does not run far inside the eastern and western sides of this bay; but beyond the sea-beach, for a considerable distance inshore, there was a succession of the most beautifully marked raised beaches or terraces, rising one over the other with a very gradual slope, which gave it a larger appearance. These were cut through in the centre by the hollow of a watercourse; and it was curious to notice how each of those terraces had successively taken the same sweep and curve along the edges of the stream as the matter forming them had been subjected to its influence, whilst it still *was* a sea-beach. The western headland is a bold and prominently marked one, very precipitous at its northern face, but a short distance inland sloping away to the southward. Beyond and over it in this direction is to be seen in the distance a low projecting point at least twenty miles off. Between this and the nearest headland, part of another bay is visible, the ice in which, at least what we could see of it, we were rejoiced to perceive was apparently free of hummocks. The sketch I endeavoured to take of this view will, perhaps, assist a little to explain it.

Looking to the northward, we could now see well round the western point of the nearest island: no land could be seen in that direction; but over and *beyond* this island, there is in two or three places high peaked hills seen, apparently on separate islands; but I do not think that this is the same land seen on the 17th, for there is in the far distance, indistinctly seen, a coast running to the eastward, which is more likely to be that which was then perceived. To the westward are seen two apparently smaller islands lying north and south of one another. On returning to the tent I found the thermometer, which had been noted when we left at + 7°, to be now + 12° (8.30 A.M.). The morning had been all along a fine one, bright sunshine and clear, with light airs from the westward. The land which we saw this morning we had no doubt Captain Penny would be able to reach without difficulty with the dog sledges; but the rapidly increasing quantity of water, and decayed state of the ice to the northward and westward, made us exceedingly anxious about his party. However, we knew that his own and Petersen's experience would not allow them blindly to incur unnecessary risks. Looking forward to a very hard day's work for the morrow, we were not long of "turning in" on this occasion, for I made it known that we should be early astir. At 5 P.M. the cook was called, and preparations for starting afoot. Our yesterday's road had been so bad at the foot of the slopes, that I walked a considerable distance out amongst the hummocks in order to see if no way could be picked out amongst them to the westward; but I soon found that it was needless to entangle ourselves amongst them, and that, however slow our progress, and hard our labour, it would be better to persevere along the shore for some distance further. Before 8 P.M. we were ready to start. The evening was fine and clear, though, if anything, too warm for the work we had in hand. The thermometer had been in the afternoon as high as + 19°, and was now + 17°. Until midnight we had a spell of the hardest work that it is possible to conceive,—dragging the heavy sledge over immense wreaths of soft snow. At last, about 1 A.M. of the 24th, we came fairly to a stand in consequence of the sledge running rapidly down the declivity of one wreath, and burying its forepart deeply in another. With all our efforts we were unable to extricate it, and there was no other course open to us but to take off part of our lading, leave it here, and return for it. A single glance at the wilderness of hummocks outside satisfied us that we must continue to stick by the shore. Half of the lading being taken off, we reached the bay with little difficulty, and returning with the empty sledge, then brought up the remainder. This is always discouraging work, having to go over the same ground twice; but we had never found it necessary to do so since the 9th, the day we parted from the eastern parties. Nevertheless, although they had already done a very hard spell of work, when I proposed to reach the western head before halting, the men at once, and most cheerfully, reloaded the sledge, and we started across the ice of the bay, which was comparatively level, although traversed in many directions with cracks, in which we sustained some awkward tumbles. It was 8.10. A.M. before the tent was pitched.

Yet I do not think, after all our hard labours, that we had accomplished more than five or six miles. From the severe nature of the work the men had been allowed to take their morning's allowance of grog at midnight; but I now reminded them that this being the morning of the Queen's birthday, I thought I would be warranted in allowing them an extra glass specially to drink her Majesty's health in. We did not forget in our thoughts the numerous bands of co-operators similarly occupied to ourselves, and, we had no doubt, similarly celebrating the day, earnestly hoping, at the same time, that some amongst them at least had been more fortunate than ourselves in the search for the lost.

Our tent was pitched upon a shingle bank close under the cliffs; a keen westerly wind was blowing, and although the sun was out, the thermometer stood at this time +2°. 24th May, 1851. Smart breeze, W. Therm. +2°.

Before turning in, I walked a short distance round the point to where some huge blocks of limestone had been precipitated to the bank beneath. From above these blocks we had a good view to the westward. The coast appears now to trend a point or two more southerly; the western point of the bay now before us, which is a large and deep one, is long, low, and outlying. No *high* land is to be seen in this direction, the shores ascending very gradually to a height, as near as I could judge, of 150 to 200 feet above the level of the sea, and, although not quite so prominently, yet well marked with those terraces characteristic of all the shores of Cornwallis Island, where they are not abrupt and precipitous. We also saw that the ice for our next journey would be very favourable, as there were no hummocks inside of the western point and the position we now occupied. A ridge of very high hummocks, however, stretched across the mouth of the bay from either point. I may mention here, that to the westward of our present position we did not fall in with any very large hummocks, every mile in that direction they became smaller, and there was less appearance of pressure. Large holes of water are seen to the northward and N.W., and farther off the scattered black clouds and patches of vapour would seem to indicate water in the distance. Our tent this day was unluckily pitched, being exposed to the keen westerly breeze without the least shelter. The thermometer was not observed to rise above +12°, and in spite of the fatigue of the last journey, almost every one of the party acknowledged that they had been prevented from sleeping soundly, and had felt the cold much more than they had done when the thermometer had ranged many degrees lower.

The slow progress we had made on our last two journeys convinced me that we must alter or curtail our operations materially, and, however irregular it might be, make another depôt at this spot. There was the prospect of better ice ahead to be sure; but still Mr. Marshall had already more than once warned me that the ice outside was evidently fast giving way, and that in a short time longer we would in all likelihood have no "*road open to us but the tops of the hills.*" I myself trusted to the narrow ledge of ice, which I argued would remain attached to the beach until a late period of the season, and which would afford us a tolerable road for the sledge, although at the expense of coasting every bight and inlet. Allowing that Mr. Marshall should prove right, and we were forced to take the "tops of the hills," there was no doubt that it would be impossible for us to take the sledge with us in that way, and that our homeward journey might prove rather a difficult and trying one. On reflection, therefore, I saw that it was absolutely necessary to make such arrangements as would enable us *now* to push on as *rapidly* and as far as was consistent with prudence.

I roused out all hands at 7 P.M., and whilst the cook was preparing our breakfast, the others were set to repack and arrange the sledge. In doing this every article was scrupulously laid aside that could be dispensed with for the remainder of the journey, and all the provisions, with the exception of sufficient for twenty-nine days, seventeen of which I intended for our use whilst still advancing, the remaining twelve I trusted would be sufficient for our return to this spot. I hoped thus to be able to make an outward journey of thirty-five days from the ships, by which time we might have examined a considerable distance of coast. The only article in which we were at all short was the fat for fuel, and which there was every reason to suspect we would run short of; upon pointing out which circumstance to the men, they every one agreed to save every ounce they possibly could on their respective cooking days. After securely covering up with gravel and large stones what we intended leaving behind, we started at 9 P.M., and keeping along the beach until we got abreast of the smooth ice of the bay, we then hauled the sledge out to the westward. The point we were now leaving, however, being the most conspicuous landmark within view, I determined before proceeding to erect a larger cairn than usual on it. Taking all the men with me, we ascended to the summit, and very soon constructed one of some height, in which I left the usual papers. This is the first place in which we have found the construction of a cairn of any size an easy matter. In our view to the northward and westward nothing new was observed in addition to what has been previously recorded. After regaining the sledge we struck right for the western point of the bay, over the best travelling ice we have had for some days back. We were not interrupted by a single hummock the whole way across the bay, the ice being perfectly smooth, and of that wavy description which indicated its being of a previous year's formation. Our quick and easy progress during this march gave rise to happier feelings than we had enjoyed for some days back.

Sunday, 25th May. Calm — We reached the point at half-past 5 A.M. of the 25th, and encamped on its western side. The morning was quite calm, and bright sunshine, the temperature where we camped being + 10°, and at midday + 25°. Before turning in we walked up to the nearest high ground. The point on which our tent was pitched is low, and outlying for about half a mile, after which the land gradually ascends to about a height of 200 feet. On gaining this elevation, we found an almost level country stretching out before us to the southward for a considerable distance; but the view in this direction was bounded by high hills. Looking to the westward, another bay, similar to the one last crossed, was now seen before us, terminated by a low point, inshore of which was an oblong hill or elevation, seemingly surrounded by very low level land. The bay itself seemed broken in two, as it were, by a small projecting point of land, which run out a short way from the bottom. The elevated land on which we stood terminated at this point; beyond it the low land commenced. Before leaving the tent we had noticed on a very conspicuous position something that had the appearance of an artificial mark or cairn; but we now found, on reaching it, that it was merely a large block of stone. We erected a small cairn on the top of it, and left the usual paper. A.M. Therm. +10° to +25°.

At 7 P.M. I roused out the cook of the day, and at 9 we were ready to start. The evening was clear and pleasant, the temperature + 19°. The ice of this march was similar to that gone over the previous day. The range of hummocks across the mouth of the bay were smaller, and at a greater distance from the shore. By midnight we were nearly half way across, or almost equidistant between the eastern and western points, and had the low land seen in the morning open to us. Had we not previously perceived its nature, we should have been inclined to judge that it was a deep inlet running in here, so little was it above the level of the ice on which we stood. The point for which we were steering our course had a number of dark coloured looking objects upon it, which afterwards turned out to be large blocks of limestone, but which, in consequence of refraction, assumed a distorted appearance. Monday, 26th May. Light airs, W. and S.W.

Report of a Journey to examine the Beaches between Capes Grinnell and Spencer, and the Neighbourhood of Caswall's Tower and Radstock Bay, by John Stuart, Assistant Surgeon, Her Majesty's Ship, "Lady Franklin."

The sledge party fitted out for the examination of the east side of Wellington Channel to the southward of Cape Grinelle, and of the beaches in Barrow's Straits in the neighbourhood of Caswall's Tower and Radstock Bay, left H.M.S. "Lady Franklin" on the night of Tuesday the 6th of May. The party consisted of six men and one officer, and was victualled for thirty days.

May 6th, 1851. Assistance Harbour.

On striking out of the bay the sledge was hauled over the east point, this being easily done, from our having four extra hands from the parties of Captain Stewart and Mr. Goodsir, who were proceeding out to their depôts of the 24th April, with one sledge and two crews each. After a march of eight hours we camped under Parry's South Bluff, close by the flagstaff of H.M.S. "Assistance."

May 7th. Cape Hotham, 2½ miles E.

The following evening we started at 7 P.M., and reached Barlow Inlet at , having seen on the road a bear, a fox, and two ravens. On the north shore of the inlet we lunched, and at 2 A.M. reached the first depôt. Here everything was found in confusion, having been disturbed, but not destroyed, by bears and foxes. The road had up to this been on the whole good with the exception of a few patches of deep snow.

May 8th. Barlow Inlet 4 miles S.

Starting at 10 P.M., with a smart breeze of wind; we still kept along the snow on the beach, and derived great advantage from our floorcloth set as a sail. In a heavy squall, however, the sledge was hove on her beam ends in passing through a gully, but luckily no damage was sustained. At 3½ A.M. we camped alongside the depôt made on the former journey. Around it were several bear marks, but it had not been disturbed. In the forenoon the dog-sledges arrived from the ships, having accomplished the journey in eight hours. I accompanied Captain Stewart to a hill four miles to the northward, and was happy to see our road across channel almost entirely clear of hummocks, being only crossed at intervals with narrow ridges.

May 9th. Barlow Inlet 12 miles S.

Starting at 8 P.M.. we proceeded along the beach through very heavy snow for more than a mile, the sledges having to be double banked all the way. Striking out to the floe from a point named Point Separation, we parted with the parties of Captain Penny and Mr. Goodsir; and the three sledges under Captain Stewart, Dr. Sutherland, and myself, set sail and stood across the channel. Though the wind was light it helped us considerably, so that by 3½ A.M. we camped, having made about eight miles of offing.

May 10th. Point Separation. W. by S. 8 miles.

After lightening Captain Stewart's sledge, which had been

dragging very heavily, we started at 8½ P.M., and made good way, deriving occasional assistance from light breezes. In the course of the march we had to cross one or two ridges of hummocks, in some of which the sledges required to be double manned. The footprints of bears were numerous, and one burgomaster was seen. We camped after eight hours' work, having made about ten miles. In the course of the day a few angles were obtained, the result of which, along with the other observation taken during the trip, is laid down in the accompanying chart. May 11th. In mid-channel.

We did not start until midnight, and then proceeded over a beautifully level floe, uninterrupted by a single hummock, till 9 A.M., when we camped. During the morning we had passed a number of recent traces of bears and foxes. The distance supposed to have been made on this march was thirteen miles. A meridian altitude gave N. lat. 75° 10′. May 12th. Cape Bowden S.E. 9 miles.

At half-past one A.M. we again got under way, and after two hours' quick march came within half a mile of the land, when we halted and carried ashore 40 lbs. of pemmican and 60 lbs. of bread, as a contingent depôt. On returning to the sledges, after having properly buried and secured the provisions, we lunched, and afterwards parted company with Captain Stewart and Dr. Sutherland. Leaving my sledge, I now struck in for the north cape of the bay I had been directed to examine, instructing the captain of the sledge to proceed within the range of hummocks stretching across the mouth of the bay, and then to pitch the tent. Immediately on landing I found the skull of a sea-horse, evidently of great age. The beach under the north cape was a short shelf at the foot of an abruptly rising terrace, on the top of which were seen the recent droppings of hare and ptarmigan. Two of the latter were seen. Following the beach I found its north shore indented with three bights, one of which was of considerable depth. The whole bay was filled with very old looking ice, the bottom of the different bights being deeply covered with snow. Nothing was seen to justify the belief that it had ever been previously visited. Continuing to follow the north shore inwards, the bottom of the bay was reached. Here the land was much lower than on either side. After having walked round fully one half the extent of the coast I was obliged to make for the tent, it having come on to blow strong with thick fog. May 13th. In Bay, Cape Bowden S.S.W. 3½ miles.

The wind continued high throughout all this day, and nothing could be done in consequence of the drift. We consequently continued camped, although the wind was fair, being unwilling to leave the bay without getting a sketch and a few bearings An opportunity occurred during a lull on Wednesday forenoon, but unfortunately the period of clearness was very short, so that nothing satisfactory could be got.

The sledge started an hour after I did, and proceeded along the inner side of the hummocks, and then hauled out of the bay. Meantime I had walked towards the bottom of the bight and examined the south shore. This was found to be formed of a long neck of land, terminated by a small square bluff. Nothing was to be seen on any part of the beach but bear and fox tracks. By the different tide marks seen in the bay the rise and fall is supposed to be about five or six feet. After leaving the usual notices on the low bluff already mentioned, I struck across a small bay formed between the peninsula and Cape Bowden. I ascended the hill, and proceeded inshore for a considerable distance towards some Esquimaux remains of considerable size. The country inshore appeared flat and rolling. Five hares were seen and fired at. At the back of Cape Bowden was found a small frozen lake in a valley intervening between this headland and the country inshore. Ascending Cape Bowden a cairn was seen, which proved to be that built by a party from the American schooners in the previous autumn. It contained a paper very indistinctly written, but nearly as follows: —

"August 28th, 1850. U.S. Brig 'Rescue.' At Cape Riley traces may be found for a winter harbour. At Whaler Point, Leopold Harbour, is a depôt of provisions for Franklin."

Rebuilding the cairn, another despatch was left, and starting I continued along the coast to the bottom of a deep sweep, but without finding any further trace. The sledge all this time continued far off on the fair floe, that inshore being covered with deep snow and hummocky.

Thursday, 15th May. Cape Bowden N.E. 5 miles.

At 5 A.M. they pitched the tent, having been nine hours under way. In an hour and a half I joined them, and was informed that they had come along footmarks on some old ice, which, from the description, I had reason to believe were those of the Americans last autumn. During the day the wind was variable; the thermometer rose to + 63° in the tent.

At about 9 P.M. we started. The wind, though light, being northerly, we set our sail, and got the floor-cloth well dried, the sledge keeping as straight a course as the ice would allow it, in order to make the shortest possible course, for Cape Spencer was a considerable distance off-shore. From our camp I re-entered the bay, holding a course for the part of the beach where I had left off the search in the morning. Having, however, noticed some low patches of land lying about half a mile from the shore, I made for these, and found them a number of shingle banks, some of them having a tide mark within them, others having only a tide mark on the outside.

A minute examination of the beach produced not the slightest trace of it having been visited by human beings, until coming within three miles of what I took for Point Innes, when a small cairn was seen about eighteen inches high. It contained a paper, of which the following is a copy: —

"A party from the U.S. brig 'Rescue,' bound to Cape Bowden in search of Sir John Franklin and his companions. August 27th, 1850."

From this I continued along the beach till past the place

where a party under Captain Penny landed from the "Lady Franklin" in August last. A remarkable cairn-like stone on the head of a hill inshore attracted my attention, and was visited. Ascending the hill above Point Innes from behind, I saw the sledge making its way through very bad ice, and not anticipating their being able to proceed much further, I pushed on to satisfy myself as to the state of things at Union Bay, Beechey Island. On the way I examined a large cairn on the site of some Esquimaux ruins, but was unable to identify it as a portion of what had been found by Captain Penny and party the preceding autumn. Union Bay was found to be full of hummocky ice, the floe pieces in it of very small size, and apparently of late formation. At and about the "Mary" everything was found as it had been left. Returning to my party I was surprised to meet them, it being then nearly 8 A.M., and the distance they had accomplished having been great even disregarding the tortuous road caused by the bad ice. We immediately camped. They informed me that on the point they had opened a mound of earth and stones which proved to be an Esquimaux grave. During the day the thermometer in the tent ranged from + 23° to + 53°.

Friday, 16th. Cape Spencer E. by S. ½ mile.

We did not start the following day till 10 P.M., and although scarcely three miles from the yacht, did not reach her till past 1 A.M., the deep snow among the hummocks making the road most laborious.

Saturday, 17th May. Cape Spencer W. 2 miles.

Pitching the tent alongside the "Mary" her stove was rigged, and while lying there all our cooking was done in the forecastle. A walk to the cairn and graves showed us that everything had been undisturbed since we left it. After making arrangements for the evening we turned in at 7 A.M. The thermometer in the tent reached + 63°. We turned out at 8 P.M. and breakfasted. I then proceeded to take a few angles in Union Bay. Meantime the boatswain and two hands were examining the graves and their neighbourhood, while another man was sent to the top of Cape Spencer, alike to examine a cairn seen on it and to report on the state of the ice to the offing. The cairn proved to be one built by Sir John Ross, and contained documents having a reference to the "Mary." The beaches along Erebus and Terror Bay and the other places already mentioned were examined, but the search produced nothing worthy of note; indeed, such was the quantity of snow that had fallen, and so greatly had the general appearance of the place altered, that it was difficult to recognise particular localities. In the middle of the day the thermometer in the tent stood for upwards of an hour at + 70°, being the greatest heat we had yet experienced.

At 9 P.M. we started with the weather close and foggy, but a westerly breeze springing up enabled us to spread our canvass, which, as usual, we found a great assistance. Our course was over the spit at the head of Union Bay, and thence to the head of Erebus and Terror Bay, where a large salt water lake, without any apparent communication with the sea, enabled us to cross with comparative ease the back of the land between Cape Riley and Gascoyne Inlet. The breeze, which by this time had increased by a gale, proved a most valuable auxiliary, the snow being on the smooth ice so deep as to cause very heavy dragging. Gascoyne Inlet was crossed on what appeared to be old ice, and at 8 A.M. we camped on its east side close by Caswall's Tower. The gale continued from W.N.W. all day, and there was much snow drift.

Monday, 19th May. Caswall's Tower N. ½ mile.

At 9 P.M., after much difficulty, I succeeded in ascending the tower; but nothing was found on its summit to repay the exertion. A small cairn was built and the usual notice left. In descending, which was found fully more difficult than the ascent, I was attracted by the ruins of an Esquimaux settlement of considerable size, and while searching about among the remains of the different huts, fell in with a bottle, then a Goldner's canister, then another bottle, and finally a tent place.

The latter was about ten feet by eight, and had a built fireplace adjacent to it. Close beside were two large and peculiarly shaped cairns, evidently built by Franklin's people, but containing no documents. Scattered about lay eight or ten tins; two marked "vegetable soup," one "carrot soup," and two or three "boiled beef." An old Esquimaux house had the appearance of having been used as a tentplace, and a small tentplace adjourned it, apparently that of Englishmen, but in neither was the least bit of twine or such article got to enable us to come to a decision on this point. The whole had the appearance of having been the station of a shooting or surveying party of the summer of 1846. Leaving notices in a cairn, we started, and the favouring gale carried us along Radstock Bay at a great speed, enabling us to reach within two miles of Cape Eardley Wilmot, although considerably retarded by thick fog. At 7 A.M. we camped on the beach. The thermometer in the tent did not rise above freezing during the day, varying from +21° to +30°.

Tuesday, 20th May. Cape Eardley Wilmot S.E. 2 miles.

At 9 P.M. I sent four of the men away in different directions to the heads of the adjacent hills in order that no beacon might be passed unobserved, but nothing was seen. While examining the beach in the neighbourhood, I found what appeared to be a cairn, but found it a large stone trap three feet by one foot, probably intended for the wolf. It had no appearance of age, though most likely it had been built by Esquimaux at least one hundred years ago. Adjoining was the site of an Esquimaux summer tent about ten feet square. The sledge did not start till nearly midnight. It then proceeded along the coast over very rough ice in the direction of Cape Hurd; but the weather coming on very thick, obliged them to haul close in for the land. I followed the beach along to Cape Eardley Wilmot, when the land suddenly breaks off to the northward for one and a half miles. The beach, which is interrupted towards the inner portion of this bluff, recommences on the opposite side of the shallow bay, caused by the angle made by the cape and the mainland. On neither was anything to be found; so, after following the coast for three or four miles, I turned, and with difficulty rejoined the sledge. We then hauled right in for the land, and pitched the tent, having found ourselves unable to pick the road through the hummocks owing to the thick fog. The thermometer in the tent ranged from +18° to +28°, and the gale continued from the W.N.W. without abatement.

Thursday, 22nd May. Cape Eardley Wilmot W. 4 miles.

It being a little more moderate at 2 A.M. I started with one of the men, and after an hour and a half's hard walking, reached Rigby Bay, having come along the whole way under the perpendicular cliffs, the snow in many places knee deep. The ice was squeezed up close to the cliffs, and was very hummocky. The bay we found filled with ice, apparently very old, and several bars of hummocks were found across the mouth of it.

Reaching Cape Hurd we found two beacons, one higher than the other, and near them was a tent-place and one preserved meat tin. Neither of the cairns was disturbed, but to the flagstaff of the lower one a cylinder was lashed containing the usual notice and a document, of which a copy follows:—

"The winter quarters of H.M.S. 'Erebus' and 'Terror' discovered at Beechey Island, but no documents have yet been found to indicate the course subsequently pursued by them.

"Cape Walker has been visited, but without affording further traces.

"Wellington Channel, Melville Island, and Bank's Land are at present being searched by travelling parties from the different ships at present at Cornwallis Island. May 22d, 1851."

At Cape Hurd.

Returning to the tent after an absence of six hours, we found those arrived whom I had sent inshore, they having seen nothing. Regarding the state of the ice as seen from Cape Hurd, there was between that promontory and Prince Leopold Island a smaller proportion of level floes than was anywhere else to be met with. The ridges of hummocks were very numerous and very broad, and the floes intervening between these hummocks had the appearance of short narrow ribands.

During Friday the gale and snow drift continued so violent up to 6 A.M. that we did not leave the tent. Moderating towards noon, we carried half a case of pemmican and 50 lbs. of pork to a low projecting point, and built over it a conspicuous cairn of large stones. A flat hill, lying immediately to the westward of the peculiar *housetop-looking* hill, noticed by Captain Parry as Table Hill, marks the commencement of the low beach on which the depôt is situated.

At 10 P.M. we started and kept for Cape Eardley Wilmot, then proceeded towards the beach and along the end of the range of hummocks stretching from the extreme capes of Radstock Bay. When sufficiently within them, we kept direct for Cape Ricketts, intending to follow the outer course in our return. Having a fair floe we made very good way, and, notwithstanding contrary winds, we were enabled to camp within four miles of Cape Ricketts shortly after 6 A.M. The tracks of bears that we had passed during this last march were more numerous than on any ice we had yet travelled over, with the exception of the bay to the northward of Cape Bowden. The cook of the day when preparing our breakfast — that is, the meal of 8 P.M.— was startled by a fox, which he afterwards shot. The animal was in good condition, but apparently very hungry. The thermometer having risen during the day as high as + 58° in the tent, everything was thoroughly soaked with the water from the young floe.

Saturday, 24th May. Cape Ricketts W. by S. 4 miles.

About 10 P.M. we started and carried the floor-cloth as a sail, more, however, to get it dried than from any good it did us. After rounding Cape Ricketts, we found the ice getting worse and worse, but keeping on the smoothest pieces we could find, disregarding the crooked road this caused us to follow, we got opposite Gascoyne Inlet, when we struck right in for it, and camped about 7 A.M. under the cliff forming a part of the west side of the inlet. Along the southern side of Cape Ricketts we had passed some very broad and lately frozen cracks, and in one place there was a crack about a foot and a half wide, communicating with a pool formed on a depressed portion of ice. This was the first water we had yet seen. What surprised us most, however, was a large number of mollymoks soaring over head, having apparently a place of residence in the adjacent cliffs. During the day the thermometer in the tent varied from + 25° to + 37°, and a smart breeze from the westward rendered it colder than we had felt it at 10°. Two ravens in the rocks above us kept up a constant croak all the latter part of the day.

Sunday, 25th May. Gascoyne Inlet E. by S. 1 mile.

On starting at 9 P.M. several bottles and canisters were found to be damaged in consequence of some rather serious capsizes we had sustained during the day. The ice we found constantly getting worse, and after the first mile travelled this day anything like a floe vanished, and the only flat ice we went over was in detached pieces among the hummocks, few of them exceeding ten acres in extent. Thus getting involved in a maze of hummocks, we were unable to accomplish more than five miles during nine hours of most fatiguing labour, two thirds of that time being at standing pulls. We camped on the land immediately below the upper beacon left by the "Assistance" on Cape Riley. In the course of the day a white hare was repeatedly seen, and numerous bear tracks of recent dates were around us in every direction.

Monday, 26th May. Cape Riley W. by S. 1 mile.

In spite of a very strong head wind and much snow drift, we started with the sledge half loaded, and got her over a ridge of hummocks on to a level piece of ice. The men then returned for the remainder of the baggage, and after a heavy pull of two hours we got clear of the hummocks and entered Erebus and Terror Bay. The wind had increased after opening out the bay, and the drift had become almost smothering, but the sky keeping clear aloft, we could see the tops of the hills ahead of us. Three hours longer brought us alongside the yacht, where we camped on our old stance.

Tuesday, 27th May. Cape Spencer W. 2 miles.

Wishing to get into the regular day during the time we remained here, instead of breakfasting on Tuesday night, we did not do so until Wednesday morning at 5 A.M., and afterwards started to examine the beaches round Erebus and Terror Bay. A fox was seen, and a mollymok was fired at but not killed. Nothing could be seen of a fire-place near where the second boarding pike was picked up : indeed in that neighbourhood the snow lay deeper than in any other part of the bay. We turned in at 8 P.M., and found the night sleeping much more comfortable than the day, the thermometer in the tent never rising above + 43°.

On Thursday one party was sent up the second ravine, another followed the course of Mary River, and a third proceeded round Cape Spencer to re-examine the ruins in that direction. Nothing was found worthy of notice. A flock of about seventy ducks passed within musket shot, flying rapidly to the north-westward.

On Friday, while part of the men were examining the top of Beechey Island, I proceeded to different parts of the bay, and made what sketches I could. Before dinner I obtained one set of angles, but a thick fog coming on with smart south-easterly breezes, prevented me from obtaining some additional bases and angles that I would have wished to get. One of the men whom I had sent to the top of Cape Spencer was unable to get a clear view of the channel, the fog having come on very suddenly. He reported the paper left in the cairn on the hill by the "Lady Franklin" in September as quite illegible from wet.

After dinner of Saturday all hands turned in to be ready for a start in the evening, although the prospect was anything but favourable, the weather continuing thick, and the wind holding from the same quarter. In the afternoon a fox had the daring to get into the sledge, and on overhauling the provisions in it we found he had regaled himself on the bolt of fat, having consumed upwards of two pounds. The fog continuing all night, we did not get under weigh, as I thought it imprudent to start through the hummocky ground that we had to go over for the first four miles at least.

There was a short clear blink at 8 A.M. on Sunday ; but it again came on thick, and continued so till 5 P.M. At 10 P.M. we started, availing ourselves of a partial clearing, and enticed by a change of wind from S.S.E. to E. We had to keep right for the centre of the bay to avoid the rough road. Such as it was, the sledge was twice capsized before she cleared Cape Spencer. The hummocks compelled us to take a much more northerly course than we otherwise should have done ; and the deep snow, softened by the late foggy weather, made the sledge

Monday, 2nd June. Cape Spencer E. by S. 6 miles.

drag very heavily. At 7 A.M. we camped, having for five hours previously been groping our way along the edge of a ridge of hummocks in thick fog.

At 10 P.M. we again started, but the fog continuing to hang over the ice, and the wind having shifted a point or two, we found at 2 A.M., when there was a partial blink, that we were keeping too far to the northward. A large burgomaster, seemingly much fatigued, and probably wounded, lighted near us repeatedly: he came from the north-westward. At 6 A.M. we camped under the lee of a large hummock, the wind being fresh from the E.S.E.; thick and murky aloft, and occasional blinks below. Towards noon the wind fell, and the heat was excessive, the thermometer in the tent standing for a considerable time at +67°. Some bearings were obtained, and several seals were seen on the ice.

Tuesday, 3rd June. In mid-channel.

At 9 P.M. we started, the sail hoisted, but scarcely drawing. The floe improved considerably for a short distance, but two ridges of hummocks detained us a little about midnight. As the sun rose a light breeze came away from N.N.E., enabling us to make longer spells. About 2 A.M. we dined close to the edge of the smooth floe, and from the top of the adjacent hummocks, a few pools of water could be seen on the top of the ice. On re-starting we made four good spells, and then camped off the mouth of Barlow Inlet about 8 A.M. A thick fog bank hung over the land, and along the hummocks inshore; while to the northward and southward the sky was beautifully clear. At noon the sun was obscure. The thermometer in the tent did not rise above 50°.

Wednesday, 4th June. Barlow Inlet W. by N. 1½ miles.

Getting under weigh at 10 P.M., we kept the outer floe till within one mile of Ragged Point. With considerable difficulty we there crossed the hummocks, and kept along the beach. A cairn and cylinder were left, according to order, in a conspicuous situation. Under the steepest part of Cape Hotham, an Esquimaux encampment, not previously observed, was seen. It had the appearance of having been recently disturbed, probably by the "Assistance's" people in the previous August. At 5 P.M. we camped, making a shorter journey than usual, in order to divide the distance to the ships. Our tent-place was one mile west of the ravine at the foot of Parry's South Bluff. During the day the thermometer in the tent ranged from +30° to +57°.

Thursday, 5th June. Parry's South Bluff 1 mile east.

Starting at 10 P.M., we had about half an hour of standing pulls to get over the hummocks along the beach, we then gained the smooth floe, and set sail with a smart breeze from the N.N.E. About 1 A.M. a party from the ships was seen within hail, having with them a boat and two sledges, hauled by fourteen men and ten dogs, in the charge of Mr. Manson, third in command of the Expedition. He informed me that a considerable water had been seen in 76° N. and 96° W., whither the boat was proceeding. Leaving my party about five miles off,

I struck overland towards the head of the harbour, and arrived at the ships at 2 A.M. on the morning of Friday the 6th June. Shortly afterwards the sledge and crew came alongside, after an absence from the ship of thirty-one days, having enjoyed the most robust health during the entire period. Of the good behaviour, and willing exertions of the whole, I cannot speak too highly; but I would beg to make particular mention of Moses Robinson, the boatswain, who was captain of the sledge, and to recommend him for his steady, willing, and careful behaviour during the journey.

I enclose a few sketches of the land, taken from the points where the most connected views could be obtained. They are necessarily very rough, but may serve to give an idea of the general characteristics of the coast gone over.

Report of the Proceedings of the Depôt Sledges Nos. 5. and 6., in their first Journey to Depôt Point, by Mr. John Stuart, Assistant Surgeon.

At half-past eight, on the morning of Thursday, the 17th April, six sledges left the ships, having to each crews of six men and one officer. On account of the sudden rise which had recently taken place in the temperature, the snow was very soft, and the sledges dragged very heavily. By 10 o'clock we bid good-bye to the "Felix's" crew, who had accompanied us to the mouth of the harbour, and assisted us through the ridges of hummocks. The ice off the mouth of the harbour, having been of March formation, was very sloppy, its recent date making it very porous. At 12 o'clock we had luncheon, during the time that Dr. Sutherland's sledge was undergoing a repair. At half-past three we camped on the ice, the whole of the party well done out by the heavy drag through the soft snow. The sledge of which I had charge had of regular weights 1,370lbs., but was well able to keep pace with the others, some of which were considerably lighter. The evening meal was cooked pretty expeditiously; but the quantity of tea afforded by the "conjuror," did not much exceed half a pint. We congratulated ourselves, however, on being much better off than some of our neighbours, and turned into the bags very contentedly. The thermometer during the day had ranged from +32° to +21°. The sun strong throughout, and very little wind.

Thursday, 17th April 1851. Assistance Harbour 6 miles W. Distance travelled, 7½ miles. Distance gained, 6 miles.

The cooks were called this morning at 5.30 A.M., and after breakfast we started at about 7 o'clock. The sledge, having sunk into the soft snow, and frozen to the ice, was very difficult to start, and the other sledges were nearly a mile ahead before

Friday, 13th April. Parry's South Bluff W. ½ mile.

Distance travelled, 7 miles. Distance gained, 6 miles.

we got moved. The floe did not at all improve, and the great want, that of water, began to show itself already; the conjuror requiring to be kept burning to keep up a supply of water, and the allowance of fuel proved quite insufficient for this purpose. A little extra fat had, however, been brought away, and it was hoped that by the time this was expended less water would be required.

We lunched off Point Dungeness, and while halted we were joined by Captain Penny and Mr. Petersen with the dog sledges, they having come along the land to this point, whence they were obliged to strike out to the floe. After proceeding a few miles further we camped at a quarter past three in a bight among the hummocks off the depôt left by the "Assistance" last autumn. Our journey of this day had, like the last, been about seven miles. At night it came on to blow, and the thermometer fell considerably. The thermometer outside ranged from $+26°$ to $+20°$, and inside the tent $+35°$ to $+40°$.

Saturday, 19th April. 1½ miles S. of Barlow Inlet. Distance travelled, 6 miles. Distance gained, miles.

Starting at half past six, the sledges were double manned to get them over the heavy hummocks inside of us. We then proceeded along the edge of the snow on the land till close under Cape Hotham, when we were obliged again to double bank the sledges for a short distance in crossing a rough floe piece. The land did not prove better than the floe, the snow being equally deep, and the surface much more irregular. On camping, however, we found the difference, the bedding being for the first time dry, though hard. The dog sledge still continue in company with us. The distance accomplished this day was nearly six miles; but for some of the sledges this appeared to be quite enough, as the frequent sinking of the low runners in the soft snow rendered "standing pulls" necessary, which soon fatigued the crews. The thermometer during the day ranged from $+20°$ to $+31°$.

Sunday, 20th April. Barlow Inlet S.W. 2 miles. Distance travelled, 7 miles. Distance gained, 4 miles.

This morning, after prayers in the open air, we again started; and after a very heavy drag through deep snow and very uneven ground, we came upon the land ice in Barlow Inlet. The dog sledges were then on ahead, and from them we understood that it was impossible to get on to the land on the north side of the inlet on account of hummocks. We accordingly hauled out to the middle, towards the most practicable looking place among the hummocks that crossed the mouth of the inlet. Three crews were then put on to each sledge, and they were roused by main strength over a very irregular piece of ice. Notwithstanding the fall of temperature, the snow on the ice continued soft and wet, and a head wind caused thirst to be felt this day more violently than ever. The most of the water bottles were frozen, and their unwieldy shape rendered them a great nuisance to any one using a drag belt.

We camped at 3 P.M. after a very heavy pull through about a mile of hummocks, in which we were only able with all hands to take two sledges at a time, consequently having to make three trips over the same ground. Our camping ground this night was wetter than any previous one, but luckily at night it began to blow very strong, with a very keen frost, and but that we were in a sheltered bight among hummocks we would have had some difficulty in keeping our tents overhead. Several frost-bites had occurred during the day, and two or three were affected with snow blindness. By midnight the thermometer had fallen considerably.

The gale continued without abatement throughout the whole of this day, and in some of the tents the thermometer fell to $-26°$. The hoar frost hung about the tents and blankets in every direction and the least motion brought down a shower of snow. The cooking had all to be done inside, and the smoke arising from the tallow was one cause which may account for one of the men getting blind. The drift outside was tremendous, and the poor dogs were hard put to it for shelter, doing, however, no small damage to whatever they could get at. Monday, 21st April. Storm stayed.

Throughout the early part of the day there were occasional lulls and squalls. No start was made till 10 A.M., when the first six days being expired I got orders to proceed on for three miles and make a depôt for the return of the extended parties. The dog sledges started first, and the others getting under weigh got over a narrow ridge of hummocks on to the land, and proceeded on to a blunt point on which the depôt was made. The other sledges pitched their tents, and, leaving a flag blowing on the depôt, we left our comrades with three cheers, and immediately commenced our return. My tent I had left at the former camp, and three disabled men, who were to return to the ships. My party then consisted of twelve men, of whom three were snow blind, and three of the remainder had been transferred to the fatigue party as proper persons to return to the ships. We had two sledges, with about three hundredweight on each, but to the thirteen hands there was only one tent made for a party of seven. There was on the other sledge a tent made of black calico; but as the dogs had been amusing themselves jumping through it every time it had been pitched, it was utterly useless. Anxious to make as short journey as possible for the sake of those suffering from snow blindness, on reaching the tent we took a hasty luncheon and packed up the sledges. In going down we kept outside the hummocks upon the smooth ice till within a mile of Cape Hotham. We then struck in over the hummocks. By this time most of the disabled half were much fatigued; accordingly, after proceeding about three miles further, we camped at the depôt of the "Assistance" about 9 P.M. Tuesday, 22nd April. Barlow Inlet S. 4 miles. Parry's South Bluff W. by S. ½ mile.

After a length of time, and getting served by divisions, we all got a little tea, and set about composing ourselves as we best might, with a view to getting a little rest. Stowing thirteen people in a space of ten feet by seven proved rather a difficult process; but by some arranging themselves for a lower tier we Distance travelled, 14 miles. Distance gained, 12 miles.

Wednesday, 23d April. Assistance Harbour.

Distance travelled, 14 miles. Distance gained, 12 miles.

managed to get three or four hours' sleep. A cold breakfast, washed down by a glass of rum, set us on our legs, and we started at a smart pace for the ships. The thermometer this day was down to – 30°, and a smart N.W. wind rendered the cold very piercing. Four or five were frequently and deeply frostbitten, but luckily without bad effects. By the time we got within five miles of the harbour, two of the men were much knocked up, and four or five more much fatigued. Having got entangled in a wrong lead among the hummocks near the point of the harbour, out of which it would have been difficult to get, I thought it advisable to leave the sledges and walk over the point; and the step proved to have been almost necessary, as one of the men, the sailmaker of the "Sophia," had to be supported in by other two.

Next morning the sledges were brought in without difficulty, and with the exception of a few trifling blisters following the frostbites no one was the worse for their journey.

Proceedings of the Expedition in charge of Mr. William Penny, Commanding Her Majesty's Ship "Lady Franklin," in 1850.

Copy of a Letter from Mr. William Penny, Commanding H.M.S. "Lady Franklin," to the Secretary of the Admiralty.

"Sir, Disco Island, 2d May, 1850.

"I have the honour to acquaint you, for the information of the Lords Commissioners of the Admiralty, that the expedition under my command arrived here at 10 P.M.; the vessels in good order, and the crews in the best of health and spirits; and will proceed immediately, after authority is obtained from the Governor, to take two Esquimaux and two Danish volunteers from the settlement of Uppernavik.

"It has been a very mild winter, and there is very much open water here, extending off seventy miles.

"I have, &c.
(Signed) "Wm. Penny."

Copy of a Letter from Mr. William Penny, Commanding H.M.S. "Lady Franklin," to the Secretary of the Admiralty.

"Her Majesty's Ship 'Lady Franklin,' off
"Sir, Uppernavik, Tuesday, 4th June, 1850.

"I have the honour to request that you will inform my Lords Commissioners of the Admiralty that the expedition under my command arrived off Uppernavik yesterday at 4 P.M., having been one month on the passage from Lievely, in consequence of the south-west winds.

"According to the arrangement before made, the services of the sub-governor, Herr Johan Carl Christian Petersen, have been retained for interpreting, at the pay of 78*l.* per annum, 1*l.* 10*s.* being paid monthly by the Governor to his wife out of this sum.

"The expedition will sail from this place at 4 A.M. to-morrow, that time being allowed the sub-governor for getting his outfit into a state of readiness, and for making the necessary arrangements with the Governor. He is a person whom I have long thought of, and I consider myself fortunate in obtaining his services, from his perfect familiarity with the English, Danish, and Esquimaux languages.

"It was necessary to grant Herr Flaskeur, the Governor, a guarantee that he should incur no risk with the Danish Government for permitting the departure of Mr. Petersen, their regulations being very strict on this point.

"I had communication with Professor Rinck (now at Omenak),

who would gladly have accompanied me, but I was unable, on account of the distance, to have a personal interview with him, which is the more to be regretted, as I believe he would have been of great service, not only as an interpreter, but also in a scientific capacity.

"I am sure their Lordships will be pleased to hear that my little vessels sustained an immense pressure, in North-east Bay, on the 18th ultimo, without the slightest damage, and that they have otherwise shown themselves all that could be wished.

"I have also the pleasure of informing their Lordships that the crew of both vessels are in good health, and that the prospect of an early north passage is still good, notwithstanding a month of prevailing S.W. winds.

"No information can be gathered regarding Her Majesty's ship 'North Star,' but it is to be hoped she has reached Lancaster Sound.

"I have, &c.
(Signed) "Wm. Penny."

Copy of a Letter from Mr. William Penny, Commanding H.M.S. "Lady Franklin," to the Secretary of the Admiralty.

"Sir, North Uppernavik, 30th June, 1850.

"I have the honour to acquaint you, for the information of my Lords Commissioners of the Admiralty, that the expedition under my command has been detained here by the prevailing S.W. winds, which have continued the greater part of the season; however, it has removed all the barriers of ice, and whenever the wind comes from the N.E. we will make rapid progress.

"Captain H. T. Austin, C.B., arrived off here 26th June, the expedition in the best of order, and all in high spirits.

"I have, &c.
(Signed) "Wm. Penny."

Copy of a Letter from Mr. William Penny, Commanding H.M.S. "Lady Franklin," to the Secretary of the Admiralty.

"H.M.S. 'Lady Franklin,' Melville Bay, 16th July, 1850.
"Sir, (lat. 75° 11′; long. 60° 8′ 30″).

"I have the honour to acquaint you, for the information of the Lords Commissioners of the Admiralty, that the expedition under my command reached this place on the 12th July, and has since been detained by the S.W. winds, which have prevailed to such an extent during the greater part of the season as to render this year backward in the extreme.

"The wind, however, is now from the N.E., and the ice is opening very fast; if it continue but for five days we shall be in the west water.

"Captain Austin's expedition is now about ten miles to the northward of us, having joined us on the 2nd July in latitude 73° 25′, and longitude 56° 20′ W.

"We have been rendering mutual services, and otherwise doing all in our power to forward the object in view.

"As yet no trace of the 'North Star' has been found, but it is to be hoped she has reached Lancaster Sound.

"The crews of the several expeditions are in the best of health and spirits, there being not one on the sick list.

"I forward this by Captain Stewart, of the 'Joseph Green,' who has rendered me many good services.

"I have, &c.
(Signed) "WM. PENNY."

Copy of a Letter from Mr. William Penny, Commanding H.M.S. "Lady Franklin," to the Secretary of the Admiralty.

"H.M.S. 'Lady Franklin,' Lancaster Sound,
"Sir, 21st August, 1850.

"I beg to acquaint you, for the information of the Lords Commissioners of the Admiralty, that the vessels under my command got clear of Melville Bay on Sunday the 11th August.

"On the following day I landed at Cape York, and had communication with the Esquimaux.

"On the 13th Captain Austin's expedition came up, and next morning I was informed of a report, said to be got from the Esquimaux I had on board for several hours; it was to the effect, that Sir John Franklin's ships had been lost forty miles to the northward, and their crews murdered.

"I immediately offered my services, together with those of my interpreter, and was happy to find that the sole foundation for the tidings was that the 'North Star' had wintered in the situation referred to.

"Immediately on the report being cleared up, Captain Austin left, with Sir John Ross's and Captain Forsyth's schooners in tow, and we were detained by calms and bay ice, so that we did not reach Jones' Sound till midnight on the 18th. We were prevented from approaching within twenty-five miles of the Sound by a chain of immense floes, and were obliged to haul out N.W. (per compass) to get clear of the ice. We entered Lancaster Sound the following night in company with the American schooners, having strong winds from the S.W. (per compass).

"For the last twenty-four hours we have been dodging in the neighbourhood of Admiralty Inlet, a heavy sea running, and very thick weather, my wish being to get intelligence of places where provisions had been landed by the 'North Star:' that vessel is now in sight ahead.

"I have prepared this despatch for their Lordships, to forward by Mr. Saunders, who will be able to inform you satisfactorily of the state of Lancaster Sound.

"From the information I have received from Mr. Saunders, it is at present my intention to put my vessels into some bight on the north shore of the Sound, allowing the ice to drive past them, and I shall then use every endeavour to push to the westward, and follow out their Lordships' instructions in that quarter.

"Before concluding, I would beg to allude to the orders transmitted to Mr. Saunders, relative to depositing his provisions on the Island of Disco.

"By such a course being pursued, an otherwise invaluable supply is rendered perfectly useless to all the expeditions at present in this quarter, and we are deprived of what we had reckoned upon,—viz. a deposit in the Sound to fall back upon, in case misfortune should compel us to abandon our vessels.

"The report received from the Esquimaux at Cape York has proved correct to the letter; and I cannot but refer to the service my interpreter, Mr. Petersen, has rendered on this occasion, in exposing a story of Sir John Ross's Esquimaux, calculated to do much mischief. "I have, &c.

(Signed) "WM. PENNY."

Mr. Penny to the Secretary of the Admiralty.

H.M.S. 'Lady Franklin,' Assistance Harbour,
Cornwallis Island, 12th April, 1851.

"Sir, (Received 11th September.)

"I have the honour to inform you, for the information of my Lords Commissioners of the Admiralty, that after parting company with H.M.S. 'North Star' on the 21st of August, I reached along the north shore of Barrow Straits until Sunday the 14th, keeping a strict look out. Being then off Beechey island I spoke the American schooner 'Rescue,' and learned that H.M.S. 'Assistance' had found traces of the Franklin expedition on Cape Riley. The 'Assistance' was then running to the westward; and, anxious to be possessed of every particular, I followed her, with the intention of going on board, but I had not that opportunity till 2 P.M., when both vessels were made fast to the land ice, two thirds of the distance across Wellington Channel, the 'Assistance' being about one mile and a half to the westward of us.

"Finding that the traces were apparently those of a retreating party, I thought it my proper course to return to the east side of Wellington Channel, which I accordingly did. The succeeding morning I landed with a party, and examined the coast from ten miles to the northward of Cape Spencer to that promontory, and an encampment was found near the latter place, seemingly that of a hunting party about three years previous.

"Joining company with the 'Advance,' the 'Rescue,' and the 'Felix' schooners the following morning, we made fast in a bight under the N.W. side of Beechey Island; and having consulted with Captain De Haven and Sir John Ross, it was agreed that the former should despatch a party to continue the search northward along the east coast of Wellington Channel, while I explored the coast to the eastward. Meantime a party of all my officers which had been despatched in the direction of Caswall's Tower discovered the quarters which had been occupied by the vessels of Sir John Franklin's expedition in the winter of 1845–6. Three graves were also found, the headboards showing them to be those of three seamen who had died early in the spring of 1846; but, notwithstanding a most careful search in every direction, no document could be found. The same evening a boat party was despatched under Captain Stewart to explore Radstock Bay and its vicinity, but no further traces were found in that direction. The 'Resolute' and the 'Pioneer' came up and made fast on Wednesday morning, and an unfavourable condition of the ice detained us all till evening, when water being open to the westward, I stood a certain distance across Wellington Channel, and in the morning sent away a party under Mr. J. Stuart to communicate with the 'Assistance.' The same evening we were again in Beechy Bay; and the party returned the following forenoon, having accomplished upwards of forty miles. By them we were acquainted, that the 'Assistance' had found no traces in about thirty miles of coast examined by her to the north and south of Barlow Inlet. The state of the ice prevented the least motion being made with the ships until Thursday the 5th of September, when we left Beechy Bay; but so little was the ice slackened off, that we were unable to reach the west side of the channel before Sunday the 8th.

"While lying under Beechey Island arrangements were made with Sir John Ross to lay up the 'Mary' yacht, and a quantity of provisions was contributed as our share of the depôt there formed.

"On Sunday the 8th I landed with a party about twelve miles to the northward of Barlow Inlet, and a cairn and pole was erected in a conspicuous situation.

"Wellington Channel being blocked up with old land ice, no alternative was left but to proceed to the westward, with a view of reaching Cape Walker, or attempting some other passage between the islands of the Parry Group, or, failing either of these, Melville Island. Following out this course, we pushed on through the bay ice, which was now so strong as to retard us greatly; but, notwithstanding that obstacle, we reached Griffith's Island on Tuesday the 10th September; and having made fast there, on account of the state of the ice, I had again a consultation with Captain Austin with a view to acting in concert.

"The following morning the more favourable appearance of the ice induced me to make an attempt to reach Cape Walker, but after proceeding twenty-five miles the ice became packed, which, with a heavy fog, caused me to put about and make for our former position. The hourly increasing thickness of the bay ice, which had now become such an obstacle that with a strong breeze the ships stayed with considerable difficulty, rendered it absolutely necessary that a place of safety should be obtained for the vessels, and I accordingly made for this harbour, a rough sketch of which I had previously obtained from the 'Assistance.' We brought up at 11 A.M. on Thursday the 12th September, and shortly afterwards the 'Felix' schooner, Captain Sir J. Ross, came in and brought up. Two boats were sent ashore, and hauled up, to fall back upon, should further progress be made; but being unable to get out by the 20th, so as to be usefully employed, preparations were commenced for wintering.

" With reference to the winter that we have spent, one fact will speak for itself, viz. that there has not been one single case of sickness in either the 'Lady Franklin' or 'Sophia.' Indeed, so completely were both the minds and bodies kept properly occupied and carefully attended to, that with the crews I have, it would have been surprising to have seen sickness. While on this subject, I cannot but make mention in terms of praise of Messrs. Sutherland, Goodsir, and Stuart,—their exertions alike to instruct and amuse the men greatly contributing to the happy issue.

Frequent communication has been held with Captain Austin's expedition, which has wintered in the strait between Griffith's and Cornwallis Islands, and arrangements were made with reference to the different routes to be taken in the coming travelling. Pursuant to these there are at present ready to start from the 'Lady Franklin' and 'Sophia' two parties of three sledges each, to explore Wellington Channel and the land which may be found at the head of that great inlet. Independent of the above, there are two dog-sledges prepared for extended search in the same direction. One of these will be conducted by the interpreter Mr. Petersen, of whom I would beg to make particular mention, trusting that his noble devotion in the cause of our countrymen may be remembered to his advantage.

" The day at present fixed for the start is Monday the 14th April, should the weather continue favourable. Previous to starting I have thought proper to make out this despatch for their Lordships' information.

" I have, &c.
(Signed) " WM. PENNY,
" Captain, &c."

Mr. Penny to the Secretary of the Admiralty.

" H.M.S. 'Lady Franklin,' at sea,
" Sir, 8th September, 1851.

" Resuming my report of proceedings from the date of my last despatch, I have to inform you, that on the 17th April six sledges, with forty-one officers and men, started from the ships, under the command of Captain Stewart of the 'Sophia;' and I could not but be gratified by seeing what our small means had put in our power to do, with these parties of men alike able and willing. The sledges were variously officered by Captain Stewart, Messrs. Marshall, Reid, and J. Stuart, and Drs. Sutherland and Goodsir. The course intended to be pursued was, to proceed so far together up the west side of Wellington Channel, and, after returning the depôt sledges, two parties to cross to the east side of the channel, while other two follow up the west coast to the head of the channel, the position of land then seen determining their future procedure. Each sledge was equipped for forty days, and the average weights per man were upwards of 200 lbs. I started from the ships on the 18th with the dog-sledges, accompanied by Mr. Petersen, and at noon on the 18th I joined the sledges. They had found the ice very heavy, in consequence of the recent snow, and the high temperature; and their journey of the previous day had not exceeded six miles and a half. The inefficient state of our cooking apparatus had already begun to cause much inconvenience. On the 19th the temperature fell, and a gale of wind faced in immediately on entering the channel, which continued with only partial intermission till the 22nd. During all this time I was continually among them; and whatever doubts the want of experience of my young officers might have warranted my entertaining, they were all removed by witnessing their management of their men on the occasion. On the 21st Mr. J. Stuart was returned with the two depôt sledges, and only one tent. In consequence of the extreme severity of the weather, I felt great anxiety for this party; however, in two marches they reached the ship with only a short interval of rest.

"Meanwhile the gale continued down the channel, with a temperature varying from $-25°$ to $-30°$. This, and the want of numerous articles, such as a sufficient supply of fuel, stronger conjurors, &c., caused me to entertain a fear of failure, if these defects were not remedied in time. I accordingly consulted my officers on the subject; and, in consequence of our unanimous opinion that a timely return was the most advisable step, I determined to deposit all the provisions and the two best sledges at this spot, returning with the other two to receive alterations. The distance travelled to this spot was forty-two miles. The dog-sledges in their return accomplished this distance in one stage.

"The other four parties, after making the depôt, returned, reaching the bay at noon on the 26th, every one in the best of health, and not a single case of frost-bite; and I cannot but state my admiration of the constant contentment and steady and willing endurance of the officers and men of the parties, under circumstances of no small hardship. From this date till the 5th of May every one was busily engaged preparing more amply for what we had found to be necessary in our first journey. On the 6th, after a short prayer to the Almighty for guidance to enable us to fulfil our duty, three sledges again started, the crews of the two that had been left up channel being distributed amongst them.

"They were again in charge of Captain Stewart till such time as I should myself join them at their upper depôt, when I was to see each party take its separate route. At 6 A.M., on the 9th of May, I started with Mr. Petersen and Thomson (one of the seamen) with the two dog-sledges; and at 2 P.M. we overtook the parties then camped at their further depôt. From Point Separation, in 75° 5′

N. lat., Captain Stewart, with his auxiliary, Dr. Sutherland, and Mr. J. Stuart of the 'Lady Franklin,' left, proceeding to Cape Grinnell, Mr. J. Stuart there separating, and proceeding along the coast to Cape Hurd, examining the various beaches, &c. for further traces, as strong opinions were still entertained that more was to be found in that quarter.

"Mr. Goodsir, with Mr. Marshall as his auxiliary, had assigned to them to examine the west side, and to follow up after the dog-sledges, receiving final instructions on reaching the head of the channel. Rapid journeys were made with the dogs to Cape De Haven in N. lat. 75° 22′. Hence the land was seen to trend N.W. ten miles, terminating in a point, afterwards named Point Decision, which was reached at 10½ P.M. on the 12th May. A hill of four hundred feet in height was ascended, and in consequence of the land being seen continuous in a north-westerly direction, instructions were left to Mr. Goodsir to take this coast along to the westward, while I myself proceeded in a N.W. by N. direction towards land seen to the northward. At 5 P.M. on the 14th we encamped on the ice, having travelled twenty-five miles N.W. by N. from Point Decision. The following day, after travelling twenty miles from this encampment in a N.W. by N. direction, we landed at 7 P.M. on an island named Baillie Hamilton Island. Ascending a hill about five hundred feet high above the headland on which we landed, the ice to the westward in the strait between Cornwallis and Hamilton Islands, was seen to be much decayed, and an island was seen to the westward, distant thirty-five or forty miles. As the decayed state of the ice prevented further progress to the westward from this point, and no trace being found, we proceeded round the island, first to the N.N.E., and afterwards, on rounding Cape Scoresby, in a N.N.W. direction, on the 16th we came upon what, to all appearance, was water; and on halting on the 17th at Point Surprise, we were astonished to open out another strait, which was twenty-five miles of clear and open water. An island was seen bearing W½ S., distant forty miles, and a headland distant fifteen miles W. by N., the dark sky over this headland indicating the presence of water to the extent of perhaps twenty miles on the other side. This point was found to be in 76° 2′ N. lat., and 95° 55′ W. long. Further progress being prevented by water, still without traces, and the dogs' provisions being exhausted, no other course remained for us but to return to the ships, which we reached after rapid journeys at midnight on the 20th May.

"The carpenters and people on board were immediately set about preparing a boat that we might endeavour to reach this water soon.

"On the 29th May the second mate arrived, having left Mr. Goodsir in 75° 36′ N., and 96° W. Water had been seen by them to the northward from their furthest station. He made a very rapid return, having run in one day from twenty-five to thirty miles. Every one on board continued actively employed, preparing the boats, provisions, &c.; and on the 4th June it started with one auxiliary sledge, and one dog sledge, the whole party being in charge of Mr. Manson.

"On the 6th of June Mr. John Stuart returned with his party from Cape Hurd, after an absence of thirty-one days, but without having found any trace either indicative of the course pursued by H.M.S. 'Erebus' and 'Terror,' or of any retreating party having subsequently passed along that coast. After thirty-six hours' rest Mr. Stuart again started to join Mr. Manson, having equipped his sledge for a twenty days' journey. He overtook the boat on the morning of the 8th of June, then one mile to the westward of Cape Hotham. The same day a dog-sledge from Mr. Manson arrived at the ship, stating that the sledge on which the boat was placed, after trial, had been found unfit for the purpose. The armourer, who was returned with the dog sledge, was immediately set about preparing a larger sledge, but having no carpenter on board, the woodwork was finished by Sir John Ross's carpenter. On the 11th, at 4 A.M., I joined the boat with the two dog-sledges; and all hands were immediately set about fitting and lashing the new sledges, and arranging the weights of the party between the two long sledges and the two dog-sledges. On the 12th Mr. Manson returned, no one then being left in the ships but the clerk in charge.

"The improvement on the boat sledge was remarkable, and the ice also was so much better, that a distance of 105 miles was accomplished in seven marches. The boat being then launched into the water and laden, the fatigue party returned, and reached the ship on the 25th of June, all in good health, the dogs dragging their light sledges the whole way.

"On our journey out we met Dr. Sutherland at Depôt Point, returning after an absence of thirty-eight days. He reported having left Captain Stewart in 76° 20′ N. in the opening of Wellington Channel, but without having yet fallen in with any traces. When off Point Griffith's on the 14th, Messrs. Goodsir and Marshall were fallen in with, having examined the northern shores of Cornwallis and Bathurst land as far 99° W., but still without having fallen in with any traces. They were obliged to return in consequence of the water.

"Resuming the boat journey, after separating from the fatigue sledges on the 17th of June, we proceeded about ten miles to the westward, when we were obliged to take shelter in an adjacent bay, in consequence of a head sea and strong westerly gale. From this date until the 20th of July, 310 miles of coast were examined by the boat, under very disadvantageous circumstances, arising from constant unfavourable winds and rapid tides. Our provisions being then within eight days of being consumed, and our distance from the ships such that prudence would not warrant further perseverance with this supply, we commenced our return, and with a strong north-west wind, succeeded in reaching Abandon Bay after fifteen hours and a half. The ice being so decayed as to preclude the launching of even an empty boat, we were compelled to haul the boat ashore and abandon her, taking with us four days' provisions.

The weather during our return was boisterous in the extreme, with continued rain, which made the streams it was necessary to ford very rapid. The constant wet caused the greatest discomfort, but from none of my men did I once hear a complaint. In 75° N. lat. we found a boat which Captain Stewart had wisely sent out in case of such a contingency as had occurred; but the ice having set into the mouth of Wellington Channel, which had up to this time been open, we were unable to fetch her down further than Barlow Inlet. Thence we walked to the ships, which we reached at 10 P.M. on the 25th July.

"Captain Stewart had returned on the 21st of June, having reached Cape Beecher, in 76° 20′ N. lat. and 97° W. long.

"He had again started on the 1st July, and carried up a depôt for my return to Cape De Haven, returning from this journey on the 17th July.

"For particulars during the different searches, I would refer you to the accompanying reports.

"On my return I was agreeably surprised to hear that Barrow Straits had been open, as far as could be seen, since the 2nd of July, an occurrence which was so far to be expected as the strait was seen to be in motion till the 11th of March. The land ice had also come out of Wellington Channel as far up as Point Separation, probably about the 5th of July; and on the 27th July, when our travelling operations coucluded, the fast edge in the Channel continued in the same position.

"The ships continued ice-bound till the 10th of August; but, had our parties returned in sufficient time to refit, and be ready to cut out from the date of water making, we would have been at liberty on the 15th of July.

"On the 11th of August, Captain Austin's ships entered our harbour in their progress to the eastward. His parties had penetrated as far as ships could hope to do, yet like our own, they were unsuccessful in finding the least trace of the missing expedition. In fact, none had been found, such as would warrant the risk of a second winter; and my orders being such as left no alternative, I determined on immediately returning to England, if no instructions to the contrary should be met with. In proceeding down the country, we landed at Cape Hay and Button Point in Ponds Bay, positions considered the most probable for despatches being left by the whaling ships. Finding none, we continued our course down along the land, crossing in 70° N. lat. through a body of one hundred and forty miles of ice. We made repeated endeavours to reach Lievly, on the island of Disco, to ascertain if any despatches had been left there for our guidance; but thick weather, and a strong northerly wind, obliged us to haul off after having made a narrow escape from a reef lying close inshore. We parted from the 'Sophia' about twenty miles off the land, expecting to rejoin her after having communicated with the Danish settlement; but the thick weather and strong gale continuing for twenty-four hours, we separated from her, and have not since seen her. Captain Stewart's instructions in case of such an event were, to make the best of his way to Woolwich, having it in his power to take either the English Channel or the Pentland Firth as his route, according as the wind might lead.

"In speaking of the services of the various officers under me, I would mention my second in command as an able and energetic coadjutor, both on board ship and in conducting the search along the east coast of Wellington Channel and the south shores of Albert Land; and his foresight in laying out depôts and a boat for the boat party greatly facilitated our safe return. Dr. Sutherland of the 'Sophia' as his auxiliary, in travelling proved himself a most indefatigable officer, and his attention while on board to natural history and meteorology will no doubt afford many useful facts. Of Mr. D. Manson, the chief mate of the 'Sophia,' an old and experienced whaling master, I cannot speak too highly. He had charge of the vessels during the absence of myself and Captain Stewart, and throughout the winter he paid the greatest attention to tidal and barometrical registers; and his services in conducting the boat to Cape Hotham, under peculiarly disadvantageous circumstances, were beyond all praise. Mr. James Reid, the second mate of the 'Sophia,' son of the ice-master of the 'Erebus,' accompanied Captain Stewart in the first journey as an auxiliary, and afterwards proceeded with him to his furthest.

"Of Messrs. Marshall and Leiper, the chief and second mates of the 'Lady Franklin,' I would make mention as experienced and skilful ice officers; and the exertions of the one in accompanying Mr. Goodsir in the whole extent of his journey, and the other as my second in the boat, were such as could not but afford me the greatest satisfaction. The whole of the duties of refitting the ship during my absence fell upon Mr. Marshall, and were accomplished in a time remarkably short, considering the few hands on board. Of Mr. John Stuart, the youngest officer under my command, I cannot speak too highly. Finding that there were no duties as assistant surgeon, he acted as third mate; and his exertions in preparing the travelling equipments, his surveys of various bays during his travels, and his assistance in preparing charts, &c., have proved of the greatest use; and for his proceedings during the search of the beaches, &c. between Cape Grinnell and Cape Hurd, I would refer you to his journal. He afterwards started as an auxiliary to the boat party, with an interval of only thirty-six hours, and was subsequently employed in numerous short journeys, conducting boats, &c.

"Mr. Goodsir, in his western search, discharged alike his duty to this expedition and his missing brother.

"Mr. Petersen, the interpreter, in conducting the dog sledges, and in affording much useful information with reference to travelling, as well as his personal exertion in the same, to the extent even of injuring his health, has afforded me the greatest satisfaction; and of his services as an interpreter on a former occasion, I have made mention in a previous despatch.

"Of the seamen of both vessels placed under my command I cannot speak too highly; for neither in winter quarters, nor while enduring the privation and fatigues of travelling, did ever one complaint or grumble reach my ears. Of their unwearied exertions a schedule is laid before you, and if success has not attended their labours they have not the less performed their duties.

"I have, &c.
(Signed) "WILLIAM PENNY,
"Commanding the Expedition."

"SCHEDULE, showing the total number of days engaged and miles travelled in the journeys of the officers and men of the 'Lady Franklin' and 'Sophia,' under the orders of Captain William Penny, during their search for Her Majesty's ships 'Erebus' and 'Terror.' 17th April to the 17th July, 1851.

"The 'Lady Franklin.'

Name.	Rate.	Total.	
		Days.	Miles.
1. Captain William Penny	- - - - - -	66	932
2. Mr. John Marshall	Mate	53	428
3. John Leiper	2nd Mate	84	862
4. John Stuart	3rd Mate	53	535
5. Robert A. Goodsir	Surgeon	53	428
6. J. Carl C. Petersen	Interpreter	26	542
7. Moses Robinson	Boatswain	59	515
8. Daniel Hendry	Carpenter	88	832
9. Alexander Robertson	Steward	- -	*
10. Richard Kitson	Captain of Hold	56	498
11. Alexander Leiper	Carpenter's Mate	53	428
12. Alexander Bain	Sailmaker	53	428
13. William Mark	Cook	21	222
14. James Leslie	Armourer	54	524
15. John Noble	Cooper	53	428
16. Alexander Thompson	Able Seaman	69	932
17. John P. Lucas	Ditto	57	702
18. Thomas Langster	Ditto	57	594
19. George Findlay	Ditto	57	540
20. William Brands	Ditto	56	498
21. Boreas A. Smith	Ditto	63	627
22. William Bruce	Ditto	84	862
23. James Hodgston	Ditto	84	862
24. J. Davidson	Ditto	88	832
25. Walter Craig	Ditto	31	347
26. George Farce	Ditto	60	557

* Left in charge of stores.

"The 'Sophia.'

Name.	Rate.	Total.	
		Days.	Miles.
1. Captain Alexander Stewart -	- - - - - -	76	625
2. Mr. Donald Manson - -	Mate - - - - -	8	33
3. Mr. James Reid - - -	2nd Mate - - -	59	560
4. Dr. Peter C. Sutherland -	Surgeon - - -	55	580
5. Alexander Samuel -	Boatswain - - -	76	705
6. Matthew Shiells - - -	Carpenter - -	31	302
7. John Gordon - - -	Captain of Hold - -	28	277
8. James Knox - - -	Cook - - -	50	837
9. Alexander Hardy - -	Steward - - -	18	136
10. John Eddie - - - -	Carpenter's Mate -	53	520
11. Donald Sutherland -	Sailmaker - - -	20	155
12. Andrew Adams - - -	Able Seamen - -	59	560
13. James M'Kenzie - - -	Ditto - - -	77	747
14. William Marshall - -	Ditto - - -	77	702
15. Alexander Smith - - -	Ditto - - -	77	737
16. John Lawson - - -	Ditto - -	56	622
17. George Knowles - - -	Ditto - - -	76	705
18. George Thomson - -	Ditto - - -	50	500
19. John Dunbar - - -	Ditto - - -	77	747
20. Andrew Robison - -	Ditto - - -	51	542

"Every officer and man has done his duty.
(Signed) "WM. PENNY."

Secretary of the Admiralty to Mr. Penny.

"Sir, Admiralty, 22nd September, 1851.

"With reference to your letters of the 12th April, and 8th September last, and to your report of the zealous assistance afforded to you by the several officers and others therein named, as well as to the general good conduct of your men, I am commanded by my Lords Commissioners of the Admiralty to acquaint you that my Lords desire to express to you, and to the officers and crews of the 'Lady Franklin' and 'Sophia,' the sense they entertain of their praiseworthy conduct throughout the service they have been employed upon; and the satisfaction of my Lords at the untiring and praiseworthy exertions of the travelling parties, as evinced in the space traversed by them, and the geographical discoveries they have made.

"My Lords are further of opinion, that great credit is due to you and Captain Stewart, and to the offcers under your orders, for the state of health maintained on board your respective ships.

"You will assure Mr. Petersen that the value of his services is fully acknowledged by their Lordships.

"I am, &c.
(Signed) "W. A. B. HAMILTON."

Director General of the Medical Department of the Navy to P. E. Sutherland, Esq., late of Captain Penny's Arctic Searching Expedition.

"Sir, Admiralty, 7th November, 1851.

"I have much pleasure in acknowledging eighty-eight zoological specimens, twenty-six botanical specimens, eighty mineralogical specimens, thirty paleontological specimens, as per margin, your contribution to the museum and library established at the Royal Naval Hospital at Haslar, for the benefit of the medical officers of the navy, and to request that you will accept my thanks for the support you thus afford to the Establishment.

"I am, &c.

(Signed) "W. Burnott,

"Director General, &c."

Sir John Richardson's Report on two pieces of Drift Wood brought home by Captain Penny of the "Lady Franklin."

"No. 1. Picked up in Robert Bay of Baillie Hamilton's Island, latitude 76° 2′ North, longitude 96° West.

"1. This piece of wood was, when found, eighteen inches long, and of very irregular width, being an inch and a half broad at the widest part, and ending each way in splintered points. It is a fragment of an inch thick elm plank, left rough on one side as it came from under the saw, and smoother on the other, which retains portions of a thin coating of tar or mineral pitch.*

"2. I entertain not the slightest doubt of the board from which this fragment has been split off having been sawn and pitched by civilized man, since neither Indians nor Esquimaux produce any work of a similar kind.

---

* A small piece was broken from the end of the fragment in carrying it to the "Lady Franklin" from the place where it was found, and another piece has since been sawn off, for the purpose of examination in the microscope. The tar coating was considered by Captain Penny and his officers to be lead-coloured or slate-coloured paint used as a priming in shipwrights' yards, but when examined through a lens it appeared to me to be mineral pitch, with bleached woody fibres shining through the interstices, giving a leaden hue to the whole surface. This opinion is partly confirmed by the solubility of the coating in ether, proving it to be either tar or petroleum. I have not been able, however, to ascertain to which of the latter two substances it is to be referred.

" 3. The roughly sawn side is every where decomposed into very fine white, shining, flax-like fibres, giving it a shaggy surface, and indicating long exposure to the weather. Similar fibres, but shorter and in smaller number, occur on the smeared side, that surface having been protected from the atmosphere by the pitch, and perhaps by its having laid undermost for a length of time. The other two sides are irregularly splintered in the direction of the woody fibre, the board having evidently been split into fragments by a hatchet. One of the sides actually bears at one end the marks of two or three blows of a rather blunt cutting instrument, and on this side the fibres of the wood are less decomposed than on the other three; whence I would infer that the board had been drifted, and exposed to the weather for some considerable time before it received these cuts. The other splintered surface has its woody fibres nearly as much decomposed as the shaggy sawn side. Since the board was split, the angles of the wood have been scarcely or not at all rounded by friction.

" 4. On the surfaces and between the interstices of the bleached fibres there are many minute black blodies (*perithecia*).

" 5. Judging from the length of time required in high northern latitudes to decompose and bleach the woody fibres to the extent that the process has advanced in the piece of drift-wood under consideration, and to develope the lichenoid bodies mentioned in paragraph 4., I am disposed to infer that it has been exposed to the weather for at least ten years, and probably for a considerably longer period, and that therefore it has no connexion with Sir John Franklin's expedition.

" 6. After having come to this conclusion from my personal observation in Arctic regions, I have, through Sir William Hooker, had an opportunity of considering the opinions of Mr. Berkely and several other eminent cryptogamists, who think that a less time would suffice to reduce wood to the condition of the drift-elm. I was thus led to examine the action of the sea and shingle on wood forming part of the sea-wall and groining off Haslar Beach, and I find that sound Norway deal exposed to the friction of gravel for part of the ebb and flood of every tide, and to the action of the sun and weather for twenty hours out of the twenty-four during a year or fourteen months, has its woody fibres considerably unravelled and bleached, though not to the extent of the drift-elm; and that oaken groining formed of old ship-timber, when exposed to the wash of the sea in ordinary tides, for periods ranging from twelve to thirty years, rots, but the fibres of even the oldest pieces are not so much disentangled and bleached as in the drift-elm. Various *perithecia* occur in the cracks of the oak; their development seeming to depend in some degree on the rotting of the woody substance. None of these bodies are found on the fir plank that had been exposed only for one year, its surface appearing quite fresh as if newly dressed, except where its prominent points are fringed by the bleached flax-like fibres disengaged by the friction of the gravel. In comparing these effects of the surf and weather on an English beach with the breaking up of the surface of a piece of drift-timber cast on the shores of Cornwallis Island, the shortness of the summer season in the latter quarter must be kept in mind. The ground there is not denuded of snow for more than two months of the year, while at Haslar the weather operates during the whole twelve months, and one year's exposure there may therefore be taken as equal to six on the shore of Victoria Channel. Moreover the low temperature of the high latitudes retards the rotting of wood, or its decay by putrefaction, for very many years. These, added to many minute circumstances which it is unnecessary to detail, lead me to adhere to the opinion expressed above, respecting the length of time during which the elm has been exposed to the weather, notwithstanding Mr. Berkely's experience of the greater effects of the open climate of Europe. Had the edges of the drift-elm been more rounded, so as to countenance the belief that it had suffered much friction in the gravel, I should have modified my opinions, so far as to think it possible that the hatchet blows which split the board for the last time had been the act of some one engaged in Franklin's expedition. That the mere exposure to the weather has not brought the more recently split surface to its present condition *within five years* is evidenced by comparing it with a chip of ash drift-timber brought home last year from Cape Riley, and then reported upon. The cut surface of that chip was then referred to a date not more distant than 1845; and the subsequent discovery of Franklin's wintering place in the neighbourhood renders its having been cut by his people prior to September 1846 nearly a certainty, yet that surface was little bleached or decomposed in comparison with the newest split side of the piece of elm.

"7. The result of the preceding investigation being such as to convince me that the piece of drift-elm had no connexion with Franklin's expedition, I was desirous of ascertaining whether some information respecting the course of the flood-tide, or main set of the currents, might not be derived from it. With this view, I requested Dr. Clark to ascertain the species of the elm, from its microscopic structure. English shipwrights make extensive use of the English elm and the American white elm.* Were it ascertained to be one of these species, its drift from the continental coast of Arctic America might be considered as disproved, for neither of these elms grow on the American rivers which fall into the Arctic Sea, or are in use with the Hudson's Bay Company in Rupert's Land. There

* The American white elm is used in our naval arsenals for paddle floats, hammock rails, boat gunwales and keels, boat timbers and knees, and for planking diagonal-built boats. When painted its first coating is white lead and oil. This information was obtained from John Fincham, Esq., master shipwright of Portsmouth Yard. To it may be added, that the sledges employed on Captain Austin's expedition were of white elm. Sir Edward Parry did not employ elm sledges.

is, however, a third kind, which has its northern limit on the banks of the Saskatchewan, whose timber is occasionally used in the construction of boats that have been sometimes, though very rarely, transported across Methy Portage to the affluents of the Mackenzie. This Saskatchewan elm is supposed to be the slippery elm of the Canadas. Boards cut from it were used in 1825 for the repair of Sir John Franklin's boats, and were found to be so porous as to allow of the transudation of water. It is the recollection of this porousness which induces me to allude to this kind of elm, since without a comparison of its wood with the drift-piece the inquiry cannot be considered to be complete. It happens, however, unfortunately, that no specimen of it is accessible to us. Franklin's boats of 1825 were payed with mineral pitch, which is universally substituted for paint or tar on the Mackenzie, in boat-building; and two of them, abandoned by me at the mouth of the Copper-mine River in 1826, and subsequently broken up by the Esquimaux, had elm foot-boards in the stern sheets so pitched. As the piece of drift-elm corresponded with the general aspect of a fragment of these foot-boards, I suspected at first that such might have been its origin; but Dr. Clark's microscopic observations cause him to refer the drift-piece to the English elm. It differs, indeed, conspicuously in its grain, even to the naked eye, from the white American elm, and closely resembles the English one, but seems to have rounder and more open pores when viewed through an ordinary eye-glass. As its microscopic structure, however, is identical with that of the English elm, its unusual porousness may be merely a variety, not amounting to a specific difference.

"8. If it be held, then, that the European origin of the wood is established, the course in which it could have drifted is next to be considered, and the probabilities seem to be greatly in favour of the opinion that it entered Wellington Strait by way of Lancaster Sound. The finding of the blade of an oar on Cape Hotham, marked with a Davis's Straits whaler's name, indicates at least an occasional drift in that direction. Those who believe in the existence of an open polar basin may infer that a piece of board may find its way into Victoria Channel, either round the north end of Greenland, or from the coasts of Lapland or Asia, or from Behring's Straits; but as yet the existence of such a basin rests only on vague conjecture.

"9. We may therefore infer, though not with absolute confidence, that this piece of elm-board drifted through Wellington Strait; and further, for reasons assigned in former paragraphs, that if it was handled by any one of Franklin's parties, which is not probable, that it was merely as a piece of drift-wood which they had split for fuel. Viewed in this light, it may be considered as evidence of open water in Wellington Strait. That the western entrance of Victoria Channel is also occasionally open, seems to be established by the presence, on the northern shores of Cornwallis Island, of a drift tree of American spruce, twelve feet long and as thick as a man's ancle, found there along with smaller pieces by Mr. Goodsir. The great scarcity or entire absence of drift-wood in the north bay of Wellington Channel, and its occurrence on the islands in Victoria Channel and on the north shore of Cornwallis Island, led the officers of the 'Lady Franklin' and 'Sophia' to believe that most of the drift-wood which they found came from the westward, a belief in accordance with their opinion of the flood-tide, or chief current, setting from the west, and the prevailing winds blowing from the north and north-west.

"No. 2. Picked up in Disappointment Bay on the north side of Cornwallis Island, in latitude 75° 36′ North, and longitude 96° West, by Mr. Goodsir.

"10. This piece of wood, which is about five inches long, has the external appearance of the American white spruce, which forms the bulk of the drift-wood found on the Arctic coasts of America; and Dr. Clark found it to correspond exactly in its minute structure with that species. It is partially rotten, has lost much of its original weight, is much rounded by friction, and two of its sides have the bleached silvery hue which drift-wood acquires. It differs, in fact, only from the ordinary morsels of drift-wood scattered over the Arctic beaches in its having been partially charred, and evidently not having been exposed to much rubbing against either ice or gravel since it was submitted to the action of fire.

"As there are no natives in that quarter, nor traces of them more recent than one or two centuries ago, I cannot but consider the charring of this small piece of wood as connected with Franklin's expedition. That it is not the remnant of a fire made on the spot may be concluded, since Mr. Goodsir found no other pieces of charcoal besides it; yet it has suffered little or no friction since it was burnt, and has not probably passed the Straits of Baillie Hamilton's Island, where the strong currents would bring it into collision with pieces of drift ice. Doubtless Franklin, in accordance with the previous practice of Arctic voyagers, and his own expressed intentions, sent out exploring parties in spring from his winter quarters at Beechey Island. By one of these this piece of wood may have been charred farther to the west in Victoria Channel, and drifted to Disappointment Bay by the currents or north-west winds. It is not likely to have been thrown overboard from the ships, as parties would scarcely have been landed in Victoria channel to pick up drift-wood without leaving some conspicuous memorials of their visit, and where wood was scarce, a piece so large would scarcely be rejected among the ashes of the galley fire. The fire-wood in use on board the ships was oak, of which a fragment was left behind on Beechey Island.

(Signed) "John Richardson,
"Medical Inspector."

Extract of Dr. Clark's Memorandum of his Microscopical Examination of the pieces of Drift-Wood referred to in the preceding Report.

"No. 1. *The drift-elm.* Perpendicular, horizontal, and tangental sections of the elm in question were compared with similarly cut sections of the English and of the American white elm. The anatomical elements of the different species are essentially the same, and it was only in the modifications of these, with respect to size, form, consistence, and colour, that a means of distinguishing the species could be found. The drift-wood differed from the American white elm in the size and character of the (*a*) *woody fibres*, (*b*) *dotted ducts*, and (*c*) *medullary rays*.

"(*a*) In the American elm the woody fibres were much elongated, narrow, acutely pointed, and had thin transparent walls without any visible contents. The woody fibres of the drift-wood were, on the other hand, rather stunted, broad, obtusely pointed, and had rough thickened walls enclosing granular contents.

"(*b*) In the American elm the dotted ducts were few in number, and about $\frac{1}{900}$th of an inch in diameter; few of them were barred or scalariform. The circular markings on their walls were irregularly disposed in rows, had each a diameter of about the $\frac{1}{2000}$th of an inch, and exhibited a minute central elliptical spot. In the drift-elm the ducts were numerous and large, the mean diameter of each being about $\frac{1}{600}$th of an inch. Almost all of them were barred or scalariform on one or two sides. The circular markings on their walls were each about the $\frac{1}{1800}$th of an inch in diameter, and exhibited a central circular diffractive spot in their interior.

"(*c*) In the American elm the perpendicular section of the medullary rays was acutely pointed, and the constituent cells contained little or no colouring matter. An analogous section of the medullary rays of the drift-piece showed that they were broader, shorter, and obtusely pointed at each extremity, and that the constituent cells contained much colouring matter.

"In the American elm the anatomical elements were closely compressed. In the elm under investigation they were loose and open.

"Those acquainted with microscopic examination of woods will perceive that the structural characteristics of the drift-wood correspond as closely as possible with those of the *English elm*, and a comparison of analogous sections of the latter wood leaves little doubt on my mind of their specific identity.

"The soft, whitish, woolly appearance of the surface of the drift-elm, having the aspect of a lichenous crust, was found by microscopic examination to depend on separation of the woody fibres from each other, their subsequent contraction and occasional interlacement, and the development on their free surface of minute granules. That this disintegration of the woody fibre has been produced by long-continued exposure and abrasion is probable, from the fact of the opposing edges of the woody fibre being ragged, as if separated by violence from each other.

"No. 2. *Drift-firwood.* The result of a comparison of this wood with Italian larch, Polish larch, Riga fir, Dantzic pine, Scotch fir, Virginian red pine, American yellow pine, pitch pine, New Zealand fir, and white spruce fir from Rupert's Land, all but the last-named in use in our naval arsenals, was its identification with the white spruce.

"Haslar Hospital, October 10th, 1851."

Extract of a Letter from the Rev. J. M. Berkely, referred to in the preceding Report.

"The wood (the elm board) has been divided transversely, and the surface has evidently been exposed some time to the atmosphere. In consequence thereof the divided ends of the woody fibres have lost their connexion, and are perfectly bleached and partly decomposed. It is very easy to trace the connexion of the bleached ends with the sound portion beneath, and there is not the slightest trace of any of those green bodies which are characteristic of lichens. The black specks which are seated on the decomposed fibres are distinct *perithecia*, thin above, but thicker and of a firmer consistence below, and furnished with a few very short brownish hairs, where they are attached to the decomposed wood. They do not contain distinct *asci*, as in perfect *verrucariæ*, but are filled with a white gelatinous mass, consisting of minute obovate oblong bodies, many of which are divided by a single septum. The production, therefore, though it comes from a species of *phoma*, an undoubted fungus, belongs to those anomalous bodies, which Acharius has placed in the genus *limboria*, and which are exactly intermediate between lichens and fungi, differing from the former in the total absence of a crust, and from the latter in their firmer, more persistent fruit. In the fissures of the wood I find a minute fungus, with distinct *perithecia*, and a highly developed *mycelium*, with very minute spores. I find, also, the *sporidia* of some lichen.

"As regards the time which such a piece of wood might be exposed to the atmosphere to assume such an appearance, I should say that in oak it would require several years, perhaps as many as Dr. Richardson mentions, viz. ten. I do not think, however, that a piece of elm wood exposed to constant changes of atmosphere could remain so long without having the subjacent wood decayed. There is nothing in the production to make one believe that it has outlived many seasons, as is undoubtedly possible with true lichens; and the presence of the fungus above mentioned in the fissures of the wood leads me to think that the wood has not been exposed more than two or three years. As I am leaving home again at five o'clock to-morrow, I have not time to compare the structure of the wood in a sound piece of elm, but the swollen ends of the vessels are peculiar.

"King's Cliff, October 12th, 1851."

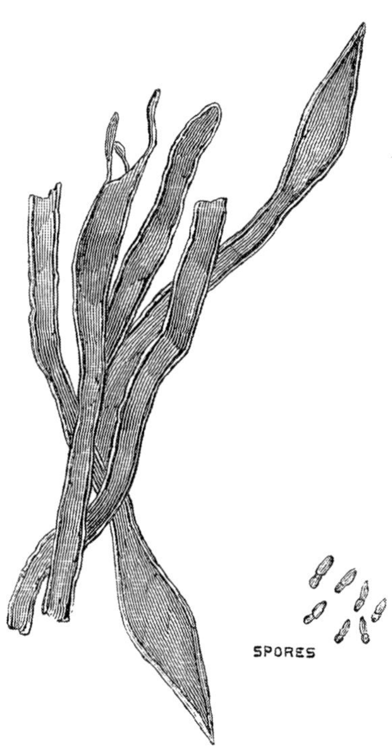

Bleached ends of the woody fibres.

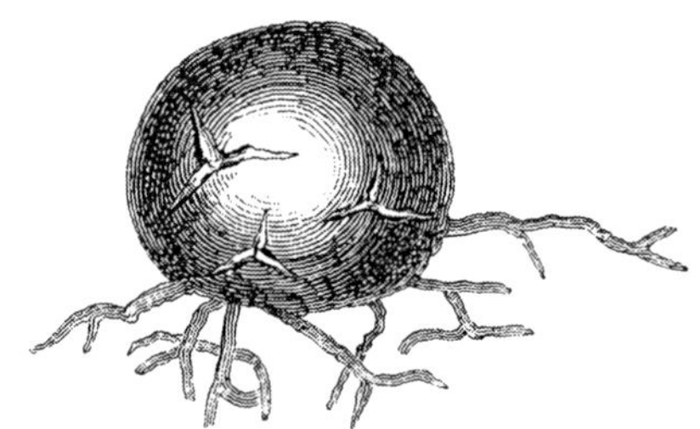

Fungus in fissures of the wood.

Perithecium splitting and pouring out its spores when pressed.

Portion of wall of perithecium, with the spores.

Spores of the fungus.

Sporidium of lichen found amongst the mycelium of the fungus.

ABSTRACTS

OF THE

THREE-HOURLY METEOROLOGICAL REGISTER,

KEPT ON BOARD HER MAJESTY'S SHIP SOPHIA,

IN THE ARCTIC REGIONS,

1850–1851.

ALSO,

AN ABSTRACT

OF

THE METEOROLOGICAL REGISTER,

KEPT IN A JOURNEY OVER THE ICE,

THROUGH THE WELLINGTON CHANNEL TO PRINCE ALFRED BAY

AND PRINCE ALBERT LAND,

1851.

Abstract of the Meteorological Journal kept on board Her Majesty's Ship Sophia.—*Davis Straits.*

1850. Month and Day.	Mean of Eight Readings of the Aneroid Barometer.	Reading of the Thermometer in the Shade at								Mean Daily Temp.
		3 A.M.	6 A.M.	9 A.M.	Noon.	3 P.M.	6 P.M.	9 P.M.	Mid-night.	
		°	°	°	°	°	°	°	°	°
May 1										
2										
3										
4										
5*										
6										
7	29·99	−1	+9	+15	+17	+23	+11	+8	+8	+9
8	·97	+10	11	15	16	16	13	8	−2	11·3
9	·75	6	17	18	21	31	25	15	+10	18
10	·75	12	24	28	30	31	30	27	22	25·5
11	·72	25	23	28	33	36	34	34	35	31
12†	·72	35	37	37	41	36	37	36	32	36
13	·75	33	36	36	38	36	34	34	34	36·4
14	·64	33	37	37	34	33	31	31	31	33
15	·88	31	31	31	44	41	39	43	29	36
16	·72	26	26	32	37	40	46	44	19	31
17	·88	...	30	31	37	41	37	35	36	35
18‡	·59	36	37	40	41	42	42	43	28	38
19	·67	37	44	44	45	40	39	32	32	39
20	30·02	32	37	40	42	40	38	36	34	38
21	·25	32	35	32	44	44	40	39	32	37
22	·30	32	44	45	42	40	36	36	36	38
23	·10	35	34	37	38	35	35	30	29	34
24§	29·87	28	32	37	40	48	36	34	31	35
25	·89	29	33	34	37	38	32	32	29	33
26	30·17	29	29	29	30	28	27	26	26	28
27	·26	26	25	25	26	26	27	27	27	26
28	·15	27	29	31	35	37	35	35	32	32
29	29·95	31	33	42	44	44	37	35	34	37
30	30·06	33	33	32	33	33	32	28	25	31
31	·01	27	33	30	33	31	34	27	23	29
Means	29·92	26·9	29·5	32·0	35·1	33·4	33·1	30·5	29·6	31·2

* The ships beset at the edge of the fixed ice.
† The ice opening out, the ships in open water.
‡ Closely beset in the pack ice, and sustaining violent pressure.
§ The ice opening out, ships in open water.

Abstract of the Meteorological Journal kept on board Her Majesty's Ship Sophia.—*Davis Straits.*

1850. Month and Day.	Mean Temp. of Sea at its Surface.	WINDS.		WEATHER.		Position at Noon.	
		Direction.	Estimated Force.	A.M.	P.M.	Latitude.	Longitude.
	°					° ′	° ′
May 1		EAST.	6			67 48	55 58
2		EAST.	5			68 40	55 50
3		S.S.W.	4	v.b.‡		70 0	56 0
4		N.W.	8	*o.v.*		71 5	54 16
5		N.N.E.	3	v.b.c.			
6		N.E.	3	v.b.c.			
7	28	N.W.	2–4	f.s.	c.m.s.		
8	28	E.S.E.	2–0	c.			
9	28	S.W.	3–0	v.c.			
10	28	S.E. to S.W.	2–5–1	v.c.b.	b.m.v.s.		
11	29	S.W.	4–1	v.c.	m.v.c.		
12	30·7	VARIABLE.	4–1	v.c.	o.v.c.		
13	32·5	VARIABLE.	1–6	v.c.	c.v.o.	71 0	55 0
14	33	N.W.	2–6	c.v.o.	o.s.		
15	33·5	N.W. to E.	1–0–2	o.s.	c.v.		
16	31·7	EASTERLY.	1–5	*v.* o.f.			
17	32	S.E. to S.W.	3–6–8	v.o.	b.q.u.	71 20	54 40
18	30·5	S.S.E.	8–0	b.c.q.u.	v.c.		
19	32·2	E. to N.W.	1–9	o.m.	s.b.m.		
20	32·5	VARIABLE.	6–1	b.m.	d.m.s.		
21	32·7	N.W. to S.W.	2–6–2	m.	o.m.		
22*	34	E.S.E.	2–8	v.	b.m.o.		
23	31·2	S.E. to N.W.	7–1–5	s.v.o.	l.m.o.		
24	31	S.E. to N.E.	2–5–9	o.b.	v.o.s.b.		
25	30·5	N.E. to N.	8–4	o.v.b.c.	o.b.s.c.	71 23	54 30
26	28·7	E.N.E.	4–10	c.b.v.	c.b.*v.*	71 35	55 45
27	28	N.E.	10–5	v.o.		71 56	56 7
28	30	N.E. to S.W.	5–1–6	o.b.c.	o.m.	72 15	55 30
29	30·7	W.S.W.	4–8	o.c.	o.c.b.		55 27
30†	30	N.E.	1–6	c.o.s.	v.c.	72 23	55 30
31	29	N.N.E.	5–2	*v.*		72 25	
Means	30·7					71 50	54 54

* Eider and long-tailed ducks in great abundance.
† Off the settlement of Proven.
‡ For an explanation of these symbols, see p. clxxviii. of the Appendix.

Abstract of the Meteorological Journal kept on board Her Majesty's Ship Sophia. — *Davis Straits.*

1850. Month and Day.	Mean of Eight Readings of the Aneroid Barometer.	Reading of the Thermometer in the Shade at								Mean Daily Temp.
		3 A.M.	6 A.M.	9 A.M.	Noon.	3 P.M.	6 P.M.	9 P.M.	Mid-night.	
		°	°	°	°	°	°	°	°	°
June 1	30·07	+22	+36	+40	+36	+39	+32	+34	+31	+33·7
2	·13	30	31	40	44	49	44	37	33	36
3	·12	33	33	34	39	43	44	41	39	38·2
4	29·98	37	39	40	44	46	46	45	31	41·1
5	·86	32	39	41	42	40	31	31	28	35·5
6	·75	29	29	30	44	50	46	37	31	37
7	·69	32	36	52	52	52	43	38	32	42·1
8	·75	32	38	47	47	51	46	36	32	41·1
9	·79	33	36	37	38	38	38	35	33	36
10	·82	32	34	38	45	46	36	34	31	37
11	·89	31	32	44	47	50	37	35	28	38
12	·89	29	36	44	46	40	35	32	32	36·7
13	·79	41	41	39	39	40	36	33	32	37·6
14	·82	34	34	34	34	34	33	32	30	33·1
15	·93	26	32	32	32	34	33	33	29	31·3
16	·84	32	34	34	34	31	34	32	31	32·7
17	·83	33	33	33	33	34	34	33	28	32·6
18	·76	34	37	36	36	34	33	33	32	34·3
19	·78	28	29	31	32	32	31	29	26	29·7
20	·79	27	27	30	33	34	30	29	27	29·6
21	·64	27	33	35	37	38	38	39	43	36·2
22	·60	37	32	34	37	38	39	34	33	35·5
23	·66	33	34	36	36	37	36	36	35	35·4
24	·60	36	36	37	36	34	35	36	35	35·6
25	·68	35	33	33	34	35	34	32	32	33·5
26	·94	33	36	37	37	37	35	35	32	35·2
27	·77	35	37	38	39	41	42	42	44	39·7
28	·55	45	45	47	44	47	45	38	38	43·6
29	·63	40	41	40	39	39	39	39	38	39·4
30*	·74	38	39	40	46	41	44	40	40	41
Means	29·80	32·6	35·7	37·7	39·7	40·1	37·6	35·4	32·6	36·3

* During this month the ships were rarely beset, but the ice was always so close and so much broken up that little advance could be made.

ABSTRACT OF THE METEOROLOGICAL JOURNAL KEPT ON BOARD HER MAJESTY'S SHIP SOPHIA.—*Davis Straits.*

1850. Month and Day.	Mean Temp. of Sea at its Surface.	WINDS.		WEATHER.		Position at Noon.	
		Direction.	Estimated Force.	A.M.	P.M.	Latitude.	Longitude.
	°					° ′	° ′
June 1	30	N.N.E.	1–2	v. : o.v.s.		72 25	56 0
2	30·5	S.E. to N.E.	3–0–4	o.s.v.c. : b.o.s.		72 30	55 45
3	31·5	E.	3–0	o.b.s. : c.v.		72 40	56 12
4	31	N.E.	1–2	v.c.		72 45	56 0
5	31·2	N.E.	3–1	v. : m.o.s.		72 48	56 6
6	30	W.S.W.	2–0	m.s. : *v.*		72 50	56 30
7	31	N.N.E.	2–1	*v.*		73 5	57 12
8	30·5	N.E.	0–4	*v.*		73 6	
9	30·5	N.E.	3–1	*v.* : o.b.		73 8	
10	30	S.S.W.	1–2	o.b. : m.o.		73 10	
11	29·5	N.N.E.	2–1	m.o. : *v.*		73 20	57 16
12*	29·5	N.N.E.	4–1	*v.*		73 22	
13	29·5	N.N.E.	3–4	*v.*			
14	30	N.N.E.	3–5	v. : m.			
15	30	N.N.E.	4	f.v. : *v.*			
16	30	N.E.	4–5	f.*v.* : *v.*			
17	30	N.E.	4–1	*v.*			
18	30	N.E.	2–4	*v.*			
19	30	N.E.	3–2	f.			
20	30	N.E.	3–5	f.			
21†	31	N.E.	3–1	f.m. : c.*v.*			
22	32	N.E. to W.	1–0–2	*v.*f. : f.		73 20	57 5
23	32	W.S.W.	2–8	f.m.s. : c.b.			
24	32	S.W.	1–10	b.c.r. : o.r.s.b.			57 0
25	31·2	S.W.	10–6	o.c.s. : c.o.b.			
26	31·2	W.S.W.	9–4	o.s.q.r. : c.v.b.			57 20
27	32	S.S.E.	3–10	c.o.g. : o.r.s.			57 0
28	32·2	SOUTHERLY.	7–1	c.o.v.		73 10	57 15
29	33	W.S.W.	1–6	o.r.c. : o.b.		73 20	57 0
30‡	33·2	NORTHERLY.	2–1	c.v.b. : c.*v.*		73 22	56 55
Means	30·8					73 10	56 56

* In the vicinity of Berry Island. Sea fowl abundant; eider ducks' eggs found upon the islands.

† Solar rays at noon, 61°. ‡ Solar rays at 3 P.M. 86°.

Abstract of the Meteorological Journal kept on board Her Majesty's Ship Sophia.—*Davis Straits.*

1850. Month and Day.	Mean of Eight Readings of the Aneroid Barometer.	Reading of the Thermometer in the Shade at								Mean Daily Temp.
		3 A.M.	6 A.M.	9 A.M.	Noon.	3 P.M.	6 P.M.	9 P.M.	Mid-night.	
			°	°	°	°	°	°	°	°
July 1	29·74	+ 42	+ 44	+ 54	+ 39	+ 44	+ 44	+ 38	+ 36	+ 42·5
2	·76	33	40	42	40	39	37	37	33	37·6
3	·90	34	34	35	34	33	32	29	29	32·5
4	·94	29	29	33	34	35	34	34	34	33·2
5*	·87	33	34	40	44	45	44	29	29	37·2
6	·75	29	39	45	44	44	35	33	33	37·7
7	·73	36	40	43	43	43	43	34	34	39·5
8	·72	34	38	37	36	35	34	34	34	35·2
9	·52	34	34	35	36	40	35	35	33	35·2
10	·60	34	32	34	35	35	34	35	34	34·1
11	·39	35	34	39	35	35	34	35	31	34·7
12	·20	34	36	38	40	34	34	34	34	35·5
13	·61	34	34	37	36	36	36	35	34	35·2
14	·73	34	38	38	38	35	36	34	34	36
15	·85	34	35	36	38	38	35	35	30	35·1
16	·78	30	31	38	37	35	34	34	34	34·3
17	·60	34	35	35	33	35	35	34	32	34·1
18	·92	33	34	36	34	37	40	36	36	35·7
19	·98	36	38	37	36	36	36	36	35	36·2
20	30·03	34	34	34	34	34	35	35	35	33·3
21	29·99	34	34	42	42	37	37	33	32	36·4
22	·83	33	32	32	33	32	32	30	30	31·8
23	·84	32	35	35	35	35	36	36	32	34·5
24	·77	30	34	34	33	35	34	34	26	32·5
25	·87	26	29	33	37	39	33	31	28	32
26	·91	28	37	37	36	36	36	35	32	34·6
27	·74	30	35	35	37	38	38	36	31	35
28	·37	30	36	37	37	37	37	35	34	35·3
29	·36	34	34	83	35	34	34	33	32	34·2
30	·59	32	33	33	34	37	37	38	35	35·5
31†	·63	35	35	37	36	36	33	30	30	34
Means	29·74	32·9	35	37	37·2	37·2	35·9	33·7	32·8	35·5

* Beset in Melville Bay. The water abundant in a brown slime; and *Entomostraca* of very large size.

† The ships were beset during the greatest part of this month.

Abstract of the Meteorological Journal kept on board Her Majesty's Ship Sophia.—*Davis Straits.*

1850. Month and Day.	Mean Temp. of Sea at its Surface.	WINDS.		WEATHER.		Position at Noon.	
		Direction.	Estimated Force.	A.M.	P.M.	Latitude.	Longitude.
	°					° ′	° ′
July 1*	32·5	VARIABLE.	0–3	c.v.b. : *v.*c.		73 35	57 0
2	34	N.E.	0–6	b.o.*v.* : b.c.v.		73 50	57 15
3	31	N.E.	6–8	b.o.v. : f.		73 55	58 0
4	31	S.W.	0–5	m.o.b. : m.r.		74 20	58 30
5	31·5	S.E.	0–1	o.c.m. : c.v.		74 37	
6†	31·5	VARIABLE.	0–1	*v.*			
7	32	S.W.	5–2	*v.*			
8	32	W.S.W.	5–1	*f.* : f.r.s.m.			
9	32	NORTHERLY.	2–5	v.c. : o.b.c.		74 45	58 40
10	31·7	S.W.	7–1	o.b.m. : f.		74 50	59 15
11‡	31·3	N.N.E.	2–5	f. : *v.*			
12	31·5	S.S.W.	3–10	o.c.b. : b.q.c.		75 16	60 8
13	31	S.S.W.	9–10	c.q.v. : c.*v.*		75 14	
14	31	W. VARIABLE.	1–0	c.b.v. : o.b.m.			
15	31	E. VARIABLE.	0–2	o.c.m. : f.*v.*			
16	31	E.N.E.	1–5	*v.*			
17	31	E.N.E.	5–0	*v.* : *v.*f.		75 20	61 0
18	32	VARIABLE.	0–1	m.o.f. : m.f.r.		75 23	61 20
19	32·7	VARIABLE.	0–1	*f.* : f.m.		75 36	61 40
20	32·5	S.S.E.	1–3	f.r. : m.c.b.		75 34	
21	32	EASTERLY.	2–1	c.m.r. : f.s.		75 32	
22	31·5	EASTERLY.	1	*f.* : b.		75 30	
23	31·7	N.E.	2–0	b.v. : c.b.v.		75 27	
24	32	N.E.	3–1	b.c.v. : *v.*b.			
25§	32·2	S.W.	1–3	*v.* : *v.*f.		75 31	61 30
26	32·3	N.E.	1–2	f.*v.* : *v.*			
27	32·5	N.E.	1	*v.*		75 32	61 25
28	32·2	E.N.E.	1–4	*v.*			
29	31	W.S.W.	4–7	v.b. : m.o.		75 34	61 20
30	30·5	W.	4–0	m.o. : m.c.v.			
31	32	VARIABLE.	0–3	c.v. : *f.*			61 15
Means	31·7					75 5	59 4

* Solar rays at noon, 108°.

† Solar rays 3 A.M., 60°; 9 A.M., 78°; noon, 88°; 6 P.M., 85°; 9 P.M., 37°. Exceedingly clear sky; intense refraction on the southern horizon.

‡ Barometer falling rapidly with a N.E. wind, lowest 28·95°; began to rise with the S.W. gale.

§ Solar rays 3 P.M., 106°.

Abstract of the Meteorological Journal kept on board Her Majesty's Ship Sophia.—*Davis Straits.*

1850. Month and Day.	Mean of Eight Readings of the Aneroid Barometer.	Reading of the Thermometer in the Shade at								Mean Daily Temp.
		3 A.M.	6 A.M.	9 A.M.	Noon.	3 P.M.	6 P.M.	9 P.M.	Mid-night.	
		°	°	°	°	°	°	°	°	°
Aug. 1	29·78	+30	+37	+37	+39	+39	31	+31	+31	+34·4
2	·79	28	34	34	34	36	35	33	28	32·6
3	·84	29	30	33	33	32	30	28	28	30·3
4	·84	27	34	34	39	40	37	29	25	33·1
5	·85	26	33	34	39	42	39	30	23	33
6	·85	26	30	36	36	38	38	38	28	33·7
7*	·86	29	36	36	36	36	36	30	27	33·2
8	·87	29	35	38	40	40	38	34	30	35·5
9	·79	32	33	38	44	42	38	35	32	36·7
10	·86	28	33	33	37	36	31	33	34	33·1
11	·94	32	34	35	34	34	34	34	30	33·3
12†	·93	34	36	32	35	36	36	33	31	34·1
13	30·01	30	33	35	35	34	33	32	30	32·7
14	29·94	31	35	37	38	39	38	36	36	36·2
15	·99	35	38	39	40	38	37	35	35	37·2
16	30·03	33	35	38	43	42	42	38	33	38
17	·05	34	37	33	34	36	35	35	32	34·1
18‡	·11	30	36	36	38	39	37	33	30	34·7
19	·13	30	32	35	37	36	35	35	33	34·1
20	29·73	33	33	32	33	34	33	33	32	32·9
21	·75	32	33	34	35	35	35	34	32	33·7
22§	·88	32	32	35	36	38	36	34	33	34·5
23	·95	32	34	36	35	36	34	34	32	34·1
24	·96	33	33	34	35	34	36	35	33	34·1
25	·96	31	31	32	32	34	32	31	30	31·6
26	·87	27	29	31	32	32	30	29	31	30·1
27	·78	33	34	36	37	34	34	31	31	33·7
28	·68	33	34	34	32	35	27	28	28	31·6
29	·59	26	26	27	30	32	28	29	27	28·1
30	·67	27	27	29	29	29	30	29	30	28·7
31	·77	30	31	31	34	34	33	32	33	32·2
Means	29·87	30·4	33·5	34·3	35·9	36·1	34·5	32·7	30·6	33·2

* In open water at the fixed ice Melville Bay.

† In the "north water," off Cape York. Young ice forming on the water among the loose pack during the night.

‡ Crossing the top of Baffin's Bay. § Enter Lancaster Sound and Barrow Straits.

ABSTRACT OF THE METEOROLOGICAL JOURNAL KEPT ON BOARD HER MAJESTY'S SHIP SOPHIA.—*Davis Straits.*

1850. Month and Day.	Mean Temp. of Sea at its Surface.	WINDS. Direction.	WINDS. Estimated Force.	WEATHER. A.M. : P.M.	Position at Noon. Latitude.	Position at Noon. Longitude.
	°				° ′	° ′
Aug. 1	32	NORTHERLY.	3–0	f.	75 34	61 12
2	31·5	E. VARIABLE.	3–0	f.*v.* : *v.*f.	75 35	61 10
3	30	W. VARIABLE.	3–1	f.*v.* : *v.*		61 5
4	31·7	E.N.E.	0–3	*v.*		
5	31·5	E. VARIABLE.	0–2	*v.* : c.*v.*		
6*	32	E. VARIABLE.	0–2	c.*v.* : *v.*	75 48	62 14
7	32·5	E. VARIABLE.	0–1	*v.*c.		62 0
8	32	E.S.E.	2–0	f. *v.* : *v.*b.c.	75 54	62 45
9	33		0	v.c.	76 0	64 0
10	31	E. VARIABLE.	2–0	f. : b.c.	76 4	66 0
11	32	SOUTHERLY.	0–3	m.o.s. : b.o.m.	76 0	66 30
12	32·5	VARIABLE.	1–2	f.v. : *v.*c.	75 54	67 15
13	33	E.N.E.	0–4	*v.*	75 55	68 15
14	35	VARIABLE.	2–0	v.c. : c.v.	76 8	69 0
15	34	VARIABLE.	0–2	v.	76 10	69 30
16	33·5	E.N.E.	0–2	v.c.	76 21	70 0
17	31·7	E.N.E.	0–2	v.f. : v.	76 24	70 30
18	33	S.E.	1–4	v.f. : v.	76 40	73 0
19	34·5	W. to S.E.	4–10	v.*f.* : b.o.c.m.	76 10	77 30
20†	32	S.E.	10–7	o.m.q.b.v.	73 47	83 20
21	31	S.E.	8–1	o.q.r : o.c.q.	74 0	
22	33	N.N.W.	0–3	o.c.v. : b.m.	74 27	86 27
23	33·2	N.N.W.	2–5	v.q. : v.b.g.	74 31	88 20
24	32·5	N.N.W.	1–5	g.c.m. : c.q.v.	74 34	91 0
25	31	N.N.E.	6–1	c.q.o. : m.o.s.	74 47	93 0
26	30	VARIABLE.	0–3	o.b.m.s.		92 15
27	30	S.W.	1–6	o.c.s. : o.c.v.	74 43	92 0
28	30	S.W. to N.E.	1–5	c.v. : c.v.q.	74 47	93 0
29	28·7	W.N.W.	2–4	o.m.q.s.	74 43	92 0
30	29·5	W.N.W.	4	o.m.q.s.		
31	30	W.N.W.	4–8	o.q. : q.m.s.		
Means	31·8				75 24	78 28

* Solar rays 3 P.M., 100°. Rotges abundant; one black whale seen; Monodons very numerous.

† Violent gale from the eastward, with a high state of the barometer.

Abstract of the Meteorological Journal kept on board Her Majesty's Ship Sophia.—*Barrow Straits.*

1850. Month and Day.	Mean of Eight Readings of the Aneroid Barometer.	Reading of the Thermometer in the Shade at								Mean Daily Temp.
		3 A.M.	6 A.M	9 A.M.	Noon.	3 P.M.	6 P.M.	9 P.M.	Mid-night.	
		°	°	°	°	°	°	°	°	°
Sept. 1	29·76	+32	+32	+32	+34	+33	+33	+33	+32	+32·7
2	·86	32	33	34	34	36	33	34	34	33·7
3	30·04	32	33	36	36	36	34	32	30	33·5
4	·09	34	33	32	32	36	32	32	32	33·
5	·15	31	31	35	38	36	35	30	29	33·
6	·19	30	30	35	36	34	33	32	32	32·7
7	·30	33	33	33	37	32	28	25	23	30·5
8	·43	23	24	24	25	26	22	23	23	23·5
9	·35	22	23	24	26	25	25	26	26	24·5
10	·12	28	29	28	30	29	27	27	25	28·
11	29·82	29	23	23	23	25	28	28	27	24·5
12	·61	23	22	20	17	16	14	13	10	17·
13	·84	9	10	10	14	14	15	13	15	12·5
14	30·00	15	16	17	19	19	18	15	14	16·5
15	29·94	14	14	14	16	19	20	21	21	17·5
16	·82	22	21	23	24	24	24	24	24	23·2
17	·67	21	22	23	26	22	20	19	20	21·7
18	·64	17	17	21	23	20	20	16	8	17·8
19	·45	15	12	12	19	19	16	19	18	16·3
20	·11	29	28	29	29	30	26	24	24	27·5
21	·52	14	15	17	19	16	14	17	17	16·
22	·72	18	21	23	21	18	14	14	16	18·
23	·61	18	18	20	23	26	25	24	21	22·2
24	·52	18	18	18	22	20	18	18	19	19·
25	·66	19	22	22	20	14	15	15	13	17·5
26	·72	9	9	11	12	12	12	13	12	11·3
27	·78	9	8	9	11	11	10	11	11	10·
28	·87	11	12	8	10	10	11	7	8	9·5
29*	·95	8	8	8	10	8	9	8	7	8·2
30	.96	8	7	6	6	8	9	9	9	7·8
Means	29·84	20·7	21·1	21·5	22·4	22·4	21·7	20·7	20·0	21·3

* The ice in the harbour one foot thick.

ABSTRACT OF THE METEOROLOGICAL JOURNAL KEPT ON BOARD HER MAJESTY'S SHIP SOPHIA.—*Barrow Straits.*

1850. Month and Day.	Mean Temp. of Sea at its Surface.	WINDS.		WEATHER.		Position at Noon.	
		Direction.	Estimated Force.	A.M.	P.M.	Latitude.	Longitude.
	°					° ′	° ′
Sept. 1	30	S.W.	9–6	o.m.q.r. : q.b.s.o.		74 43	92 0
2	30	S.W. to S.E.	6–1	q.b.m. : o.c.b.q.			
3	30	NORTHERLY	0–2	o.b.c.m.			
4	30	WESTERLY	0–4	o.v. : c.*v.*			
5	30	VAR. N.E.	0–2	c.*v.*		74 47	92 54
6	29·7	S.S.E.	1–8	c.*v.* : c.q.m.			
7	29·5	S.E. to N.E.	3–8	m.o.b.r. : c.v.			
8	28·5	N.E.	7–2	c.v.q.			
9	28	N. to W.	1–5	c.b.o.m.		74 35	94 0
10	28·2	W.N.W.	5–1	o.q.s. : o.m.c.s.		74 27	95 30
11	28	S.E.	2–8	n.q.s. : o.q.s.		74 7	95 50
12	28·3	N.W.	3–8	o.c.q.*s.*		74 34	94 10
13	28·3	N.W.	8–1	q.u.s.g.		74 40	94 16*
14	28·5	VARIABLE	1–2	o.c.b. : o.c.v.			
15	28·5	W.S.W.	2–8	o.c.m.s.q.			
16	28·5	S.S.W.	6–4	o.m.q.u.s.			
17	28·7	S. to S.E.	6–3	o.m.s. : o.m.c.			
18	28·8	E.N.E.	2–1	m.c. : o.m.c.s.			
19	29	N.E.	3–6	o.m.q.s.u.			
20	29·2	S.E.	9–3	o.m.q. : o.s.q.			
21	29·3	S.W.	6–2	q.v.c. : o.m.s.			
22	29·2	N.E.	1–8	o.c.s. : c.v.q.			
23	29·3	N.E.	8–4	o.m.q.u.s.			
24	29·2	E.S.E.	4–1	o.c.m. : o.c.b.			
25	29·5	E.S.E.	2–1	o.m.c.b.			
26	29·5	S.W.	1	o.m.c.b.			
27	29·5	S.S.E.	1–2	o.m.c.b.			
28	29·5	S.W.	1–3	o.m.c.b.s.			
29	29·5	S.W.	1–2	o.m.c.s.			
30	29·5	WESTERLY.	1–2	o.c.v.s. : o.m.c.s.			
Means	29·1	Temperature in the shade, monthly				Max. +38°	Min. +6°

* The ships brought to anchor in winter quarters.

Abstract of the Meteorological Journal kept on board Her Majesty's Ship Sophia. — *Barrow Straits.*

1850. Month and Day.	Mean of Eight Readings of the Aneroid Barometer.	Reading of the Thermometer in the Shade at							
		3 A.M.	6 A.M.	9 A.M.	Noon.	3 P.M.	6 P.M.	9 P.M.	Mid-night.
		°	°	°	°	°	°	°	°
Oct. 1	29·92	+*10	+10	+12	+13	+12	+12	+12	+10
2	·77	11	12	15	15	14	3	−½	7
3	·88	9	10	11	12	11	9	+1	−2
4	·94	−5	−5	3	3	1	0	−5	5
5	·93	+1	4	−3	−6	−5	−3	2	2
6	·71	−1	+4	+6	+6	+7	+7	+7	+7
7	·73	+5	7	6	6	7	6	5	8
8	·89	2	2	5	5	4	3	3	7
9	30·01	9	10	10	18	14	13	11	10
10	29·75	9	9	10	8	5	5	5	5
11	·81	4	4	3	2	4	3	−2	−3
12	·93	7	10	11	13	12	8	+9	11
13	30·21	11	14	13	17	15	14	6	6
14	·34	4	4	10	11	8	3	2	4
15	·36	3	3	5	10	3	4	8	2
16	·19	2	2	7	2	4	2	−1	1
17	·01	−1	−1	−1	0	2	2	+5	7
18	29·90	+9	+1	+6	5	5	8	9	9
19	·84	10	8	6	4	0	−1	−5	−5
20	·71	−6	−6	−1	0	0	+8	+9	+8
21	·71	+5	+3	4	−4	−3	−4	−3	0
22	·90	−1	−1	1	3	7	8	7	−7
23	·86	5	2	2	1	1	1	0	+1
24	·82	+1	+1	+1	2	5	1	+4	3
25	·89	−6	−8	−10	2	2	7	−9	−9
26	·98	9	6	3	3	4	4	0	1
27	30·04	8	10	12	11	7	11	13	13
28	·00	13	14	14	13	13	11	10	7
29	29·90	10	11	10	10	12	9	10	9
30	·79	9	10	3	2	+1	0	+1	1
31†	·79	4	8	9	9	−9	9	−9	10
Means	29·92	+1	+1	+2·2	+2·7	+1·5	+1·3	+0·6	+1

* The thermometer placed on the ice at a distance of upwards of thirty yards from the ships.

† The ice in the harbour two feet two inches thick.

ABSTRACT OF THE METEOROLOGICAL JOURNAL KEPT ON BOARD HER MAJESTY'S SHIP SOPHIA. — *Barrow Straits.*

1850. Month and Day.	Mean Daily Temp.	WINDS.		WEATHER.	
		Direction.	Estimated Force.	A.M.	P.M.
	°				
Oct. 1	+ 11·5	S.S.W.	1–3	o.m.*s.*	
2	9·5	S.E.	1–2	o.m.s.b. : c.v.	
3	8	N.E. to N.W.	3–5	o.m.c.v. : v.	
4	– 1·5	N.N.E.	3–6	v. b. : m. c.o.s.	
5	3	N.E	6–8	c.q.*s.* v.	
6	+ 5·5	N.E. to N.W.	2–10	o.m.s.	
7	6·3	N.N.E.	5–9	m.s.q. : v.q.s.	
8	4	E.N.E.	1–4	v. *q.* : c.*v.*	
9	11·7	VARIABLE S.E.	0–4	c.v. : o.m.c.	
10	7	N. to N.W.	5–1	o.m.c. : o.m.c.b.	
11	2	S.W.	1–3	o.c.b.m. : v.c.	
12	10	S.E.	5–1	o.c.s.q.	
13	12	S.E.	1–2	o.*s.*m.c.	
14	5·7	S. to N.E.	1–4	c.v.m. : c.v.	
15	4·8	N.E.	4–3	c.v.m. : c.*v.*	
16	2·5	N.N.W.	8–4	r.q.s. : *v.*q.	
17	1·5	N. to W.	5–1	*v.* q. : c.b.v.	
18	6·2	E. to N.	1–9	c.*v.* : c.b.v.	
19	2	N.N.W.	8–1	c.*v.* : *v.*	
20	1·5	N.W.	4–2	*v.* : c.*v.*	
21*	– 1·2	N.W.	3–1	c.o.*v.*	
22	4·5	N.W.	2–1	c.*v.*	
23	1·3	N.W.	1–4	c.*v.*	
24	0·3	W.S.W.	3–4	o.m.s.	
25	– 6·5	N.W.	2–5	o.m.s.q.	
26	3·7	W.	4–0	v. : v.o.c.	
27	10·8	W. to N.	2–1	o.c.m. : m.s.*v.*	
28	12·2	N.W.	1–0	r.m. : *v.*	
29	10	VARIABLE N.E.	0–1	*v.* : m.s.	
30	2	VARIABLE S.E.	0–1	v.c. : o.m.	
31†	8·5	NORTH.	1–4	o.m. : v.c.	
Means	+ 1·5	Temperature in the shade, monthly - -		Max. + 18°; Min. – 14°	

* The ice on Kate Austin Lake two feet thick.

† The weather during this month has been very unsteady, and generally violent, with long-continued and dense falls of snow.

ABSTRACT OF THE METEOROLOGICAL JOURNAL KEPT ON BOARD HER MAJESTY'S SHIP SOPHIA. — *Barrow Straits.*

1850. Month and Day.	Mean of Eight Readings of the Aneroid Barometer.	Reading of the Thermometer in the Shade at							
		3 A.M.	6 A.M.	9 A.M.	Noon.	3 P.M.	6 P.M.	9 P.M.	Mid-night.
		°	°	°	°	°	°	°	°
Nov. 1	29·77	−10	−11	−11	−14	−15	−17	−12	−14
2	·82	14	18	13	11	9	9	13	14
3	·79	15	15	14	13	13	11	11	9
4*	·81	18	9	7	7	5	6	3	2
5	·89	7	7	6	5	4	2	2	2
6	·64	2	2	2	2	2	2	4	4
7	·62	2	2	2	2	3	4	7	10
8	·79	10	14	12	12	12	13	13	16
9	·67	16	17	17	17	7	5	3	0
10	·29	2	+4	+5	+6	+8	+8	+8	+9
11	·47	+9	13	13	12	11	8	6	3
12	·81	3	−5	−8	−11	−13	−17	−17	−19
13	·98	−20	18	14	11	14	10	10	15
14	·94	18	12	18	11	10	9	7	7
15	·86	6	5	3	3	3	3	3	8
16	·93	8	6	4	3	3	5	8	5
17	30·04	5	4	3	3	6	6	8	8
18	·15	10	7	8	13	17	18	19	11
19	29·98	10	9	8	6	6	3	3	3
20	·75	3	3	1	+1	+1	+0	+1	0
21	·91	+1	3	4	−5	−6	−8	−8	9
22†	·90	−6	6	6	1	0	0	4	2
23	30·01	+1	2	2	4	5	9	10	9
24	·06	−10	10	12	12	12	12	10	9
25	·21	10	7	4	3	7	4	3	2
26	·24	6	10	13	14	13	10	7	7
27	·09	7	8	6	7	7	11	15	11
28	·00	11	11	8	7	8	8	6	5
29	29·91	5	4	3	0	1	2	2	1
30	·97	2	4	5	6	8	10	21	24
Means	29·88	−6·9	−6·8	−6·6	−6·7	−6·3	−6·5	−7·1	−7·0

* Sun beneath the horizon at noon.
† The ice in the bay three feet thick.

ABSTRACT OF THE METEOROLOGICAL JOURNAL KEPT ON BOARD HER MAJESTY'S SHIP SOPHIA. — *Barrow Straits.*

1850. Month and Day.	Mean Daily Temp.	WINDS.		WEATHER.	
		Direction.	Estimated Force.	A.M.	P.M.
	°				
Nov. 1	−13	W.N.W.	4–3	v.c.	
2	12·5	N.E.	3–1	o.c.m.	*v.*
3	12·6	E.S.E.	1–7	v.c.	v.
4	5·9	E. to S.W.	2–1	r.	m.o.s.
5	4·3	S.W. to S.E.	1–9	m.o.s.	m.o.c.s.
6	2·5	S.E.	10–4	o.q.*s.*	v.c.
7	4	S.E. to N.E.	3–1	o.m.c.	v.
8	12·7	W.N.W.	1–2	*v.*c.	
9*	10·5	S.E.	8–11	v.	o.m.c.*s.*
10	+6·2	S.E.	11	*o.q.s.*	
11	9·4	S.E. to N.W.	10–7	*o.q.s.*	
12	−10·9	N.E. to N.W.	3–9	v.c.m.	*v.*
13	14	N.N.W.	3–2	v.o.c.	v.
14	11·5	S.W.	2–1	v.c.	c.o.s.
15	4·7	S.E. to N.	1–4	c.o.s.	o.c.v.
16	5·2	N.E.	2–5	c.o.m.	c.v.
17	5·4	E. VARIABLE.	2–1	c.v.b.	c.*v.*
18	11·6	N.E. VARIABLE.	3–0	*v.*c.	*v.*
19	6·3	S.E.	7–9	q.o.s.c.b.	
20	0·5	S.E.	9–1	q.s.c.	q.v.c.
21	5·4	NORTHERLY.	1–4	c.o.v.	*v.*b.
22	3·2	NORTHERLY.	2–1	b.v.o.c.	
23†	5	N.N.W.	1–5	m.o.c.	*v.*
24	10·9	N.W.	1–3	v.b.	v.m.
25	5	S.E.	1–2	b.o.m.	
26	10	S.E.	5–0	c.o.b.v.	m.o.c.
27	9	VARIABLE.	0–1	m.o.	v.m.
28	8·1	N. to S.W.	1–5	o.m.	o.m.s.
29	2·4	S.W.	5–2	m.o.s.	
30	10	VARIABLE N.	1–4	m.o.s.	c.v.
Means	−6·7	Temperature in the shade, monthly - - -		Max. +13°	Min. −24°

* Sudden gale at half-past 2 P.M. White appearance on the S.W. horizon last night.

† Brilliant paraselenæ.

Abstract of the Meteorological Journal kept on board Her Majesty's Ship Sophia. — *Barrow Straits.*

1850. Month and Day.	Mean of Eight Readings of the Aneroid Barometer.	Reading of the Thermometer in the Shade at							
		3 A.M.	6 A.M.	9 A.M.	Noon.	3 P.M.	6 P.M.	9 P.M.	Mid-night.
		°	°	°	°	°	°	°	°
Dec. 1	30·04	−27	−30	−34	−35	−35	−35	−37	−33
2	·00	33	30	30	28	27	25	21	22
3	29·88	22	22	23	20	20	20	18	19
4	·78	22	24	23	21	19	15	20	19
5	·79	17	17	20	21	21	21	18	17
6	·89	15	16	17	18	20	21	20	20
7	·90	22	21	19	20	22	21	10	21
8	30·02	18	18	20	18	18	17	19	15
9	29·98	16	17	17	20	17	18	16	19
10	·96	21	24	26	28	29	28	26	26
11	·85	30	30	30	32	32	34	34	34
12	·73	35	34	34	32	34	32	34	33
13	·69	34	35	30	28	26	25	24	23
14	·75	23	19	16	15	16	19	20	19
15	·89	25	23	26	22	24	26	23	23
16	·93	20	24	27	27	16	15	15	14
17	·80	12	10	8	6	6	10	8	15
18	·86	19	17	19	20	21	20	17	15
19*	·83	17	17	22	20	23	20	26	29
20	·57	29	28	28	25	23	24	23	25
21	·65	17	17	16	20	22	20	15	13
22	·76	19	9	7	4	6	8	12	10
23	·78	12	5	5	6	10	12	12	13
24	·90	19	16	16	15	12	16	17	20
25	·94	20	20	21	23	21	21	22	23
26	·75	22	19	18	17	13	10	10	12
27	·84	16	13	13	12	20	21	21	23
28	·94	24	23	23	20	12	9	8	37
29	·77	7	11	21	28	28	30	30	31
30†	·64	35	35	37	34	35	36	37	34
31	·46	36	35	35	35	35	33	25	24
Means	29·84	22	21·3	22	21·3	21·3	21·3	20·9	21

* The ice in the bay three feet eleven inches thick.

† Open water always in Barrow Straits.

ABSTRACT OF THE METEOROLOGICAL JOURNAL KEPT ON BOARD HER MAJESTY'S SHIP SOPHIA. — *Barrow Straits.*

1850. Month and Day.	Mean Daily Temp.	WINDS.		WEATHER.	
		Direction.	Estimated Force.	A.M.	P.M.
	°				
Dec. 1	−33·2	N.N.W.	4–1	v.c. : v.	
2	27	N.W.	5–1	v. : m.o.s.v.	
3	20·5	N.N.W.	7–1	v.c. : v.m.c.	
4	20·4	N.W.	4–1	v.f. : m.o.s.*v.*	
5	19	N.W.	1–4	v.c.s. : v.c.	
6	18·7	N. to S.E.	2–4	v.	
7	20·6	N.E. to W.	1–5	v.m. : v.m.	
8	17·5	S.E.	5–2	v.m. : *v.*	
9	18	N.	2–4	v.b. : *v.*	
10	26	N.W.	1–5	*v.* : v.c.	
11	32	N.W.	1–4	v.c.b. : v.c.q.	
12	33·4	N.N.W.	6–1	v.m. : *v.*	
13	28·1	N.W.	1–4	v.c.	
14	18·4	N.W. to N.E.	3–4	c.b.o. : v.c.	
15	24·3	VARIABLE.	1–3	v.b. : v.c.	
16	19·7	N.W.	4–3	c.o.v. : c.s.o.	
17	9·4	W.S.W.	4–1	o.m.s q.	
18	18·5	W. to N.E.	1–4	o.m. : *v.*c.	
19	22·5	N.N.E.	4–5	*v.*	
20*	25·6	N.W.	5–1	v.o.c.q. : v.o.c.	
21	17·8	N.W.	3–1	v.o.c. : m.o.c.	
22	8·1	S.S.W.	1–2	m.o.c.s. : v.o.c.	
23	9·3	S.E.	1–2	v.c.m. : v.c.	
24	16·4	N.W. to S.E.	1–2	v.c.b. : v.m.	
25	21·6	VARIABLE.	1–2	*v.*c.b. : v.c.	
26	15·3	N.	1–2	v.c. : o.m.c.	
27	17·3	N.W.	1–3	o.m.c. : *v.*	
28	15·7	N.E.	3–2	*v.* : m.o.s.	
29	23·3	S. to N.W.	7–2	v.o.c. : v.q.	
30	35·4	N.N.W.	4–7	v.q. : v.q.s.	
31†	32·2	N.N.W.	8–6	v.q.s. dft.	
Means	21·4	Temperature in the shade, monthly - - -		Max. −4°; Min. −37°	

* Paraselenæ 20° to 22° from the moon, deficient in colours, except a slight blush of red at the lunar edge.

† Chloride and iodide of silver freely exposed to the southern horizon for two months, and to the light of the moon, do not become changed in colour.

Abstract of the Meteorological Journal kept on board Her Majesty's Ship Sophia. — *Barrow Straits.*

1851. Month and Day.	Mean of Eight Readings of the Aneroid Barometer.	Reading of the Thermometer in the Shade at							
		3 A.M.	6 A.M.	9 A.M.	Noon.	3 P.M.	6 P.M.	9 P.M.	Mid-night.
		°	°	°	°	°	°	°	°
Jan. 1	29·31	−28	−30	−32	−35	−36	−36	−34	35
2	·32	36	36	36	36	37	36	36	35
3	·44	35	32	33	31	31	30	32	34
4	·56	34	36	34	31	30	29	29	27
5	·60	26	25	24	26	24	24	26	23
6	·60	26	26	26	26	28	29	33	32
7	·79	33	33	33	31	32	32	28	25
8	·88	22	19	19	23	18	16	16	17
9	·81	20	24	25	26	28	24	24	25
10	·68	25	26	22	18	20	16	15	11
11	·71	12	15	19	20	20	20	21	20
12	·71	19	15	14	14	16	26	31	35
13	·84	36	37	39	40	40	38	37	39
14	·90	35	35	36	34	35	34	32	36
15	·95	33	32	35	36	36	36	38	38
16	·97	39	36	37	35	35	38	38	38
17	·87	36	37	37	38	38	38	36	37
18	·71	37	38	36	33	36	37	38	38
19	·71	39	39	39	39	39	39	39	40
20	·79	41	40	40	39	39	38	39	37
21	·76	35	31	30	30	29	25	26	26
22	·74	29	33	32	34	36	33	34	32
23	·47	31	29	32	33	34	36	38	38
24*	·51	39	37	36	30	28	30	29	37
25	·86	29	26	24	25	24	23	18	20
26	30·01	15	19	17	16	16	21	20	21
27	·08	23	25	23	24	20	17	20	23
28	29·93	26	20	20	21	19	15	13	17
29	·86	19	18	20	16	18	19	18	18
30	·89	24	20	17	19	21	26	29	29
31	·53	30	30	32	36	32	26	26	29
Means	29·73	29·4	29	29	29	29	29·9	28·8	29·3

* The ice in the bay four feet ten inches thick. The open water in Barrow Straits yielding a copious supply of vapour to the atmosphere.

ABSTRACT OF THE METEOROLOGICAL JOURNAL KEPT ON BOARD HER MAJESTY'S SHIP SOPHIA. — *Barrow Straits.*

1851. Month and Day.	Mean Daily Temp.	WINDS.		WEATHER.	
		Direction.	Estimated Force.	AM.	P.M.
	°				
Jan. 1	−33·2	N.N.W.	3–4	v.q.s. :	*v.*
2	36	N.N.W.	2	v.c.	
3	22·6	N.N.W.	2–3	v.c. :	v.c.b.
4	31·1	N.N.W.	4–7	*v.*q.	
5	24·8	N.W.	10–7	q.o.s.g. :	q.v.c.
6	28·2	N.W.	4–5	v.c.m. :	v.c.q.
7	31	NORTHERLY.	4–1	*v.*	
8	18·8	N.N.E.	1–4	*v.*	
9	24·5	VARIABLE.	1–2	*v.*	
10	19	VARIABLE.	1–2	*v.* :	m.o.s.
11	18·3	NORTHERLY.	2–3	v.m. :	v.c.m.
12	21·5	N.N.W.	1–6	m.o.s. :	v.b.c.
13*	38·3	N.W.	4–3	v.c.m. :	v.m.c.
14	33·8	N.W.	3–4	v.m. :	v.c.q.m.
15	35·5	N.N.W.	5–6	v.c.q. :	v.q.
16	37	N.N.W.	4–6	v.q. :	v.c.q.
17	37·1	N.W.	3–1	v.q.m. :	v.c.
18	36·6	N.W.	3–1	v.c. :	v.m.
19	39·1	N.N.W.	3–1	*v.*m. :	*v.*
20	39·2	N.W.	2–5	*v.*m. :	*v.*q.
21	29	N.W. to S.W.	2–1	v.m. :	o.s.*v.*
22	32·8	N.N.W.	1–3	*v.* :	v.b.m.
23	33·8	N.W.	1–3	v.b.m. :	*v.*
24	33·3	N.N.E.	1–4	v.m. :	v.c.m.
25	23·7	N.N.E.	3–10	v.c. :	v.q.s.p.
26	18·2	NORTH.	9–4	v.q.s.p. :	*v.*q.
27	22·1	NORTH.	4–2	*v.*q. :	v.c.m.
28	18·8	N.W.	3–5	v.o.c.m. :	v.s.m.
29	18·2	W.S.W.	4–1	c.s. :	c.v.m.
30	23·1	N.W.	1–3	v.c. :	*v.*m.
31†	30·2	N.W.	2–5	v.m. :	v.c.m.
Means	−29	Temperature in the shade, monthly - -		Max. −10°	Min. −41°

* Mercury, exposed to the air, became frozen for the first time this season.
† Aurora Borealis often present, but not very brilliant or diversified in colour.

ABSTRACT OF THE METEOROLOGICAL JOURNAL KEPT ON BOARD HER MAJESTY'S SHIP SOPHIA. — *Barrow Straits.*

1851. Month and Day.	Mean of Eight Readings of the Aneroid Barometer.	Reading of the Thermometer in the Shade at							
		3 A.M.	6 A.M.	9 A.M.	Noon.	3 P.M.	6 P.M.	9 P.M.	Mid-night.
		°	°	°	°	°	°	°	°
Feb. 1	29·31	−28	−34	−32	−31	−32	−32	−34	−33
2	·43	33	33	36	26	27	32	33	35
3	·56	35	32	33	32	32	29	24	27
4	·49	31	29	29	26	23	22	22	23
5	·68	23	30	31	33	33	35	35	35
6	·77	35	34	33	27	27	29	30	29
7*	·75	31	37	39	39	38	40	41	40
8	·89	40	39	38	39	36	36	30	28
9	·69	30	35	35	37	37	36	36	34
10	·94	30	30	30	27	31	31	32	33
11	·88	32	32	31	30	31	31	30	25
12	·78	24	25	27	28	28	28	25	28
13†	·76	26	29	28	24	22	24	23	22
14	·58	20	17	17	18	19	20	21	19
15	·39	18	17	18	17	17	14	13	12
16	·42	10	11	14	12	14	12	15	15
17	·67	15	17	27	29	29	24	24	24
18	·76	22	25	27	26	27	28	29	30
19	·84	29	29	29	27	27	28	29	30
20	·85	29	28	26	27	30	30	33	34
21	·92	36	36	37	39	34	36	38	36
22	30·05	37	38	37	37	41	41	41	41
23	·13	39	39	38	32	37	41	40	41
24	·16	41	41	41	40	39	39	39	45
25	·08	37	36	36	34	30	31	26	27
26	·09	29	29	29	24	27	37	34	38
27	·30	38	38	38	33	40	43	39	37
28	·15	37	32	29	30	32	29	29	25
Means	29·80	29·8	30·4	30·9	29·2	29·8	30·6	30·1	30·2

* The sun seen, after an absence of ninety-five days.
† The ice in the harbour five feet eight inches thick.

ABSTRACT OF THE METEOROLOGICAL JOURNAL KEPT ON BOARD HER MAJESTY'S SHIP SOPHIA. — *Barrow Straits.*

1851. Month and Day.	Mean Daily Temp.	WINDS.		WEATHER.	
		Direction.	Estimated Force.	A.M.	P.M.
	°				
Feb. 1	−32·4	N.W.	5–3	o.m.s. : v.m.	
2	31·8	VARIABLE.	1–3	m.s. : v.b.m.	
3	30·6	NORTH.	2–4	v.c.m. : v.m.	
4	25·6	N.W.	4–6	o.m.s. : o.q.s.	
5	31·8	N.N.W.	7–8	o.q.s.	
6	30·6	N.N.W.	2–5	m.q. : *v*.b.	
7	38·3	NORTH.	3–5	v.m. : *v*.	
8	35·7	N. to W.	3–6	*v*.m. : v.q.m.	
9	35	N.W.	2–5	o.m.s. : *v*.m.c.	
10	30·5	N.N.E.	4–6	v.q.c.	
11	30·3	N.N.E.	3–1	v.c.	
12	26·8	N.N.W.	1–3	v.c. : v.c.m.	
13	24·8	N.W.	2–3	o.m. : o.m.s.	
14	18·8	S.W.	4–5	o.m.s.	
15	15·8	S.E.	4–10	o.m.q.s.	
16	13·3	E.S.E.	9–5	m.o.q.s. : v.q.c.	
17	23·6	N.E.	1–3	v.q.c. : v.c.	
18	26·7	NORTH.	2–3	v.m.	
19	28·5	N.N.W.	1–2	v.b.m. : *v*.m.	
20	29·7	N.N.W.	1–3	o.m. : v.c.m.	
21	24·4	NORTHERLY.	3–1	v.c.m. : v.m.	
22	39·2	WESTERLY.	1	o.m. : v.m.	
23	38·7	NORTHERLY.	1–2	v.m.	
24	40·6	NORTHERLY.	1–3	v.m.	
25	32·2	N.E.	4–6	v.m. : v.q.s.m.	
26	31·1	NORTH.	6–1	v.q.s.m. : o.m.s.	
27	38·3	VARIABLE.	1–2	*v*.b.m. : v.c.m.	
28*	30·3	N.E.	2–11	o.q.s. : q.s.	
Means	29·8	Temperature in the shade, monthly - -		Max. −10°; Min. −45°	

* Greatest rise and fall of tide observed, 6 feet 2 inches; least, 1 foot 2⅛ inches; average, 3 feet 2 inches.

ABSTRACT OF THE METEOROLOGICAL JOURNAL KEPT ON BOARD HER MAJESTY'S SHIP SOPHIA. — *Barrow Straits.*

1851. Month and Day.	Mean of Eight Readings of the Aneroid Barometer.	Reading of the Thermometer in the Shade at							
		3 A.M.	6 A.M.	9 A.M.	Noon.	3 P.M.	6 P.M	9 P.M.	Mid-night.
		°	°	°	°	°	°	°	°
March 1	29·85	−23	−22	−22	−22	−16	−15	−15	−11
2	·49	10	10	9	9	11	16	20	23
3*	·45	28	27	26	23	22	23	22	14
4	·65	15	17	14	19	20	22	22	21
5	·52	20	20	23	21	20	21	23	29
6	·46	27	30	28	28	29	32	32	33
7	·54	31	26	26	24	26	30	32	34
8	·58	33	33	32	30	30	35	35	35
9	·70	36	36	36	30	31	36	38	39
10	·81	37	21	28	25	26	28	29	30
11	·89	32	30	31	30	28	34	36	35
12	·99	35	38	28	24	24	25	22	23
13	·89	22	20	17	15	15	12	8	12
14	·82	12	7	8	8	7	9	9	9
15	30·00	8	8	8	13	15	20	29	29
16	·34	33	30	28	22	26	29	30	30
17	·48	37	30	26	21	22	28	30	32
18	·36	29	30	22	11	19	17	15	15
19†	·10	14	14	10	6	6	8	8	8
20	29·99	10	11	11	10	18	23	26	26
21‡	30·13	30	35	39	40	41	36	31	32
22	·29	32	30	25	19	21	20	22	22
23	·09	22	22	20	13	10	14	20	17
24	29·96	20	22	20	21	23	29	30	30
25	·91	31	28	23	20	17	21	20	24
26	·69	24	22	18	17	15	19	19	21
27	·97	22	16	18	18	19	23	26	26
28	·94	28	20	25	14	16	21	27	32
29	·81	25	22	17	12	12	16	15	16
30	·87	19	16	12	4	6	7	17	21
31	30·05	20	18	15	11	12	13	24	24
Means	29·89	24·7	23	21·4	18·7	19·6	21·3	23·6	24·3

* Thickness of the ice 6 feet 1 inch. Temperature of the water 29·5°.

† Open water in Barrow Straits up to this time.

‡ The lowest temperature observed during this gale was −41·75, after eighteen consecutive hours of thick snow and a strong wind from N.N.W.

ABSTRACT OF THE METEOROLOGICAL JOURNAL KEPT ON BOARD HER MAJESTY'S SHIP SOPHIA. — *Barrow Straits.*

1851. Month and Day.	Mean Daily Temp.	WINDS.		WEATHER.	
		Direction.	Estimated Force.	A.M.	P.M.
	°				
March 1	− 18·2	N.N.W.	11–8	q.s.	
2	16	N.E. to N.W.	10–4	q.s.	
3	24·3	N. to S.E.	4–7	v.c.q.m.	
4	18·8	S.E. to N.E.	7–4	q.c.v :	q.m.v.
5	22·1	N.N.W.	5–7	q.v.b.c.m.	
6	30	VARIABLE.	4–1	o.m.	
7	28·9	VARIABLE.	1–5	v.b.c. :	b.q.*v*.c.
8	32·8	N.E.	1–3	*v*.	
9*	35·3	NORTH.	2–4	*v*.b.	
10	28	N.N.E.	3–4	o.m. :	*v*.b.
11	32	N.N.W.	1–3	*v*.b.	
12†	27·3	N.W. to E.	1–6	*v*.b. :	*v*.o.u.
13	15·1	E.S.E.	6–9	q.c.v. :	q.o.s.
14	8·6	E.S.E.	7–2	q.o.s. :	o.*s*.
15	16·2	N.N.E.	1–8	o.s. :	c.s.q.
16	28·5	W.S.W.	3–1	*v*.q.b :	*v*.
17	28·4	VARIABLE.	1–3	*v*.	
18‡	19·7	N.W. to S.E.	2–5	*v*.c.b. :	o.q.s.
19	9·2	E.S.E.	5–6	o.m.s.q. :	o.s.
20	17	N.E. to N.W.	6–2	c.m.s. :	b.m.s.
21	35·5	N.W.	10–7	b.o.q.m.s.	
22	24	N.W.	10–7	o.m.q.s.	
23	17·2	N.W.	7–3	o.q.s. :	m.q.b.c.
24	24·7	N.W.	6–2	v.q.c.b. :	b.*v*.
25	23	VARIABLE.	1–2	b.c.v. :	b.m.s.
26	19·3	VARIABLE.	2–3	b.m. :	v.b.c.
27	21	NORTH.	3–4	b.*v*.	
28§	23	VARIABLE.	1–3	b.*v*. :	b.c.v.
29	16·8	N.E.	1–6	b.c.v. :	o.m.s.
30	12·7	N.E. to N.W.	4–6	b.c.m.q. :	b.v.q.
31	17·1	N.W.	2–6	o.m.q. :	b.m.c.q.
Means	22·4	Temperature of the air in the shade, monthly		Max. − 4°	Min. − 41°

* Solar rays at 1 P.M., +2°; 3 P.M., −12°.
† Solar rays at 9 A.M., +2°; 11 A.M., +7°; noon, +5°; 1 P.M., −3°.
‡ Solar rays at 11 A.M., +22°; noon, +15°; 1 P.M., −12°.
§ Solar rays at noon, +35°; 1½ P.M., +40°.

ABSTRACT OF THE METEOROLOGICAL JOURNAL KEPT ON BOARD HER MAJESTY'S SHIP SOPHIA. — *Barrow Straits.*

1851. Month and Day.	Mean of Eight Readings of the Aneroid Barometer.	Reading of the Thermometer in the Shade at							
		3 A.M.	6 A.M.	9 A.M.	Noon.	3 P.M.	6 P.M.	9 P.M.	Mid-night
		°	°	°	°	°	°	°	°
April 1	30·11	−25	−20	−22	−16	−16	−17	−21	−24
2	·15	25	23	18	15	10	23	28	31
3*	29·84	25	19	15	10	5	10	9	8
4	·86	10	7	3	+2	+1	1	3	5
5	30·04	9	10	2	3	−5	12	21	17
6	·10	19	18	9	−9	5	12	21	14
7	·21	11	5	12	5	2	6	11	16
8	·10	21	23	19	12	5	16	17	15
9	·05	19	15	7	0	0	4	16	18
10	.00	22	14	8	11	+3	13	18	19
11	·12	20	18	14	10	−8	15	18	21
12	·29	27	17	15	7	14	14	14	14
13	·38	8	6	5	+8	+10	+10	1	5
14	·36	1	+6	+6	10	11	9	+9	+7
15	·36	+7	10	17	26	23	15	13	13
16	·37	13	17	22	28	29	12	13	12
17	·39	14	17	24	30	34	34	34	30
18	·24	22	25	27	30	32	25	20	18
19	·00	19	22	26	29	30	29	25	20
20†	29·96	22	25	29	32	29	26	16	14
21	30·18	13	12	4	4	6	2	−7	−8
22	·22	−12	−12	−11	−8	−5	−7	14	15
23	·08	21	20	20	17	16	20	23	23
24	·11	20	18	14	3	+1	2	2	3
25	·16	4	0	+4	+6	4	+1	12	18
26	·28	20	17	−14	−9	3	+3	13	12
27	·25	12	18	16	5	−2	−5	13	21
28	·06	19	19	9	2	2	6	8	12
29	·16	13	10	2	+5	+10	6	12	14
30	·32	19	19	5	−2	2	7	13	14
Means	30·16	−8·7	−6·5	−2·4	+2·4	+4·4	−1	−6·1	−7·6

* Thickness of the ice in the bay, seven feet one inch; on Kate Austin Lake, about eight feet. Temperature of the sea 29·5°.

† Seals seen on the ice for the first time this season.

ABSTRACT OF THE METEOROLOGICAL JOURNAL KEPT ON BOARD HER MAJESTY'S SHIP SOPHIA. — *Barrow Straits.*

1851. Month and Day.	Mean Daily Temp.	WINDS.		WEATHER.	
		Direction.	Estimated Force.	A.M.	P.M.
	°				
April 1	−20·1	N.W.	1–6	b.c.q. :	b.v.q.
2	21·7	N.W.	1–2	v.b. :	b c.v.
3*	12·6	S.E.	2–5	o.m. :	o.m.c.
4	3·2	E.S.E.	4	b.m.s. :	b.c.v.
5	9·1	N.W. to S.W.	1–2	v.c.m. :	o.c.m.
6	13·4	N.N.W.	1	v.b.c. :	b.m.o.c.
7	8·2	NORTH.	1–2	o.m.s. :	s.b.c.m.
8	14·7	N.W. to S.W.	1–3	v.b.m. :	o.m.c.
9	9·8	W.S.W.	1–2	o.m.c. :	c.b.o.
10	12·8	N.N.E.	3–1	*v*.b.o.c. :	b.v.c.
11	15·5	N.N.W.	1–2	v.b.m. :	*v.b.*
12	15·2	N.W. to S.E.	2–1	v.b.m.	
13	+0·3	S.E.	4–8	g.o.m.c.s.	
14	7·1	S.E.	7–8	g.o.m.s.	
15	15·5	S.E.	3–6	o.m.s.	
16	18·2	S.E.	3–6	o.m.s. :	c.b.o.v.
17	25·2	VAR. SOUTH.	1–0	o.m.s. :	b.v.c.
18	24·9	S.E.	1–3	b.v. :	o.m.s.
19	25	VAR. EAST.	1–2	o.m.s. :	o.m.b.
20	26·2	N.W.		o.s.	
21	3·2	N.W.		m.s.	
22	−10·5	N.W.		s. dft. :	s.q.c.
23	20	N.N.W.		s.dft.q.c.b.	
24	7·6	N.N.W.		s.dft.q.c.b.	
25†	2·3	N.W. to S.E.		s.b.c.v.	
26	9·9	E.S.E.	3–5	v.b.c.	
27	11·7	N.N.E.	4–8	q.v.b.c.s.dft.	
28	7·2	S.E.	1–3	*v.b.*c.	
29	5	S.E.	1–4	*v.*b.	
30	7·3	N.E. to S.E.	4–1	b.*v.* :	b.v.q.
Means	−3·2	Temperature of the air in the shade, monthly -		Max. + 34° Min. − 31°	

* Solar rays at noon +34°. The snow upon the ice and the land glazed by the action of the sun's rays, although the temperature in the shade has not yet been up to zero.

† Bright and prismatic parhelia and parhelic circles.

Abstract of the Meteorological Journal kept on board Her Majesty's Ship Sophia. — *Barrow Straits.*

1851. Month and Day.	Mean of Eight Readings of the Aneroid Barometer.	Reading of the Thermometer in the Shade at							
		3 A.M.	6 A.M.	9 A.M.	Noon.	3 P.M.	6 P.M.	9 P.M.	Mid-night.
		°	°	°	°	°	°	°	°
May 1	30·36	−15	−10	−2	−2	−2	−3	−15	−19
2*	·42	20	14	+3	+3	4	+2	+2	+2
3	·19	+2	0	1	18	+17	7	4	3
4	29·89	4	+9	12	18	19	11	7	3
5	·78	2	9	9	12	12	12	3	−3
6	·74	−5	−5	−2	9	11	9	5	+2
7	·79	2	+5	+9	11	14	7	4	3
8	·91	+7	7	11	15	18	16	13	11
9	30·32	1	1	3	5	7	5	3	2
10	·46	4	1	12	16	11	12	8	6
11†	·49	5	11	21	21	22	13	5	3
12	·50	6	6	7	7	10	7	2	2
13	·43	1	9	12	10	12	13	7	8
14	·36	9	8	13	15	13	9	5	4
15	·25	5	10	15	18	19	15	8	3
16	·06	12	11	12	18	19	12	9	3
17	·02	9	11	11	19	22	23	16	15
18	·06	19	17	20	29	32	29	26	21
19	·00	17	13	10	13	14	13	10	10
20	·00	7	14	13	13	19	16	13	8
21	·82	12	14	18	21	13	13	12	6
22	30·01	10	10	13	12	14	15	10	12
23	·04	10	10	11	16	18	18	14	10
24	·09	11	10	14	23	22	14	12	9
25	·02	17	24	24	19	18	15	14	12
26	29·86	23	22	23	26	24	28	26	19
27	30·00	14	14	16	18	19	17	15	10
28	·05	11	26	23	23	22	23	16	13
29	·06	14	12	18	22	23	23	24	20
30	·18	19	20	26	34	29	28	27	22
31	·26	22	27	34	42	40	31	27	27
Means	30·11	7·4	9·7	14	17	17	14·4	10·7	8

* The ice in the bay, seven feet nine inches thick.

† The land around the harbour beginning to assume a black appearance, from the action of the sun melting the snow where there was but a thin coating, on slopes with a southern exposure.

Abstract of the Meteorological Journal kept on board Her Majesty's Ship Sophia. — *Barrow Straits.*

1851. Month and Day.	Mean Daily Temp.	WINDS.		WEATHER.	
		Direction.	Estimated Force.	A.M.	P.M.
	°				
May 1	− 7·2	N. to S.W.	5–1–4	b.v.q.m. : b.v.	
2	− 3·2	S.W. to S.E.	2–4	o.m.g.s.	
3	+ 7·7	S.E.	4–7	o.s.m.	
4	10·3	S.E.	7–2	o.s.m. : q.o.s.m.	
5	·7	N.E. to N.W.	5–1	o.b.q.m.s.	
6	3	W. to S.	3–1	*v.b.*c. : v.b.m.s.	
7	5·1	N.W.	2–3	v.b.c.s. : v.b.o.s.	
8	12·2	S.S.W.		o.m.s. : b.v.	
9	3·3	S.W.		b.v.c.	
10	8·7	W.S.W.		o.m.c.	
11	12·6	N.N.W.		o.m.s. : b.v.c.	
12	6	N.W.		c.q.b.	
13	9	N.N.W.		b.c.q. s.dft.	
14*	9·5	N.W.		q.c.b. : b.v.c.	
15	11·6	S.W.		b.v.c.	
16	12	VARIABLE.		*b.v.*	
17	15·7	VARIABLE.		*v.b.*	
18	24·1	WEST		o.s.m.	
19	12·5	N.W. to S.W.		o.m.s.q. : b.v.c.	
20	12·8	W.N.W.		s.dft. q.	
21	13·6	N.W.		s.dft. p.q.	
22†	12	N.N.W.		s.dft. q.	
23	13·3	N. to W.		q.v.b.c.	
24	14·3	VARIABLE.		b.c.q.v.	
25	17·8	N.N.W.		v.b.	
26	22·7	N.N.W.		q.s.p.dft.	
27	15·3	N.W.		q.s.p. : v.b.c.	
28	20	N.W.		o.m.c. : v.b.c.	
29	19·5	N.N.W.		q.p.s. : c.o.m.	
30	25·6	N.W.		o.m.s.	
31‡	30	VARIABLE.		o.m.s.	
Means	12·5	Temperature of the air in the shade monthly - -		Max. + 42° Min. − 20°	

* On this, and the three following days, the meridian altitude was 33° 49′, 34° 2′, 34° 18′, and 34° 39′ respectively.
† At midnight, a parhelion east of the sun.
‡ Bears frequently seen in Barrow Straits.

Abstract of the Meteorological Journal kept on board Her Majesty's Ship Sophia. — *Barrow Straits.*

1851. Month and Day.	Mean of Eight Readings of the Aneroid Barometer.	Reading of the Thermometer in the Shade at							
		3 A.M.	6 A.M.	9 A.M.	Noon.	3 P.M.	6 P.M.	9 P.M.	Mid-night.
		°	°	°	°	°	°	°	°
June 1	30·26	+23	+31	+34	+32	+22	+23	+22	+23
2	·26	22	25	34	40	33	28	26	25
3	·36	27	28	27	25	23	25	20	16
4	·33	16	25	28	32	32	31	26	25
5	·25	26	35	35	39	35	31	30	30
6*	29·97	30	31	32	40	40	37	34	32
7	30·08	31	30	34	36	35	35	34	32
8	·22	32	45	42	45	44	43	45	40
9	·30	40	44	47	47	40	41	39	37
10	·32	41	45	45	45	45	45	40	39
11	·31	43	44	46	49	46	43	43	42
12†	·28	33	35	37	39	40	39	38	35
13	·24	35	36	38	39	36	39	39	39
14	·09	35	32	39	40	40	38	36	36
15	29·88	37	40	43	43	46	38	38	38
16	·87	33	33	33	35	36	35	30	37
17	30·03	32	33	41	41	41	36	31	31
18	29·88	37	38	39	33	38	38	38	34
19	·85	33	35	34	34	35	34	34	31
20	30·01	28	29	31	32	34	34	34	31
21	·08	29	30	34	33	32	32	32	28
22	·06	28	29	30	33	35	33	32	31
23	·14	31	32	32	33	34	34	33	27
24	·09	28	30	30	34	36	32	32	31
25	29·84	30	34	34	35	35	33	33	33
26‡	·81	33	32	31	32	34	39	34	33
27	·98	32	33	35	36	37	34	32	31
28	30·06	35	35	33	40	47	42	34	32
29	·07	32	34	36	36	36	35	37	36
30	·21	32	35	36	39	39	38	33	31
Means	30·07	31·4	33·4	33·5	37·2	36·7	35·5	33·5	32·8

* The surface of the ice very soft: blue spots and water appearing upon it.
† Rain for the first time this season.
‡ Small streams beginning to seek their seaward channels through the dense snow in the ravines.

Abstract of the Meteorological Journal kept on board Her Majesty's Ship Sophia. — *Barrow Straits.*

1851. Month and Day.	Mean Daily Temp.	WINDS.		WEATHER.	
		Direction.	Estimated Force.	A.M.	P.M.
	°				
June 1	+ 26	S.W.		o.m.s.: v.b.c.	
2	29·1	S.E.		o.m.s.	
3*	24	S.S.E.		o.m.s.: v.b.c.	
4	26·1	S.E.		*v*.b.c.	
5	32·7	S.W. to N.E.		v.b.c.	
6†	34·5	E.S.E.		v.b.c.	
7	33·3	S.S.W.		o.m.s.	
8	42	SOUTH		b.o.m.s.	
9	41·9	S.S.W.		b.o.m.v.	
10	43·1	S.E.		v.b.c.	
11	44·5	S.W.		v.b.c.	
12	37	N.N.W.		v.b.c.	
13	37·6	S.W.		v.b.c.	
14	37	S.W. to S.E.	3–2	o.m.s.r.	
15‡	40·3	S.E. to S.W.	4–1	o.m.c.s.	
16	34·9	S.W. to N.W.	3–1	g.o.m.r.	
17	35·7	W.S.W.	2–5	v.b.c.: o.m.s.	
18	36·8	S.W.	6–9	o.m.q.r.s.	
19	33·7	NORTH.	6–2	v.b.c.	
20	31·6	N.W.	2–5	v.b.c.	
21	31·5	W.N.W.	4–6	b.c.q.s.p.	
22	31·3	N. to N.E.	4–6	v.b.c.: v.b.c.q.	
23	32	NORTH.	5–3	v.b.c.q.	
24	31·6	N.W.	3–6	v.b.c.q.g.	
25	33·3	N.W.	6–5	q.o.s.r.p.	
26	33·5	N.W.	4–5	b.c.p.r.	
27	33·7	N.W.	2–1	v.b.c.	
28§	37·2	N.N.W.	1–2	b.v.: o.m.f.	
29	35·2	N.N.W.	2–4	b.v.	
30	35·3	N.N.W.	2–4	b.v.	
Means	34·3	Temperature in the shade monthly - - -		Max. + 49° / Min. − 16°	

* Flocks of brent geese migrating northward.

† The ice in the top of Wellington reported to have shifted northward, leaving a wide crack.

‡ Fissures in the floe at Cape Hotham.

§ Open water in Barrow Straits; abundance of sea-fowl, white whales, narwhals, walruses and seals.

Abstract of the Meteorological Journal kept on board Her Majesty's Ship Sophia. — *Barrow Straits.*

1851. Month and Day.	Mean of Eight Readings of the Aneroid Barometer.	Reading of the Thermometer in the Shade at							
		3 A.M.	6 A.M.	9 A.M.	Noon.	3 P.M.	6 P.M.	9 P.M.	Mid-night.
		°	°	°	°	°	°	°	°
July 1*	30·24	+30	+33	+35	+42	+43	+41	+36	+31
2	·23	33	35	38	42	44	47	40	36
3	·26	35	35	44	44	49	48	39	37
4	·24	36	36	39	50	50	36	40	35
5	·18	37	40	46	50	45	41	40	39
6†	·08	37	38	42	43	43	39	39	37
7	29·91	38	40	43	46	42	40	36	34
8	·87	35	34	37	45	47	37	34	31
9	·91	30	35	37	39	44	39	35	32
10	·88	32	33	39	44	45	39	37	34
11	·77	39	36	36	38	41	40	37	31
12	·79	32	38	38	33	37	33	33	31
13	·81	32	33	33	35	37	36	35	35
14	·97	34	34	37	38	38	37	35	34
15	30·00	34	34	43	40	37	36	35	32
16	·04	33	34	42	44	46	41	42	42
17	·02	40	42	44	44	46	45	43	41
18	·02	42	42	43	41	39	38	36	38
19	·02	39	39	39	45	44	41	36	33
20	·02	33	34	36	41	42	38	36	33
21	·04	33	34	39	40	40	42	35	33
22	·12	35	35	42	43	39	35	32	30
23	·16	29	31	37	43	42	41	35	35
24	·12	35	38	38	35	35	40	38	39
25	29·91	34	36	39	39	38	36	37	35
26	30·02	36	36	37	38	44	35	36	36
27	29·91	36	36	38	40	38	37	36	34
28	·57	48	49	46	41	38	39	34	33
29	·82	32	35	36	39	36	36	33	32
30	·79	33	34	35	42	38	34	33	32
31‡	·80	32	33	40	39	39	39	34	33
Means	29·98	35·1	36·2	39·6	41·4	41·5	38·5	36·3	34·4

* The ice in the bays and channels relieving itself from the water on its surface.

† Violent débâcles entering Assistance Bay from the lakes. The pools on the floe, where the water is comparatively fresh, freeze over at night during clear weather.

‡ The ice has been diminished in thickness, by four feet of its upper surface wasting away under the direct influence of the sun.

ABSTRACT OF THE METEOROLOGICAL JOURNAL KEPT ON BOARD HER MAJESTY'S SHIP SOPHIA. — *Barrow Straits.*

1851. Month and Day.	Mean Daily Temp.	WINDS.		WEATHER.	
		Direction.	Estimated Force.	A.M.	P.M.
	°				
July 1	+36·3	N.N.W.	4–1	v.b.c.	
2	39·3	VARIABLE.	1–2	v.b.c.	
3	41·3	VARIABLE.	1–3	v.b.c.	
4	40·2	VARIABLE.	2	*v.b.*c. : o.b.c.	
5*	42·2	S.S.E.	1–7	o.m.c. : c.v.q.	
6	39·7	VARIABLE.	1–3–7	o.c.q.r. : m.c.r.	
7	40	S.E.	7–5	o.v.c.q.g.p.r.	
8	37·5	W.N.W.	1–4	o.c.v. : b.v.	
9	36·3	N.W. to S.W.	3–1	b.v. : o.m.a.	
10	37·9	S.W. VARIABLE.	4–1	b.v.c.	
11	37·2	NORTH.	6–3	o.e. : c.b.v.	
12	34·3	W.S.W.	6–3	f.o.g. : p.s.c.q.	
13	34·5	N.W.	5–6	s.o.q. : r.p.o.q.	
14	35·8	N.W.	5–0	q.r.p.o. : v.b.c.	
15	36·3	S.E. VARIABLE.	0–3	v.b.c. : v.b.c.m.	
16	40·5	S. VARIABLE.	2–0	v.b.c. : o.m.	
17	43·1	N.W.	2–4	b.c.v.f.m.o.	
18	39·9	N.W.	2–4	m.o. : *v*.b.c.	
19	39·4	S.E.	1–6	v.b.c. : v.b.q.m.	
20	36·6	S.E.	9–1	g.o.m. : c.b.v.	
21†	35·7	S.E.	3–4	v.b.c.	
22	36·1	VARIABLE.	4–0	b.c.v. : f.b.c.v.	
23	36·6	S.W.	1–2	f.c.b. : f.d.r.	
24	37·2	SOUTHERLY.	1–7	f.d.r. : m.o.v.	
25	38	S.E.	8–1	u.o.q.r.	
26	37·2	W.	5–2	b.m.q.c.r.	
27	37	S.W.	2–4	o.r.m. : b.v.c.	
28	40	S.E. to N.W.	5–8	*o.r.*m. : b.c.q.p.r.	
29	34·9	N.W.	8–5	b.c.q.v. : q.p.r.o.	
30	35·1	W.N.W.	3–6	q.b.c.m.p.r.s.	
31	36·2	W.N.W.	6–3	q.b.c.p.r.s.	
Means	37·8				

* Barrow Straits remarkably free from ice ; a sort of commotion in the water at the free edge of the ice in the harbour : it arises from the admixture of comparatively freshwater with sea water of mean density.

† South-east winds beginning to prevail ; Barrow Straits often full of loose drifting ice.

Abstract of the Meteorological Journal kept on board Her Majesty's Ship Sophia. — *Davis Straits,* &c.

1851. Month and Day.	Mean of Eight Readings of the Aneroid Barometer.	Readings of the Thermometer in the Shade at 3 A.M.	6 A.M.	9 A.M.	Noon.	3 P.M.	6 P.M.	9 P.M.	Mid-night.	Mean Daily Temp.
		°	°	°	°	°	°	°	°	°
August 1	29·97	+33	+33	+34	+39	+37	+39	+37	+33	+35·6
2*	·61	32	32	32	32	34	32	32	32	32·3
3	·40	31	33	36	37	37	37	36	35	35·2
4	·73	33	37	38	40	41	40	36	34	37·3
5	·88	32	32	34	35	36	38	35	32	34·2
6	30·16	32	34	35	38	40	39	36	31	35·6
7	·29	32	33	40	41	42	33	32	31	35·5
8	·34	31	33	37	40	38	38	37	33	35·9
9	·39	31	33	38	39	37	34	33	32	34·6
10	·50	34	35	41	45	46	42	39	38	40
11†	·47	34	35	43	42	40	40	39	38	38·9
12	·37	32	32	32	31	31	33	34	34	32·3
13	·31	34	33	35	35	35	35	36	35	34·7
14	·21	35	34	35	35	35	35	34	35	34·8
15	·22	35	35	35	36	35	37	37	37	35·9
16	·17	37	35	35	36	37	37	37	36	36·2
17	·12	37	37	32	35	35	37	37	37	35·8
18	29·96	34	35	35	35	36	35	32	31	34·1
19‡	·90	32	34	34	38	34	32	32	32	33·4
20	30·14	32	36	36	40	38	37	36	38	36·6
21	·16	39	41	44	44	41	37	35	35	39·5
22	·15	36	36	38	37	38	35	35	35	36·2
23	·05	36	38	41	41	42	42	41	41	40
24	29·87	39	39	40	41	41	39	39	39	39·6
25	·87	40	40	40	48	47	44	45	46	43·7
26§	·97	45	44	45	47	51	45	43	43	45·3
27	·91	44	44	45	45	45	44	47	46	45
28	·38	47	48	49	48	47	50	46	46	47·3
29	·54	45	47	47	47	47	45	46	45	46·1
30	·82	46	45	47	49	49	47	46	46	46·8
31	·76	47	46	47	49	50	45	45	44	46·6
Means	30·02	36·4	37·1	38·7	40·1	40	39·9	37·9	37·4	38·4

* Snow and rain very frequent. Large streams, the result of long continued rainy weather.
† The river beds drying up; young ice forming on the surface of the sea at night.
‡ Among a heavy, but loose, pack.
§ Brilliant Aurora Borealis over all the sky, colours much diversified.

ABSTRACT OF THE METEOROLOGICAL JOURNAL KEPT ON BOARD HER MAJESTY'S SHIP SOPHIA. — *Davis Straits*, &c.

1851. Month and Day.	Mean Daily Temp. of Sea at its Surface.	WINDS.		WEATHER.		Position at Noon.	
		Direction.	Estimated Force.	A M.	P.M.	Latitude.	Longitude.
August 1		N.N.W.	6–3	q.b.c.p.r.s.		Winter	Quarters
2		S.W.	2–1	q.v.b.c. : *o.s.*		° ′	° ′
3		N.E.	3–8	o.s.b. : b.c.v.q.		74 40	94 16
4		N.W.	4–1	b.c.v.q. : b.o.a.			
5		N.W.	1–6	b.p.s. : q.p.r.c.			
6		N.N.W.	6–1	b.v.c.q.			
7		SOUTH.	1–2	v.b.o. : f.			
8*		S.E.	1–6	v.b.c. : *v.b.*c.			
9		E.S.E.	6–4	q.o.f. : *o.m.*			
10		N.E.	5–0	o.m.f.			
11		VARIABLE.	1–2	o.m. : *v.*b.c.			
12	32·3	VARIABLE.	1–2	*v.b.*c.		74 35	93 40
13	34·7	N.W.	3–0	*v.*b.c.		74 22	90 45
14	35	N. to S.W.	1–6–0	*v.b.*c. : v.b.f.		74 0	84 0
15	36	N.W.	2–3	f. : v.b c.		73 50	80 45
16†	36	N.W.	4–7	b.c.m. : v.b.c.		73 15	76 0
17	36	N.N.W.	5–1	f.m.o.r.f.		72 10	71 15
18	33·3	W.N.W.	3–6	o.m.r. : f.		71 20	68 0
19	32·8	N.W.	3	f.m.o. : m.o.r.		70 45	64 30
20‡	35·8	S.W. to S.E.	3–4	m.o.s. : v.r.		69 56	59 30
21	39·2	VARIABLE.	0–4	f. : f.p.d.		69 20	57 40
22	39·4	NORTH.	4–6	o.v. : o.v.m.		68 10	56 15
23§	40·3	NORTH.	2–6	b.v.c. : b.v.c.m.		66 34	55 8
24	40·1	NORTH.	6–5	v.o.		64 19	55 0
25	45	N. to S.W.	5–2	v.b.c. : v.b.r.		61 58	54 40
26	43·7	S.W. to N.	4–1–4	v.b.c. : *v.b.*c.		61 37	52 0
27	46·3	N. to S.E.	4–9	v.b.e. : g.o.b.*v.*		60 48	50 0
28	46·8	S.E.	10	m.o.g. : m.o.p.g.		60 0	52 0
29	47	S.E. to S.W.	10–5–6	m.o.p.q.		59 55	51 10
30	47·5	S.W. to S.E.	5–1–2	v.b.c. : o.b.v.		59 17	49 30
31	47·2	W.N.W.	1–6	o.b.v. : v.b.c.		59 0	49 0
Means	39·7	Temperature of the Sea in Mean lat. 67° 15′ and Mean long. 63° 23′.				69 56	74 21

* The ice in Assistance Bay broke loose and set the ships at liberty.
† Entering Baffin's Bay. ‡ Approach the coast of West Greenland.
§ Cross the Arctic Circle.

Abstract of the Meteorological Journal kept on board Her Majesty's Ship Sophia.—*Crossing the Atlantic, &c.*

1851. Month and Day.	Mean of Eight Readings of the Aneroid Barometer.	Readings of the Thermometer in the Shade at								Mean Daily Temp.
		3 A.M.	6 A.M.	9 A.M.	Noon.	3 P.M.	6 P.M.	9 P.M.	Mid-night.	
		°	°	°	°	°	°	°	°	°
Sept. 1	29·80	+44	+43	+45	+47	+46	+46	+46	+46	+45·3
2*	30·11	47	46	47	50	51	49	48	47	48·1
3	·29	48	50	49	50	53	50	50	49	50
4	·38	51	52	53	57	57	55	53	52	53·7
5	·41	53	52	54	57	55	54	55	55	54·3
6	·43	55	55	55	55	55	55	54	54	54·8
7	·54	55	55	55	57	55	55	55	53	55
8†	·52	55	54	55	57	55	53	53	53	54·3
9	·50	53	53	54	55	57	54	54	54	54·3
10	·51	56	55	55	55	58	56	55	55	55·6
11	·54	55	55	55	56	54	55	55	55	55·5
12	·51	55	53	55	55	61	58	53	53	55·3
13	·52	52	52	52	55	55	54	50	50	52·5
14	·56	50	50	53	53	53	52	51	51	51·6
15	·68	55	52	52	52	53	51	50	50	51·9
16‡	·68	50	50	49	53	54	51	51	51	50·3
17	·64	53	51	53	53	53	53	53	52	52·7
18	·54	52	52	52	53	53	53	52	53	52·5
19	·40	53	51	51	55	53	52	51	51	52·2
20	·37	53	52	55	55	57	57	57	57	55·3
21	·30	57	57	59	59	59	59	58	55	57·9

* The sea very abundant in *Entomostraca* and *Acalephæ*, which invariably render it luminous during the night when agitated, as in a storm or in a vessel in the dark.

† Sea-fowl common on the British coasts seen in great abundance.

‡ Entomostracous and other crustacea of minute size in the surface of the water.

Abstract of the Meteorological Journal kept on board Her Majesty's Ship Sophia.—*Crossing the Atlantic, &c.*

1851. Month and Day.	Mean Temp. of Sea at its Surface.	WINDS.		WEATHER.		Position at Noon.	
		Direction.	Estimated Force.	A.M.	P.M.	Latitude.	Longitude.
	°					° ′	° ′
Sept. 1	48·5	W.N.W.	7	q.v.b.c.p.r.		58 11	43 5
2	50	W.N.W.	7–6	q.v.b.c.p.			36 25
3	52·1	W.S.W.	5–3	o.v.p.q.		57 45	32 0
4	54·1	W.S.W.	5–3	o.v.p.q.b.c.		58 0	26 0
5	55·1	S.W. to S.E.	3–6	v.q.	*v*.b.c.	58 3	22 0
6	54	S.E.	6–7	v.b.c.	v.o.c.	59 4	16 40
7	54·1	S.E.	6–7	*v*.b.c.	v.b.c.	60 2	13 50
8	53	S.S.E.	5–6	v.b.c.		60 12	9 10
9	53·8	SOUTH.	6–7	v.b.c.q.r.m.		59 35	4 9
10*	53·3	S.S.W.	4–3	b.c.v.	b.c.v.o.	59 12	1 30
11	54·1	SOUTHERLY.	2–0	v.b.o.c.	*v*.b.c.		
12	53·6	VARIABLE W.	1–0	v.b.c.		57 50	2 0
13	54	VARIABLE N.	1–2	*v*.b.f.		57 30	1 40
14	54	VARIABLE.	2–0	f.		57 12	1 30
15	54	VARIABLE.	2–0	f.		56 35	
16†	54·7	VAR. S.E.	1–2	f.	b.c.m.	56 10	On the English Coast.
17	55	E.S.E.	3–1	m.o.	v.o.	55 30	
18	55	E.N.E.	1–3	m.o.r.	d.v.e.		
19	54·8	NORTHERLY.	1–2	v.c.	b.v.c.o.	54 34	
20	56·2	N. to E.	1–5	v.b.c.			
21‡	59	E.N.E.	6–2	m.o.q.	m.o.		

* Saw the land and sailed through the Roost.
† Baffling calms and very fine weather ; occasional fogs and generally misty.
‡ Arrived in the Thames and dropped anchor off Gravesend.

ABSTRACT OF A METEOROLOGICAL JOURNAL KEPT IN THE BY A TRAVELLING PARTY FROM HER MAJESTY'S

1851. Month and Day.	Temperature of the air in the shade.			Mean temp. at the same hours in the harbour.	Difference warmer + or colder − at the ships.	WINDS.		WEATHER.	
	Max.	Min.	Mean.			Direction.	Force.	A.M.	P.M.
	°	°	°	°	°				
April 17	+35	+14	+25·1	+25·5	+0·4	VARIABLE.	1–2	o.m.s. :	b.v c.
18	31	20	22·5	23·2	+0·7	S.S.W.	2–1	b.v.c. :	o.m.s.
19	31	19	25·2	26·6	+1·4	S.W to N.W.	3–1	o.m.s. :	m.b.o.
20	30	15	21·4	24·6	+3·2	N.N.W.	2–5	b.o.v. :	o.m.s.
21	5	−25	−10	−2	+8	N.N.W.	6–8	g.q.o. :	m.s.dft.
22	−8	30	19·5	10	+9·5	NORTH.	8–4	q.b.c.s.dft.	
23	13	30	23·2	21	+2·2	NORTH.	4	q.v.b.c.s.dft.	
24	5	22	10·7	10	+0·7	NORTH.	4–5	b.v.s.dft.q.c.	
25	+5	22	8	4	+4	N. to E.	6–2	m.s.o. :	v.b.c.
26	−8	19	13·5	13	+0·5	S.E.	3–5	v.b.c.s.dft.	
May 6	1	4	2·5	+3·5	+6	N.N.W.	1–2	v.b.s.dft.	
7	+12	7	+2	6	+4	N.W.	2–6	b.v.q.s.dft.m.	
8	22	4	9	12·4	+3.4	S.E. to S.W.	6–8	*e.m.s.g.*	
9	−3	9	−5·1	3·3	+8.4	S.W.	1–3	*v.b.c.* :	c.m.
10	+9	9	+0·6	7·6	+7	S.S.W.	1–3	c.b.v. :	m.o.
11	26	2	10	11	+1	S.E.	2–1	m.c. :	v.b.o.
12	6	1	2	4·4	+2.4	N.N.W.	3–2	v.b.c. :	m.o.s.
13	11	5	5·2	8	+2.8	NORTH.	2–4	v.b.q. :	s.dft.
14	14	+2	5·7	9	+3.3	NORTH.	3–1	q.*b.v.*	
15	22	−2	10·2	10·2		S.S.E.	2	v.o.b.	
16	22	+3	9	10·5	+1·5	S.W.	1	v.b.c.	
17	35	1	10·8	14	+3·2	N. to E.	1–2	v.b.c.	
18	25	9	16·3	22	+5·7	S.W.	1–4	*m.o.s.*	
19	15	9	11	12·1	+1·1	N.W.	6–4	*o.m.s.*	
20	14	9	11·3	12·8	+1·5	N.W.	4	o.m.s.dft.	
21	31	2	12	13·8	+1·8	NORTH.	4–1	v.b.s.dft.m.b.	
22	21	4	11·5	11·1	−0·4*	N.N.E.	4–9	v.b.q.s.dft.c.	
23	16	6	11·1	13·3	+2·2	N.W.	4–7	v.b.q.s.dft.	
24	18	6	13·2	13·4	+0·2	E. VAR.	1–5	*v.b.c.*	
	+35	−30	+5·2	+8·1	+2·9	Maximum Minimum and Means.			

* It is rather a remarkable fact that the first difference of temperature warmer to the northward than at the ships occurred during a north wind, and after nearly four consecutive days of west and northwest winds.

WELLINGTON CHANNEL, BARING BAY, AND PRINCE ALFRED BAY, SHIPS LADY FRANKLIN AND SOPHIA.

Position.		REMARKS.
Latitude.	Longitude.	
° ′	° ′	
74 37	94 0	Leaving the harbour. The ice very soft. Snow water brackish.
74 40	93 50	The ice about four feet thick ; evidently of recent formation.
74 43	93 45	A white misty haze over all the sky.
74 48*		Snow-blindness of frequent occurrence. Violent weather.
		Detained from the violence of the weather.
		Temperature in the tents $-16°$ to $-25°$.
74 58		The clear sky opening out. Frost-bites common, but very slight.
75 5		Invalids recovering rapidly from snow-blindness.
74 45	93 50	Remarkable parhelia and parhelic circles at noon.
74 36	94 0	Arrival on board. Threatening appearance of the weather.
74 40	94 16	Leave the ships a second time. Pleasant weather.
	93 50	The sun's rays reflected from the hummocky ice.
74 48	93 45	The snow that falls now generally very soft.
75 5		Parhelia in the evening. Crossing the channel.
	93 30	Misty and hazy weather.
75 8	93 0	About the middle of the channel. Old ice seen.
75 10	92 15	The ice about seven and half feet thick, the growth of last season. Generally rough, close to the land.
75 21*	92 30	Smooth ice at a distance from the land.
75 30	92 20	Saw a ptarmigan for the first time this season.
75 34*	91 40	Snow-blindness occurring. Foxes and bears seen.
75 41*	91 30	Hares seen and also ptarmigan. The hares burrow in the snow
	91 20	not far from the surface.
75 47		Journey made over a portion of the land, which is very flat, at the coast for a few miles inland.
75 55*	92 0	Very changeable weather.
76 3*		In the vicinity of Point Hogarth. Violent weather. Detention owing to the storm.
76 9*	92 40	Pleasant weather, intense refraction to westward.
75 12	92 50	Mean Latitude and Longitude.

* The latitudes marked with the asterisk are by observation.

Abstract of a Meteorological Journal kept in the by a Travelling Party from Her Majesty's

1851. Month and Day.	Temperature of the air in the shade. Max.	Min.	Mean.	Mean temp. at the same hours in the harbour.	Difference warmer or colder at the ships.	WINDS. Direction.	Force.	WEATHER. A.M.	P.M.
	°	°	°	°	°				
May 25	+21	+4	+12·2	+19·2	+7	VAR. E.	1–5	v.c.b.	s.dft.g.o.
26	32	17	23·1	23·1	0	NORTH.	6–9	q.g.o.m.s.dft.	
27	21	8	15·1	15·3	+0·2	NORTH.	9–2	v.b.q.s.dft.	
28	16	5	11	19·1	+8·1	E.N.E.	0–2	*v*.b.c.	
29	30	9	19·5	19	−0·5	N.E. to N.W.	3–1	*v.b.*	o.m.s.
30	25	7	15·4	25·4	+10	S.E.	1–2	b.m.	o.m.s.
31	31	15	19·6	30	+10·4	S.E.	2–7	*o.m.s.*	
June 1	32	16	22·6	26	+3·4	S.E.	7–3	*o.m.s.*c.	
2	40	14	24·1	29·1	+5	S.S.E.	3–5	o.m.s.	
3	39	16	25·3	24	−1·3	S.S.W.	3–2	o.m.s.b.v.	
4	25	10	16	26·1	+10·1	S.S.E.	2–3	*b.v.*	
5	36	20	28·6	32·7	±4·1	S. to S.S.E.	3–4	*b.v.*	
6	41	24	33·2	34·5	+1·3	E.S.E.	1–9	m.o.s.q.	
7	32	29	31	33·3	+2·3	S.S.W.	5–7	m.o.s.q.	
8	31	29	29.7	42	12·3	S.W.	7–3	m.o.s.	v.b.c.
9	40	29	34·2	41·9	7·7	S.S.W.	1–3	b.m.o.s.	m.s.
10	34	31	32·2	43·1	10·9	S.W. to S.E.	2–4	m.o.b.v.	*v.b.*
11	*55	31	38·4	44·5	±6·1	N.W.	2–1	v.b.c.	b.m.c.
12	55	29	39·5	37	−2·5	VARIABLE.	2–1	b.v.	b.v.m.
13	40	31	34·8	37·6	+2·8	S.W.	2–4	b.v.m.	o.m.r.
14	37	32	34	37	+3	S.W.	3–4	o.m.r.	m.r.o.
Maxima and Minima transferred from the foregoing table.	55	4	−25·6	30	+4·4	Highest and lowest temperatures observed by the party, and the means of 610 simultaneous observations entered in the registers kept at the ships and on the journey to the northward.			
	35	−30	5·2	8·1	+2·9				
	55	−30	15·4	19·0	3·6				

* The highest temperature for the season occurred on this and the subsequent day, but not the highest daily mean.

Wellington Channel, Baring Bay, and Prince Alfred Bay, Ships Lady Franklin and Sophia.

Position. Latitude.	Position. Longitude.	REMARKS.
° ′	° ′	
76 15	92 50	Crossing Prince Alfred Bay. The ice suffered from pressure
76 20	93 0	when it was about one foot thick. Polar bears and foxes going to the north-westward.
76 17	92 20	Division of the party ; of which the one half returns.
76 10	92 45	Polar bears and foxes seen. The ice thirteen to fourteen feet
76 1*	92 20	thick ; cracks open out in it. Sea-fowl seen.
75 49*	91 55	Measured the ice through a seal hole : eleven feet thick. Snow buntings common, on a small island.
75 41*	91 20	There has been a great fall of snow from the southward.
75 42	91 30	Low temperatures. Frosty weather best adapted for travelling.
75 36	91 48	Old ice with rounded hummocks crossed over.
75 27	92 23	The ice at Cape Osborne about nine feet thick.
75 18	92 30	Broad fissures in the ice 9½ feet thick. Sea-fowl seen. The
75 8	92 15	first time this season mean temp. above the freezing point. Several bears and brent geese and other birds seen.
75 10	93 0	Seals abundant upon the ice. Water on the surface of the
	93 30	ice. The highest temperature for the season occurred on
75 5	93 45	the 11th and 12th. Position in the vicinity of a very pre-
74 48		cipitous coast. Running water.
74 42	93 50	Rain and thick misty weather. The surface of the ice covered
74 40	94 16	with water. Surface of the land very soft.
75 38	92 40	Mean latitude and longitude of the positions of the party every day at noon.
75 12	92 50	
75 20	92 45	

* The latitudes marked with the asterisk are by observation.

TABLES drawn up with a view to exhibit the ANNUAL MEAN TEMPERATURES and their Variations in different Seasons, according to the Latitude and Longitude, the Extremes of Heat and Cold, and the hottest and coldest Days of each Month and Year observed within the Arctic Circle.*

1850 and 1851.	Monthly.				Daily Means.				Monthly Means.	Ranges of Max. and Min.	Ranges of Mean Daily Max. and Min.	Position.
	Max.	Dates.	Min.	Dates.	Max.	Dates.	Min.	Dates.				
	°		°		°		°		°	°	°	
September -	+ 38	5	6	30	+ 33·7	2	+ 7·8	30	+ 21·3	32	26	Barrow Straits, Cornwallis Island, Assistance Bay, lat. 74° 40', long. 94° 16'.
October -	18	9	– 14	28	11·7	9	– 12·2	28	1·5	32	23	
November -	13	11	24	30	6·2	10	12·7	30	– 6·7	37	19	
December -	– 4	4	37	30	– 8	22	35·4	30	21·4	33	27	
January -	10	10	41	20	18·2	29	39·2	19	29	31	21	
February -	10	10	45	24	13·3	16	40·6	24	29·8	35	27	
March -	6	19	41	21	8·6	14	35·5	21	22·4	35	27	
April - -	+ 34	17	31	2	+ 26·2	20	21·7	2	3·2	65	48	
May - -	42	31	20	2	30	31	7·2	1	+ 12·1	65	37	
June - -	49	11	+ 16	4	44·5	11	+ 24	3	34·3	33	20	
July - -	50	5	29	23	43·1	17	34·3	12	37·8	21	9	
Aug. to 10th	46	10	31	10	40	10	32·3	2	35·6	15	8	
Year - -	+ 50		– 45		+ 44·5		– 40·6		+ 2·5	95	85	
Annual mean temp. and ranges, Sheriff Harbour -									+ 2·4	113	105	
Difference warmer, lower ranges, Assistance Bay -									0·1	18	20	

* This table is the result of observations extending over the whole year, except the last twenty-one days of August; and these observations comprehend upwards of 2,652 regular three-hourly readings of the thermometer.

TABLES drawn up with a view to exhibit the ANNUAL MEAN TEMPERATURES and their Variations in different Seasons according to the Latitude and Longitude, the Extremes of Heat and Cold, and the hottest and coldest Days of each Month and Year, observed within the Arctic Circle.*

1819 and 1820.	Monthly.				Daily Means.				Monthly Means.	Ranges of Max. and Min.	Ranges of Mean Daily Max. and Min.	Position.
	Max.	Dates.	Min.	Dates.	Max.	Dates.	Min.	Dates.				
	°		°		°		°		°	°	°	Barrow Straits, Melville Island, winter quarters, lat. 74° 47′, long. 110° 48′.
September -	+ 37	3	− 1	26	+ 33	1	+ 5	26	+ 22·5	38	28	
October -	17	2	28	31	6·3	1	−26·1	30	−3·4	45	32	
November -	6	6	47	19	5·5	4	43·7	20	20·6	41	49	
December -	6	31	43	20	− 4·3	17	38·9	30	21·8	37	34	
January -	− 2	1	47	12	10·2	18	45·2	13	30·1	45	35	
February -	17	1	50	15	20·7	6	46·3	14	32·2	33	26	
March -	+ 6	11	40	1	2·2	11	31·3	1	18·1	46	29	
April - -	32	30	32	10	+ 20·3	30	22·9	10	8·3	64	43	
May - -	47	27	4	7	39·1	27	+ 0·8	7	16·6	51	38	
June - -	51	22	+ 28	6	44·3	22	29·6	7	36·2	23	14	
July - -	60	7	32	4	51	17	34·5	29	42·4	28	16	
Aug. to 12th.	42	1	30	10	36	8	31·2	10	34·5	12	5	
Year - -	+ 60		− 50		+ 51		−46·3		+ 1·4	110	97	
Annual mean temp. and ranges, Assistance Bay -									+ 2·5	95	85	
Difference colder, higher ranges, Melville Island -									1·1	15	12	

* This table is drawn up from the Meteorological Abstracts in the account of Sir W. E. Parry's "First Voyage of Discovery in search of a North-west Passage."

TABLES drawn up with a view to exhibit the ANNUAL MEAN TEMPERATURES and their Variations in different Seasons according to the Latitude and Longitude, the Extremes of Heat and Cold, and the hottest and coldest Days of each Month and Year, observed within the Arctic Circle.*

1824 and 1825.*	Monthly.				Daily Means.				Monthly Means.	Ranges of Max. and Min.	Ranges of Mean Max. and Min.	Position.
	Max.	Dates.	Min.	Dates.	Max.	Dates.	Min.	Dates.				
	°		°		°		°		°	°	°	
September -	+34	27	+16	18	+32·7	27	+18·7	18	+25·8	16	14	Prince Regent Inlet, Port Bowen, lat. 73° 13′, long. 88° 56′.
October -	31	6	−12	28	26·2	5	−8·9	30	10·8	43	35	
November -	17	27	26	26	12·1	27	19·4	20	−5	43	31	
December -	−4	7	35	15	−9·2	8	33·2	16	19	31	24	
January -	14	19	42	26	17·6	19	40·1	25	28·9	28	23	
February -	8	12	45	21	10·1	27	40·3	21	27·3	37	30	
March -	9	27	47	2	18	27	43	2	28·3	38	25	
April - -	+20	22	37	1	+10·8	21	29·5	1	6·5	57	40	
May - -	39	28	7	5	31·8	28	+3·4	5	+17·6	46	28	
June - -	48	6	+23	3	41·5	27	31·8	4	36·1	45	9	
July - -	50	3	30	21	41·5	23	33·9	19	37·3	20	7	
August -	51	15	25	30	44·8	15	27·5	30	31·3	26	17	
Year - -	+51		−47		+44·8		−43		+3·1	98	87	
Annual mean temp. and ranges, Igloolik - -									+5·6	106	96	
Difference colder, lower ranges at Port Bowen -									2·5	8	9	

* This table is drawn up from the Meteorological Abstracts in the account of Sir W. E. Parry's "Third Voyage of Discovery in search of a North-west Passage."

Tables drawn up with a view to exhibit the Annual Mean Temperatures and their Variations in different Seasons according to the Latitude and Longitude, the Extremes of Heat and Cold, and the hottest and coldest Days of each Month and Year, observed within the Arctic Circle.*

1830 and 1831.*	Monthly.				Daily Means.				Monthly Means.	Ranges of Max. and Min.	Ranges of Mean Daily Max. and Min.	Position.
	Max.	Dates.	Min.	Dates.	Max.	Dates.	Min.	Dates.				
	°		°		°		°		°	°	°	
September	+ 43	15	+ 5	29	+ 38	13	+ 11·4	27	+ 27·4	38	27	Boothia Gulf, Sheriff Harbour, lat. 70° 2′, long. 91° 52′.
October	24	31	− 12	27	20·7	23	− 3·8	27	10·9	36	24	
November	24	5	41	25	21·3	1	39	25	− 11·4	65	60	
December	6	3	47	31	3·4	3	43	31	20·2	53	46	
January	2	16	59	5	1·1	16	55·5	5	25·4	51	56	
February	9	2	49	20	6·9	2	47·9	20	32·4	58	54	
March	− 8	31	51	21	− 15·7	31	44·2	21	34·7	43	28	
April	+ 30	21	25	1	+ 19	21	16·9	10	6·4	65	36	
May	36	27	16	1	27·2	25	0·4	1	+ 16	46	27	
June	52	23	+ 14	3	40·9	23	+ 19·9	1	31·5	38	21	
July	50	30	31	2	42·7	19	33·2	5	37·9	19	9	
August	54	2	24	29	47	2	27·9	29	36·5	30	20	
Year	+ 54		− 59		+ 47		− 55·5		+ 2·4	113	105	
Annual mean temp. and ranges, Port Bowen									+ 3·1	98	87	
Difference warmer, lower ranges, Port Bowen									0·7	15	18	

* This table is drawn up from the Meteorological Abstracts in the account of Sir John Ross's "Second Voyage of Discovery in search of a North-west Passage."

TABLES drawn up with a view to exhibit the ANNUAL MEAN TEMPERATURES
gitude, the Extremes of Heat and Cold, and the hottest and coldest

1846 and 1847.*	Monthly.				Daily Means.				Monthly Means.	Ranges of Max. and Min.	Ranges of Mean Daily Max. & Min.	Position.
	Max.	Dates.	Min.	Dates.	Max.	Dates.	Min.	Dates.				
	°		°		°		°		°	°	°	
September -	+45	15	+16	23	+45	15	+19·7	30	+28·5	29	26	Repulse Bay, Fort Hope, Lat. 66° 32′, Long. 86° 56′.
October -	38	14	−15	27	38	4	−10·6	27	12·5	53	48	
November -	28	10	25	24	26·3	3	22·5	24	0·6	55	49	
December -	17	10	40	29	15·7	10	36·8	24	−19·2	57	52	
January -	−10	11	47	8	−10	10	46·7	8	29·3	37	36	
February -	8	11	42	15	11·6	11	39·8	15	26·8	34	28	
March -	6	31	45	1	8·6	31	37·5	1	28·1	39	39	
April -	+21	13	25	19	+9·6	30	16·3	17	3·9	46	26	
May - -	45	29	4	5	30·67	30	+3·3	4	+17·8	50	27	
June - -	46	24	+12	1	38·7	24	19·3	1	31·3	34	19	
July - -	60	28	29	1	51·8	28	33·6	1	41·4	31	18	
Aug. to 10th	59	7	34	5	49·8	6	36·9	4	44·7	25	13	
Year - -	+60		−47		+51·8		−46·7		+3·3	107	98	
Annual mean temp. and ranges, Assistance Bay -									+2·5	95	85	
Difference warmer, high ranges, Fort Hope -									0·8	12	13	

AN ABSTRACT of Six of the preceding Tables, showing the ANNUAL MAXIMUM, MINIMUM, AND MEAN TEMPERATURES at various positions within the Arctic Circle.

Years.	Positions.					Temperature.			Ranges of Max. and Min.	Ranges of Mean Max. and Min.
	Monthly.	Lat.		Long.		Max.	Min.	Mean.		
1850–51	Assistance Bay -	74	40	94	16	+50	−45	+2·5	95	85
1846–47	Fort Hope - -	66	32	86	56	60	47	3·3	107	98
1830–31	Sheriff Harbour -	70	2	91	52	54	59	2·4	113	105
1824–25	Port Bowmen - -	73	13	88	54	51	47	3·1	98	87
1822–23	Igloolik - -	69	23	81	45	59	45	5·6	104	96
1819–20	Melville Island -	74	47	110	48	60	50	1·4	110	97
Means, &c. - - - -		71	29	92	25	+60	−59	+3·4	113	105

* This table is drawn up from the Meteorological Abstracts in Dr. Rae's "Narrative of an Expedition to the shores of the Arctic Sea."

and their Variations in different Seasons, according to the Latitude and Lon-
Days of each Month and Year, observed within the Arctic Circle.

1822 and 1823.*	Monthly.				Daily Means.				Monthly Means.	Ranges of Max. and Min.	Ranges of Mean Daily Max. & Min.	Position.
	Max.	Dates.	Min.	Dates.	Max.	Dates.	Min.	Dates.				
	°		°		°		°		°	°	°	Melville Peninsula, Igloolik, Lat. 69° 23′, Long. 81° 45′.
September -	+ 37	12	+ 11	18	+ 31·8	2	+ 13·2	18	+ 24·4	26	17	
October -	24	13	− 9	23	24·1	10	− 5·3	23	12 7	38	29	
November -	8	9	32	25	1·4	9	31·5	25	− 19·3	40	32	
December -	− 10	24	43	31	− 13·2	24	40·4	10	27·8	33	27	
January -	+ 22	15	45	3	+ 17·5	14	44	3	17	67	61	
February -	21	3	43	16	13·5	3	40·5	16	20·4	64	54	
March -	4	25	41	2	− 3·8	25	36·7	4	19·7	45	34	
April - -	32	29	25	7	+ 18·9	29	15·3	7	1·6	57	34	
May - -	49	26	8	1	38·2	26	+ 5·3	26	+ 24·8	57	33	
June - -	52	30	+ 8	1	42·3	30	19·2	2	32·1	44	23	
July - -	59	19	30	2	51·8	18	36·1	31	40·4	19	15	
August -	55	3	24	31	45·9	4	31·5	31	37·7	31	14	
Year - -	+ 59		− 45		+ 51·8		− 44		+ 5·6	104	96	
Aug. to 10th	55	3	+ 31	1	45·9	4	+ 36·8	9	41·5	24	9	
Year - -	59		− 45		+ 51·8		− 44		+ 5·8	104	96	
Annual mean temp. and ranges, Melville Island -									+ 1·4	110	97	
Difference colder, higher ranges, Melville Island -									4·4	6	1	

* This table is drawn up from the Meteorological Abstracts in the account of Sir W. E. Parry's "Second Voyage of Discovery in search of a North-west Passage."

A TABLE drawn up with a view to exhibit the MEAN TEMPERATURE of the Surface of the Sea, and the Atmosphere in the Shade, during the Summer Months within the Arctic Circle.

Date.		Positions.					Mean Temp.	
Year.	Month.	Names.	Mean Lat.		Mean Longitude.		Water.	Atmosphere.
			°	′	°	′	°	°
1819	July	Davis Straits, east side	70	0	59	0	32·6	33·5
1824	July	Davis Straits, east side	70	0	58	0	33·0	34·8
1850	May	Davis Straits, east side	71	50	54	54	30·7	30·6
„	June	Davis Straits, east side	73	10	56	56	30·8	36·6
„	July	Davis Straits, east side	75	5	59	4	31·7	34·9
1851	Aug. 20. to 23.	Davis Straits, east side	68	30	57	8	38·7	38·1
		Means -	71	26	57	20	32·9	34·7
1850	Aug. 11. to 19.	Top of Baffin's Bay	76	7	67	57	33·2	34·6
1820	September	Davis Straits, west side	69	0	62	0	31·9	31·3
1824	August	Davis Straits, middle ice	72	17	62	17	29	30·3
1825	September	Davis Straits, west side	68	38	65	17	34	34·3
1851	Aug. 16. to 19.	Davis Straits, west side	71	52	70	11	34·5	34·8
		Means -	70	27	64	56	32·3	32·6
1819	August	Lancaster Sound and	74	20	90 to 110		31·9	33·6
1824	September	Barrow Straits	73	54	79	24	28·1	26·5
1825	August	Prince Regent's Inlet	72	50	91	56	31·6	36·9
1850	Aug. 20. to 31.	Lancaster Sound and	74	32	90	0	31·0	31·7
„	September	Barrow Straits	74	39	93	52	29	21·3
1851	Aug. 12. to 15.		74	12	87	27	34·5	34·2
		Means -	74	4	91	16	31·0	30·7
1821	June 12. to 30.	Off the entrance of Hudson Straits	62	0	63	0	33·1	34·4
„	July	Middle of Hudson Straits	63	0	77	0	31·8	35·3
„	August	Off Vansittart Island	66	0	83	0	32·2	36·6
		Means -	63	40	77	40	32·7	35·4

A TABLE drawn up with a view to exhibit the MEAN TEMPERATURE of the Surface of the Sea, and of the Atmosphere in the Shade, during the Summer Months within the Arctic Circle.

Date.		Positions.			Mean Temp.	
Year.	Month.	Names.	Mean Lat.	Mean Longitude.	Water.	Atmosphere.
			° ′	° ′	°	°
1827	May	Greenland Seas	77 45	11 50E.	30·1	26·1
„	June	Greenland Seas	79 44	15 53	31·5	35·8
„	July	Hecla Cove, Greenland Seas	79 55	16 48	35·4	40·1
„	August	Hecla Cove, Greenland Seas	79 46	13 30	36·8	38·3
„	Sept. to 10.	Greenland Seas	68 14	1 3	46·6	45·6
„	June 25. to Aug. 10.	Greenland Seas, Boat Expedition	82 3	20 30	32·6	33
		Means -	77 54	13 25E.	35·5	36·5
1826	July 20. to 31.	Kotzebue Sound, Behring's Straits	67 30	165 30W.	50·2	53·5
			„	„	45·5	45·6
„	August	Kotzebue Sound	„	„	46·9	46·6
„	September	Kotzebue Sound	„	„	40·5	37·2
„	October to 14.	Kotzebue Sound	„	„	44·3	42·9
1827	August	Port Clarence	65 30	168 „	38·9	27·3
„	Sept. to 5.	Kotzebue Sound	67 30	165 30	40·6	39·3
„	Sept 6. to 30.	Kotzebue Sound	„	„	36·0	30·8
„	October to 14.					
		Means -	67 15	165 47	42·8	40·4

* In drawing up this table some of the voyages quoted on the preceding pages have been used, and, in addition to them, Sir W. E. Parry's "Narrative of an Attempt to reach the North Pole," and the "Narrative of a Voyage to the Pacific and Behring's Straits" by Captain T. W. Beechey, have also been used.

THE following is an explanation of the abbreviations used in the METEOROLOGICAL REGISTER kept on board Her Majesty's Ship "Sophia," according to Admiral Sir Francis Beaufort's system.

In the column with the heading Winds and sub-column Estimated Force;—

0 denotes *calm;*
1, *light air*, just perceptible;
2, *light breeze*, in which a ship, clean full, in smooth water, would go from one to two knots;
3, *gentle breeze* (from two to four knots);
4, *moderate breeze* (from four to six knots);
5, *fresh breeze*, in which a ship could just carry on a wind royals, &c.;
6, *stormy breeze* (single-reefed topsails and top-gallant sails);
7, *moderate gale* (double-reefed, &c.);
8, *fresh gale* (triple-reefed and courses);
9, *stormy gale* (close-reefed, &c.);
10, *whole gale* (close-reefed main-topsail and reefed foresail);
11, *storm* (storm staysails);
12, *hurricane* (no canvas can stand);

In the column with the heading Weather:—

b denotes *blue sky*, be the atmosphere clear or heavy.
c, *clouds* (detached passing clouds).
d, *drizzling rain.*
f, *foggy.*
g, *gloomy*, dark weather.
h, *hail.*
l, *lightening.*
m, *misty*, hazy atmosphere.
o, *overcast*, (the whole sky covered with thick clouds).
p, *passing*, temporary showers.
q, *squally.*
r, *rain* (continued rain).
s, *snow.*
s.dft. *snowdrift.*
t, *thunder.*
u, *ugly*, threatening appearance.
v, visibility of objects (clear atmosphere).
w, *wet* (dew).
Any letter in italic denotes a great degree.

REGISTER OF THE TIDES.

On the following pages I have given a register of the tides in Assistance Harbour. It extends over nearly six months and a half, and shows the time of high and low water and the rise and fall throughout the whole of that time, with the exception of two or three short intervals arising from derangement of the gauge, or from extremely violent weather. It is computed from the register of the gauge kept on board the "Sophia," under the immediate superintendence of Mr. Manson, mate, a person well qualified for such a duty, inasmuch as both precision and punctuality were necessary to arrive at uniform, and consequently so far correct, results. The gauge was read off every hour, and, as frequently as it could be accomplished the exact time of slack tide was observed, and noted together with the rise or fall since the preceding low or high water. My original intention was to have applied the times of the Meridian passage of the moon, and to have laid down the lunitidal intervals, working them out in detail; but as this is scarcely the proper place for so much calculation, all ideas of such a course were given up, and the only substitute that I give for it is the phases of the moon computed to civil time, which will enable any person, desirous of information on a subject of so much importance, to ascertain the "vulgar establishment."

Register of the Tides kept in Assistance Harbour, Barrow Straits, on board Her Majesty's Ship Sophia.—*October*, 1850.

Day of Month.	Forenoon.								Afternoon.							
	High Water.				Low Water.				High Water.				Low Water.			
	Time.		Rise.		Time.		Fall.		Time.		Rise.		Time.		Fall.	
	h.	m.	ft.	in.	h.	m.	ft.	in.	h.	m.	ft.	in.	h.	m.	ft.	in.
1	*	*	*	*	*	*	*	*	*	*	*	*	2	30	*	*
2	10	0	*	*	*	*	*	*	10	30	3	7	4	0	*	*
3	10	45	2	5½	5	30	3	7	11	15	*	*	5	30	4	5½
4	11	30	4	5	6	0	4	4½	*	*	*	*	*	*	*	*
5*					6*	0	4	1	0	40	4	0	7	0	4	0½
6	0	30	5	2½	6	40	5	2½	1	0	5	1	7	30	4	4
7	1	30	5	5½	8	30	4	11	1	45	4	9½	8	30	4	10
8	1	45	4	6	8	45	4	7	3	0	4	10	9	30	4	6½
9	3	0	3	11	9	30	4	5	3	0	4	9	9	30	3	8
10	2	45	3	8	10	0	3	8	4	0	4	3	10	30	3	3
11	4	0	2	1½	10	0	3	7½	4	30	3	11	11	45	2	1½
12	6	0	1	0	12	0	1	10	6	0	2	10				
13	6	30	1	0	0	20	2	0	7	30	2	4	0	30	1	9½
14	7	30	0	3½	1	30	1	7½	9	0	1	11½	2	30	1	0
15	9	15	1	3	4	0	2	4	9	30	2	1	3	0	0	11
16	11	0	1	4½	5	0	2	3	11	0	2	5	5	0	1	3½
17	11	15	1	8	5	0	2	3½	11	30	2	10	5	15	1	10½
18	11	30	2	5½	5	30	3	0	12	0	3	0	5	45	2	3½
19					6	20	3	2½	0	30	2	5½	6	45	2	5½
20	0	45	3	0½	6	45	3	5	0	45	3	4½	6	45	3	1
21	1	10	3	10	7	15	4	1½	1	30	3	10	7	30	4	1
22	1	30	3	8½	7	30	4	1½	1	30	4	3½	7	30	4	0
23	1	30	3	3	7	30	4	2½	1	45	5	0½	8	15	5	0
24	2	30	3	0	8	15	4	0	2	45	4	10	9	0	3	6½
25	2	45	2	9½	8	45	3	9	3	0	3	6½	9	30	2	6½
26	3	30	2	1	9	45	2	10	3	50	3	2½	9	50	3	4
27	3	50	1	10	10	15	1	7	4	30	3	10	11	0	2	9½
28	5	15	1	3	11	30	2	0	6	0	3	5				
29	6	15	1	2½	0	15	2	4	7	0	2	8	0	15	2	0½
30	9	15	1	6½	3	0	2	5	9	30	3	5	3	15	2	0½
31	9	30	1	9	3	0	2	11	9	30	3	2	3	0	2	0

Phases of the Moon.

Full Moon ○ 21st 3 h. 11 m. A.M.

New Moon ● 5th 2 h. 55 m. P.M.

Last Quarter ☾ 28th 4 h. 59 m. A.M.

First Quarter ☽ 13th 2 h. 29 m. A.M.

* The blanks occur when only three half-tides take place in twenty-four hours. Where blanks are filled up with asterisks the observations were deficient from accidents to the gauge, or other causes.

Register of the Tides kept in Assistance Harbour, Barrow Straits, on board Her Majesty's Ship Sophia.—*November*, 1850.

Day of Month.	Forenoon.								Afternoon.								Phases of the Moon.
	High Water.				Low Water.				High Water.				Low Water.				
	Time.		Rise.		Time.		Fall.		Time.		Rise.		Time.		Fall.		
	h.	m.	ft.	in.	h.	m.	ft.	in.	h.	m.	ft.	in.	h.	m.	ft.	in.	
1	10	30	2	7	3	30	3	1	10	30	2	11	4	30	2	9	Full Moon ☉ 19th 4 h. 34 m. P.M. New Moon ● 4th 2 h. 40 m. A.M.
2	11	30	3	8	5	15	3	10	11	30	3	11	5	15	3	8	
3	12	0	4	9	5	30	4	4	12	0	4	2	6	0	4	2	
4	12	0	4	5	5	45	4	4					6	15	4	7	
5	0	15	3	8	6	0	3	10	1	15	6	9	7	15	4	4	
6	1	20	4	0	7	30	4	10	1	15	5	6	7	45	4	3	
7	1	45	3	1	7	45	4	0	1	45	4	11	7	45	4	7	
8	1	45	4	1	7	50	4	6½	2	0	4	4½	8	0	3	1	
9	2	30	1	8	9	0	3	0½	3	15	4	3	9	20	2	7	
10	3	30	1	9½	9	15	2	1	3	45	3	9	9	30	3	9	
11	3	30	2	8	9	45	2	10	4	0	3	6	10	30	2	10	
12	5	0	1	3	11	0	1	9	5	15	2	0	10	45	2	0	
13	5	30	1	2	12	0	1	4½	7	30	2	0½					
14	8	0	1	1	2	0	2	5	8	30	2	6	2	15	0	8	
15	9	30	2	0½	3	0	3	2½	9	30	2	4½	5	30	1	6½	Last Quarter ☾ 26th 0 h. 32 m. P.M. First Quarter ☽ 11th 11 h. 15 m. P.M.
16	10	0	2	9	4	0	3	4	11	0	2	6	4	30	2	0	
17	11	15	3	2	5	0	3	1	11	45	2	9½	5	45	2	10	
18	12	0	4	1	5	45	4	2	12	0	3	3	6	0	3	2	
19	13*	0	5	2	6	15	4	4	12	0	3	9	7	0	3	11	
20					7	0	4	6	1	15	5	3½	7	20	4	6½	
21	1	30	3	2	8	0	4	6	2	10	5	5	8	0	4	6	
22	2	0	3	4	8	10	4	6	3	0	5	7	9	10	4	4	
23	2	45	3	7	9	0	3	9	3	15	5	0½	9	50	4	2½	
24	3	15	2	5	9	30	3	7	4	0	5	1	10	30	3	5	
25	4	0	1	6	10	0	2	9	5	0	4	6	11	0	3	2	
26	4	45	1	3	11	0	2	4	6	30	3	10					
27	7	20	1	7	1	0	3	1	7	20	2	11	0	50	1	9	
28	8	30	2	0	2	0	3	4	8	20	3	2	1	50	1	5	
29	9	20	2	7	3	0	3	5	9	15	3	2	3	0	2	3	
30	10	15	3	6	4	0	3	10	9	40	3	0	3	45	2	10	

* This irregularity of the times of high water is owing probably to a strong gale from S.E. See Meteorological Abstract. (13h. 0m. is the same as 1h. 0m. P.M.)

REGISTER OF THE TIDES KEPT IN ASSISTANCE HARBOUR, BARROW STRAITS, ON BOARD HER MAJESTY'S SHIP SOPHIA.—*December*, 1850.

Day of Month.	Forenoon.								Afternoon.								Phases of the Moon.
	High Water.				Low Water.				High Water.				Low Water.				
	Time.		Rise.		Time.		Fall.		Time.		Rise.		Time.		Fall.		
	h.	m.	ft.	in.	h.	m.	ft.	in.	h.	m.	ft.	in.	h.	m.	ft.	in.	
1	11	0	4	0	4	30	4	0	11	0	3	8½	5	45	3	10	Last Quarter 25th, 9h. 23m. ☾ P.M. Full Moon ◯ 19th, 5h. 2m. A.M. First Quarter ☽ 11th, 8h. 36m. P.M. New Moon ● 3d, 5h. 16m. P.M.
2	11	30	4	8	5	10	4	5	11	45	2	11	5	45	3	4½	
3	12	0	4	9	6	0	3	7½					6	0	3	7	
4	0	20	2	6	6	20	3	8	0	30	5	1	7	0	3	9	
5	1	5	2	8	7	10	4	0	1	30	5	4	7	30	3	11	
6	1	40	2	7	8	0	3	0	3	0	5	6	9	0	4	0	
7	2	45	2	3½	8	45	3	2½	3	10	4	9	9	15	3	8	
8	3	0	1	9	9	0	3	2	3	40	4	7	9	30	2	6	
9	3	30	1	1	9	30	2	5	4	45	3	8	11	0	2	10	
10	5	0	0	10	11	0	2	1	5	15	3	10	11	30	2	10	
11	6	0	1	1	12	0	1	5	6	0	3	2					
12	7	0	1	2½	1	0	2	5	7	15	2	4½	1	0	1	5	
13	8	30	1	4	2	0	2	6	8	30	2	2	2	15	1	2	
14	8	50	1	6	2	45	2	6	8	50	2	1	2	30	1	6	
15	10	20	2	0	3	45	2	5	10	30	1	9	4	30	1	6	
16	11	0	3	8	4	15	3	3	11	0	2	1½	5	15	2	4	
17	12	0	4	2	5	30	3	3½	12	0	2	6½	6	0	3	1½	
18					6	0	3	10	1	0	4	9	7	0	3	6	
19	1	0	2	7	7	30	4	5	1	15	5	3	7	40	3	11	
20	1	40	2	8	7	30	4	2½	2	15	6	0½	8	30	4	2	
21	1	30	2	9	8	0	4	2½	2	30	6	1½	8	40	4	8	
22	2	30	2	4	8	40	4	0	2	45	6	2	9	30	4	8	
23	3	10	2	6	9	20	3	9	4	0	5	6	10	30	4	4	
24	4	10	2	1	10	0	3	3	5	0	5	0	12	0	4	3	
25	6	0	2	2	12	0	3	3	6	10	3	2					
26	6	15	2	1	0	20	1	10	6	20	4	0	0	15	2	8	
27	7	0	2	5	1	30	3	6	7	0	2	9	1	0	2	4	
28	9	0	2	8	3	0	3	1	9	0	2	2	3	0	1	11	
29	9	0	3	2½	3	0	3	0½	10	0	2	2½	4	0	2	0	
30	10	0	3	11	4	0	3	2½	10	0	2	2	4	30	2	6	
31	*	*	*	*	*	*	*	*	*	*	*	*	*	*	*	*	

REGISTER OF THE TIDES KEPT IN ASSISTANCE HARBOUR, BARROW STRAITS, ON BOARD HER MAJESTY'S SHIP SOPHIA.—*January*, 1851.

Day of Month.	Forenoon.								Afternoon.								Phases of the Moon.
	High Water.				Low Water.				High Water.				Low Water.				
	Time.		Rise.		Time.		Fall.		Time.		Rise.		Time.		Fall.		
	h.	m.	ft.	in.	h.	m.	ft.	in.	h.	m.	ft.	in.	h.	m.	ft.	in.	
1	*	*	*	*	*	*	*	*	*	*	*	*	*	*	*	*	Full Moon ◯ 17th 4 h. 42 m. P.M. New Moon ● 2nd 10 h. 43 m. A.M. Last Quarter ☾ 24th 8 h. 16 m. A.M. First Quarter ☽ 10th 4 h. 21 m. P.M.
2	*	*	*	*	*	*	*	*	*	*	*	*	*	*	*	*	
3	*	*	*	*	*	*	*	*	1	0	3	4½	7	0	3	4½	
4	1	0	1	10	7	30	3	4	2	0	3	6½	8	30	3	5½	
5	2	0	2	6	8	0	2	7	3	0	5	0	9	0	3	11	
6	3	0	2	2½	9	0	3	1½	3	0	4	7	10	0	3	7	
7	4	0	1	4	10	10	2	8	4	0	4	2	10	0	3	2	
8	4	0	0	6	9	30	2	4½	4	0	3	6½	10	0	2	11	
9	4	0	1	3	10	0	1	7	5	0	3	0	11	0	2	4	
10	5	0	1	1	11	0	1	7½	6	0	2	9½					
11	7	0	1	4	1	0	1	5	6	0	2	7½			1	3	
12	7	0	1	5	1	0	2	2	7	30	1	6	1	0	0	10½	
13	10	0	2	6	3	0	2	10	9	0	1	4	3	0	1	7	
14	10	30	2	11	3	15	2	6½	11	0	1	10½	5	0	1	8	
15	11	15	3	5	5	0	2	10	11	15	1	5½	5	0	2	9	
16	12	0	5	2	6	0	2	7½	12	0	2	0	6	0	3	2	
17					6	0	3	5	0	20	5	1	7	0	4	4	
18	1	30	2	9	8	0	2	8	1	0	4	10	7	0	4	7	
19	1	30	2	7	8	0	4	3	2	0	6	4	8	0	3	10	
20	2	0	2	8	8	30	4	7	3	0	6	1½	8	15	4	10½	
21	3	0	3	2	9	0	4	1½	3	0	5	9½	9	0	4	9	
22	3	0	2	11½	9	15	3	9½	4	0	5	2	10	15	4	5	
23	4	0	3	0	10	30	3	2	5	0	4	7½	11	0	3	8½	
24	6	0	2	7	12	0	2	6	6	0	1	1	12	0	1	2½	
25	*6	40	1	1½					7	30	2	2	0	45	1	9	
26	9	0	2	9	2	0	3	0	9	0	1	7	3	0	2	0	
27	9	30	2	6	3	0	2	5	9	40	1	2	3	30	1	8	
28	10	0	3	4	4	0	2	4	10	40	1	3	4	0	1	9	
29	11	0	3	10	4	30	2	7	11	40	1	2	5	50	2	6	
30	12	0	4	3	5	30	2	5	12	0	1	7	6	0	3	1	
31					6	0	2	8½	0	45	4	4½	7	0	2	11	

* The irregularity in this instance may be owing to strong north-west winds. See Meteorological Abstracts, January 25th, 1851.

Register of the Tides kept in Assistance Harbour, Barrow Straits, on board Her Majesty's Ship Sophia.—*February*, 1851.

Day of Month.	Forenoon.								Afternoon.								Phases of the Moon.
	High Water.				Low Water.				High Water.				Low Water.				
	Time.		Rise.		Time.		Fall.		Time.		Rise.		Time.		Fall.		
	h.	m.	ft.	in.	h.	m.	ft.	in.	h.	m.	ft.	in.	h.	m.	ft.	in.	
1	1	0	1	6	7	0	3	3	1	30	5	0	7	15	3	6	*Last Quarter* ☾ 22nd, 9h. 38m. P.M. Full Moon ○ 16th, 3h. 28m. A.M. *First Quarter* ☽ 9th, 8h. 55m. A.M. New Moon ● 1st, 6h. 2m. A.M.
2	1	0	1	10	7	15	2	3	2	0	4	10	8	0	3	10	
3	2	0	2	5	8	0	3	5	2	30	5	1	9	0	4	4	
4	3	0	2	11	9	0	3	5	3	20	5	3½	9	0	4	7	
5	3	15	3	3½	9	0	3	5½	3	30	4	1	9	20	3	6	
6	4	0	2	2	10	0	3	0	4	0	4	2	10	15	3	4	
7	4	20	2	8	9	20	2	10	4	0	3	10	10	0	2	6	
8	4	40	2	0	11	0	2	3	5	0	2	6	11	0	3	0	
9	6	0	2	5	12	0	1	6	6	0	2	4	12	0	2	8	
10	7	0	1	8½					7	20	1	3	1	0	1	2½	
11	9	0	2	6	2	0	2	2	9	15	1	8	3	0	1	3	
12	9	15	3	3	3	0	2	5	10	0	1	3	4	0	2	2	
13	10	30	4	0	4	0	2	9	11	0	1	10	5	0	2	0	
14	11	0	4	7	5	0	3	0	11	30	1	2½	6	0	2	5½	
15	12	0	5	10	6	0	3	6					7	0	5	3	
16	0	30	2	8	7	0	4	0	1	20	5	10	8	0	5	6	
17	1	0	3	5½	8	0	4	8½	2	0	6	2	8	0	5	7	
18	2	0	3	11	8	20	4	10½	3	0	5	11	9	0	5	3	
19	3	0	4	0½	9	0	4	8	3	0	5	10	9	0	4	9	
20	3	45	2	11	9	40	2	8	3	45	3	1	10	0	2	10	
21	4	0	2	8	10	0	3	8	4	0	0	8	10	45	3	7	
22	5	0	1	2	11	0	0	11	5	45	2	10	12	0	2	11	
23	6	0	2	10					6	20	1	7½	0	30	1	11	
24	7	0	2	8	0	30	2	5½	7	30	0	9	1	0	1	4	
25	9	25	2	6	2	15	1	7	9	0	0	9	3	0	1	4	
26	10	0	2	9	3	15	1	8	10	0	0	10	4	0	2	0	
27	11	0	3	2	4	30	2	0	11	0	0	11	5	0	2	9	
28	12	0	3	11	5	0	1	10	12	0	1	10	6	0	2	9	

Register of the Tides kept in Assistance Harbour, Barrow Straits, on board Her Majesty's Ship Sophia.—*March*, 1851.

Day of Month.	Forenoon.								Afternoon.								Phases of the Moon.
	High Water.				Low Water.				High Water.				Low Water.				
	Time.		Rise.		Time.		Fall.		Time.		Rise.		Time.		Fall.		
	h.	m.	ft.	in.	h.	m.	ft.	in.	h.	m.	ft.	in.	h.	m.	ft.	in.	
1					6	0	2	1	0	50	3	11	6	45	3	6	Full Moon ⊙ 17th 1h. 18m. P.M. New Moon ● 3rd 1h. 14m. A.M. *Last Quarter* ☽ 24th 1h. 25m. P.M. *First Quarter* ☾ 10th 9h. 44m. P.M.
2	0	45	2	1	6	45	2	0	1	0	4	10	7	0	3	5	
3	1	0	2	3½	7	0	3	4½	1	40	4	7	7	40	4	0	
4	1	40	2	9	7	45	3	9	2	0	4	7	8	0	4	0	
5	2	0	3	1	8	10	3	8	2	30	4	7	8	45	3	9	
6	2	30	3	1	8	45	3	9	3	0	4	1	9	0	3	6	
7	3	0	3	4	9	30	3	8	3	45	3	7	9	50	3	9	
8	3	30	3	6	9	45	3	4	3	50	3	3	10	0	3	5	
9	4	0	3	1½	10	0	2	9½	4	30	2	8	10	30	3	4	
10	5	0	3	5	11	0	2	1½	5	0	1	7½	11	50	1	7½	
11	6	0	2	6½	12	0	1	8	6	30	1	1					
12	7	45	1	4½	0	40	1	9½	8	20	0	8	1	50	1	6	
13	9	0	3	0½	2	10	1	7½	9	20	0	10	3	50	2	1	
14	10	0	3	7½	3	40	0	8½	10	30	1	5	4	30	2	11	
15	10	50	4	3	4	20	2	6	11	40	2	3	5	45	3	11	
16	12	0	4	8	5	45	3	1	12	0	3	1	6	0	4	8	
17					6	0	4	2	0	30	5	7	6	45	5	0	
18	0	30	3	10	6	50	4	7	1	10	5	8	7	0	5	2½	
19	1	45	4	7½	8	0	4	8	2	0	5	6	8	0	5	4	
20	2	0	5	6	8	10	5	2	2	30	5	1	8	30	5	4	
21	3	0	4	11	9	0	4	6½	3	0	4	10	9	0	5	9	
22	3	30	5	4	10	0	4	9	4	0	4	7	10	0	3	10	
23	*	*	*	*	*	*	*	*	*	*	*	*	*	*	*	*	
24	*	*	*	*	*	*	*	*	*	*	*	*	*	*	*	*	
25	*	*	*	*	*	*	*	*	*	*	*	*	*	*	*	*	
26	7	0	2	0½	1	0	1	1½	8	0	1	0	2	0	1	11	
27	8	45	1	11	2	0	1	2	9	30	1	6	3	0	1	7	
28	10	0	2	4	4	0	1	2	10	30	1	1	4	0	2	3	
29	11	0	2	11	5	0	1	6	11	30	1	8	5	0	2	8	
30	12	0	3	2	6	0	2	2	12	0	2	2	6	0	3	2	
31	12	0	3	0	6	0	2	8					6	50	2	11	

REGISTER OF THE TIDES KEPT IN ASSISTANCE HARBOUR, BARROW STRAITS, ON BOARD HER MAJESTY'S SHIP SOPHIA.—*April*, 1851.

Day of Month.	Forenoon.								Afternoon.								Phases of the Moon.
	High Water.				Low Water.				High Water.				Low Water.				
	Time.		Rise.		Time.		Fall.		Time.		Rise.		Time.		Fall.		
	h.	m.	ft.	in.	h.	m.	ft.	in.	h.	m.	ft.	in.	h.	m.	ft.	in.	
1	0	30	3	3½	7	0	3	8½	1	0	3	8½	7	0	3	9½	*First Quarter* ☽ 9th, 7h. 2m. P.M. New Moon ● 1st, 6h. 32m. P.M.
2	1	0	3	2	7	0	3	4½	1	0	3	8	7	0	3	10	
3	1	0	3	8	7	0	3	4½	2	0	3	11	8	0	3	6	
4	2	0	3	6½	8	0	3	6½	2	0	3	6	8	30	4	0	
5	2	30	3	11	8	15	4	0	2	30	3	1	9	0	3	6	
6	3	0	4	0½	9	20	3	2½	3	0	2	3	9	20	3	0	
7	4	0	3	8	10	0	3	0	4	0	1	11	10	30	2	9	
8	5	0	3	5	11	0	2	5	5	0	1	3½	11	30	1	2½	
9	6	0	3	6	12	0	2	0	6	0	1	7	12	0	1	8½	
10	7	0	3	2½					8	0	1	3	1	0	2	2	
11	8	30	2	7½	2	0	1	10	9	0	1	2½	3	0	2	8	
12	10	0	2	8	4	0	1	4½	*	*	*	*	*	*	*	*	

The register of the tides was given up at this time, in consequence of all hands, with the exception of two or three persons, having to leave the ships on travelling parties: it was fully intended that it should be resumed as soon as circumstances would permit: unhappily, however, owing to the protracted character of our explorations in and beyond the Wellington Channel, we were unable to commence it again.

SKETCHES

OF THE

NATURAL HISTORY AND GEOLOGY

OF THE

REGIONS VISITED DURING THE VOYAGE,

WITH ILLUSTRATIONS.

BOTANY.

PLANTS COLLECTED DURING THE VOYAGE,

AND NAMED BY

SIR W. J. HOOKER, K.H., D.C.L. F.R.A. & L.S.

ETC.

1. Ranunculus frigidus *Willd.* Assistance Bay.
2. Papaver nudicaule *L.* Assistance Bay.
3. Cochlearia fenestralis *Br.* Assistance Bay.
4. Parrya arctica *Br.* Assistance Bay.
5. Cardamine bellidifolia *De.* Assistance Bay.
6. Braya glabella *Richardson.* Assistance Bay.
7. Draba rupestris *Br.* Assistance Bay.
8. glacialis *Adams*, var. Assistance Bay.
9. alpina *L.* Assistance Bay.
10. Arenaria Rossii ? *Br.* Assistance Bay.
11. rubella *Hook.* Assistance Bay.
12. Cerastium alpinum *L.* var. glabatum. Assistance Bay.
13. alpinum *L.* Assistance Bay.
14. alpinum *L.* Bushman Island.
15. Stellaria longipes *Goldie.* Northumberland Inlet.*
16. longipes *Goldie.* Assistance Bay.
17. Lychnis apetala *L.* Assistance Bay.
18. Potentilla nana *Lehm.* Berry Island and other islands in Davis' Straits.
19. Dryas integrifolia *L.* Assistance Bay, Berry Island, and adjacent islands.
20. Cruciferæ ?
21. Epilobium latifolium *L.* Northumberland Inlet.
22. Saxifraga pauciflora ? *Stev.* Bushnan Island.
23. oppositifolia *L.* Assistance Bay, Berry Island.
24. nivalis *L.* Assistance Bay.
25. cernua *L.* Northumberland Inlet.

---

* Known also by the name Hogarth Sound, which was given by Captain Penny, its original discoverer.

26. Saxifraga cernua *L.* Assistance Bay.
27. cæspitosa *L.* Assistance Bay.
28. flagellaris *Willd.* Assistance Bay.
29. tricuspidata *De.* Northumberland Inlet.
30. hirculus *De.* Northumberland Inlet.
31. Pyrola rotundifolia *L.* Northumberland Inlet.
32. Cassiope tetragona *Don.* Bushnan Island.
33. Vaccinium Vitis Idæa *L.* Bushnan Island.
34. Arctostaphylos alpina *Spr.* Northumberland Inlet.
35. Polygonum viviparum *L.* Assistance Bay.
36. Oxyria reniformis *L.* Assistance Bay.
37. reniformis *L.* Northumberland Inlet.
38. Empetrum nigrum *L.* Northumberland Inlet.
39. Vaccinium uliginosum *L.* Northumberland Inlet.
40. Salix cordifolia *Parsh.* Assistance Bay.
41. arctica *Pall.* Assistance Bay.
42. arctica *Pall.* Bushnan Island.
43. Juncus biglumis *L.* Assistance Bay.
44. Carex Hepburnii *Boott.* Berry Island.
45. Luzula hyperborea *Br.* Berry Island, Davis' Straits.
46. Eriophorum polystachyum *L.* Assistance Bay.
47. Phippsia monandra *Trin.* Assistance Bay.
48. Alopecurus alpinus *Sm.* Bushnan Island.
49. alpinus *Sm.* Assistance Bay.
50. 51. } Poa cenisia *All.* Bushman Island, Assistance Bay.
52. Hierochloe alpina *Wahl.* Bushnan Island.
53. Luzula hyperborea *Br.* Bushnan Island.
54. Woodsia glabella *Br.* Berry Island and other islands Davis' Straits.

NOTES ON THE ALGÆ,

BY DR. DICKIE,

PROFESSOR OF NATURAL HISTORY, QUEEN'S COLLEGE, BELFAST.

⁎ The following Notes on Arctic Algæ have been contributed in accordance with a request recently made by my friend and former pupil, Dr. Sutherland.

MELANOSPERMEÆ.

SPOROCHNACEÆ.

Desmarestia aculeata *Lamour.* A few imperfect specimens, dredged in three fathoms, rocky bottom. N. lat. 73° 20′, W. long. 57° 20′.

LAMINARIEÆ.

Laminaria saccharina *De la Pyl.* Young specimens, dredged in fifteen fathoms, Assistance Bay. N. lat. 74° 40′.

L. Fascia *Ag.* An imperfect specimen, apparently this species, was received, having been dredged in Union Bay.

Agarum Turneri *Post. & Rupr.* Dredged in fifteen fathoms, rocky bottom, Assistance Bay; and also dredged in Union Bay.

ECTOCARPEÆ.

Chætopteris plumosa *Kutz.* Dredged in three fathoms, rocky bottom. N. lat. 73° 20′, W. long. 57° 20′.

RHODOSPERMEÆ.

HALYMENIEÆ.

Dumontia sobolifera *Lamour.* A single imperfect specimen was received by me; referred by Professor Harvey to the above species. Dredged in three fathoms, rocky bottom. N. lat. 73° 20′, W. long. 57° 12′.

POLYSIPHONIEÆ.

Polysiphonia urceolata *Grev.* Upon Chætopteris plumosa.

Corallineæ.

Melobesia polymorpha *Harv.* Upon stones, in fifteen fathoms, Union Bay, between Beachey Island and Cape Spencer.

In Assistance Bay, along with the Laminaria and Agarum, fragments of a plant were procured, which I supposed might be referred to Iridæa: Professor Harvey thought they more resembled Rhodymenia in structure, but now refers them to the genus Kallymenia, viz.:—

Kallymenia Pennyii *Harvey MSS.* This interesting addition to the genus is named in compliment to Captain Penny, the energetic and intrepid commander of the Expedition.

An account of it will appear in the next part of the "Nereis Boreali Americana."

Dr. Sutherland describes it as abundant at the shingly bottom, in fifteen to twenty fathoms, in the entrance of Assistance Bay. Dredged July 12, 1851.

CHLOROSPERMEÆ.

Confervaceæ.

Cladophora lanosa *Kutz.* From rocky bottom in two to six fathoms. N. lat. 73° 20′, W. long. 57°.

On the west coast of Greenland, lat. 66° 53′, a minute species of Cladophora was found, forming a greenish coating upon driftwood. It is probably a new species; but the small fragment at my disposal is scarcely sufficient to enable me to speak with confidence respecting it. Its general characters are these: "Filaments very slender, short; ramuli few, alternate; axils very acute; joints twice or thrice as long as broad."

Conferva melagonium *Web. & Mohr.* Dredged in Assistance Bay, muddy bottom; sometimes attaining five feet in length.

C. glacialis *Kg.?* Plant forming a matted crust upon stones in a stream, Prospect Hill, winter quarters; it seems to me identical with that species.

Conferva aerea *Dillw.* It is with some doubt I refer the plant to this species, the specimens sent, preserved in spirits, being rather fragmentary. The nature of the endochrome is peculiar, forming a thin layer on the cell wall, and arranged like a network with tolerable regularity. The plant was dredged along with C. melagonium, &c. in two fathoms. N. lat. 73° 20′, W. long. 57° 16′.

Ulothricheæ.

Ulothrix zonata *Kg.* On a rock moistened by water oozing from melting snow and ice, on an island. N. lat. 73° 20′, W. long. 57° 16′. June 18, 1850.

Ulothrix æqualis *Kg.* A few fragments of a plant apparently identical with this species, from a stream of water fed by melting snow, south side of an island. N. lat. 73° 20′, W. long. 57°. June 22, 1850.

SCYTONEMEÆ.

Sirosiphon ocellatus *Kg.* Associated with the two last.

RIVULARICÆ.

Rivularia microscopica, *n. s.* Basal joint spherico-elliptical, others mostly depressed.

This minute plant, only to be detected by the microscope, forms small radiating tufts upon Enteromorpha compressa, from Assistance Bay and other localities. Each tuft consists of ten to twelve very minute radiating filaments having the above characters: they are dark green at the base, hyaline and capillary at the points.

If the hair-splitting method of Professor Kutzing be followed, our plant might be placed in his genus Physactis.

OSCILLATORIEÆ.

Oscillatoria —— ? Forming a thin green crust upon moist calcareous rocks, on Seal Island, in Wellington Channel. N. lat. 75° 49′. The specimens were so imperfect and fragmentary that I can only indicate the genus.

ULVACEÆ.

Prasiola arctica, *n. s.* Frond oblong, linear; margin entire, with a few short linear ramuli, mostly opposite.

It is with some hesitation that I venture to define this very minute plant, having only been able to detect a few fragments mixed with Nostoc microscopicum; from south side of the harbour, winter quarters.

Enteromorpha compressa *Hook.* After careful examination of specimens from different localities, I have come to the conclusion that all must be referred to the species in question.

Dr. Sutherland has the following notes of localities:—

"From dried pools on the shore, near high-water mark, Beachey Island 3rd. Sept. 1850."

"Assistance Bay; from a small pool of fresh water on the beach; very abundant, and infested by larvæ of flies and gnats; 4th July, 1851. Also in dry masses on the beach, on 14th Sept. 1850.

"In Baring Bay, dry upon the beach, six to eight feet above the level of the sea; 17th May, 1851.

NOSTOCHINEÆ.

Nostoc microscopicum *Carm.* On stones in a small stream on the south side of the harbour, winter quarters, thirty to forty feet above the level of the sea; 26th July, 1851.

Nostoc Sutherlandi *n. s.* Discoid, coriaceous; filaments crowded; cells mostly spherical.

The plant is one to two inches in diameter, attached by one point of the margin. Plicato-venose beneath, the plicæ radiating chiefly from the point of attachment; faintly venose above, especially near the point of adhesion; towards the margin, reticulately venose.

This beautiful species I have dedicated to its discoverer, who found it on the south side of the harbour, winter quarters, in July, 1851. Its habitat was distinct from that of the next species. Following Kutzing's arrangement, it would be placed in his genus Hormosiphon.

Nostoc arcticum *Berk.* This species has been recently described by the Rev. M. J. Berkeley, in a paper read before the Linnæan Society. He refers it to Hormosiphon, expressing a doubt whether the latter genus is anything but a young or abnormal state of Nostoc. It appears to grow in great profusion in the localities where it occurs, and Dr. Sutherland communicates the following notes respecting it: —

"It grows upon the soft, and almost boggy slopes around Assistance Bay; and when these slopes become frozen, at the close of the season, the plant lying upon the surface in irregularly plicated masses becomes loosened, and if it is not at once covered with snow, which is not always the case, the wind carries it about in all directions. Sometimes it is blown out to sea, where one can pick it up on the surface of the ice, over a depth of probably one hundred fathoms. It has been found at a distance of two miles from the land, where the wind had carried it. Each little particle lay in a small depression in the snow, upon the ice: this tendency to sink commenced early in June, owing to the action of the sun. At this distance from the land it was infested with Poduræ; and I accounted for this fact by presuming that the insects of the previous year had deposited their ova in the plant upon the land, where, also, the same species could be seen in myriads upon the little purling rivulets, at the sides of which the Nostoc was very abundant."

Dr. Sutherland found this plant to be edible, and superior to the Tripe de Roche, in connection with which it may be worthy of remark here that Nostoc edule (*Berk. & Mont.*) is used as food in China.

PALMELLEÆ.

Hæmatococcus minutissimus *Hass.* A minute plant, which I have ventured to refer to this species, was found on stones moistened by melting snow, on a small island, north side of Baring Bay; north latitude 75° 49′.

Protococcus nivalis *Ag.* Very fine examples of this interesting species were found in the form of a red crust upon stones in a stream, south side of the harbour, winter quarters, July, 1851. The red colour communicated by it to snow and ice fields in the Arctic regions is a fact too well known to require more special notice here.

DESMIDIEÆ.

This beautiful and interesting family is but poorly represented in the collection made by Dr. Sutherland; others would doubtless have occurred if proper means had been employed for collecting them in such localities as generally produce them.

Cosmarium crenatum *Ralfs.* A few examples were found in muddy matter adhering to the surface of Nostoc Sutherlandi.

Cosmarium pyramidatum *Bréb.* Mixed with the last; both of them I have detected at a considerable elevation in the north-east of Scotland.

Arthrodesmus minutus *Kutz.* Two specimens of a very small species, apparently identical with this, were observed, mixed with Diatoma flocculosum &c., in fresh water from melting snow, at an elevation of one hundred feet above the sea, upon an island in N. lat. 73° 20′, W. long. 57°; 22nd June, 1850.

DIATOMACEÆ.

At my request, made previous to the departure of the Expedition, Dr. Sutherland paid special attention to the colouring matters of ice and sea-water; samples of such from different localities were carefully collected and forwarded for my inspection. They were found to consist almost solely of Diatomaceæ; and in some instances fresh-water forms were detected, though rather sparingly, intermixed with others exclusively marine. This is not surprising when we consider the copious discharges of fresh water from the land, occasioned by the melting of snow and ice during the brief summer.

The contents of the alimentary canal of examples of Leda, Nucula and Crenella dredged in Assistance Bay, consisted of mud in a fine state of division, including also numerous Diatomaceæ identical with those colouring the ice and the water.

Though not a new fact, it is one of some interest in relation to the existence of animal life in those high latitudes. Where Diatomaceæ abound, certain Mollusca obtain sure supplies of food; these in turn are the prey of fishes; these last contribute to the support of sea mammalia and birds.

After bestowing considerable pains on this family, still I cannot write with full confidence regarding some of the species. Improvements in high powers of the microscope reveal the necessity of paying greater attention to the minute markings of the surface in addition to mere external form. The recent investigations of the Rev. W. Smith in reference to such characters of British species, show the importance of this, and in some measure detract from the general value of Professor Kutzing's useful work, the only one on the subject to which I have access here.

Some of the forms are certainly new: descriptions of such must be deferred to another time, in order that more careful examination than can be bestowed at present may lead to more matured opinions respecting them.

Many of the species enumerated have also been found in other parts of the world, and this confirms the ideas entertained respecting their wide distribution, and the very general diffusion of these minute organisms.

On the south side of an island, N. lat. 73° 20′, W. long. 57°, at an elevation of one hundred feet, in water from melting snow and ice, the following species were found :—

Achnanthes minutissima *Ag.*
Diatoma flocculosum *Ag.*
Eunotia monodon *Ehr.*
Eunotia diodon *Ehr.*
Navicula affinis *Ehr.*
Navicula lanceolata *Ehr.*
Navicula, new species?

—the first, second, and fifth of which I have met with at high altitudes in Scotland.

On Desmarestia aculeata a few fragments of a Schizonema were observed, probably allied to, if not identical with, S. Grevillii *Ag.*

Micromega Stewartii *n. s.* Gelatinous; sparingly and alternately branched. Branches clavate, apiculate; internal tubuli delicate and hyaline; frustules in front, rectangular, thrice as long as broad; lateral view elliptico-lanceolate.

The frustules are large and crowded in the tips of the branches. The whole plant is about an inch in length. Dredged in N. lat. 73° 20′, W. long. 57° 16′; 18th June, 1850. I have named this in compliment to Captain Stewart of the "Sophia"

Grammonema Jurgensii *Ag.* Upon Desmarestia aculeata, and dredged abundantly in two fathoms, along with myriads of minute crustacea, N. lat. 73° 20′, W. long. 57° 16′; 18th June, 1850.

Melosira arcticum *n. s.* Frustules transversely elliptical; central line rather faint.

The young frustules are nearly spherical. At first I supposed it to be a variety of M. Borreri; but, on more careful examination, I now agree with Rev. W. Smith in believing it to be new.

Dr. Sutherland describes it as n ix with the two last, and communicating a brown tinge to the water in Melville Bay, off the Devil's Thumb, in shreds of mucilaginous consistence, and infested with numerous microscopic animals; N. lat. 74° 40′; 11th July, 1850.

Triceratium striolatum *Ehr.* Dredged in fifteen fathoms, Union Bay; 3rd September, 1850. Plentiful, and unmixed with any other Diatomaceæ.

Fragilaria ——? This is probably a new species; but at present I cannot venture to write more confidently respecting it. "Taken from the sea-water, when there was no ice, in the form of rounded pellicles of a brown colour, near the eastern extremity of an island, in N. lat. 73° 20′, W. long. 57° 16′."

The matter deposited from the water in which the Kallymenia already mentioned had been macerated, was found, on careful examination, to contain the following species ; some of these are fresh-water forms, but they were less abundant than the marine.

Amphora hyalina *Kg.*
Cocconeis borealis *Ehr.*
Coscinodiscus striatus *Kg.*
 minor *Ehr.*
 subtilis *Ehr.*
And another of the same genus, probably new.

Cyclotella ——— new species.
Cymbella Helvetica *Kg.*
Epithemia Zebra *Kg.*
 Westermanni *Kg.*
Gomphonema acuminatum *Ehr.*
 curvatum *Kg.* var. marinum.
Grammatophora stricta *Ehr.*
 anguina *Ehr.*
Navicula quadrifasciata *Ehr.* ?
 didyma *Ehr.*
Odontella obtusa *Kg.*
 aurita *Kg.*
Rhabdonema minutum *Kg.* ?
Stauroneis aspera *Kg.*
Synedra curvula *Kg.* ?
 pulchella *Sm.*
Triceratium striolatum *Ehr.*

The following additional species were detected by the Rev. W. Smith :—

Pleurosigma prolongatum *Sm.*
 elongatum *Sm.*
 Fasciola *Sm.*

The following species were procured from the washings of Desmarestia aculeata and Chætopteris plumosa, dredged in N. lat. 73° 20′, W. long. 57° 20′.

Cyclotella, new species ? already mentioned.
Cymbella Helvetica.
Grammatophora anguina.
Navicula didyma.
Odontella obtusa.
Rhabdonema minutum.
Stauroneis aspera.
Synedra pulchella.
Triceratium striolatum.

All these are mentioned above as found in Assistance Bay.

The washings of Agarum Turneri, from Union Bay, yielded eight species identical with those already noticed as found in Assistance Bay, viz.:

Synedra pulchella.
    curvula.
Stauroneis aspera.
Odontella obtusa.
Grammatophora anguina.
Cyclotella —— ?
Cymbella Helvetica.
Triceratum striolatum.

On 29th May, 1850, in N. lat. 72° 15′, Dr. Sutherland states that "A slimy substance was found on the surface of the water and beneath the ice, which was generally decayed and rotten, very abundant in Davis' Straits along the eastern shore, but especially in deep bays where the water is still. When violent pressure happens among the ice, the broken-up floes reduced to the condition of pack ice have a dirty appearance from the presence of this substance." The following species were detected.

Grammonema Jurgensii *Ag.*
Pleurosigma Thuringica *Kg.*
    Fasciola.
Navicula, new species?
Surirella, new species?
Triceratium striolatum.

A substance very similar to the last, but with a frothy appearance, was collected on 8th June, 1850, N. lat. 73° 17′; it contained the following: the tissue of all the species was of excessive tenuity:—

Achnanthidium delicatulum *Kg.*
Cocconeis Rhombus *Ehr.*
Coscinodiscus marginatus *Ehr.*
Grammonema Jurgensii.
Melosira Orcticum *n.s.*
Navicula Oxyphyllum *Kg.*
    Thuringica.
Nitzchia —— new?
Synedra pulchella.

Among rotten ice in N. lat. 73° 40′, W. long. 57°, in July, 1851, a flocculent substance was collected; I found it to consist of the following five species:—

Denticula obtusa *Kg.*?
Melosira arcticum.
Navicula Oxyphyllum.
Pleurosigma Fasciola.
    angulatum *Sm.*

"On 2nd July, 1850, in Hinkson's Bay N. lat. 73° 50′, W. long. 57°, to the southward of Sugar-loaf Hill, a substance scarcely slimy was collected in great abundance, water still, ice very rotten, decaying where it had formed without drifting, the colour brown, sometimes white, and resembling an oily film on the surface of the calm sea."

It contains the following species, all remarkable for the tenuity of their tissue, and most of them destroyed by the action of nitric acid; the Dictyocha, Melosira, Triceratium, and two or three others alone resisting it.

Amphora hyalina.
Amphiprora alata *Kg.*
Ceratoneis closterium *Ehr.*
Cocconeis Rhombus.
Denticula obtusa.
Dictyocha gracilis *Kg.*
Grammonema Jurgensii.
Melosira arcticum.
Navicula Oxyphyllum.
Nitzschia, new species?
Pleurosigma Fasciola.
Thuringica.
Schizonema, new species, in fragments.
Triceratium striolatum.

In lat. 75° 42′, May, 1850, a matter taken from the surface of the hummocky ice along the beach, in one or two fathoms water, was found to contain the following species:—

Cocconeis Rhombus?
Navicula didyma.
Semen, *Ehr.*
new species?
Nitzschia, new species.
Odontella obtusa.
aurita.
Rhabdonema minutum?
Stauroneis aspera.
Synedra curvula
pulchella.
Triceratium striolatum.

It may be worthy of remark here, that the colouring matter of ice in the Arctic regions sometimes consists of the remains of Algæ either in a state of decomposition, or reduced to a pulp by the abrading action of drifting bergs, &c.; such at least was the nature of specimens examined by me several years ago.

In conclusion, it may be observed how few species there are of the olive-coloured and red Algæ; such as are recorded may be considered as fairly representing these plants in the parts visited by the Expedition. The number of littoral species in such regions must be few, or in many places altogether absent; the continual abrading influence of bergs and pack ice would effectually prevent their growth.

In the thinning out of Algæ in such latitudes, it is a point of interest to ascertain what genera and species resist longest the influence of conditions inimical to the development of vegetable organisms. Only five of the olive-coloured series are recorded here, four of which are British; the fifth, viz. the Agarum, being exclusively an American form. Of the red series there are only three: one of them, the Polysiphonia, being a common species in Britain; the Dumontia is an American form, the third new.

The green Algæ are better represented, six being marine, and fourteen from fresh water or moist places on land, confirming the opinions entertained respecting the more general diffusion of the green than of the olive and red. Of the twenty enumerated, about a third are British.

Of Desmidieæ only three were detected in Dr. Sutherland's collection, two of which are British; and the Arthrodesmus has been found in France and Germany.

The Diatomaceæ, as might have been expected, are numerous. Their importance in reference to the existence of animal life in high latitudes has been already alluded to; an importance out of proportion to their size, the generality of them being so minute that their presence can only be detected by the microscope; or rather it may be remarked that their minuteness renders them important, since they are readily conveyed to the digestive organs of mollusca by currents produced by the numerous cilia on the mantle and gills of these animals. By a wise arrangement, their numbers compensate for their small size. The climate is so unfavourable, that gigantic Algæ, such as occur in more favoured regions, cannot exist; the organisms in question, the representatives of the individual cells of which the larger species are composed, supply their place; and the silicious matter which they have the power of separating from the medium in which they live, renders them better fitted to resist the injuries to which they are exposed.

ZOOLOGY.

In bringing together the following lists and descriptions, it may be proper to state, that many of the marine species, and some of the insects collected during the voyage, are left out, owing to want of opportunity, and other difficulties that stood in the way of a more detailed examination. Among the *Crustacea* a few undetermined species are omitted, and the *Annelides* are not so much as alluded to ; the difficulty of preserving many of the latter, and of examining them even when well preserved, is so great, that however interesting an account of them might prove, this is hardly the place for it. The following is a list of *Mollusca*, which I have been able to make out by comparison with the valuable and well-arranged collections in the British Museum, to which I was kindly permitted access by J. E. Gray, Esq., the conservator of the zoological department, and Dr. Baird.

GASTEROPODA.

Buccinum glaciale. *Hab.* Muddy bottom of Assistance Bay, seven to ten fathoms.

B. cyaneum. *Hab.* Coast of West Greenland, rocky bottom, fifteen to twenty fathoms.

Turbo corneus of Keiner. *Hab.* Assistance Bay, muddy bottom, seven to fifteen fathoms.

Trichotropis costellatus. *Hab.* Assistance Bay, shingly bottom, fifteen fathoms.

Margarita undulata,
glauca,
arctica,
vahlii
umbilicalis, were very abundant. *Hab.* Assistance Bay, and the coast of W. Greenland, rocky bottom, twelve to twenty fathoms.

M. helicina. *Hab.* Coast of W. Greenland, rocky bottom, fifteen to twenty fathoms.

Bulla corticata. *Hab.* Assistance Bay, muddy bottom, seven to ten fathoms. Not abundant.

Chiton lævigatus. *Hab.* Barrow Straits, shingly bottom, twelve to fifteen fathoms.

Patella rubella,
cerea,
Sottia testudinalis. *Hab.* Assistance Bay, twelve to fifteen fathoms, shingly bottom.

CONCHIFERÆ.

Modiola (Lanistina) discors,
Astarte arctica,
Spitzbergensis,
Nucula (Yoldia) arctica,
(Leda) fluviatilis,
radiata,
caudata,
Hiatella arctica,
minuta,
Tellina (Psammobia) fusca,
calcarea,
Cardium (Aphrodite) Grœnlandicum,
Saxicava rugosa,
Mya truncata,
Pandora glacialis,
Montacuta substriata, were also abundant. *Hab.* Assistance Bay and the shores of Barrow Straits, muddy and shingly bottom, seven to twenty fathoms.

In addition to the above, the following were made out by Prof. E. Forbes and J. H. Huxley, Esq.

CEPHALOPODA.

Philonexis ——— ? This undetermined species was found in a cavity on the surface of the ice in Melville Bay, Davis Straits. July, 1850.

Sepia ——— ? Found abundantly, but in a very imperfect state, in the stomach of a narwhal, killed in Melville Bay. July, 1850.

Sagita bipunctata. This creature, whose true position among various classes of the mollusca is so doubtful, is most widely distributed. During the late voyage it was found over the whole Atlantic, Davis Straits, Baffin's Bay, and Barrow Straits. It attains to a large size in Davis Straits; some of the specimens obtained there exceeding two inches in length, while those in the Atlantic and the North Sea rarely exceeded half that length. Its quickness of motion and transparency render it safe from the hands of the collector, unless it is included in a large quantity of water.

CRUSTACEA.

Entomostraca.

Of this division the following species were collected : —

Arpacticus Kronii. (*fig.* 4.) Davis Straits, lat. 66° 34′, long. 55° 8′. *Kroyer Voyages en Scandinav. Lappon, Zoologie Crustaces, t.* xliii. f. 3.

A. chelifer. Davis Straits; lat. 73° 20′, long. 57° 16′. *Baird's British Entomostraca.*

Cypridina Brenda. Assistance Bay. *Baird's British Entomostraca.*

Cyclopsina ——— ? Davis Straits; lat, 73° 20′, long. 57° 16′. *Baird's British Entomostraca.*

Cyclops ——— ? Davis Straits; lat 73° 20′, long. 57° 16′.

Cetochilus septentrionalis. North Sea. *Baird's British Entomostraca.*

Two new species, for the following description of which I am indebted to Dr. Baird, F.L.S.R. of the British Museum, author of the above work on the British Entomostraca.

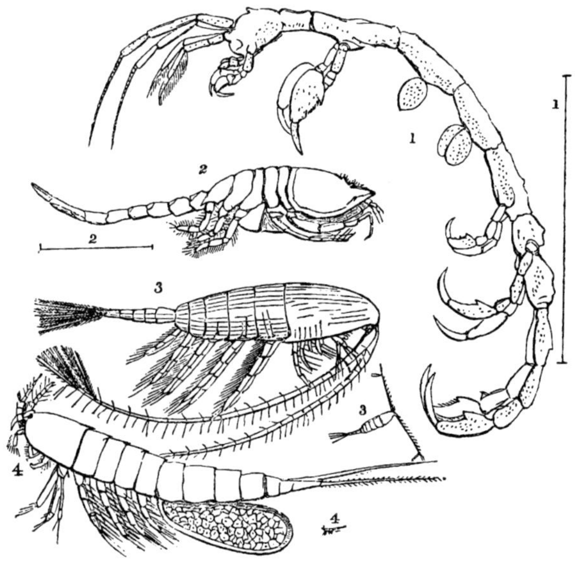

" *Cetochilus arcticus,* (*fig.* 3). Body oval, of six articulations; the first, which contains head and first segment of thorax very much the largest; abdominal portion much narrower and smaller, consisting of five articulations, the last being bilobed. Each lobe gives off four or five stout setæ, which are closely and beautifully plumose, and are of a fine brilliant rose colour. The antennæ are very long, exceeding the whole length of the animal. They consist of about twenty-four segments, gradually diminishing in size as they reach the extremity. From the base of the penultimate and the second last articulations on the inner side arise a number of strong and long setæ, equal in diameter to the last joint, but much longer. These are beautifully and distinctly feathered, or plumose, and, like the tail setæ, are of a brilliant rose colour. From the base of the penultimate joint, on the outer side, rises one long simple seta; and from the extremity of the last, three or four are given off. The animal is of a translucent snow colour, the legs of a reddish brown, while the brilliant rosy hue of the tail setæ, and those of the antennæ, renders it very striking. It is of about five lines in length.

This appears to be a very common species in the Arctic seas, having been taken in lat. 71° 21′, off Cape Desolation, in lat. 64° 19′, and in Melville Bay. "The motions of this little creature," says Dr. Sutherland in his notes, "are exceedingly quick and graceful, and it eludes its pursuer by a sudden spring forward. To this succeeds a moment of perfect quiescence. When watched in the water, it will be seen with the long, oar-like antennæ, at right angles with the body, and after a sudden spring they are seen thrown towards the tail, and forming an arc on each side." In one place, the water from which they were taken was very luminous at night. The specimens taken at that time (off Cape Desolation), are smaller than the generality of those taken elsewhere. One specimen, taken in Melville Bay, is of a dark brown colour, and is fully $\frac{3}{4}$ of an inch in length, possessing the same plumose setæ on caudal segment and antennæ, and differing only in general colour and in size. I am not prepared to consider it a distinct species, although the antennæ themselves appear smaller and shorter in comparison with the length of the animal, than in the other specimens.

Alauna uncinata (*fig.* 2.). Body oval; rostrum short, broad and pointed at extremity; dorsal margin of thoracic portion of body armed with seven or eight short stout hooked spines, the three first being close together; a number of short hairs are given off along the dorsal edge of the carapace. Abdomen long and slender, seven jointed, the last joint produced into a long and rather sharp conical spine, beset with short sharp spines on each side. The caudal styles are similar to those of A. rostrata. From half an inch to nearly one inch long. The colour is of a very light pale brown. *Hab.* From the bottom of Assistance Bay; seven to fifteen fathoms. August 7th, 1851.

For the following list I am indebted to Arthur Adams, Esq., surgeon, R.N.

Order DECAPODA (Macroura).

Family CRANGONIDÆ.

Genus CRANGON *Fabricius.*

96. *Crangon boreas* Fabr. Zool. Dan. iv. p. 14. pl. 132. f. 1.; Suppl. Parry's First Voy. p. 235. *Cancer boreas*, Phipps' Voy. p. 194. pl. 11. f. 1. *Cancer homaroides*, O. Fabr. F. G. 241. *Hab.* Assistance Bay, twelve to fifteen fathoms, shingly bottom. July, 1851.

64? *Crangon septemcarinatus* Sabine, Suppl. to Parry's First Voy. p. 236. pl. 2. f. 11—13. *Hab.* Assistance Bay, muddy and shingly bottom, seven to fifteen fathoms. August, 1851.

Genus PALÆMON.

Four specimens unidentified.

Genus ALPHEUS *Fabricius.*

101. *Alpheus aculeatus*, O. Fabr.
Cancer aculeatus O. Fabr. Faun. Grœnl. No. 217. Suppl. to Parry's First Voy. p. 237. pl. 2. f. 9—10. *Astacus Greenlandicus*, I. C. Fabr. Ent. Syst. vol. ii. p. 484. This beautiful species was found in lat. 66° 34′, long. 55° 8′, on the 23rd August, 1851, in the maw of a cod killed in forty fathoms.

Genus HIPPOLYTE *Leach.*

96. *Hippolyte polaris* Sab.
Alpheus polaris Sab. Append. to Parry's First Voy. p. 238. pl. 2. f. 5—8. *Hippolyte polaris*, J. C. Ross, App. to Ross's Second Exp. 85. *Lebbeus orthorynchus* Leach. *Hab.* Assistance Bay, muddy and shingly bottom, seven to fifteen fathoms. July, 1852.

Order STOMAPODA.

Family MYSIDÆ.

Genus MYSIS *Latreille.*

50. *Mysis flexuosus* Müll.
Cancer flexuosus Müll. Zool. Dan. 2. p. 34. pl. 66. *Mysis flexuosus* Lamck, v. p. 200.; Kroyer, Voy. en Scandinavie, pl. 9. *Hab.* Union Bay, Beechey Island, shingly bottom, fifteen fathoms.

Order AMPHIPODA.

Family GAMMARIDA.

Genus GAMMARUS *Fabricius.*

19. *Gammarus nugax* Sab. Suppl. to Parry's First Voy. p. 229. *Cancer nugax*, Phipps' Voy. pl. 12. f. 3. *Talitrus nugax*, Ross, App. Parry's Third Voy. p. 119. *Hab.* W. coast of Greenland, rough sand and rocky bottom, four to twenty fathoms.

Genus ACANTHONOTUS *Owen & Ross.*

Acanthonotus tricuspis Kroy. Voy. en Scandinavie, pl. 18. f. 1.

19. *Acanthonotus Sabinii* Leach.
Amphithœ Sabinii Leach. App. Ross. Voy. ii. p. 178., Sabine, App. Ross. Voy. p. 54. t. 1. f. 8—11. *Hab.* Same as above species.

Genus AMPHITHŒ *Leach.*

50. *Amphithœ Edvardsii* Sabine.
Talitrus Edvardsii Sab. Suppl. to Parry's First Voy. p. 232. pl. 2. f. 1—4. *Amphithœ Edvardsii.* Ross in Ross's Second Voy. Suppl. p. 90. *Hab.* Assistance Bay, muddy bottom, seven fathoms. September, 1850.

Genus STEGOCEPHALUS *Kroyer.*

64. *Stegocephalus inflatus* Kroyer, Naturhistorik Tidsokrift, vol. iv. p. 150.; new series, vol. i. pl. 7. f. 3.; Gaimard's Voy. en Scandinavie, tab. 20. f. 2. *Hab.* Same as that of the above species.

Genus ANONYX *Kroyer.*

Five specimens unidentified.

Order ISOPODA.

Family IDOTEIDÆ.

Genus ARCTURUS *Latr.*

50. *Arcturus Baffini* Sab.
Idotea Baffini Sab. Suppl. to Parry's First Voy. p. 228. pl. 1. f. 4—6. *Arcturus Baffini*, M. Edwards, pl. 31. f. 1. *Hab.*

Union Bay, Beechey Island, fifteen fathoms, shingly bottom. September 5th, 1850.

GENUS SADURIA *Leach.*

62. *Saduria entomon* Linn.
Oniscus entomon Linn. Syst. Nat. ii. 1060. *Idotea entomon*, Latr. Hist. Crust. vi. 36. tab. 58. f. 23. Sab. Suppl. Parry's First Voy. p. 227. *Entomon pyramidale*, Klein. *Squilla entomon*, Degeer. *Oniscus marinus*, Penn. *Hab.* Assistance Bay, seven fathoms, muddy bottom; most abundant. August, 1851.

FOR the following descriptions of some of the species of the crustaceæ not identified by Mr. ADAMS, and of some of the insects collected, I am indebted to ADAM WHITE, Esq., F.L.S. &c., British Museum.

Fig. 1. represents a *Caprella* found by Dr. Sutherland, and which may be named *Caprella cercopoides* from some resemblance which it has to the *Cercops Hölbölli*, a læmodipodous crustacean, figured and described by Kroyer in his "Tidschrift," and also in the "Voyages en Scandinavie," &c. of Gaimard (pl. 24.); it may be distinguished by the strong spine, somewhat blunt at the end and directed forwards, which exists on the crown of the head and about the middle of it.

The subcheliform leg has the long and sharp chela when closed against the swollen joint, reaching somewhat beyond the point of a spinous projection which exists on the under side near its base. The back of two or three of the longest vesicle-bearing segments, seem to be slightly sinuated here and there, so as to make them look somewhat nodulous above, but this may be the result of contraction in the spirits.

Mr. Wing's figure, which is considerably magnified, shows the peculiarities of this species. It was found by Dr. Sutherland in lat. 73° 16′ N., long. 57° 16′ W., on the coast of West Greenland, four to twenty fathoms, rocky bottom.

Fig. 5. represents a species of *Nymphon*, which seems to differ in many respects from any species described by Otho Fabricius in his "Fauna Grœnlandica." It may be called *Nymphon crassipes*, in allusion to its thick legs; there seem to be only four joints to the palpi, unless the short balls, by which the palpus is united to the head, be regarded as a joint; in that case the second joint is as long as the third and fourth taken together; the two terminal joints are about equal in length, and with the third are covered with minute hairs.

The chelæ have their basal joint long, cylindrical, and somewhat bent; the fixed claw is swollen on the under side where it receives the moveable claw, which is sharp and hooked, like the terminal portion of the other. The figure represents it of the natural size.

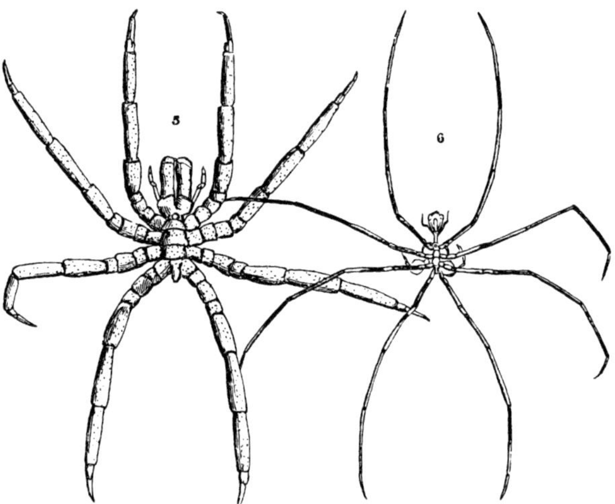

Fig. 6. represents a species of Nymphon agreeing in many respects with the *Pycnogonum grossipes* described so elaborately by Otho Fabricius, in his "Fauna Grœnlandica." It seems, however, to be smaller and more slim than his species, and as the specimens found by Dr. Sutherland seem to be some of them mature, from the condition of the ovaries, they may prove to be distinct. From an inspection of the figures of Kroyer in the "*Voyage en Scandinavie, &c.*" of Captain Gaimard, I am inclined, however, to think it may prove only to be a variety of Strom's species, his specimen, as Fabricius records (l. c. p. 229.), differing in some particulars from those described by the accurate author of the "Fauna Grœnlandica."

Both these species were taken with the dredge in Union Bay, Beechey Island, September, 1851.

INSECTS AND APTERA.

Figs. 7 and 8, are profile figures, much magnified, of two species of *Poduræ* found by Dr. Sutherland. *Fig.* 7. is a hairy species of a greyish black colour, with a squarish head which is abrupt behind. The antennæ are thick and four jointed, the terminal joint longer than the penultimate, which, again, is longer than the second joint. The dorsal abdominal plates have longer hairs on the posterior edge than on the other parts.

This species, which may be named *Desoria arctica*, is interesting from its resemblance in many particulars to a species found by

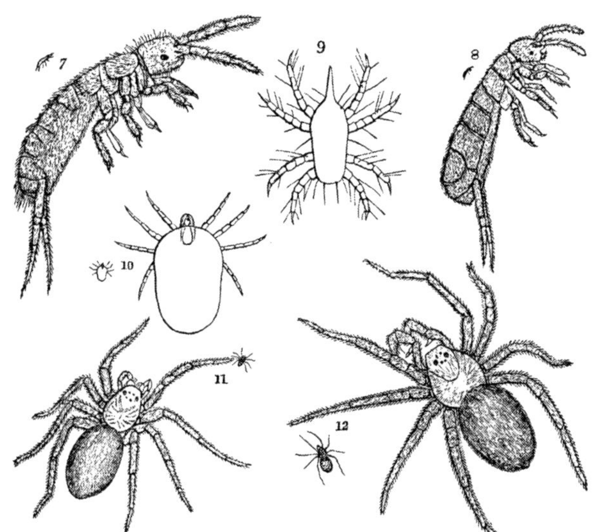

Desor and Agassiz among the Alps of Switzerland, and named by Agassiz *Desoria saltans*, a name changed by Nicolet in the " Neuchâtel Memoirs " into *Desoria glacialis*. This species, which is of a deep black, has a distinct somewhat swollen neck and cylindrical thorax, the abdomen is slightly fusiform, and the third joint of the antennæ is somewhat ovoid. M. Desor first met with it on the surface of some holes on the glacier of Zermatt, to which M. Agassiz at first fancied the insects were brought by the wind, but the discoverer believed that the glaciers were their proper home. In turning over stones (See Desor, " Excursions sur la Mer de Glace du Lauteraar et du Finsteraar," in the " Bibliothèque Universelle du Génève," No. xxxii. p. 125.) he and his friend found countless numbers, sometimes many thousands in the space of a square foot. He found them generally under stones. MM. Desor, Pourtales, and Agassiz saw them running into ice apparently very compact, and, on breaking off a piece, the ice was seen to be pierced with numerous canals in which the Desoriæ leaped and ran like drops of blood.

Fig. 8. is a species with a short and truncate head, and the abdomen somewhat clavate, it is much smoother than the D. arctica. the scale-like hairs with which it is covered being very minute and close to each other. Neither this species nor the preceeding seem to be known to the able monographer of the Podurellæ, H. Nicolet. "Mémoires pour servir a l'histoire des Podurelles," in the 6th volume of the "Nouveaux Mémoires de la Société Helvétique des Sciences Naturelles.")

Dr. Sutherland found this latter species on the patches of nostoc blown off on the ice, and also on the land associated with nostoc and conferve. Dr. Sutherland tells me that he has alluded in his Journal to the circumstances under which these interesting Poduræ were found.

Fig. 9. is a figure of a mite of the genus *Bdella* of Latreille, in which the sucker projects into a beak, and the palpi are elbowed. The beak in the species, found by Dr. Sutherland, is nearly half the length of the rest of the body, and is grooved longitudinally down the middle. Its palpi (not shown in the cut) are seemingly three-jointed, being elbowed after the first joint, which is nearly three times as long as the two other joints taken together. There are two bristles at the end of the terminal joint. The four legs of each side are placed in pairs, two being directed forwards and two backwards; the femoral part of these is much thickened. The body is blunt behind, and is thickest just behind the two first pairs of legs. As this curious little red species is found on Cornwallis Island associated with the Podura, and as it does not seem to be described, it may be called *Bdella podurophila.*

Fig. 10. represents a small species of *Ixodes*, a genus of Acaridæ in which the palpi close the sucker as in a sheath, and form with it a projecting truncated beak. The species are very numerous and are parasitic on vertebrata, neither the huge rhinoceros among the mammalia, nor the immense boa constrictor among the reptiles, being free from the attacks of members of the genus.

The species found by Dr. Sutherland in the Arctic regions was parasitic on the Loom (*Uria troile*). It seems strange that an adult bird which lives nearly constantly in the sea should be infested by a parasite of this nature.

It is of a greyish black colour, and is rather wider in front than behind; the lateral margins are somewhat sinuated, and the legs appear to be long compared with other species of the genus. It does not seem to be described or alluded to by Professor Gervais in the 3rd volume of the "Aptères," where fifty species are recorded, neither is it mentioned by Otho Fabricius in the "Fauna Grœnlandica." It may be called *Ixodes uriæ*, many of the species being named from the animals to which they are attached as parasites.

The small figure by the side represents it of the natural size.

Fig. 12. is the male of a species of spider of the genus *Micryphantes*; and *Fig.* 11. seems to me to represent an immature female of the same species. The cephalothorax is somewhat depressed behind, and rather attenuated and elevated in front, ending abruptly above the chelicera. The eyes, which are eight in number, are placed on the most elevated parts of the cephalothorax; there are four in the middle, the two front ones being placed closer to each other than the posterior pair; the two eyes on each side are close together, the hindmost is rather remoter than its neighbour from either of the posterior pair. In the male, the first joint of the palpus is long and somewhat sigmoid, the end of the second joint is subclavate and has a sharp and longish spine proceeding from it nearly at right angles and directed downwards. The legs, the second and fourth pairs of which appear to be rather longer than the first and third pairs, are of an ochraceous yellow, while the cephalothorax, and abdomen are of a blackish brown colour.

This species may be named, *M. Arcticus.* Dr. Sutherland tells me he found it abundantly around Assistance Bay, running about among the tufts of vegetation.

ASCIDIANS AND ECHINODERMS.

REMARKS upon some specimens collected and preserved in spirits by Dr. SUTHERLAND, by THOMAS H. HUXLEY, Esq., F.R.S., Assistant Surgeon R.N.

Having been requested by Dr. Sutherland to examine some specimens of animals preserved in spirits, procured by him at Assistance Bay, I beg to furnish the following short notes of the results at which I have arrived. A more detailed description, with illustrative figures, will appear in another place.

The specimens were very few in number, but they belong to highly interesting forms. With the exception of one or two Annelides, which were not in a fit state for examination, they were entirely Echinoderms and Ascidians.

Echinoderms.

There were four specimens belonging to this class, and to the subdivision of the footless Holothuriadæ.

The animal was $\frac{1}{2}$ to $\frac{3}{4}$ of an inch long, and $\frac{3}{8}$ to $\frac{1}{2}$ of an inch thick, so as to be more or less ovoid. The anterior extremity was surrounded by a circle of twelve short retracted tentacula, which were slightly plaited at their edges, and surrounded by a circular mouth; the posterior extremity was more pointed.

The integument was delicate, and of a greyish brown colour. It was dotted over with minute white spots, which, on careful microscopical examination, turned out to be calcareous deposits in the shape of wheels. These wheels were about $\frac{1}{130}$th of an inch in diameter; eighteen to twenty spokes radiated from the centre to the rim, which was somewhat thickened opposite their insertion. The spokes were concave on one side, convex on the other, so that the whole wheel was concave externally. Twenty to twenty-six large regular triangular teeth were set, pointing almost horizontally inwards upon the outer face of the rim.

The wheels were not continued in rows, nor attached upon a common connecting thread.

Ten flattened calcareous plates surrounded the œsophagus. There was a single Polian vesicle, and a single very small ($\frac{1}{45}$ inch) curved calcareous one, which lies in the mesenteric fold, connecting the œsophagus with the generative cœca. The latter were two, united above, as long as the body, and branched below.

The intestinal canal makes a double bend, and terminates in a cloacal sac, which possesses neither pulmonary nor Cuvierian appendages.

Five projecting muscular bands run down the inner surface of the inner muscular tunic, which is very readily separated from the outer integument.

According to Müller, the only genus of footless and lungless Holothuriadæ which possesses the calcareous wheels, is Chiridota —(Ueber dei Larven d. Holothurien, &c.). Of this genus Eschscholz, its institutor, found several species on the shores of the Island of Sitcha. These, however, as well as all others which I have seen described, differ from the present in being long and wormlike, and in having the tentacles long and digitated. The latter is, indeed, made the diagnosis of the genus by Eschscholz, but it must, I think, give way before the far more definite character of the calcareous wheels.

Under these circumstances, this singular Holothurian may be regarded as a new species under the name of *Chiridota brevis.*

Ascidians.

There were six specimens of this class. Two presented no marks of previous attachment, and were oblong, with the apertures four-cleft, but very indistinct. They were about $\frac{3}{4}$ of an inch long. The tail was membranaceous and corrugated. Prof. E. Forbes informed me that they were undistinguishable externally from *Pelonaia corrugata.*

One of the other Ascidians was much larger, $1\frac{5}{8}$ inch in length. It had evidently been attached by one extremity. The apertures were closely approximated at the other extremity, indistinct, and four-cleft. The test resembled that of the foregoing, but was more corrugated and thicker. Two other Ascidians were attached to the surface of the test of the preceding. They were about half an inch in length, and more oval in shape than the form which supported them. The test was membranaceous, corrugated, and thin. The apertures two, four-cleft, and obscure.

Notwithstanding the close resemblance of the first mentioned of these forms to *Pelonaia*, the internal anatomy showed that they were all Cynthiæ.

In all the external tunics adhered closely to the test, so as to be with some difficulty separated. I have observed this circumstance in many other Ascidians, so that it must be given up as a characteristic of Pelonaia.

In all there was a circlet of numerous filiform branchial tentacles, and there were four more or less marked folds to the branchial sac, with a large and characteristic "ciliated sac," or "tubercule anterieure" of Savigny.

The generative organs in the first form consisted of four or five sacs, placed transversely on each side of the body towards the branchial aperture.

In the two latter forms, which, notwithstanding their dissimilarity, I strongly suspect to be only modifications of the same species dependent upon age, the generative organ consists of several dendritic sacs placed upon the left side of the animal only. Each sac consists externally of a racemose seminal gland, investing and inclosing a band-like ovary.

In these three forms the structure and arrangement of the hepatic organ is very interesting. It consists of a network of fine tubes, terminating in pyriform secreting cells, and investing the stomach and intestines. The tubes unite into three or four larger ducts, which open into the stomach. This observation appears to me clearly to show that the problematical "tubular system" which I have described in Salpa (Phil. Transactions, 1851) is a peculiar form of liver.

This circumstance of the occurrence of a dendritic ovo-testis upon the left side only, refers this species to the section Dendrodon of Mac Leay. Until a more complete examination of the Ascidians has enabled me to estimate the exact value of characters drawn from the generative organs, I prefer to leave these species unnamed.

The sixth Ascidian, about 1½ inches long, by 1 inch broad, had a subgelatinous dark yellowish brown wrinkled and irregular test, of a flattened form, with the apertures six-cleft, sub-prominent and approximated upon its upper surface. The tunics were stained deep red about the two apertures.

The animal has the branchial sac and general anatomy of a Phallusia; but the circumstance most worthy of note is, that the visceral mass, instead of being placed as usual on the right side, is altogether beneath the branchial sac, an arrangement which appears also to obtain in *Chelyosoma*, according to Eschricht's description. As a result of this arrangement, the vessels for the test do not come off on the side opposite to the apertures, but near them, towards the right anterior extremity (in the ordinary position of the animal).

I propose to give to this species (to be more fully described and figured hereafter) the name *Phallusia Sutherlandii*, after its zealous discoverer. It is the most remarkable modification of the *Phallusia* type with which I am acquainted.

NOTES on animals of the class ECHINODERMATA collected by Dr. SUTHERLAND in Assistance Bay, by Professor EDWARD FORBES, F.R.S.

Some very interesting species of Echinodermata, collected during this voyage, throw much light on the Radiate fauna of the Polar regions. They include one sea-urchin, two star-fishes, several brittle-stars, two *Holothuriæ* and a *Chirodota.*

The sea-urchin (the only one met with) was taken in considerable numbers in Assistance Bay, in depths from seven to fifteen fathoms. It is the *Echinus neglectus*, a species well known as a member of the Scandinavian fauna and having its southern limits at the extreme north of Scotland. This is the only member of the genus of which we find fossil remains in the northern drift or pleistocene formation; where it is associated with a molluscous fauna in many respects comparable with that of the Arctic seas. Of the *Holothuriadæ* the most common is *Cucumaria Hyndmanni*, taken in Assistance Bay, Barrow Straits, muddy bottom, seven to ten fathoms water, September 1850, and August 1851. This is a Scandinavian species and a member of the boreal type of our British fauna. In some of Dr. Sutherland's specimens, the suckers become quadriserial in the avenues instead of the usually alternating or biserial arrangement. The other appears to be *Cucumaria fucicola*, a Zetland species regarded by some naturalists as the young of the large *Cucumaria frondosa.* The *Chirodota* has been examined by Mr. Huxley and is regarded by him as new.

The star-fishes are *Ctenodiscus polaris*, taken in from seven to fifteen fathoms, Assistance Bay; a young form which appears to belong to *Uraster violacea*, and a young *Solaster papposa.*

The brittle-stars are the most interesting part of the collection. There are no fewer than seven species. Of these, four are species of *Ophiura* (in the restricted sense), three of *Ophiolepis*, and one of *Ophiocoma.*

Of the species of *Ophiura*, one resembles at first glance the well known *O. texturata.* It differs from that species in having finer and larger spines upon the ray joints. It was taken in fifteen fathoms in Assistance Bay. The remaining three are also new.

Of the species of Ophiolepis, one is a slight variety of *O. filiformis*, a species generally distributed through the European seas; a second appears to be my *O. punctata*; the third is closely allied to *O. Ballii.* The *Ophiocoma* is nearly allied to, but quite distinct from *O. nigra.*

CHARACTERS OF NEW SPECIES.

Ophiura fasciculata. Nov. Sp.

Disc subpentagonal, covered by naked scales which are not very unequal, with no conspicuous central rosette. Two broadly subtriangular approximated but diverging disc plates at the origins of the arms. Pectinated scales clasping the bases of the arms, covered by irregularly grouped short stout conical spines. Upper arm-scales very thick, broadly fan-shaped, with truncated bases. Lateral arm-scales bearing three stout and one minute spine, the uppermost spines largest, thick, conic, smooth, longer than an arm joint, but not equal in length to the breadth of a ray. Under arm-scales broadly heptagonal, emarginated above. Genital openings with tuberculated margins. Inferior intermediate plates broadly and regularly shield-shaped.

Breadth of disc $0\frac{4}{10}$ths inch. Length of arms as compared with diameter of disk 3 – 1.

Ophiura glacialis. N. S.

Disc round, distinctly notched at the arm-insertions, covered by regularly rosulated smooth scales, not very unequal and conspicuous. Two subtriangular, approximated diverging plates opposite the base of each arm, hiding the comb-scales on which are about nine very short stout papillary spines. Upper arm-scales subhexagonal; side scales bearing three spines each, the uppermost stout, conic, as long as an upper arm-scale, and nearly equal to the breadth of a ray. Under arm-scales fan-shaped. Borders of genital openings fringed with regular minute papillæ. Inferior intermediate plates very broadly shield-shaped, rather short. First inferior arm-plate *remarkably large.*

Diameter of disc $0\frac{1}{4}$ inch. Length of ray as compared with diameter of disk 3 – 1.

Ophiura sericea. N. S

Disc very round, soft and tender, not notched for the insertion of the arms, and seeming as if naked when moist, covered by very minute smooth scales, among which are regularly arranged large ones forming a central rosette. Opposite the base of each arm are two distant oblong plates, much concealed. The combs at the superior origins of the arms fringe the margins of the disk, and are confluent; in each there are about nine stout minute spines. The upper arm-scales are broadly tile-shaped and subcarinated; the under ones are greatly concealed by the overlapping of the side scales, each of which bears four spines, the uppermost slender and longest, one and a half times as long as an arm-joint. The inferior intermediate plates are regularly shield-shaped. The genital slits have papillose margins.

Diameter of a disc $\frac{1}{2}$ an inch. Length of arms as compared with breadth of disk as 5 – 2.

Ophicoma echinulata. N. S.

Disc subpentangular, rough with stout short clavate echinulated spines, rising from punctated scales. Opposite the origin of each arm are two triangular scales, much hidden, small, distant and irregular. The upper arm-scales are triangular, and pointed below, except the lowermost ones. The under arm-scales are shield-shaped, The lateral arm-scales bear six or seven slender striated and echinated spines, longer than the rays are broad. The inferior intermediate plates are very broad and short, truncate above and angulated below.

This species approaches *O. nigra*, but differs in having fewer and larger spines on the disc, and differently shaped arm-scales and inferior intermediate plates.

Diameter of disc ½ an inch. Length of ray as compared with diameter of disc 3 – 1.

GEOLOGY.

BY

J. W. SALTER, Esq., F.G.S., &c., &c.

ASSISTANT NATURALIST OF THE GEOLOGICAL SURVEY OF GREAT BRITAIN.

Humboldt has remarked, that "while on entering a new hemisphere we change all other familiar and accustomed objects,— while in the plains around we survey entirely new forms of vegetable and animal being, and in the heavens over our heads we gaze on new constellations, — in the rocks under our feet alone we recognise our old acquaintances:" and, with regard to the primordial rocks, there is undoubtedly much truth in this pointed remark.*

This conclusion of the great father of Physical Geography is undoubtedly true, if applied, as he intended it, to the physical characters and mineralogical constitution of the masses forming our earth's crust. The same influences of internal heat and chemical affinity have everywhere produced the same crystalline materials; and the same physical agents — water and the atmosphere — have everywhere stratified them : the rocks themselves, therefore, are the same under all climates and in the most remote localities.

But with regard to the organic remains imbedded in the rocks, the case is widely different. The variety which Humboldt saw in each new region among living plants and animals, is scarcely less conspicuous among those whose remains lie beneath the surface. We do not yet know whether climate and latitude affected the species of former epochs in the same degree as at the present day ; but that there was a geographical distribution of life, then, as now, is evident. The fact that the same stratum at remote points yields only similar and not the same fossils, is too well proved to admit of doubt. The similarity which enables us to recognise them in widely-separated regions, as from the same formation, is maintained by the presence of the same genera and families, and not of the same species. The geographical districts marked out in the present day, by the presence of peculiar groups of species, are sometimes small, — at other times very extensive ; and although we have by no means a like facility for judging of the extent of such provinces in past time, yet, as far as we know, the case was similar.

---

* Conybeare's "Report on Geology, Brit. Association, 1832," 411.

These general observations are only introduced in preface to a few descriptions of Arctic Silurian fossils, because the Palæozoic strata in the Northern hemisphere seem a little at variance with this general rule. From the eastern borders of Europe to the Rocky Mountains, and from the southern States of America to the Polar regions, there is a general similarity of fossil contents in the old rocks, and several of the most common species are the same. But, on close examination, it will be found that even over this wide area, the seas of which must certainly have communicated with each other, there are great local differences; that Europe contains a multitude of species not found in America; and that the northern districts are wanting in many forms characteristic of the southern; and, besides, each separate country contains also its peculiar species, which never appear to have ranged beyond. The Arctic species, in like manner, brought home by the late Expedition, while a few of them appear identical with European and American forms, show, even in the scattered gleanings yet obtained, a distinct character of their own.

The few notices hitherto given of the fossils of these Arctic Silurian rocks, are those appended to Captain Parry's voyages by Mr. König and Professor Jameson. From their accounts, the north shore of Barrow Straits and the coasts of both sides of Prince Regent's Inlet, are occupied by a transition limestone of an ash-grey or yellowish and grey colour, often fœtid, and sometimes crystalline or compact. It is described as filled with zoophytes and shells, and in certain places, as noticed by Mr. König, quite made up of the detritus of encrinites, the fragments of which are so comminuted, that it might readily be mistaken for a granular limestone. He found in it a chain coral, resembling that from the transition limestone of Gothland, Sweden; but thought he saw a strong resemblance both in mineral character and fossils between some of the fœtid varieties, and the equally fœtid mountain limestone of Derbyshire. Professor Jameson gives a more complete list of organic remains from Port Bowen: —

Entrochites — joints of Encrinite stems,
Catenulariæ, — chain coral,
Spiropore, — ?
Turbinoliæ, — Cyathophyllum, Calophyllum, Strephodes, &c.,
Favosites, — several species,
Terebratulæ, — Rhynconellæ,
Turritellæ, — smooth Murchisoniæ, and
Orthoceratites, — several species; —

and showed that this rock (Port Bowen limestone) extends eastward to Cape York, Admiralty Inlet, and even Possession Bay, and southward as far as the coasts of Regent's Inlet were explored. In addition to these fossils, with which we are now familiar, Professor Jameson described those obtained by Captain Parry from the north shore of Melville Peninsula, Igloolik, Amherst Island, &c. But it does not appear clear that these were from rocks of the same age as those further north. They contained among the Trilobites, corals, and producti, a *Maclurite*, and also a coral regarded as a new genus by Mr. Stokes. This coral, which is evidently the *Receptaculites*, frequently occurs in the older rocks of America. In Upper Canada, Sir John Richardson found it associated with fossils of the same or younger date than those of Barrow Straits; but in Lower Canada it and the *Maclurite* are characteristic, as in New York, of the Lower Silurian; the age, therefore, of the limestone of Igloolik is not quite certain. Nor can the age of the limestone of Melville Island, so famous for its fossil plants, be gathered from the notice given by König of the transition rocks of Table Hill. Favosites and Terebratulæ * were found, but it is not clear that the limestone is of the Silurian age, or whether it is connected with the coal; the sandstone of that island appears to be of Carboniferous date, and in addition to the flora, of which it shows the impressions, it contains *Trilobites*, *Encrinites* and *Aviculæ*.

I ought not to omit to mention the notice given by Professor Ansted, in his " Elementary Course of Geology, &c." of the Silurian fossils found in a whitish crystalline limestone, brought to this country from Prince Leopold Island in 1849 as ballast, by the Expedition under the command of Sir James Clark Ross. By the kindness of Captain James, R. E., who had selected the specimens from the heaps at Woolwich Dockyard, we have been able to examine them, and a few are noticed in the following descriptions.

The late Expeditions in search of Sir John Franklin have, however, thanks to the zeal and labours of the officers and gentlemen engaged in them, brought much more copious materials, sufficient to point out the exact geological place of the fossils, and to show that the same great formation of Silurian limestone covers an enormous area in these cold regions, and that in general it is as little disturbed from its horizontal position, as in the American continent.

The principal localities from which these highly interesting remains were gathered lie near the entrance of the Wellington Channel, but they were found to extend northward on both sides of that Channel, and the newly discovered Queen's Channel, by Dr. Sutherland and the officers and seamen of Captain Penny's Expedition, who were engaged in travelling parties; and it was observed that they were very abundant in Seal Island in lat. 75° 49′, on the north side of Baring Bay, and the islands to the eastward of Queen's Channel. Cape Riley and Beechey Island on the east, and Cornwallis Island on the west entrance of Wellington Strait, are very rich in fossils; and Captain Ommanney, Mr. Pickthorne, Mr. Donnett, and Dr. Sutherland, have each contributed series from these localities. Griffith's Island, lat. 74° 30′, long. 95° 30′, was found, by the officers

* Dr. Conybeare says, *Catenipora* and *Caryophylliæ*; so that it is very probably the same with that from the other parts of Barrow Straits.

of Captain Austin's squadron, to be equally rich in fossils. Mr. Donnett collected a specimen of coral from Somerville Island, and limestone with some shells was also obtained by travelling parties at Cape Walker, still farther to the southwest. The fossils brought home in ballast from Prince Leopold Island are in a white crystalline limestone like those from Baring Bay ; and the collections made by Parry render it probable that this same 'secondary limestone' with similar fossils occurs at Port Bowen, and extends far down the shores of Cockburn Island.

Dr. Conybeare, in the report above alluded to, has noticed the great similarity between the fossils from the Arctic regions and those of our own country. He says, "it would often puzzle a practised eye, if two groups of specimens — one from Dudley and another from Melville Island — were placed before him, to say which specimen came from which locality : the same *Cateniporæ*, *Caryophylliæ*, and *Encrinites* being present in both."*

One fossil at least will be familiar to all, as occurring in our own Silurian strata — the *Halysites catenulatus* † *Linn*. Pl 6., *fig*. 11., — the chain coral of collectors. This is truly a cosmopolite coral, at least over the northern hemisphere. It was brought from Griffith's Island, by Messrs. Donnett and Pickthorne. Dr. Sutherland brought it from Cape Riley. It appears from the specimens now collected to be identical with the common chain coral.

Favosites Gothlandicus and *F. polymorpha*, Goldf., both well known British species, were met with — the former at Griffith's and Cornwallis Islands, the latter at Griffith's Island only.

The *Pentamerus*, figured at pl. 5., *figs*. 9, 10., appears not to differ in any essential characters from the *P. Conchidium* of Dalman, a species from Gothland, Sweden. It was found at Assistance Harbour, both by Dr. Sutherland and Mr. Donnett.

The common and almost the only *Trilobite* which has occurred in these collections, seems also to be a Swedish species — the *Encrinurus* (or *Cryptonymus*) *lævis* of Anselm, also found in Gothland. It has been brought from of Cornwallis and Griffith's Islands, and Cape Riley ; and Dr. Sutherland found it, associated with many other fossils, in the rocks at the top of Seal Island, Baring Bay. There is found in Cornwallis Island, too, the *Leperditia Baltica*, which is also found with the above Trilobite in Gothland.

Lastly, the universal *Atrypa reticularis*, which ranges from America to Armenia, and is found both in the Lower and Upper Silurian and Devonian rocks, — occurs of diminished size, in the white limestone of the solitary islet last mentioned, in company

---

* We can as yet only identify four or five as actually the same species with those common in our own Upper Silurian strata, and two or three more that occur in limestones of a like age on the continent.

† *Catenipora Parrii*, König, Supp. Append. 1st Voyage.

with what appears to be another European species, the *Terebratula sublepida*, De Verneuil, from the Ural Mountains.

With these few exceptions, the species are not known European forms; and as they appear to be equally distinct from those yet known or published from North America, I am compelled to give a few new names, intended to commemorate the self-denying labours of the gentlemen who collected them.

CRUSTACEA.

Encrinurus (Cryptonymus) lævis, Anselm? Pl. 5. *figs.* 14. 14*a*, magnified. — Palæontologia Suecica, Part I. Fasc. 1., Pl. 4. *fig.* 10.?

A fine and perhaps undescribed species of a genus more frequently found in the Upper than in Lower Silurian rocks. This Trilobite somewhat resembles *E. variolaris*, Brongniart, in its blunt tail, thick body rings, and compact form, but differs from it and from several other species by the rings on the axis of the tail being continuous across, and not interrupted or with a central row of tubercles. *E. (Crypt.) obtusus*, Anselm, has, like this, ten side ribs to the tail, but it differs at a glance by the row of coarse tubercles down the middle of that part. But his *E. lævis*, from the Upper Silurian of Gothland, has so much the habit of ours, that although his figure shows only eight side ribs to the tail, and the eyes are smaller than in ours, it is probable that both are of the same species; should it prove otherwise, the name *E. Arcticus* would be appropriate.

The eyes are rather large and depressed for the genus; the glabella and cheeks covered with large coarse tubercles: the hypostome (preserved in one specimen) is gently convex, and has the usual cucullate base. The body rings and tail are quite smooth. The ten side ribs of the tail are strongly bent down, and towards the blunt apex become crowded, a small ovate convex appendage filling up the space between the two last. The ribs on the axis of the tail, about nine or ten in number and of large size (not small and crowded as usual in the genus), and the three or four upper ones, are continuous across with the first four side ribs: the rest are very slightly interrupted in the middle.

Localities. — Cape Riley: Griffith's Island, in plenty; Cornwallis and Seal Islands; Dundas Island, lat. 76° 15′.

Proetus ——, sp. Pl. 5. *fig.* 15.

A characteristic portion of the head (the free cheek) of a species very like those in the Dudley limestone of England.

Locality. Cornwallis Island.

Leperditia baltica, Hisinger sp. var *arctica*, Jones. Pl. 5. *fig.* 13. *Cytherina baltica*, Hisinger Lethæa Suecica. Pl. 1. *fig.* 2.

Nearly half an inch long, and four lines broad, not very convex; general form bean-shaped, the straight dorsal edge or hinge being much less than the entire length, and the ends obliquely truncated rather than rounded. The dorsal edge is thickened and separated from the end of the valve by a short furrow, which is nearly parallel to the margin; this only occurs on the left-hand valve, the front edge of which is also lapped over by the thickened and bent edge of the other. This furrow is the only point in which the species differs from *C. baltica;* and I am indebted to T. R. Jones, Esq., of the Geological Society, for identifying it with that species. The greatest convexity of the valve is nearer the anterior than the posterior end, the former being indicated by a minute pimple or tubercle placed in advance of the convexity at about one-third of the length. The exterior surface is minutely punctate, and the interior is beautifully radiated from a central impressed spot.

Localities. — Cape Hotham, Assistance Bay; and Seal Island, Baring Bay. In some parts abundant.

MOLLUSCA.

Of the Cephalopods, the genus *Orthoceras*, so common in the Silurian rocks of Europe and America, is also here abundant, and with similar forms: — one other interesting species of this class has occurred, viz.: —

Lituites ——, *n. sp.*

Quite discoid, and the general form flat. Whorls, in a shell one inch and three-quarters broad, six or seven at least, only just touching each other, compressed and bluntly keeled on the back. Their sides very convex and ribbed across from the inner margin nearly to the keel. The ribs are prominent, a little curved backwards.

This pretty shell much resembles *L. articulatus* Sow. (Silur. Syst. t. 11. f. 7.); but the number of whorls is much greater, the sides are more convex, and the back not so sharp. We regret that want of space has obliged us to omit a figure of it.

Locality. — Cornwallis Island; Mr. Pickthorne.

Orthoceras Ommanneyi, Pl. 5. *figs.* 16, 17.

Fig. 16. is a view of the septum, with its large siphon. *Fig.* 17. a young specimen.

This fine large species seems to be frequently met with, and will easily be recognised by its large lateral siphuncle, and its waved and close septa. It must have been a foot long, and one inch and three-quarters wide. The shell tapers slowly, and has a round transverse section. The septa are placed obliquely, the side farthest from the mouth of the shell being that in which the large siphuncle is placed, and externally they show a downward course in this side. They are very closely placed; in a specimen of an inch and a quarter diameter there are nine in the space of barely an inch. The septa are flattish, and the large siphon is placed less than half its own diameter from the edge. It would belong to the section *Cameroceras*.

The young specimen figured shows the septa waved upwards, — it is viewed on the side.

Localities. — Assistance Bay (Mr. Donnett and Dr. Sutherland). Dedicated to Captain Ommanney, of H. M. S. "Assistance," who collected many specimens which he kindly presented to us.

Orthoceras ——, sp. 1.

One specimen of a species with the waved and flattish septa rather close, as in the last, but not oblique, and with the siphon of small size and central.

Locality. — Cornwallis Island (Mr. Pickthorne).

Orthoceras ——, sp. 2.

Long and very slowly tapering. The septa much more distant than in the two last. In the largest specimen, three-quarters of an inch wide, they are frequently more than two lines apart, and very convex. The siphon is considerably out of the middle, and is small where it joins the septum, but is swelled into a bead-like shape between them. It is probably an *Ormoceras*.

Localities. — Plentiful in Griffith's and Cornwallis Islands.

Large fragments of other species occur also on Cornwallis Island.

Bellerophon Nautarum. Pl. 5. *fig*. 20.

Though only an internal cast, this interesting species differs from any Silurian one with which I am acquainted. It is less keeled than many, and too much so for others. It resembles a good deal some of the species of the mountain limestone, such as *B. apertus*, but has a smaller umbilicus, and a less rounded back. I must be pardoned for naming it, although imperfect, in honour of James Knox, a hardy seaman of the "Sophia," who, amid all his fatigue, found time to collect it and the *trilobite* before mentioned, on the extreme northern point from which fossils have been brought.

Diameter 15 lines, thickness 13 lines. The whorls are rounded, and very obscurely keeled on the back. The umbilicus small; its sides steep but rounded off into the whorl, and not more than $2\frac{1}{2}$ lines broad even in the cast. Aperture crescent-shaped; its sides rounded; its width 13 lines; its length, taken in the middle, which is the widest part, 6 lines.

Locality.—Dundas Island, Victoria Channel, lat, 76° 15′; long. 96° 50′.

Spiral shells are not common; we have only three species.

Murchisonia ——, sp. 1. Pl. 5. *fig*. 18.

This looks very like *M. gracilis* (Hall, Palæontology New York), but it is too imperfect to name; and there are so many species of this form in all the Silurian rocks. It is sometimes longer, — of 8 or 9 whorls.

Locality.—Cornwallis Island, many specimens on the shores of Assistance Bay, and inland.

Murchisonia, —— sp. 2. Pl. 5. *fig.* 19.

Different from the last; it is figured to show the great number of whorls, which are more closely packed than in the other species. There was probably a broad band on the middle of each whorl of this and the preceding species.

Locality.—Cape Riley (Mr. Donnett.)

A small *Euomphalus* occurs at Point Separation, Cornwallis Island.

Of ordinary bivalve shells, one only has yet been found. It appears to be a species of *Modiola*, of a transverse oval shape, and with no sinus in the front margin; it is only gently convex. It is from Beechey Island.

Brachiopodous shells are the most common, we have 11 species.

Strophomena Donnetti. Pl. 5. *figs.* 11, 12.

About an inch and a quarter broad. Transverse when young, as long as wide when older, the large valve concave, the upper or dorsal one quite convex, and with a very gentle depression down its middle. The area is moderately broad and inclined backwards, the deltidial triangle convex, and the opening filled by a semicircular projection from the upper valve. The hinge line is equal to the entire width of the shell. Towards the front margin the lines of growth are strong, and the shell becomes antiquated and thickened at the edge (*see fig.* 12.). Surface covered by radiating striæ, which are fine and regular in the young shell, and increase in size, but not greatly in number, on the older portion. The striæ are not of equal size, — the young shell being radiated by eight or ten much stronger than the rest, each with two or three of the finer ones between; these are chiefly in the middle and front of the shell. These larger ribs become more numerous towards the edge, but are not so distinct, on account of the increasing size of the intermediate striæ. On the ears the striæ are of equal size. All are crossed by fine concentric lines of growth, which are close and thread-like between the striæ, and give a somewhat eticulate appearance when the surface is perfect. *Fig.* 11. shows a young specimen, *fig.* 12. an old one.

Orthisina plana, and O. inflexa, Pander, are a good deal like this, more especially the latter, but besides wanting a central furrow down the smaller valve, our shell differs from that species by the strong striæ, regularly interlined by one or two fainter ones. The shape, too, is not transverse, but as long as broad. From general analogy it is placed in the genus *Strophomena*, but not having the interior, it may possibly be an *Orthisina*, to which genus I would have referred it, but that none are yet described from Upper Silurian rocks.

Locality.— Griffith's Island (Mr. Donnett).

Strophomena ——, sp.

Another elegant species, with the lower or receiving valve

convex, and with projecting ears; it is finely striated, and with sharp raised ribs at regular intervals. Width at the ears, three-quarters of an inch.

Localities.—Point Separation, Cornwallis Island: and Leopold Island.

Orthis ——, sp. A large, rather flattened species, closely but irregularly striated, and measuring more than an inch across. It occurs at Griffith's Island, and is the only one of the genus I have seen from these countries.

Spirifer crispus Linnæus ?. Pl. 5. *fig.* 8. Hisinger, Leth. Suec. Pl. 21. *fig.* 5.

These small shells, of which there are many on one slab, cannot be distinguished from English specimens, but they may be the young of a larger *Spirifer* found by Mr. Pickthorne at Griffith's Island, and which, except that it has one more side rib, closely resembles *S. elevatus* of Dalman.

Locality. — Assistance Bay (associated with *Terebratula phoca*). Dr. Sutherland has presented these and many other specimens to the Museum of Practical Geology.

Chonetes ——, sp. A small specimen, very like *Leptæna lata* of the Ludlow rock, but not quite perfect enough to identify it.

Locality.—Cornwallis Island.

Atrypa reticularis Linn. sp. Pl. 5. *fig.* 7.

Locality. — Seal Island, lat. 75° 49′. Small specimens frequent.

Pentamerus Conchidium Dalman, sp. Pl. 5. *figs.* 9, 10. — De Vern. Geol. Russ. Pl. 1. *fig.* 2.

There are two or three varieties of this shell at Cornwallis Island which differ from each other just as various specimens of the *P. Knightii* in England, do. One variety is coarse ribbed, and seen on the back looks exactly like Gothland specimens. The other which we have figured, has more numerous ribs; and a third, of which the interior (*fig.* 10.) is given, has the ribs still more close and irregular in size. I do not doubt they are all the same species. The beak is sometimes more incurved than at others. The internal median plate which supports the V-shaped chamber is about equal in breadth to the chamber itself, and as in *P. Conchidium* and *P. Vogulicus*, De Vern, the lines of growth on it are straight across (or a little curved back at their origin, and then straight across). Those on the V-shaped chamber itself, instead of being a regular sigmoid curve as in *P. Knightii*, are bent at an obtuse angle in the middle. The upper edge of the chamber retreats considerably, and its lower edge does not project forwards beyond the supporting median plate:—in these respects it resembles *P. Vogulicus*. It has also the lower angle of the chamber ribbed lengthwise, and the median plate puckered. *P. Vogulicus*, however, is very large and ventricose, and the resemblance is more close with the Swedish species.

Locality.—Cornwallis Island (Mr. Donnett, Dr. Sutherland).

Rhynconella phoca, n. sp. Pl. 5. *figs.* 1, 2, 3. —Variety of *F. subcamelina* De Vern. Geol. Russ. vol. 2. Pl. 9. *fig.* 4.?

All the *Terebratulæ* of the older rocks, being without a perforation in the beak, are supposed to belong to the genus *Rhynconella*.

Descr.— Rounded, globose, valves longer than broad, their greatest breadth at about the middle of the shell, thence rapidly narrower towards the front, which is somewhat truncated. Valves equally convex in middle age; in old specimens the smaller one rather gibbous near the beak, but not raised into a ridge. Beak small but prominent, incurved in full-grown specimens. Front not at all raised, but indented by a broad shallow sinus. The large valve has a distinct narrow median sulcus in the depression. Surface concentrically striated, often interrupted by lines of growth.

Except for the imperforate beak, this might be taken for an oolitic Terebratula. It is so like the general shape of the species above quoted, that I can hardly think it distinct; however, the narrow distinct sinus that runs down the larger valve appears constantly to distinguish it from that species, and from *T. camelina*. M. De Verneuil, who has seen our specimens, pronounces the species distinct. *F. Prunum*, of Dalman, from Gothland, is nearly allied, but still quite another species.

Localities. — Cape Riley, abundant. We have figured a middle aged specimen, *figs.* 1. and 2., a full grown and convex specimen, *fig.* 3. Cornwallis, Leopold, Griffith's and Seal Islands.

Rhynconella sublepida De Vern. Pl. 5. *figs.* 6, 6*a*. magnified. Syn. *T. sublepida*, Vern. Geol. Russ. Pl. 10. *fig.* 14.

In referring the small shell figured in the plate to the Russian species, it is necessary to state that the ribs on the middle are not all of equal size, and that the surface is not well enough preserved to show if the scales of growth were so numerous as in De Verneuil's figure: the ribs, too, seem rather more prominent; otherwise the general shape, sharply depressed centre with small ribs, and keeled back to the large valve, as well as the scaly lines of growth, are very much alike in both, — and the size is equal.

Locality. — Leopold Island (collected from ballast by Captain James, R. E.), also S. W. end of Seal Island, in a white limestone, where it is associated with the next species:—

Rhynconella Mansonii, n. sp. Pl. 5. *fig.* 5.

Descr.—Lenticular, nearly round, smooth, with fine concentric lines of growth. In the young shell the growth is nearly even; then raised and recurved; lastly, elevated into an oblong sinus, which is notched above by a short median furrow. On the sides, the edge of the upper valve is bent down, and that of the lower valve undulated at the origin of the sinus on each side. The beak of the lower valve projects very little, and the valve itself is convex when young, bent (not depressed) towards the sinus, and with a gentle swelling in the sinus itself, to correspond with the median notch in the upper valve.

Dedicated to Mr. Manson, mate of the " Sophia," long familiar with Arctic service, a zealous observer, and a most experienced navigator.

Locality. — S. W. end of Seal Island.

Rhynconella ——, n. sp. Pl. 5. *fig.* 4.

Without perfect and numerous specimens, it would be idle to give a name to one of this numerous group of ribbed Terebratulæ. Such species are frequent in all the old rocks. It is not at all unlike species in our own Wenlock limestone.

Localities.—Griffith's, and Cornwallis Islands. A similar, but not the same species, occurs at Leopold Island.

RADIATA (Encrinites and Corals.)

Although remains of Encrinites are so abundant in the limestone as often to constitute large masses of it, no perfect remains have been found.* There are two kinds of stem joints found at Griffith's Island,—one with cylindrical narrow joints and a small perforation, —the other with broad rings and a wide central canal. Similar stems are found at Beechey Island. and also on Cornwallis Island.

At Seal Island, Baring Bay, a large cylindrical stem, very like that of *Crotalocrinus rugosus* of the Wenlock limestone,—it most probably belongs to that genus. Each joint is studded with large, perforate tubercles (rudimentary roots or auxiliary arms), which alternate on different rings. A portion of a body (probably of an *Actinocrinus*) was found by Mr. Donnett on Griffith's Island. It has a very small pelvis of three plates, and the next row consists of six, the corners of which are all deeply indented.

Fenestella ——, sp. Pl. 6. *fig.* 1.

A pretty species, with the meshes nearly all of equal size. The threads (interstices as they are called) do not radiate in straight lines, but are curved and zigzag, leaving roundish oval spaces (fenestrules) which are nearly twice as long as broad. The cross pieces, or dissepiments, are a little less in thickness than the threads.

Locality. — Seal Island, at the S.W. extremity.

A small specimen, probably of the same species with the above, shows the poriferous side. The pores are small and but little prominent, and only two along the side of each fenestrule.

Locality. — Leopold Island. Captain James, R.E.

Corals are exceedingly abundant; twenty or twenty-five species have been collected, of which I can only describe a few here. They include some European species. Want of space in our plate compels the omission of several very interesting ones; among others a

---

* M. König, in his " Supplement to Parry's Voyage," mentions the rock composed of the detritus of *Encrinites*. Dr. Sutherland brought such masses home from Cape Riley.

large *Ptychophyllum**, three inches across, *Cyathophyllum*, *Cœnites*, *Syringopora*, *Aulopora*, *Cystiphyllum*, *Heliolites*, *&c.* These may be illustrated at some future time.

Favosites polymorpha Goldf. Pl. 6. *figs.* 9. 9*a*. magnified. Goldfuss. Petrefacta Germ. t. 27. f. 2—4.

Well preserved specimens are frequent; and both the polymorphous (*fig.* 9.) and branched varieties are found at Griffith's Island. The tubes are by no means of equal size,—numerous small ones occurring between the others. The edges are somewhat thickened. Internally the tubes are sometimes cylindrical and smooth, at others more prismatic. They are sometimes faintly striated inside. The pores occur in single rows at wide distances apart. The transverse diaphragms are not visible in these specimens.

But another specimen, with all the same external characters as the rest, and having the internal diaphragms very plain and rather close, about two in the diameter of a tube, and the pores in two rows on each face, agrees well with *F. crassa* of M'Coy.

Localities. — Griffith's Island. Cape Riley and Beechey Island. Leopold's Island (frequent).

Favosites Gothlandica Linn. sp. *Corallium Gothlandicum* Linn., *Calamopora Gothlandica* Goldfuss. Pet. Germ. t. 26. f. 3., and *C. baltica*, fig. 4.

This very common species we have not figured, as it appears to be quite identical with the beautiful figure of Goldfuss. On the same specimens, a single or double alternating row of pores may be seen on each face; and the distance between the transverse partitions (diaphragms) varies much; in the same tube we have, within a very short distance, 5, 4, 3, 2, and 1½ diaphragms in the space of one diameter. The columns also vary much in size.

Localities. — Griffith's, Cornwallis, and Leopold Islands.

Another very elegant species, with smaller tubes than *F. Gothlandica*, with very closely set diaphragms and three rows of pores, is found in Cornwallis Island. It may probably be a small variety of *F. Troostii*, Milne Edw., or *F. perplexa*, mentioned by him in the same description.

Halysites Catenulatus Linn. sp. Pl. 6. *fig.* 11. *Catenipora Parrii*, König. Supp. Append. Parry's 3d Voyage.

Here, as everywhere else, the large and small varieties are found together, some with meshes not a quarter of an inch broad, others an inch and more (*C. labyrinthica*, Goldfuss); and the individual polypes vary equally in size. We have represented on the right-hand side of the figure one of the tubes cut through to show the close transverse plates, "dissepimentis confertissimis," König —

* Contrary to the usual arrangements in the calyx of a coral, it has twice the number of lamellæ toward the centre to that which the broad margin shows — and should be called *P. contrarium*.

whose *C. Parrii*, from Prince Regent's Inlet, agrees perfectly with ours. His specimens were "tubes converted into carbonate of lime, internally drused with crystals of the same;" ours are silicified, in a magnesian limestone.

Locality. — Griffith's Island.

Favistella reticulata, n. sp. Pl. 6. *figs.* 2, 2*a*. magnified.

Our specimen is three inches high by four or five inches broad, but the species grows much larger. The surface is not well preserved; the horizontal fracture shows flat, thick walled hexagonal cells, two lines broad, with slightly wavy diaphragms occupying all the centre; the edges fringed with about thirty-six stout lamellæ, alternately long and short,—the longer ones not reaching more than half-way to the centre; the length of the smaller ones about equal to the thickness of the cell walls. In the vertical rough fracture the walls appear to be very thick; but this appearance is due to the breadth of the two or three lamellæ on each side being added to them. Under a lens the real thickness is easily seen, the diaphragms, (which are wavy and very close, four or five in the space of a line) crossing all the lamellæ, but stopping against the real outer wall. The appearance of the rough vertical section is rendered very elegant by the numerous longitudinal threads or lamellæ crossing the diaphragms, and giving a strongly reticulate character.

Tubes about the size of *F. Stellata*, from the Lower Silurian rocks of America, but easily distinguished from it by the much shorter lamellæ, which never reach more than half-way to the centre, while in that they meet. The transverse diaphragms, too, in *F. Stellata*, are distant about two or three in the diameter of a tube.

Locality.—Cape Riley. Dr. Sutherland.

Favistella Franklini, n. sp. Pl. 6. *figs.* 3, 3*a*. magnified.

Masses a foot in diameter, composed of long polygonal tubes, nearly two lines broad, of very nearly equal size on the surface, the growth is by interposition of young tubes, which soon attain the adult size. The walls of the tubes are as thick in reality as those of the last species, but appear much thinner from the absence of lamellæ; these are reduced to mere longitudinal striæ, seldom projecting at all into the tube, and in general scarcely visible to the naked eye. The diaphragms are very closely packed, about four in the space of a line, throughout the largest specimen,—those in the figured fragment are more distant, especially towards the base of the young tubes. They are seldom quite flat, usually a little waved up or down, as in the last species.

There is a beautiful *Favastrea* from the Lower Silurian of Canada, which resembles this in the short rudimentary lamellæ, but the tubes are twice the diameter, and the diaphragms quite flat and very distant.

Dedicated to Sir John Franklin, whose return we all ardently expect, but scarcely dare hope for.

Locality. Cape Riley. Dr. Sutherland.

Calophyllum Phragmoceras, n. sp. Pl. 6. *figs.* 4, 4*a*.

Growing in large loosely aggregate clusters of broad conical tubes. The young buds, six or eight in a group, spring from within the edge of the old tubes, which are frequently an inch and a quarter in diameter at top, acquiring this diameter rapidly. The surface is coarsely striated lengthwise, the interior showing (either by rough fracture or polishing) strong transverse plates set closely at nearly equal distances from each other, and flat, or but very little concave; in some specimens, however, especially in the younger part, they are depressed and almost funnel-shaped. The edges of these plates are not crenulated, but show in their substance thin lamellæ, corresponding in number to the outside striæ; half of them project more than the rest, but all are very thin and short; they are shown in *fig.* 4*a*.

This seems to correspond well with Dana's genus, *Calophyllum*, in the calyculato-ramose growth and transverse plates; it is evidently a close ally of *Amplexus*.

Locality. — In a white crystalline limestone, Seal Island, Baring Bay.

Strephodes Pickthornii, n. sp. Pl. 6. *fig.* 5.

The coral here figured is one out of very numerous specimens, some of which are larger. It probably grows to a much more considerable size. The tube is short, conical, and longitudinally striated; sometimes annulated and rugose in growth: and it grows rapidly in breadth, — in the length of an inch and a half attaining an inch in diameter. The cup is very deep, its sides formed of about 56 narrow lamellæ of equal size, connected by cross bars, which are the edges of vesicular plates. Half of these lamellæ stop short at the bottom of the cup, but the rest cross a shallow depression, and are then twisted a little into bundles, and united on the crown of a low boss, which is not nearly elevated enough to constitute it a *Clisiophyllum*. At first sight the coral looks like a *Petraia*, but the vesicular plates between the numerous lamellæ removes it from that genus.

Mr. Pickthorne, surgeon of the "Pioneer," has added several interesting fossils to the Arctic list.

Localities. — Cape Riley and Beechey Island, Griffith's Island and Cornwallis Island.

Strephodes? Austini, n. sp. Pl. 6. *figs*. 6, 6*a*. magnified.

This fine coral, which we dedicate with great pleasure to the gallant commander of the Expedition, is one of the most frequent species. It occurs in the form of rounded masses from an inch to several inches in diameter, covered on all sides with stellate cells — at first sight looking very like the *Astreæ* of the present seas. The internal structure, however, as of nearly all the corals of the older rocks, is quite of another order. Prof. M'Coy, to whom I submitted these figures of the corals with drawings and notes, has kindly given me his opinion on several of them. He would prefer to regard this as *Clisiophyllum* rather than *Strephodes* from the internal structure; it is however so imperfectly shown in the sections I was able to make—and the twisting of the lamellæ is so conspicuous—that I leave it here for the present.

Surface covered by hexagonal or pentagonal cells, of various sizes, the larger ones frequently four lines across, the smaller ones in groups of two, three, or more at the angles of the others. The extreme edges of the cups are thin and crenulated, their sides thickened and sloping steeply. In a large star they are radiated by about 30 or 40 equal blunt lamellæ, which extend to the base, and about half of them are there united in bundles of three or four, and are twisted upon the surface of a low boss which rises from the centre. The lamellæ are united everywhere by frequent vesicular plates. A transverse section below the cup shows narrow but distinct divisional walls between the cells; and the lamellæ twisted in the middle and united loosely by the vesicular tissue. The intermediate ones in the section appear shorter than they are in the cup. A longitudinal section shows the vesicular plates arched a little upwards in the middle under the boss, then downward, and again inclined upwards in the outer area in two or three rows of cells. In these sections both the lamellæ and the transverse plates are thin, and the former are wavy.

Localities.—Cornwallis, Beechey, and Griffith's Islands.

Clisiophyllum ——, sp. Pl. 6. *fig.* 7.

A mass some inches over, with the surface not preserved, is all we possess of this coral; but the structure of these fossils is fortunately so well understood from sections, that we can refer it to this genus without doubt. The tubes are $\frac{1}{4}$ inch broad, tolerably straight, ending in polygonal stars of very unequal size and shape; young ones, in groups of two and three, occur very frequently between the large stars. The walls of the cells, as seen in a transverse section, are rather thick and straight; and the lamellæ, forty in number even in the smaller stars. are stout, straight, and half of them meet in the middle without twisting, the rest extend but half-way, and all are connected by close vesicular plates. In the longitudinal section, best seen by a rough fracture, the vesicular plates are quite distinct; they are closely placed, and arch upwards in the middle into a conical boss; in the intermediate space they are flat across, and then incline steeply upwards to the sides in four or five rows of oval cells. The stout, straight, and more numerous lamellæ distinguish this species easily from the last; the whole structure is closer and more compact.

Locality.—Cape Riley, in a whitish limestone. (Dr. Sutherland.)

Columnaria Sutherlandi, n. sp. Pl. 6. *fig.* 8.

Long, cylindrical, free tubes, a quarter of an inch broad. They are of equal breadth at each end of our specimen, which is three or four inches long, and imperfect at both ends. A thin outer coat, or epitheca, is seen by polished sections, and within it no lamellæ, or even striæ. The whole interior is occupied by vesicular plates, convex upwards, and which curve downward from the walls toward the centre, but few of them appear to reach the middle of the tube, being met and interrupted by others from the opposite sides; and frequently a plate occupies only the middle, stretching across a hollow left between two neighbouring plates.* The sides are occupied by shorter and more numerous plates than the middle, where, from the downward curvature of the larger plates, a set of funnel-shaped cavities is produced. This would, I suppose, fall under the genus *Beaumontia* of Milne Edw. (*Columnaria* of Goldfuss and M'Coy); but the tubes are more widely separated, and the diaphragms are more convex than in any described species.

Locality.—This beautiful and rare coral was found by Dr. Sutherland at Seal Island, which he and his party alone explored, and also at Beechey Island. We trust he may soon meet with it again on his return to the latter locality after a successful survey of the north of Baffin's Bay with Captain Inglefield.

Arachnophyllum Richardsonii, n. sp. Pl. 6. *figs.* 10, 10*a.* magnified.

In the distant, regularly-placed, and small cell-mouths, this species appears to differ from any published ones. It is named in honour of the accomplished naturalist and explorer, the Inspector of Haslar Hospital. It belongs to the genus *Phillipsastrea* of Milne Edw.; but I follow Professor M'Coy, who has placed similar fossils in the genus *Arachnophyllum*. The form figured is such as is more usually found in the Carboniferous rocks. Coral an expanded tabular mass four inches broad, gently convex, (flat below, and concentrically rugged); composed in this specimen of several layers or laminæ which do not adhere very strongly together. The cells are circular, very small, sharp edged holes, with their margins gently raised above the surface, and standing twice or generally three times their diameter apart from each other. The edges of the cells, which are not a line in diameter, are regularly serrated by about twenty equal teeth forming the termination of so many wavy lines of equal thickness, which radiate on all sides from the cell. Some of these lamellæ run in a definite direction across the coral from one cell to another, each ridge terminating as a tooth at the edge of the two contiguous cells.

Others, on the contrary, running transverse to this direction, are interrupted by the rays of the next cell, and are either shortened or deflected, so as to pass in a direction parallel with the prevailing one. This linear arrangement, though conspicuous over a large surface, as represented in our figure, is not constantly in one direction over the same surface, and on the next layer the direction is

* To use a familiar illustration, the plates tile over one another like the convex valves of oysters in a boy's grotto — leaving hollow spaces between.

often quite opposite, although the two surfaces are but the upward growth of the same coral cells.

Within the cell-cup the lamellæ are vertical, and become much thinner; and about half of them are united below into a complicated bundle, which forms the boss or style in the bottom of the cup. The cells are not quite so deep as they are broad.

Locality.—Point Eden, south side of Baring Bay, 200 feet above the sea coast. (Collected by Dr. Sutherland).

I have taken no notice of the igneous and metamorphic rocks found along the coasts of Baffin's Bay, and for some distance on the north side of Barrow's Strait. Several specimens of these were collected during the late Expeditions, and they had been previously mentioned by Professor Jameson and Mr. König. Coal was picked up as usual in Winter Harbour, Melville Island, and at Byam Martin's Island; and a fragment occurred in the detritus, 350 feet above the sea, at Kate Austin's Lake, Cornwallis Island. Both at Griffith's and Browne Islands fragments of iron ore were found.

Nor is there space here to do more than notice the occurrence, already remarked on in the body of the work, of pleistocene drift with marine shells of existing Arctic species (*Mya truncata*, *Saxicava rugosa*, &c.) which was found on every elevation up to 500 feet, on Beechey and Cornwallis Islands.

The great formation which occupies the Arctic lands, or at least skirts their icy shores, is a limestone, which, from all that can be gathered from the fossils, is of Upper Silurian age.

THE END.

London:
Spottiswoodes and Shaw,
New-street-Square.